BCOM
Are you in?

an innovative concept in teaching and learning solutions designed to best reach today's students

MW00565095

54%

Percentage of Fortune 100 companies who use **Twitter to market to customers.**

4.5 OUT OF 5

Employers rank communication skills (written and verbal) as **what they look for in top skills or qualities in job candidates.**

Statistics taken from the following sites:
• Source: http://www.examiner.com/x-828-Entry-Level-Careers-Examiner~y2009m8d19-Potential-employers-are-looking-at-your-social-networking-habits
• Source: http://www.armhr.am/AdviceDetail23.aspx
• Source: http://www.nacweb.org/press/display.asp?year=&prid=254
• Source: http://www.dmconfidential.com/blogs/column/Marketing/2371/

SOUTH-WESTERN
CENGAGE Learning·

BCOM2 2010–2011 Edition
Carol M. Lehman
Debbie D. DuFrene

EVP/Publisher: Jonathan Hulbert

VP/Editorial Director: Jack W. Calhoun

VP/Director of Marketing: Bill Hendee

Editor-in-Chief: Melissa Acuña

Acquisitions Editor: Erin Joyner

Developmental Editor: Laura Rush,
    B-books, Ltd.

Product Development Manager, 4LTR
    Press: Steven E. Joos

Project Manager, 4LTR Press:
    Clara Goosman

Executive Brand Marketing Manager,
    4LTR Press: Robin Lucas

Editorial Assistant: Kayti Purkiss

Sr. Marketing Communications Manager:
    Sarah Greber

Production Director: Amy McGuire,
    B-books, Ltd.

Managing Media Editor: Pam Wallace

Media Editor: John Rich

Manufacturing Coordinator:
    Miranda Klapper

Production Service: B-books, Ltd.

Art Director: Stacy Jenkins Shirley

Internal Designer: Ke Design, Mason, OH

Cover Designer: KeDesign, Mason, OH

Cover Image: ©Veer/Shutterstock

Photography Manager: Deanna Ettinger

Photo Researcher: Charlotte Goldman

For product information and technology assistance, contact us at
Cengage Learning Academic Resource Center, 1-800-423-0563

For permission to use material from this text or product,
submit all requests online at **www.cengage.com/permissions**
Further permissions questions can be emailed to
permissionrequest@cengage.com

© 2011 Cengage Learning. All Rights Reserved.

Library of Congress Control Number: 2009943351

SE ISBN-13: 978-0-538-75335-7
SE ISBN-10: 0-538-75335-8

South-Western Cengage Learning
5191 Natorp Boulevard
Mason, OH 45040
USA

Cengage Learning products are represented in Canada by
Nelson Education, Ltd.

For your course and learning solutions, visit **www.cengage.com**
Purchase any of our products at your local college store or at our
preferred online store **www.CengageBrain.com**

Printed in the United States of America
2 3 4 5 6 7 13 12 11 10

Brief Contents

Communication Foundations and Analysis 2

1 Establishing a Framework for Business Communication 2

2 Focusing on Interpersonal Communication 22

3 Focusing on Group Communication 38

4 Planning Written and Spoken Messages 54

Communication Through Electronic, Voice, and Written Messages 74

5 Communicating Electronically 74

6 Preparing Good- and Neutral-News Messages 88

7 Preparing Bad-News Messages 106

8 Preparing Persuasive Messages 126

9 Revising Written Messages 146

Communication Through Reports and Business Presentations 166

10 Understanding the Report Process and Research Methods 166

11 Managing Data and Using Graphics 188

12 Organizing and Preparing Reports and Proposals 204

13 Designing and Delivering Business Presentations 224

Communication for Employment 248

14 Preparing Résumés and Application Messages 248

15 Interviewing for a Job and Preparing Employment Messages 278

Contents

Part 1 Communication Foundations and Analysis   2

1 Establishing a Framework for Business Communication   2

Purpose of Business Communication   2

The Communication Process   3
Encoding the Message   4
Channel Selection and Message Transmission   4
Causes of Interference   5
Decoding the Message   6
Giving Feedback   6

Communicating Within Organizations   6
Levels of Communication   6
Communication Flow in Organizations   7

External Influences on Business Communication   10
Legal and Ethical Constraints   11
Diversity Challenges   14
Team Environment   18
Changing Technology   19

2 Focusing on Interpersonal Communication   22

Foundations   22
Communication and the Self   22
Impression Management   26

Communication Styles or Modes   26

Interpersonal Influence   28

Nonverbal Communication   29
Metacommunication   29
Kinesic Messages   29
Understanding Nonverbal Messages   30

Listening as a Communication Skill   33
Listening for a Specific Purpose   33
Poor Listening Habits   35
Suggestions for Effective Listening   36

3 Focusing on Group Communication   38

Increasing Focus on Groups   38
Flat Organizational Structures   38
Heightened Focus on Cooperation   40

Characteristics of Effective Groups   40
Common Goals   40

Role Perception   40
Longevity   40
Size   40
Status   41
Group Norms   41
Leadership   41
Group Roles   41

From Groups to Teams   42

Group Decision Making   44

Group Conflict   45

Personal Conflict   46
Substantive Conflict   46
Procedural Conflict   46
Competitive versus Cooperative Orientation   46
Social Dilemmas   47
Conflict Resolution   47
Groupthink   49

Meeting Management   50

Face-to-Face Meetings   50
Electronic Meetings   51
Suggestions for Effective Meetings   51

4 Planning Written and Spoken Messages   54

Writing – A Ticket to Work   54

Step 1: Determining the Purpose and Type of Message   56

Communicating to Inform   56
Communicating to Persuade   56
Communicating to Establish Credibility   57
Communicating to Convey Goodwill   60

Step 2: Envision the Audience   61

Position in or Relation to the Organization   63
Generational Differences   65
Personality Differences   65

Step 3: Consider the Context   66

Step 4: Choose a Channel and Medium   67

Richness versus Leanness   67
Need for Interpretation   68
Speed of Establishing Contact   68
Time Required for Feedback   68
Cost   69
Amount of Information Conveyed   69
Need for a Permanent Record   69
Control over the Message   69

Step 5: Adapt the Message to the Audience   70

Step 6: Organize the Message   71

Outline to Benefit the Sender and the Receiver   71
Sequence Ideas to Achieve Desired Goals   72

Step 7: Prepare the First Draft   73

Part 2 Communication Through Electronic, Voice, and Written Messages   74

5 Communicating Electronically   74

Appropriate Use of Technology   74

Determine the Purpose of the Message   74

Determine Whether the Information is Personal or Confidential   75

Decide Whether Positive Human Relations are Sacrificed   76

Electronic Mail Communication   76

Advantages of Email   76

Guidelines for Preparing Email Messages   76

Effective Use of Email   79

Instant Messaging   80

Email and the Law   81

Web Page Communication   82

Writing for a Website   83

Writing for Weblogs   84

Voice and Wireless Communication   84

Voice Mail Communication   85

Cell Phone Communication   85

Wireless Communication and the Future   86

6 Preparing Good- and Neutral-News Messages   88

Choosing the Channel or Medium   88

The Deductive Organizational Approach   88

Good-News Messages   90

Positive News   90

Thank-You and Appreciation Messages   91

Routine Claims   93

Claim Message   93

Favorable Response to a Claim Message   94

Routine Requests   96

Routine Request   96

Favorable Response to a Routine Request   96

Favorable Response to a Favor Request   99

Form Letters for Routine Responses   99

Routine Messages About Orders and Credit   101

Acknowledging Customer Orders   101

Providing Credit Information   101

Extending Credit   101

Procedural Messages   104

7 Preparing Bad-News Messages 106

Choosing an Appropriate Channel and Organizational Pattern 106
Channel Choice and Commitment to Tact 106
Cultural Concerns 108
Use of the Inductive Approach to Build Goodwill 108
Advantages of the Inductive Approach 109
Exceptions to the Inductive Approach 109

Developing a Bad-News Message 109
Writing the Introductory Paragraph 110
Presenting the Facts, Analysis, and Reasons 110
Writing the Bad-News Statement 111
Offering a Counterproposal or "Silver Lining" Idea 113
Closing Positively 114

Refusing a Request 115

Denying a Claim 117
Denying Credit 118

Delivering Constructive Criticism 119
Communicating Negative Organizational News 121

8 Preparing Persuasive Messages 126

Persuasion Strategies 126
Plan Before You Write 127
Apply Sound Writing Principles 129

Use the Inductive Approach 130
Gain Attention 130
Gain Interest by Introducing the Product, Service, or Idea 132
Create Desire by Providing Convincing Evidence 133
Motivate Action 136

Persuasive Requests 137
Making a Claim 137
Asking a Favor 139
Requesting Information 139
Persuading Within an Organization 139
Sales Messages 142

9 Revising Written Messages 146

Cultivate a Frame of Mind for Effective Revising and Proofreading 146

Use Systematic Procedures for Revising 148

Check the Content to Ensure Ethical Communication 150

Check for Logical Development and Unity 151
Develop Coherent Paragraphs 152

Craft Powerful Sentences   154

Use Correct Sentence Structure   154

Rely on Active Voice   155

Emphasize Important Ideas   156

Improve Readability   157

Understand Readability Measures   157

Use Contemporary Language   158

Use Simple, Informal Words   159

Communicate Concisely   160

Apply Visual Enhancements to Improve Readability   161

Project a Positive, Tactful Tone   163

Be Sensitive to International Audiences   165

Part 3 Communication Through Reports and Business Presentations   166

10 Understanding the Report Process and Research Methods   166

Characteristics of Reports   166

Types of Reports   167

Proposals   169

The Problem-Solving Process   170

STEP 1: Recognizing and Defining the Problem   170

STEP 2: Selecting a Method of Solution   172

STEP 3: Collecting and Organizing the Data   177

STEP 4: Arriving at an Answer   184

11 Managing Data and Using Graphics   188

Communicating Quantitative Information   188

Using Graphics   190

Effective and Ethical Use of Graphics   190

Types of Graphic Aids   191

Including Graphics in Texts   201

Pattern for Incorporating Graphics in Text   201

Positioning of Graphics in Text   201

12 Organizing and Preparing Reports and Proposals   204

Parts of a Formal Report   204

Preliminary Parts   205

Report Text   208

Addenda 208
Organization of Formal Reports 209
Writing Convincing and Effective Reports 209
Choosing a Writing Style for Formal Reports 212
Short Reports 214
Memorandum, Email, and Letter Reports 214
Form Reports 214
Parts of a Proposal 216
Structure 216
Proposal Preparation 221
Collaborative Skills for Team Writing 221

13 Designing and Delivering Business Presentations 224

Planning an Effective Business Presentation 224
Identify Your Key Message 225
Know Your Audience 226
Organizing the Content 226
Introduction 226
Body 227
Close 229
Designing Compelling Presentation Visuals 229
Types of Presentation Visuals 230
Design of Presentation Visuals 230
Space Design and Typography 234
Refining Your Delivery 236
Delivery Method 236
Vocal Qualities 238
Delivery Style 240
Special Presentation Situations 243
Speaking to Culturally Diverse Audiences 243
Team Presentations 244
Distance Presentations 246

Part 4 Communication for Employment 248

14 Preparing Résumés and Application Messages 248

Preparing for the Job Search 248
Gathering Essential Information 249
Identifying Potential Career Opportunities 250
Using Traditional Sources 251
Using Electronic Job Searches 252
Planning a Targeted Résumé 253
Standard Parts of a Résumé 254
Qualifications 255
Types of Résumés 258

Preparing Résumés   259

   Preparing a Print (Designed) Résumé   260

   Preparing a Scannable Résumé   261

   Adapting to Varying Electronic Submission
      Requirements   266

Supplementing a Résumé   268

   Professional Portfolios   268

   Employment Videos   269

Composing Application Messages   270

   Persuasive Organization   271

   General Writing Guidelines   274

   Finishing Touches   275

15 Interviewing for a Job and Preparing Employment Messages   278

Types of Employment Interviews   278

   Structured Interviews   278

   Unstructured Interviews   280

   Stress Interviews   280

   Team Interviews   280

   Virtual Interviews   280

Preparing for an Interview   281

   Study the Prospective Employer   281

   Study Yourself   282

   Plan Your Appearance   282

   Plan Your Time and Materials   283

Practice the Interview   283

Conducting a Successful Interview   287

   The Opening Formalities   287

   The Information Exchange   288

   The Closing   288

Preparing Other Employment Messages   289

   Application Forms   289

   Follow-Up Messages   289

   Thank You Messages   289

   Job-Acceptance Message   290

   Job-Refusal Message   290

   Resignations   292

   Recommendation Requests   292

Grammar and Usage Appendix   295

Endnotes   311

Index   317

REVIEW

HE DID

BCOM2 puts a multitude of study aids at your fingertips. After reading the chapters, check out these resources for further help:

- **Chapter in Review cards**, found in the back of your book, include all learning outcomes, definitions, and visual summaries for each chapter.

- **Online printable flash cards** give you three additional ways to check your comprehension of key concepts.

Other great ways to help you study include **interactive games, podcasts, audio downloads, and online tutorial quizzes with feedback**.

You can find it all at **4ltrpress.cengage.com/bcom**.

SPEAK UP! THEY DID

BCOM2 was built on a simple principle: to create a new teaching and learning solution that reflects the way today's faculty teach and the way you learn.

Through conversations, focus groups, surveys, and interviews, we collected data that drove the creation of the version of **BCOM2** that you are using today. But it doesn't stop there—in order to make **BCOM2** an even better learning experience, we'd like you to SPEAK UP and tell us how **BCOM2** worked for you.

What did you like about it? What would you change? Are there additional ideas you have that would help us build a better product for next semester's students?

At **4ltrpress.cengage.com/bcom** you'll find all of the resources you need to succeed – **videos, audio downloads, flash cards, interactive quizzes** and more!

Speak Up! Go to **4ltrpress.cengage.com/bcom.**

Establishing a Framework for Business Communication

Purposes of Business Communication

objective ①
Define communication and describe the main purpose for communication in business.

We communicate to satisfy needs in both our work and nonwork lives. Each of us wants to be heard, appreciated, and wanted. We also want to accomplish tasks and achieve goals. Obviously, then, a major purpose of communication is to help people feel good about themselves and about their friends, groups, and organizations. The classic purposes of communication are to inform, to persuade, and to entertain. However, in business, entertainment is often limited to celebratory occasions and products or services that are being marketed to customers and clients. Two additional purposes of communication in an organizational setting are establishing credibility and goodwill or positive and productive relationships with others.

What is communication? Communication is the process of exchanging information and meaning between or among individuals through a common system of symbols, signs, and behavior. Other words used to describe the communication process include expressing feelings, conversing, speaking, corresponding, writing, listening, and exchanging. Studies indicate that managers typically spend 60 to 80 percent of their time involved in communication. In your career activities, you may communicate in a wide variety of ways, including:

objectives

① Define communication and describe the main purpose for communication in business.

② Explain the communication process model and the ultimate objective of the communication process.

③ Discuss how information flows in an organization.

④ Explain how legal and ethical constraints, diversity challenges, team environment, and changing technology influence the process of business communication.

© David Meharey/iStockphoto.com

- Attending meetings and writing reports related to strategic plans and company policy.
- Collaborating with others to make decisions and accomplish tasks.
- Establishing productive working relationships with coworkers, supervisors, clients, customers, and outside vendors.
- Presenting information to large and small groups.
- Explaining and clarifying management procedures and work assignments.
- Coordinating the work of various employees, departments, and other work groups.
- Evaluating and counseling employees.
- Promoting the company's products/services and image.

The Communication Process

objective ②
Explain the communication process model and the ultimate objective of the communication process.

Effective business communication is essential to success in today's work environments. Recent surveys of executives document that abilities in writing and speaking are major determinants of career success in many fields.[1] Although essential to personal and professional success, effective business communication does not occur automatically.

Your own experiences have likely taught you that a message is not interpreted correctly just because you transmitted it. An effective communicator anticipates possible breakdowns in the communication process—the unlimited ways the message can be misunderstood. This mind-set provides the concentration to design the initial message effectively and to be prepared to intervene at the appropriate time to ensure that the message received is on target. However, the responsibility to ensure effective communication does not end with the sender. The receiver of the message is also responsible for ensuring that he or she received the message as intended by providing feedback, asking for clarification, and checking for correct understanding.

Consider the communication process model presented in Figure 1-1. The seemingly simple steps actually represent a very complex process.

Encoding the Message

The sender carefully designs a message by selecting (1) words that clearly convey the message and (2) when using channels other than writing, choosing nonverbal signals (gestures, stance, tone of voice, and so on) that reinforce the verbal message. The process of selecting and organizing the message is referred to as **encoding**. The sender's primary objective is to encode the message in such a way that the message received

encoding
the process of selecting and organizing the message

is as close as possible to the message that is intended. Knowledge of the receiver's educational level, experience, viewpoints, culture, and other information aids the sender in encoding the message in such a way that it is received as intended. If information about the receiver is unavailable, the sender can put himself or herself in the receiver's position to gain fairly accurate insight for encoding the message.

Communication Breakdown

Various behaviors can cause breakdowns in the communication process at the encoding stage, such as when the sender uses:

- Words not present in the receiver's vocabulary.
- Ambiguous, nonspecific ideas that distort the message.
- Nonverbal signals that contradict the verbal message.
- Expressions such as "uh" or grammatical errors, mannerisms (excessive hand movements, jingling keys), or dress styles that distract the receiver.

Channel Selection and Message Transmission

To increase the likelihood that the receiver will understand the message, the sender carefully selects an appropriate channel for transmitting the message. Three typical communication channels are two-way, face-to-face; two-way, not face-to-face; and one-way, not face-to-face.

Selecting an inappropriate channel can cause the message to be misunderstood and can adversely affect human relations with the receiver. In some cases, to ensure clarity, it is also a good idea to choose one channel and to follow up with another. For example, for a complex subject, a sender might begin with a written message and follow up with a face-to-face or telephone discussion after the receiver has had an opportunity to review the information.

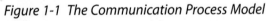

Figure 1-1 The Communication Process Model

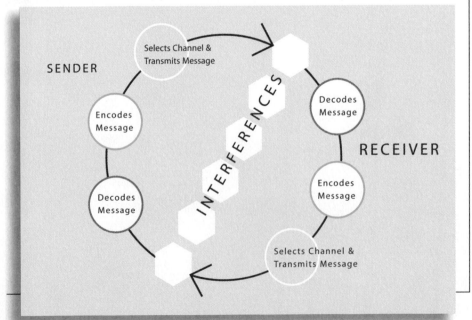

Two-Way, Face-to-Face

Examples of two-way, face-to-face communication include informal conversations, interviews, oral presentations, speeches, and videoconferences. Two-way, face-to-face communication has several advantages. It provides instant feedback, the potential to establish a personal connection, and information from nonverbal signals. For these reasons, two-way, face-to-face communication is the richest channel of communication. (Experts say that more than 90 percent of two-way, face-to-face communication can be transmitted nonverbally.) Because of these advantages, two-way, face-to-face communication can be especially appropriate and effective for conveying sensitive or unpleasant news.

Two-Way, Not Face-to-Face

Two-way, not face-to-face communication includes telephone conversations, online chats, and text messaging, all of which provide instant feedback using a real-time connection. Often, this type of communication is a comparably inexpensive form of communication, particularly when communicating over long distances. Physical absence creates disadvantages, however. Nonverbal elements are lacking, so the message must be particularly clear and forms of feedback and clarification should be used to ensure correct understanding. That means this channel of communication is not a good choice for certain situations, such as conveying sensitive or unpleasant news.

One-Way, Not Face-to-Face

One-way, face-to-face communication includes letters, memos, reports, and electronic communications, such as email, fax, voice mail, and web pages, and has the advantage of being considered more permanent and official. Thus written documents are required when legal matters are involved and written records must be retained. However, because nonverbal elements and the chance for instant feedback are missing, possible confusion must be anticipated and prevented by ensuring that the message is very well written.

Causes of Interference

Senders and receivers must anticipate other factors that may hinder the communication process and attempt to eliminate or reduce their effect. These factors are referred to as **interferences** or **barriers** to effective communication. Interferences may occur at various stages of the communication process. For example:

- Differences in educational level, experience, culture, and other characteristics of the sender and the receiver increase the complexity of encoding and decoding a message.
- Physical interferences occurring in the channel include a noisy environment, interruptions, and uncomfortable surroundings.
- Mental distractions, such as preoccupation with other matters and developing a response rather than listening, interfere with decoding a message.

Both the sender and the receiver of messages should be aware of these additional barriers to communication and attempt to remove them by changing the setting or even making arrangements to communicate at a different time when fewer distractions exist.

interferences (barriers)
other factors that may hinder the communication process

Decoding the Message

The receiver's task is to interpret the sender's message, both verbal and nonverbal, with as little distortion as possible. The process of interpreting the message is referred to as **decoding**. Because words and nonverbal signals have different meanings to different people, countless problems can occur at this point in the communication process:

- The receiver does not understand the words being used or the words are ambiguous or nonspecific.
- The nonverbal signals may be distracting or contradict the verbal message.
- The receiver is intimidated by the position or authority of the sender, resulting in tension that prevents the receiver from concentrating effectively on the message and failing to ask for needed clarification.
- The receiver may be from another culture and may not interpret the message as intended because of differing values and practices.
- The receiver prejudges the topic as too boring or difficult to understand and does not attempt to comprehend the message.
- The receiver is close-minded and unreceptive to new and different ideas.
- The receiver may have preconceptions about the sender or his or her organization or product that interfere with his or her ability to be open-minded and receptive.

The infinite number of breakdowns possible at each stage of the communication process makes it challenging for effective, mutually satisfying communication to occur. The complexity of the communication process amplifies the importance of the next stage in the communication process—feedback to clarify understanding.

Giving Feedback

When the receiver responds to the sender's message, the response is called **feedback**. The feedback may prompt the sender to modify or adjust the original message to make it clearer to the receiver. Feedback may be verbal or nonverbal. A remark such as "Could you clarify . . ." or a perplexed facial expression provides clear feedback to the sender that the receiver does not yet understand the message. Conversely, a confident "Yes, I understand" and a nod of the head likely signal understanding or encouragement.

Communicating Within Organizations

objective ③
Discuss how information flows in an organization.

To be successful, organizations must create an environment that energizes and provides encouragement to employees to accomplish tasks by encouraging genuine openness and effective communication. **Organizational communication** is concerned with the movement of information within the company structure. Regardless of your career or level within an organization, your ability to communicate will affect not only the success of the organization but also your personal success and advancement within that organization.

Levels of Communication

Communication can involve sending messages to both large and small audiences. **Internal messages** are intended for recipients within the organization. **External messages** are directed to recipients outside the organization. When considering the intended audience, communication can be described as taking place on five levels: intrapersonal, interpersonal, group, organizational, and public.

Intrapersonal Communication

Intrapersonal communication is within oneself. Because it does not involve a separate sender and receiver, some do not consider intrapersonal communication to be true communication. Others, however, believe that intrapersonal communication when conceived of as the degree of our self-awareness is an important foundation of effective communication. Accurate perception of our self and an understanding of how others see us is the first building block of effective communication. Self-awareness is generally achieved through self-reflection or what might be thought of as intrapersonal communication.

---

decoding
the process of interpreting the message

feedback
the response the receiver gives to the sender of a message

organizational communication
communication concerned with the movement of information within the company structure

internal messages
messages intended for recipients within the organization

external messages
messages directed to recipients outside the organization

intrapersonal communication
communication that occurs within oneself

Interpersonal Communication

Interpersonal communication is communication that occurs between two people. Its goals are to (1) accomplish the tasks (task goal) and (2) to help the participants feel better about themselves and each other because of their interaction (maintenance goal). Examples of interpersonal communication include that occurring between a supervisor and subordinate and that occurring between two coworkers.

Group Communication

Group communication occurs among more than two people, generally in a small group. It's the goal of group communication to achieve greater output through the collaboration of several individuals than could be produced through individual efforts. Examples of this include communication within a committee or a work team.

Organizational Communication

Organizational communication generally involves large groups working together in such a way as to accomplish complex, ambitious tasks. The goal of organizational communication is to provide adequate structure, communication flow, and channels and media for communication to allow that to happen. More on organizational communication follows.

Public Communication

Public communication is intended to help the organization reach out to its public to achieve its external communication goals. Examples of public communication include advertisements, public relations, crisis management, and website communication about the company

and its products and services. Some forms of public communication, such as advertisements and public relations, might be characterized as mass communication since they are often transmitted using mass media. Public communication is not within the scope of this text, although many of the communication principles addressed here are applicable.

Communication Flow in Organizations

Communication flows in a variety of ways in an organization. Some flows are planned and structured; others are not. Some communication flows can be formally depicted, whereas some defy description. The flow of communication within an organization occurs both formally and informally. The **formal network flow** often follows a company's formal organization chart, which is created by management to control individual and group behavior and to achieve the organization's goals. The formal system is dictated by the cultural, technical, political, and economic environment of the organization. By contrast, the **informal network flow** develops as people interact within the formal communication system and certain behavior patterns emerge—patterns that accommodate social and psychological needs. Because the informal network undergoes continual changes, it generally cannot be depicted accurately by graphic means.

Formal Network Flow

The direction in which communication flows formally within an organization may be downward, upward, or horizontal, as shown in Figure 1-2 on the next page. Although the concept of flow seems simple, direction has meaning for those participating in the communication process.

Downward Communication. **Downward communication** flows from supervisor to employee, from policy makers to operating personnel, or from top to bottom on the organization chart.

interpersonal communication
communication that occurs between two people
group communication
communication that occurs among more than two people
public communication
communication intended to help the organization to reach out to its public to achieve its external communication goals
formal network flow
communication that often follows a company's formal organization chart
informal network flow
flow of communication that develops as people interact within the formal communication system
downward communication
communication from supervisor to employee

Figure 1-2 Flow of Information Within an Organization

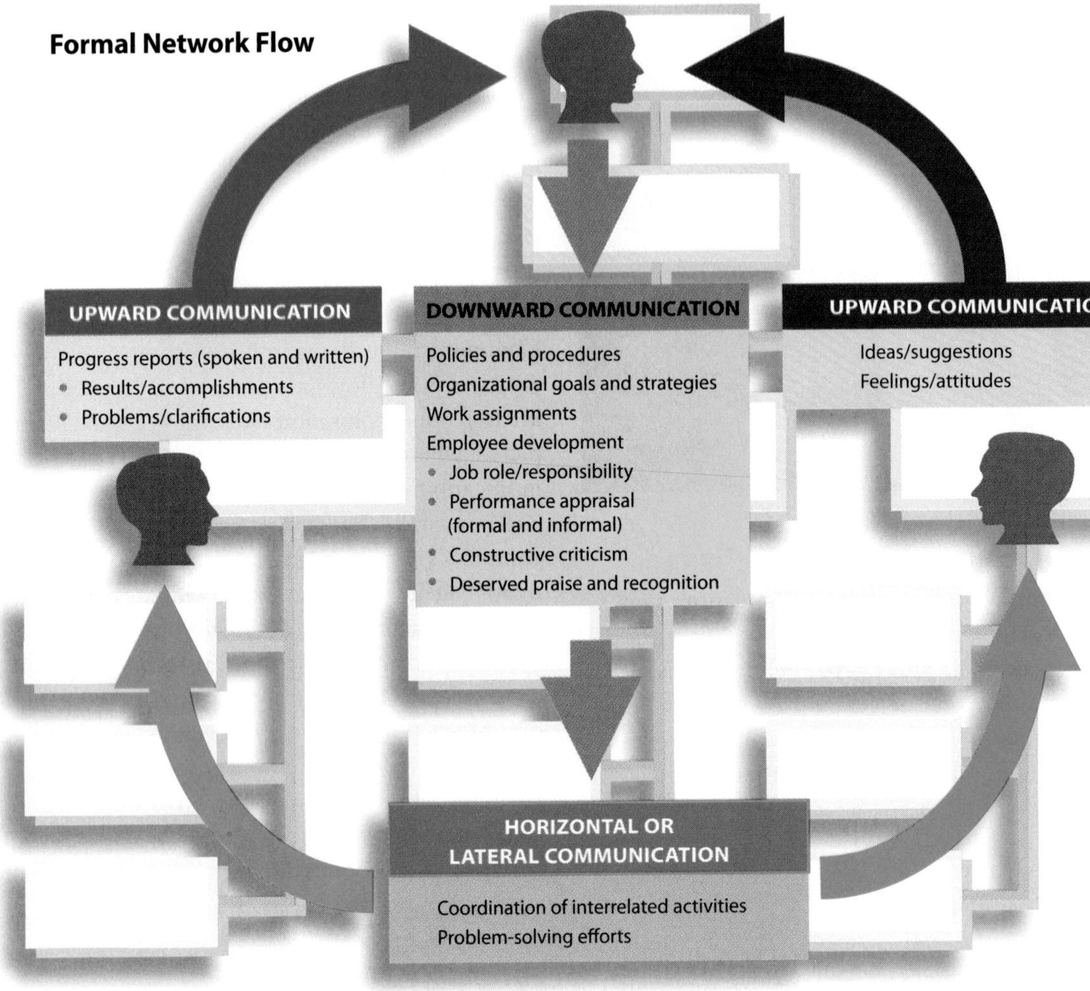

Formal Network Flow

UPWARD COMMUNICATION	DOWNWARD COMMUNICATION	UPWARD COMMUNICATION
Progress reports (spoken and written) • Results/accomplishments • Problems/clarifications	Policies and procedures Organizational goals and strategies Work assignments Employee development • Job role/responsibility • Performance appraisal (formal and informal) • Constructive criticism • Deserved praise and recognition	Ideas/suggestions Feelings/attitudes

HORIZONTAL OR LATERAL COMMUNICATION

Coordination of interrelated activities
Problem-solving efforts

A simple policy statement from the top of the organization may grow into a formal plan for operation at lower levels. Teaching people how to perform their specific tasks is an element of downward communication. Another element is orienting employees to a company's rules, practices, procedures, history, and goals. Employees also learn about the quality of their job performance through downward communication.

Upward Communication. **Upward communication** is generally feedback to downward communication. Although necessary and valuable, upward communication involves risks. When management requests information from lower organizational levels, the resulting information becomes feedback to that request. Employees talk to supervisors about themselves, their fellow employees, their work and methods of completing it,

upward communication
communication from employees to supervisors

Go with the Flow

Downward communication normally involves both written and spoken methods and makes use of the following guidelines:

- People high in the organization usually have greater knowledge of the organization's broad, long-range goals than do people at lower levels.

- Both spoken and written messages tend to become larger as they move downward through organizational levels. This expansion results from attempts to prevent distortion and is more noticeable in written messages.

- Spoken messages are subject to greater changes in meaning than are written messages because of the potential distortion that occurs as the information is transmitted from person to person.

and their perceptions of the organization. These comments are feedback to the downward flow transmitted in both spoken and written form by group meetings, procedures or operations manuals, company news releases, the company intranet, and the grapevine.

Accurate upward communication keeps management informed about the feelings of lower-level employees, taps the expertise of employees, helps management identify both difficult and potentially promotable employees, and paves the way for even more effective downward communication. Employees reporting upward are aware that their communications carry the risk of putting them on the spot or committing them to something they cannot handle.

Although employees typically appreciate and welcome genuine opportunities to send information to management, they will likely resent any superficial attempt to provide an open communication network with management.

Upward Communication:

- Is primarily feedback to requests and actions of supervisors.
- May occur in more progressive organizations as a mechanism for upper management to acquire information about specific processes at the production level or front line.
- May be misleading because lower-level employees often tell the superior what they think the superior wants to hear. Therefore, their messages might contradict their true observations and perceptions.
- Is based on trust in the supervisor.
- May involve risk to an employee, depending upon the corporate culture of the organization.
- Must be sincere (employees will reject superficial attempts by management to obtain feedback from employees).

Horizontal Communication. **Horizontal** or **lateral** **communication** describes interactions between organizational units on the same hierarchical level. These interactions reveal one of the major shortcomings of organizational charts: They do not allow much room for horizontal communication when they depict authority relationships by placing one box higher than an-

other and define role functions by placing titles in those boxes. Yet management should realize that horizontal communication is the primary means of achieving coordination in a functional organizational structure. Units coordinate their activities to accomplish task goals just as adjacent workers in a production line coordinate their activities. So, for horizontal communication to be maximally effective, the people in any system or organization should be available to one another.

Today, the traditional hierarchy organized around functional units is inadequate for competing in increasingly competitive global markets. Companies use work teams that integrate work-flow processes rather than having specialists who deal with a single function or product. These cross-functional work teams break down the former communication barriers between isolated functional departments. Communication patterns take on varying forms to accommodate team activities. Therefore, in an organization divided into cross-functional teams, horizontal communication among the team members is extremely important to achieve individual and team goals.

Informal Network Flow (the Grapevine)

The *grapevine,* often called the *rumor mill,* is perhaps the best-known part of the informal communication system. As people talk casually during coffee breaks and lunch periods, the focus usually shifts from topic to topic. One of the usual topics is work—job, company, supervisor, fellow employees. Even though the formal system has a definite pattern of communication flow, the grapevine tends to emerge spontaneously and operates within all organizations. Consider these points concerning the accuracy and value of grapevine communication:

- The grapevine has a reputation for being speedy but inaccurate. In the absence of alarms, the grapevine may be the most effective way to let occupants know that the building is on fire. It certainly beats sending a written memorandum or an email.
- Although the grapevine is often thought of as a carrier of inaccurate communication, in reality it is no more or less accurate than other channels. Even formal communication may become inaccurate as it passes from level to level in the organizational hierarchy.
- The inaccuracy of the grapevine has more to do with the message input than with the output. For example, the grapevine is noted as a carrier of rumor,

horizontal (lateral) communication
interactions between organizational units on the same hierarchical level

primarily because it carries informal messages. If the input is rumor and nothing more, the output obviously will be inaccurate. But the output may be an accurate description of the original rumor.

- In a business office, news about promotions, personnel changes, company policy changes, and annual salary adjustments is often communicated by the grapevine long before being disseminated by formal channels. The process works similarly in colleges, where information about choice instructors typically is not published but is known by students from the grapevine. How best to prepare for examinations, instructor attitudes on attendance and homework, and even future faculty personnel changes are messages that travel over the grapevine.

- A misconception about the grapevine is that the message passes from person to person until it finally reaches a person who can't pass it on—the end of the line. Actually, the grapevine may work to spread information to a huge number of people in a short time. That is, one person tells two or three others, who each tell two or three others, who each tell two or three others, and so on.

- The grapevine has no single, consistent source. Messages may originate anywhere and follow various routes.

Due at least in part to widespread downsizing and corporate scandals during the last few years, employees in many organizations are demanding to be better informed. Some companies have implemented new formal ways for disseminating information to their internal constituents, such as newsletters and intranets. Company openness with employees, including financial information, means more information in the formal system rather than risking its miscommunication through informal channels. An employee of The Container Store—named to *Fortune* magazine's list of best companies to work for in America—said that the company's willingness to divulge what it makes each year and its financial goals builds her trust in management.[2]

An informal communication system will emerge from even the most carefully designed formal system. Managers who ignore this fact are attempting to manage blindfolded. Instead of denying or condemning the grapevine, the effective manager will learn to *use* the informal communication network. The grapevine, for instance, can be used to counteract rumors and false information.

External Influences on Business Communication

Communication is often a complicated process that does not take place in a vacuum but rather is influenced by a number of factors in the environment. The effective communicator carefully considers each of these environmental influences when developing messages. Another word for the environmental influences that may affect our communication is *context*. (Context is discussed in more detail in Chapter 4.) As shown in Figure 1-3, four principal factors are constantly at work shaping this context: legal and ethical constraints, diversity challenges, team environment, and changing technology.

© John Lund/Blend Images/Jupiterimages

Figure 1-3 *External Factors Influencing Business Communication*

LEGAL & ETHICAL CONSTRAINTS	DIVERSITY CHALLENGES	TEAM ENVIRONMENT	CHANGING TECHNOLOGY
• International Laws	• Cultural Differences	• Trust	• Accuracy and Security Issues
• Domestic Laws	• Language Barriers	• Team Roles	• Telecommunications
• Code of Ethics	• Gender Issues	• Shared Goals and Expectations	• Software Applications
• Stakeholder Interests	• Education Levels	• Synergy	• "High-touch" Issues
• Ethical Frameworks	• Age Factors	• Group Reward	• Telecommuting
• Personal Values	• Nonverbal Differences	• Distributed Leadership	• Databases

Legal and Ethical Constraints

Legal and ethical constraints affect business communication because they set boundaries in which communication can occur. International, federal, state, and local laws affect the way that various business activities can be conducted. For instance, laws specify that certain information must be stated in letters that reply to credit applications and those dealing with the collection of outstanding debts. Furthermore, one's own ethical standards will often influence what he or she is willing to say in a message. For example, a system of ethics built on honesty may require that the message provides full disclosure rather than a shrouding of the truth. Legal responsibilities, then, are the starting point for appropriate business communication. One's ethical belief system, or personal sense of right and wrong behavior, provides further boundaries for professional activity.

The press is full of examples of unethical conduct in the business and political communities, but unethical behavior is not relegated to the papers—it has far-reaching consequences. Those affected by decisions, the **stakeholders**, can include people inside and outside the organization. Employees and stockholders are obvious losers when a company fails. Competitors in the same industry also suffer, because their strategies are based on what they perceive about their competition. Beyond that, financial markets as a whole suffer due to erosion of public confidence. Business leaders, government officials, and citizens frequently express concern about the apparent erosion of ethical values in society. Even for those who want to do the right thing, matters of ethics are seldom clear-cut decisions of right versus wrong, and they often contain ambiguous elements. In addition, the pressure appears to be felt most strongly by lower-level managers, often recent business school graduates who are the least experienced at doing their jobs.

Many find defining ethics challenging. Most people immediately associate ethics with standards and rules of

Matters of ethics are seldom clear-cut decisions of right versus wrong

conduct, morals, right and wrong, values, and honesty. Dr. Albert Schweitzer defined *ethics* as "the name we give to our concern for good behavior. We feel an obligation to consider not only our own personal well-being, but also that of others and of human society as a whole."[3] In other words, **ethics** refers to the principles of right and wrong that guide you in making decisions that consider the impact of your actions on others as well as yourself.

Good reasons exist for a business to make ethical decisions. According to James E. Perrella, executive vice president of Ingersoll-Rand Company:[4]

Many people, including many business leaders, would argue that such an application of ethics to business would adversely affect bottom-line performance. I say nay. . . . Good ethics, simply, is good business.

stakeholders
those affected by decisions
ethics
the principles of right and wrong that guide decision making

In March 2009, Bernard Madoff admitted to operating the largest investor fraud ever committed by an individual. Madoff paid returns to investors from their own money or money paid by other investors rather than any actual profit made through investments. Once Madoff's assets were frozen, businesses and charities around the world felt the effects; several foundations were forced to close as a consequence of the fraud.

© AP Images/Kathy Willens

Good ethics will attract investors. Good ethics will attract good employees. You can do what's right. Not because of conduct codes. Not because of rules or laws. But because you know what's right.

Identifying ethical issues in typical workplace situations may be challenging, however, since coworkers and superiors may apply pressure to violate our ethical principles for seemingly logical reasons.

Deal with Pressure to Compromise Your Ethics

Your fundamental morals and values provide the foundation for making ethical decisions. Yet even minor concessions in day-to-day decisions can gradually weaken an individual's ethical foundation.

You can take steps now to prepare for dealing with pressure to compromise personal values:

- **Consider your personal value system.** Only if you have definite beliefs on a variety of issues and the

courage to practice them will you be able to make sound ethical judgments. Putting ethical business practices first will also benefit your employing firm as its reputation for fairness and good judgment retains long-term clients or customers and brings in new ones.

- **Become aware of a tendency to rationalize.** When we are asked to do something that goes against our personal value system but that would allow us to get something we want, we may have a tendency to rationalize that behavior. This tendency may occur outside of our conscious thought processes. When we rationalize, we are acting solely on our emotional needs rather than including our rational, logical abilities to make a decision. The best way to combat a tendency to rationalize unethical actions is to try to step outside of ourselves when making decisions and ask what other people would say or think about such behavior. What would an admired spiritual leader or a respected parental figure say about the behavior on its own standing apart from its benefit to us?

- **Learn to analyze ethical dilemmas.** Knowing how to analyze ethical dilemmas and identify the consequences of your actions will help you make decisions that conform to your own value system. Thus, unless you know what you stand for and how to analyze ethical issues, you become a puppet, controlled by the motives of others and too weak to make a decision on your own.

Causes of Illegal and Unethical Behavior

Understanding the major causes of illegal and unethical behavior in the workplace will help you become sensitive to signals of escalating pressure to compromise your values. All of the causes discussed below might easily put us in the position of rationalizing an unethical activity. Unethical corporate behavior can have a number of causes:

- **Excessive emphasis on profits.** Business managers are often judged and paid on their ability to increase business profits. This emphasis on profits may send a message that the end justifies the means. According to former Federal Reserve chairman Alan Greenspan, "infectious greed" ultimately pushed companies such as Enron, Global Crossing, and WorldCom into bankruptcy.[5]

- **Misplaced corporate loyalty.** A misplaced sense of corporate loyalty may cause an employee to do what seems to be in the best interest of the company, even if the act is illegal or unethical.

- **Obsession with personal advancement.** Employees who wish to outperform their peers or are working for the next promotion may feel that they cannot afford to fail. They may do whatever it takes to achieve the objectives assigned to them.

- **Expectation of not getting caught.** Employees who believe that the end justifies the means often believe that the illegal or unethical activity will never be discovered. Unfortunately, a great deal of improper behavior escapes detection in the business world. Believing no one will ever find out, employees are tempted to lie, steal, and perform other illegal acts.

- **Unethical tone set by top management.** If top managers are not perceived as highly ethical, lower-level managers may be less ethical as a result. Employees have little incentive to act legally and ethically if their superiors do not set an example and encourage and reward such behavior. The phrase "the speed of the leader is the speed of the pack" illustrates the importance of leading by example.

- **Uncertainty about whether an action is wrong.** Many times, company personnel are placed in situations in which the line between right and wrong is not clearly defined. When caught in this gray area, the perplexed employee asks, "How far is too far?"

- **Unwillingness to take a stand for what is right.** Often employees know what is right or wrong but are not willing to take the risk of challenging a wrong action. They may lack the confidence or skill needed to confront others with sensitive legal or ethical issues. They may remain silent and then justify their unwillingness to act.

Framework for Analyzing Ethical Dilemmas

Determining whether an action is ethical can be difficult. Learning to analyze a dilemma from both legal and ethical perspectives will help you find a solution that conforms to your personal values. Figure 1-4 shows the four conclusions you might reach when considering the advisability of a particular behavior.

Figure 1-4 Four Dimensions of Business Behavior

DIMENSION 1 Behavior that is illegal and unethical	**DIMENSION 2** Behavior that is illegal yet ethical
DIMENSION 3 Behavior that is legal yet unethical	**DIMENSION 4** Behavior that is both legal and ethical

© Stockbyte/Getty Images

Dimension 1: Behavior That Is Illegal and Unethical.
When considering some actions, you will reach the conclusion that they are both illegal and unethical. The law specifically outlines the "black" area—those alternatives that are clearly wrong—and your employer will expect you to become an expert in the laws that affect your particular area. When you encounter an unfamiliar area, you must investigate any possible legal implications. Obviously, obeying the law is in the best interest of all concerned: you as an individual, your company, and society. In addition, contractual agreements between the organization and another group provide explicit guidance in selecting an ethically responsible alternative. Frequently, your own individual sense of right and wrong will also confirm that the illegal action is wrong for you personally. In such situations, decisions about appropriate behavior are obvious.

Dimension 2: Behavior That Is Illegal yet Ethical.
Occasionally, a businessperson may decide that even though a specific action is illegal, there is a justifiable reason to break the law. A case in point is a recent law passed in Vermont that makes it illegal for a pharmaceutical company to give any gift valued at $25 or more to doctors or their personnel.[6] Those supporting the law charge that the giving of freebies drives up medical costs by encouraging doctors to prescribe new, more expensive brand-name drugs. The law's opponents contend that the gifts do not influence doctors and are merely educational tools for new products. Although a pharmaceutical firm and its employees may see nothing wrong with providing gifts worth an excess of $25, they would be well advised to consider the penalty of $10,000 per violation before acting on their personal ethics. A better course of action would be to act within the law while possibly lobbying for a change in it.

Dimension 3: Behavior That Is Legal yet Unethical.
If you determine that a behavior is legal and complies with relevant contractual agreements and company policy, your next step is to consult your company or profession's **code of ethics**. This written document summarizes the company or profession's standards of ethical conduct. Some companies refer to this document as a *credo* or *standards of ethical conduct*. If the behavior does not violate the code of ethics, then put it to the test of your own personal integrity. You may at times reject a legal action because it does not "feel right." Most Americans were appalled to learn that many leading figures in recent corporate scandals were never convicted of a single crime. Although they may have acted legally, their profiting at the expense of company employees, stockholders, and the public hardly seemed ethical.

Dimension 4: Behavior That Is Both Legal and Ethical. Decisions in this dimension are easy to make. Such actions comply with the law, company policies, and your professional and personal codes of ethics.

The Pagano model offers a straightforward method for determining whether a proposed action is advisable.[7] For this system to work, you must answer the following six questions honestly:

- Is the proposed action legal—the core starting point?
- What are the benefits and costs to the people involved?
- Would you want this action to be a universal standard, appropriate for everyone?
- Does the action pass the light-of-day test? That is, if your action appeared on television or others learned about it, would you be proud?
- Does the action pass the Golden Rule test? That is, would you want the same to happen to you?
- Does the action pass the ventilation test? Ask the opinion of a wise friend with no investment in the outcome. Does this friend believe the action is ethical?

Diversity Challenges

Diversity in the workplace also influences communication. Differences between the sender and the receiver in areas such as culture, age, gender, and education require sensitivity on the part of both parties so that the intended message is the one that is received.

Understanding how to communicate effectively with people from other cultures has become more integral to the work environment as many U.S. companies are increasingly conducting business with international companies or becoming multinational. Successful communication must often span barriers of language and requires a person to consider differing worldviews resulting from societal, religious, or other cultural factors. When a person fails to consider these factors, communication suffers and the result is often embarrassing and potentially costly.

McDonald's is an example of a large U.S. company that has expanded its operations to include most major countries in the world. To be successful on an international scale, managers had to be aware of cultural differences and be willing to work to ensure that effective communication occurred despite these barriers.

Occasionally, however, a whopper of an intercultural communication faux pas occurs. That is what happened when McDonald's began its promotional campaign in Great Britain for the World Cup soccer championship. It seemed like a clever (and harmless) idea to reproduce the flags of the 24 nations participating in the event and print them on packaging—two million Happy Meal bags to be exact. What marketing personnel failed to consider was that words from the *Koran* are printed on the Saudi flag. The idea that sacred words from Islam's holy book were mass printed to sell a product with the knowledge that the packages would be thrown into the trash angered and offended many Muslims, who immediately complained. McDonald's apologized for the gaffe and agreed to cooperate with the Saudis in finding a solution to the problem.[8]

code of ethics
a written document summarizing the company or profession's standards of ethical conduct

The McDonald's example shows how much "homework" is involved in maintaining good relations with customers or clients from other cultures. The potential barrier of language is obvious; however, successful managers know that much more is involved in communicating with everyone—across cultures, genders, ages, abilities, and other differences.

Communication Opportunities and Challenges in Diversity

As world markets expand, U.S. employees at home and abroad will be doing business with more people from other countries. You may find yourself working abroad for a large American company, an international company with a plant in the United States, or a company with an ethnically diverse workforce. Even in homogeneous environments, you will be working with people of different genders, different ages, and different life experiences that affect their perceptions, values, and communication practices. Consequently, regardless of the workplace, your **diversity skills**—that is, your ability to communicate effectively with both men and women of all ages and with people of other cultures or minority groups—will affect your success in today's culturally diverse, global economy.

Workplace diversity can lead to misunderstandings and miscommunications, but it also poses opportunities to improve both workers and organizations. Managers must be prepared to communicate effectively with workers of different nationalities, genders, races, ages, abilities, and so forth.

Managing a diverse workforce effectively will require you to communicate with *everyone* and to help all employees reach their fullest potential and contribute to the company's goals. To avoid miscommunication, which inevitably occurs, increasing numbers of companies have undertaken *diversity initiatives* and are providing diversity-training seminars to help workers understand and appreciate gender and age differences and the cultures of coworkers.

Culture and Communication

Managers with the *desire* and the *skill* to conduct business in new international markets and manage a diverse workforce effectively will confront problems created by cultural differences. The way messages are decoded and encoded is not just a function of the experiences, beliefs, and assumptions of the person sending or receiving those messages but also are shaped by the society in which he or she lives.

People learn patterns of behavior from their **culture**. The culture of a people is the product of their living experiences within their own society. Culture could be described as "the way of life" of a people and includes a vast array of behaviors and beliefs. These patterns affect how people perceive the world, what they value, and how they act. Differing patterns can also create barriers to communication.

A good deal of research has been done on cultural differences. One of the most recognized studies was conducted by social scientist Geert Hofstede, who defined four dimensions of cultural difference. These dimensions can be useful in understanding and communicating with people from different cultures.

- **Power distance. Power distance** describes the extent to which less powerful people expect and accept the fact that power is unequal within the country or an organization. Hofstede found that people in Malaysia, Panama, the Philippines, and Mexico were most accepting of power distance, while Austrians, Israelis, Danes, New Zealanders, and the Irish were the least accepting of power distance.

- **Individualism versus collectivism.** Individualistic cultures are those that emphasize individual goals and behaviors, while collectivist cultures emphasize group goals and behaviors. In individualist cultures, people are supposed to look out for themselves and their family only, while in collectivist cultures, people belong to groups and collectivities that are supposed to look after them in exchange for their loyalty. The United States, Australia, Great Britain, Canada, and the Netherlands are more individualistic cultures, while Japan, China, Korea, and parts of Latin America are more collectivist in their value orientations.

- **Masculinity versus femininity.** Cultures that are high in masculinity enforce distinctly different roles for men and women, while those that are more feminine allow for the blurring of roles between men and women. Middle Eastern cultures are generally high in masculinity, while the Scandinavian countries allow men and women to share roles and personal characteristics and behaviors.

- **Uncertainty avoidance.** In some cultures, people are more comfortable accepting risk. In the United States, for example, it does not seem unusual for people to

diversity skills
the ability to communicate effectively with both men and women of all ages and with people of other cultures or minority groups

culture
"the way of life" of a people, which includes a vast array of behaviors and beliefs

power distance
the extent to which less powerful people expect and accept the fact that power is unequal within the country or an organization

leave their jobs to start businesses, even though the odds of failure are high. In contrast, people in some countries, such as France, prefer jobs with a lifetime guarantee of employment.

In addition to Hofstede's four dimensions of culture, it is also helpful to view communication as being either low context or high context, depending upon whether the culture is individualistic or collectivist in its value orientation. Individualist cultures tend to be low context in their communication practices, which means that people from those cultures pay less attention to the context of the communication. In other words, they attribute most of the meaning of an interaction to the explicit, transmitted code or the specific words. In contrast, people from collectivist cultures tend to be more high context in their communication practices, which means that they pay a good deal of attention to the surroundings and context of the communication, including nonverbal elements. The United States is a low-context culture, while Japan, China, and Korea are examples of high-context cultures.

Barriers to Intercultural Communication

Because cultures give different definitions to such basics of interaction as values and norms, people raised in two different cultures may clash in various ways. Barriers to intercultural communication include ethnocentrism, stereotypes, chronemics, proxemics, haptics, kinesics, and language.

Ethnocentrism. Problems occur between people of different cultures primarily because people tend to assume that their own cultural norms are the right way to do things. They wrongly believe that the specific patterns of behavior desired in their own cultures are universally valued. This belief, known as ethnocentrism, is certainly natural, but learning about other cultures and developing sensitivity will help minimize ethnocentric reactions when dealing with other cultures.

Stereotypes. We often form a mental picture of the main characteristics of another group, creating preformed ideas of what people in this group are like. These pictures, called **stereotypes**, influence the way we interact with members of the other group. When we observe a behavior that conforms to the stereotype, the validity of the preconceived notion is reinforced. We often view the other person as a representative of a class of people rather than as an individual. People of all cultures have stereotypes about other cultural groups they have encountered. These stereotypes can interfere with communication when people interact on the basis of the imagined representative and not the real individual.

Interpretation of Time. The study of how a culture perceives time and its use is called **chronemics**. In the United States, we have a saying that "time is money." Canadians, like some northern Europeans who are also concerned about punctuality, make appointments, keep them, and do not waste time completing them. In some other cultures, time is the cheapest commodity and an inexhaustible resource; time represents a person's span on earth, which is only part of eternity. To these cultures, long casual conversations prior to serious discussions or negotiations is time well spent in establishing and nurturing relationships. Examples of such cultures can be found in Latin America, Asia, and the Middle East. On the other hand, the time-efficient American businessperson is likely to fret about the waste of precious time.

Personal Space Requirements. Space operates as a language just as time does. The study of cultural space requirements is known as **proxemics**. In all cultures, the distance between people functions in communication as "personal space" or "personal territory." In the United States, for example, for intimate conversations with close friends and relatives, individuals are willing to stay within about a foot and a half of each other; for casual conversations, up to two or three feet; for job interviews and personal business, four to twelve feet; and for public occasions, more than twelve feet. Figure 1-5 illustrates these zones of distance. However, in many cultures outside the United States, closer personal contact is accepted or greater distance may be the norm. Generally speaking, people of the United States tend to need more space than those from Greece, Latin America, or the Middle East, while the Japanese prefer a greater distance than people of the United States in social situations.

Touching. Touch, or **haptics**, communicates a great deal. What is appropriate and people's tendency to touch differ by culture and gender. Sidney Jourard

ethnocentrism
belief that the specific patterns of behavior desired in one's own culture are universally valued

stereotype
a mental picture of the main characteristics of another group, creating preformed ideas of what people in this group are like

chronemics
the study of how a culture perceives time and its use

proxemics
the study of cultural space requirements

haptics
the study of touch

Figure 1-5 Personal Space Requirements

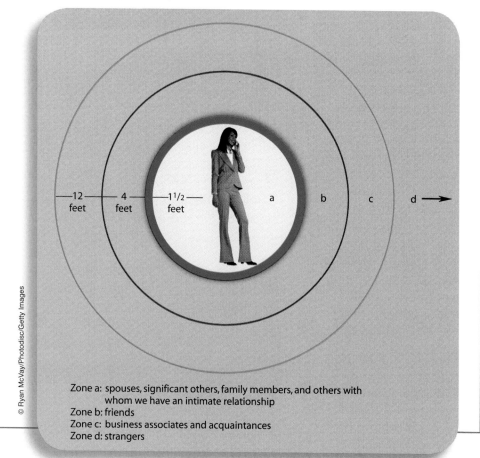

© Ryan McVay/Photodisc/Getty Images

—12—   —4—   —1½—
feet   feet   feet   a   b   c   d →

Zone a: spouses, significant others, family members, and others with
         whom we have an intimate relationship
Zone b: friends
Zone c: business associates and acquaintances
Zone d: strangers

that a translator is working with a second language and must listen to one language, mentally cast the words into another language, and then speak them. This process is difficult and opens the possibility that the translator will fall victim to one or more cultural barriers.

Instead of ignoring cultural factors, employees and employers can improve communication by recognizing them, working to understand them better, and considering people as individuals rather than as members of stereotypical groups.

Commonsense Approach. Minimize the barriers to intercultural communication by applying a few commonsense guidelines.

- **Learn about and experience other cultures.**
  Many sources of information are available, including books, Internet sites, and workshops. But more fun avenues for learning about other cultures exist, such as meeting people from other cultures, getting to know them and their culture, and traveling to other countries and spending time in local communities.

- **Cultivate patience with yourself and with others.** Conversing with someone from another culture, when one of you is likely to be unfamiliar with the language being used, can be difficult and time consuming. By being patient with mistakes, taking your time, and asking and answering questions carefully, you are more likely to communicate effectively. It is also helpful to become comfortable with ambiguity. Being able to respond to new, different, and unpredictable situations with little visible discomfort or irritation can be invaluable.

- **Get help when you need it.** If you are not sure what is being said or why something is being said in a certain way, ask for clarification. If you feel uneasy about communicating with

conducted a study in which he found that adults in Puerto Rico touched 180 times per hour; those in Paris touched about 110 times per hour; those in Gainesville, Florida, touched 2 times per hour; and those in London touched 1 time per hour.

Body Language. The study of body language is known as **kinesics**. Body language is not universal but instead is learned from one's culture. Even the most basic gestures have varying cultural meanings—the familiar North American symbol for "okay" means zero in France, money in Japan, and an expression of vulgarity in Brazil. Similarly, eye contact, posture, and facial expressions carry different meanings throughout the world. In China, for example, people rarely express emotion, while the Japanese may smile to show a variety of emotions, such as happiness, sadness, or even anger.

Translation Limitations. Words in one language do not always have an equivalent meaning in other languages, and the concepts the words describe are often different as well. Translators can be helpful, but keep in mind

kinesics
the study of body language

someone from another culture, bring along someone you trust who understands that culture.

Team Environment

A team-oriented approach is replacing the traditional top-down management style in some of today's organizations. Firms around the world are facing problems in decreasing productivity, faltering product quality, and worker dissatisfaction. Work teams are being examined as a way to help firms remain globally competitive. Although worker involvement in the management process has long been the hallmark of Japanese business, many U.S. businesses as well as those of other countries are experimenting with self-directed work teams.[9] The list of companies using self-directed work teams is diverse, including such firms as Hunt-Wesson, the Internal Revenue Service, and the San Diego Zoo. Other companies using the team concept include Hewlett-Packard, Southwest Airlines, Toyota, Motorola, General Electric, and Corning.

Work Team Defined

The terms *team, work team, group, work group, cross-functional team,* and *self-directed team* are often used interchangeably.[10] Whatever the title, a **team** is a small group of people with complementary skills who work together for a common purpose. Team members set their own goals in cooperation with management and plan how to achieve those goals and how their work is to be accomplished. The central organizing element of a team is that it has a common purpose and measurable goals for which the team can be held accountable, independent of its individual members. Employees in a self-directed work team handle a wide array of functions and work with a minimum of direct supervision.[11]

A key element in team success is the concept of *synergy,* defined as a situation in which the whole is greater than the sum of the parts. Teams provide a depth of expertise that is unavailable at the individual level. Teams open lines of communication that then lead to increased interaction among employees and between employees and management. The result is that teams help companies reach their goals of delivering higher-quality products and services faster and with more cost-effectiveness.

Communication Differences in Work Teams

In the past, most businesses were operated in a hierar-

team
a small group of people with complementary skills who work together for a common purpose

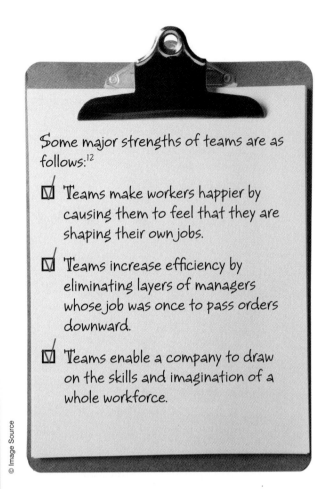

Some major strengths of teams are as follows:[12]

☑ Teams make workers happier by causing them to feel that they are shaping their own jobs.

☑ Teams increase efficiency by eliminating layers of managers whose job was once to pass orders downward.

☑ Teams enable a company to draw on the skills and imagination of a whole workforce.

© Image Source

chical fashion, with most decisions made at the top and communication following a top-down pattern. Communication patterns are different in successful team environments as compared to traditional organizational structures:

- Trust building is the primary factor that changes the organization's communication patterns.
- Open meetings are an important method for enhancing communication as they educate employees about the business while building bridges of understanding and trust.
- Shared leadership, which involves more direct and effective communication between management and its internal customers, is common.
- Listening, problem solving, conflict resolution, negotiation, and consensus become important factors in group communication.
- Information flows vertically up to management and down to workers as well as horizontally among team members, other teams, and supervisors.

Communication is perhaps the single most important aspect of successful teamwork. Open lines of communication increase interaction between employees and management. All affected parties should be kept informed as projects progress.

Maximization of Work Team Effectiveness

Grouping employees into a team structure does not mean that they will automatically function as a team. A group must go through a developmental process to begin to function as a team. Members need training in such areas as problem solving, goal setting, and conflict resolution. Teams must be encouraged to establish the "three R's"—roles, rules, and relationships.[13]

The self-directed work team can become the basic organizational building block to best ensure success in dynamic global competition. Skills for successful participation in team environments are somewhat different from those necessary for success in old-style organizations:

- The ability to give and take constructive criticism, listen actively, clearly impart one's views to others, and provide meaningful feedback are important to the success of work teams.
- Emotional barriers, such as insecurity or condescension, can limit team effectiveness.
- Process barriers, such as rigid policies and procedures, can also interfere by stifling effective team functioning.
- Cultural barriers, such as stereotyped roles and responsibilities, can separate workers from management and each other.[14] Understanding of the feelings and needs of coworkers is needed so that members feel comfortable stating their opinions and discussing the strengths and weaknesses of the team.
- The emergence of leadership skills that apply to a dynamic group setting lead to team success. In the dynamic team leadership, referred to as **distributed leadership**, the role of leader may alternate among members, and more than one leadership style may be active at any given time.[15]

Gender, cultural, and age differences among members of a team can present barriers to team communication. Knowing what behaviors may limit the group process is imperative to maximizing results. Team members may need awareness training to assist in recognizing behaviors that may hinder team performance and in overcoming barriers that may limit the effectiveness of their communication.

Changing Technology

Electronic tools have not eliminated the need for basic communication skills; they can, in fact, create new obstacles or barriers

distributed leadership
when the role of leader alternates among members, and more than one leadership style may be active at any given time

To improve group communication, time needs to be set aside to assess the quality of interaction. Questions to pose about the group process might include the following:

What are our common goals?

Is the group dealing with conflict in a positive way?

What in the group process is going well?

What about the group process could be improved?

What roles are members playing? Is one person dominating while others contribute little or nothing?

© Rachel Epstein/PhotoEdit

to communication that must be overcome. These tools, however, also create opportunities, which range from the kinds of communications that are possible to the quality of the messages themselves. Using various communication technologies, individuals can often work in their homes and send and receive work from the office electronically. *Telecommuting* offers various advantages, including reduced travel time and increased work flexibility. Laptops and PDAs provide computing power for professionals wherever they may be—in cars, hotel rooms, airports, or clients' offices.

Electronic tools can help people in various ways, such as (1) collecting and analyzing data, (2) shaping messages to be clearer and more effective, and (3) communicating quickly and efficiently with others over long distances.

Tools for Data Collection and Analysis

Knowing how to collect information from the Internet and communicate in a networked world is critical. Generally, electronic communication provides researchers with two distinct advantages: time savings and greater quantity of information. Researchers can then develop better solutions to problems faster. There are three types of electronic networks:

1. **Internet.** The vast "network of networks" links computers throughout the world. Information in the form of text, images, audio, and video is quickly available and easily searchable.

2. **Intranets.** Password-protected resources available via the Internet allow companies to post information and resources for employees.

3. **Extranets.** Protected information and resources on the company's website are made available to customers, partners, or others with need to know.

Data are collected for a purpose, so the ability to find information quickly and easily is essential to organizational and personal success. Whereas the public Internet is accessible to everyone and offers a wide array of information, private databases provide specialized and advanced information on specific topics. The specialized functions of databases allow businesspeople to analyze information quickly and in myriad ways so that they can make the best possible decisions.

Internal databases contain proprietary information that is pertinent to the particular business or organization and its employees. External databases (networks) allow users to access information from remote locations literally around the world and in an instant transfer that information to their own computers for further

manipulation or storage. Information is available on general news, stocks, financial markets, sports, travel, weather, and a variety of publications.

Advantages of Databases

- **Data organization**—the ability to organize large amounts of data.
- **Data integrity**—assurance that the data will be accurate and complete.
- **Data security**—assurance that the data are secure because access to a database is controlled through several built-in data security features.

Tools for Shaping Messages to Be Clearer

Documents that took days to produce during the b.c. (before computers) era can now be created in hours and with a wide array of creative elements. These include document production software, electronic presentation tools, web publishing tools, and collaborative software.

Document Production Software. Document production software provides a number of benefits, including the following:

- Production of documents is expedited by the ability to save, retrieve, and edit.
- Quality of messages is improved through spell-check, thesaurus, writing analysis software, and print features.
- Report preparation is simplified by automatic generation of contents page, indexes, and documentation references.
- The mail merge feature allows for personalization of form letters. Typography and design elements can be used to create persuasive, professional communications.

Electronic Presentation Tools. Electronic presentation software provides a number of benefits, including the following:

- Multimedia presentations can include visuals that combine text, images, animation, sound, and video.
- Quality royalty-free multimedia content is available from third-party sources.
- Images can be scanned or captured with digital cameras and recorders or generated using specialized software.
- Interactive whiteboards give speakers direct control over computer applications from the board, facilitate interaction using electronic ink to annotate visuals or record brainstorming ideas, and record annotated files for electronic distribution or later use.

Legal and Ethical Implications of Technology

In addition to its many benefits, technology poses some challenges for the business communicator. For instance, technology raises issues of ownership, as in the case of difficulties that arise in protecting the copyright of documents transmitted over the Internet. Technology poses dilemmas over access—that is, who has the right to certain stored information pertaining to an individual or a company.

Technology threatens our individual privacy, our right to be left alone free from surveillance or interference from other individuals or organizations. Common invasions of privacy caused by technology include:

- Collecting excessive amounts of information for decision making and maintaining too many files.

- Monitoring the exact time employees spend on a specific task and between tasks, and the exact number and length of breaks, and supervisors' or coworkers' reading of another employee's email and computer files.

- Integrating computer files containing information collected from more than one agency without permission.[16]

Web Publishing Tools. Web publishing tools provide a number of benefits, including the following:

- Pages can be created without need for extensive knowledge of hypertext markup language, or HTML.

- Hyperlinks to other documents and websites can be included in the design.

- Formatted web pages may be viewed using a variety of web browsers.

- Weblogs (blogs) are websites that are updated on a frequent basis with new information about a particular subject(s). Information can be written by the site owner, gleaned from other websites or other sources, or contributed by users.

Collaborative Software. Collaborative software provide a number of benefits, including the following:

- Groups can write collaboratively, with each author marking revisions and inserting document comments for distribution to all coauthors.

- Some collaborative software programs allow multiple authors to work on documents at the same time.

- When placed on an electronic whiteboard, drawings or information written on its surface can be displayed simultaneously on team members' computer screens.

Tools for Communicating Remotely

Technology networks have placed the world at our fingertips. To exploit the possibilities, whole new media for communication have emerged. These include smartphones, email, instant messaging, electronic conferences, Voice over Internet Protocol (VoIP), and social networking sites. Most of these technologies are probably quite familiar to you since they not only are used in business but also are popular as a personal means of communication. The one exception may be electronic conferences, which are primarily used in the business arena. Teleconferencing and videoconferencing are cost-efficient alternatives to face-to-face meetings for people in different locations. Using collaborative software with web camera technology, users can see each other. This technology thus restores the nonverbal elements lost with telephone, email, and instant messaging.

Focusing on Interpersonal Communication

Foundations

nterpersonal communication is the foundation of all successful communication with others in face-to-face situations and some mediated forms of communication, such as with telephones. Interpersonal communication begins with our own self-concept and our attitudes toward others. These, in turn, affect our style of communication with others and our ability to influence them, which is an important role of interpersonal communication in the workplace. Because the majority of the message in many interpersonal communication situations is communicated via nonverbal signals, it is also important to develop an awareness of our nonverbal communication behaviors and align them with our verbal message to reduce confusion. Finally, effective listening practices also affect our ability to communicate interpersonally and are another important area of skill development. Remember, you will spend most of your time in the workplace listening to others.

objective ①
Explain how the foundational element of intrapersonal communication is an understanding of ourselves.

Communication and the Self

Because of the increased interdependency of people around the world and the diversity in the workplace, successful communication requires recognition of the contested nature of reality and our interpretation of it. It thus requires openness to others' views and opinions if we are to communicate effectively. This required openness creates some challenges. It requires recognition that because of the contested nature of reality, reaching understanding may take more time and effort.

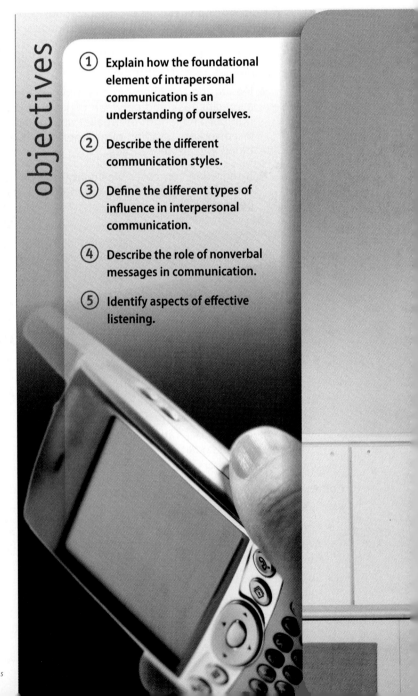

objectives

1. Explain how the foundational element of intrapersonal communication is an understanding of ourselves.

2. Describe the different communication styles.

3. Define the different types of influence in interpersonal communication.

4. Describe the role of nonverbal messages in communication.

5. Identify aspects of effective listening.

It requires recognition that others' views and perceptions may be as valid as our own. Finally, and perhaps most challenging, is the need to be open to the views and perceptions of others. This situation may be challenging because in these cases our personal identities (how we believe ourselves to be) may be threatened.

Interpersonal communication thus begins with our own **self-concept**. *Self-concept* is our subjective description of who we think we are. Our self-concept is developed in two ways: by communicating with ourself and by communicating with others. That is, we develop our self-concept by reflecting on our thoughts and actions to understand what motivates those thoughts and ac-

tions. We also learn about ourselves by observing how others respond to us.

For young people, much of their self-concept may be based on the responses and expectations of others, particularly parents and later on, peers. The more you learn about yourself, the better you will understand how and why you communicate with others. Self-understanding allows us a more realistic view of ourselves that includes both our strengths and weaknesses; we need to be able to feel good about who we are despite that knowledge—or perhaps because of it. Our professional

self-concept
our subjective description of who we think we are

© David Oliver/Taxi/Getty Images

success depends so much upon relationships with others and their perceptions of us, so we must also be knowledgeable about how others perceive us.

The second part of self-concept is **self-esteem**, or how you feel about yourself—how well you like and value yourself. Perception and communication are both affected by self-esteem. People with high self-esteem tend to view others who are motivated as bright people and those who are not motivated as less bright.[1] People with low self-esteem do not make this distinction. In the contemporary business world, high levels of self-awareness and self-esteem may help us be more open to the opinions and perspectives of others. Without high levels of self-awareness and self-esteem, we may feel threatened when we meet others who are different from ourselves, and that feeling may get in the way of our ability to be open to listening to them and considering their perspectives and opinions. A high level of self-esteem is also important because we must be willing to admit that perhaps we don't know everything; we always have opportunities to learn. To engage in dialogue, we must be able to take "the stance that there is something that I don't already know,"[2] and engage with others "with a mutual *openness* to learn."[3]

As has been discussed, how you view yourself can make a great difference in your ability to communicate and achieve your purposes. Many scholars believe that communication forms our self-concept. In other words, people are the products of how others treat them and of the messages others send them. That is, individuals "construct" themselves through the relationships they have, wish to have, or perceive themselves as having.[4] We can count six persons in every two-person communication.[5] These six persons emerge from:

- How you view yourself.
- How you view the other person.
- How you believe the other person views you.
- How the other person views himself or herself.
- How the other person views you.
- How the other person believes you view him or her.

Through the interactions of these six persons, you can see the relational nature of communication and the centrality of the self and our perception of the self in communication. From this model comes the notion of the **self-fulfilling prophecy**, or the idea that you behave and see yourself in ways that are consistent with how others see you.[6]

Another term that refers to the way you think about yourself is *self-awareness*, which is an understanding of the self, including your attitudes, values, beliefs, strengths, and weaknesses.[7] As the six-person model indicates, self-awareness develops through our communication with ourself as well as our interaction with others. Communication with ourselves is called **intrapersonal communication**, which includes "our perceptions, memories, experiences, feelings, interpretations, inferences, evaluations, attitudes, opinions, ideas, strategies, images, and states of consciousness."[8] A related concept is **intrapersonal intelligence**, or the capacity to form an accurate model of one's self and to be able to use that model to operate effectively in life.[9]

Self-awareness is important for communication because it can affect how well we communicate with others and how we are perceived by others. Intrapersonal intelligence is a correlative ability to **interpersonal intelligence**, which is the ability to understand other people, such as what motivates them, how they work, and how

- How you view yourself.
- How you view the other person.
- How you believe the other person views you.

© Inspirestock/Jupiterimages

self-esteem
how you feel about yourself—how well you like and value yourself
self-fulfilling prophecy
the idea that you behave and see yourself in ways that are consistent with how others see you
intrapersonal communication
includes "our perceptions, memories, experiences, feelings, interpretations, inferences, evaluations, attitudes, opinions, ideas, strategies, images, and states of consciousness"
intrapersonal intelligence
the capacity to form an accurate model of one's self and to be able to use that model to operate effectively in life
interpersonal intelligence
the ability to understand other people, such as what motivates them, how they work, and how to work cooperatively with them

to work cooperatively with them.[10] So, we must have self-awareness in order to be able to understand others.

For example, if our self-concept does not match the perception that others have of us, we may misinterpret their responses to our messages. We may also misinterpret the way that our communication is interpreted by others. For instance, we may believe that we are highly reliable; however, others may believe the opposite about us. These contradictions can negatively impact our ability to work with others and in groups. If we are unaware of these contradictions, then we are unable to change our communicative behaviors, both verbal and nonverbal, to better correspond with the message we want to send about ourselves. People are more likely to believe nonverbal cues, so it is important that the messages we send through our actions correspond to those we send verbally and in writing.

Understanding subtle verbal and nonverbal cues is indicative of **emotional intelligence**, which is an assortment of noncognitive skills, capabilities, and competencies that influence a person's ability to successfully cope with environmental demands and pressures.

Not all researchers believe emotional intelligence can be measured scientifically. However, as a construct, it can be useful in thinking about the importance of our relationships with others as well as our credibility in effective business communication. In fact, many organizations now test employees' level of emotional intelligence for hiring and promotion.

For example, having the ability to manage and control our emotions can contribute to the creation of a credible and professional image and support successful relationships. Emotional control or the ability to delay gratification and resist impulses can greatly affect our career success and ability to communicate with others. Studies have shown that those who are able to resist temptation as small children were more socially competent as adolescents.[11] They were more personally effective, self-assertive, and better able to cope with life's frustrations. They were less likely to be negatively affected by stress or to become disorganized when pressured; they embraced challenges, were self-reliant and confident, trustworthy and dependable, and took initiative. More than a decade later, they were still able to delay gratification. Those who were less able to delay gratification were more likely to shy away from social contacts, to be stubborn and indecisive, to be easily upset by frustrations, to think of themselves as unworthy, to become immobilized by stress, to be mistrustful and resentful about not getting enough, to be prone to jealousy and envy, and to overreact to irritations with a sharp temper, thus provoking arguments.

Additional factors affect our ability to forge the relationships businesspeople depend upon so much: valuing relationships, assertiveness, and active listening.[12] The first

emotional intelligence
an assortment of noncognitive skills, capabilities, and competencies that influence a person's ability to successfully cope with environmental demands and pressures

- How the other person views himself or herself.
- How the other person views you.
- How the other person believes you view him or her.

The **5** Dimensions of Emotional Intelligence:

1. **Self-awareness.** The ability to be aware of what you are feeling.

2. **Self-management.** The ability to manage one's emotions and impulses.

3. **Self-motivation.** The ability to persist in the face of setbacks and failures.

4. **Empathy.** The ability to sense how others are feeling.

5. **Social skills.** The ability to handle the emotions of others.

© Jasper James/Stone+/Getty Images

step in building interpersonal relationships at work is learning to *recognize the importance of relationships* in business (if you haven't already). For many individuals, interpersonal communication is the work, particularly among managers.

Impression Management

Impression management is the control (or lack of control) of communication information through performance. In impression management, people try to present an "idealized" version of themselves in order to reach desired ends.

All of us attempt to manage our impression to varying degrees in various situations. For example, when you are with your friends, you probably try to dress like them and act like them so as to be seen as part of the group. When you go out on a date, you are likely to be on your "best behavior" to reduce the risk of doing or saying something that may not be viewed as attractive by your date. In small group situations, you might often hold back during the forming stage of the group process for the same reason.

High self-monitors are those individuals who are highly aware of their impression management behavior.[13] By contrast, **low self-monitors** communicate with others with little attention to the responses to their messages. They have little idea about how others perceive them and

know even less about how to interact appropriately with others.

Impression management is one aspect of a natural and productive process called **anticipatory socialization**. Anticipatory socialization is the process through which most of us develop a set of expectations and beliefs concerning how people communicate in particular occupations and in formal and informal work settings.[14] The business communication course you are now enrolled in as well as some of the other university courses you are now taking are part of that process. If you are involved in internships or other job-related activities, these also contribute to that process. In fact, learning how to work in a position probably begins in early childhood.

For that reason, anticipatory socialization is also a part of our self-concept. Most discussions of anticipatory socialization recognize that as people mature, they use the information they gather about jobs from their environment to compare against their self-concept. This comparison helps them to make judgments about choosing occupations and specific jobs.[15] This process may be likened to a self-inventory to determine career opportunities that best match an individual's skills and attitudes.

Some people believe that impression management is unethical or deceptive. However, it is to varying degrees a normal social process that can help others and ourselves save face or embarrassment. When we act in ways that are appropriate to the situation, we are respecting the expectations of others. In these cases, impression management is a matter of politeness. Like many matters of communication, the ethics of impression management comes down to intent and to degree. If we change our behaviors and presentation style in an attempt to deceive or mislead others, then such actions can be judged as unethical. At the least, we may be seen as superficial, pretentious, inauthentic, lacking integrity, or a "suck-up."

Communication Styles or Modes

Our self-concept, self-esteem, and self-awareness affect how we communicate with others. One dimension of the self that is particularly relevant to our interactions with others is our communication style. Styles or modes of communication can be separated into three types: avoiding, aggressive, and assertive.

objective ②
Describe the different communication styles.

---

impression management
the control (or lack of control) of communication information through performance

high self-monitors
individuals who are highly aware of their impression management behavior

low self-monitors
individuals who communicate with others with little attention to the responses to their messages

anticipatory socialization
the process through which most of us develop a set of expectations and beliefs concerning how people communicate in particular occupations and in formal and informal work settings

6 Steps to Communicating Assertively

1. **Describe how you view the situation.** When being assertive, it may be necessary to describe how you view the situation, since the other person may not be sensitive to your needs or concerns. To communicate assertively, it is important to monitor nonverbal elements, particularly your voice. You should avoid negative emotions, such as sarcasm or frustration. You should then describe the situation from your perspective. "I have noticed that you have missed two of our group meetings."

2. **Disclose your feelings.** After you inform the other person of your perspective, you should let him or her know how this situation makes you feel. As a follow-up to the previous example, you might state, "I feel that you don't take our meetings seriously." The purpose of disclosing your feelings is to help build empathy to avoid lengthy arguments.

3. **Identify effects.** The next step is to describe the effects of the person's behavior on you and others. "When you miss meetings, it affects the quality of our group process since we don't get your input and ideas."

4. **Wait for a response.** Be silent so that the other person may respond to your statement. During this time, monitor your nonverbal behavior so that your facial expressions do not contradict your verbal message.

5. **Paraphrase the other's response.** After the other person responds, paraphrase the other's statement, paying attention to both content and feeling. For example, the other person might have responded, "I'm sorry. I am just very busy right now with several group projects, and it is difficult for me to make time for all the meetings." Your response might be, "So the key problem is time conflicts with your other commitments. It can be stressful to manage too many projects."

6. **Ask for or suggest a solution.** Depending on the responsiveness of the other person, you should, at some point, ask for or suggest a solution to the problem. Asking the other person for a solution is generally a better approach, since he or she will be more likely to comply with an idea that is his or hers. In some cases, though, you may need to be prepared to suggest a solution. A solution should be sensitive to your own needs and those of the other person to improve the chances that it will be accepted.

The avoiding, passive-aggressive individual whines, complains, and frets about problems at work but when asked directly what is wrong says nothing.[16] This strategy, known as **avoidance**, is defined as a conscious attempt to avoid engaging with people in the dominant group.[17] Avoidance is considered *passive*, which is an attempt to separate by having as little to do as possible with the dominant group. The result of an avoiding, passive approach is a consistent inability to raise and resolve problems, needs, issues, and concerns.

At the other extreme, aggressive individuals sabotage their ability to meet their needs and to establish supportive relationships by creating defensiveness and alienating others.[18] Aggressive behaviors include those perceived as hurtfully expressive, self-promoting, and assuming control over the choices of others.[19] Aggressive individuals are also described as argumentative. Not only are such individuals more aggressive, they are more insecure and less likely to be well regarded or happy at work.[20]

In contrast to avoidance and aggression, **assertiveness** is defined as "self-enhancing, expressive communication that takes into account both self and others' needs."[21] Assertiveness involves clearly articulating what you want from others in terms of behavior. It is direct yet nonattacking or blaming. The second component of

avoidance
a conscious attempt to avoid engaging with people in the dominant group

assertiveness
"self-enhancing, expressive communication that takes into account both self and others' needs"

assertiveness is what is called *responsiveness,* or the tendency to be sensitive to the needs of others. Assertiveness is associated with positive impressions and overall quality of work experience.

In some cases, the other person may not be responsive and may be evasive or even aggressive. In these cases, you should repeat the steps, clearly describing the situation, your feelings, and the effects, then waiting for an appropriate response.

Like assertiveness, *listening* is a learned skill and one that very few individuals ever master. Talking to someone who really knows how to listen actively makes you feel valued, important, and free to speak your mind.[22] (Active listening is discussed in more detail below.) In an ideal communication situation, assertiveness and active listening go hand in hand as people are able to express their own perceptions and desires and, at the same time, attend to the perceptions and desires of others.

Interpersonal Influence

n interpersonal and small group communication situations, influencing others is often the goal of communication. **Influence** is the power that a person has to affect other people's thinking or actions.[23]

In the area of interpersonal influence, one area of research focuses on compliance-gaining and compliance-resisting behaviors. **Compliance-gaining** involves attempts made by a communicator to influence another to "perform some desired behavior that the [other person] otherwise might not perform."[24] Compliance-gaining occurs whenever we ask someone to do something for us. For example, we may ask our supervisor to give us a raise or promotion or a coworker to switch days off with us. Research into compliance-gaining shows that its success also often involves a series of attempts.

Studies show that people generally prefer socially acceptable, reward-oriented strategies when attempting to gain compliance.[25] In other words, people are more apt to be influenced if they are offered some kind of reward or benefit for doing so. Conversely, people do not respond well to negative, threatening, or punishing strategies to gain compliance. Compliance-gaining behaviors that rely upon coercion and threats can be seen as abuses of power rather than the ethical pursuit of influence. Studies indicate that as more resistance is encountered, compliance-gaining efforts generally move from positive tactics to more negative ones.

Compliance-resisting is the refusal to comply with influence attempts.[26] When resisting requests, people tend to offer reasons or evidence to support their refusal.[27] People who are more sensitive to others and who are more adaptive are more likely to engage in further attempts to influence.[28] They may address some of the obstacles they expect when they initiate their request and adapt later attempts to influence by offering counterarguments.

For example, if you are preparing to ask your supervisor for a raise, you might consider some of the reasons he or she might refuse. Your supervisor might respond by saying money isn't available, you don't deserve a raise compared to your peers' contributions, or you have not performed in such a manner as to deserve a raise. In such a case, a person who is adaptive and sensitive to his or her audience's needs and concerns will respond with information or evidence intended to counter these claims.

Those who use communication to achieve influence or control over another have what is called **interpersonal dominance.**[29] Even though dominance is often viewed negatively, especially when the objective is to control others, it may include positive qualities that include aspects of social competence.

There are four dimensions of interpersonal dominance. *Persuasiveness* and *poise* refer to a person's ability to act influentially and to behave with dignity. *Conversational control* and *panache* refer to the individual's presence and expressiveness. *Task focus* refers to an individual's ability to remain focused on the task at hand, and *self-assurance* refers to a person's level of confidence and ability to avoid either arrogance or timidity.

Because of recent changes in the workplace, such as the team environment discussed in Chapter 1, influence is becoming more important in building relationships. That's because positional authority is no longer sufficient to get the job done, so as a businessperson, you'll need to develop a web of influence, or a balanced web of relationships, that includes people in several different interest groups—superiors, peers, and outsiders as well as subordinates.[30]

Just as managers must learn how to foster and orchestrate relationships between people, often through

objective ③
Define the different types of influence in interpersonal communication.

influence
the power that a person has to affect other people's thinking or actions
compliance-gaining
attempts made by a communicator to influence another to "perform some desired behavior that the [other person] otherwise might not perform"
compliance-resisting
refusal to comply with influence attempts
interpersonal dominance
the achievement of influence or control over another via communication

the process of influence, so must subordinates. **Rational explanation** is the most frequently used type of influence that subordinates use on superiors.[31] Rational explanation includes some sort of formal presentation, analysis, or proposal. A host of other tactics, such as arguing without support, using persistence and repetition, threatening, and manipulation were not found to be effective. In fact, one team of researchers found that subordinates who used these tactics usually failed miserably.[32] Nevertheless, no one influence tactic will be best in all situations; instead, the subordinate must learn to tailor his or her approach to the audience he or she is attempting to influence and the objective that is sought.[33]

Similarly, the primary skill individuals must cultivate in managing their boss is **advocacy**—the process of championing ideas, proposals, actions, or people to those above them in the organization.[34] Advocacy requires learning how to read your superior's needs and preferences and designing persuasive arguments that are most likely to accomplish your goals.

Nonverbal Communication

objective ④
Describe the role of nonverbal messages in communication.

Managers use verbal and nonverbal messages to communicate an idea to a recipient. *Verbal* means "through the use of words," either written or spoken. *Nonverbal* means "without the use of words." Although major attention in communication study is given to verbal messages, studies show that nonverbal messages can account for over 90 percent of the total meaning.[35] Nonverbal communication includes *metacommunication* and *kinesic* messages.

Metacommunication

A **metacommunication** is a message that, although *not* expressed in words, accompanies a message that *is* expressed in words. For example, "Don't be late

for work" communicates caution; yet the sentence may imply (but not express in words) such additional ideas as "You are frequently late, and I'm warning you" or "I doubt your dependability" (metacommunication). "Your solution is perfect" may also convey a metacommunication, such as "You are efficient" or "I certainly like your work." Whether you are speaking or writing, you can be confident that those who receive your messages will be sensitive to the messages expressed in words and to the accompanying messages that are present but not expressed in words.

Kinesic Messages

People constantly send meaning through kinesic communication, an idea expressed through nonverbal behavior. In other words, receivers gain additional meaning from what they see and hear—the visual and the vocal:

- **Visual**—gestures, winks, smiles, frowns, sighs, attire, grooming, and all kinds of body movements.

- **Vocal**—intonation, projection, and resonance of the voice.

On the next page, Table 2-1 gives possible kinesic messages for a range of actions.

rational explanation
a type of influence that includes some sort of formal presentation, analysis, or proposal
advocacy
the process of championing ideas, proposals, actions, or people to those above them in the organization
metacommunication
a message that, although not expressed in words, accompanies a message that is expressed in words

6 Steps to Successful Advocacy

1. **Plan.** Think through a strategy that will work.
2. **Determine why your boss should care.** Connect your argument to something that matters to your boss, such as a key objective or personal value.
3. **Tailor your argument to the boss's style and characteristics.** Adapt your evidence and appeal to those things that are persuasive to your boss, not those things that are persuasive to you.
4. **Assess prior technical knowledge.** Do not assume too much about your boss's level of knowledge and vocabulary or jargon.
5. **Build coalitions.** Your arguments need the support of others in the organization.
6. **Hone your communication skills.** An articulate, well-prepared message is critical to build your credibility with your boss.

© Ryan McVay/Photodisc/Getty Images

Table 2-1 *Interpreting Kinesics*

Action	Possible Kinesic Message
A wink or light chuckle follows a statement.	*"Don't believe what I just said."*
A manager is habitually late for staff meetings.	*"My time is more important than yours. You can wait for me." Alternately, the action may be ordinary for a non-U.S.-born manager.*
A supervisor lightly links his arm around an employee's shoulders at the end of a formal disciplinary conference.	*"Everything is fine; I'm here to help you solve this problem." Alternately, the action may be sexually motivated or paternalistic—comforting a child after necessary discipline.*
A job applicant submits a résumé containing numerous errors.	*"My language skills are deficient." Alternately, "I didn't care to do my best."*
The supervisor looks up but then returns his or her attention to a current project when an employee arrives for a performance appraisal interview.	*"The performance appraisal interview is not an important process. You are interrupting more important work."*
A group leader sits at a position other than at the head of the table.	*"I want to demonstrate my equality with other members."*
An employee's clothing does not comply with the company's dress code.	*"Rules are for other people; I can do what I want." Alternately, "I do not understand the expectations."*
A manager hesitates when asked to justify a new rule for employees.	*"I don't have a good reason." Alternately, "I want to think this through to be sure I give an understandable answer."*

Understanding Nonverbal Messages

Metacommunications and kinesic communication have characteristics that all communicators should take into account. Nonverbal messages:

- **Cannot be avoided.** Both written and spoken words convey ideas in addition to the ideas contained in the words used. All actions—and even the lack of action—have meaning to those who observe them.

- **May have different meanings for different people.** If a team member smiles after making a statement, one member may conclude that the speaker was trying to be funny, another may conclude that the speaker was pleased about having made such a great contribution, and another may see the smile as indicating friendliness.

- **Vary between and within cultures.** Not only do nonverbal messages have different meanings from culture to culture, but men and women from the same culture typically exhibit different body language. As a rule, U.S. men make less body contact with other men than do women with women. Acceptable male body language might include a handshake or a pat on the back, while women are afforded more flexibility in making body contact with each other.

- **May be intentional or unintentional.** "You are right about that" may be intended to mean "I agree with you" or "You are right on *this* issue, but you have been wrong on all others discussed." The sender may or may not intend to convey the latter and may or may not be aware of doing so.

- **Can contradict the accompanying verbal message and affect whether your message is understood or believed.** If the verbal and nonverbal messages contradict each other, which do you suppose the receiver will believe? The old adage "Actions speak louder than words" provides the answer. Picture a person who says "I'm happy to be here" but looks at the floor, talks in a weak and halting voice, and clasps his hands together in front of his body in an inhibited "fig leaf" posture. Because his verbal and nonverbal messages are contradictory, his audience may not trust his words. Similarly, consider the negative effect of a sloppy personal appearance by a job candidate.

- **May receive more attention than verbal messages.** If a supervisor rhythmically taps a pen while making a statement, the words may not register in the employee's mind. An error in basic grammar may receive more attention than the idea that is being transmitted.

- **Provide clues about the sender's background and motives.** For example, excessive use of big words may suggest that a person reads widely or has an above-average education; it may also suggest a need for social recognition or insecurity about social background.

- **Are influenced by the circumstances surrounding the communication.** Assume that two men, Ganesh and Sam, are friends who work for the same firm. When they are together on the job, Ganesh sometimes puts his hand on Sam's shoulder. To Sam, the act may mean nothing more than "We are close friends." But suppose Ganesh is a member of a committee that subsequently denies a promotion for Sam. Afterward, the same act could mean "We are still friends," but it could also arouse resentment. Because of the circumstances, the same act could now mean something like "Watch the hand that pats; it can also stab."

- **May be beneficial or harmful.** Words or actions can be accompanied by nonverbal messages that help or hurt the sender's purpose. Metacommunications and kinesic communications can convey something like "I am efficient in my business and considerate of others," or they can convey the opposite. They cannot be eliminated, but they can be made to work for communicators instead of against them.

- **May vary depending upon the person's gender.** Gender is a social construction. This means that men and women learn the behaviors that correspond to their gender from their culture. Just as with other cultural differences, nonverbal messages and their meaning may vary depending upon the person's gender.

Let's look more closely at the challenges of understanding the nonverbal signals of people of differing cultures and genders.

Nonverbal Communication and Culture

Numerous research studies point out the importance of nonverbal communication in international negotiations. A 15-year study of negotiation styles in 17 cultures revealed that Japanese negotiators behaved least aggressively, typically using a polite conversation style with infrequent use of "no" and "you" as well as more silent periods. The style of French negotiators was most aggressive, including more threats and warnings as well as interruptions, facial gazing, and frequent use of "no" and "you." Brazilians were similarly aggressive, with more physical touching of their negotiating partners. Germans, the British, and Americans fell somewhat in the middle.

Removing words from a negotiation might at times give the process additional strength by avoiding many of the problems raised by verbal communication in a multicultural context. The negotiation process is the sum of such factors as the number of parties, existence of external audiences, issues to be discussed, deadlines, laws, ethics, customs, physical setting, and so on. The emphasis on nonverbal cues is often lost on American negotiators who rely on the inherent advantage provided by their mastery of global languages. Cultural awareness includes both education and sensitivity concerning behaviors, expectations, and interpretations of persons with different backgrounds and experiences.[36]

Some examples of the differences in nonverbal behavior associated with different cultures include the following:

- The Japanese greet with a respectful bow rather than the traditional handshake. Middle Easterners may exchange kisses on the cheek as the preferred form of greeting.

South America, not okay

United States, okay

Other places, better check first

- While North Americans believe that eye contact is an indicator of interest and trust, the Japanese believe that lowering the eyes is a sign of respect. Asian females and many African Americans listen without direct eye contact. Extended facial gazing is typified by the French and Brazilians but often seen by Americans as aggressive.

- The time-conscious North American can expect to be kept waiting for an appointment in Central America, the Middle East, and other countries where the North American sentiment "time is money" is not accepted.

- North Americans, who often slap each other on the back or put an arm around the other as a sign of friendship, receive disapproval from the Japanese, who avoid physical contact. Japanese shopkeepers place change on a plastic plate to avoid physical contact with customers.[37]

Nonverbal Communication and Gender

Research on communication patterns in mixed-gender work groups shows that the traditional behaviors of men and women may restrict the richness of discussion and limit the productivity of the group. In the United States, the basic male approach to work tasks is confrontational and results oriented. By contrast, the female method of working is collaborative and oriented toward concern for individuals. The adversarial male style leads to respect from other males, while the collaborative female style engenders rapport. Differences in male and female behavior that accentuate gender differences are often so subtle that group members may not be aware of what is happening.

Until recently, most research on differences between the communication styles of men and women focused on face-to-face interactions. Current research

Communication Differences Between Men and Women

A Partial List

- Men are more likely to control discussion through introducing topics, interrupting, and talking more than women.

- Women not only talk less but often assume supportive rather than leadership roles in conversation and receive less attention for their ideas from the group.

- Both men and women may expect group members to follow gender-stereotyped roles that can limit each individual's contributions (e.g., always selecting a man as leader or a woman as note taker).

- Either women or men may use exclusionary language that reinforces gender stereotypes and that others in the group find offensive.

- Women may exhibit verbal characteristics of submissiveness (allowing sentence endings to trail off or using a shrill voice), while men communicate in ways that restrict and control a group (raising the voice or ignoring ideas generated by women).

- Men's nonverbal behavior (extended eye contact, a condescending touch, or overt gestures) may convey messages of dominance, while women's nonverbal behavior (smiling, hair twirling, or primly crossed legs) may suggest a lack of self-confidence and power.

- Men and women may sit separately, thereby limiting cross-gender interaction.

has also addressed computer-mediated communication (CMC), such as email, instant messaging, and electronic meetings. Such studies indicate differences in the communication patterns of men and women when they use technology. For example, women using CMC with other women develop more disclosure and a sense of community, whereas men using CMC with other men seem to ignore the socioemotional aspects of group functioning and are more likely to use mild flaming (emotional language outbursts). Overall, men are less satisfied with the CMC experience and show lower levels of group development than do women.

While caution is advised concerning stereotyping of men and women in communication situations, knowing what behaviors may limit the group process is imperative to maximizing results. Group members may need awareness training to assist in recognizing behaviors that may hinder team performance and in overcoming barriers that may limit the effectiveness of their communication. Differences can also be used to productive advantage.

Listening as a Communication Skill

objective ⑤
Identify aspects of effective listening.

Most managers spend a major part of their day listening and speaking with supervisors, employees, customers, and a variety of business or industry colleagues and associates. Listening commonly consumes more of business employees' time than reading, writing, and speaking combined. The ability to listen effectively is consistently rated as one of the most important skills necessary for success in the workplace. A survey of North American executives reveals that 80 percent believe that listening is one of the most important skills needed in the corporate environment. The same survey participants, however, also rated the skill as one of the most lacking. Effective listening is crucial to providing quality service, facilitating groups, training staff, improving teamwork, and supervising and managing for improved performance. In times of stress and change, effective listening is the cornerstone of workplace harmony because it furthers interpersonal and intercultural understanding. Listening is more than just hearing. It is an interactive process that takes concentration and commitment.

Effective listening habits pay off in several ways:

- Good listeners are liked by others because they satisfy the basic human needs of being heard and being wanted.
- People who listen well are able to separate fact from fiction, cope effectively with false persuasion, and avoid having others use them for personal gain. In other words, good listeners don't "get taken" very often.
- Listening opens doors for ideas and thus encourages creativity.
- Effective listeners are constantly learning—gaining knowledge and skills that lead to increased job performance, advancement, and satisfaction.
- Job satisfaction increases when people know what is going on, when they are heard, and when they participate in the mutual trust that develops from good communication.

Listening depends on your abilities to receive and decode both verbal and nonverbal messages. The best-devised messages and sophisticated communication systems will not work unless people on the receiving end of spoken messages actually listen. Senders of spoken messages must assume their receivers can and will listen, just as senders of written messages must assume their receivers can and will read.

Listening for a Specific Purpose

Individuals satisfy a variety of purposes through listening: (1) interacting socially, (2) receiving information, (3) solving problems, and (4) sharing feelings with others. Each activity may call for a different style of listening or for a combination of styles.

Casual Listening

Listening for pleasure, recreation, amusement, and relaxation is casual listening. Some people play music all day long to relax the brain and mask unwanted sounds during daily routines, work periods, and daily commutes. Aspects of casual listening are as follows:

- It provides relaxing breaks from more serious tasks and supports our emotional health.
- It illustrates that people are selective listeners. You listen to what you want to hear. In a crowded room in which everyone seems to be talking, you can block out all the noise and engage in the conversation you are having with someone.
- It doesn't require much emotional or physical effort.

Listening for Information

Listening for information involves the search for data or material. In the classroom, for example, the instructor usually has a strategy for guiding the class to desired goals. The instructor will probably stress several major points and use supporting evidence to prove or to reinforce them. When engaged in this type of listening, you could become so focused on recording every detail that you take copious notes with no organization. When listening for information:

- Use an outlining process to help you capture main ideas and supporting subpoints in a logical way.
- Watch the speaker as well as listen to him or her, since most speakers exhibit a set of mannerisms composed of gestures and vocal inflections to indicate the degree of importance or seriousness that they attach to portions of their presentation.
- Separate fact from fiction, comedy from seriousness, and truth from untruth.

Intensive Listening

When you listen to obtain information, solve problems, or persuade or dissuade (as in arguments), you are engaged in intensive listening. Intensive listening involves greater use of your analytical ability to proceed through problem-solving steps. When listening intensively:

- Gain an understanding of the problem, recognize whatever limitations are involved, and know the implications of possible solutions.
- Become a good summarizer.
- Trace the development of the discussion and then move from there to your own analysis.
- Feel free to "tailgate" on the ideas of others; creative ideas are generated in an open discussion.

Empathetic Listening

Empathy occurs when a person attempts to share another's feelings or emotions. Counselors attempt to use empathetic listening in dealing with their clients, and good friends listen empathetically to each other. Empathy is a

empathy
when a person attempts to share another's feelings or emotions

valuable trait developed by people skilled in interpersonal relations. When you take the time to listen to another, the courtesy is usually returned. When listening empathetically:

- Avoid preoccupation with your own problems. Talking too much and giving strong nonverbal signals of disinterest destroy others' desire to talk.
- Remember that total empathy can never be achieved simply because no two people are exactly alike. However, the more similar our experiences, the better the opportunity to put ourselves in the other person's shoes. Listening with empathy involves some genuine tact along with other good listening habits.
- Whenever possible, listen in a one-to-one situation. Close friends who trust each other tend to engage in self-disclosure easily. Empathetic listening is enhanced when the participants exhibit trust and friendship.

Many people in positions of authority have developed excellent listening skills that apply to gaining information and to problem solving. However, an equal number of people have failed to develop good listening practices that work effectively in listening for feelings. An "open door" policy does not necessarily indicate an "open ear." A supervisor's poor listening habits may interfere with problem solving and reduce employee morale.

Overlistening

Allowing disruptions

Faking attention

© Image Source

Frequently, you may have to combine listening intensively and listening for feelings. Performance appraisal interviews, disciplinary conferences, and other sensitive discussions between supervisors and employees require listening intensively for accurate understanding of the message and listening empathetically for feelings, preconceived points of view, and background. The interviewing process also may combine the two types of listening. Job interviewers must try to determine how someone's personality, as well as skill and knowledge, will affect job performance. Whatever the situation, good listeners stay focused on their intended purpose.

Poor Listening Habits

Physicians must first diagnose the nature of a person's medical problems before prescribing treatment. In the same way, you can't improve your listening unless you understand some of the nonphysical ailments of your own listening. Most of us have developed poor listening habits in one or more of the following areas:

- **Faking attention.** Have you ever left a classroom lecture and later realized that you had no idea what

Failing to use nonverbal aids

Dismissing subject as uninteresting

went on? Have you ever been introduced to someone only to realize 30 seconds later that you missed the name? If you had to answer "yes" to these questions, join the huge club of "fakers of attention." Isn't it amazing that we can look directly at a person, nod, smile, and pretend to be listening?

- **Allowing disruptions.** Listening properly requires both physical and emotional effort. As a result, we welcome disruptions of almost any sort when we are engaged in somewhat difficult listening. The next time someone enters your classroom or meeting room, notice how almost everyone in the room turns away from the speaker and the topic to observe the latecomer.

- **Overlistening.** Overlistening occurs when listeners attempt to record in writing or in memory so many details that they miss the speaker's major points. Overlisteners "can't see the forest for the trees."

- **Stereotyping.** Most people use their prejudices and perceptions of others as a basis for developing stereotypes. As a result, we make spontaneous judgments about others based on their appearances, mannerisms, dress, speech delivery, and whatever other criteria play a role in our judgments. If a speaker doesn't meet our standards in any of these areas, we simply turn off our listening and assume the speaker can't have much to say.

- **Dismissing subjects as uninteresting.** People tend to use "uninteresting" as a rationale for not listening. Unfortunately, the decision is usually made before the topic is ever introduced. A good way to lose an instructor's respect when you have to miss class is to ask, "Are we going to do anything important in class today?"

- **Failing to observe nonverbal aids.** Good listening requires the use of eyes as well as ears. To listen effectively, you must observe the speaker. Facial expressions and body motions always accompany speech and contribute much to messages. If you do not watch the speaker, you may miss the meaning.

In addition to recognizing poor listening habits and the variety of barriers to effective listening, you must recognize that listening isn't easy. Many poor listening habits develop simply because the speed of spoken messages is far slower than our ability to receive and process them. Normal speaking speeds are between 100 and 150 words a minute. The human ear can actually distinguish words in speech in excess of 500 words a minute, and many people read at speeds well beyond 500 words a minute. Finally, our minds process thoughts at thousands of words a minute.

Because individuals can't speak fast enough to challenge our ability to listen, listeners have a responsibility to make spoken communication effective. Good listening typically requires considerable mental and emotional effort.

Suggestions for Effective Listening

Because feedback and nonverbal signs are available, there are several ways you can enhance the effectiveness of your face-to-face listening. First, be prepared to listen. Minimize environmental and mental distractions by moving to a quiet area where you are not distracted by noise or other conversation. Avoid becoming so preoccupied with thoughts of other projects or what you will say next that you fail to listen. In preparation for listening, you should also reflect on what you know about the speaker. Through experience, you will begin to recognize the unique speaking and organizing traits of particular individuals. Some people seem to run on and on with details before making the point. With this speaker, you will learn to anticipate the major point but not pay much attention to details. Other speakers give conclusions first and perhaps omit support for them. In this case, you will learn to ask questions to obtain further information.

As you listen, try to get in touch with the speaker. You can do this by maintaining an open mind while attempting to understand the speaker's background, prejudices, and points of view. Listen for emotionally charged words and watch for body language, gestures, facial expressions, and eye movements as clues to the speaker's underlying feelings. Part of effective listening is, well, listening, so do not interrupt the speaker. Try to understand the speaker's full meaning, and wait patiently for an indication that you should enter the conversation. When appropriate, ask reflective questions that assess understanding by restating in your own words what you think the other person has said. This paraphrasing will reinforce what you have heard and allow the speaker to correct any misunderstanding or add clarification. You can also use probing statements or questions to help the speaker define the issue more concretely and specifically.

Kinesics play a role in active listening. Show genuine interest by remaining physically and mentally involved; for example, avoid daydreaming, yawning, frequently breaking eye contact, looking at your watch or papers on your desk, whispering, or allowing numerous interruptions (phone calls, etc.). Encourage the speaker to continue by providing appropriate feedback, either orally or nonverbally.

Listening carefully should be your primary focus; however, you can think ahead at times as well. Thinking ahead can help you develop a sense of the speaker's logic, anticipate future points, and evaluate the validity of the speaker's ideas. Making written or mental notes allows you to provide useful feedback when the opportunity arises. If you cannot take notes during the conversation, record important points as soon as possible so that you can summarize the speaker's key points. Listening skills can have a dramatic effect on your personal and professional success. By listening, you get listened to. Listening builds relationships and wins trust.[38]

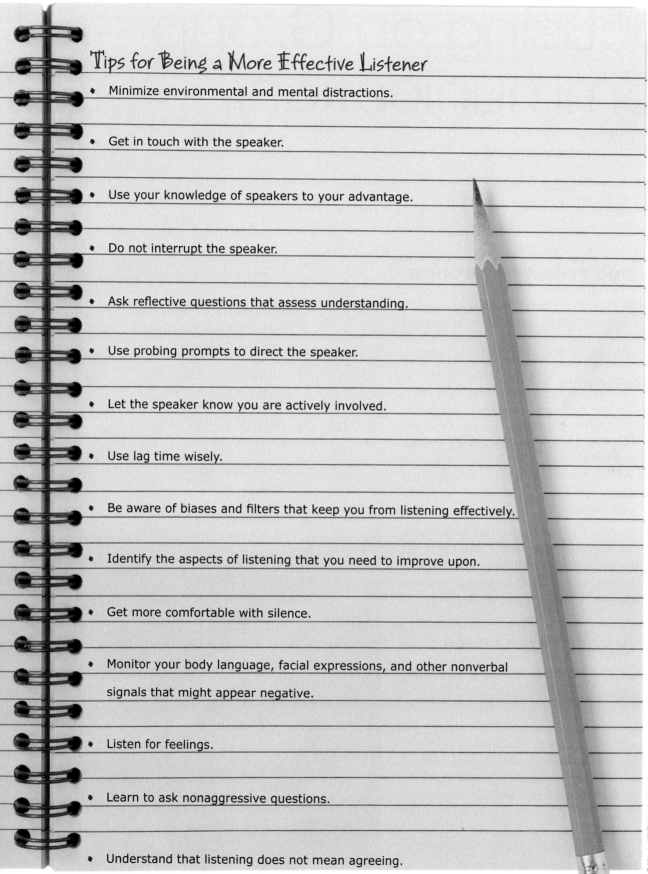

Tips for Being a More Effective Listener

- Minimize environmental and mental distractions.

- Get in touch with the speaker.

- Use your knowledge of speakers to your advantage.

- Do not interrupt the speaker.

- Ask reflective questions that assess understanding.

- Use probing prompts to direct the speaker.

- Let the speaker know you are actively involved.

- Use lag time wisely.

- Be aware of biases and filters that keep you from listening effectively.

- Identify the aspects of listening that you need to improve upon.

- Get more comfortable with silence.

- Monitor your body language, facial expressions, and other nonverbal signals that might appear negative.

- Listen for feelings.

- Learn to ask nonaggressive questions.

- Understand that listening does not mean agreeing.

Focusing on Group Communication

Increasing Focus on Groups

Although much of your spoken communication in business will occur in one-to-one relationships, another frequent spoken communication activity will likely occur when you participate in groups, primarily groups within the organizational work environment. The work of groups, committees, and teams has become crucial in most organizations.

objective ①
Explain the factors influencing the increasing importance of group communication.

As discussed in Chapter 1, developments among U.S. businesses in recent years have shifted attention away from the employment of traditional organizational subunits as the only mechanisms for achieving organizational goals and toward the increased use of groups.

Flat Organizational Structures

Many businesses today are downsizing and eliminating layers of management. Companies implementing Total Quality Management programs are reorganizing to distribute the decision-making power throughout the organization. The trend is to eliminate functional or departmental boundaries. Instead, work is reorganized in cross-disciplinary teams that perform broad core processes (e.g., product development and sales generation) and not narrow tasks (e.g., forecasting market demand for a particular product).

In a flat organizational structure, communicating across the organization chart (among the cross-

objectives

① Explain the factors influencing the increasing importance of group communication.

② Describe the characteristics of effective groups.

③ Explain the difference between groups and teams.

④ Outline the group decision-making process.

⑤ Discuss group conflict and conflict resolution.

⑥ Discuss aspects of effective meeting management.

disciplinary teams) becomes more important than communicating up and down in a top-heavy hierarchy. An individual may take on an expanded role as important tasks are assumed. This role may involve power and authority that surpasses the individual's **status**, or formal position in the organizational chart. Much of the communication involves face-to-face meetings with team members rather than numerous, time-consuming "hand-offs" as the product moves methodically from one department to another.

The time needed to design a new card at Hallmark Cards decreased significantly when the company adopted a flat organizational structure. Team members representing the former functional areas (graphic artists, writers, marketers, and others) now work in a central area, communicating openly and frequently, solving problems and making decisions about the entire process as a card is being developed. For example, a writer struggling with a verse for a new card can solicit immediate input from the graphic artist working on the team rather than finalizing the verse and then "handing it off" to the art department.[1]

status
formal position in the organizational chart

Heightened Focus on Cooperation

Competition has been a characteristic way of life in U.S. companies, not only externally with other businesses but also internally. Organizations and individuals compete for a greater share of scarce resources, for a limited number of positions at the top of organizations, and for esteem in their professions. Such competition is a healthy sign of the human desire to succeed, and in terms of economic behavior, competition is fundamental to the private enterprise system. At the same time, when excessive competition replaces the cooperation necessary for success, communication may be diminished, if not eliminated.

Just as you want to look good in the eyes of your co-workers and supervisors, units within organizations want to look good to one another. This attitude may cause behavior to take the competitive form, a *win-lose philosophy*. When excessive competition has a negative influence on the performance of the organization, everyone loses.

Although competition is appropriate and desirable in many situations, many companies have taken steps through open communication and information and reward systems to reduce competition and to increase cooperation. Cooperation is more likely when the competitors (individuals or groups within an organization) have an understanding of and appreciation for others' importance and functions. This cooperative spirit is characterized as a *win-win philosophy*. One person's success is not achieved at the expense or exclusion of another. Groups identify a solution that everyone finds satisfactory and is committed to achieving. Reaching this mutual understanding requires a high degree of trust and effective interpersonal skills, particularly empathetic and intensive listening skills, and the willingness to communicate long enough to agree on an action plan that is acceptable to everyone.

Characteristics of Effective Groups

G roups form for synergistic effects; that is, through pooling their efforts, group members can achieve more collectively than individually. At the same time, the social nature of groups contributes to the individual goals of members. Communication in small groups leads to group decisions that are generally superior to individual decisions. The group process can

objective ②
Describe the characteristics of effective groups.

motivate members, improve thinking, and assist attitude development and change. The emphasis that a particular group places on task and maintenance activities is based on several factors.

Common Goals

In effective groups, participants share a common goal, interest, or benefit. This focus on goals allows members to overcome individual differences of opinion and to negotiate acceptable solutions. Nothing can be more devastating to the accomplishment of group tasks than personal agendas taking precedent over the goal of the larger group.

Role Perception

People who are invited to join groups have perceptions of how the group should operate and what it should achieve. In addition, each member has a self-concept that dictates how he or she will behave. Those known to be aggressive will attempt to be confrontational and forceful; those who like to be known as moderates will behave in moderate ways by settling arguments rather than initiating them. In successful groups, members play a variety of necessary roles and seek to eliminate nonproductive ones.

Longevity

Groups formed for short-term tasks, such as arranging a dinner and program, will spend more time on the task than on maintenance. However, groups formed for long-term assignments, such as an audit of a major corporation by a team from a public accounting firm, may devote much more effort to maintenance goals. Maintenance includes division of duties, scheduling, record keeping, reporting, and assessing progress.

Size

The smaller the group, the more its members have the opportunity to communicate with each other. Conversely, large groups often inhibit communication because the opportunity to speak and interact is limited. When broad input is desired, large groups may be good. When extensive interaction is the goal, smaller groups may be more effective. Interestingly, large groups generally divide into smaller groups for maintenance purposes, even when the large group is task oriented. Although much research has been conducted in the area of group size, no optimal number of members has been identified. Groups of five to seven members are thought to be best for decision-making and problem-solving tasks. An odd number of members is often preferred because decisions are possible without tie votes.

Status

Some group members will appear to be better qualified than others. Consider a group in which the chief executive of the organization is a member. When the chief executive speaks, members agree. When members speak, they tend to direct their remarks to the one with high status—the chief executive. People are inclined to communicate with peers as their equals, but they tend to speak upward to their supervisor and downward to lower-level employees. In general, groups require balance in organizational power, status, and expertise.

Group Norms

A **norm** is a standard or average behavior. All groups possess norms. An instructor's behavior helps establish classroom norms. If an instructor is generally late for class, students will begin to arrive late. If the instructor permits talking during lectures, the norm will be for students to talk. People conform to norms because we are social animals who desire to be part of the group for safety and social reasons. Conformity leads to acceptance by other group members and creates communication opportunities. However, conformity can get in the way of effective decision making if it becomes more important than openness to new information. Pressure to conform or *groupthink* is discussed more below.

Leadership

The performance of groups depends on several factors, but none is more important than leadership. Some hold the mistaken view that leaders are not necessary when an organization moves to a group concept. The role of leaders changes substantially, but leaders still have an important part to play. The ability of a group leader to work toward task goals while contributing to the development of group and individual goals is often critical to group success. Leadership activities may be shared among several participants, and leadership may also be rotated, formally or informally. The leader can establish norms, determine who can speak and when, encourage everyone to contribute, and provide the motivation for effective group activity.[2]

Group Roles

Groups are made up of members who play a variety of roles, both positive and negative. Negative roles detract from the group's purposes and include the following:

- Isolate—one who is physically present but fails to participate
- Dominator—one who speaks too often and too long
- Free rider—one who does not do his or her fair share of the work
- Detractor—one who constantly criticizes and complains
- Digresser—one who deviates from the group's purpose
- Airhead—one who is never prepared
- Socializer—one who pursues only the social aspect of the group

© Radius Images/Jupiterimages

Perhaps you recognize one or more of the negative roles, based on your personal group experiences. Or perhaps your group experiences have been positive as a result of members' playing positive group roles that promote the group's purposes:

- Facilitator (also known as *gatekeeper*)—one who makes sure everyone gets to talk and be heard
- Harmonizer—one who keeps tensions low
- Record keeper—one who maintains records of events and activities and informs members
- Reporter—one who assumes responsibility for preparing materials for submission
- Leader—one who assumes a directive role

norm
a standard or average behavior

In healthy groups, members may fulfill multiple roles, which rotate as the need arises. Negative roles are extinguished as the group communicates openly about its goals, strategies, and expectations. The opinions and viewpoints of all members are encouraged and expected.

From Groups to Teams

objective ③
Explain the difference between groups and teams.

While some use the terms *group* and *team* interchangeably, others distinguish between them. The major distinction between a group and a team is in members' attitudes and level of commitment. A team is typified by a clear identity and a high level of commitment on the part of members. A variety of strategies have been used for organizing workers into teams:

- A **task force** is generally given a single goal with a limited time to achieve it.
- A **quality assurance team**, or **quality circle**, focuses on product or service quality, and projects can be either short- or long-term.

- A **cross-functional team** brings together employees from various departments to solve a variety of problems, such as productivity issues, contract estimations and planning, and intradepartmental difficulties.
- A **product development team** concentrates on innovation and the development cycle of new products and is usually cross-functional in nature. Consider the impact of team structures, as shown in Figure 3-1.
- A **virtual team** has members in more than one location. Although separated geographically, virtual teams are still highly effective in a number of areas.

While chain of command is still at work in formal organizational relationships and responsibilities, team structures unite people from varying portions of the organization. Work teams are typically given the authority to act on their conclusions, although the level of authority varies depending on the organization and the purpose of the team. Typically, the group supervisor retains some responsibilities, some decisions are made completely by the team, and the rest are made jointly.

Merely placing workers into a group does not make them a functional team. A group must go through a developmental process to begin to function as a team. The four stages of team development are **forming**, when members become acquainted with each other and the

task force
a team given a single goal with a limited time to achieve it
quality assurance team (quality circle)
a team that focuses on product or service quality
cross-functional team
a team that brings together employees from various departments to solve a variety of problems
product development team
a team that concentrates on innovation and the development cycle of new products
virtual team
a team with members in more than one location
forming
the stage of team development when members become acquainted with each other and the assigned task

© Thinkstock Images/Jupiterimages

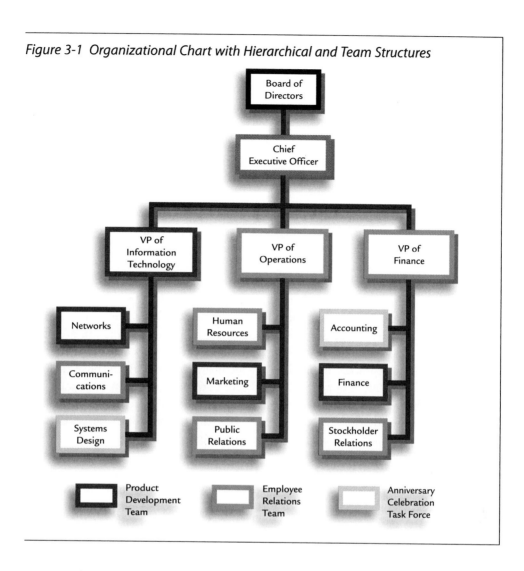

Figure 3-1 *Organizational Chart with Hierarchical and Team Structures*

assigned task; **storming**, when members deal with conflicting personalities, goals, and ideas; **norming**, which involves developing strategies and activities that promote goal achievement; and **performing**, when the team reaches its optimal performance level.

For a variety of reasons, teams are often unable to advance through all four stages of development. Even long-term teams may never reach the optimal performing stage, settling instead for the acceptable performance of the norming stage.

Research into what makes workplace teams effective indicates that training is beneficial for participants in such areas as problem solving, goal setting, conflict resolution, risk taking, active listening, and recognizing the interests and achievement of others. Participants need to be able to satisfy one another's basic needs for belonging, personal recognition, and support. Team members at the performing stage of team development exhibit the following behaviors:

- **Commitment.** They are focused on the mission, values, goals, and expectations of the team and the organization.

- **Cooperation.** They have a shared sense of purpose, mutual gain, and teamwork.

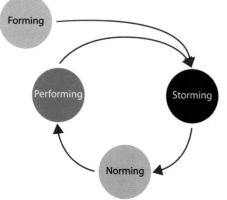

storming
the stage of team development when members deal with conflicting personalities, goals, and ideas
norming
the stage of team development during which members develop strategies and activities that promote goal achievement
performing
when the team reaches its optimal performance level

- **Communication.** They know that information must flow smoothly between top management and workers. Team members are willing to face confrontation and unpleasantness when necessary.
- **Contribution.** All members share their different backgrounds, skills, and abilities with the team.[3]

Group Decision Making

objective ④
Outline the group decision-making process.

One of the most common tasks associated with groups in the workplace is making decisions. However, group decision making can be less than effective if some thought and planning is not given to the decision-making process. Groups process information in four or more stages that appear consistently in many groups.

- **Orientation stage.** The group identifies the problem to be solved and plans the process to be used in reaching the decisions.
- **Discussion stage.** The group gathers information about the situation, identifies and weighs options, and tests its assumptions.
- **Decision stage.** The group relies on an implicit or explicit social decision scheme to combine individual preferences into a collective decision. Common schemes include delegating, averaging inputs, voting with various proportions needed for a decision, and consensus.
- **Implementation stage.** The group carries out the decision and assesses its impact. Members are more likely to implement decisions when they were actively involved in the decision-making process.

Although group decision making can have productive outcomes, group members should be aware of some the challenges and limitations of such a process. One problem is the tendency for groups to spend too much of their discussion time examining shared information—details that two or more of the group members know in common—rather than unshared information.[4] This tendency is called **oversampling.** Oversampling

oversampling
the tendency of groups to examine information they already know

of shared information leads to poorer decisions when a hidden profile would be revealed by considering the unshared information more closely. Oversampling of shared information increases when tasks have no demonstrably correct solution and when group leaders do not actively draw out unshared information.

In addition, the usefulness of group discussion is limited, in part, by members' inability to express themselves clearly and by their limited listening skills. Not all group members have the interpersonal skills a discussion demands. When researchers asked 569 full-time employees what happened during a meeting to limit its effectiveness, they received 2,500 answers. The problems identified are shown in Table 3-1.[5]

Sometimes, groups use discussion to avoid making decisions. In addition, judgment errors that cause people to overlook important information and overuse unimportant information are often exacerbated in groups. These errors occur more frequently when group members are cognitively busy (i.e., they are trying to work on too many tasks at once).

Common sense suggests that groups are more cautious than individuals, but early studies found that group discussion generates a shift in the direction of the more risky alternative. When researchers later found evidence of cautious shifts as well as risky ones, they concluded that the responses of groups tend to be more extreme than individual members' responses (the group polarization hypothesis).[6] Polarization is sustained by the desire to evaluate one's own opinions by comparing them to those of others (social comparison theory), by exposure to other members' pro-risk and pro-caution arguments (persuasive arguments theory), and by groups' implicit reliance on a "risk-supported wins" social decision scheme.[7] This approach is adopted by groups whose members are initially more risk prone than cautious. In such groups, if one person supports a risky alternative, the group will not adopt it. But if two people support it, the group often accepts the risky recommendation.[8]

Group decision making can be challenging because it requires the ability to consider and accommodate multiple interpretative frameworks—multiple versions of reality—and to emerge with a single recommendation or course of action.[9] This means that we must be willing to accept the inevitability of differences and to make a commitment to dialogue. Groups also can be more effective at decision making if they pay more attention to the procedure that they use to solve problems.[10]

Group Conflict

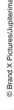

T here are three types of group conflict: personal conflict, substantive conflict, and procedural conflict. Conflict can also be increased by other factors, such as competition within a group and the social dilemmas that groups can create for their members. Just as there are various types of conflict, there are several approaches that group members use to resolve conflict.

objective (5)
Discuss group conflict and conflict resolution.

Personal Conflict

Personal conflict is rooted in individuals' dislike of other group members. For example, group members who treat others unfairly or impolitely create more conflict than those who are polite.[11]

The relationship between dislike and conflict explains why groups with greater diversity sometimes display more conflict than homogeneous groups. Just as similarity among members increases interpersonal attraction, dissimilarity tends to increase dislike and conflict.[12] Groups whose members have dissimilar personalities (e.g., differences in authoritarianism, cognitive complexity, and temperament) generally do not get along as well as groups composed of people whose personalities are similar.[13] Groups whose members vary in terms of ability, experience, opinions, values, race, personality, ethnicity, and so on can capitalize on their members' wider range of resources and viewpoints, but these groups often suffer high levels of conflict.[14]

Substantive Conflict

When people discuss their problems and plans, they sometimes disagree with one another's analyses. These

Table 3-1 Problems When Groups Make Decisions

Problem (Frequency)	Description
Poor communication skills (10%)	Poor listening skills, ineffective voice, poor nonverbals, lack of effective visual aids, misunderstood or no clearly identified topic, repetitive, use of jargon
Egocentric behavior (8%)	Dominating conversation and group, behaviors that are loud and overbearing, one-upmanship, show of power, manipulation, intimidation, filibustering, talk to hear self talk, followers or brown-nosers, clowns and goof-offs
Nonparticipation (7%)	Passive, lack discussion, silent starts; not all participate, speak up, or volunteer
Sidetracked (6.5%)	Leave main topic
Interruptions (6%)	Members interrupt speaker, talk over others, socialize, allow phone calls/messages from customers/clients
Negative leader behavior (6%)	Unorganized and unfocused, not prepared, late, has no control, gets sidetracked, makes no decisions
Attitudes and emotions (5%)	Poor attitude, defensive or evasive, argumentative, personal accusations, no courtesy or respect, complain or gripe, lack of control of emotions

© Pixland/Jupiterimages

minimize procedural conflict by adopting formal rules that specify goals, decisional processes, and responsibilities.[16] Rules, however, can be overly formalized, which can hinder openness, creativity, and adaptability to change. Sometimes, creating formal rules for the functioning of the group can also minimize personal conflict because they can help the group focus more on the task and less on various types of disagreement.

Competitive Versus Cooperative Orientation

Conflict is more likely when group members compete against each other for resources such as money, power, time, prestige, or materials instead of working with one another to reach common goals. When people compete, they must look out for their own interests instead of the group's interests or their comembers' interests. Because competing members can only succeed when others fail, they may even sabotage others' work, criticize it, and withhold information and resources that others might need.[17] Looking out for our own interest instead of focusing on the broader group goal is sometimes referred to as pursuing a *personal agenda*. In the United States, because of our individualistic culture, the emergence of personal agendas is common in groups.

In contrast, members of cooperative groups enhance their outcomes by helping other members achieve success. Work units with high levels of cooperation have fewer latent tensions, personality conflicts, and verbal confrontations.[18]

Few situations involve pure cooperation or pure competition; the motive to compete is often mixed with the motive to cooperate. Furthermore, as the **norm of reciprocity** suggests, cooperation begets cooperation while competition begets competition.

People's personalities contribute to conflict. Some people seem to be natural competitors, whereas others are more cooperative or individualistic.[19] **Competitors** view group disagreements as win-lose situations and find satisfaction in forcing their ideas on others.

Individuals with competitive value orientations are more likely to find themselves in conflicts. Furthermore, competitors rarely modify their behavior in response to the complaints of others because they are relatively unconcerned with maintaining smooth interpersonal relations.

Two other value orientations are those of cooperator and individualist. **Cooperators** value accommodative interpersonal strategies, while **individualists** are concerned only with their own outcomes. They make decisions based on what they personally will achieve with

substantive conflicts, however, are integrally related to the group's work. Substantive conflict does not stem from personal disagreements between individuals but from disagreements about issues that are relevant to the group's real goals and outcomes. In other words, of the three types of conflict, substantive conflict has the potential to provide the most positive outcomes, such as making plans, increasing creativity, solving problems, deciding issues, and resolving conflicts of viewpoints.[15] Substantive conflict, in fact, is one of the reasons that groups are used to complete tasks.

Even though substantive conflicts help groups reach their goals, these impersonal conflicts can turn into personal ones. Members who disagree with the group, even when their position is a reasonable one, often provoke considerable animosity within the group. The dissenter who refuses to accept others' views is less liked. Group members who slow down the process of reaching consensus are often responded to negatively. Such pressures to conform can lead to what is called *groupthink*. (This concept is discussed in more detail below.) To avoid this aspect of groupthink, groups should encourage members to take on the role of devil's advocate.

norm of reciprocity
cooperation begets cooperation while competition begets competition
competitors
individuals who view group disagreements as win-lose situations
cooperators
individuals who value accommodative interpersonal strategies
individualists
people concerned only with their own outcomes

Procedural Conflict

While substantive conflicts occur when ideas, opinions, and interpretations clash, procedural conflicts occur when strategies, policies, and methods clash. Many groups can no concern for others' outcomes. They neither interfere with nor assist others' attempts to reach their goals.

As discussed in Chapter 1, social values vary across cultures. Western societies, such as the United States, tend to value competition, while more cooperative and peaceful societies devalue individual achievement and avoid competitive games.[20]

Social Dilemmas

Groups create social dilemmas for their members. The members, as individuals, are motivated to maximize their own rewards and minimize their costs. Conflicts arise when individualistic motives trump group-oriented motives and the collective intervenes to redress the imbalance.

One cause of conflict is the division of resources. When group members feel they are receiving too little for what they are giving, they sometimes withdraw from the group, reduce their effort, and turn in work of lower quality. Group members who feel that they are receiving too much for what they are giving sometimes increase their efforts.

Many studies of groups working on collective tasks find that members do not work as hard as when they are working for themselves. Such **free riding** occurs most frequently when individuals' contributions are combined in a single product and these products aren't monitored.

Free riding can cause conflict in a group. To make the problem of free riding worse, some individual group members may reduce their own contributions or withdraw from the group to counter the inequity of working in a group with free riders.

As conflicts escalate, group members often become more committed to their positions instead of more understanding of the positions taken by others. Conflict is exacerbated by members' tendency to misperceive others and to assume that the other party's behavior is caused by personal rather than situational factors. This tendency is called the **fundamental attribution error**. As conflict worsens,

© Immagine/Inspirestock/Jupiterimages

group members will shift from weak to strong tactics, such as threats, punishment, and bullying.

Conflict Resolution

Most of the tactics that people use to deal with conflict can be classified into one of five basic categories, as shown in Figure 3-2 on the following page.

In group and teamwork situations, the first dysfunction that occurs is a lack of **trust**, or the confidence among group members that their peers' intentions are good.[21] In other words, we must believe that those with whom we work will not act opportunistically or take advantage of us and others to narrowly pursue their own self-interest or personal agendas. Without trust, individuals are unable to use what is generally considered the most effective approach to conflict resolution: collaboration. Collaboration is built on trust.

The styles of conflict resolution can be understood by comparing how each relates in the areas of concern for others and concern for self as well as level of aggressiveness and cooperation.[22]

- **Competition.** This style is characterized by high aggressiveness and low cooperation. Some people see conflict as a win-lose situation and use competitive and aggressive tactics to intimidate others. Fighting can take many forms, including authoritative mandate, challenges, arguing, insults, accusations, complaining, vengeance, and even physical violence.[23] An individual who uses a competing style exhibits a high concern for self and low concern for others.

- **Collaboration.** An individual who exhibits this style shows a high concern for others and for self. Because of this orientation, this style is characterized by assertive communication and high levels of cooperation. As such, it is considered a win-win approach since a solution should be found that satisfies both parties. The disadvantage of collaboration is that it can take a significant amount of time and energy to reach a solution that all parties support.

- **Compromise.** This style is a middle ground. The emphasis is on achieving workable but not necessarily

free riding
the tendency of group members to not work as hard as when they are working for themselves

fundamental attribution error
the assumption that the other party's behavior is caused by personal rather than situational factors

trust
the confidence among group members that their peers' intentions are good

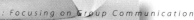

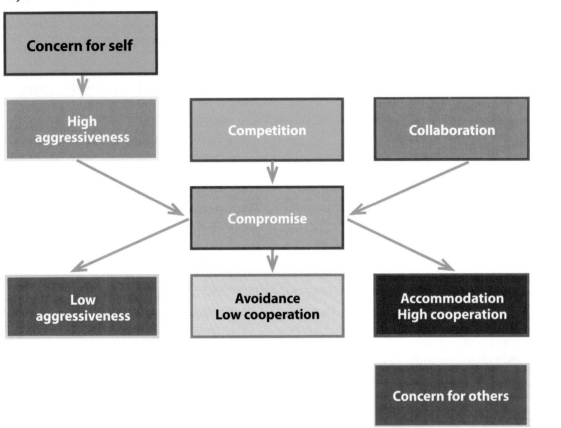

Figure 3-2 Styles of Conflict Resolution

Concern for self

High aggressiveness

Competition

Collaboration

Compromise

Low aggressiveness

Avoidance
Low cooperation

Accommodation
High cooperation

Concern for others

© PhotoAlto/JupiterImages

optimal solutions. Some consider this a lose-lose approach to conflict resolution. This strategy is often used in organizational settings because it requires less time.

- **Avoidance.** Individuals who practice this style show little concern for relationships or for task accomplishment. By avoiding conflict, they hope it will disappear. When students in small groups talked about their disagreements, they often said they adopted a "wait-and-see" attitude, hoping the problem would eventually go away.[24] Sometimes, however, avoiding is appropriate if you are a low-power person and the consequences of confrontation are risky and potentially harmful to you.

- **Accommodation.** This style is characterized by a high concern for relationships but a low concern for task accomplishment. Like avoiding, this can be a useful approach in groups that have shown a high degree of conflict. Accommodating others in this situation provides for an opportunity for tempers to cool and steps toward resolution to occur. It can also be appropriate if the risk of yielding is low. For example, a group of your friends may disagree about where to eat dinner. The choice may be between two of your favorite restaurants, but the one that most of your friends prefer is your second choice. However, since you like that restaurant, too, you have little to lose by yielding.

Of these five basic ways of resolving conflict, collaborating is more likely to promote group unity. Unfortunately, it often takes a much bigger investment in time and so it often is not used in an organizational setting because of the costs associated with it.

Groupthink

Our dislike of conflict and the need to promote cohesiveness can lead to an additional danger: **groupthink**. Groupthink occurs when group members dominate interaction, are intimidated by others, or care more about social acceptability than reaching the best solution. Groupthink occurs at the highest levels and can have serious consequences. It has been cited as causing the Bay of Pigs fiasco in the 1960s, the Challenger disaster in the 1980s, the Enron debacle, and the lack of effective preparation and response by the U.S. government to terrorism in the 21st century.

In summary, it is useful to understand the benefits and potential problem areas of group work since we will all work in groups during our lives. The issues surrounding such concerns as group structure and development, conflict, performance, and decision making should be understood and considered when working in groups or deciding whether a group approach is appropriate for a task. The type of task that needs to be accomplished should guide the decision as to whether to achieve it through group means.

groupthink
when group members avoid conflict rather than pursue the best solution

8 Ways
to Avoid Groupthink

1. The leader should encourage participants to voice objections and critically evaluate ideas.
2. Members should take an impartial stance and not get wrapped up in ego and emotions, affording a more objective view of the decision. However, trying to view a situation from an outsider's perspective can be challenging.
3. More than one group can work on a problem, which may lead to radically different recommendations.
4. Each member can be encouraged to discuss the group's deliberations with people outside the group and get their feedback.
5. Outside experts can be invited into the group for their input and feedback.
6. One of the group members can be appointed as devil's advocate to assure that all sides of each issue are explored.
7. The group can be divided into subgroups, each of which works the problem separately and then reports back.
8. A "second-chance" meeting can be held after a preliminary consensus is reached to allow members to express doubts and concerns that may have come up.

Source: Jane Gibson and Robert Hodgetts (1986).

Meeting Management

M eetings are essential for communication in organizations. They present opportunities to acquire and disseminate valuable information, develop skills, and make favorable impressions on colleagues, supervisors, and subordinates. U.S. businesses spend more money on conducting meetings than any other country in the world. In fact, estimates of the cost for a meeting of eight managers range from $300 to $700 an hour. U.S. workers also spend more time in meetings than do people of other countries.[25]

objective ⑥
Discuss aspects of effective meeting management.

Workers frequently have a negative attitude toward meetings because they perceive them as a waste of time. Studies support this opinion, revealing that as much as one third of the time spent in meetings is unproductive. Negative attitudes toward meetings can be changed when meetings are used and conducted properly, giving attention to correct procedures and behavior. Successful meetings don't just happen; rather, they occur by design. Careful planning and attention to specific guidelines can help ensure the success of meetings, whether they are conducted in a face-to-face format or electronically.

Face-to-Face Meetings

Face-to-face meetings continue to be the most-used meeting format in most organizations. One of the keys to holding a productive meeting is knowing when such a channel of communication is appropriate. The first question to ask before planning a meeting is, "Could this information be conveyed in writing just as effectively as meeting face-to-face?" It is appropriate to hold a face-to-face meeting in the following situations:

- When you need the richest nonverbal cues, including body, voice, proximity, and touch.
- When the issues are especially sensitive.
- When the participants don't know one another.
- When establishing group rapport and relationships are crucial.
- When the participants can be in the same place at the same time.
- When no other channel or medium of communication would suffice.[26]

8 managers + 1 meeting =

© Medioimages/Jupiterimages

Face-to-face meetings may be enhanced through the use of various media tools, such as flipcharts, handouts, and electronic slide shows. While face-to-face meetings provide a rich nonverbal context and direct human contact, they also have certain limitations. In addition to the obvious logistical issues of schedules and distance, face-to-face meetings may be dominated by overly vocal, quick-to-speak, and high-status members. In these cases, formal rules for communicating and a skilled leader are necessary to keep the meeting on track.

Electronic Meetings

A variety of technologies is available to facilitate electronic meetings. Participants may communicate with one another through telephones, personal computers, or video broadcast equipment using groupware or meeting management software applications. Electronic meetings offer certain advantages. They facilitate geographically dispersed groups because they provide the choice of meeting at different places/same time, different places/different times, same place/same time, or same place/different times. Electronic meetings also speed up meeting follow-up activities because decisions and action items may be recorded electronically.

Electronic meetings also have certain limitations:[27]

- They cannot replace face-to-face contact, especially when group efforts are just beginning and when groups are trying to build group values, trust, and emotional ties.

- They may make it harder to reach consensus, because more ideas may be generated and because it may be harder to interpret the strength of other members' commitment to their proposals.

- The success of same-time meetings is dependent on all participants having excellent keyboarding skills to engage in rapid-fire, in-depth discussion. This limitation may be overcome as voice input systems become more prevalent.

Suggestions for Effective Meetings

Whether you engage in face-to-face or electronic meetings, observing the following guidelines may help to ensure that your meetings are productive:

- **Limit meeting length and frequency.** Any meeting held for longer than an hour or more frequently than once a month should be scrutinized. Ask yourself whether the meeting is necessary. Perhaps the purpose can be achieved in another way, such as email, instant messaging, or telephone.

- **Make satisfactory arrangements.** Select a date and time convenient for the majority of expected participants. For face-to-face meetings, plan the meeting

site with consideration for appropriate seating for attendees, media equipment, temperature and lighting, and necessary supplies. For electronic meetings, check hardware and software and connectivity components.

- **Distribute the agenda well in advance.** The **agenda** is a meeting outline that includes important information: date, beginning and ending time, place, and topics to be discussed and responsibilities of those involved. Having the agenda prior to the meeting allows participants to know what is expected of them and to better prepare so that the meeting is more effective. A sample agenda template is provided in Figure 3-3 on the following page.

- **Encourage participation.** While it is certainly easier for one person to make decisions, the quality of the decision making is often improved by involving the team. Rational decision making may begin with **brainstorming**, the generation of many ideas from among team members without judgment. Brainstormed ideas can then be discussed and ranked, followed by some form of decision-making process.

- **Maintain order.** Proper parliamentary procedure may be followed in formal meetings to help maintain order, as outlined in sources such as *Robert's Rules of Order* and *Jones' Parliamentary Procedure at a Glance*. For less formal meetings, a more relaxed approach may be taken to ensure that everyone has an opportunity to share in the decision making. However, a lack of structure or order may negatively affect the perceived usefulness of the meeting as well as the leader.

- **Manage conflict.** In an autocratic organization, conflict may be avoided because employees are conditioned to be submissive. Such an environment, however, leads to smoldering resentment. On the other hand, conflict is a normal part of any team effort and can lead to creative discussion and superior outcomes. Maintaining focus on issues and not personalities helps ensure that conflict is productive rather than destructive.

- **Seek consensus.** While unanimous agreement on decisions is an optimal outcome, total agreement cannot always be achieved. **Consensus** (or compromise, discussed earlier) represents the collective opinion of the group, or the informal rule that all team members can live with at least 70 percent of what is agreed upon.

- **Prepare thorough minutes.** Minutes provide a concise record of meeting

agenda
a meeting outline that includes important information: date, beginning and ending time, place, and topics to be discussed and responsibilities of those involved
brainstorming
the generation of many ideas from among team members without judgment
consensus
the collective opinion of the group

actions, ensure the tracking and follow-up of issues from previous meetings, and assist in the implementation of previously reached decisions.

Meetings are an important management tool and are useful for idea exchange. They also provide opportunities for you, as a meeting participant, to communicate impressions of power and status. Knowing how to present yourself and your ideas and exhibiting knowledge about correct meeting management will assist you in your career advancement.

© Nicole Waring/iStockphoto.com

Figure 3-3   SAMPLE   *Formal Generic Agenda for Meetings*

Agenda for [name of group] Meeting
Prepared on [date agenda created]
By [name of author of agenda]

Attendees: [those invited to attend, often in alphabetical order]
Date and time of meeting:
Location of meeting:
Subject: [major issues to be discussed or purpose of meeting]
Agenda items:

1. Call to order
2. Routine business [procedural or administrative matters]   (10–15 minutes)
    a. Approval of agenda for this meeting
    b. Reading and approval of minutes of last meeting
    c. Committee reports
3. Old business [unfinished matters from previous meeting]   (15–20 minutes)
    a. Discussion of issue(s) carried over from previous meeting
    b. Issue(s) arising from decision(s) made at previous meeting
4. New business   (20–25 minutes)
    a. Most important issue
    b. Next most important issue
    c. Other issues in decreasing order of importance
    d. Business from the floor not included on the agenda
        [only as time permits; otherwise, these issues should be
        addressed in the next meeting]
5. Adjournment

82% of students surveyed on a 4LTR Press Solution find it is designed more closely to match the way they naturally study.

LISTEN UP! SHE DID

BCOM2 was designed for students just like you—busy people who want choices, flexibility, and multiple learning options.

BCOM2 delivers concise, focused information in a fresh and contemporary format. And...

BCOM2 gives you a variety of online learning materials designed with you in mind.

At **4ltrpress.cengage.com/bcom,** you'll find electronic resources such as **videos, audio downloads,** and **interactive quizzes** for each chapter.

These resources will help supplement your understanding of core concepts in a format that fits your busy lifestyle. Visit **4ltrpress.cengage.com/bcom** to learn more about the multiple resources available to help you succeed!

Planning Written and Spoken Messages

Writing—A Ticket to Work

In a report entitled "Writing: A Ticket to Work . . . or a Ticket Out," the National Commission on Writing reported that two thirds of salaried employees in large companies have some writing responsibilities, and getting hired and promoted in many industries demands this skill. Writing is important; however, the commission also concluded that one third of employees in corporate America writes poorly. Knowing that effective communication is tied to the corporate bottom line and many employees can't write well, businesses are investing $3.1 billion annually to train employees to write.[1] Remedies are needed to prevent confusion, waste, errors, lost productivity, and damaged corporate image—all caused by employees, customers, and clients muddling their way through unreadable messages.

As a capable communicator, you can immediately add value to your organization and set yourself apart from your peers who are struggling to articulate ideas in writing and presentations. Communication that commands attention and can be understood easily is essential for survival in today's information explosion. As an effective communicator, you will be expected to process volumes of available information and shape useful messages that respond to the needs of customers or clients, coworkers and supervisors, and other key business partners. Additionally, increased use of electronic communication will require you to be technologically savvy and capable of adapting the rules of good communication to the demands of emerging technology.

How can you learn to plan and prepare powerful business messages? The systematic analysis pro-

objectives

1. Identify the purpose and type of message.

2. Develop clear perceptions of the audience to enhance the impact of the communication and human relations.

3. Consider the context of the message and any environmental influences that may affect its delivery.

4. Determine the appropriate channel and media for communicating the message.

5. Apply techniques for adapting messages to the audience.

6. Recognize the importance of organizing a message before writing the first draft and select the appropriate message outline (deductive or inductive) for developing messages to achieve the desired response.

7. Prepare the first draft.

cess outlined in Figure 4-1 on the following page will help you develop messages that save you and your organization valuable time and money and portray you as a capable, energetic professional. A thorough analysis of the audience and your specific communication assignment will empower you to write a first draft efficiently and to revise and proofread your message for accuracy, concision, and appropriate tone. You will focus on the planning process in this chapter and then learn to prepare various types of messages in Chapters 5 through 8. Revising written messages is covered in Chapter 9.

Communication that commands attention and can be understood easily is essential for survival in today's information explosion.

Figure 4-1 Process for Planning and Preparing Spoken and Written Messages

STEP 1	STEP 2	STEP 3	STEP 4	STEP 5	STEP 6	STEP 7
Determine the purpose and select an appropriate channel	Envision the audience	Consider the context	Choose a channel and the medium	Adapt the message to the audience's needs and concerns	Organize the message	Prepare the first draft

Step 1: Determining the Purpose and Type of Message

f you are to speak or write effectively, you first must think through what you are trying to say and understand it thoroughly before you begin.

Hundreds of years ago, the Greek philosopher and writer Aristotle identified three purposes of communication: to inform, to persuade, and to entertain. Although entertainment is the purpose of much of the communication that occurs in the culture of the United States today, particularly mediated forms, it is not highly emphasized in communication for business purposes. In fact, communication that is intended to entertain can have a negative effect on the relationship you have with others or can damage your credibility. For example, if you use humor in oral presentations or email messages at work, you take the risk of offending others who might not share your sense of humor or creating an image of yourself as unprofessional. Some attempts at humor may even violate the law if they are considered racist, sexist, ageist, or otherwise discriminatory.

For these reasons, entertainment will not be considered one of the foundational purposes of communication in organizational settings. However, four purposes of communication still exist in the professional workplace. They are:

- To inform
- To persuade
- To convey goodwill
- To establish credibility

Many textbook writers group credibility and goodwill into a single category, but those purposes have been separated here to emphasize the importance of both aspects in achieving your purposes of communication in organizational settings and to help you better understand their nuances.

After determining the broader purposes for communicating, you can determine even more specific purposes for a particular message. For example, informative messages can be categorized as good-news, neutral, or bad-news messages. Good-news messages include those that deliver positive news and messages of appreciation or thank-you notes. Neutral messages include a variety of routine messages, such as requests and claims, and those dealing with customer orders and credit as well as procedures. Bad-news messages include refusals of requests and claims, denials of credit, and those that handle problems with customer orders. Persuasive messages include sales messages and persuasive requests, such as those for a favor or for information.

Communicating to Inform

A major purpose of many business messages is to deliver routine types of information needed to complete daily tasks. Informative messages are used to explain instructions to employees, announce meetings and procedures, acknowledge orders, accept contracts for services, and so forth. Another informative type of message delivers bad news, and these, because of the potential for damaging your relationship with your audience, deserve special attention.

Communicating to Persuade

Most messages also have a persuasive element—to influence or change the attitudes or actions of the receiver in some way. These messages include promoting a product or service and seeking support for ideas and worthy causes presented to supervisors, employees, stockholders, customers/clients, and other stakeholders of an organization.

Although we may believe that most of our communication is intended to inform others, in the business

objective 1
Identify the purpose and type of message.

world almost all communication is persuasive. In other words, you are trying to get another person to do or believe something. In business, you are almost always selling: selling your ideas, yourself, your products, or your services. Selling and persuading are nearly synonymous in the business world. You may be trying to persuade your supervisor to give you a raise, attempting to persuade a colleague to change a portion of a project on which you are both working, or trying to sell a customer your company's service or product. All of these are examples of persuasion at work. (Persuasion, in an interpersonal context, is referred to as influence in Chapter 2.)

In order to succeed at persuasion, you must generally give good reasons for the person you are communicating with to do or believe what you intend. That is one reason why it is generally important to identify your purposes for communicating in the workplace before you communicate. If you believe you are only informing, you may fail to provide the good reasons or evidence necessary to persuade, if that is indeed your primary purpose. Evidence consists of a variety of types of information, such as facts, anecdotes, examples, and statistics. (We will explore evidence in more detail in Chapter 8.)

Unless you are making a simple request, successful persuasion usually involves more than writing or delivering a single message. In fact, persuasion is often a difficult and time-consuming activity.[2] But it is a skill that is necessary in today's business environment where the old "command-and-control" managerial model now often generates poor or unwanted outcomes. AlliedSignal's CEO Lawrence Bossidy once put it this way, "The day when you could yell and scream and beat people into good performance is over. Today you have to appeal to them by helping them to see how they can get from here to there by establishing some credibility and by giving them some reasons and help to get there. Do all those things, and they'll knock down doors."[3]

Effective persuasion involves four essential steps. First, you must establish credibility through building expertise and cultivating relationships. Second, you need to thoroughly understand your audience and its needs and concerns. This will help strengthen the appeal of your proposal. Third, effective persuaders make their positions come alive by providing evidence—numerical data, examples, stories, metaphors, and analogies. Finally, because emotions are always involved to some extent in every decision we make, effective persuaders will connect emotionally with the audience and adjust their arguments to their audience's emotional state.[4]

Persuasion is more than the act of convincing and selling: It is a process of learning and negotiating that relies heavily on dialogue. Dialogue must happen before and during the persuasive process. "A persuader should make a concerted effort to meet one-on-one with all the key people he or she plans to persuade."[5] In some cases, through this dialogue, effective persuaders may find that they need to adjust their positions in order to better achieve their goals.

Communicating to Establish Credibility

To persuade effectively, you should also put some energy forth establishing or maintaining your credibility. Credible people demonstrate that they have strong emotional character and integrity; they are known to be honest, steady, and reliable. On organizational and individual levels, reputation is increasingly important to the success of a firm and the personal success of the employees who work there. (Public relations has developed as a functional area to manage the reputations of companies.) Savvy employees are aware of the applicability of these concepts in their own careers. One study indicates that 92 percent of more than 2,300 executives said that if a person loses credibility with them, it would be very difficult to gain it back.[6]

Steps to Effective Persuasion

1. Establish credibility.
2. Frame for common ground.
3. Provide evidence.
4. Connect emotionally (convey goodwill).

© Medioimages/Jupiterimages

Most managers overestimate their own credibility considerably.[7] In the worst-case scenario, they may revert to the old "command-and-control" style of leadership that studies have shown damage productivity and morale in skilled, well-educated workers and create frustrated, silenced employees who steal all the pencils and sabotage the company's computer system. Credibility no longer comes from authority but from having expertise and competence, being trustworthy (strong integrity), controlling emotions, and developing and maintaining a professional image.

Expertise and Competence

Clearly, your knowledge about your job and ability to perform your job well affect your credibility. Likewise, your communication competence reflects on your credibility. Speaking correctly and articulately generally enhances our credibility by indicating to others that we are well educated and intelligent. The same goes for our written communication. If our written messages are full of errors, we may be perceived as undereducated, lazy, or not detail oriented. All of these negative judgments can affect our credibility. In one case, a résumé or letter with a grammatical error eliminated an applicant from consideration; in another, the same company asked an applicant with a doctoral degree to provide samples of reports and other documents he had written.[8]

One way you can positively distinguish yourself from others in today's competitive business environment is by demonstrating excellent communication skills. Employees who can write clearly can create a better impression of a firm with customers, suppliers, and outsiders than any public relations program ever devised. "If you send out a sales letter that is filled with errors, you're losing credibility. You send the image that your company is careless," says Dawn Josephson, president of Cameo Publications, an editorial and publishing services firm based in Hilton Head, South Carolina.[9]

Effective business writing skills have become crucial for both personal performance and organizational productivity. With the proliferation of personal computing, more and more employees at all levels in the company are producing documents that represent an organization, and the quality of this written material can have a significant impact on both perceptions and performance. For that reason, focusing on improving the quality of your communication is critical. There is no quick fix for grammar and mechanical problems, however. Achieving correct grammar usage takes time and some effort; it also takes practice. By exerting some

time and energy toward the goal of achieving correctness, you will be rewarded with greater confidence, competence, and credibility.

To Improve the Correctness of Your Writing

1. Read—often and about diverse topics. Reading helps us to subconsciously recognize and internalize correct grammar usage in writing.

2. Solve word games and puzzles. These activities can help you build your vocabulary and learn the meanings of words.

3. Become aware of the common mistakes you make in your writing. This knowledge will streamline the process of proofreading if you can more quickly identify the areas that you need to double-check for correctness.

4. Edit other's writing. This activity can improve your analytical skills, which are necessary to proofread your own writing.

5. Learn how to properly operate and then use the spell-checking and grammar-checking tools available in most word-processing programs. It is important to recognize that these computer tools do not recognize all writing errors. You will also need to proofread your written messages carefully, so it is essential to keep a good writing handbook and dictionary on hand.

6. For very important messages, it is often a good idea to ask a literate friend or colleague to review and provide feedback as to their correctness.

Personal Ethics and Integrity

Ethics is involved whenever people interact with one another because communication by nature involves some degree of manipulation of the audience and the message.[10] Therefore, not upholding a high standard of personal integrity can compromise or greatly reduce your credibility. Table 4-1 gives some examples of unethical messages that can occur in organizations.

To keep unethical communication practices in check, both senders and receivers of messages need to act responsibly. That is, they should carefully analyze claims, assess probable consequences, and weigh relevant values.[11] In addition, responsible communicators should respond to the needs and communication of others in sensitive, thoughtful, fitting ways.[12] Finally, both parties in an interaction bear mutual responsibility to participate actively in the process.

Table 4-1 Typology of Unethical Messages

Type	Examples
Coercive	An employee criticizes the boss's "pet" development program in a meeting and is fired on the spot for her remarks.
Destructive	A supervisor makes a sexist joke at the expense of an employee.
Deceptive	Federal Aviation Administration employees falsify employee work records to justify the firing of air traffic controllers during their 1981 strike.
Intrusive	Electronic surveillance of employees is conducted through hidden video cameras.
Secretive	The asbestos industry suppresses information that leaves little doubt about the health hazards posed by its product.
Manipulative/ Exploitative	Management threatens union members with a plant closing if they don't ratify a contract.

Source: Redding, W.C. (1991). Unethical Messages in the Organizational Context. Paper presented at the Annenberg Convention of the ICA, Chicago, IL.

Emotional Control

Our ability to control our emotions greatly affects our credibility. According to a study done by the University of Missouri–Columbia, "many employees do not want their coworkers to express any type of strong emotion—positive or negative."[13] Employees in the study were asked to describe situations where they believed coworkers acted appropriately and inappropriately. The consensus of the employees was that negative emotion should never be expressed, and positive emotion should be shown in moderation.

Anger is one of the more common negative emotions that cloud communication; when you allow anger to control your communication, the results are generally unproductive. Outbursts of anger tend to make people uncomfortable, especially when the person exhibits irrational forms of anger. If construed as harassment in the workplace, excessive displays of anger can lead to disciplinary measures.

Anger also comes through in written communication. We should never write a message when we are feeling a negative emotion but should wait until we have calmed down to express ourselves. Although it can feel good to vent negative feelings, we should immediately delete or erase messages written in anger. Such negative emotions can affect the tone of the message, which may have a negative impact on our relationship with the receiver or our ability to convey goodwill. Unfortunately, with the popularity and proliferation of email, it is easy to pound out our frustrations and quickly send them. "Then we click 'send.' In a frenzied span of 15 minutes we have managed to do some real psychological damage, usually more to ourselves than to anyone else."[14]

However, negative emotions can be tamed. Kristin Anderson, president of Say What? Consulting, recommends that you maintain a neutral body and voice. Keeping your body loose and your voice tone neutral will help to maintain a calm demeanor.[15] A second tactic is to listen without trying to judge if the situation is good or bad.

© Randolph Pamphrey/iStockphoto.com

If confronted by anger, you may feel like retreating or become defensive. However, being defensive and yelling back may cause more harm. Instead, empathize with the person. Doing so will help you maintain your credibility by showing that you act reasonably, rationally, and respectfully in stressful situations.

Developing a Professional Image

Expertise and competence, emotional control, and integrity are all components of your professional image. Likewise, our communication skills, both written and oral, can enhance our image as a professional. Personality traits can also contribute to a more credible and professional image. If we show ourselves to be dependable, reliable, careful, thorough, able to plan, organized, hard working, persistent, and achievement oriented, we are more likely to be perceived as professional and competent.

Our appearance through dress and posture also communicates to others. Every time you walk into a room, you communicate who you are before you speak, through your appearance.[16] For example, it would not be expected for your company president to walk into a business meeting wearing Bermuda shorts. On the other hand, a fishing guide would not show up for work in three-piece suit. Dressing appropriately for a particular situation can affect whether others perceive you as professional and credible. It also sends the message that you are a part of the group and that you belong. This message can help you in the relationship or goodwill area of communication.

Some people are better able to consciously cultivate a professional image. Recall from Chapter 2 that impression management is the control (or lack of control) of communicating information through performance. In impression management, people try to present an "idealized" version of themselves in order to reach desired ends.

goodwill
the ability to create and maintain positive, productive relationships with others

All of us attempt to manage our impression to varying degrees in various situations. The key to successful impression management is to accurately assess the social expectations for particular contexts and to do our best to match those expectations through our appearance, body language, emotional control, and use of language.

Communicating to Convey Goodwill

According to *Webster's College Dictionary*, goodwill has three definitions: "1. friendly disposition; kindly regard; benevolence. 2. cheerful acquiescence or consent. 3. an intangible, salable asset arising from the reputation of its business and its relations with its customers." For those of you who have taken accounting courses, you are probably familiar with the third definition of goodwill; in business contexts, goodwill is considered an asset. As a purpose of business communication, **goodwill** is the ability to create and maintain positive, productive relationships with others.

Many of you who have work experience would probably agree with this statement: The ability to establish and maintain relationships is indeed what makes the business world go around. Establishing and maintaining relationships with others, or networking, is the heart of much of business. One of the key elements of positive relationships is trust and vice versa. You are more likely to trust someone with whom you have a positive relationship and to have a positive relationship with someone you trust.

From an organizational perspective, relationships can play an important role in producing effective supervision, promoting social support among employees, building personal influence, and ensuring productivity through smooth work flow. The need for good interpersonal relationships in organizations is particularly important from both the standpoint of the individual, who requires social support in an increasingly turbulent world, and the organization, which

More Tips on Anger Management

1. Put yourself in the other person's shoes. See if you can imagine how he or she feels.

2. Exercise to get rid of the tension. Ride your bike, play soccer, or, if you are at work, go for a long walk.

3. Do not jump to conclusions. Listen carefully to what the other person says.

4. Take a time out. Give yourself time and space to calm down so that you can think clearly and communicate rationally.

Following these simple techniques can help any aggressive situation turn positive.

© Comstock Images/Jupiterimages

must maintain high levels of cooperation among employees to meet customer demands and remain competitive. Most decision makers rely heavily on verbal information from people they trust. *Trust* can be understood as the confidence that our peers' intentions are good.[17] In other words, we must believe that those with whom we work will not act opportunistically or take advantage of us and others to narrowly pursue their own self-interest.

Step 2: Envision the Audience

objective ②
Develop clear perceptions of the audience to enhance the impact of the communication and human relations.

Perception is the part of the communication process that involves how we look at others and the world around us. It's a natural tendency to perceive situations from our own limited viewpoint. We use the context of the situation and our five senses to absorb and interpret the information bombarding us in unique ways.

Individual differences in perception account for the varied and sometimes conflicting reports given by eyewitnesses to the same accident. The popular television series *Monk* focuses on Monk, the "defective" detective who can see things that scores of trained police workers cannot see, although they've all been looking at the same crime scene.

Perception of reality is also limited by previous experiences and our attitudes toward the sender of the message. We filter messages through our own frames of reference and tend to only see things that we want to see. Our frames of reference are affected by our backgrounds, experiences, and cultural values. If we come from different backgrounds or cultures or have had different life experiences than our audience or the receiver of our message, then our perceptions are likely different from theirs. To make this situation more challenging, we tend to support ideas that are in line with our own thinking. We may simply refuse to hear a message that doesn't fit into our view of the world.

Much of the confusion in communication is caused by these differences in both the sender and receiver's perceptions. For example, team members may clash when some members perceive the task to be of greater importance than do other people involved in the work.

Overcoming perceptual barriers is difficult but essential if you are to craft messages that meet the needs and concerns of your audience. To help you envision the audience, first focus on relevant information you know about the receiver. The more familiar you are with the receiver, the easier this task will be. When communicating with an individual, you immediately recall a clear picture of the receiver—his or her physical appearance, background (education, occupation, religion, culture), values, opinions, preferences, and so on. Most importantly, your knowledge of the receiver's reaction in similar, previous experiences allows you to anticipate how this receiver is likely to react in the current situation. Consider the following audience characteristics:[18]

- **Economic level.** A banker's collection letter to a customer who pays promptly is not likely to be the same form letter sent to clients who have fallen behind on their payments for small loans.

- **Educational/occupational background.** The technical jargon and acronyms used in a financial proposal sent to bank loan officers may be inappropriate in a proposal sent to a group of private investors.

- **Needs and concerns of the receiver.** Just as successful sales personnel begin by identifying the needs of the prospective buyer, an effective manager attempts to understand the receiver's frame of reference as a basis for organizing the message and developing the content.

- **Culture.** As was discussed in Chapter 1, the vast cultural differences between people (language, expressions, customs, values, religions) increase the complexity of the communication process. An email containing typical American expressions (e.g., "The proposal was *shot down*," "projections are *on par*," and "*the competition is backed to the wall*") would likely confuse a manager from a different culture. Differences in values also influence communication styles and message patterns. For example, Japanese readers value the beauty and flow of words and prefer an indirect writing approach, unlike Americans who prefer clarity and concision.[19]

- **Rapport.** A sensitive message written to a long-time client may differ significantly from a message written to a newly acquired client. The rapport created by previous dealings with the client aids understanding in a current situation.

- **Expectations.** Because accountants, lawyers, and other professionals are expected to meet high standards, a message from one of them containing errors in grammar or spelling would likely cause a receiver to question the credibility of the source.

You may find that envisioning an audience you know well is often such an unconscious action that you may not even recognize that you are doing it. On the other hand, envisioning those you do not know well requires additional effort. In these cases, simply assume an empathetic attitude toward the receiver to assist you in identifying his or her frame of reference (knowledge, feelings, emotions). In other words, project mentally how you believe you would feel or react in a similar situation and then use that information to communicate understanding back to the person.

Consider the use (or lack) of empathy in the following workplace examples:

Sample Message

Example 1: A U.S. manager's instructions to a new employee from an Asian culture:

"Please get to work right away <u>inputting</u> the financial data for the Collier proposal. Oh, I need you to get this work out <u>ASAP</u>. Because this proposal is just a <u>draft</u>, just plan to give me a <u>quick-and-dirty</u> job. You can clean it up after we <u>massage the stats</u> and get <u>final blessings</u> from the <u>top dog</u>. Do you have any questions?"

Example 2: An excerpt from a letter sent to Mr. Sandy Everret:

Dear <u>Ms. Everett:</u>

The wireless iPod kit that you expressed an interest in is now available <u>in</u> at your local car dealer. This innovative Bluetooth technology can be demonstrated at <u>you convience</u>. Please call your local sales representative to schedule <u>a</u> appointment. <u>I remain</u>

<u>Respectfully yours,</u>

Dana Merrill
Dana Merrill, Manager

Problem Analysis

- *The use of acronyms and expressions peculiar to the U.S. environment confuse and intimidate.*

- *Final open-ended question indicates that the writer does not understand the importance of saving face to a person from an Asian culture. Deep cultural influences may prevent this employee from asking questions that might indicate lack of understanding.*

- *Misspelling the receiver's name (and misinterpreting the gender) and overlooking mechanical errors imply incompetence or carelessness and disrespect for the receiver.*

- *The outdated closing and omission of contact information reduce the writer's credibility and show lack of genuine concern for meeting the sender's needs.*

communication and people's feelings about you, your ideas, and themselves.

2. **Permits you to address the receiver's needs and concerns.** This knowledge allows you to select relevant content and to communicate in a suitable style.

3. **Simplifies the task of organizing your message.** From your knowledge of yourself and from your experiences with others, you can predict (with reasonable accuracy) receivers' reactions to various types of messages. To illustrate, ask yourself these questions:

- Would I react favorably to a message saying my request is being granted or that a new client is genuinely pleased with a job I'd just completed?

- Would I experience a feeling of disappointment when I learn that my request has been refused or that my promised pay raise is being postponed?

- Would I need compelling arguments to convince me to purchase a new product or support a new company policy or an employer's latest suggestion for improvement?

Your commitment to identifying the needs and concerns of your audience before you communicate is invaluable in today's workplace. Organizations must focus on providing quality customer service and developing work environments supportive of talented, diverse workers. Alienating valuable customers and talented employees as a result of poor audience analysis is not an option in today's competitive environment.

However, audience analysis is often not given the attention it deserves, and when it is performed, it is not done well. This problem arises because of the difficulty of getting outside of our own perceptual world. In other words, it is very difficult to get outside of our

Taking the time and effort to obtain a strong mental picture of your audience through firsthand knowledge or your empathetic attitude *before* you write will enhance your message in the following ways:

1. **Establishes rapport and credibility needed to build long-lasting personal and business relationships.** Your receivers will appreciate your attempt to connect and understand their feelings. A likely outcome is mutual trust, which can greatly improve

own skins and to look at the world as others do because of the limits created by our own experiences, beliefs, and worldviews. We tend to be attracted to those who are like us and to spend our time with people like ourselves, which limits our ability to understand those who may be different. This phenomenon was shown in the 2008 primary presidential campaigns when people under 29 years of age tended to prefer Barack Obama, the youngest candidate in the race; older women tended to prefer Hillary Clinton; and those describing themselves as fundamentalists or born-again Christians preferred Michael Huckabee, a former Baptist minister. Overcoming these constraints can thus take significant effort and time.

Because of these challenges, it is helpful to have additional mechanisms for understanding audiences. These include their position within an organization or relation to it, which can affect their communication needs, and generational and personality differences.

Position in or Relation to the Organization

Business audiences are often quite different from those you may be familiar with in your academic experience. For example, most of your writing in school is probably intended for a teacher, who knows a great deal about the subject and who is required to read or listen to your message. However, this situation may not be true in the workplace. You may communicate with audiences who have little understanding of your topic, and it is very likely that you will write or speak to people who are not obligated to spend time reading or listening to your messages.

Another difference between communication in an academic setting and that in the workplace is that you may be communicating with a variety of people rather than a single person (i.e., your instructor). If you are communicating with a number of people, they may have varying knowledge and needs. They may also differ in the strategies they use and skills they have for listening, reading, and processing information.

In the workplace, you will generally be communicating with five types of audiences: managerial, nonexpert, expert, international/multicultural, and mixed.[20]

Managers will often be your most important audiences because they have decision-making ability and power over your future. According to Henry Mintzberg, managers fulfill three types of roles that affect the way they communicate: *interpersonal, informational,* and *decisional* roles.[21] The demands of these various roles

It can be difficult to see the world as others do.

force managers to deal with enormous time pressures. They have little time to listen or read carefully. Mintzberg's study found that 50 percent of the activities that executives engaged in lasted less than nine minutes. Many also treat message processing as a burden to be dispensed with as quickly as possible.

To ensure that your messages are received by managers, you can use a few strategies. For example, you can put key information up front where it is easily accessible. One study looked at how managers read reports and found that all of them read the executive summary while most read the introduction, background, and conclusions sections. Only 15 percent read the body of the report. In general, managers look for the "big picture" and tend to ignore details.[22]

Nonexpert audiences may be the most difficult to address since they know little about a subject and will need more details. (Managers are also nonexperts, but they ignore details.) If you are communicating with a customer or client or perhaps a fellow employee from another department, you are probably communicating with a nonexpert audience.

The problem with communicating with a nonexpert audience is that you probably think like a specialist. That is, you may think about your topic differently than a nonexpert and use different terminology than they might to discuss that topic. In addition, you may have difficulty identifying exactly what it is that a nonexpert audience doesn't know since you are so familiar with the topic.

Expert audiences are those who know as much about the topic as you do. Generally, expert audiences, who may be your peers, speak the same language as you do—that is, they understand the jargon associated with your profession. They also understand the same concepts, so you don't need to provide as much explanation and examples. In other words, they can fill in the gaps by making inferences about material that is common knowledge to both of you.

The global economy and the growing diversity of the workplace means that we will likely communicate with *international or multicultural audiences.* Members of these audiences may not speak English as a first language and may have differing cultural interpretations of symbols and behaviors.

The most challenging audiences are those composed of a variety of people, or *mixed audiences:* managers, nonexperts, experts, and nonnative speakers or some combination of these. For example, you may be writing marketing literature that will be read by experts, nonexperts, and nonnative speakers or speaking to a group composed of the same individuals. To overcome the challenges presented by a mixed audience, you can use a *layered approach,* which entails targeting parts of the communication to different members of the mixed audience. An example of the layered approach is a formal report. Such a report might include an executive summary, background information, and recommendation sections aimed at managers, while the body and appendixes contain the details needed by specialists who are charged with implementing the report.

Alternatively, you can use the *democratic strategy.* In this case, you primarily aim your message at the most important audience, but you add information in appropriate places that is needed for understanding by the other audiences. Although this approach is similar to the "layered" one, it differs in that you add in examples, definitions, and explanations throughout the message that are needed for understanding by all audiences.

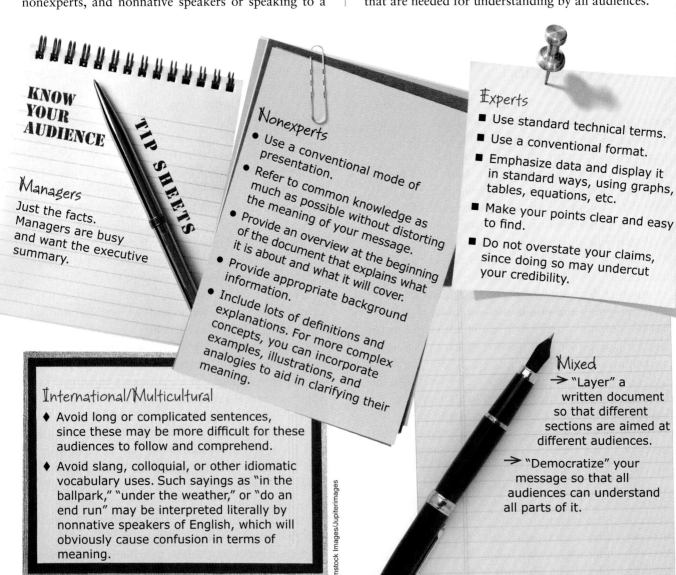

KNOW YOUR AUDIENCE

TIP SHEETS

Managers
Just the facts. Managers are busy and want the executive summary.

Nonexperts
- Use a conventional mode of presentation.
- Refer to common knowledge as much as possible without distorting the meaning of your message.
- Provide an overview at the beginning of the document that explains what it is about and what it will cover.
- Provide appropriate background information.
- Include lots of definitions and explanations. For more complex concepts, you can incorporate examples, illustrations, and analogies to aid in clarifying their meaning.

Experts
- Use standard technical terms.
- Use a conventional format.
- Emphasize data and display it in standard ways, using graphs, tables, equations, etc.
- Make your points clear and easy to find.
- Do not overstate your claims, since doing so may undercut your credibility.

International/Multicultural
- Avoid long or complicated sentences, since these may be more difficult for these audiences to follow and comprehend.
- Avoid slang, colloquial, or other idiomatic vocabulary uses. Such sayings as "in the ballpark," "under the weather," or "do an end run" may be interpreted literally by nonnative speakers of English, which will obviously cause confusion in terms of meaning.

Mixed
→ "Layer" a written document so that different sections are aimed at different audiences.
→ "Democratize" your message so that all audiences can understand all parts of it.

Generational Differences

Age diversity is a reality in the U.S. workforce today, and the span of age continues to increase. Older workers are working longer or re-entering the job market after retirement even as increasing numbers of younger workers enter the workplace. In fact, there are four generations spanning 60 years working side by side in today's workplace:

- **Matures or seniors.** Americans over 60 years of age whose survival of hard times caused them to value hard work, sacrifice, and a strong sense of right and wrong. They like the idea of re-entering the job market after retirement or remaining there for the long haul.

- **Baby boomers.** Set squarely in middle age, they are referred to as the "Me" generation because they grew up in boom times and were indulged and encouraged by their parents to believe their opportunities were limitless. They will work longer than their parents because of greater financial strain and a limited retirement budget.

- **Generation Xers.** Members of the "latchkey" generation were born between 1965 and 1976 and are fiercely independent, self-directed, and resourceful. They also tend to be skeptical of authority and institutions because they entered the workforce in a time of downsizing and cutbacks. Gen-Xers expect immediate and ongoing feedback and are equally comfortable giving feedback to others. They are pragmatic and desire some fun in the workplace. They do not see progression in their careers as a ladder but as a career "lattice." Their careers are more fluid, since they are comfortable moving laterally and stopping and starting.

- **Millennials (also called Generation Yers).** The children and grandchildren of the boomers' children, born between 1977 and 1998, are technologically savvy, active, and visually oriented due to their lifetime experience in a high-tech world. Because they grew up in structured parenting situations, they prefer structured situations at work. They also are demanding and have high expectations. They work well in groups, preferring this to individual endeavors.

Recognizing generational differences provides insights into the expectations and concerns of others and enables us to shape our messages to be more effective. When properly managed, companies with a strong mix of older and younger workers have a distinct competitive edge. Each generation has something to offer—younger workers bring new ideas; older workers bring experience.

© Image Source

Personality Differences

More and more companies are using personality tests in their hiring and promotion decisions. According to the Association of Test Publishers, a nonprofit association for providers of tests and assessment tools, those participating in employment testing reported 10 to 15 percent growth over the last three years. These tests are used to try to identify potential employees who will be a good fit for the organization and the position.

Personality tests are not only useful for corporations; they also can be used by individuals to identify their best fit with a particular occupation. Knowing one's own personality type as well as being able to use a schema to obtain insights about others' preferences can help us shape our communication to meet

Even though personality is individual, the following guidelines can help you deal with different personality types more generally:

☑ **Act.** Communication is often based on assumptions. To break the assumption trap, find out what you don't know by asking questions. An example is the question, "How much detail do you prefer in these reports, or what form should data take—anecdotal or facts only?"

☑ **Collaborate.** Divide up projects to take advantage of other people's strengths. An example is the statement, "I'm a detail-oriented person. I would be happy to handle the number crunching for this project."

☑ **Appreciate.** Be proactive in thanking people for contributing different perspectives. An example is the statement, "I hadn't really thought of how that software change would affect others. Thanks for helping me see it from their angle."

☑ **Speak the Right Language for Your Audience.** For example, when communicating with a sensor, provide the details and a step-by-step breakdown. In contrast, when communicating with intuitors, emphasize each step (the bigger picture by comparison).

Source: McIntosh, P. & Luecke, R. (2007). Interpersonal Communication Skills in the Workplace. New York: AMACOM Books.

them. As you might expect, different personality types have different communication preferences.[23] A failure to recognize and manage those differences can lead to communication difficulties, resulting in a drop in productivity and a growth in general workplace tension. By contrast, appreciating the complementary nature of these different approaches can lead to better decisions and complementary work relationships. Having a schema that we can use to better understand others and their preferences can also help us to create messages that better meet their needs.

Step 3: Consider the Context

objective ③
Consider the context of the message and any environmental influences that may affect its delivery.

The next step in planning a message is to consider the context of the situation and whether that will affect how and what is communicated. The context of the message refers to the environmental influences that affect its content and, in some cases, the decision as to whether to even send a message. As we discussed in Chapter 1, some important environmental factors influence business communication: legal and ethical constraints, considerations regarding technology, intercultural or diversity issues, and the team environment. Additionally, financial or economic considerations may affect the decision to send a message. For example, if the company's financial picture is weak and layoffs are being discussed, it might not be the appropriate time to ask your supervisor for a raise or to ask for financial support to go to a professional conference or training program.

Multiple issues within an organization might affect the content of a message, how it is delivered, and more importantly whether it is even appropriate to send a message. Organizational considerations include the corporate culture and the flow of communication within the company. A company's policies, programs, and structures can support or interfere with good communication. The context within which communication occurs can also affect how, what, when, and whether we should communicate. In short, the corporate culture of an organization can affect the quality of communication that occurs within it. The flow of communication can affect choices about how communication should best occur.

There are several dimensions to context, including physical, social, chronological, and cultural. The *physical* context or setting can influence the content and quality of interaction. For example, if you were to ask your boss for a raise, the effect of the setting might dramatically affect your chances for success. How might the following settings affect such an interaction: In the boss's office? At a company picnic? Over lunch at a restaurant? In your work area, with others' observing?

The *social* context refers to the nature of the relationship between the communicators as well as who is present. In the same situation mentioned above, imagine how the relationship between your manager and yourself might affect your request for a raise if:

- You and the manager have been friends for several years as opposed to a situation in which you and your manager have no personal relationship.
- You are the same age as your manager *or* she or he is 15 years older (or younger) than you.
- You and the manager have gotten along well in the past compared to a situation in which you and the manager have been involved in an ongoing personal conflict.

The *chronological* context refers to the ways time influences interactions. For example, how might the time of day affect the quality of an interaction? How might the communicator's personal preferences regarding time affect an interaction? Is it a busy time of year for employees and managers? Has there just been a major layoff, downsizing, or profit loss? In this last case, you might want to put off your request for a raise until conditions improve.

The *cultural* context includes both the organizational culture as well as the cultural backgrounds of the people with whom you may be communicating. **Organizational culture** refers to a system of shared meanings and practices held by members that distinguish the organization from other organizations. Organizational culture can affect the means and style of communication that takes place in an organization.

For example, if a company is resistant to innovation and risk taking, you may be taking a risk in putting forth proposals that support such goals. In this case, you might consider whether such a message would be received well and its effect on your credibility and support within the organization. If a corporate culture expects precision and attention to detail, then all of your messages should reflect these values in terms of their quality and correctness. Knowing whether an organi-

organizational culture
a system of shared meanings and practices held by members that distinguish the organization from other organizations

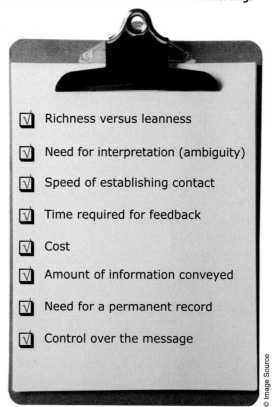

<<Be sure to consider culture when communicating.

☑ Richness versus leanness

☑ Need for interpretation (ambiguity)

☑ Speed of establishing contact

☑ Time required for feedback

☑ Cost

☑ Amount of information conveyed

☑ Need for a permanent record

☑ Control over the message

zation is outcome, people, or team oriented may help select evidence that would improve the potential for success of persuasive messages.

Step 4: Choose a Channel and Medium

objective ④ Determine the appropriate channel and media for communicating the message.

Channels of communication were discussed in Chapter 1. These channels were two-way, face-to-face; two-way, not face-to-face; and one-way, not face-to-face. Each channel also has various media associated with it that can be used to conduct the actual communication. For example, the media most often used in the workplace for two-way, face-to-face communication

consist of in-person or interpersonal communication, meetings, and video- and teleconferencing. When choosing the appropriate channel and media for communication, the following things should be considered.

Richness Versus Leanness

Some channels of communication provide more information than others. The richest channels of communication provide nonverbal information in addition to that provided in written or oral form. For this reason, the richest channel of communication is two-way, face-to-face or what is often called *interpersonal communication.*

Two-way, face-to-face communication provides participants a rich source of information, including vocal cues, facial expressions, bodily movement, bodily appearance, the use of space, the use of time, touching, and clothing and other artifacts. In addition, two-way, face-to-face communication provides opportunities to facilitate feedback and to establish a personal focus. These aspects also contribute to the richness of interpersonal communication as a channel of communication.

One-way, not face-to-face communication or written communication may provide less access to nonverbal forms of communication. However, tone can be communicated in writing and can be an indicator of the writer's attitude. For this reason, you should never write messages when you are experiencing negative emotions that may adversely affect your relationship with your audience. If you are experiencing negative emotions in response to a workplace situation, you should wait until you have calmed down before you respond in writing.

Perhaps one of the leanest media of communication is a printed form. Most forms ask for information that is very specific and limited in scope. Furthermore, forms often provide a limited amount of space in which to provide information. Because of the specificity and space limitations, forms usually provide little opportunity to gather information other than the least amount needed to fulfill a particular task.

Need for Interpretation

Some channels and media of communication are more ambiguous or leave more room for interpretation of the message being sent than others. Nonverbal communication may be the most ambiguous channel of communication since it requires the audience to interpret almost the entirety of the message. Nonverbal communication is difficult to interpret for a variety of reasons. First of all, one nonverbal code may communicate a variety of meanings. For example, you may stand close to someone because you are in a crowded room, you are having difficulty hearing him or her, or you are attracted to the person.

Similarly, nonverbal communication can be difficult to interpret because a variety of codes may communicate the same meaning. This problem is particularly apparent when cultural differences come into play in a communication situation. In a public speaking situation, for example, you might show respect for the speaker by looking directly at the speaker, while in some cultures respect is shown by the listeners when they avert their eyes from the speaker.

Another issue that may affect a person's ability to interpret nonverbal codes accurately is intentionality. Some nonverbal codes are sent intentionally while others are unintentional. If you smile at a friend, you are intentionally showing that you are glad to see that person. However, the same nonverbal cue may be sent unintentionally yet interpreted as intentional. You might be thinking about a pleasant experience you had the night before and unintentionally smile. But if this occurs while you are walking down the street, the stranger approaching you may interpret this unintentional signal as an intentional cue of interest in him or her. For this reason, two-way, face-to-face communication may be more ambiguous than other channels of communication. Furthermore, depending on our sensitivity to

nonverbal communication codes, we may overreact to certain nonverbal messages or may be somewhat or completely unaware of such information.

In contrast, written communication has the potential for being the least ambiguous channel of communication, particularly if it is prepared by a highly skilled writer who is able to precisely encode such a message. In other words, such a writer has an excellent command of the language and its correct usage. For this reason, many official or legal messages are delivered in the form of a written document. Similarly, instructions are often provided in written form.

Speed of Establishing Contact

Another important consideration, particularly in the business world, is the time it will take for a message to be delivered. As the old saying goes, time is often money. That's why electronic forms of communication have become so popular. Using the telephone, writing an email message, and sending a fax are almost instantaneous media for communication. In contrast, sending a written message or package by mail may take days. If you wish to communicate with someone who lives or works in another state or nation, it may also take days to arrange a face-to-face meeting. For these reasons, electronic channels of communication have become extremely useful in the modern workplace.

Time Required for Feedback

Even though the most rapid forms of communication are generally electronic, they may not produce the most prompt feedback. If you need a response immediately and your audience is in the cubicle next to yours, face-to-face communication may be the fastest means of receiving the information you need. Regardless, response time depends on the person with whom you are communicating, his or her personality, and your relationship. In other words, people generally have communication channel and media preferences and differing communication practices. Some people may prefer face-to-face communication and thus may be more responsive to messages delivered using this channel. Others may prefer the telephone, while still others may prefer to be contacted by email. Just because you prefer email does not mean that the person you are communicating with has a similar preference and will respond to your message immediately.

For these reasons, you should take into consideration your audience's preferences when selecting a communication channel and medium.

Cost

Many communication media are relatively inexpensive for business users. Mail, email, telephones, and faxes are generally considered inexpensive forms of communication. Face-to-face communication, although the richest channel, can be quite expensive if those you wish to communicate with are located at a distance from yourself in another city, state, or country. If you wish to communicate with a large number of people who are not in close proximity, the costs of communicating interpersonally can be quite high. This is because such meetings involve the costs of travel, accommodations, and lost productivity. In these situations, many businesses use teleconferencing, and larger companies have even begun investing in videoconferencing systems.

Amount of Information Conveyed

The best channel for conveying large amounts of information is generally a written one. That's because most of us are poor listeners. Studies indicate that we retain only about 10 percent of what we hear. Therefore, if you want people to have the opportunity to process and remember the information you have to deliver, particularly if the message is long or complex, it is best delivered using the written channel. Typically, less information is delivered by electronic, oral media like television newscasts or radio programs because they appeal to people who do not have much time to invest in such information or do not wish to invest much time, have short attention spans, or do not like to read. Bottom

line, these channels generally deliver less information about the topics they address.

For these reasons, if you have a fairly large quantity of complex or detailed information to deliver, the written communication channel is the best because it provides readers the opportunity to take the time necessary to process that information, oftentimes at their own convenience.

Need for a Permanent Record

A related consideration is the need to keep a permanent record. Businesspeople are often involved in situations where they must keep records of what occurred during various work activities throughout the day or week. These situations include the need to record what occurred at a department meeting, an employee's work history, the findings of an audit of a client's financial records, and an employee's travel expenses. Most legal documents, including contracts, use the written channel of communication for this reason: the need to maintain a record. Email messages that are stored and backed up properly can also serve as a record.

Control over the Message

The written channel of communication, or one-way, not face-to-face, is also the best choice when you wish to maintain greater control of the message that you send. The reason is this: If information is presented orally and interpersonally, you have a greater chance of people who disagree with you or who wish to discredit you speaking out. These displays of disagreement or displeasure can interfere

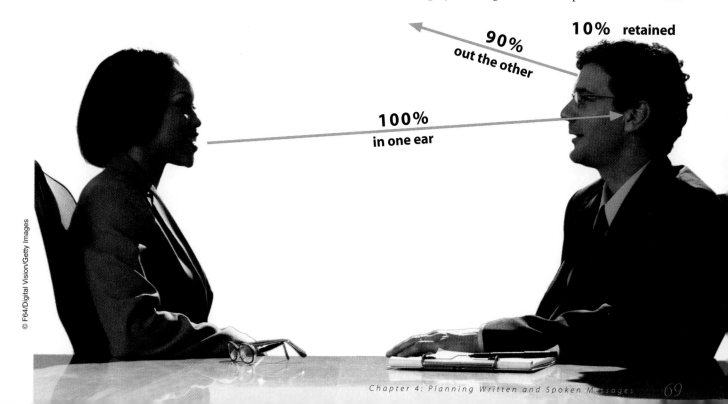

with the clarity of the message and the assurance that it is delivered as intended. That is why many negative messages are sent using the written channel of communication.

For example, if you must tell a job applicant that he was not selected for the position for which he recently interviewed, you can maintain control over the act of delivering that information by doing so in the form of a letter. Although calling the person to deliver the message might exhibit greater goodwill on your part because you have taken the time to interact using a channel and medium that enables you to utilize some nonverbal cues, you also risk a situation that might spin out of control if the person does not take the news well or wishes to take more of your time to find out why he was not selected. In this case, you also may be put in a position to explain the decision more fully. However, by sending a polite letter, you are able to convey the same basic message without the risk of losing control of the situation.

Similarly, in crisis situations, some companies refuse to speak to the media for fear of losing control of the message or releasing information that may be damaging. These situations may be handled by using the written communication channel to send a press release to the media. The press release delivers information but does not provide an opportunity for the receiver to question the communicator and potentially lose control of the message that the company intends to convey. Oral channels of communication are often riskier because they expose the speaker to differences of opinion, conflict, and personalities that may be difficult to control.

attempt to choose content and language that will promote goodwill or help you to maintain or establish a lasting, positive relationship with him or her.

Ideas are more interesting and appealing to the receiver if they are expressed from his or her viewpoint. Developing a "you attitude" rather than a "me attitude" involves thinking in terms of the other person's interests and trying to see a problem from the other's point of view. A letter, memo, email, or phone call reflecting a "you attitude" sends a direct signal of sincere concern for the receiver's needs and interests.

The use of the word *you* (appropriately used) conveys to receivers a feeling that messages are specifically for them. If the first-person pronoun *I* is used frequently, especially as the subject, the sender may impress others as being self-centered—always talking about self. Compare the following examples of sender-centered and receiver-centered statements.

I- or Sender Centered	Receiver Centered
I want to take this opportunity to offer my congratulations on your recent promotion to regional manager.	Congratulations on your recent promotion to regional manager.
We allow a 2-percent discount to customers who pay their total invoice within 10 days.	Customers who pay within 10 days may deduct 2 percent from their total invoice. (*You* could be the subject in a message to a customer.)
I am interested in ordering . . .	Please send me . . . (*You* is the understood subject.)

Step 5: Adapt the Message to the Audience

objective ⑤

Apply techniques for adapting messages to the audience.

After you have envisioned your audience, considered the context of the communication, and chosen the most effective channel and medium with which to communicate, you are ready to adapt your message to fit the specific needs of your audience. As was discussed earlier in this chapter, adaptations should take into consideration the receiver's point of view and

Concentrating on cultivating a "you attitude" will boost the receiver's confidence in the sender's competence and will communicate nonverbally that the receiver is valued enough to merit your best effort. For people who practice courtesy and consideration, the "you attitude" is easy to incorporate into written and spoken messages.

Compliments (words of deserved praise) are another effective way of increasing a receiver's receptiveness to ideas that follow. Give sincere compliments judiciously, as they can do more harm than good if paid at the wrong time, in the wrong setting, in the presence of the wrong people, or for the wrong reasons. Likewise, avoid flattery (words of undeserved praise). Although the recipient may accept your flattery as a sincere compliment, chances are the recipient will interpret your undeserved praise as an attempt to seek to gain favor or special attention. Suspicion of your motive makes effective communication less likely.

How to Cultivate a "You Attitude"

To cultivate a "you attitude," concentrate on the following questions:

- Does the message address the receiver's major needs and concerns?
- Would the receiver feel this message is receiver centered? Is the receiver kept clearly in the picture?
- Will the receiver perceive the ideas to be fair, logical, and ethical?
- Are ideas expressed clearly and concisely (to avoid lost time, money, and possible embarrassment caused when messages are misunderstood)?
- Does the message promote positive business relationships—even when the message is negative? For example, are *please, thank you,* and other courtesies used when appropriate? Are ideas stated tactfully and positively and in a manner that preserves the receiver's self-worth and cultivates future business?
- Is the message sent promptly to indicate courtesy?
- Does the message reflect the high standards of a business professional: quality paper, accurate formatting, quality printing, and absence of misspellings and grammatical errors?

© Image Source

Step 6: Organize the Message

objective ⑥

Recognize the importance of organizing a message before writing the first draft and select the appropriate message outline (deductive or inductive) for developing messages to achieve the desired response.

After you have identified the specific ways you must adapt the message to your specific audience, you are ready to organize your message. In a discussion of communication, the word *organize* means dividing a topic into parts and arranging them in an appropriate sequence. Before undertaking this process, you must be convinced that the message is the right message— that it is complete, accurate, fair, reasonable, ethical, and logical. If it doesn't meet these standards, it should not be sent. Good organiza-

tion and good writing or speaking cannot be expected to compensate for a bad decision.

If you organize and write simultaneously, the task seems hopelessly complicated. Writing is much easier if questions about the organization of the message are answered first: What is the purpose of the message, what is the receiver's likely reaction, and should the message begin with the main point? Once these decisions have been made, you can concentrate on expressing ideas effectively.

Outline to Benefit the Sender and the Receiver

When a topic is divided into parts, some parts will be recognized as central ideas and the others as minor ideas (details). Another way to think about this type of organization is from general to specific. The process of identifying these ideas and arranging them in the right sequence is known as **outlining**. Outlining *before* communicating provides numerous benefits:

- **Encourages accuracy and brevity.** Outlining reduces the chance of leaving out an essential idea or including an unessential idea.
- **Permits concentration on one phase at a time.** Having focused separately on (1) the ideas that need to be included, (2) the distinction between major and minor ideas, and (3) the sequence of ideas, total concentration can now be focused on the next challenge—expressing.
- **Saves time in structuring ideas.** With questions about which ideas to include and their proper sequence already answered, little time is lost in moving from one point to the next.
- **Provides a psychological lift.** The feeling of success gained in preparing the outline increases confidence that the next step—writing or speaking—will be successful, too.
- **Facilitates emphasis and de-emphasis.** Although each sentence makes its contribution to the message, some sentences need to stand out more vividly in the receiver's mind than others. An effective outline ensures that important points will appear in emphatic positions.

The preceding benefits derived from outlining are sender oriented. Because a message has been well outlined, receivers benefit as well:

- The message is more concise and accurate.
- Relationships between ideas are easier to distinguish and remember.

outlining
the process of identifying ideas and arranging them in the right sequence

- Reaction to the message and its sender is more likely to be positive.

A receiver's reaction to a message is strongly influenced by the sequence in which ideas are presented. A beginning sentence or an ending sentence is in an emphatic position. (Other emphasis techniques are explained in Chapter 8.) Throughout this text, you will see that outlining (organizing) is important.

Sequence Ideas to Achieve Desired Goals

When planning your communication, you should strive for an outline that will serve you in much the same way a blueprint serves a builder or an itinerary serves a traveler. Organizing your message first will ensure that your ideas are presented clearly and logically and all vital components are included. To facilitate your determination of an appropriate sequence for a business document or presentation, follow the three-step process illustrated in Figure 4-2. This process involves answering the following questions in this order:

deductive sequence
when a message begins with the major idea
inductive sequence
when a message withholds the major idea until accompanying details and explanations have been presented

1. *What is the central idea of the message?* Think about the *reason* you are writing or speaking—the first step in the communi-

cation process. What is your purpose—to extend a job offer, decline an invitation, or seek support for an innovative project? The purpose is the central idea of your message. You might think of it as a message condensed into a one-sentence telegram.

2. *What is the most likely receiver reaction to the message?* Ask, "If I were the one receiving the message I am preparing to send, what would *my* reaction be?" Because you would react with pleasure to good news and displeasure to bad news, you can reasonably assume a receiver's reaction would be similar. Recall the dual goals of a communicator: clarity and effective human relations. By considering anticipated receiver reaction, you build goodwill with the receiver. Almost every message will fit into one of four categories of anticipated receiver reaction: (1) pleasure, (2) displeasure, (3) interest but neither pleasure nor displeasure, or (4) no interest, as shown in Figure 4-2.

3. *In view of the predicted receiver reaction, should the central idea be listed first in the outline or should it be listed as one of the last items?* When a message begins with the major idea, the sequence of ideas is called **deductive**. When a message withholds the major idea until accompanying details and explanations have been presented, the sequence is called **inductive**.

Consider the receiver to determine whether to use the inductive or deductive sequence. If a receiver might be antagonized by the main idea in a deductive message, lead up to the main idea by making the message inductive. If a sender wants to encourage receiver in-

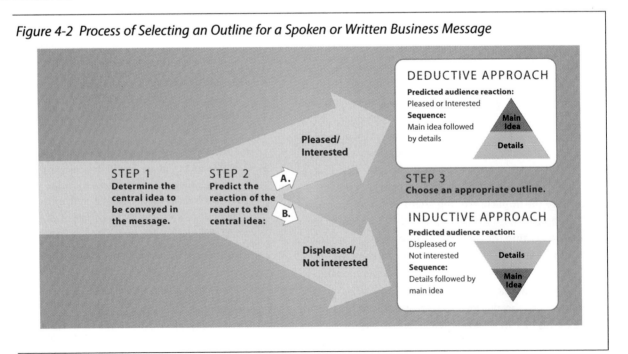

Figure 4-2 *Process of Selecting an Outline for a Spoken or Written Business Message*

volvement (to generate a little concern about where the details are leading), the inductive approach is recommended. Inductive organization can be especially effective if the main idea confirms the conclusion the receiver has drawn from the preceding details—a cause is worthy of support, an applicant should be interviewed for a job, a product/service should be selected, and so on. As you learn in later chapters about writing letters, memos, and email messages and about planning spoken communications, you will comprehend the benefits of using the appropriate outline for each receiver reaction:

Deductive Order (main idea first)	Inductive Order (details first)
When the message will *please* the receiver	When the message will *displease* the receiver
When the message is *routine* (will not please or displease)	When the receiver *may not be interested* (will need to be persuaded)

Sequencing Minor Ideas

Here are some common ways for determining the sequence of minor ideas that accompany the major idea:

- **Time.** When writing a memo or email about a series of events or a process, paragraphs proceed from the first step through the last step.
- **Space.** If a report is about geographic areas, ideas can proceed from one area to the next until all areas have been discussed.
- **Familiarity.** If a topic is complicated, the presentation can begin with a known or easy-to-understand point and proceed to progressively more difficult points.
- **Importance.** In analytical reports in which major decision-making factors are presented, the factors can be presented in order of most important to least important or vice versa.
- **Value.** If a presentation involves major factors with monetary values, paragraphs can proceed from those with greatest values to those with least values or vice versa.

These organizational patterns work for both written and spoken communication and are applicable in email messages, letters, memos, and reports.

© Mark Vicker/Iconica/Getty Images

Step 7: Prepare the First Draft

objective (7)
Prepare the first draft.

Once you have determined the purpose and type of message, considered the audience's needs and perspectives, chosen the proper channel and medium for communication, determined whether the message should be presented deductively (main idea first) or inductively (explanation and details first), and planned the logical sequence of points, you are ready to begin composing the message. Before doing so, however, you should read Chapters 5 through 8 for specific guidelines for the preparation of electronic communication, neutral and good-news messages, bad-news messages, and persuasive messages.

As for the process of drafting itself, once you are confident about the organization and approach to the draft, you are ready to write. Normally, writing rapidly (with intent to rewrite certain portions, if necessary) is better than slow, deliberate writing (with intent to avoid any need for rewriting portions). The latter approach can be frustrating and can reduce the quality of the finished work. Time is wasted on details that are better addressed in the revising and proofreading stage of writing, such as thinking of a particular way to express an idea, discarding it either before or after it is written, waiting for new inspiration, and rereading preceding sentences.

Concentrating on getting your ideas down as quickly as you can is an efficient approach to writing. During this process, remember that you are preparing a draft and not the final copy. If you are composing at the computer, you can quickly and easily revise your draft throughout the composition process. This seamless approach to writing allows you to continue to improve your "working draft" until the moment you are ready to submit the final copy. Numerous electronic writing tools are available to help with this process, and technology will continue to unfold to enhance it.

Communicating Electronically

Appropriate Use of Technology

Technology offers numerous advantages, but a technological channel is not always the communication method of choice. Before sending a message, be certain the selected channel of communication is appropriate by considering the message's purpose, confidentiality issues, and human relations factors.

objective ①
Identify the appropriate use of communication technology, including its legal and ethical implications.

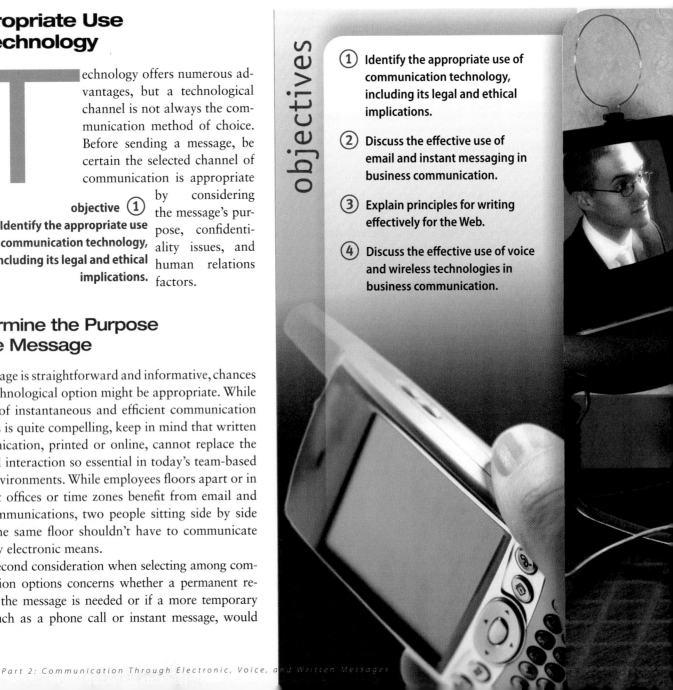

objectives

① Identify the appropriate use of communication technology, including its legal and ethical implications.

② Discuss the effective use of email and instant messaging in business communication.

③ Explain principles for writing effectively for the Web.

④ Discuss the effective use of voice and wireless technologies in business communication.

Determine the Purpose of the Message

If a message is straightforward and informative, chances are a technological option might be appropriate. While the use of instantaneous and efficient communication methods is quite compelling, keep in mind that written communication, printed or online, cannot replace the personal interaction so essential in today's team-based work environments. While employees floors apart or in different offices or time zones benefit from email and web communications, two people sitting side by side or on the same floor shouldn't have to communicate solely by electronic means.

A second consideration when selecting among communication options concerns whether a permanent record of the message is needed or if a more temporary form, such as a phone call or instant message, would suffice.

Determine Whether the Information Is Personal or Confidential

As a general guideline, keep personal correspondence off-line if you don't want it to come back and haunt you. The content of an email message could have embarrassing consequences since such documents often become a part of public records and wireless communications might be unexpectedly intercepted. Your company technically "owns" your electronic communications and thus can monitor them to determine legitimate business use or potential abuse. Undeliverable email messages are delivered to a mail administrator, and many networks routinely store backups of all email messages that pass through them.

Even deleted messages can be "resurrected" with little effort, as several public figures discovered when investigators retrieved archived email as evidence in court cases. For sensitive situations, a face-to-face encounter may be preferred.

Decide Whether Positive Human Relations Are Sacrificed

Be wary of using an electronic communication tool as an avoidance mechanism. Remember, too, that some people may not regularly check their email or voice mail, and some have unreliable systems that are slow or prone to lose messages. Some news will be received better in person than through an electronic format that might be interpreted as cold and impersonal.

Additionally, some people, especially those of certain cultures, may prefer a personal meeting even if you perceive that an electronic exchange of information would be a more efficient use of everyone's time. Choose the communication channel carefully to fit both your purpose and the preference of the receiver.

Before composing electronic messages, study carefully the guidelines presented in Chapters 6 through 9 for preparing various types of written communications and revising and proofreading them. Then, study the specific suggestions in the "Check Your Communication" checklist on this chapter's review card. Compare your work with this checklist after you have written a rough draft, making any needed corrections.

Electronic Mail Communication

objective ②
Discuss the effective use of email and instant messaging in business communication.

A vital factor in successful global business and economic development is the effective use of knowledge and information. Companies must not only provide the means for their workers to access important information and communicate it internally but also must provide them with the tools to communicate with audiences who have decided to pay attention via websites and electronic messages. As you read in Chapter 1, the continuous evolution of technology has expanded communication options. Email, instant messaging (IM), web communications, and voice and wireless technologies are important tools for accomplishing company goals.

Advantages of Email

Electronic mail, known as email, has quickly become the most used communication tool in many organiza-

tions. Its ready availability, convenience, and ease of use have resulted in its skyrocketing popularity over the last decade. The advantages of email are numerous:

- **It facilitates the fast, convenient flow of information among users at various locations and time zones.** Mail service is often too slow for communicating timely information, and the telephone system is inconvenient and costly when communicating with people located in several locations and time zones. For these reasons, email is especially effective when sending a single message to several recipients and when needing to communicate 24 hours a day, 365 days a year.

- **It increases efficiency.** Email reduces "telephone tag" and unnecessary telephone interruptions caused when delivering messages that are unlikely to require a verbal response.

- **It reduces costs.** Sending email messages represents a substantial savings to companies in long-distance telephone costs and postal mail-outs.

- **It reduces paper waste.** Often, an electronic message can be read and immediately discarded without the need for a printed copy.

© Digital Vision/Getty Images

SEND

Guidelines for Preparing Email Messages

The principles of written style and organization that you learn throughout this book are applicable to email messages. Other techniques are specific to email. All of these tools will assist you in using informal communication channels more efficiently without jeopardizing the effectiveness of your message or damaging relationships with valued coworkers and outside parties.

Standard Heading

Email systems automatically show a heading format that includes *To:, From:, Date:,* and *Subject:* but the sender need only provide information for the *To:* and the *Subject:* lines. Sending an email message to multiple recipients simply involves keying the email address of each recipient into a distribution list and selecting the distribution list as the recipient.

Useful Subject Line

The subject line expedites the understanding of the message by (1) telling the receiver what the following message is about, (2) setting the stage for the receiver to understand the message, and (3) providing meaning when the document is referenced at a later date. Additionally, a well-written subject line in an email message will help a receiver sort through an overloaded mailbox and read messages in priority order. The following suggestions should be helpful in wording subject lines.

- **Provide a useful subject line that has meaning for you and the receiver.** Identifying key words will help you develop good subject lines. Think of the five W's—Who, What, When, Where, and Why—to give you some clues for a useful subject line. Consider the following examples:

General and Ineffective	Precise and Informative
Report of Meeting	**Meeting Report on Dublin Plant Relocation**
	Provides specific information that will identify the exact purpose of the message
Product Launch	**Product Launch Snafu**
	Pinpoints a problem and will provoke an immediate response

- **Restate the subject in the body of the message.** Opening sentences should not include wording such as "This is . . ." and "The above-mentioned subject . . ." The body of the message should be a complete thought and should not rely on the subject line for elaboration. A good opening sentence might be a repetition of most of the subject line. Even if the reader were to skip the subject line, the message would still be clear, logical, and complete.

SUBJECT: Budget Meeting at Crystal Bluff

Arrange your schedule to attend a day-long meeting to finalize the 2008 budget on Friday, February 24. We're meeting in the conference room at the Crystal Bluff Conference Center . . .

Single Topic Directed Toward the Receiver's Needs

What do you hope to accomplish as a result of the message? Being clear in your purpose will enable you to organize and develop the content of your message and tailor your message to show how the receiver will benefit.

An email message is generally limited to one idea rather than addressing several issues. If you address more than one topic in a single email message, chances are the recipient will forget to respond to all points discussed. Additionally, discussing one topic allows you to write a descriptive subject line that will accurately describe your purpose and effectively compete for the receiver's attention—especially when the subject line appears in an overcrowded inbox. The receiver can transfer the single subject message to a separate mailbox folder for quick, accurate access.

Lengthy messages may be divided into logical sections. Using headings to denote the divisions will capture receiver attention and simplify comprehension.

Sequence of Ideas Based on Anticipated Reader Reaction

Use empathy to determine a logical, efficient sequence of information that will gain the reaction you want from the receiver. As you learned previously, ideas should be organized deductively when a message contains good news or neutral information; inductive organization is recommended when the message contains bad news or is intended to persuade.

In addition, email messages may use other bases for determining the sequence of ideas—for example, time (reporting events in the order in which they happened), order of importance, and geography. As a general rule of thumb, present the information in the order it is likely to be needed. For example, describe the nature and purpose an upcoming meeting before giving the specifics (date, place, time). Otherwise, the receiver may have to reread portions of the email to extract the details.

Careful Use of Jargon, Technical Words, and Shortened Terms

You are more likely to use jargon and technical terms in email messages than in business letters. Because people doing similar work are almost sure to know the technical terms associated with it, jargon will be understood, will not be taken as an attempt to impress, and will save time. For the same reasons, acronyms, abbreviations, and shortened forms, such as *info*, *rep*, *demo*, *pro*, and *stat*, are more useful in email messages than in letters. In practicing empathy, however, consider whether the receiver will likely understand the terms. Remember that an in-

ternational receiver or an external business partner may not understand your jargon or shortened language.

Graphic Highlighting

Graphical treatment is appropriate whenever it strengthens your efforts to communicate. Enumerated or bulleted lists, tables, graphs, pictures, or other images may be either integrated into the content of the email or attached as supporting material.

The email message in Figure 5-1 illustrates guidelines for using this informal communication channel effectively in a professional setting. The director of loan compliance begins her email message to the loan officer with a short sentence alerting the loan officer to the new mortgage policies. The short paragraphs that follow include timely information and refer to the attachment. The message

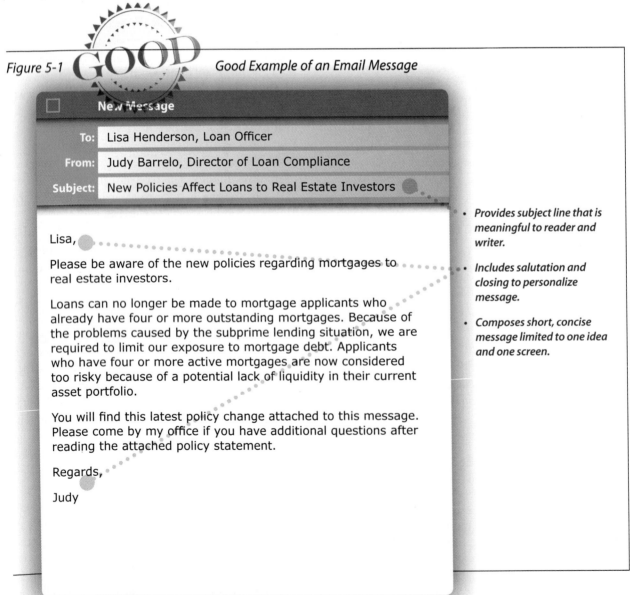

Figure 5-1 **GOOD** *Good Example of an Email Message*

New Message

To: Lisa Henderson, Loan Officer
From: Judy Barrelo, Director of Loan Compliance
Subject: New Policies Affect Loans to Real Estate Investors

Lisa,

Please be aware of the new policies regarding mortgages to real estate investors.

Loans can no longer be made to mortgage applicants who already have four or more outstanding mortgages. Because of the problems caused by the subprime lending situation, we are required to limit our exposure to mortgage debt. Applicants who have four or more active mortgages are now considered too risky because of a potential lack of liquidity in their current asset portfolio.

You will find this latest policy change attached to this message. Please come by my office if you have additional questions after reading the attached policy statement.

Regards,

Judy

- *Provides subject line that is meaningful to reader and writer.*
- *Includes salutation and closing to personalize message.*
- *Composes short, concise message limited to one idea and one screen.*

closes by inviting the reader to stop by the director's office if she has any questions.

While email offers various advantages in speed and convenience, problems arise when it is used inappropriately. The following guidelines will direct you in the effective use of email messages.

Effective Use of Email

Established standards of online behavior have emerged to help online communicators send and receive email messages that are courteous while enhancing communication effectiveness *and* productivity. Learning fundamental **netiquette**, the buzzword for proper behavior on the Internet, will assure your online success.

- **Check mail promptly.** Generally, a response to email is expected within 24 hours. Ignoring messages from coworkers can erode efforts to create an open, honest, and cooperative work environment. On the other hand, responding every second may indicate that you are paying more attention to your email than your job.
- **Do not contribute to email overload.** To avoid clogging the system with unnecessary messages, follow these simple guidelines:

- Be certain that individuals need a copy of the email, and forward an email from another person only with the original writer's permission.
- Never address an email containing action items to more than one person to ensure a response. This practice supports the old adage "Share a task between two people, and each takes 1% responsibility."[1]
- Avoid sending formatted documents. Messages with varying fonts, special print features (e.g., bold, italics, etc.), and clip art take longer to download, require more storage space, and may be unreadable on some computers. In addition, enhancing routine email messages does not support the goals of competitive organizations, and employees and clients/customers may resent such frivolous use of time.
- Edit the original message when you reply to email if the entire body of the original message is not needed for context. Instead, you can cut and paste pertinent sections within a reply that you believe will help the recipient understand your reply. You can also key brief comments in all caps below the original section.
- Follow company policy for personal use of email, and obtain a private email account if you are job hunting or sending many private messages to friends and relatives.

- **Use email selectively.** Send short, direct messages for routine matters that need not be handled immediately (scheduling meetings, giving your supervisor quick updates, or addressing other uncomplicated issues).

- **Do not send messages when you are angry.** Email containing sensitive, highly emotional messages may be easily misinterpreted because of the absence of nonverbal communication (facial expressions, voice tone, and body language). Sending a **flame**, the online term used to describe a heated, sarcastic, and sometimes abusive message or posting, may prompt a receiver to send a retaliatory response. Email messages written in anger and filled with emotion and sarcasm may end up as evidence in litigation. Because of the potential damage to relationships and legal liability, read email messages carefully before clicking "Send." Unless a response is urgent, store a heated message for an hour until you have cooled off and thought about the issue clearly and rationally. When you *must* respond immediately, you might acknowledge that your response is emotional and has not been thoroughly considered. Give this warning by using words such as

netiquette
the buzzword for proper behavior on the Internet
flame
a sarcastic, sometimes abusive message or posting that may prompt a receiver to send a retaliatory response

"I need to vent my frustration for a few paragraphs" or "flame on—I'm writing in anger."[2]

- **Exercise caution against email viruses and hoaxes.** An ounce of prevention can avert the problems caused by deadly *viruses* that destroy data files or annoying messages that simply waste your time while they are executing. Install an *antivirus software program* that will scan your hard drive each time you start the computer or access external devices, and keep backups of important files. Be suspicious of email messages from people you don't know that contain attachments. Email text is usually safe to open, but the attachment may contain an executable file that can affect your computer's operations. *Social networking sites,* such as Facebook and MySpace, are also common sources of viruses and spyware.

  Additionally, be wary of *computer hoaxes*—email messages that incite panic typically related to risks of computer viruses or deadly threats and urge you to forward them to as many people as possible. Forwarding a hoax can be embarrassing and causes inefficiency by overloading email boxes and flooding computer security personnel with inquiries from alarmed recipients of your message.

  If a hoax is forwarded to you, reply to the person politely that the message is a hoax. This action allows you to help stop the spread of the malicious message and will educate one more person about the evils of hoaxes.

- **Develop an effective system for handling email.** Some simple organization will allow you to make better use of your email capability:
  - Set up separate accounts for receiving messages that require your direct attention.
  - Keep your mailbox clean by deleting messages you are not using and those not likely to be considered relevant in a lawsuit.
  - Set up folders to organize messages for quick retrieval. If you receive many messages, consider purchasing an email handler to sort and prioritize messages, send form letters as replies to messages received with a particular subject line, automatically forward specified email, and sound an alarm when you receive a message from a particular person.

Instant Messaging

IM or chat, represents a blending of email with conversation. This real-time email technology allows you to maintain a list of people with whom you want to interact. You can send messages to any or all of the people on your list as long as the people are online. Sending a message opens up a window in which you and your contact can key messages that you both can see immediately. Figure 5-2 illustrates a sample IM conversation that occurred as a follow-up to the loan compliance director's email message in Figure 5-1.

Gift Card Hoax

Imagine opening an email that tells you in two weeks several stores from which you purchased gift cards will not honor those cards because of mass store closures. Before you hurry out to redeem the cards in question, you forward this email to everybody in your address book to make sure they don't get cheated either.

Now imagine you are the manager of Eddie Bauer, inundated with calls from irate customers demanding their money back for unredeemable gift cards. You spend most of the coming days trying to reassure these customers that their cards are still good, are redeemable at any store and online, and that, as far as you know, that won't change.

This scenario came true for several retailers mentioned in a hoax email that flooded inboxes in November and December 2008. The news of unredeemable gift cards spread like wildfire, causing holiday gift card sales to drop further than anticipated. Stores like Eddie Bauer and Talbots released messages from their CEOs attempting to debunk the rumors of closure and unredeemable gift cards, but the damage was done. Holiday gift card sales are a significant source of income and repeat business for retailers. A decrease in those sales is difficult to recover.

Before forwarding emails, check the facts. Several websites, such as the following, devote themselves to separating fact from fiction and give tips on how to identify a potential hoax:

- *Urban Legends:* **www.urbanlegends.com**
- *Snopes:* **www.snopes.com**
- *Truth or Fiction:* **www.truthorfiction.com**

Figure 5-2 Good Example of an Instant Message

- Opens message by "knocking" to ask if she is interrupting.

- Keeps conversation brief by limiting it to a few short sentences.

- Uses a few easily recognized abbreviations and acronyms but avoids informal slang that could be confusing and detract from professional nature of message.

- Uses instant messaging for a few quick questions but agrees to make critical decisions during meeting.

Output Interaction Box

Judy:>>Is this a good time to talk about changes in loan policy?
Lisa:>>Sure. Shoot.
Judy:>>I've just received the latest lending policies from the banks that supply our mortgage loans.
Lisa:>>Great. Are there big changes?
Judy:>>Yes. We can no longer loan to investors with four or more outstanding mortgages.
Lisa:>>IC. Why?
Judy:>>With the real estate downturn, their assets now lack liquidity. Too risky.
Lisa:>>Is there anything else we need to do?
Judy:>>No. I'll send u the new policy electronically.
Lisa:>>Ok.
Judy:>>We can talk this afternoon if u have questions. I'll be in.

Users Logged On

Judy Barrelo
Lisa Henderson

☐ Entry Chime

Enter your message below

Send URL
Quit

Business use of IM has experienced phenomenal growth. Analysts estimate that in 90 percent of companies some employees use IM, whether to close a sale, collaborate with a colleague, or just trade pleasantries with a colleague.[3] The best-known IM programs are free and require no special hardware and little training. With some programs, users can exchange graphics and audio and video clips. Many of the guidelines that apply to the use of email for business purposes apply also to IM. With IM, however, spelling and grammar matter less when trading messages at high speed. IM users often use shorthand for common words and phrases. IM and telephone communication also share common challenges: being sure that the sender is who he or she claims to be and that the conversation is free from eavesdropping.

Some managers worry that employees will spend too much work time using IM to chat with buddies inside and outside the company. They also emphasize that IM is not the right tool for every business purpose; employees should still rely on email when they need a record and use the telephone for the personal touch.

Email and the Law

Remember that you are responsible for the content of any electronic message you send. Because email moves so quickly between people and often becomes very informal and conversational, individuals may not realize (or may forget) their responsibility. If a person denies commitments made via email, someone involved may produce a printed copy of the email message as verification.

Email communicators must also abide by copyright laws. Be certain to give credit for quoted material and seek permission to use copyrighted text or graphics from printed or electronic sources. Unless you inform the reader that editing has occurred, do not alter a message you are forwarding or re-posting, and be sure to ask permission before forwarding it.

The courts have established the right of companies to monitor the electronic mail of an employee because they own the facilities and intend them to be used for job-related communication only. On the other hand, employees typically expect that their email messages should be kept private.

Email has often become the prosecutor's star witness—the corporate equivalent of DNA evidence, as it and other forms of electronic communication are subject to subpoena in litigation. Several perils of "evidence" mail that companies must address are illustrated in these cases:[4]

- Including inappropriate content can humiliate and lead to conviction. Emails such as the one sent by a JPMorgan Chase banker

Destroying evidence mail is like playing with fire.

© ImageState-Pictor/ImageState/Jupiterimages

warning a colleague to "shut up and delete this email" or the emails exchanged by Wall Street investment houses discussing increasing stock ratings to "please investment clients" are likely to be used in court as evidence of inappropriate business behaviors.

- Failing to preserve or destroying email messages in violation of securities rules is a sure path to destruction. Arthur Andersen's destruction of Enron-related messages led to a criminal conviction and eventually to Enron's implosion.

- Using inability to locate emails and other relevant documents demanded by the courts (negligence) is unacceptable to the courts. Penalties have included monetary fines, assessment of court costs or attorney's fees, and dismissal of the case in favor of the opposing side.

On the other hand, evidence mail can protect a company from lawsuits. A company being sued by a female employee because a male executive had allegedly sexually abused her retrieved a trail of emails with lurid attachments sent by the female employee to the male executive named in the case.[5]

To avoid the legal perils of email, employees must be taught not to write loose, potentially rude, and informal email messages; to avoid casually deleting emails; and to take the time to identify and organize relevant emails for quick retrieval.

Web Page Communication

objective ③
Explain principles for writing effectively for the Web.

The World Wide Web is truly a universal communication medium, reaching a broad audience in diverse locations. The familiar web platform may be used for offering a company *intranet* to distribute various types of information to employees at numerous locations. Avenue A and Razorfish won the 2007 WebAward for outstanding achievement in website development for its intranet design.

Business partners such as vendors, suppliers, and customers can utilize the Web to access a company's *extranet*. Both intranets and extranets restrict access to those visitors with authorization such as a password. An organization can also establish a *public web presence* to extend its reach significantly and provide potential customers or clients with an always-available source of information and contact. While effective web page development is a highly specialized activity, understanding of the process will be useful to any business communicator. Organizations can use the Web not only to communicate with customers and clients but also to interact with business partners.

In product design and building projects, a project team is typically comprised of various company personnel and a variety of outside parties that provide goods and services necessary for project completion. Completion is often delayed unnecessarily by misunderstandings between different vendors or plant personnel. Compounding the problem are the differences in computer systems, terminology, and processes. Fortunately, the Web can now provide a neutral environment to bridge those gaps and get work done correctly and on time.

Web-based project software applications allow information to be viewed from any computer with Internet access, as long as the user has the proper security clearance and passwords. This means you don't necessarily have to own the same kind of system as the people with whom you are sharing data. Comfort with the familiar Internet platform means that users can be trained in a matter of minutes. The web-based software provides a quick, convenient, and controlled way to exchange information with colleagues and vendors. Project team members have easy access regardless of their technical ability, location, application, or computer platform.[6]

A successful example of web-based project software is ActiveProject by Framework Technologies Corporation, a subsidiary of Centric Software.[7] The application, used largely for design, engineering, and manufacturing projects, comes with preformatted website templates that allow users to set up their project management communications quickly. The integrated system uses the Web as a communication mechanism to enable a team of people to work together on a project. They don't need a shared system or shared software applications to exchange information, comment on each other's information, and proceed with the project.[8]

When a new project is planned, documents, drawings, photos, key performance indicators (KPIs), and other requirements are posted online by the host company to share with the various vendors of equipment, materials, and labor. Files on the server are instantly available to everybody on the project team. Now all of the vendors have the shop-floor drawings and can start adding information. Various members of the team can visit the site, post their information, make comments, and ask questions. Access can also be controlled, so information can be shared with various people without opening it to everyone.

KPIs collected at the project level can be governed with Centric Charter, a web-based form that enables collaboration using a spreadsheet interface. The managed KPIs can be merged with KPIs exposed by other systems to do project portfolio analysis with Centric Decision Center.

The software allows users to comment directly about various aspects of the project, either verbally or by marking up the charts and diagrams on the site. Comments and requests for information are tracked automatically, so the project manager can see all of the communication in a log form. If the manager notices that an issue is causing problems, a deadline is falling behind schedule, or a team member is not responding to requests for information, then proper action can be taken to resolve the problem quickly.

A web page is fundamentally an ordinary text or ASCII file, so special tools are not necessary, although it is easier to create web pages using dedicated editors. What turns ordinary text into a web page is a web browser (such as Internet Explorer or Mozilla Firefox) and instructions or tags written in hypertext markup language (HTML). The browser interprets the HTML and displays the page. Hyperlinks on a page can link to web pages or other types of files, such as sound, video, or interactive programs.

Writing for a Website

Many standard rules for writing apply whether for the Web or print. However, some important differences exist between readers of paper material and web users:[9]

- Web users do not want to read. They skim, browse, and hop from one highlighted area to another trying to zero in on the word or phrase that relates to their search.

- English-speaking readers typically start scanning at the top left-hand side of the main content area. They move top to bottom, left to right. Given this pattern, it is important to put frequently accessed items close to the top of the content area. Information should follow the pyramid style of writing common in newspaper

TIP SHEET:

For Composing Appropriate Web Content[10]

- **Be brief.** A rule of thumb is to reduce the wording of any print document by 50 percent when you put it on the Web.

- **Keep it simple.** Use short words that allow for fast reading by people of various educational backgrounds. Use mixed case, since all caps are slower to read.

- **Consider appropriate jargon.** If all of your site users share a common professional language, then use it. Otherwise, keep to concise yet effective word choices.

- **Use eye-catching headlines.** They may catch interest, ask a question, present the unusual, or pose a conflict.

- **Break longer documents into smaller chunks.** Provide ways to easily move through the document and return to the beginning.

- **Use attention-getting devices judiciously.** Bold, font changes, color, and graphics do attract attention but can be overdone, causing important ideas to be lost.

- **Avoid placing critical information in graphic form only.** Many users are averse to slow-loading graphics and skip over them.

Digital Footprint

Whether writing an email or a posting on your company's internal blog, every step you take in cyberspace leaves a footprint. Your computer's hard drive, your connection to the Internet, even footage on security cameras contribute to your digital footprint and are a public archive of your electronic activity. Even "anonymous" blog posts can be traced back to you. When everything you do on the computer leaves a traceable mark, it is important to use all electronic communications ethically and wisely to protect yourself and others.

writing: The main idea or conclusion is presented first, and subsequent sections and pages expand upon it.

- Users can more quickly scan items in columns rather than rows, especially if they are categorized, grouped, and have headings. You can have more lists on the Web than in a typical print document.

- Users refer infrequently to directions. It is unlikely that they will read little notes, sidebars, and help files, so directions must appear in simple, numbered steps.

In recognition of these web-user characteristics, writers should tailor their styles accordingly. Effective web writing involves moving beyond the paper mode into the web mode of thinking. Understanding the distinctive expectations of web readers will allow you to structure your ideas effectively and efficiently.

Writing for Weblogs

A **weblog**, or **blog** for short, is a personal journal published on the Web that can take many forms. Some of the millions of blogs now populating the Web are online scrapbooks for posting links, information, and quotes. Some resemble personal diaries, often illustrated with digital snapshots; others serve as digital soapboxes, providing a platform for airing opinions and commentary about the world at large or on a special topic of interest. Users (known as *bloggers*) add entries (referred to as *posts*) using a simple online form in their browsers, while the weblog publishing software takes care of formatting the page layout and creating archive pages.[11]

Blogs differ from websites in that blogs are dy-

weblog (blog)
a personal journal published on the Web that can take many forms

namic, with rapidly changing content that does not require authorization to post. The creator of the message does not have to be familiar with special coding and uploads a message simply by clicking the "Publish" button.[12] Blogging allows average citizens to become publishers. Bloggers, however, should write each post with the realization that it is publicly available.

Blog formats have been adapted for business uses, including commercial publishing and marketing, and as a knowledge management tool. Blogs can store knowledge in searchable archives for future use. This function can be helpful, for example, for service teams as they search past communications to troubleshoot current problems. Many companies, such as Microsoft, Sun Microsystems, and General Motors, encourage blogging among employees.[13] An effective corporate blog begins with a clear goal, such as winning business or building customer loyalty, and then provides relevant, frequently updated information for the target audience to return to regularly. Like other effective web communications, blogs must be promoted creatively to attract avid readers.[14]

Internal blogs can be established that are not published to anyone outside the company. They present similar legal issues to those surrounding email and IM. One of the most important considerations is whether posts are truly anonymous. The potential for anonymous speech creates an atmosphere that can encourage irresponsible behavior, such as harassment, defamation, and gossip. To reduce this problem, information technology professionals can configure internal blogs so that all users can be identified, at least by the company.[15]

Voice and Wireless Communication

We live in an age of technological miracles. Communication capabilities that were considered science fiction 25 years ago are now commonplace. Not so long ago, voice communication referred to telephone usage, and using the telephone effectively is still an important skill in any profession. While the traditional telephone still plays an important role in business activity, voice communication extends to voice mail systems

objective ④
Discuss the effective use of voice and wireless technologies in business communication.

and cell phone usage. Both voice and data can be transmitted now using wireless communication systems.

Voice Mail Communication

Voice mail technology allows flexibility in staying in touch without the aid of a computer. Just as email communication can be enhanced by adhering to some basic principles, voice mail communication can be more effective by following recommended guidelines:[16]

- Update your greeting often to reflect your schedule and leave special announcements.
- Leave your email address, fax number, or mailing address on your greeting if this information might be helpful to your callers.
- Encourage callers to leave detailed messages. If you need certain standard information from callers, then use your greeting to prompt them for it. This information may eliminate the need to call back.
- Instruct callers on how to review their message or be transferred to an operator.
- Check your voice mail regularly, and return all voice messages within 24 hours.

When leaving a message, you can improve your communication by following these tips:[17]

- Speak slowly and clearly, and repeat your name and phone number at the beginning and end of the message.
- Spell your name for the recipient who may need the correct spelling.

- Leave a detailed message, not just your name and number, to avoid prolonged phone tag.
- Keep your message brief, typically 60 seconds or less.
- Ensure that your message will be understandable. Don't call from places with distracting background noise; when using a cell phone, consider whether your connection is adequate to complete the message.

The sound of your voice makes a lasting impression on the many people who listen to your greeting or the messages you leave. To ensure that the impression you leave is a professional one, review your voice greeting before you save it. Rerecord to eliminate verbal viruses ("um," "uh," stumbles), flat or monotone voice, and garbled or rushed messages that are difficult to understand. Consider scripting the message to avoid long, drawn-out recitations. As you are recording, stand, smile, and visualize the person receiving the message; you'll hear the added energy, enthusiasm, and warmth in your voice.[18]

Remember that the voice mail message you leave should be seen as permanent. In some systems, the digital files are backed up and stored for possible retrieval by managers or other company personnel. A voice mail message can also be used as evidence in a lawsuit or other legal proceeding.[19]

Cell Phone Communication

Mobile telephones, once a rarity, are now a standard accessory for many people throughout the world. In the

United States, cell phones are as commonplace as land-line phones, and the number continues to rise.

Cell Phone Calling

The popularity of cell phones has outstripped the development of rules for proper cell phone etiquette. Cell phone abuse causes much annoyance, and your attention to a few commonsense guidelines will help assure that you are not seen as a rude phone user.[20]

- **Observe wireless-free quiet zones.** This obviously includes theaters, performances, and religious services but may also include meetings, restaurants, hospitals, and other public places. Exercise judgment about silencing your ringer or turning off your phone.
- **Respect others in crowded places.** Speak in low conversational tones, and consider the content of your conversation.
- **Think safety.** Some states and municipalities have banned the use of cell phones while driving. Others allow the use of hands-free devices only. Even if not illegal, cell phone usage increases the risk of accident by distracting the driver.

Cell phone users should remember that the technology is not secure. Perhaps you have overheard another party's phone conversation when using your cell phone. The radio frequencies that transmit the voice signals can be picked up by other equipment. For this reason, information that is confidential or sensitive should be shared using an alternate communication channel.

Text Messaging

Text messaging on a cell phone or personal digital assistant (PDA) is a refinement of computer IM. But because the typical cell phone screen can accommodate no more than 160 characters, and because the keypad is far less versatile, text messaging puts an even greater premium on conciseness. An entire codebook of acronyms and abbreviations has emerged, ranging from CWOT (complete waste of time) to DLTBBB (don't let the bed bugs bite). The use of emoticons has also advanced far beyond the traditional smiley face and includes drooling (:-)...) and secrecy (:X). Inventive and

young users frequently insert their own style, substituting "z" for "s," or "d" for "th." While text messaging is generally a social communication tool, it does have some applications for business when the sender needs to get a quick and silent message to the recipient, such as in a meeting. Refer to Figure 5-3, which compares the completeness and relative formality of the email message to the informal nature of the instant message and the abbreviated style of the text message. Each medium requires its own appropriate writing style to maximize effectiveness and social expectations.

The United States lags behind much of the rest of the world in the use of text messaging because voice calls are inexpensive and in many cases easier. Some of the most avid text-messagers are clustered in Southeast Asia. The Chinese language is particularly well suited to text messaging, because in Mandarin the names of the numbers are also close to the sounds of certain words.[21]

Both abroad and at home, text messaging can be used as an avoidance mechanism that preserves the feeling of communication without the burden for actual intimacy or substance. The majority of text messages are superficial greetings often sent when the two parties are within speaking distance of each other. Like a wave or nod, they are meant to merely establish a connection without getting specific.

Wireless Communication and the Future

With the many communication innovations that have occurred in the last 20 years, one can only wonder what the next 20 years will hold. Whatever the breakthroughs, one particular technology will figure strongly in the changes—wireless communication. For many years, wireless communication has freed us from the necessity of being literally plugged in while enabling us to

© Edyta Pawlowska/iStockphoto.com

Figure 5-3 Levels of Formality Required by Various Technology

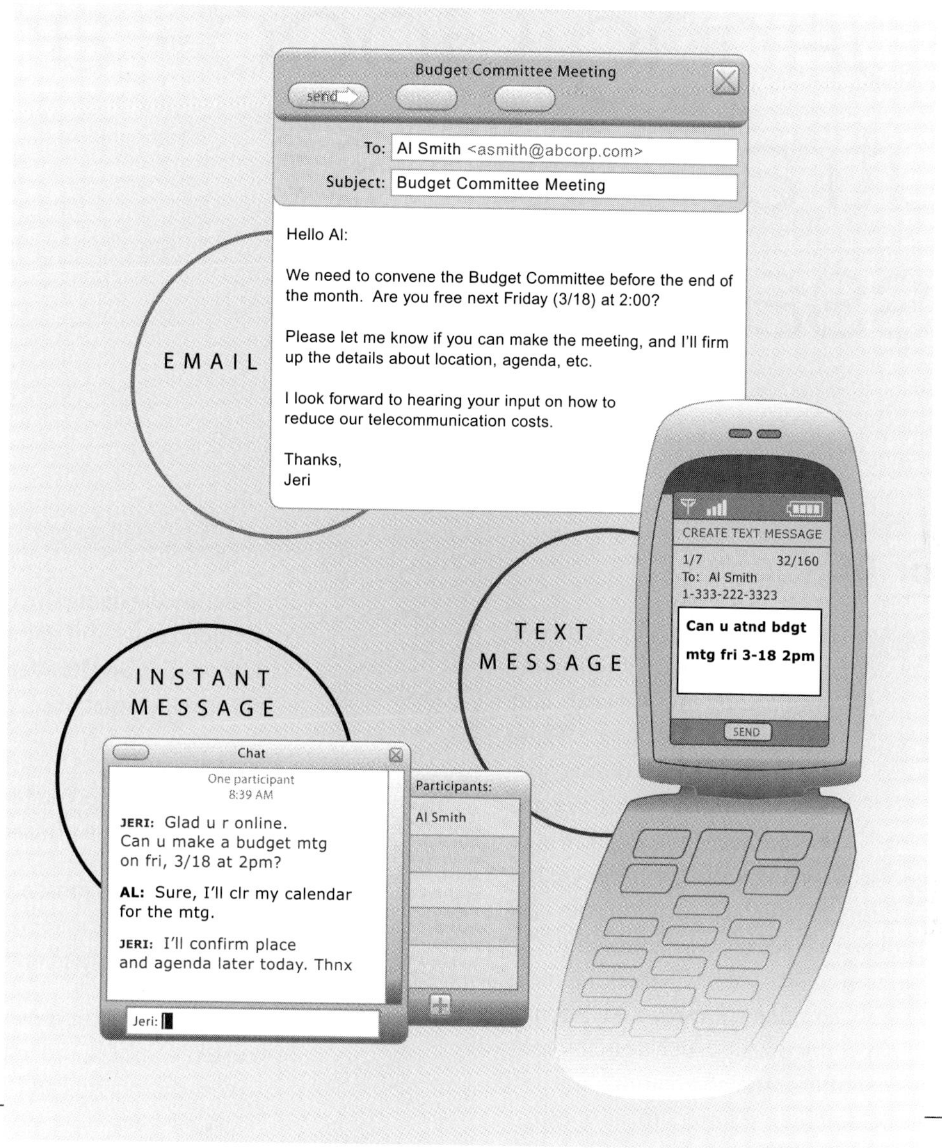

EMAIL

To: Al Smith <asmith@abcorp.com>
Subject: Budget Committee Meeting

Hello Al:

We need to convene the Budget Committee before the end of the month. Are you free next Friday (3/18) at 2:00?

Please let me know if you can make the meeting, and I'll firm up the details about location, agenda, etc.

I look forward to hearing your input on how to reduce our telecommunication costs.

Thanks,
Jeri

TEXT MESSAGE

CREATE TEXT MESSAGE
1/7   32/160
To: Al Smith
1-333-222-3323

Can u atnd bdgt mtg fri 3-18 2pm

SEND

INSTANT MESSAGE

Chat
One participant
8:39 AM

JERI: Glad u r online. Can u make a budget mtg on fri, 3/18 at 2pm?

AL: Sure, I'll clr my calendar for the mtg.

JERI: I'll confirm place and agenda later today. Thnx

Participants:
Al Smith

communicate virtually anytime and anywhere. But wireless is no longer merely voice technology over a cell phone; it can now accommodate high-speed data transmission as well.

Wireless technology is driving many of the significant changes that are affecting today's business. PDAs combine computing, telephone/fax, Internet, and networking features. A typical PDA can function as a cellular phone, fax sender, web browser, and personal organizer. Most PDAs are pen based, using a stylus rather than a keyboard for input. This means that they also incorporate handwriting recognition features. Some PDAs can also react to voice input by using voice recognition technologies.

The impact of wireless communication will become even more significant as voice-to-text and text-to-voice technology continues to develop. Voice-to-text and vice-versa technology offers the ability to communicate with a computer system without a keyboard. While such technology has been around for more than two decades, newer systems have more powerful processors, are more miniaturized, and tolerate variances in speakers' accents and inflections without sacrificing speed and accuracy. Wireless capability will increase the timeliness of key business decisions, resulting in greater revenues and profitability.

However, just being able to make decisions quickly does not ensure that they are the right decisions. As in the past, workers will need to have correct and timely information for making decisions. A second challenge for the wireless era will be balancing electronic communication capabilities with the need for human interaction.

Preparing Good- and Neutral-News Messages

Choosing the Channel or Medium

People in organizations use a number of channels to communicate with internal and external audiences. When sending a message that is positive or neutral, you have numerous choices, as shown in Figure 6-1 on page 91. Depending on the message, the recipient, and constraints of time and location, the best channel might be spoken or electronic. In addition to the electronic and verbal tools discussed in Chapter 5 (email, instant messaging, web communications, and phone), companies also use paper documents, such as memorandums and letters, to communicate information.

Memorandums (commonly referred to as *memos*) provide a tangible means of sharing information with people inside an organization. Letters are more formal because they are used to convey information to external audiences, such as customers, clients, business partners, or suppliers. Regardless of whether the audience is an internal or external one, communication should be carefully planned and prepared to achieve the desired purposes.

The Deductive Organizational Approach

As discussed in Chapter 4, you can organize business messages either deductively or inductively depending on your assessment of the receiver's reaction to your main idea. Learning to or-

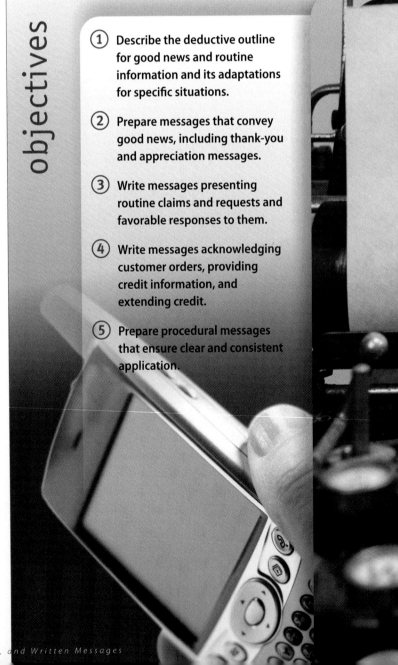

objectives

(1) Describe the deductive outline for good news and routine information and its adaptations for specific situations.

(2) Prepare messages that convey good news, including thank-you and appreciation messages.

(3) Write messages presenting routine claims and requests and favorable responses to them.

(4) Write messages acknowledging customer orders, providing credit information, and extending credit.

(5) Prepare procedural messages that ensure clear and consistent application.

objective ①
Describe the deductive outline for good news and routine information and its adaptations for specific situations.

ganize business messages according to the appropriate organizational approach will improve your chances of preparing a document that elicits the response or action you desire.

In this chapter, you will learn to compose messages that convey ideas that a receiver likely will find either *pleasing* or *neutral*. Messages that convey pleasant information are referred to as **good-news messages**. Messages that are of interest to the receiver but are not likely to generate an emotional reaction are referred to as **neutral messages**.

Because message expectations and social conventions differ from culture to culture, the effective writer will adapt as necessary when writing for various audiences. Asians, for example, typically use indirect patterns of writing, even when writing about good news; they avoid negative messages or

good-news message
message that conveys pleasant information
neutral message
message of interest to the receiver but unlikely to generate an emotional reaction

Good News..

Once they understand the important idea, they can move rapidly through the supporting details.

As you study sample deductive messages in this chapter, note the *bad example* notation that clearly marks the examples of poor writing. Detailed comments highlight important writing strategies that have been applied or violated. While gaining experience in developing effective messages, you will also learn to recognize standard business formats. Fully formatted messages are shown as printed documents (letters on company letterhead or paper memos) or as electronic formats (email messages or online input screens). Details about formatting letters, memos, and email messages are included in the style cards at the end of the book.

In the following sections, you will find considerations for preparing a variety of good- and neutral-news messages and examples of each. More specifically, you will find a discussion of:

- Good-news messages, including positive news, thank-you, and appreciation messages.
- Routine claims and their responses.
- Routine requests and their responses.
- Routine messages about orders and credit.
- Procedural messages.

Good-News Messages

Messages delivering good news are organized using a direct approach, as illustrated in Figure 6-1. You'll study examples of messages that convey positive news as well as thank-you and appreciation messages that generate goodwill.

objective ②
Prepare messages that convey good news, including thank-you and appreciation messages.

camouflage them so expertly that the reader might not recognize them. On the other hand, Germans tend to be more direct than North Americans, even with bad news.

In North America, good-news or neutral messages follow a **deductive** or **direct sequence**—the message begins with the main idea. To present good news and neutral information deductively, begin with the major idea, followed by supporting details as depicted in Figure 6-1. In both good-news and neutral messages, the third point (closing thought) may be omitted without seriously impairing effectiveness; however, including it unifies the message, avoids abruptness, and if written well can help to build goodwill with your audience.

The deductive pattern has several advantages:

- The first sentence is easy to write. After it is written, the details follow easily.
- The first sentence gets the attention it deserves in this emphatic position.
- Encountering good news in the first sentence puts receivers in a pleasant frame of mind, and they are more receptive to the details that follow.
- The arrangement may save receivers some time.

deductive sequence (direct sequence)
when the message begins with the main idea

Positive News

The memo sent to all employees in Figure 6-2 on page 92 begins directly with the main idea—the implementation of a new process for requesting vacation days. The discussion that follows includes a brief review of the old process and ends positively by encouraging employees to take advantage of the new system as well as offers contact information if they encounter problems.

Figure 6-1 Direct Outline Used in Good- and Neutral-News Messages Sent in Written, Electronic, or Spoken Form

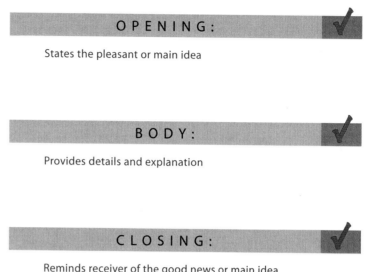

Letters
Memos

Written

Email
Instant message
Website
Blog
Text message

Electronic

In person
Telephone
Voice mail

Spoken

OPENING:

States the pleasant or main idea

BODY:

Provides details and explanation

CLOSING:

Reminds receiver of the good news or main idea and includes a future-oriented closing thought

Thank-You and Appreciation Messages

Empathetic managers take advantage of occasions to write goodwill messages that build strong, lasting relationships among employees, clients, customers, and various other groups. People usually are not reluctant to say "Thank you," "What a great performance," "You have certainly helped me," and so on. Despite good intentions, however, often people don't get around to sending thank-you and appreciation messages. Because of their rarity, written appreciation messages are especially meaningful—even treasured—and can positively distinguish you as a person who values others.

Thank-You Messages

After receiving a gift, being a guest, attending an interview, or benefiting in various other ways, a thoughtful person will take the time to send a written thank-you message. A simple handwritten or electronically sent note is sufficient for some social situations, such as a follow-up to a job interview. However, when written

from a professional office to respond to a business situation, the message may be printed on company letterhead. Your message should be written deductively and reflect your sincere feelings of gratitude. The following thank-you messages (1) identify the circumstances for which the writer is grateful and (2) provide specific reasons the action is appreciated.

To express thanks for a gift

> After conducting your strategic planning seminar, I was pleasantly surprised to receive a certificate to your online music site. Downloading music added some "jazz" to my day while giving me more insight into your business model. Thanks for your kindness and for this useful gift.

To extend thanks for hospitality

> Ray and I thoroughly enjoyed the weekend excursion you hosted at Lake Douglas for our work team. Since we moved here from Myrtle Beach, sailing has become a rare pleasure. You were kind to invite us. Thanks for a delightful time.

Figure 6-2   **GOOD**   *Good Example of a Good-News Message*

INTEROFFICE MEMORANDUM

TO: All Employees
FROM: Randy House, Human Resources Manager   *RH*
DATE: January 1, 2010
SUBJECT: New Policy for Requesting Vacation Days

A new system for requesting vacation days has been implemented by the Human Resources department. The new system is now available, and you should use it to request your vacation days for the coming year.

The new system replaces the old policy of requesting vacation days in writing from your supervisor. The new system is designed to save you time, ensure a quick confirmation of your request, and help the company maintain better records and coordinate resource needs better.

To use the new system, follow the steps below:

1. Log on to the human resources website at www.Luna/HR.com.
2. Click on the link that appears in the upper right-hand corner of your computer screen, "vacation request."
3. Type in the days you are requesting. You should use the following format: "06/05/10" in both the start date and end date boxes.
4. You will receive a confirmation via email if your vacation is approved within one week. If there is a problem with your request, you will receive an email message from human resources explaining the problem and providing you additional instructions on what to do next.

Please visit the HR website to make your vacation request soon. The earlier your request is made, the more likely it is to be approved without potential complications due to staffing needs. If you have problems with the electronic system, please contact our technical support staff at ext. 001.

- Announces approval of new vacation request policy.

- Provides clear explanation to ensure policy is understood. Formats as numbered list for quick, easy reference for specific details.

- Continues with a reason to try the new system soon.

- Provides additional information for readers who may have problems with the new system.

Format Pointers
Uses a template with standard memo headings for efficient production. Review other formatting guidelines on your style cards at the end of the book.

Includes writer's initials after printed name and title.

© Comstock Images/Jupiterimages

Appreciation Messages

An appreciation message is intended to recognize, reward, and encourage the receiver; however, the sender also gains happiness from commending a deserving person. Such positive thinking can be a favorable influence on the sender's own attitude and performance. In appropriate situations, you may wish to address an appreciation message to an individual's supervisor and send a copy of the document to the individual to share the positive comments.

For full potential value, follow these guidelines for appreciation messages:

- **Send in a timely manner.** Sending the appreciation message within a few days of the circumstance will emphasize the genuineness of your efforts. Appreciation letters sent long overdue may arouse questions about the sender's motive.

- **Avoid exaggerated language.** You may believe the exaggerated statements to be true, but the recipient may find them unbelievable and insincere. Strong language with unsupported statements arouses questions about your motive for the message.

- **Make specific comments about outstanding qualities or performance.** The following cold, mechanical message may have only minimal value to a speaker who has worked hard and has not been paid for the engagement. While the sender cared enough to say thank you, the message could have been given to any speaker, even if its sender had slept through the entire speech. Similarly, a note merely closed with *sincerely* does not necessarily make the ideas seem sincere. Including specific remarks about understanding and applying the speaker's main points makes the message meaningful and sincere and helps the writer to better convey goodwill.

Original: Your speech to the Lincoln Jaycees was very much appreciated. You are an excellent speaker, and you have good ideas. Thank you.

Improved: This past week I have found myself applying the principles you discussed last week at your speech to the Lincoln Jaycees.

When I completed the time analysis you suggested, I easily identified a number of areas for better management. Taking time to prioritize my daily tasks will be a challenge, but I now see its importance for accomplishing critical goals. Thank you for an informative and useful seminar.

The appreciation message in Figure 6-3 on the next page was sent from a manager to an employee who gave a seminar on improving interpersonal communication.

It conveys a warmer, more sincere compliment than a generic, exaggerated message. The net effects of this message are positive: The sender feels good for having passed on a deserved compliment, and the employee is encouraged by the manager's satisfaction with her initiative as well as her training sessions.

An apology is written much like an appreciation message. A sincere written apology is needed to preserve relationships when regrettable situations occur. While often difficult for the writer to prepare, the recipient will usually respond favorably to a well-written apology. See the Model Document card for this chapter for an example.

Routine Claims

objective ③
Write messages presenting routine claims and requests and favorable responses to them.

A claim is a request for an adjustment. When business communicators ask for something of which they think they are entitled (such as a refund, replacement, exchange, or payment for damages), the message is called a *claim message*.

Claim Message

Requests for adjustments can be divided into two groups: **routine claims** and **persuasive claims**. Persuasive claims, which are discussed in Chapter 8, assume that a request will be granted only after explanations and persuasive arguments have been presented. Routine claims (possibly because of guarantees, warranties, or other contractual conditions) assume that a request will be granted quickly and willingly, without persuasion. Because you expect routine claims to be granted willingly, a forceful, accusatory tone is inappropriate.

When the claim is routine, the direct approach shown in Figure 6-1 will be followed. Let's consider the situation referred to in Figures 6-4 and 6-5 on page 95. Clearly, the copier company intends to fix the copiers because it is in their contract and they have already sent a worker out. Because of the specific terms of the contract, WorkPartners, Inc. can expect the copiers to be fixed without persuasion. Thus,

claim
a request for an adjustment
routine claim
claim granted quickly, willingly, and without persuasion
persuasive claim
claim granted only after explanations and persuasive arguments have been presented

Figure 6-3

New Message

To: Ellen Meyer <emeyer@techno.com>
From: Martha Riggins <mriggins@techno.com>
Subject: Appreciation for Outstanding Contribution

Ellen,

Thank you for spearheading the initiative to improve interpersonal communication within the office and for arranging for the training sessions to achieve that goal. It was a big commitment on your part in addition to your regular duties.

Your efforts are already paying off. I have observed the techniques we learned in the training sessions being used in the department on several occasions already. In times of uncertainty, anxiety can often spill over into people's professional lives, so the seminar was very timely in helping to ensure a collaborative and civil workplace where everyone is treated respectfully.

You have proven yourself a dedicated and insightful employee, a true asset to the continued success of our organization.

Best regards,
Martha

- Extends appreciation for employee's efforts to improve departmental communication.

- Provides specific evidence of worth of experience without exaggerating or using overly strong language or mechanical statements.

- Assures writer of tangible benefits to be gained from training session.

Format Pointers
Uses short lines, mixed case; omits special formatting such as emoticons and email abbreviations for improved readability.

---

the administrative assistant can ask for a service person *before* providing an explanation, as shown in Figure 6-5. Beginning with the request for an adjustment gives it the emphasis it deserves. The message in Figure 6-4 is written using an indirect approach—the details are presented before the main idea, and the tone is unnecessarily forceful. Such an indirect approach may frustrate the reader since it takes longer to determine the purpose of the message and the tone is potentially insulting. Such an effect may result in a negative relationship and a less positive, conscientious response to the request.

Favorable Response to a Claim Message

Well-run businesses *want* their customers to communicate when merchandise or service is not satisfactory. They want to learn of ways in which goods and services can be improved, and they want their customers to receive value for the money they spend. With considerable confidence, they can assume that writers of claim letters think their claims are valid. By responding fairly to legitimate requests in **adjustment messages**, businesses can gain a reputation for standing behind their goods and services. A loyal customer may become even more loyal after a business has demonstrated its integrity.

When the response to a claim letter is favorable, present ideas using the deductive or direct sequence. Although the word *grant* is acceptable when talking about claims, its use in adjustment messages is discouraged. An expression such as "Your claim is being granted" unnecessarily implies that the sender is in a position of power.

Because the subject of an adjustment is related to the goods or services provided, the message can include a brief sales message. **Resale** refers to a discussion of goods or services already bought. It reminds customers and clients that they made a good choice in selecting a company with which to do business, or it reminds them of the good qualities of their purchase. **Sales promotional material** refers to statements made about related merchandise or service. For example, a message

adjustment message
message that adjusts the terms of a sale in the customer's favor
resale
a discussion of goods or services already bought
sales promotional material
statements made about related merchandise or service

Figure 6-4  Poor Example of a Routine Claim

- *Uses writer-centered, ~~forceful~~ tone to convey details receiver already knows.*

- *Continues discussion of problem but shows no empathy for receiver.*

- *Uses second person with negative language that emphasizes receiver is at fault.*

- *States claim that should have appeared in first paragraph and continues forceful tone damaging to human relations, including a threat.*

Mr. Kelly,

Three of our copiers have been out of service for a week. One of your service people came out three days ago to work on the copiers, but they still are not working properly. In all three cases, the copiers jam when used. This has caused us to have to go down the street to get our copying done with a loss of time and at additional expense to us.

Could you please send a competent service person immediately to fix the three copiers that still are not working? Our contract with your company says that all copier repairs will be made satisfactorily within three working days of the initial request for service. If you cannot honor that contract, we will be forced to look elsewhere for our copier servicing needs.

Figure 6-5   Good Example of a Routine Claim

- *Provides subject line that is meaningful to reader and writer.*

- *Emphasizes main idea by placing it in first sentence.*

- *Provides explanation and relevant information, including work order number.*

- *Ends on positive note, reminding reader that company has immediate need for working copiers.*

Format Pointers
Limits message to single idea—the claim request.

Composes short, concise message that fits on one screen.

Includes salutation and closing to personalize message.

Reflects other formatting guidelines covered on your style cards.

New Message

To: John Kelly <jkelly@copyhelp.com>

From: David Betty <dbetty@workpartners.com>

Subject: Immediate Service Needed for Broken Copiers

Mr. Kelly,

Please send us a service person immediately to fix three copiers that are not working at our office at 3970 West Vista Street.

The copiers have been out of service for a week. One of your service people came out three days ago to work on the copiers, but they still are not working properly. In all three cases, the copiers jam when used. The work order for that visit was number 39K402.

Our contract with your company says that all copier repairs will be made satisfactorily within three working days of the initial request for service, so we would appreciate your immediate attention to this matter.

Thanks,

David Betty
Administrative Assistant
WorkPartners, Inc.

Figure 6-6

- *Uses a defensive tone and content that attempts to take any blame away from the service firm.*

- *Implies that the reader has made a mistake or is at fault, potentially putting him or her on the defensive or angering him or her.*

- *Continues discussion of problem but shows no empathy for receiver.*

- *States claim that should have appeared in first paragraph at end of second paragraph.*

- *Closes with a generic conclusion that ignores earlier negative tone of the message.*

Thank you for your email of May 30. It has been referred to me for reply.

I have reviewed the work report made by our service person, and it looks as if the problem you refer to was repaired on May 27, the day of his last visit to your office. The operating issues that you now report experiencing with your copiers thus appear to be a new problem. We will honor our contract with your firm by sending out a service person this afternoon—under the three-day period outlined in our contract with your company.

We at CopyHelper are dedicated to providing excellent copier repair service to our valued customers.

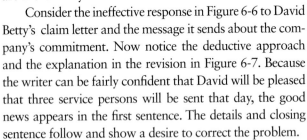

about a company's recently purchased office furniture might also mention its office equipment offerings. These subtle sales messages may be more effective than direct sales messages, since they are more likely to be read.

Consider the ineffective response in Figure 6-6 to David Betty's claim letter and the message it sends about the company's commitment. Now notice the deductive approach and the explanation in the revision in Figure 6-7. Because the writer can be fairly confident that David will be pleased that three service persons will be sent that day, the good news appears in the first sentence. The details and closing sentence follow and show a desire to correct the problem.

Routine Requests

Like claims, requests are divided into two groups: *routine requests* and *persuasive requests*. Routine requests and favorable responses to them follow the deductive sequence. Persuasive requests, which are discussed in Chapter 8, assume that action will be taken after persuasive arguments are presented.

Routine Request

Requests for information about people, prices, products, and services are common. Because these requests from customers and clients are door openers for future business, well-run businesses accept them optimistically. Follow the steps in the deductive sequence for preparing effective requests you are confident will be fulfilled.

Figure 6-8 does not follow the deductive outline that is appropriate for a routine request. Note that the revision in Figure 6-9 on page 98 starts with a direct request for specific information. Then, as much detail as necessary is presented to enable the receiver to answer specifically. The revision ends confidently with appreciation for the action requested. The message is short, but because it conveys enough information and has a tone of politeness, it is effective.

Favorable Response to a Routine Request

The message in Figure 6-10 on page 99 responds favorably but with little enthusiasm to an online request for detailed information related to more specific information about CommunicationCounts! With a little

Figure 6-7   *Good Example of a Favorable Response to a Routine Claim*

- *Begins with good news (main idea) for deserved emphasis; assures receiver that action is being taken.*

- *Expresses appreciation for being informed about problem.*

- *Presents explanation and assurance of company's process for assuring quality service.*

- *Attempts to regain possible lost goodwill by offering personalized assistance.*

New Message

To: David Betty <dbetty@workpartners.com>

From: John Kelly <jkelly@copyhelp.com>

Subject: Service Persons Will Arrive at 1 p.m. Today

Mr. Betty,

Please expect three service people to arrive at your offices at 1 p.m. today to make the repairs you requested this morning.

Thank you for bringing this situation to my attention so quickly, because we are dedicated to providing our clients the highest quality repair services. As part of that goal, we will happily reimburse your company for the additional copying costs you may have had over the past three days if you will submit copies of those receipts to one of our service people visiting today. A check will be in the mail tomorrow to reimburse you for those costs.

Thanks,

John Kelly
Service Manager

Figure 6-8   *Poor Example of a Routine Request*

- *Provides vague subject line that provides no meaningful reference to topic.*

- *Delays request (main idea of letter).*

- *Presents request vaguely using writer-centered language and rambles needlessly.*

- *Lacks logical organizational structure for easy readability.*

- *Closes with weak cliché that provides no incentive for quick response.*

Subject: Need training information

Our company appears to be having problems with its communication process. These problems appear to be affecting productivity and morale. For example, a major change in our policy for dealing with client financing was not communicated properly to the sales staff, and this mistake has cost the company thousands of dollars and may cause the company to lose some of its most valued clientele. In addition, our employees have had to deal with the frustration and anger of those clients, and this has not gone as well as it might. Some of our most valued employees are threatening to leave, and we are afraid that the fallout will cause a loss of productivity in those that remain.

I found your company on the Internet, and it looks like you might be the answer that we need. I don't know much about communication at the organizational level, but I think we may need an audit of the sort that you describe on your website. We need to look at the process for disseminating messages from management to the lower levels in the organization as well as how feedback gets transmitted upward. I am sure there is more to it than that, though.

I look forward to receiving your reply soon.

Figure 6-9 **Good Example of a Routine Request**

New Message

To:	Rosalind LeBlanc <rleblanc@commcounts.com>
From:	Mitchell Lewis <mlewis@vmi.com>
Subject:	Please Send Information About Communication Auditing Services

Dear Ms. LeBlanc:

The excellent information on your website describing your communication audit services suggests your company might be able to assist VMI, Inc. in improving its organizational communication practices and processes.

To assist us in selecting a consulting firm to achieve these goals, please provide the following information:

• A detailed explanation of the services that you provide, the procedure used to gather the information that you need, an anticipated project schedule, a brief explanation of the deliverables you will provide, and a cost sheet.

• Contact information for past clients so that we might get some information on the effectiveness of the services that your company provides.

• A copy of your standard contract for our legal department to review.

The information you provide could likely confirm our expectation that CommunicationCounts! can assist our company in meeting its communication improvement goals. Should you wish to contact me directly, please call (310) 555-3910, Ext. 120.

Thank you,

Mitchell Lewis
Director, Strategic Planning
VMI, Inc.

Annotations (left margin):

• *States request plainly.*

• *Asks for specific items with necessary explanation; uses list for emphasis.*

• *Expresses appreciation and alludes to benefits of quick action.*

• *Opens door for personal dialogue by providing telephone number.*

Format Pointers
Provides salutation appropriate for company.

- *Provides general subject line.*

- *Opening tone too informal and inappropriate to create a professional business impression.*

- *Focuses on writer and does not address request directly and thoroughly.*

- *Uses empty cliché and doesn't show a concerted interest in helping reader.*

From: Rosalind LeBlanc <rleblanc@commcounts.com>

RE: Information Needed

Mr. Lewis:

Holy cow! It sounds like you could really use our help! Communication is often undervalued by companies, particularly as to its potential effects on the bottom line. But it sounds as if you found this out the hard way.

We can certainly help, though. We have been in the communication consulting business for more than ten years, and our clients include large and small businesses alike, including *Fortune* 500 companies.

The way that our company works is that we will send out a sales team to make a presentation to you that outlines our procedure and explains the deliverables and provides examples. If you like what you see, we will prepare a project schedule and a cost estimate for your review.

We are happy you're considering CommunicationCounts! for your consulting needs. Please give me a call, and we will schedule a time for a sales visit.

planning and consideration for Mr. Lewis, the message in Figure 6-11 on the next page could have been written just as quickly. Note the specific answers to Mitchell's questions and the helpful, sincere tone.

Favorable Response to a Favor Request

As a business professional, you may occasionally be asked for special favors. You may receive invitations to speak at various civic or education groups, spearhead fund-raising and other service projects, or offer your expertise in other ways. If you say "Yes," you might as well say it enthusiastically. Sending an unplanned, generic acceptance suggests that the quality of contribution will be similar.

If you find yourself responding to invitations frequently, you can draft a form message that you'll revise for each invitation you receive. This well-written acceptance illustrates that individualized form messages sent by mail or electronically enable businesses to communicate quickly and effectively with clients or customers.

Form Letters for Routine Responses

Form letters are a fast and efficient way of transmitting frequently recurring messages to which receiver reaction is likely favorable or neutral. Inputting the customer's name and address and other variables (information that differs for each receiver) personalizes each letter to meet the needs of its receiver. Companies may use form paragraphs that have been stored in separate word processing files. Perhaps as many as five versions of a paragraph related to a typical request are available for use in a routine request letter. The originator selects the appropriate paragraph for the receiver's request. After assembling the selected files on the computer screen, the originator inputs any additional variables (e.g., name and address). A copy of the personalized letter is printed on letterhead and sent to the receiver.

Form letters have earned a negative connotation because of their tendency to be impersonal. Many people simply refuse to read such letters for that reason. Personalizing a form letter can circumvent this problem.

Figure 6-11

GOOD

Good Example of a Favorable Response to a Routine Request

- Revises subject line after clicking "Reply" to communicate enthusiasm for providing exceptional personalized service.

- Shows sincere interest in request and person.

- Highlights specific answers to recipient's questions using an articulate, concise writing style.

- Encourages direct call and provides more useful information that communicates genuine interest in person and requested service.

Format Pointer
Uses Q&A format to enhance readability of response to series of detailed questions.

New Message

To: Mitchell Lewis <mlewis@vmi.com>

From: Rosalind LeBlanc <rleblanc@commcounts.com>

Subject: Assistance for Improving Communication Effectiveness at VMI

Mr. Lewis:

Thank you for your interest in the services of CommunicationCounts! We can assist you in meeting your goals to improve your corporate communication processes and practices. Studies have shown that well-conceived communication plans can add as much as 30 percent to an organization's bottom line.

You will find attached a detailed proposal that addresses your request. For your added convenience, you will find a summary response to your request below.

Q: A detailed explanation of the services that you provide, the procedure used to gather the information that you need, an anticipated project schedule, a brief explanation of the deliverables you will provide, and a cost sheet.

A: CommunicationCounts! is a comprehensive consulting company that customizes its service to meet client communication needs. Since you are requesting a plan to help your entire organization, we recommend a complete audit of your organization, which would entail trained consultants visiting your company to gather information about your current communication practices, using three different tools: observation, confidential interviews with employees, and questionnaires.

The results of these data-gathering methods will then be provided in a report to you that identifies the aspects of your communication process that appear to be working well and those that appear to need attention. The report will then provide detailed recommendations for addressing those processes that need improvement. If desired, our firm will provide experienced personnel to implement the plan and to assess the effectiveness of its implementation.

Communication audits typically take about two weeks for a firm of your size, while implementation of a plan may take as long as six months, with a quality control check coming at the end of a year. Depending upon the level of service requested, costs can range from $25,000 for an audit of a company your size to $100,000 for implementation and an effectiveness review.

Q: Contact information for past clients so that we might get some information on the effectiveness of the services that your company provides.

A: A number of our past clients have agreed to speak with new clients about their experience with CommunicationCounts! A full listing is provided in the attached proposal, but I recommend that you start with a call and visit with Renee Warner at First Bank, since she is within easy driving distance of your firm. Her phone number is (310) 555-9103. She is expecting your call.

Q: A copy of your standard contract for our legal department to review.

A: Please find a copy of our standard contract attached to this message in a separate file for your convenience.

Please call my direct line (213) 555-8401 if you have additional questions about our services after reading the attached proposal. I would be happy to schedule a personal meeting with you if you would like to proceed with the creation of a customized plan to help VMI better meet its corporate communication goals.

Best regards,

Rosalind LeBlanc, Senior Consultant
CommunicationCounts!

© Image Farm/Jupiterimages

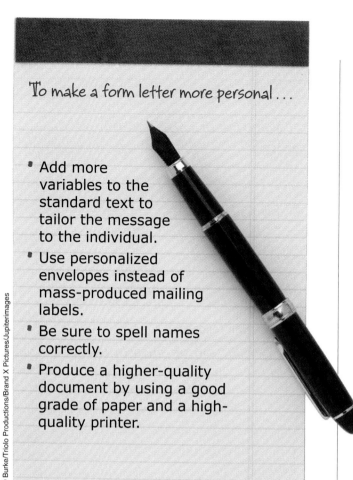

To make a form letter more personal . . .

- Add more variables to the standard text to tailor the message to the individual.
- Use personalized envelopes instead of mass-produced mailing labels.
- Be sure to spell names correctly.
- Produce a higher-quality document by using a good grade of paper and a high-quality printer.

© Burke/Triolo Productions/Brand X Pictures/Jupiterimages

Routine Messages About Orders and Credit

objective ④
Write messages acknowledging customer orders, providing credit information, and extending credit.

Routine messages, such as customer order acknowledgments, are written deductively. Normally, credit information is requested and transmitted electronically from the national credit reporting agencies to companies requesting credit references. However, when companies choose to request information directly from other businesses, individual credit requests and responses must be written.

Acknowledging Customer Orders

When customers place orders for merchandise, they expect to get exactly what they ordered as quickly as possible. Most orders can be acknowledged by shipping the order; no message is necessary. For an initial order and

for an order that cannot be filled quickly and precisely, companies send an **acknowledgment message**, a document that indicates the order has been received and is being processed. Typically, acknowledgment messages are preprinted letters or copies of the sales order. An immediate email message acknowledges an order placed online and confirms the expected date of shipment, as shown in Figure 6-12 on the next page. Individualized letters are not cost-effective and will not reach the customer in a timely manner. Although the form message is impersonal, customers appreciate the company acknowledging the order and giving them an idea of when the order will arrive.

Non-routine orders, such as initial orders, custom orders, and delayed orders, require individualized acknowledgment messages. When well written, these messages not only acknowledge the order but also create customer goodwill and encourage the customer to place additional orders. Because saying "Yes" is easy, writers may develop the habit of using clichés and selecting words that make messages sound cold and mechanical. The acknowledgment letter shown as a model document on the cards for this chapter confirms shipment of goods in the first sentence, includes concrete resale on the product and company, and is sincere and original. When communication with the customer has occurred electronically, an acknowledgment by email is often appropriate.

Providing Credit Information

Replies to requests for credit information usually are simple—just fill in the blanks and return the document. If the request does not include a form, follow a deductive sequence when writing the reply: the major idea first, followed by supporting details.

When providing credit information, you have an ethical and legal obligation to yourself, the credit applicant, and the business from which credit is requested. You must be able to document any statement you make to defend yourself against a defamation charge. Thus, good advice is to stick with facts; omit any opinions. "I'm sure he will pay promptly" is an opinion that should be omitted, but include the documented fact that "His payments are always prompt." Can you safely say a customer is a good credit risk when all you know is that he or she had a good credit record when a purchase was made from you?

Extending Credit

A timely response is preferable for any business

acknowledgment message
a document that indicates the order has been received and is being processed

Figure 6-12  Good Example of an Online Order Confirmation

---

New Message

To: Terry Gross <biggestdog@hotmail.com>

From: customerservice@killergames.com

Subject: Order Confirmation from www.killergames.com

Terry,

Thank you for shopping online at www.killergames.com. Your order (shown below) has been shipped via UPS with delivery expected on Monday, March 3. Your tracking number is 345K7099.

A summary of your order information follows:

Order No: 6418243370   Order Date: Feb. 25, 2010 10:12 AM

Billed and shipped to:
Terry Gross
619 Apple Street
Deer Park, WA 86045
USA
Day Phone: 513 555-3211
Evening Phone: 513 555-4561
Email: biggestdog@hotmail.com

Thank you for shopping with us. If you have questions about your order, please chat online with a customer service specialist at http://www.killergames/service/ or call us at 1-800-555-3198. You can reach us 24 hours a day, 7 days a week.

Customer.service@killergames.com

- *Acknowledges receipt and delivery of customer's online order with convenient link to company's website.*

- *Confirms expected shipment date and provides number for easy tracking of delivery at company's website.*

- *Itemizes specific merchandise ordered and billing and shipping information for verification.*

- *Closes with offer of assistance and expectation of future business.*

---

document, but it is especially important when communicating about credit. The Equal Credit Opportunity Act (ECOA) requires that a credit applicant be notified of the credit decision within 30 days of receipt of the request or application. The party granting the credit must also disclose the terms of the credit agreement, such as the address for sending or making payments, due dates for payments, and the interest rate charged. (You will learn more about other legal implications related to credit when you study credit denials in Chapter 7.)

When extending credit, follow these guidelines as you write, using the deductive sequence:

1. **Open by extending credit and acknowledging shipment of an order.** Because of its importance, the credit aspect is emphasized more than the acknowledgment of the order. In other cases (in which the order is for cash or the credit terms are already clearly understood), the primary purpose of writing may be to acknowledge an order.

2. **Indicate the basis for the decision to extend credit, and explain the credit terms.** Indicating that you are extending credit on the basis of an applicant's prompt-paying habits with present creditors may encourage this new customer to continue these habits with you.

3. **Present credit policies.** Explain policies (e.g., credit terms, authorized discounts, payment dates). Include any legally required disclosure documents.

4. **Communicate a genuine desire to build a strong business relationship.** Include resale, sales promotional material, and comments that remind the customer of the benefits of doing business with you and encourage additional orders.

Figure 6-13  **Good Example of Letter Extending Credit**

- *Acknowledges customer's electronic access to product and implies credit extension.*

- *Recognizes dealer for earning credit privilege and gives reason for credit extension.*

- *Introduces credit terms and encourages taking advantage of discount in terms of profits for dealer.*

- *Presents resale to remind of product benefits and encourage future business.*

- *Includes sales promotion for repeat business; assumes satisfaction with initial order and looks confidently for future orders.*

Legal Issue
Provides answer to request for credit within required time frame (within 30 days of receipt of request) and mentions terms of credit that will be provided, as required by law.

Endure Paint

July 20, 2010

Sam Becker
Custom Painters
613 Avocado Street
Tampa, FL 33310

Dear Sam:

You now have access to the hundreds of colors and finishes of the finest quality paint available in the United States. Endure Paint provide paints and supplies for every type of material, including wood, plastic, fiberglass, concrete, metal, and even fabrics.

Because of your favorable current credit rating, we are pleased to provide you with a $10,000 credit line subject to our standard 2/10, n/30 terms. By paying your invoice within ten days, you can save 2 percent on your paint purchases.

You can access our quick and easy-to-use online ordering service at www. endurepaint.com. Our website also provides lists and samples of all the colors, finishes, and types of paint available to our valued customers. You will receive your paint order within five working days, guaranteed.

The highest quality of paint with the widest range of choices is just a click away.

Sincerely,

Tina Wagner

Tina Wagner
Credit Manager

Enclosure

The letter in Figure 6-13 was written to a retailer; however, the same principles apply when writing to a consumer. Each letter should be written so as to address the receiver's interests. Dealers are concerned about markup, marketability, and display; consumers are concerned about price, appearance, and durability. Consumers may require a more detailed explanation of credit terms because they may be less knowledgeable about these issues.

Companies receive so many requests for credit that the costs of individualized letters are prohibitive; therefore, most favorable replies to credit requests are form letters. To personalize the letter, however, the writer should merge the customer's name, address, amount of loan, and terms into the computer file containing the form letter information. Typically, form messages read something like this:

Dear [TITLE] [LAST NAME]:
Worldwide Industries is pleased to extend credit privileges to you. Initially, you may purchase up to [CREDIT LIMIT] worth of merchandise. Our credit terms are [TERMS]. We welcome you as a credit customer at Worldwide Industries and look forward to serving your needs for fine imported goods from around the world.

Although such form messages are effective for informing the customer that credit is being extended, they do little to promote sales and goodwill. Managers can effectively prepare and personalize form letters so that recipients do not perceive the messages as impersonal, generic responses.

Procedural Messages

objective ⑤
Prepare procedural messages that ensure clear and consistent application.

Memos or email messages are the most frequently used methods of communicating procedures and instructions, changes related to personnel or the organization, and other internal matters for which a written record is needed.

Instructions to employees must be conveyed clearly and accurately to facilitate the day-to-day operations of business, to increase productivity, and to prevent negative feelings that occur when mistakes are made and work must be redone. Managers must take special care in writing standard operating procedures to ensure that all employees complete the procedures accurately and consistently.

Before writing instructions, perform the procedure, breaking it down into its individual steps. Doing so can also help you locate potential trouble spots about which you might need to elaborate. Then attempt to determine how much employees already know about the process and anticipate any questions or problems.

As you write instructions that require more than a few simple steps, follow these guidelines:

1. **Begin each step with an action statement to create a vivid picture of the employee completing the task.** Using an action verb and the understood subject *you* is more vivid than a sentence written in passive voice. For example, a loan officer attempting to learn new procedures for evaluating new venture loans can understand "*identify* assets available to collateralize the loan" more easily than "assets available to collateralize the loan should be identified."

2. **Itemize each step on a separate line to add emphasis and to simplify reading.** Number each step to indicate that the procedures should be completed in a particular order. If the order is not important, use bullets for the steps.

3. **Consider preparing a flowchart depicting the procedures.** The cost and effort involved in creating a sophisticated flowchart may be merited for extremely important and complex procedures.

4. **Complete the procedure by following your instructions step-by-step.** Correct any errors you locate.

5. **Ask a colleague or employee to walk through the procedures.** This walk-through will allow you to identify ambiguous statements, omissions of relevant information, and other sources of miscommunication.

The procedures in Figure 6-14 include clear, consistent instructions for downloading pay stubs that were written after the manager anticipated potential problems and walked through a draft of the procedures. The policy is being sent as an email attachment and is posted to the company website for easy reference.

Figure 6-14

Good Example of a Procedural Email with an Attachment

- Introduces main idea.

- Explains new procedures that are outlined in attached file.

- Includes attached file for document requiring involved formatting.

- Provides descriptive title that clearly identifies procedures.

- Enumerates to direct attention to each step and emphasizes need for sequence.

- Begins each item with an action verb to help employees visualize themselves completing procedures.

- Includes date of last revision to ensure currency.

New Message

To: All Employees

From: Manuel Ruiz <mruiz@westerngeneral.com>

Subject: New Procedures for Downloading Pay Stubs

Everyone,

To reduce paper and administrative costs, we have moved many of our personnel functions online. Beginning January 1, all payroll information, including your pay stubs, will be accessible from the Human Resources website.

To view your most recent pay stub or to review your pay history, please follow the procedure outlined in the attached file and posted to the company website under Human Resources. This process may be completed from any computer.

Sincerely,

Manuel Ruiz, Payroll Specialist
Attachment: Procedures for Downloading Pay Stubs

Procedures for Downloading Pay Stubs

1. Access http://www.westerngeneral.com/HR, and click the "Payroll" option.

2. Create a username and a PIN number for your account, then click "Submit."

3. Fill in the form that appears with your name and contact information. You will need a current check stub to provide your employee number and department number in the appropriate boxes. Click "Submit" when completed.

4. In the window that appears, click "Payroll Information." Your most recent pay stub information should appear on your computer screen.

Revised 05/20/10

Preparing Bad-News Messages

Choosing an Appropriate Channel and Organizational Pattern

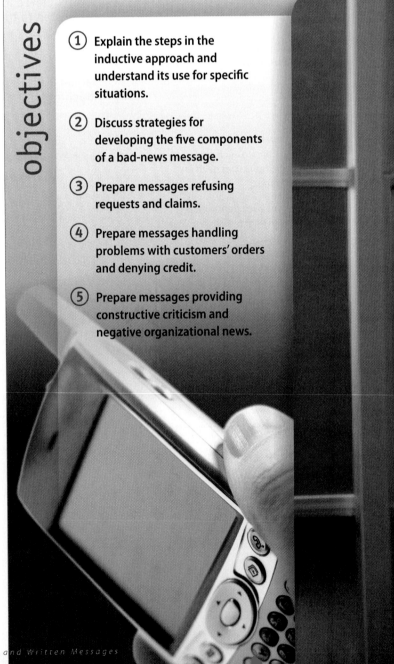

objective ①
Explain the steps in the inductive approach and understand its use for specific situations.

Perceptions of employees, local citizens, and the public at large are closely tied to an organization's ability to handle difficult situations with tact and empathy. A skilled communicator will attempt to deliver bad news in such a way that the recipient supports the decision and is willing to continue a positive relationship. To accomplish these goals, allow empathy for the receiver to direct your choice of an appropriate channel and use an inductive approach for presenting a logical discussion of the facts and the unpleasant information. The use of tactful and effective language will further aid you in developing a clear yet sensitive message.

Channel Choice and Commitment to Tact

Personal delivery has been the preferred medium for relaying bad news because it signals the importance of the information and shows empathy for the recipient. Face-to-face delivery also provides the benefit of nonverbal communication and immediate feedback, which minimizes the misinterpretation of these highly sensitive messages. Personal delivery, however, carries a level of discomfort and the potential for escalation of emotion. A voice on the telephone triggers the same discomfort as a face-to-face meeting, and the increased difficulty of interpreting the intensity of nonverbal cues over the telephone only adds to the natural discomfort associated with delivering negative information.

The widespread use of electronic media for organizational communication and studies related to the interaction dynamics of various communication media may challenge the current practice of delivering bad news in person. A study by the Institute for Operations Research and the Management Sciences concluded that negative messages delivered by email rather than personally or by telephone are more honest and accurate and cause less discomfort for the sender. While inappropriate for extremely personal or potentially legal situations, such as firing an employee, email can be a viable communication channel for facilitating the delivery of bad news when face-to-face interaction is not possible due to geographic separation. Furthermore, the straight talk fostered by email may also improve upward communication and thus the performance of the company, as reluctant employees may feel more comfortable relaying unpopular news to their superiors.[1]

You must be cautious when you deliver bad news electronically, whether by email or electronic postings.

While you may feel more comfortable avoiding the discomfort of facing the recipient, the impersonal nature of the computer may lead to careless writing that is lacking in tact and empathy, and perhaps even defamatory. When sending electronic messages, stay focused and follow the same communication strategies you would apply if you were speaking face-to-face or writing a more formal letter or memo.

Cultural Concerns

Effective message organization varies among cultures because of values held by each society. While U.S. businesspeople prefer the indirect style for delivering bad news, Germans, for instance, prefer the direct pattern for positive and negative messages. Asians and Latinos may avoid saying "No" or give a qualified "No" in order to save face. Understanding value differences can aid in interpreting messages from people of other cultures.

Use of the Inductive Approach to Build Goodwill

Because of the potential negative effects on goodwill, special consideration should be made when planning bad-news messages to ensure they are delivered with tact. Doing so often requires a less direct approach. For example, if the bad news is presented in the first sentence, the reaction is likely to be negative: "They never gave me a fair chance"; "That's unfair"; "This just can't be." Having made a value judgment on reading the first sentence, receivers are naturally reluctant to change their minds before the last sentence of the message—even though the intervening sentences present a valid basis for doing so. Once disappointed by the idea contained in the first sentence, receivers are tempted to concentrate on *refuting* (instead of *understanding*) supporting details. Therefore, an inductive approach should be used when delivering bad news.

An inductive approach to the ordering of a message differs from the more direct, deductive approach that is generally preferred in many Western cultures. Deductive ordering works from the general to the specific. It is generally implemented by stating the purpose of the message and then supporting or explaining that purpose with details. The inductive approach is just the opposite. It begins with details and then works to the more general. In the case of a bad-news message, this approach is implemented by stating the reasons for the bad news before the bad news itself.

As with good-news messages, the details that support or provide the reasoning for a refusal also are very important. If the supporting details are understood and believed, the message may be readily accepted and good business relationships preserved. Because the reasons behind the bad news are so important, the communicator needs to organize the message in such a way as to emphasize the reasons rather than the bad news.

If the bad news precedes the reasons, (1) the message might be discarded before this important portion is even read or (2) the disappointment experienced when reading the bad news might interfere with the receiver's ability to comprehend or accept the supporting explanation.

The five steps for organizing bad-news messages are shown in Figure 7-1.

Figure 7-1 Inductive Sequence Used in Bad-News Messages

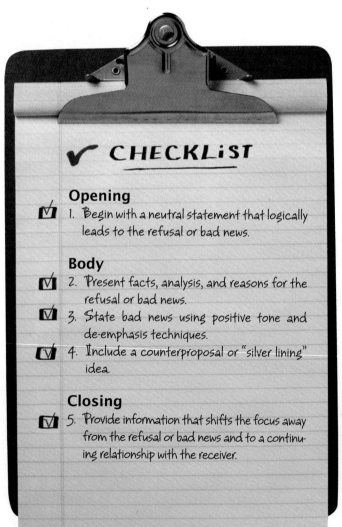

✔ CHECKLIST

Opening

☑ 1. Begin with a neutral statement that logically leads to the refusal or bad news.

Body

☑ 2. Present facts, analysis, and reasons for the refusal or bad news.

☑ 3. State bad news using positive tone and de-emphasis techniques.

☑ 4. Include a counterproposal or "silver lining" idea.

Closing

☑ 5. Provide information that shifts the focus away from the refusal or bad news and to a continuing relationship with the receiver.

Although the outline has five steps, a bad-news message may or may not have five paragraphs. More than one paragraph may be necessary for conveying supporting reasons. In the illustrations in this chapter, note that the first and final paragraphs are seldom longer than two sentences. In fact, one-sentence paragraphs (as beginnings) look easier and thus more inviting to read.

Advantages of the Inductive Approach

Use of the inductive approach to bad-news messages has the following advantages:

- It sufficiently identifies the subject of the message without initially turning off the receiver.

- It presents the reasons *before* the refusal, where they are more likely to be received and understood with the appropriate emphasis.

- It avoids a negative reaction. By the time the reasons are read, they seem sensible and the refusal is foreseen. Because it is expected, the statement of refusal does not come as a shock.

- It de-emphasizes the refusal by closing on a neutral or pleasant note. By showing a willingness to cooperate in some way, the sender conveys a desire to be helpful.

You may speculate that receivers may become impatient when a message is inductive in its organization. Concise, well-written explanations are not likely to make a receiver impatient. They communicate empathy for the receiver's problem, present information not already known, and help the receiver understand. However, if a receiver becomes impatient while reading a well-written explanation, that impatience is less damaging to understanding than would be the upset that may result from encountering bad news in the first sentence.

Exceptions to the Inductive Approach

Normally, the writer's purpose is to convey a clear message and retain the recipient's goodwill; thus, the inductive approach is appropriate. In the rare circumstance in which a choice must be made between the two, clarity is the better choice. When the deductive or direct approach will serve a communicator's purpose better, it should be used. For example, if you submit a clear and tactful refusal and the receiver submits a second request, a deductive presentation may be justified in the second refusal. In this case, the refusal may need the emphasis

on the bad news provided by a deductive outline. Placing a refusal in the first sentence can be justified when one or more of the following circumstances exist:

- The message is the second response to a repeated request.

- A very small, insignificant matter is involved.

- A request is obviously ridiculous, immoral, unethical, illegal, or dangerous.

- A sender's intent is to "shake" the receiver.

- A sender–recipient relationship is so close and long standing that satisfactory human relations can be taken for granted.

- The sender *wants* to demonstrate authority.

In most situations, the preceding circumstances do not exist. When they do, a sender's goals may be accomplished by stating bad news in the first sentence.

Developing a Bad-News Message

objective ②
Discuss strategies for developing the five components of a bad-news message.

Developing a bad-news message following the inductive approach can be challenging. The following suggestions will aid you in writing the introductory paragraph, explanation, bad-news statement, counterproposal or silver lining idea, and closing paragraph.

Delivering bad news can often feel like walking a tightrope between tact and truth.

Writing the Introductory Paragraph

The introductory paragraph in the bad-news message should accomplish the following objectives: (1) providing a buffer to cushion the bad news that will follow, (2) letting the receiver know what the message is about without stating the bad news, and (3) serving as a transition into the discussion of reasons for the bad news. If these objectives can be accomplished in one sentence, then that sentence can be the first paragraph. Avoid the following when writing the introductory paragraph:

- **Empty acknowledgments of the obvious.** *"I am writing in response to your letter requesting . . ."* or *"Your letter of the 14th has been given to me for reply"* wastes space to present points of little value. Beginning with *I* signals the message may be writer centered.

- **Signaling the bad news too early.** *"Although the refund requested in your letter of May 1 cannot be approved . . ."* may cause an immediate emotional reaction, resulting in the message being discarded or interfering with understanding the explanations that follow. The neutral statement *"Your request for an adjustment has been considered. However . . ."* does not reveal whether the answer is "Yes" or "No," but the use of "however," signals the answer is "No" before the reasons are presented. Such a beginning has about the same effect as an outright "No."

- **Starting too positively so as to build false hopes.** Empathetic statements, such as *"I can understand how you felt when you were asked to pay an extra $54,"* may lead the receiver to expect good news. When a preceding statement has implied that an affirmative decision will follow, a negative decision is all the more disappointing.

Several ideas that can be used to create effective beginning paragraphs include:

- **Compliment.** A message denying a customer's request could begin by recognizing the customer's promptness in making payments.

- **Point of agreement.** A sentence that reveals agreement with a statement made in the message could get the message off to a positive discussion of other points.

- **Good news.** When a message contains a request that must be refused and another that is being answered favorably, beginning with the favorable answer can be effective.

- **Resale.** A claim refusal could begin with some favorable statement about the product.

- **A review.** Refusal of a current request could be introduced by referring to the initial transaction or by reviewing certain circumstances that preceded the transaction.

- **Gratitude.** Although an unjustified request may have been made, the receiver may have done or said something for which you are grateful. An expression of gratitude could be used as a positive beginning.

Presenting the Facts, Analysis, and Reasons

The reasons section of the bad-news message is extremely important because people who are refused want to know why. When people say "No," they usually do so because they think "No" is the better answer for all concerned. They can see how recipients will ultimately benefit from the refusal. If a message is based on a sound decision and if it has been well written, recipients will understand and accept the reasons and the forthcoming refusal statement as valid.

Study the following examples that use transitions to achieve a coherent opening:

Your application was reviewed separately by two loan officers.	• *Reveals topic as reply to recipient's loan application.*
Each officer considered . . .	• *Uses "officer" to transition from first to second sentence. Discusses officers' review to satisfy expectation presented in first sentence.*
Following your request for permission to pick up food left over from the buffets served in our conference center, we reviewed our experiences of recent years.	• *Reveals subject of message as reply to humanitarian organization's request.*
Last year, two incidents . . .	• *Uses "year" to tie second paragraph to first and transitions into discussion of "experiences" mentioned in first paragraph.*

Both writers and readers benefit from the explanation of the reasons behind the refusal. For writers, the explanation helps to establish fair-mindedness; it shows that the decision was not arbitrary. For receivers, the explanation not only presents the truth to which they are entitled but also has guidance value. From it they learn to adjust habits and, as a result, may be more likely to avoid refusals in the future.

When presenting the reasons, begin with a well-written first paragraph that transitions the receiver smoothly into this section. Then, develop the reasons section following these guidelines:

- **Provide a smooth transition from the opening paragraph to the explanation.** The introductory paragraph or buffer should help set the stage for a logical movement into the discussion of the reasons.

- **Include a concise discussion of one or more reasons that are logical to the reader.** Read the section aloud to identify flaws in logic or the need for additional explanation.

- **Show reader benefit and/or consideration.** Emphasize how the receiver will benefit from the decision. Avoid insincere, empty statements such as "To improve our service to you . . . ."

- **Avoid using "company policy" as the reason.** Instead, disclose the reason behind the policy, which likely will include benefits to the receiver. For example, a customer is more likely to understand and accept a 15-percent restocking fee if the policy is not presented as the "reason" for the refusal. The letter in Figure 7-2 on the next page presents specific benefits to the receiver for the company's cancellation policy.

The principles for developing the reasons section are illustrated in Figure 7-3 on page 113 in the body of a letter written by a bank refusing an additional mortgage on a customer's property.

Writing the Bad-News Statement

A paragraph that presents the reasoning behind a refusal may partially convey the refusal before it is stated directly or indirectly. Still, one sentence needs to convey (directly or by implication) the conclusion to which the preceding details have been leading. A refusal (bad news) needs to be clear; however, you can subordinate the refusal so that the reasons get the deserved emphasis. The following techniques will help you achieve this goal.

- **Position the bad-news statement strategically.** Using the inductive approach places the bad-news statement in a less important position—sandwiched between an opening buffer statement and a positive closing. Additionally, the refusal statement should be included in the same paragraph as the reasons, since placing it

in a paragraph by itself would create too much emphasis on the bad news. Because the preceding explanation is tactful and seems valid, the sentence that states the bad news may cause little or no resentment. Positioning the bad-news statement in the dependent clause of a complex sentence will also cushion the bad news. In the sentence "Although our current personnel shortage prevents us from lending you an executive, we do want to support your worthy project," the emphasis is directed toward a promise of help in some other form.

- **Use passive voice, general terms, and abstract nouns.** Review the *emphasis techniques* that you studied in Chapter 3 as you consider methods for presenting bad news that helps to preserve goodwill.

- **Use positive language to accentuate the positive.** Simply focus on the good instead of the bad, the pleasant instead of the unpleasant, and what can be done instead of what cannot be done. Compared with a negative idea presented in negative terms, a negative idea presented in positive terms is more likely to be accepted. When you are tempted to use the following terms, search instead for words or ideas that sound more positive:

complaint	failure	lied	regrettable
error	inexcusable	neglect	wrong

To businesspeople who conscientiously practice empathy, such terms may not even come to mind when communicating the unpleasant. Words in the preceding list evoke negative feelings that contrast sharply with the positive feelings evoked by words such as these:

accurate	concise	enthusiasm	productive
approval	durable	generous	
recommendation		assist	energetic
gratitude	respect		

To increase the number of pleasant-sounding words in your messages, practice thinking positively. Strive to see the good in situations and in others.

- **Imply the refusal when the receiver can understand the message without a definite statement of the bad news.** By *implying* the "No" answer,

Figure 7-2  Good Example of a Claim Denial

Imperial Mountain

1803 Winter Road • Lake Tahoe, Nevada 70123 • 1-800-555-0101

August 14, 2010

Gena Little
Mitron, Inc.
3406 Pennsylvania Street
Reno, NV 87801

Dear Ms. Little:

You will find a check enclosed for the refund that you requested for the block of rooms you reserved for your summer sales meeting. We regret that your staff was not able to visit Lake Tahoe and the premier resort property, Imperial Mountain, to take advantage of our many amenities and the outdoor wonders of the area.

Our refund policy provides corporate guests the opportunity for a full refund for conference bookings made during the high seasons if cancellations are made 30 days prior to the scheduled event. (The high seasons run from June 1–August 30 and from November 15–March 30.) For cancellations of events scheduled during high seasons and that occur after the 30-day period, a 20-percent fee is charged to help provide a more accurate report of room availability to guests during these highly desirable periods. The enclosed check for $16,100.76 covers the cost of the 30 rooms that were canceled on July 30.

As the economic climate improves, we hope that you will consider Imperial Mountain for future corporate events. Please take advantage of the 5-percent reduction in booking price for events of more than 25 people for a period of three days or more.

Sincerely,

Chris Hays

Chris Hays
Reservation Manager

Enclosure: Check
Legal and Ethical Constraints

- *Uses resale to cushion bad news and lead into explanation.*

- *Presents explanation of cancellation policy with emphasis on ways reader benefits from policy.*

- *Implies refusal by stating amount of enclosed check.*

- *Shifts emphasis away from refusal by presenting silver lining sales promotion for future bookings.*

Avoids corrective language that might insult, belittle, or offend.

Format Pointers
Specifies enclosure to emphasize importance of exact items.

the response achieves several purposes: (1) it uses positive language, (2) it conveys reasons or at least a positive attitude, and (3) it seems more respectful. For example, during the noon hour one employee says to another, "Will you go with me to see this afternoon's baseball game?" "No, I won't" communicates a negative response, but it seems unnecessarily direct and harsh. The same message (invitation is rejected) can be clearly stated in an *indirect* way (by implication) by saying "I must get my work done" or even "I'm a football fan." Note the positive tone of the implied refusals on the looseleaf paper to the right.

Implied Refusal	Underlying Message
I wish I could.	• *Other responsibilities forbid, but recipient would like to accept.*
Had you selected the variable mortgage rate, you could have taken advantage of the recent drop in interest rates.	• *States condition under which answer would have been "Yes" instead of "No." Note use of "had" and "could."*
By accepting the arrangement, Donahoo Industries would have tripled its insurance costs.	• *States obviously unacceptable results of complying with request.*

Figure 7-3 Developing the Components of a Bad-News Message

- *Begins with statement with which both can agree. Sets stage for reasons for bad news.*

- *Reveals subject of message and transitions into reasons.*

- *Provides rule and clearly applies rule to situation.*

- *States refusal positively and clearly using complex sentence and positive language.*

- *Includes counterproposal as alternative.*

- *Closes with sales promotion for other services, inferring a continuing business relationship.*

The current subprime mortgage situation and its subsequent effects on the economy have provided an opportunity to better educate loan seekers about the types of financial risk they might safely assume. For this reason, mortgage seekers may be restricted in the number of mortgage loans they might hold.

As part of the effort to help loan seekers reduce their financial risk, banks now limit the number of mortgages a person might judiciously hold to no more than four. Because of current sluggishness in the housing market, house sellers now have more difficulty selling homes in a timely manner, making such assets much less liquid. If a mortgage holder gets into trouble, he/she will have less ability to resell the property and recover the loan amount. This puts the mortgage holder and the lender at greater financial risk.

In order to secure an additional mortgage, you must first pay off one of your current mortgages. Alternately, our affiliated real estate brokers are available to help you sell one of your properties so that you might secure another. Please call me at 213-555-3400 to discuss these services.

Offering a Counterproposal or "Silver Lining" Idea

Following negative news with an alternative action, referred to as a *counterproposal*, will assist in preserving a relationship with the receiver. Because it states what you can do, including a counterproposal may eliminate the need to state the refusal directly. The counterproposal can follow a refusal stated in a tactful, sensitive manner. For example, when Best Buy faced the possibility of massive layoffs, it offered a voluntary buyout package to over 4,000 employees. In return for voluntarily leaving, employees received 7.5 months of pay plus 1 year of health care, life insurance, and outplacement services. Nearly 500 employees accepted the offer.[2]

While the counterproposal may represent a tangible benefit, it is generally more intangible in nature. For instance, in a letter that informs a job applicant that he or she was not selected to fill the vacant position, the counterproposal might be an offer to reconsider the applicant's résumé when other appropriate positions become available. Any counterproposal must, of course, be reasonable. For instance, when informing a customer of an inability to meet a promised delivery deadline, an unreasonable counterproposal would be to offer the merchandise at no charge. A reasonable counterproposal might be to include some additional items at no charge or to offer a discount certificate good on the customer's next order.

When no reasonable counterproposal is apparent, the sender may be able to offer a "silver lining" thought that turns the discussion back in a

Best Buy's silver lining: 7.5 months' pay

positive direction. For instance, a statement to tenants announcing an increase in rent might be followed by a description of improved lighting that will be installed in the parking lot of the apartment complex. When offering a counterproposal or silver lining statement, care must be taken to assure that the idea does not seem superficial or minimize the recipient's situation.

Closing Positively

After presenting valid reasons and a tactful refusal followed with a counterproposal or silver lining, a closing paragraph should demonstrate empathy without further reference to the bad news. A pleasant closing paragraph should convey an empathetic tone and achieve the following goals:

- **De-emphasize the unpleasant part of the message.** End on a positive note that takes the emphasis away from the bad news previously presented. A statement of refusal (or bad news) in the last sentence or paragraph would place too much emphasis on it. Preferably, *reasons* (instead of bad news) should remain uppermost in the receiver's mind. Placing bad news last would make the ending seem cold and abrupt.

- **Add a unifying quality to the message.** Make your final sentence an *appropriate* closing that brings a unifying quality to the whole message. Repetition of a word or reference to some positive idea that appears early in the message serves this purpose well. Avoid restatement of the refusal or direct reference to it. This paragraph is usually shorter than the preceding explanatory paragraphs, often one or two sentences.

- **Include a positive, forward-looking idea.** This idea might include a reference to some pleasant aspect of the preceding discussion or a future aspect of the business relationship, resale or sales promotion, or an offer to help in some way. Consider the following closures that apply these suggestions:

Reference to some pleasant aspect of the preceding discussion

"Your addition of the home mortgage rider to your policy last year was certainly a wise decision." Home mortgage and other provisions had been mentioned in the early part of a letter to a client who was refused a double-indemnity settlement.

Use of resale or sales promotional material

"According to a recent survey, an advanced resolution 24-bit DVD produces sound qualities that are far superior; it was an ideal choice." A reminder that the DVD has a superior feature will assist in regaining goodwill after a customer's request for free repair has been refused.

An expression of willingness to assist in some other way

Specifically, you may offer an alternative solution to the receiver's problem or useful information that could not be presented logically with the bad news.

"Our representative will show you some samples during next week's sales call." The samples are being proposed as a possible solution to the receiver's problem.

When Writing Your Closing Paragraph:

- **AVOID trite statements that may seem too generic or impersonal.** The well-worn statement *"Thank you for your interest"* is often used thoughtlessly. It may seem shallow and superficial. *"When we can be of further help, please do not hesitate to call or write"* is also well worn and negative. *Further* help may seem especially inappropriate to someone who has just read a denial.

- **AVOID statements that could undermine the validity of your refusal.** The statement *"We trust this explanation is satisfactory"* or *"We hope you will understand our position"* could be taken as a confession of doubt about the validity of the decision. Use of *position* seems to heighten controversy; positions are expected to be defended. Saying *"We are sorry to disappoint you"* risks a negative reply: "If it made you feel so bad, why did you do it?" It can also be interpreted as an apology for the action taken. If a decision merits an apology, its validity may be questionable.

- **AVOID statements that encourage future controversy.** Statements such as *"If you have questions, please do not hesitate to let us know"* could also be perceived as doubt and possibly communicate a willingness to change the decision. If the decision is firm, including this type of closing could result in the writer having to communicate the negative message a second time.

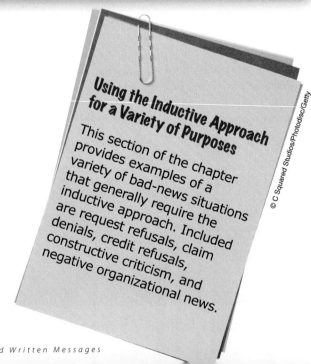

Using the Inductive Approach for a Variety of Purposes

This section of the chapter provides examples of a variety of bad-news situations that generally require the inductive approach. Included are request refusals, claim denials, credit refusals, constructive criticism, and negative organizational news.

© C Squared Studios/Photodisc/Getty

Figure 7-4
 **Good Example of a Refusal for a Favor**

MONTGOMERY & BANKS

188 Green Street, Boise, ID 83301
Telephone: 800-555-4309

September 12, 2010

Sarah Nichols
Boise Girls and Boys Club
534 State Street
Boise, ID 83301

Dear Sarah:

You are to be commended for your commitment to supporting the families and children of the greater Boise area. Our children are our future, and you and your organization are working hard to ensure that future is a bright one for all of us.

The success of your organization and its goals depend on volunteers who have the passion and time to commit to the children you serve. The last year has brought many changes for me. We have a new baby at home, my husband's mother has moved in with us, and I have taken on more duties at work. Although I believe the work that your organization does is invaluable, I can't with good conscience accept your invitation, because I don't believe I can devote the time and energy it deserves right now.

However, Susan Wadsworth, a new account executive with us, has just moved here from Georgia. She misses her big family back home and would be delighted to work with your organization for the coming year. If you are interested, Susan can be reached at 208-555-2104.

Sincerely,

Mina

Mina Edwards
Sales Manager

- *Introduces subject without revealing whether answer will be "Yes" or "No."*

- *Gives reasons that will seem logical to reader.*

- *Subordinates refusal by placing it in dependent clause of complex sentence.*

- *Closes on positive note by offering counterproposal. Summarizes another's willingness to volunteer and provides her telephone number to increase genuineness of offer.*

Format Pointer
Signs first name only because writer knows receiver well.

Refusing a Request

t's a good idea to use the inductive approach, or to provide the reasons before the refusal, when refusing requests for a favor, an action, or even a donation. You can examine a refusal to volunteer for the Girls and Boys Club in Figure 7-4. The letter in this figure—which is a *response* to prior correspondence—uses the same principles of sequence and style that are recommended for messages that *initiate* communication about unpleasant topics. The same

objective ③
Prepare messages refusing requests and claims.

principles apply whether the communication is a letter, memo, email, or spoken message sent to an employee within a company.

Companies have learned that building employee relationships is just as important as developing customer goodwill. Refusing employees' requests requires sensitivity and complete, honest explanations—qualities not included in the poor email in Figure 7-5 on the next page. The department manager's hasty and vague response to a valued employee's request to purchase smartphones for her staff uses a direct, blunt approach. In the revision illustrated in Figure 7-6 on page 117, the department manager takes the time to think about the impact her message will have on Clova.

Question

Which suggested techniques were used to cushion this bad-news statement?

Although the Trammell Road property was selected as the building site, nearness to the railroad was considered a plus for the Drapala property.

Answer

The de-emphasis techniques used in the example are:

1. States what was done rather than what was not done.
2. Includes a positive idea (nearness to the railroad) to accentuate a positive aspect and thus cushion the bad news.
3. Uses passive voice (property was selected) to depersonalize the message.
4. Places the bad news in the dependent clause of a complex sentence ("although the Trammell property was selected"). The positive idea in the independent clause (nearness to the railroad) will receive more attention.

© Ann Marie Kurtz/iStockphoto.com / © Michal Rozanski/iStockphoto.com

---

Figure 7-5 **BAD** *Poor Example of a Refusal to an Employee's Request*

- Reveals refusal in subject line. Uses insensitive language.

- States refusal before explanation.

- Uses negative language and condescending tone.

- Offers possible alternative, but reluctant tone doesn't seem sincere.

- Doesn't include a closing or signature, suggesting a hasty reply.

New Message

To:	Clova Smith
From:	Judith Roswell
Subject:	No Crackberries on company payroll!

Clova,

We can't afford to provide smartphones for our employees.

I would really like to enable you to access your Internet in your car and as you run errands, but the cost of buying smartphones for everyone is too high—as much as $300 per person—and paying for monthly service is totally out of the question. The main issue is that we don't work with outside clients, so there is no guarantee that you will be using the device for work-related tasks.

If economic conditions improve, I will keep your request in mind and will pass it on to upper management.

Figure 7-6

Good Example of a Refusal to an Employee's Request

- Sends message by email—medium preferred by recipient.

- Cushions bad news with sincere compliment for suggestion.

- Transitions to reasons and provides complete explanation for refusal.

- Restates reason for saying "No" to de-emphasize refusal.

- Includes logical alternative that indicates this is a company issue, not a personal one.

Format Pointers
Includes .sig file to identify writer and provide additional contact information.

	New Message
To:	Clova Smith
From:	Judith Roswell
Subject:	Request for the Purchase of Smartphones for Employees

Clova,

Because providing our employees the tools they need to do their job effectively and productively is a priority, your suggestion to purchase smartphones for the department has been carefully considered. Being able to check your email and respond to messages while running errands or away from your computer is one way to make workplace communication more efficient and convenient.

Purchasing such a device can be expensive. Each device costs about $250 and monthly plans are about $50 a month, for a total of $600 a year per employee. The company is experiencing a bit of a slowdown right now, but I may be able to work out a deal with upper management in which interested employees can take part of their yearly cost-of-living raise and use it toward smartphones and service.

At our next department meeting, I will ask employees to indicate whether they would be interested in getting a smartphone and gather suggestions for paying for them if there is an interest. We might also be able to cover the cost by diverting money from other department expenditures. Based upon that discussion, I would be happy to draft a proposal to present to upper management.

Later,

Judith

Judith Roswell
Department Manager
2650 Imperial Blvd.
Los Angeles, CA 90053
(213) 555-6300, Ext. 59 Fax (213) 555-6306

Denying a Claim

objective ④
Prepare messages handling problems with customers' orders and denying credit.

Companies face a challenging task of refusing claims from customers while maintaining goodwill and developing customer loyalty. Claim refusals are necessary when a warranty does not apply, a warranty has expired, or a customer has misused the product. Companies must also write refusals when customers ask for something that a company simply can't do. For example, many retailers charge cus-

tomers a $25 to $40 fee on returned checks. A retailer who receives a customer's request to waive the charge must refuse because the claim is inconsistent with the retailer's policies and objectives.

The inductive approach is helpful in communicating this disappointing news to customers. Presenting the explanation for the refusal first leads customers through the reasoning behind the decision and helps them *understand* the claim is unjustified by the time the refusal is presented. Tone is especially important when denying claims. Present the reasons objectively and positively without casting blame or judgment on the customer for the problem. Avoid lecturing a customer on the actions he or she should have taken to have avoided the problem. (An example: *The warning was printed in bold print in the User's Manual, and the toll-free operator informed you of this stipulation when you called.*) Finally, close the message with resale or sales promotion material that indicates you expect future business. Although disappointed with your decision, customers continue doing business with companies who make fair, objective decisions and communicate the reasons for those decisions in a positive, respectful manner.

Assume a resort receives the following email from a customer:

New Message

To: Chris Hays
From: Gena Little
Subject: Reservation Refund Error

Please issue a credit to my account for the full cost of all 30 room reservations. Although you accepted my payment of $20,125.95, you have only returned $16,100.76 upon my cancellation. Because I could find no explanation for the discrepancy, I assume an error has been made.

The resort's cancellation policy allows customers to receive a full refund up to 30 days prior to their scheduled event. This policy is stated in the contract signed by the customer and was mentioned by the sales manager over the phone.

The customer's inquiry shows a lack of understanding of the cancellation policy. Although a frustrated company representative may question why the customer didn't understand the cancellation policy, the response must be more tactful than that illustrated in Figure 7-7. If you return to Figure 7-2 on page 112, it reveals the subject of the letter in the first sentence and leads into a discussion of the reasons. Reasons for the cancellation policy, including customer benefits, precede the refusal. The tone is positive and respectful. The refusal statement uses several de-emphasis techniques to cushion its impact, and the final sentence turns the discussion away from the refusal with reference to future business with the customer.

Denying Credit

Companies are also challenged when they must refuse an order for a variety of reasons yet still maintain goodwill and develop customer loyalty.

Once you have evaluated a request for credit and have decided "No" is the better answer, your primary writing problem is to refuse credit tactfully so that you might keep the business relationship on a cash basis. When requests for credit are accompanied with an or-

Figure 7-7   *Poor Example of a Claim Denial*

- *Begins with obvious idea (receipt of request could be implied).*

- *Includes unnecessary apology for justified decision and provides refusal before reasons.*

- *Uses patronizing tone that may offend receiver.*

- *Presents explanation that focuses on sender.*

- *Uses clichés that may undermine decision and may lead to unnecessary correspondence.*

Your message questioning the amount of our refund has been received. I am sorry, but we cannot adjust your refund account as you requested.

The contract that you signed with us to reserve 30 rooms for your sales meeting clearly states that cancellations later than 30 days prior to the reservation date are subject to a 20-percent penalty. You are responsible for reading the contract carefully before signing. Our event sales manager also says that she stated the policy to you in a phone conversation in April. You must surely appreciate the cost associated with the lost business associated with late cancellations.

Thank you for doing business with us. If you have any further questions, please do not hesitate to call or message us.

der, your credit refusals may serve as acknowledgment letters. Prospective customers will be disappointed when they cannot buy on a credit basis. However, if you keep them sold on your goods and services, they may prefer to buy from you on a cash basis instead of seeking credit privileges elsewhere or may be potential customers when their credit improves. Of course, every business message is directly or indirectly a sales message.

In credit refusals, as in other types of refusals, the major portion of the message should be an explanation for the refusal. You cannot expect your receiver to agree that your "No" answer is the right answer unless you give the reasons behind it. Naturally, those who send you credit information will expect you to keep it confidential. If you give the reasons without using the names of those from whom you obtained your information, you are not violating a confidence. You are passing along the truth as a justification for your business decision.

Because of the legal implications involved in refusing credit, a legal counsel should review your credit refusal letters to ensure that they comply with laws related to fair credit practices. For example, the Equal Credit Opportunity Act (ECOA) requires that the credit applicant be notified of the credit decision within 30 calendar days following application. Applicants who are denied credit must be informed of the reasons for the refusal. If the decision was based on information obtained from a consumer reporting agency (as opposed to financial statements or other information provided by the applicant), the credit denial must include the name, address, and telephone number of the agency. It must also remind applicants that the Fair Credit Reporting Act provides them the right to know the nature of the information in their credit file. In addition, credit denials must include a standard statement that the ECOA prohibits creditors from discriminating against credit applicants on the basis of a number of protected characteristics (race, color, religion, national origin, sex, marital status, and age). (For more information about fair credit reporting, visit **http://www.privacyrights.org/fs/fs6-crdt.htm**.)

To avoid litigation, some companies choose to omit the explanation from the credit denial letter and invite the applicant to call or come in to discuss the reasons. Alternately, they may suggest that the receiver obtain further information from the credit reporting agency whose name, address, and telephone number are provided.

Assume that a retailer of electronic devices has placed an initial order and requested credit privileges. After examining financial statements that were enclosed, the wholesaler decides the request should be denied. Review the letter in Figure 7-8 on the next page to

© Hill Street Studios/Blend Images/Jupiterimages

identify techniques used to refuse credit while preserving relations with this customer—who may very well have good credit in the near future.

The credit refusal in Figure 7-8 provides an explanation for the refusal. Credit scores on which the decision was based provide legitimacy to the credit denial. It makes no apology for action taken that would only cause the applicant to speculate that the decision was arbitrary.

Including resale material in a credit refusal letter is helpful because it:

- Might cause credit applicants to prefer your brand and perhaps be willing to buy on a cash basis.
- Suggests that the writer is trying to be helpful.
- Makes the writing easier—negative thoughts are easier to de-emphasize when cushioned with resale material and when you seem confident of future cash purchases.
- Can confirm the credit applicant's judgment. (Suggesting the applicant made a good choice of merchandise is an indirect compliment.)

Delivering Constructive Criticism

A person who has had a bad experience as a result of another person's conduct may be reluctant to write or speak about that experience. However, because one person took the time to communicate, many could benefit. Although not always easy or pleasant, communicating constructive criticism can be thought of as a civic responsibility. For example,

Figure 7-8 Good Example of a Credit Denial

Legal and Ethical Constraints
Assures compliance with laws by including reason for denial.

- *Thanks applicant for his interest in company's service and confirms his good choice.*

- *Leads to discussion of basis for refusal and continues with explanation.*

- *De-emphasizes refusal by using positive language to suggest a possible solution.*

- *Looks confidently to future by encouraging subsequent application and thus implies continued business.*

- *Closes with sales promotion.*

 PHOENIX FEDERAL BANK
2307 Desert Boulevard, Phoenix, AZ 85042
Tele.: 800-555-3400 ···· Fax: 800-555-3419

April 8, 2010

Randall Soto
412 Bayou Way
Tallahassee, FL 33074

Dear Mr. Soto:

Thank you for choosing Phoenix Federal Bank for your credit needs. After checking your credit rating with the three national credit reporting firms, we are unable to fulfill your request for a Phoenix Platinum Credit Card at this time.

Your credit scores were 640, 645, and 642, for an average score of 640. In order to get a Phoenix Platinum Card, your credit score must be 700 or above.

We are eager to fulfill your credit needs and encourage you to obtain your credit report so that you can discover whether there are errors in your credit history that you might be able to correct. You can obtain a free credit report via the Internet at www.creditrating.com.

Once your credit rating has improved, please reapply for your Phoenix Platinum Card. Phoenix Platinum provides many benefits to its users, including a competitive interest rate and special offers for discounts at the best hotels, resorts, and rental car agencies.

Sincerely,

Roberto Ramírez

Roberto Ramirez
Customer Service Manager

a person who returns from a long stay at a major hotel might, upon returning home, write a letter or email to the management commending certain employees. If the stay had not been pleasant and weaknesses in hotel operation had been detected, a tactful message pointing out the negatives would probably be appreciated. Future guests could benefit from the effort of that person.

Before communicating about the problem, an individual should recognize the following risks: being stereotyped as a complainer, being associated with negative thoughts and perceived in negative terms, and appearing to challenge management's decisions concerning hotel operations. Yet such risks may be worth taking because of the benefits:

- The communicator gets a feeling of having exercised a responsibility.
- Management learns of changes that need to be made.
- The hotel staff about whom the message is written modifies techniques and is thus more successful.
- Other guests will have more enjoyable stays in the hotel.

In the decision to communicate negative information, the primary consideration is intent. If the intent is to hurt or to get even, the message should not be sent. Including false information would be *unethical* and *illegal*. To avoid litigation charges and to respond ethically, include only specific facts you can verify and avoid evaluative words that present opinions about the person's character or ability. For example, instead of presenting facts, the message in Figure 7-9 judges the salesman sent to the medical office. Overall, the message is short, general, and negative. By comparison, the revision in Figure 7-10 has positive intent, is factual, uses positive language, and leaves judgment to the recipient.

Communicating Negative Organizational News

Being able to *initiate* messages that convey bad news is as important as responding "No" to messages from customers/clients and others outside the company. Employees and the public are seeking, and expecting, *honest* answers from management about situations adversely affecting the company—slumping profits, massive layoffs as a result of downsizing, a variety of major changes in the organization, and negative publicity that affects the overall health of the business and retirement plans, to name a few.

Managers who can communicate negative information in a sensitive, honest, and timely way can calm fears and doubts and build positive employee and public relations. Effective managers recognize that employee morale as well as public goodwill is fragile—easily damaged and difficult to repair. If handled well, these bad-news messages related to the organization can be opportunities to treat employees, customers, and the general public with respect, thus building unity and trust.

Strong internal communication is a key to involving employees in corporate strategies and building an important sense of community. The best companies use a variety of communication tools that promote an open exchange of honest, candid communication and welcome input from employees. Newsletters, email updates,

Figure 7-9   *Poor Example of a Constructive Criticism*

- *Lacks adequate buffer to create fair-minded tone.*

- *Uses judgmental terms and overly negative words.*

- *Ends with negative tone and patronizing comments.*

Roger Dickenson, a sales associate with your company, regularly visits our medical office, and his conduct around our female staff is absolutely unacceptable. He makes lewd jokes and comments inappropriately about their appearance and parts of their anatomy. He creates enormous discomfort among my staff whenever he enters the office.

Although he has an adequate understanding of your product line, his sexist attitude makes him an unwelcome visitor to our office. I hope you can either replace him or get him some training to at least educate him about the dangers of sexual harassment.

Figure 7-10

- *Provides a context for discussion.*

- *Tries to convey fair-mindedness and establish credibility by acknowledging good as well as bad points.*

- *Presents verifiable statements without labeling them in negative, judgmental terms.*

- *Ends on pleasant note that seeks to add credibility to preceding negatives.*

Legal and Ethical Constraints
Conveys positive intent to help—not to hurt or get even.

Avoids potential litigation charges by including specific, verifiable facts and avoiding negative evaluative statements.

Uses "confidential" as safeguard; information is intended for professional use only, not designed to hurt or to be thought of as gossip.

Paradise Day Spa and Cosmetic Center

ATLANTIC CITY, NJ 08499   800-555-2100

November 17, 2010

Charles Lamkin
Wideworld Pharmaceuticals Corp.
1001 West 5th Avenue
New York, NY 11008

Dear Mr. Lamkin:

Roger Dickenson, a sales associate with your company, visits our office on a monthly basis to keep us up to date with your product line. He is a proficient salesperson who is very knowledgeable about your products and can always answer our questions about the medications' efficacy and potential side effects.

His demeanor, while friendly and open, has caused some of our employees to complain that he may be a bit too friendly, particularly around our young female employees. There have been reports of inappropriate jokes of a sexual nature and comments about employees' appearance and anatomical features.

Roger is obviously a skilled salesperson, but I felt it was appropriate to confidentially inform you about his behavior so that he would have the opportunity to get the training he needs to avoid a more serious situation.

Sincerely,

Teresa Favor

Teresa Favor
Office Manager
Paradise Day Spa and Cosmetic Center

---

town hall or focus meetings, videoconferencing, phone calls, and discussion boards deliver relevant messages and allow employees to pose questions to management. This quality, two-way communication involves employees in corporate strategies; employees who are aware of company goals and potential problems feel connected and accountable. Informed employees are also better prepared for bad news than employees who only receive dire pronouncements of bad news.

Assuming this long-term commitment to keep employees informed, the following suggestions provide guidance in breaking bad news to employees and the public:

- **DO convey the bad news as soon as possible.** Timeliness will minimize damage caused by rumors

and will give employees the concern and respect they deserve.

- **DO give a complete, rational explanation of the problem.** Be candid about what is happening, why, and its effect on employees, customers, and the public. Provide enough detail to establish your credibility, and provide context so your audience can understand the situation. Stressing positive aspects will provide needed balance. However, avoid sugarcoating or minimizing the severity of the news to the point that the message is misunderstood.

- **DO show empathy and respond to the feelings.** Allow people adequate time to react to the bad news. Listen attentively for understanding and then address the concerns, issues, and potential problems presented.

- **DO follow up.** Let people know what will happen next—what is expected of employees or customers, and what the company will do and when. Plan to repeat your explanations and assurances that you are available to respond to concerns in several communications that extend over a given time.

Consider the company president who emailed employees about the plant closing in Figure 7-11. The president should not be surprised to learn that employees are resisting the closure; some perceive the company to be an enemy for threatening their families' livelihoods. The president's revision, in Figure 7-12 on page 124, anticipates the employees' natural resistance to this stunning announcement and crafts a sensitive message.

A printed memo is a more effective channel for communicating this sensitive and official information than the efficient, yet informal, email message.

Before developing a bad-news message, review the specific suggestions in this chapter's "Check Your Communication" checklist on the student review card. Compare your work with this checklist again after you have prepared a rough draft, and make any revisions.

Figure 7-11

BAD

Poor Example of a Bad-News Message
Announcing Negative Organizational News

- *Reveals bad news before explanation.*

- *Begins bluntly with bad news.*

- *Explains reason for decision but lacks adequate explanation that might help employees understand or accept decision.*

- *Is clear on next step but shows no empathy for employees' feelings.*

Format Pointer
Sends highly sensitive message through email without prior communication to prepare employees.

New Message

To: <company employees>

From: Germain Crocker

Subject: FACTORY CLOSING

February 14, 2010

Effective May 1, 2010, we will close our plant facility. The current economic crisis has given management no other option as our sales have dropped 30 percent for the last six months.

All employees will be eligible for unemployment benefits. A representative from the state unemployment insurance agency will visit the company next week to explain the process and help you fill out the necessary forms. More information about this meeting will be forthcoming.

Figure 7-12

GOOD

Good Example of a Bad-News Message
Announcing Negative Organizational News

- *Uses subject line to introduce topic but does not reveal bad news.*

- *Uses buffer to introduce topic familiar to employees through previous communication and leads into reasons.*

- *Provides rational explanation for bad news.*

- *Presents bad news and provides an immediate solution for employees.*

- *Provides hope by informing employees of next steps to solve the company's problem and by association, theirs.*

- *Follows up assuring continued exchange of timely information.*

- *Ends with positive appeal for unity.*

Legal and Ethical Constraints
Uses the more formal memo channel rather than email for conveying sensitive message.

INTEROFFICE MEMORANDUM

TO: All Employees
FROM: Germain Crocker, Plant Manager
DATE: February 14, 2010
SUBJECT: Proposed Plan for Dealing with Current Economic Conditions

The current recession has hit the automobile industry hard. Consumers are having difficulty getting the credit they need to finance new-car purchases. Continued discussion of the country's deepening recession in the media has reinforced consumers' fears about the future, resulting in increased cutbacks in their spending.

The immediate effect upon Lincoln Automotive has been a drastic reduction in our sales of 30 percent over the past six months. This has depleted our operating income, and recent attempts to get government help have fallen on deaf ears.

These developments have led to a decision by our board of directors to close several plants to reduce costs and give the company time to turn the situation around. As a result, temporary plant layoffs will commence May 1. All employees will be eligible for full unemployment benefits at that time. A meeting will be held at 8 a.m. on February 16 in the company cafeteria to explain the process for applying for benefits and to help you to fill out the proper paperwork.

We are hoping that these cutbacks will allow the company to get back on its feet in the next few months and will lead to the eventual reopening of the plant. A corporate team has been assembled to look at every aspect of the company's operations to come up with a plan to improve operational efficiencies as well as our product to increase demand. You will be kept up to date of the company's progress in reaching these goals and any decision to resume plant operations. It is our goal to restore Lincoln Automotive to financial solvency so that we can continue our tradition of great people making great cars for great people.

Preparing Persuasive Messages

Persuasion Strategies

Persuasion is the ability to influence others to accept your point of view. It is not an attempt to trick or manipulate someone into taking action favorable to the communicator. Instead, it is an honest, organized presentation of information on which a person may choose to act. In all occupations and professions, rich rewards await those who can use well-informed and well-prepared presentations to persuade others to accept their ideas or buy their products, services, or ideas.

objective ①
Develop effective outlines and appeals for messages that persuade.

How do you learn to persuade others through spoken and written communication? Have you ever made a persuasive request, written a cover letter, completed an application for a job, or written an essay for college entry or a scholarship? If so, you already have experience with this type of communication. While the persuasive concepts discussed in this chapter are directed primarily at written communication, they can also be applied in many spoken communication situations.

For persuasion to be effective, you must understand your product, service, or idea; know your audience; anticipate the arguments that may come from the audience; and have a rational and logical response to those arguments. Remember, persuasion need not be a hard sell; it can simply be a way of getting a client or your supervisor to say "Yes."

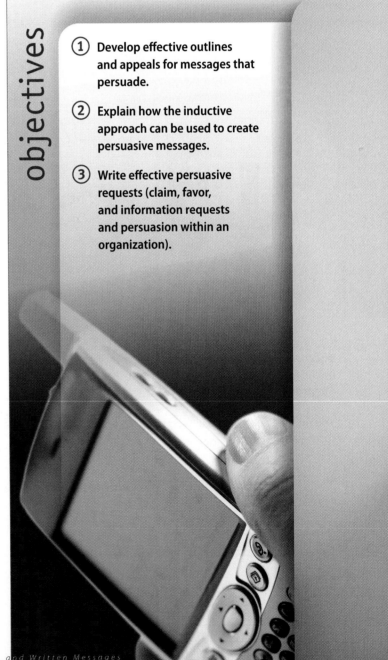

objectives

① Develop effective outlines and appeals for messages that persuade.

② Explain how the inductive approach can be used to create persuasive messages.

③ Write effective persuasive requests (claim, favor, and information requests and persuasion within an organization).

Plan Before You Write

Success in writing is directly related to success in preliminary thinking. If the right questions have been asked and answered, the composing will be easier and the message will be more persuasive. Specifically, you need information about (1) your product, service, or idea; (2) your audience; and (3) the desired action.

Know the Product, Service, or Idea

You cannot be satisfied with knowing the product, service, or idea in a general way; you need details. Get your information by (1) reading all available literature; (2) using the product and watching others use it; (3) comparing the product, service, or idea with others; (4) conducting tests and experiments; and (5) soliciting reports from users.

Before you write, you need concrete answers to such questions as these:

- What will the product, service, or idea do for the receiver(s)?
- What are its superior features (e.g., design and workmanship or receiver benefit)?
- How is the product or service different from its competition? How is the proposed idea superior to other viable alternatives?
- What is the cost to the receiver?

Similar questions must be answered about other viable alternatives or competing products. Of particular importance is the question, "What is the major difference?" People are inclined to choose an item (or alternative) that has some distinct advantage. For example, some people may choose a particular car model because of its style and available options; still others may choose the model because of its safety record.

Know the Receiver

Who are the people to whom the persuasive message is directed? What are their wants and needs? Is a persuasive message to be written and addressed to an individual or to a group? If it is addressed to a group, what characteristics do the members have in common? What are their common goals, their occupational levels, their educational status? To what extent have their needs and wants been satisfied? How might cultural differences affect your message?

The easiest way to persuade someone is to show how the product, service, or idea will benefit him or her. Benefits might include convenience, durability, efficiency, or serviceability. Others may respond favorably to appeals to the social status or the need to be loved, entertained, remembered, popular, praised, appreciated, or respected.

In deciding how to best persuade a particular audience, it might be helpful to consider the three appeals identified centuries ago by the Greek philosopher Aristotle. Aristotle claimed that there are three general types of appeals that might be made to persuade an audience: ethical, logical, and emotional.

A logical appeal, or **logos**, consists of such information as facts and statistics. It is a fact, for example, that most plants require sunshine to grow. A *fact* is any information that is broadly accepted as true. Business audiences tend to be persuaded by logical information, particularly numbers, dollars, and statistics. They also often prefer that such information is presented visually, using tables or graphs.

An ethical appeal, or **ethos**, does not generally refer to ethics as we normally think of the concept but rather to information or an association that provides credibility for ourselves, our product, or position. One of the easiest ways to make an ethical argument is to cite recognized authorities in the subject of discussion. The writer or speaker can also establish him or herself as an expert in the subject. Credibility can be established by being fair-minded, balanced, and objective in the discussion of a topic.

An emotional appeal, or **pathos**, generally works by eliciting an emotional response from the audience and is the most common type of appeal used in advertisements. Examples of pathos include appeals to the desire for social status or to be loved, admired, popular, attractive, or respected.

To be a successful persuader, it is important to identify the concerns of the receiver. Consider the varying appeals used in a memo to employees and to supervisors seeking support of telecommuting. The memo to employees would appeal to the need for greater flexibility, reduced stress, and reduced cost of transportation and office apparel. Appeals directed at supervisors would focus on increased productivity and morale, reduced costs for office space, and compliance with the Clean Air Act, a federal law requiring companies to reduce air pollution and traffic congestion.

When dealing with audiences who are not receptive to your message, additional considerations may need to be made. For example, you may need to anticipate their objections to your proposal and then be prepared to subtly respond to each of these objections with the purpose of eliminating them. Doing so may be necessary to place these audiences in a position where they might *begin* to consider your proposal, let alone accept it. It may take time to persuade some audiences; you may first need to establish a trusting relationship with them before they are willing to consider your proposals.

© Walter Bibikow/Index Stock Imagery/Jupiterimages

logos
a logical appeal that consists of such information as facts and statistics
ethos
an appeal based on information or an association that provides credibility for ourselves, our product, or position
pathos
an emotional appeal that works by eliciting an emotional response from the audience

Identify the Desired Action

What do you want the receiver to do? Change an office policy? Allow you to purchase new equipment for your department? Complete an order form and enclose a personal check? Receive a demonstration version for trial examination? Return a card requesting a representative to call? Email for more information? Approve a request? Accept a significant change in service, style, and procedures? Whatever the desired action, you need to have a clear definition of it before composing your message.

Apply Sound Writing Principles

The principles of unity, coherence, and emphasis are just as important in persuasive messages as in other messages. In addition, some other principles seem to be especially helpful in preparing persuasive messages:

- **Keep paragraphs short.** The spaces between paragraphs show the dividing place between ideas, improve appearance, and provide convenient resting places for the eyes. Hold the first and last paragraph to three or fewer lines; a one-line paragraph (even a very short line) is acceptable. You can even use paragraphs less than one sentence long by putting four or five words on the first line and completing the sentence in a new paragraph. Be careful to include key attention-getting words that either introduce the product, service, or idea, or lead to its introduction.

- **Use concrete nouns and active verbs.** Concrete nouns and active verbs help receivers see the product, service, or idea and its benefits more vividly than do abstract nouns and passive verbs.

- **Use specific language.** General words won't mean much unless they are well supported with specifics. Specific language is space consuming (saying that something is "great" is less space consuming than telling what makes it so); therefore, persuasive messages are usually longer than other messages. Still, persuasive messages need to be concise; they should say what needs to be said without wasting words.

- **Let receivers have the spotlight.** If receivers are made the subject of some of the sentences, if they can visualize themselves with the product in their hands, if they can get the feel of using it for enjoyment or to solve problems, then the chances of creating a desire are increased.

- **Stress a central selling point or appeal.** A thorough analysis ordinarily will reveal some feature that is unique or some benefit that is not provided by other viable alternatives. This point of difference can be developed into a theme that is woven throughout

Ethical persuasion should include these elements:[1]

- **Clear definition.** Present products and their characteristics with clear explanation.

- **Scientific evidence.** Provide the source and nature of your evidence.

- **Context for comparison.** Better, faster, cleaner, easier, and similar terms imply a comparison. Better than what? Better than it once was? Better than the competition? Or better than using nothing at all?

- **Audience sensitivity.** Consider who might be offended by your message and revise.

the entire message. Or, instead of using a point of difference as a central selling point, a writer may choose to stress a major satisfaction to be gained from using the item or doing as asked. A central selling point (theme) should be introduced early and reinforced throughout the remainder of the message.

You will see how to apply sound writing principles and blend the steps in the four-step outline presented on the next page in Figure 8-1 to prepare effective persuasive messages.

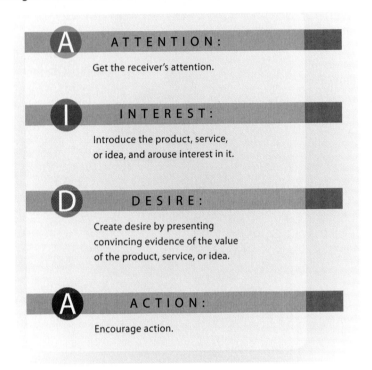

Figure 8-1 *Inductive Outline Used in Persuasive Messages Sent in Written, Electronic, or Spoken Form*

A ATTENTION:
Get the receiver's attention.

I INTEREST:
Introduce the product, service, or idea, and arouse interest in it.

D DESIRE:
Create desire by presenting convincing evidence of the value of the product, service, or idea.

A ACTION:
Encourage action.

Use the Inductive Approach

objective ②
Explain how the inductive approach can be used to create persuasive messages.

ver 100 years ago, Sherwin Cody summarized the persuasive process into four basic steps called **AIDA**.[2] The steps have varied somewhat and have had different labels, but the fundamentals remain relatively unchanged. The persuasive message illustrated in Figure 8-1 is inductive. The main idea, which is the request for action, appears in the *last* paragraph after presenting the details—convincing reasons for the receiver to comply with the request.

Each step is essential, but the steps do not necessarily require equal amounts of space. Good persuasive messages do not require separate sentences and paragraphs for each phase of the outline. The message *could* gain the receiver's attention and interest

AIDA
a four-step inductive process that involves gaining attention, generating interest, creating desire, and motivating action

in the same sentence, while creating desire *could* require many paragraphs.

Gain Attention

The same principles apply in writing a *solicited sales letter,* with one exception: Because the solicited sales letter is a response to a request for information, an attention-getter is not essential. However, when writing an unsolicited sales message, various techniques can be used to successfully convince receivers to consider it. Some commonly used attention-getting devices include:

- **A personal experience.** When a doctor gives you instructions, how often have you thought "I wish you had time to explain" or "I wish I knew more about medical matters"?

- **A solution to a problem (outstanding feature/benefit).** Imagine creating a customized multimedia presentation that . . . .

- **A startling announcement.** More teens die as a result of suicide each month than in auto accidents in the same time period.

- **A what-if opening.** What if I told you there is a savings plan that will enable you to retire three years earlier?

- **A question.** Why should you invest in a company that has lost money for six straight years?

- **A story.** Here's a typical day in the life of a manager who uses Wilson Enterprise's Pager.

- **A proverb or quote from a famous person.** Vince Lombardi, one of the most successful coaches in the history of football, once said, "If winning isn't everything, why do they keep score?" At Winning Edge, we specialize in making you the winner you were born to be.

- **A split sentence.** Sandy beaches, turquoise water, and warm breezes . . . it's all awaiting you on your Mesa cruise.

- **An analogy.** Like a good neighbor, State Farm is there.

Other attention-getters include a gift, an offer or a bargain, or a comment on an enclosed product sample. Regardless of the technique used, the attention-getter should achieve several important objectives:

- **Introduce a relationship between the receiver and the product, service, or idea.** Remaining sentences grow naturally from this beginning sentence. If receivers do not see the relationship between the first sentence and the sales appeal, they may react negatively to the whole message—they may think they have been tricked into reading. For example, consider the following poor attention-getter:

Would you like to be the chief executive officer of one of America's largest companies? As CEO of Barkley Enterprises, you can launch new products, invest in third-world countries, or arrange billion-dollar buyouts. Barkley Enterprises is one of several companies at your command in the new computer software game developed by Creative Diversions Software.

The beginning sentence is emphatic because it is a short question. However, it suggests the message will be about obtaining a top management position, which

it is not. All three sentences combined suggest high-pressure techniques. The computer software game has relevant virtues, and one of them could have been emphasized by placing it in the first sentence.

- **Focus on a central selling feature.** Almost every product, service, or idea will in some respects be superior to its competition. If not, factors such as favorable price, fast delivery, or superior service may be used as the primary appeal. This central selling point must be emphasized, and one of the most effective ways to emphasize a point is by position in the message. An outstanding feature mentioned in the middle of a message may go unnoticed, but it will stand out if mentioned in the first sentence. Note how the following opening sentence introduces the central selling feature and leads naturally into the sentences that follow:

One of the Soviet Georgia's senior citizens thought Dannon was an excellent yogurt. She ought to know. She's been eating yogurt for 137 years.

Dannon Yogurt is a part of healthy nutrition plan that can add years to your life, too. It's high in important nutrients including calcium, protein, vitamin B12, potassium, phosphorus, and riboflavin as well as being a great way to reduce fat and calories from your meals.

- **Use an original approach.** To get the reader's attention and interest, you must offer something new and fresh. Thus, choose an anecdote likely unfamiliar to your receiver, or use a unique combination of words to describe how a product, service, or idea can solve the receiver's problem:

I step into my favorite restaurant, and the waiters all dive for cover. Only the restaurant owner has the guts to take my order—as if she really needs to ask. "I'll have the usual," I say. "Give me . . . the *All You Can Eat Buffet*." For the next two hours, I stuff myself. I indulge at the salad bar and gorge at the taco bar. As much as I consume, though, I haven't tried everything—I just don't have room.

In many ways, WordPerfect is like that gigantic buffet. The new WP is packed with powerful, useful features. . . .[3]

Gain Interest by Introducing the Product, Service, or Idea

A persuasive message is certainly off to a good start if the first sentences cause the receiver to think "Here's a solution to one of my problems," "Here's something I need," or "Here's something I want." You may lead the receiver to such a thought by introducing the product, service, or idea in the very first sentence. If you do, you can succeed in both getting attention and arousing interest in one sentence. An effective introduction of the product, service, or idea is cohesive and action centered and continues to stress a central selling point.

- **Be cohesive.** If the attention-getter does not introduce the product, service, or idea, it should lead naturally to the introduction. Note the abrupt change in thought and the unrelatedness of the attention-getter to the second paragraph in the following example:

Employees appreciate a company that provides a safe work environment.

DON'T The Adcock Human Resources Association has been conducting a survey for the last six months. Their primary aim is to improve the safety of office work environments.

The last words of the first sentence, "safe work environment," are related to "safety of office work environments"—the last words of the last sentence. No word or phrase in the first sentence connects the words of the second sentence, which creates an abrupt, confusing change in thought. In the following revision, the second sentence is tied to the first by the word "that's." "Safety" in the second sentence refers to "protection" in the third. The LogicTech low-radiation monitor is introduced as a means of providing a safe work environment. Additionally, notice that the attention-getter leads smoothly to the discussion of the survey results.

Employees appreciate a company that provides a safe work environment.

DO That's one thing the Adcock Human Resources Association learned from its six-month survey of the safety of the office work environment. For added protection from radiation emissions, more companies are purchasing LogicTech's low-radiation computer monitors. . . .

- **Be action oriented.** To introduce your offering in an interesting way, you must place the product, service, or idea in your receivers' hands and talk about their use of it or benefit from accepting your idea. They will get a clearer picture when reading about something happening than when reading a product description. Also, the picture becomes all the more vivid when the receiver is the hero of the story—the person taking the action. In a sense, you do not sell products, services, or ideas—you sell the pleasure people derive from their use. Logically, then, you have to focus more on that use than about the offering itself. If you put receivers to work using your product, service, or idea to solve problems, they will be the subject of most of your sentences.

Some product description is necessary and natural. In the following example, the writer focuses on the product and creates an uninteresting, still picture: *The Body Solid Endurance treadmill has an oversized running surface. It has a shock-absorbent deck for added comfort.* In the revision, a person is the subject of the message and is enjoying the benefits of the treadmill.

When you step onto the Body Solid Endurance 8K Treadmill, the oversized 21" x 53" running surface will inspire you to go for an all-out marathon session. Go ahead. That's what the 8K was made for. The shock-absorbent deck will keep you comfortable and your run smooth. The powerful 2.5 HP continuous duty (7.5 HP peak duty) motor will keep your pace fluid and consistent whether you are a beginner or a professional athlete.[4]

- **Stress a central selling point.** If the attention-getter does not introduce a distinctive feature, it should lead to it. You can stress important points by position in the message and space allocation. As soon as receivers visualize the product, service, or idea, they need to have attention called to its outstanding features. If you want to devote much space to the outstanding features, introduce them early. Note how the attention-getter introduces the distinctive selling feature (ease of operation) and how the following sentences keep the receivers' eyes focused on that feature:

If you know how to write a check and record it in your checkbook, then you can operate Easy Accounting. It's that easy to use. Just click the check icon to display a blank check. Use the number keys to enter the amount of the check and Easy Accounting fills in the word version of the amount. Doesn't that sound easy?

Now click on the category box and conveniently view a complete listing of your accounts. Move the arrow to the account of your choice and click. The account is written on the check and posted to your records automatically.

>>Apple is one company that knows how to create desire through persuasive marketing messages. Shown are customers waiting in line to purchase the iPhone the day it was released.

AP Images/M. Spencer Green

By stressing one point, you do not limit the message to that point. For example, while ease of operation is being stressed, other features are mentioned. A good film presents a star who is seen throughout most of the film; a good term paper presents a thesis idea that is supported throughout; a school yearbook develops a theme; a sales message should stress a central selling point.

Create Desire by Providing Convincing Evidence

After you have made an interesting introduction to your product, service, or idea, present enough supporting evidence to satisfy your receivers' needs. Keep one or two main features uppermost in the receivers' minds, and include evidence that supports these features. For example, using appearance as an outstanding selling feature of compact cars while presenting abundant evidence to show economy of operation would be inconsistent.

Present and Interpret Factual Evidence. Few people will believe general statements without having supporting factual evidence. Simply saying that a certain method is efficient is not enough. You must say how it is efficient and present some data to illustrate how efficient. Providing evidence also has the secondary advantage of making the claims about a product, feature, or benefit clearer to the receiver.

Because of the importance of evidence for being persuasive, it can be helpful to understand the difference between two basic components of a persuasive message: the **claim** and the **evidence** that supports it. A claim is often a general or abstract statement, while evidence is specific. In the following example, the claim is implied. Can you identify the claim?

> The Honda Accord sedan has a 255 horsepower engine, versus the 240 horsepower of the gasoline V-6. Boasting excellent fuel economy, it's rated at 38 miles per gallon on the highway and 32 in town. The cylinder shutoff feature allows the Accord to run on just three of its six cylinders to save even more fuel, with the electric motor kicking in when additional power is needed.

If you guessed that the claim was that the Honda Accord gets excellent gas mileage, you would be correct. Presenting hard facts and figures to support your statements is one way to increase your chances of convincing your audience. Presenting results of a research study takes space but makes the message much more convincing than general remarks about superior durability and appearance. Facts and figures are even more impressive if they reflect comparative advantage, as shown in the example above.

Providing specific evidence also has the advantage of increasing the credibility of the writer by making him or her sound well informed. Talking about pages treated with special protectants to retard aging and machine-sewn construction suggests the writer is knowledgeable about the product, which increases receiver confidence.

Naturally, your receivers will be less familiar with

claim
a general or abstract statement
evidence
specific, supportive statement

the product, service, or idea and its uses than you will be. Not only do you have an obligation to give information, but also you should interpret it if necessary and point out how the information will benefit the receiver. Notice how the following example clearly explains why infrared technology is superior to that used in traditional keyboards. The interpretation makes the evidence understandable and thus convincing.

General Statement Without Explanation	Specific, Interpreted Fact
Wireless keyboarding is superior to traditional keyboarding.	*With wireless keyboarding, you are no longer tied to your computer. Infrared technology uses infrared light to transmit information between the keyboard and the computer in the same way your remote control communicates with your television. You can now move your keyboard for greater comfort and flexibility.*

This example uses a valuable interpretative technique—the comparison. You can often make a point more convincing by comparing something unfamiliar with something familiar. Most people are familiar with the television remote, so they can now visualize how the wireless keyboard will work. Comparison can also be used to interpret prices. Advertisers frequently compare the cost of sponsoring a child in a third-world country to the price of a fast-food lunch. An insurance representative might write this sentence: *The annual premium for this 20-year, limited-payment policy is $360, or $1 a day—about the cost of a cup of coffee.*

Do not go overboard and bore or frustrate your receivers with an abundance of facts or technical data. Never make your receivers feel ignorant by trying to impress them with facts and figures they may not understand.

Be Objective and Ethical. Use language that people will believe. Specific, concrete language makes your message sound true. Excessive superlatives, exaggerations, flowery statements, unsupported claims, and incomplete comparisons all make your message sound like high-pressure sales talk. Just one such sentence can destroy confidence in the whole message. Examine the following statements to see whether they give convincing evidence. Would they make a receiver want to buy? Or do they merely remind the receiver of someone's desire to sell? *This antibiotic is the best on the market today. It represents the very latest in biochemical research.*

Identifying the best-selling antibiotic requires gathering information about all antibiotics marketed and then choosing the one with superior characteristics. You know the sender is likely to have a bias in favor of the particular drug being sold. However, you do not know whether the sender actually spent time researching other antibiotics or whether he or she would know how to evaluate this information. You certainly do not know whether the sender knows enough about biochemical research to say truthfully what the very latest is.

Similarly, avoid preposterous statements *(Gardeners are turning handsprings in their excitement over our new weed killer!)* or subjective claims *(Stretch those tired limbs out on one of our luscious water beds. It's like floating on a gentle dream cloud on a warm, sunny afternoon. Ah, what soothing relaxation!)*. Even though some people may be persuaded by such writing, many will see it as an attempt to trick them.

Note the incomplete comparison in the following example: *SunBlock provides you better protection from the sun's dangerous ultraviolet rays.* Is SunBlock being compared with *all* other sunscreens, *most* other sunscreens, *one* unnamed brand, or others? Unless an additional sentence identifies the other elements in the comparison, you do not know. Too often, the writer of such a sentence hopes the receiver will assume the

comparison is with *all* others. Written with that intent, the incomplete comparison is *unethical*. Likewise, statements of certainty are often inaccurate or misleading.

In order for persuasive messages to be ethical, you should use concrete evidence to substantiate all claims that are made. Legal guidelines related to truth in advertising provide clear guidance for avoiding misrepresentation. Further, if you exaggerate or mislead in a letter delivered by the U.S. Postal Service, you can be charged with the federal offense of mail fraud and incur significant fines or even imprisonment.

Being objective also means that you do not omit, distort, or hide important information that does not support your argument or claims. Consider the truthfulness of a message disclosing the financial benefits of a plant closing but omitting the fact that 3,000 employees were laid off in a town where the plant is the primary employer. The investor may realize the impact of the omission and lose faith in the CEO's credibility.

Include Testimonials, Guarantees, and Enclosures. One way to convince prospective customers that they will like your product, service, or idea is to give them concrete evidence that other people like it. Tell what others have said (with permission, of course) about the usefulness of your offering. Guarantees and free trials convey both negative and positive connotations. By revealing willingness to refund money or exchange an unsatisfactory unit, a writer confesses a negative: The purchase could be regretted or refused. However, the positive connotations are stronger than the negatives: The seller has a definite plan for ensuring that buyers get value for money spent. In addition, the seller exhibits willingness for the buyer to check a product, service, or idea personally and compare it with others. The seller also implies confidence that a free trial will result in a purchase and that the product will meet standards set in the guarantee. A long or complex guarantee can be included in an enclosure.

A message should persuade the receiver to read an enclosure, attachment, or file link that includes more detailed information. Thus, refer to the added material late in the message after the major portion of the evidence has been given. An enclosure or link is best referred to in a sentence that is not a cliché ("Enclosed you will find," or "We have enclosed a brochure") and says something else:

> The enclosed annual report will help you understand the types of information provided to small- and medium-sized companies by Lincoln Business Data, Inc.

> Click here to view the huge assortment of clearance-priced items and other end-of-season specials.

the grass is greener

Incomplete comparisons are unethical.

Subordinate the Price. Logically, price should be introduced late in the message—after most of the advantages have been discussed. Use the following techniques to overcome people's natural resistance to price:

- **Introduce price only after creating a desire for the product, service, or idea and its virtues.** Let receivers see the relationship of features and benefits to the price.

- **Use figures to illustrate that the price is reasonable or that the receiver can save money.** Example: Purigard saves the average pool owner about $10 in chemicals each month; thus, the $150 unit pays for itself in 15 months.

- **State price in terms of small units.** Twelve dollars a month seems like less than $144 a year.

- **Invite comparison of like products, services, or ideas with similar features.**

- **Consider mentioning price in a complex or compound sentence that relates or summarizes the virtues of the product, service, or idea.** Example: For a $48 yearly subscription fee, Medisearch brings you a monthly digest of recent medical research that is written in nontechnical language.

Motivate Action

For proper clarity and emphasis, the last paragraph should be relatively short. Yet it must accomplish three important tasks: specify the specific action wanted and present it as easy to perform, encourage quick action, and ask for the action confidently.

- **Make the action clear and simple to complete.** Define the desired action in specific terms that are easy to complete. For example, you might ask the receiver to complete an order blank and return it with a check, place a telephone call, or order online. General instructions such as "Let us hear from you," "Take action on the matter," and "Make a response" are ineffective. Make action simple to encourage receivers to act immediately. Instead of asking receivers to fill in their names and addresses on order forms or return cards and envelopes, do that work for them by preprinting the information on the form. Otherwise, they may see the task as difficult or time-consuming and decide to procrastinate.

- **Restate the reward for taking action (central selling point).** The central selling point should be introduced early in the message, interwoven throughout the evidence section, and included in the last paragraph as an emphatic, final reminder of the reason for taking action.

- **Provide an incentive for quick action.** If the receiver waits to take action on your proposal, the persuasive evidence will be harder to remember and the receiver will be less likely to act. Therefore, you prefer the receiver to act quickly. Reference to the central selling point (assuming it has been well received) helps to stimulate action. Commonly used appeals for getting quick action are to encourage customers to buy while prices are in effect, while supplies last, when a rebate is being offered, when it is a particular holiday, or when they will receive benefits.

- **Ask confidently for action.** If you have a good product, service, or idea and have presented evidence effectively, you have a right to feel confident. Demonstrate your confidence when requesting action: "To save time in cleaning, complete and return. . . ." Avoid statements suggesting lack of confidence, such as "If you want to save time in cleaning, complete and return. . . ," "If you agree. . . ," and "I *hope* you will. . . ."

Observe how the following closing paragraph accomplishes the four important tasks: refers to the central selling point, makes a specific action easy, provides an incentive for quick action, and asks confidently for action.

Simply dial 1-800-555-8341. Then input the five-digit number printed in the top right corner of the attached card. Your name and address will be entered automatically into our system—a speedy way to get your productivity software to you within five working days along with a bill for payment. When you order by August 12, you will also receive a free subscription to *Time Resource Magazine*. TMC's new productivity software is as easy to use as it is to order!

Persuasive Requests

The preceding discussion of sales messages assumed the product, service, or cause was sufficiently worthy to reward the receiver for taking action. The discussion of persuasive requests assumes requests are reasonable—that compliance is justified when the request is for an adjustment and that compliance will (in some way) be rewarded when the request is for a favor.

objective ③ Write effective persuasive requests (claim, favor, and information requests and persuasion within an organization).

Common types of persuasive requests are claim messages and messages that request special favors and information. Although their purpose is to get favorable action, the messages invite action only after attempting to create a desire to take action and providing a logical argument to overcome any anticipated resistance.

Making a Claim

Claim messages are often routine because the basis for the claim is a guarantee or some other assurance that an adjustment will be made without need of persuasion. However, when an immediate remedy is doubtful, persuasion is nec-

essary. In a typical large business, the claim message is passed on to the claims adjuster for response.

Often, any reasonable claim will be adjusted to the customer's satisfaction. Therefore, expressing negative emotions or displeasure in the claim message is of little value. It can alienate the claims adjuster—the one person whose cooperation is needed. Remember, adjusters may have had little or nothing to do with the manufacture and sale of the product or direct delivery of the service. They did not create the need for the claim.

Companies should welcome claims. First, research indicates two important facts: (1) complainers are more likely to continue to do business with a company than those who do not complain, and (2) businesses that know how to resolve claims effectively will retain 95 percent of the complainers as repeat customers.[5] Second, only a small percentage of claims are from unethical individuals; the great bulk is from people who believe they have a legitimate complaint. Thus, the way an adjuster handles the claim determines, to a large extent, the goodwill of the company.

For the adjuster, granting a claim is much easier than refusing it. Because saying "No" is one of the most difficult writing tasks, the sender of a persuasive claim message has an advantage over the adjuster.

Like sales messages, persuasive claims should use an inductive sequence. Unlike routine claim messages, persuasive claims do not begin by asking for an adjustment. Two major changes would improve the poor example in Figure 8-2 on the next page: (1) writing inductively (to reduce the chance of a negative reaction in the first sentence) and (2) stressing an appeal throughout the message (to emphasize an incentive for taking favorable action). In a persuasive claim, an appeal serves the same purpose that a central selling feature does in a sales message. Both serve as a theme; both remind the receiver of a benefit that accrues from doing as asked. Note the application of these techniques in the revision in Figure 8-3.

Knowledge of effective claim writing should never be used as a means of taking advantage of someone. Hiding an unjustifiable claim under a cloak of untrue statements is difficult and strictly unethical. Adjusters typically are fair-minded people who will give the benefit of the doubt, but they will not satisfy an unhappy customer simply to avoid a problem.

My complaint = potential business

Figure 8-2

Poor Example of a Persuasive Claim

- Begins with an implied request before presenting reasons.

- Uses writer-oriented language to present limited facts. Provides no appeal or incentive for taking requested action.

- Sounds demanding without presenting persuasive appeal.

We've just reviewed the first draft of the proposed plan for revitalizing Palmdale Galleria and find it lacks imagination and attention to the latest trends of creating a total shopping experience for consumers. As such, it is totally unacceptable to us.

We made it clear that today's consumers expect to be immersed in a world that takes them away from their daily lives, transported to a fantasy world where they can feel special, pampered, and entertained by the latest in technological advances. This world should provide a total sensual experience that includes sights, sounds, enticing aromas, unique food offerings from around the world, and numerous entertainment elements. The expectation that we had was the creation of an upscale fantasy land, where shoppers could escape and be made to feel special and unique, with an experience that would draw them back to the Galleria time and time again to shop and attempt to sate their every desire.

We hope that you can provide us a new vision for the mall. Please call if you are unclear about our expectations for the redesign.

Figure 8-3

Good Example of a Persuasive Claim

- Seeks attention by giving sincere compliment that reveals subject of message.

- Continues central appeal—commitment to creative redesign—while providing needed details.

- Presents reasoning that leads to request and subtle reminder of central appeal.

- Connects specific request with firm's commitment to develop a creative redesign.

Legal and Ethical Considerations
Uses letter rather than less formal email format to emphasize importance of these differences regarding contractual agreement.

October 27, 2010

Samantha Reynolds
Senior Architect
Primera Design
3400 Wilshire Boulevard
Los Angeles, CA 90052-3674

Dear Samantha:

When Palmdale Galleria selected your firm to redesign our retail space, we were impressed by the work that you had done in a number of hotels and mall properties in Las Vegas and other upscale developments throughout the country. We were most impressed with the fantasy world that you created for the Insight Hotel's shopping galleria, a space that attended to every aspect of the consumer's shopping experience, including sight, sound, smell, taste, and sensation, through the implementation of the latest technological and design advances.

In our meeting with your creative team, we asked for attention to the visual design, the entertainment elements, and the creation of an ambiance that addressed all aspects of the consumers' sensual experience. After reviewing the initial plan for our redesign, we find the degree of incorporation of entertainment and sensual experiences for consumers to be disappointing. The redesign incorporates the latest trends in architectural design but needs more attention to entertainment features, including spaces for "street" entertainers, mini-concerts, and amusement park rides, including bungee jumping, etc. We also expected a more complete integration of water features, such as fountains, waterfalls, and streams, with the associated opportunities for entertainment, such as a simulated river rafting experience. In the tropical forest region of the mall, we hoped to have a better integration of spaces for zoo animals and an apparatus to create the "smells" and "sounds" of the jungle. Consumers no longer go to malls to simply shop but to want to be transported to a world of leisure, pampering, and entertainment, one that appeals to all of their senses.

With Primera Design's reputation for creative productions, we are confident the redesign plan for the Palmdale Galleria will be revised to incorporate these elements. Please let us know if you would like to meet to discuss and clarify any of the design issues raised here. Because of the importance of this project, I am at your disposal. Please call me at 444-1920 to schedule a meeting.

Sincerely,

Martinique Cole

Martinique Cole
General Manager
Palmdale Galleria

Figure 8-4   *Poor Example of a Persuasive Request (asking a favor)*

- *Begins with announcement that is already known.*

- *Asks favor before presenting reason for accepting.*

- *Sounds somewhat doubtful; is wordy and overuses first person pronoun "I."*

The entertainment that you provide in your restaurant is too loud to allow for conversation among diners. It's clear to me that you are a family restaurant that caters to those wishing to have a special get-together or to dine to celebrate such occasions as birthdays. Have you ever considered scheduling the entertainment for later in the evening for those customers who have finished dining and wish to stay for the music?

I'm probably not telling you anything you don't already know, but I wanted to make sure you were aware of some of your current customers' views on the entertainment in your restaurant.

Asking a Favor

Occasionally, everyone has to ask someone else for a special favor—an action for which there is little reward, time, or inclination. For example, suppose a professional association wants to host its annual fund-raiser dinner at an exclusive country club. The program chair of the association must write the club's general manager requesting permission to use the club. Will a deductive message be successful?

When a deductive approach is used in a persuasive situation, chances of getting cooperation are minimal. For example, what might be a probable reaction to the following beginning sentence? *Please send me, without charge, your $450 interactive CD on office safety.*

If the first sentence gets a negative reaction, a decision to refuse may be made instantly. Having thought "No," the receiver may not read the rest of the message or may hold stubbornly to that decision despite a well-written persuasive argument that follows the opening sentence. Note that the letter in Figure 8-4 asks the favor before presenting any benefit for doing so.

The letter illustrated in Figure 8-5 on the next page uses an inductive approach. Note the extent to which it applies principles discussed earlier. As this message shows, if the preceding paragraphs adequately emphasize a receiver's reward for complying, the final paragraph need not shout loudly for action.

Requesting Information

Requests for information are common in business. Information for research reports frequently is obtained by questionnaire, and the reliability of results is strongly influenced by the percentage of return. If a message inviting respondents to complete a questionnaire is written carelessly, responses may be insufficient.

The most serious weakness is asking too quickly for action and providing no incentive for it. Sometimes the reward for taking action is small and indirect, but the message needs to make these benefits evident. Note the reward and the appeal to the manager's social responsibility in the sample document shown in Figure 8–6 on page 141.

Persuading Within an Organization

The majority of memos are of a routine nature and essential for the day-to-day operation of the business—for example, giving instructions for performing work assignments, scheduling meetings, providing progress reports on projects, and so on. In many organizations, such matters are handled through the use of email rather than paper memos. These routine messages, as well as messages conveying good news, are written deductively. However, some circumstances require that a supervisor write a persuasive message that motivates employees to accept a change in their jobs that might have a negative effect on the employees or generate resistance in some form (e.g., being transferred to another position or office, automating a process that has been performed manually, changing computer software programs, etc.).

For example, in order for Ford Motor Company to avoid taking government loans, Ford had to negotiate with and persuade the United Auto Workers union to make some concessions, such as cutting overtime and layoff benefits. Executive Chairman Bill Ford and Executive Officer Alan Mulally used the grapevine strategically to leak their agreement to voluntarily forgo all cash compensation. By demonstrating their

Figure 8-5

Good Example of a Persuasive Request

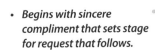

Sally Jenson

671 Linden St., Apt 13 | Tucson, AZ 85706-0671 | 913-555-0987

June 8, 2010

Tomas Rivera, Manager
Scallopino's Restaurante
897 Speedway
Tucson, AZ 85076-8976

Dear Mr. Rivera:

As a regular customer of Scallopino's Restaurante, my family and I have enjoyed the fine food, service, and family ambiance you and your staff have provided for many years. For these reasons, Scallopino's has become well-known throughout the community as an affordable place for special family occasions. Many have also developed a fondness for your regular entertainer, Carmine, who sings the traditional songs of Italy nightly.

On different occasions, I have noticed that the schedule for the entertainment differs. Some nights Carmine begins singing at 7 p.m., while on other nights he doesn't begin singing until 9 p.m. Because so many of your customers come to celebrate family and to converse and enjoy those interpersonal connections, the later 9 p.m. starting time for the entertainment might better provide for those opportunities.

By providing time for families to reconnect over Scallopino's fine food and allowing those who come for the entertainment to enjoy the singing of Carmine, you could meet the needs of all your customers, ensuring their continued patronage of your fine restaurant.

Sincerely,

Sally Jenson
Sally Jenson

- Begins with sincere compliment that sets stage for request that follows.

- Explains rationale for request with discussion of benefits to restaurant and its customers.

- Connects specific action to rewards for taking action.

Figure 8-6

- Begins with sincere compliment that sets stage for the request that follows.

- Explains rationale for request with discussion of benefits to the bank.

- Provides details for proposed change.

- Provides additional benefits of change.

INTEROFFICE MEMORANDUM

TO: Gloria Martinello, Human Resources Manager
FROM: Martin Rose
DATE: April 8, 2010
SUBJECT: Proposal to Improve Customer Relations

First National Bank had always viewed itself as a hometown bank that takes pride in knowing its customers on a first-name basis. With that goal in mind, we have been successful in establishing warm and lasting relationships with many of our clients.

First National Bank can go even further to make our employees appear even more friendly and approachable to our customers by adopting a "business casual" dress policy. Most of our customers are small business owners, working in the construction trades, or parents running household errands, who are dressed in "business casual" or more comfortably. Adopting a "business casual" policy would enable employees to continue conveying a professional appearance to the community while at the same time seeming more like a part of it.

To maintain our traditional professional image while creating a more relaxed atmosphere at the bank, I propose we follow the guidelines below:

Men	Women
Sport or polo shirt, with collars	Pantsuit
Khakis or corduroys	Sweater or blouse with pants or skirt
Loafers with socks	Low heels with hosiery

Added benefits of this policy would be savings to employees for clothing costs and dry cleaning fees. Reducing the need for dry cleaning also benefits the environment by reducing the use of toxic chemicals. Not only might the new dress policy create a friendlier atmosphere at the bank but also it would increase employees' spendable income and make the bank a "greener" business.

willingness to sacrifice, Ford and Mulally encourage the workers to compromise. In their memo to the workers, Ford and Mulally indicate their full awareness of the unpleasant situation: "We know these are challenging times and we all are affected by the tough actions we are taking. However, these are necessary actions to help us emerge as an even stronger, profitably growing Ford Motor Company for the benefit of us all." Through their shared sacrifice, contact, with their workers, appropriate tone, and straightforward language, Ford's top executives persuaded the United Auto Workers to make concessions to avoid taking government loans.

Similarly, employees must often make persuasive requests of their supervisors. For example, they may recommend a change in procedure, acquisition of equipment or software, or attendance at a training program to improve their ability to complete a job function.

Figure 8-7  *Good Example of a Persuasive Memo*

To: Maxine Burke, President
From: Jennifer Hastings
Date: May 6, 2010
Subject: Proposal to Decrease Sick Days and Company Health Costs

Barnard Products has always prided itself on its "employee-centric" culture and its related efforts to make the company the best place to work in the entire city. As part of that goal, you have created an "open-door" policy, inviting employees to make suggestions for further improvements to the workplace.

One of the biggest costs to employers is that of health insurance coverage and absenteeism. But there is a well-documented solution to these two problems: the creation of on-site exercise facilities for employees. Studies have shown that on-site exercise facilities reduce employer health care costs by 15 percent and decrease absenteeism from illness by as much as 20 percent.

An on-site exercise facility could easily be created in our building. An unused space exists on the first floor, where the industrial products design team used to be located. This space could easily be converted into an exercise center with the inclusion of variety of exercise machines and equipment. There are a number of ways to acquire this equipment. One way would be to use a portion of the savings from lost productivity and health care costs to purchase the equipment. If that is not financially feasible at this time, we could ask employees to donate their unused exercise equipment to the company until the savings from healthier employees became available.

With your approval, I will volunteer my spare time to help set up the facility. I worked as a personal trainer while in college and would happily volunteer my expertise to the company to help get this project off the ground.

- **Opens with discussion of company goal and alludes to proposal without revealing specifics.**

- **Links company strength that will lead logically to proposed change.**

- **Builds interest by providing benefits to the company.**

- **Reduces resistance by explaining how proposed change might easily be put in place.**

- **Closes with specific action to be taken to get started.**

They may justify a promotion or job reclassification or recommendation. Persuasive memos and email messages are longer than most routine messages because of the extra space needed for developing an appeal and providing convincing evidence.

When preparing to write the memo in Figure 8-7, the employee recognizes that limited company resources could affect the president's reaction to her proposal to add an on-site exercise facility to their building. An-ticipating resistance, the employee writes inductively and builds a logical, compelling argument for her proposal.

Sales Messages

The four-point persuasive outline also is appropriate for an *unsolicited sales message*—a letter, memo, or email message written to someone who has not requested it.

Figure 8-8  Poor Example of a Sales Message Promoting a Product

- Uses deductive approach inappropriately by stating request before gaining receiver's attention or providing convincing evidence.

- May erode reader confidence through overconfident attitude and claims with no explanation.

- Uses exaggerated language that may potentially diminish receiver interest and trust.

- Discusses features without showing receiver benefit.

- States desired action with no mention of benefit, and uses demanding tone and choppy sentence structure.

- Entire message lacks central selling point that responds to receiver's needs.

- Provides no unity for numerous details presented.

Dear Tommy:

Buy a $199 Jack smartphone from Global Communications, and we will automatically enter you in our December Sweepstakes with a grand prize of a cruise to Mexico!

There is nothing like the Jack on the market today! It is exactly what you have been waiting for. Jack provides the best features available, including a camera, built-in GPS, media player, video recording, wireless email, an organizer, a browser, a phone, corporate data access, SMS/MMS, and Wi-Fi support.

The display is the greatest, with half VGA resolution and 480 x 360 pixels. It incorporates a transmissive TFT LCD, backlighting, and a light-sensing screen that displays over 65,000 colors. The Jack also provides many security features, including password protection and keyboard lock, and support for AES or Triple DES encryption when integrated with the Jack Galaxy Server. It is FIPS 140-2 compliant, and support for S/MIME is an option.

To buy the Jack at the low price of $199, go to our website at www.globalcom.com and key in the enclosed authorization number. And if you do it before December 30, we will automatically enter you into the Mexico Trip Sweepstakes.

A *solicited sales message* has been requested by a potential buyer or supporter—that is, the message is prepared to answer this interested person's questions. With the use of persuasive email on the rise, potential customers can also indicate willingness to receive electronic communication about products and services.

Someone who has invited a persuasive message has given some attention to the product, service, or idea already; an attention-getting sentence is hardly essential. However, such a sentence is essential when the receiver is not known to have expressed an interest previously. The very first sentence, then, is deliberately designed to make a receiver put aside other thoughts and concentrate on the rest of the message.

Figures 8-8 and 8-9 (on the next page) illustrate poor and good unsolicited sales messages for a product. Figure 8-10 on page 145 presents an unsolicited sales message promoting a service. The same principles apply in writing a solicited sales letter, except an attention-getter is not essential.

Figure 8-9  *Good Example of a Sales Message Promoting a Product*

Global Communications
www.globalcom.com

November 20, 2010
Tommy LaTour
150 Goldrun Ave.
Carson City, NV 87703

Dear Tommy:

How would you like to have all the features of a camera, a GPS, a media player, a phone, a video recorder, and a laptop computer all in a device that is less than five by three inches in size? And what's more, what if you could buy such a device for less than two hundred dollars? Well you can—the new Jack by Global Communications.

You can immediately take advantage of the many features the Jack provides, including updating your social networking site and keeping in touch with friends. With the camera feature, you can instantly share and tag funny pictures you just took and post on your friends' walls from wherever you are!

The built-in camera allows you to just snap or record and send via email. You get

- Digital zoom
- Built-in flash
- 1.3MP or 2.0MP
- Self-portrait mirror

The Jack also provides instant and text messaging. You can add up to ten supported personal and work email addresses to your Jack, and each mailbox is automatically updated whenever you send, delete, file, or read messages on your Jack. Last-minute change of plans? Fire off a quick text message to keep everyone up-to-speed.

In addition to helping you keep in touch with friends, the Jack also provides a media player that allows you to play video and music files. You can shuffle your downloaded songs and enjoy your favorite playlist anywhere and anytime or watch sports clips while working out at the gym.

Visit www.globalcom.com today, and key in the enclosed authorization number with your order to automatically be entered in the December Sweepstakes for the grand prize of a Mexican cruise. With any luck, you will be text messaging your friends from the Mexican Rivera and sending them photos of all the great fun you are having with Jack!

Sincerely,

Andrea Riggins

Andrea Riggins
Sales Manager
Enclosure

- *Gains attention by introducing attractive product features at an attractive price.*

- *Uses easy-to-read bulleted list to present information.*

- *Explains benefits and uses of the features that will most likely be attractive to this particular reader.*

- *Keeps focus on receiver by use of second person, active-voice sentences.*

- *States specific action with reward. Makes action easy and provides incentive for quick response.*

Figure 8-10

☐   **New Message**

To: Traci Lim <tlim@hotmail.com>

From: Dr. Anita Byron <info@paradise.com>

Subject: Stop the March of Time

Traci,

How would you like to look 25 years old forever? How would you like to erase the tiny lines around your eyes and the creases in your forehead? How would you like to retain the smooth, healthy skin of your youth? You can with the radical new technology of the Thermage laser system.

Paradise Day Spa is eager to inform you about the immediate benefits of this remarkable skin rejuvenating treatment. Please take a moment to visit our website at www.paradise.com to see the amazing results of just one Thermage treatment on women just like you. Many of your questions will be answered by reading about the improvements you can realistically expect, testimonials of satisfied clients, and the experience and certification of our well-qualified staff of clinicians.

You are also invited to attend a special Evening of Beauty at Paradise on January 20 at 7 p.m. The Thermage laser treatment will be demonstrated, and I will be on hand to answer your questions about Thermage and our other skin care options. Light refreshments will be served.

Would you like to preserve your youthful looks for years to come? Get started today by going to our website, www. paradise.com, and registering for our Evening of Beauty on January 20. The first 30 people to register will receive a free sample of Porcelana eye cream, a $30 value. Stop the march of time now by learning more about Thermage laser system.

Sincerely,

Dr. Anita Byron
Dr. Anita Byron

Margin notes:

- Sends customized email message to patients who are considered potential candidates for procedure.

- Gains attention by introducing familiar concerns and their elimination as a central selling point.

- Introduces laser treatment as a potential solution to reader's concerns.

- Builds interest by providing easy access to detailed information and inviting reader to a demonstration of the technology.

- Reduces resistance by indicating one treatment is all that is necessary for results.

- Requests specific action and associates it with central selling point.

Revising Written Messages

As the sender of a message, you are responsible for evaluating the effectiveness of each message you prepare. However, this task has become more challenging with the speed and convenience of today's electronic communication, which have caused many communicators to confuse informality with sloppiness. Sloppy messages contain misspellings, grammatical errors, unappealing and incorrect formats, and confusing content—all of which create a negative impression of the writer and the company and affect the receiver's ability to understand the message. Some experts believe the increased use of email is leading to bosses becoming ruder. To combat against the brusque tone that sets in when managers must respond to 300 to 500 emails weekly, Unilever is providing writing training and urging staff to think before they press the send button.[1]

You must not use informality as an excuse to be sloppy. Instead, take one consultant's advice: "You can still be informal and not be sloppy. You can be informal and correct."[2] Take a good hard look at the messages you prepare. This effort may save you from being embarrassed or jeopardizing your credibility.

Cultivate a Frame of Mind for Effective Revising and Proofreading

The following suggestions will guide your efforts to develop business documents that achieve the purpose for which they are intended.

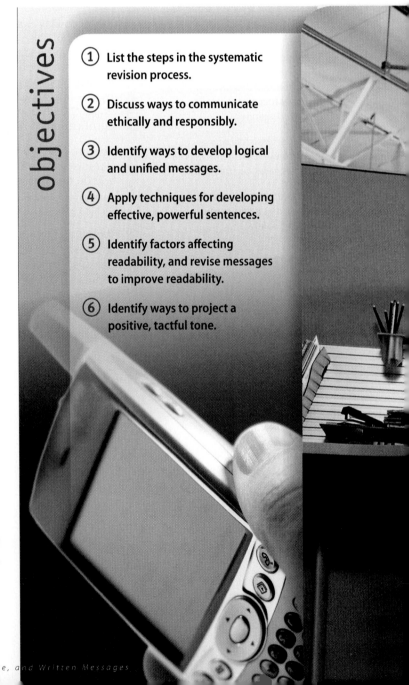

objectives

1. List the steps in the systematic revision process.

2. Discuss ways to communicate ethically and responsibly.

3. Identify ways to develop logical and unified messages.

4. Apply techniques for developing effective, powerful sentences.

5. Identify factors affecting readability, and revise messages to improve readability.

6. Identify ways to project a positive, tactful tone.

- **Attempt to see things from your audience's perspective rather than from your own.** That is, have empathy for your audience. Being empathetic isn't as simple as it seems, particularly when dealing with today's diverse workforce. Erase the mind-set of "I know what *I* need to say and how *I* want to say it." Instead, ask "How would my audience react to this message? Is this message worded so that my audience can easily understand it?"

- **Revise your documents until you cannot see any additional ways to improve them.** Resist the temptation to think of your first draft as your last draft. Instead, look for ways to improve and be willing to incorporate valid suggestions once you have completed a draft. Experienced writers believe that there is no such thing as good writing, but there is such a thing as good rewriting. Author Dorothy Parker, writer for *Vanity Fair* and *Esquire,* once said, "I can't write five words that I change seven."[3] Skilled speech writers might rewrite a script 15 or 20 times. Writers in public relations firms revise brochures and advertising copy until perhaps only a comma in the final draft is recognizable from the first draft. Your diligent revising will yield outstanding dividends.

- **Be willing to allow others to make suggestions for improving your writing.** Because most of us consider our writing personal, we may feel reluctant to share it with others and may be easily offended if

they suggest changes. This syndrome, called *writer's pride of ownership,* can prevent us from seeking needed assistance from experienced writers—a proven method of improving communication skills. On the job, especially in today's electronic workplace, your writing will be showcased to your supervisor, clients/customers, members of a collaborative writing team, and more. You have nothing to lose but much to gain by allowing others to critique your writing. This commitment is especially important considering that the mistake hardest to detect is your own. However, you have the ultimate responsibility for your document; don't simply trust that someone else will catch and correct all of your errors.

Use Systematic Procedures for Revising

objective ①
List the steps in the systematic revision process.

Errors in writing and mechanics may seem isolated, but the truth is that revising and proofreading are important. You don't have to look too far to see silly typos or obvious instances of writers relying only on the computer spell-check. The classifieds in a small-town newspaper advertised "fully fascinated and spade damnation puppies." The advertisement was for fully vaccinated and spayed Dalmatian puppies. These errors clearly illustrate how spell-check can fail; it will identify misspelled words most of the time but wrong words never. Goofs like these are not limited to small-town newspapers.

It was not a spelling error but a simple transposition in a telephone number that created an unbelievably embarrassing situation for a telecommunications giant. AT&T customers calling to redeem points earned in a True Rewards program were connected to pay-by-the-minute erotic phone entertainment.[4] Mistakes ranging from printing ordinary typos to running entirely erroneous ads have forced newspapers to refund $10.6 million to dissatisfied advertisers and to print $10.5 million in free, make-good ads.[5] These mistakes illustrate that inattention to proofreading can be potentially embarrassing and incredibly expensive.

Following systematic revision procedures will help you produce error-free documents that reflect positively on the company and you. Using the procedures that follow, you will see that effective proofreading must be

done several times, each time for a specific purpose. Also, using standard proofreading marks will simplify your proofreading method and will allow others who know these marks to understand your corrections easily. Study the standard proofreaders' marks shown in the rough draft in Figure 9-1.

© Image Farm/Jupiterimages

Follow these simple procedures to produce a finished product that is free of errors in (1) content, organization, and style; (2) mechanics; and (3) format and layout:

1. **Print a draft copy of the document.** Errors on a computer screen are difficult to locate; therefore, print a draft copy on plain paper and proofread carefully. Proofreading solely from the screen may be adequate for brief, routine documents.
2. **Proofread once concentrating on errors in content, organization, and style.** To locate errors, ask the following questions:

   Content: Is the information complete? Have I included all the details the receiver needs to understand the message and to take necessary action? Is the information accurate? Have I checked the accuracy of any calculations, dates, names, addresses, and numbers? Have words been omitted?

   Organization: Is the main idea presented appropriately, based on the receiver's likely reaction (deductive or inductive organization)? Are supporting ideas presented in a logical order?

   Style: Is the message clear? Will the receiver interpret the information correctly? Is the message concise and written at an appropriate level for the receiver? Does the message reflect a considerate, caring attitude and focus primarily on the receiver's needs? Does the message treat the receiver honestly and ethically?
3. **Proofread a second time concentrating on mechanical errors.** You are searching for potentially damaging errors that a spell-check cannot detect. These problem areas include:
   - *Grammar, capitalization, punctuation, number usage, abbreviations.* Review the grammatical principles presented in the Appendix if necessary.
   - *Word substitutions.* Check the proper use of words such as *your* and *you* and words that sound alike *(there, they're, or their; affect or effect).*
   - *Parts of the document other than the body.* Proofread the entire document. Errors often appear in

Figure 9-1 Rough Draft of a Letter (excerpt)

- *Adds mailing notation.*
- *Uses two-letter state abbreviation.*
- *Corrects spelling of name.*
- *Adds smooth transition to next paragraph.*

- *Divides into two sentences to enhance readability.*
- *Recasts from receiver's viewpoint.*
- *Corrects grammatical error.*

- *Includes specific action ending.*
- *Corrects grammatical error.*
- *Eliminates redundancy.*

Errors Undetectable by Spell-Check
Spelling of receiver's name, "Munoz."

Correct word substitutions: "you're" for "your."

August 23, 2010
Fax Transmission

Tina Munoz, CEO
Hospital Technology Solutions
3405 Elm Street
Cedar Rapids, ~~Iowa~~ IA 68009

Dear Ms. ~~Numoz:~~ Munoz

⌐ With your years of experience training hospital staff in the use of XENOG software, our goal of using the latest technology to create more efficient and effective healthcare solutions will surely be accomplished. We are excited to explore other ways our companies may benefit through shared expertise.

⌐ One of the objectives of our new administrator Johna Fitzgerald ~~are~~ is to review all of the hospital's current technology and to create a plan to update it, if necessary, and to add capabilities where needed. As part of that process, Ms. Fitzgerald has asked me to form a planning committee ~~whose~~ The committee's primary ~~basic~~ functions ~~is~~ are to perform the review of our current systems and write a report containing its recommendations for improvement. The committee thus should consist of representatives from all areas of the hospital that ~~is~~ are currently involved in the use of technology.

⌐ Since you will be an important part of the implementation of some of ~~those~~ that improvements, ~~we need you're~~ your is essential input. The time that you serve on the committee will be added to our current contract with your firm. Please ~~advise~~ let me ~~that~~ know by September 15 whether or not you will serve on the Technology Steering Committee. A meeting will be scheduled as soon all ~~members'~~ members have been selected.

the opening and closing sections of letters (e.g., date line, letter address) because writers typically begin proofreading at the first paragraph.

4. **Proofread a third time if the document is nonroutine and complex.** Read from *right to left* to reduce your reading speed, allowing you to concentrate deliberately on each word. If a document is extremely important, you may read the document aloud, spelling names and noting capitalization and punctuation, while another person verifies the copy.

5. **Edit for format and layout.** Follow these steps to be certain the document adheres to appropriate business formats:

   - Format according to a conventional format. Compare your document to the conventional business formats shown on your Style and Formatting cards and make any revisions. Are all standard parts of the document included and presented in an acceptable format? Are all necessary special letter parts (e.g., attention line, enclosure) included? Does the message begin on the correct line? Should the right margin be justified or jagged?

   - Be sure numbered items are in the correct order. Inserting and deleting text may have changed the order of these items.

   - Evaluate the visual impact of the document. Could you increase the readability of long, uninterrupted blocks of texts by using enumerated or indented lists, headings, or graphic borders or lines? Would adding graphics or varying print styles add visual appeal?

   - Be certain the document is signed or initialed (depending on the document).

6. **Use the spell-check to locate simple keying errors and repeated words.** The last proofreading step you should take is to check one last time for typographical errors that might have been introduced during the revision process. When the software cannot guess the correct spelling based on your incorrect attempt, you will need to consult a dictionary, other printed source, or online reference such as the Merriam Webster's online language center at **http://m-w.com**.

7. **For documents to be delivered on paper, print on high-quality paper.** The envelope and second-page paper (if needed) should match the letterhead. The printing should read in the same direction as the watermark (the design imprinted on high-quality paper).

The message in Figure 9-1 has been revised for (1) content, organization, and style; (2) mechanics; and (3) format and layout. Changes are noted using proofreaders' marks, a standard, simplified way to indicate changes. The commentary makes it easy to see how revising this draft improved the document's quality.

In the sections that follow, these steps are discussed in more detail.

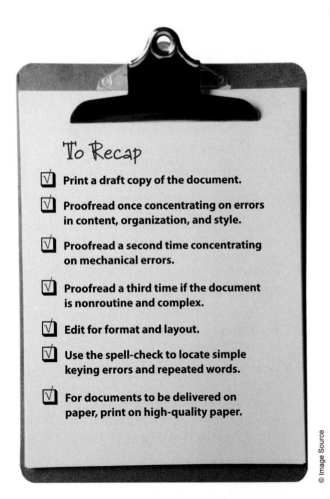

To Recap

☑ **Print a draft copy of the document.**

☑ **Proofread once concentrating on errors in content, organization, and style.**

☑ **Proofread a second time concentrating on mechanical errors.**

☑ **Proofread a third time if the document is nonroutine and complex.**

☑ **Edit for format and layout.**

☑ **Use the spell-check to locate simple keying errors and repeated words.**

☑ **For documents to be delivered on paper, print on high-quality paper.**

© Image Source

Check the Content to Ensure Ethical Communication

objective ②
Discuss ways to communicate ethically and responsibly.

The familiar directive "with power comes responsibility" applies especially to your use of communication skills. Because business communication affects the lives of many, you must accept responsibility for using it to uphold your own personal values and your company's standards of ethical conduct. Before speaking or writing, use the following guidelines to help you communicate ethically and responsibly.

- **Is the information stated as truthfully, honestly, and fairly as possible?** Good communicators recognize that ensuring a free flow of essential information is in the interest of the public and the organization. One example of the negative effect of withholding information is that of Merck, the manufacturer of the prescription pain reliever Vioxx. It was sued by thousands of patients and patients' families for withholding information about known heart risks associated with taking the drug.[6] Your honor, honesty, and credibility will build strong, long-lasting relationships and lead to the long-term success of your company. Sending complete, accurate, and timely information, regardless of whether it supports your views, will help you build that credibility.

- **Does the message embellish or exaggerate the facts?** Legal guidelines related to advertising provide clear guidance for avoiding *fraud,* the misrepresentation of products or services; however, overzealous sales representatives or imaginative writers can use language skillfully to create less-than-accurate perceptions in the minds of readers. Businesses have learned the hard way that overstating the capabilities of a product or service (promising more than can be delivered) is not good for business in the long run. Researchers are at times tempted to overstate their findings to ensure continued funding or greater publicity. Eric T. Peohlman, a medical researcher, acknowledged that while at the University of Vermont he fabricated data in 17 applications for federal grants to make his work seem more promising. Under a plea agreement, he was barred for life from receiving federal funding and had to pay back $180,000 as well as ask scientific journals to retract and correct ten articles he had authored.[7] Developing skill in communicating persuasively will be important throughout your profession; however, these techniques should *not* be used if your motive is to exploit the receiver.

- **Are the ideas expressed clearly and understandably?** If a message is to be classified as honest, you must be reasonably confident that the receiver can understand the message accurately. Ethical communicators select words that convey the exact meaning intended and that are within the reader's vocabulary. Consider a plumber's frustration with the following message from the Bureau of Standards: "The effect of HCL is incompatible with the metallic piping" and "We cannot assume responsibility for the production of toxic and noxious residues with HCL." Finally the Bureau sent a message the plumber could understand: "Don't use HCL. It eats the heck out of pipes!"[8] To protect consumers, some states have passed "Plain English" laws that require certain businesses and agencies to write policies, warranties, and contracts in language an average reader can understand.

- **Is your viewpoint supported with objective facts?** Are facts accurately documented to allow the reader to judge the credibility of the source and to give credit where credit is due? Can opinions be clearly distinguished from facts? Have you evaluated honestly any real or perceived conflict of interest that could prevent you from preparing an unbiased message?

© PRNewsFoto/Shock Magazine

- **Are ideas stated with tact and consideration that preserves the receiver's self-worth?**

libel
written defamatory remarks
slander
spoken defamatory remarks

The metaphor "An arrow, once it is shot, cannot be recalled" is used to describe the irrevocable damage caused by cruel or unkind words.[9] Ego-destroying criticism, excessive anger, sarcasm, hurtful nicknames, betrayed secrets, rumors, and malicious gossip pose serious ethical problems in the workplace because they can ruin reputations, humiliate, and damage a person's self-worth. Serious legal issues arise when negative statements are false, constituting defamation. Written defamatory remarks are referred to as **libel**, and similar spoken remarks are referred to as **slander**. If you choose to make negative statements about a person, be sure the facts in question are supported. Additionally, you'll hone your abilities to convey negative information and to handle sensitive situations in a constructive, timely manner rather than ignoring them until they get out of control. For considerate, fair, and civilized use of words, follow this simple rule: Communicate with and about others with the same kindness and fairness that you wish others to use when communicating with you.

- **Are graphics carefully designed to avoid distorting facts and relationships?** Communicating ethically involves reporting data as clearly and accurately as possible. Misleading graphics result either from the developers' deliberate attempt to confuse the audience or from their lack of expertise in constructing ethical graphics. You will study the principles of creating graphics that show information accurately and honestly in Chapter 11.

Check for Logical Development and Unity

objective ③
Identify ways to develop logical and unified messages.

Receivers expect the first paragraph of a message to introduce a topic, additional paragraphs to discuss that topic, and a final paragraph to tie them together. A letter, report, or email message with unity covers its topic adequately but will not include extraneous material. A report or presentation with unity begins with an introduction that identifies the topic, reveals the thesis, and previews upcoming points. The introduction may also include some background, sources of information, and the method of treating data. Between the beginning and the ending, a unified message will have paragraphs arranged in a systematic sequence. A summary or conclusion brings all major points together.

Develop Coherent Paragraphs

Well-constructed sentences are combined into paragraphs that discuss a portion of the topic being discussed. To write effective paragraphs, you must learn to (1) develop deductive or inductive paragraphs consistently, (2) link ideas to achieve coherence, (3) keep paragraphs unified, and (4) vary sentence and paragraph length.

Position the Topic Sentence Appropriately

Typically, paragraphs contain one sentence that identifies the portion of the topic being discussed and presents the central idea. That sentence is commonly called a **topic sentence**.

When the subject matter is complicated and the details are numerous, paragraphs sometimes begin with a main idea, follow with details, and end with a summarizing sentence. In this case, the paragraphs are **deductive** in their organizational approach—that is, the topic sentence *precedes* details. Most business messages use this organizational approach to make them easier to read.

When topic sentences *follow* details, the paragraphs are **inductive** in their organizational approach. As discussed previously, the receiver's likely reaction to the main idea (pleased, displeased, interested, not interested) aids in selecting the appropriate sequence.

Whatever approach is used, receivers appreciate consistency in the placement of topic sentences. Once they catch on to the writer's pattern, they know where to look for main ideas. Regardless of which organizational approach is selected, topic

topic sentence
the one sentence that identifies the portion of the topic being discussed and presents the central idea of the paragraph
deductive
an organizational approach in which the topic sentence precedes the details
inductive
an organizational approach in which the topic sentence follows the details

sentences are clearly linked with details that precede or follow.

Link Ideas to Achieve Coherence

Careful writers use coherence techniques to keep receivers from experiencing abrupt changes in thought. Although the word *coherence* is used sometimes to mean "clarity" or "understandability," it is used throughout this text to mean "cohesion." If writing or speaking is coherent, the sentences stick together; each sentence is in some way linked to the preceding sentences. Avoid abrupt changes in thought, and link each sentence to a preceding sentence.

The following techniques for linking sentences are common:

1. **Repeat a word that was used in the preceding sentence.** The second sentence in the following example is an obvious continuation of the idea presented in the preceding sentence.

    . . . to take responsibility for the decision. This responsibility can be shared . . .

2. **Use a pronoun that represents a noun used in the preceding sentence.** Because "it" means "responsibility," the second sentence is linked directly with the first.

    . . . to take this responsibility. It can be shared . . .

3. **Use connecting words.** Examples include *however, therefore, yet, nevertheless, consequently, also,* and *in addition.* "However" implies "We're continuing with the same topic, just moving into a different phase." Remember, though, that good techniques can be overused. Unnecessary connectors are space consuming and distracting. Usually they can be spotted (and crossed out) in proofreading.

    . . . to take this responsibility. However, few are willing to . . .

Just as sentences within a paragraph must link, paragraphs within a document must also link. Unless a writer (or speaker) is careful, the move from one major topic to the next will seem abrupt. A good transition sentence can bridge the gap between the two topics by summing up the preceding topic and leading a receiver to expect the next topic:

Cost factors, then, seemed prohibitive until efficiency factors were investigated.

© Inspirestock/Jupiterimages

This sentence could serve as a transition between the "Cost" and "Efficiency" division headings. Because a transition sentence comes at the end of one segment and before the next, it emphasizes the central idea of the preceding segment and confirms the relationship of the two segments. While transition sentences are helpful if properly used, they can be overused, creating redundancy.

Vary Paragraph and Sentence Length

A paragraph can be from one line in length to a dozen lines or more. However, average paragraph length in business writing should be kept short, as appropriate to the document type:

- Paragraphs in business letters, memos, and email messages are typically shorter than paragraphs in business reports.

- First and last paragraphs are normally short (one to four lines), and other paragraphs are normally no longer than *six lines*. A short first paragraph is more inviting to read than a long first paragraph, and a short last paragraph enables a writer to emphasize parting thoughts.

- The space between paragraphs is a welcome resting spot. Long paragraphs are difficult to read and make a page appear unattractive. Paragraph length will vary depending on the complexity of the subject matter. However, as a general rule paragraphs should be no longer than *eight to ten lines*. This length usually allows enough space to include a topic sentence and three or four supporting statements. If the topic cannot be discussed in this space, divide the topic into additional paragraphs.

To observe the effect large sections of unbroken text has on the overall appeal of a document, examine the memos in Figure 9-2 that contain identical information. Without question, the memo with the short, easy-to-read paragraphs is more inviting to read than the memo with one bulky paragraph.

Just as paragraphs should generally be kept shorter in business writing, sentences of short or average length also are easy to read and preferred for communicating clearly. However, keeping *all* sentences short is

Figure 9-2 Contrast the Readability and Appeal of Bulky Versus Broken Text

New Message

To: All employees
From: Freda Wilcox, HR Manager
Subject: Membership Discounts at Golden's Gym

Imagine finding two additional hours in your day to read, catch up on your email, watch movies, write a book, or just relax. It's possible if you park your car and let Metrotrak do the driving for you. Not only will you be gaining more time in your day for other activities (besides driving), but you will be saving money and wear and tear on your car, increasing your safety, and helping to reduce the negative effects of global warming. To encourage you to take advantage of Metrotrak, you can buy an annual pass at the low corporate rate at our Human Resource offices. In addition, with every purchase of a Metrotrak annual pass, you will receive a discounted membership to Golden's Gym, located conveniently across the street from our facility. Not only can you save money and help save the environment, but you can get healthier at the same time.

New Message

To: All employees
From: Freda Wilcox, HR Manager
Subject: Membership Discounts at Golden's Gym

Imagine finding two additional hours in your day to read, catch up on your email, watch movies, write a book, or just relax. It's possible if you park your car and let Metrotrak do the driving for you. Not only will you be gaining more time in your day for other activities (besides driving), but you will be saving money and wear and tear on your car, increasing your safety, and helping to reduce the negative effects of global warming.

To encourage you to take advantage of Metrotrak, you can buy an annual pass at the low corporate rate at our Human Resource offices located on the third floor in Room 302. In addition, with every purchase of a Metrotrak annual pass, you will receive a discounted membership to Golden's Gym, located conveniently across the street from our facility.

Not only can you save money and help save the environment, but you can get fit at the same time. What a great way to start the New Year!

undesirable because the message may sound monotonous, unrealistic, or elementary. Just as sentences should vary in length, they should also vary in structure. Some complex or compound sentences should be included with simple sentences.

Craft Powerful Sentences

objective ④
Apply techniques for developing effective, powerful sentences.

Well-developed sentences help the receiver understand the message clearly and react favorably to the writer or speaker. In this section, you will learn about correct sentence structure, predominant use of active voice, and emphasis of important points that affect the clarity and human relations of your message.

Use Correct Sentence Structure

The following discussion identifies common problems and techniques that business writers encounter.

All sentences have at least two parts: *subject* and *verb*. In addition to a subject and a verb, a sentence may have additional words to complete the meaning. These words are called **complements**.

Subject	Verb	Complement
Sid	transferred	overseas.
Chien	transferred	to our Hong Kong office.

© Rubberball/Getty Images

A group of words that is not a complete sentence is called a **phrase** or a **clause**. A phrase does not include a subject and a verb; a clause does. In the following, the phrases are underlined in the left column. In the clauses on the right, the subject is underlined once and the verb is underlined twice:

Phrases	Clauses
Some of the employees were opposed to the new policy.	As the president reported this morning . . .
Workplace stress is increasing the cost of health care.	If construction is begun soon . . .
The engineer was injured while conducting stress tests.	Although the production schedule is incomplete . . .

Clauses are divided into two categories: dependent and independent. A **dependent clause** does not convey a complete thought. The preceding examples are dependent. An **independent clause** conveys a complete thought; it could be a complete sentence if presented alone.

Dependent Clause	Independent Clause
As the president reported this morning,	sales increased in May.

The independent clause "sales increased in May" can be stated as a separate sentence. The dependent clause "As the president reported this morning" does not convey a complete thought and should not be presented without the remainder of the sentence. When a **sentence fragment** (a portion of a sentence) is presented as a separate sentence, receivers become confused and distracted.

Sentences fall into four categories: simple, compound, complex, and compound-complex.

In the following examples, note the use of punctuation to separate one clause from another. When no punctuation or coordinating conjunction appears between the

complements
additional words in a sentence that help complete the meaning
phrase (clause)
a group of words that is not a complete sentence
dependent clause
a clause that does not convey a complete thought
independent clause
a clause that conveys a complete thought and could be a complete sentence if presented alone
sentence fragment
a portion of a sentence which when presented as a separate sentence causes receivers to become confused and distracted

Simple:	Independent Clause
	The union has gone on strike.

Compound:	Independent Clause	Independent Clause
	The union has gone on strike, and all manufacturing lines have stopped production.	

Complex:	Dependent Clause	Independent Clause
	Because contract terms cannot be reached, the union has gone on strike.	

Compound-Complex:	Dependent Clause	Independent Clause
	Because contract terms cannot be reached, the union has gone on strike;	
	Independent Complex	
	but a settlement is expected at the end of the week.	

Run-On or Fused Sentence	Corrected Sentence
A new printer has been ordered it should be delivered tomorrow.	A new printer has been ordered. It should be delivered tomorrow.
	A new printer has been ordered, and it should be delivered tomorrow.
	A new printer has been ordered; it should be delivered tomorrow.
	A new printer, which was ordered last week, should be delivered tomorrow.

Comma Splice	Corrected Sentence
The number of questions has been reduced, the survey will require require less time to complete.	Because the number of questions has been reduced, the survey will require less time to complete.

run-on sentence (fused sentence)
when no punctuation or coordinating conjunction appears between clauses

comma splice
when clauses are joined only with a comma instead of a comma and coordinating conjunction or a semicolon

active verbs
when the subject is the doer of action

passive verbs
when the subject is the receiver of action

clauses, the result is a **run-on sentence** or **fused sentence**. Another problem is the **comma splice**, in which the clauses are joined only with a comma instead of a comma and coordinating conjunction or a semicolon.

Rely on Active Voice

Business communicators normally use active voice more heavily than passive voice because active voice conveys ideas more vividly. In sentences in which the subject is the *doer* of action, the verbs are called **active**. In sentences in which the subject is the *receiver* of action, the verbs are called **passive**. In the following example, the sentence in the left column uses passive voice; the sentence in the right column uses active voice:

Passive Voice	Active Voice
Reports are transferred electronically from remote locations to the home office.	Our sales reps transfer reports electronically from remote locations to the home office.

The active sentence invites the receiver to see the sales reps using a computer to complete a report. The passive sentence draws attention to a report. Using active voice makes the subject the actor, which makes the idea easier to understand. Sentences written using passive voice give receivers a less-distinct picture. In the passive sentence, the receiver becomes aware that something was done to the reports, but it does not reveal who did it.

Even when a passive sentence contains additional words to reveal the doer, the imagery is less distinct than it would be if the sentence were active: *Reports compiled by our sales representatives are transferred electronically from remote locations to the home office.* "Reports" gets the most attention because it is the subject. The sentence seems to let a receiver know the result of action before revealing the doer; therefore, the sentence is less emphatic.

Although active voice conveys ideas more vividly, passive voice is useful:

- In concealing the doer. *("The reports have been compiled.")*
- In placing more emphasis on *what* was done and what it was *done* to than on who *did* it. *("The reports have been compiled by our sales representatives.")*
- In subordinating an unpleasant thought. *("The Shipping Department has not been notified of this delay" rather than "You have not notified the Shipping Department of this delay.")* In bad-news messages, using passive voice to avoid a blaming tone is sometimes a good strategy. The use of passive voice to de-emphasize negative ideas is discussed further in the "Project a Positive, Tactful Tone" section found later in this chapter.

Emphasize Important Ideas

A landscape artist wants some features in a picture to stand out boldly and others to get little attention. A musician sounds some notes loudly and others softly. Likewise, a writer or speaker wants some ideas to be *emphasized* and others to be *de-emphasized*. Normally, pleasant and important ideas should be emphasized; unpleasant and insignificant ideas should be de-emphasized. Emphasis techniques include sentence structure, repetition, words that label, position, and space and format.

Sentence Structure

For emphasis, place an idea in a simple sentence. The simple sentence in the following example has one independent clause. Because no other idea competes with it for attention, this idea is emphasized.

Simple Sentence Is More Emphatic	Compound Sentence Is Less Emphatic
Nicole took a job in insurance.	Nicole took a job in insurance, but she really preferred a job in accounting.

For emphasis, place an idea in an independent clause; for de-emphasis, place an idea in a dependent clause. In the compound sentence below, the idea of taking a job is in an independent clause. Because an independent clause makes sense if the rest of the sentence is omitted, an independent clause is more emphatic than a dependent clause. In the complex sentence, the idea of taking a job is in a dependent clause. By itself, the clause would not make complete sense. Compared with the independent clause that follows ("Nicole really preferred . . ."), the idea in the dependent clause is de-emphasized.

Compound Sentence Is More Emphatic	Complex Sentence Is Less Emphatic
Nicole accepted a job in insurance, but she really preferred a job in accounting.	Although she accepted a job in insurance, Nicole really preferred a job in accounting.

Repetition

To emphasize a word, let it appear more than once in a sentence. For example, a clever advertisement by OfficeMax used the word *stuff* repeatedly to describe generically several types of office needs ranging from paper clips to color copies and then ended succinctly with "OfficeMax . . . for your office stuff." Likewise, in the following example, "success" receives more emphasis when the word is repeated.

Less Emphatic	More Emphatic
The project was successful because of . . .	The project was successful; this success is attributed to . . .

Words That Label

For emphasis or de-emphasis, use words that label ideas as significant or insignificant. Note the labeling words used in the following examples to emphasize or de-emphasize an idea:

But most important of all . . .
A less significant aspect was . . .

Position

To emphasize a word or an idea, position it first or last in a sentence, clause, paragraph, or presentation. Words that appear first compete only with words that follow; words that appear last compete only with words that precede. Note the additional emphasis placed on the words *success* and *failure* in the examples in the right column because these words appear as the *first* or the *last* words in their clauses.

Less Emphatic	More Emphatic
Your efforts contributed to the <u>success</u> of the project; otherwise, <u>failure</u> would have been the result.	<u>Success</u> resulted from your efforts; failure would have resulted without them.
The project was <u>successful</u> because of your efforts; without them, <u>failure</u> would have been the result.	The project was a <u>success</u>; without your efforts, it would have been a <u>failure</u>.

In paragraphs, the first and last words are in particularly emphatic positions. An idea that deserves emphasis can be placed in either position, but an idea that does not deserve emphasis can be placed in the middle of a long paragraph. The word *I*, which is frequently overused in messages, is especially noticeable if it appears as the first word. *I* is more noticeable if it appears as the first word in *every* paragraph. *However* is to be avoided as the first word in a paragraph if the preceding paragraph is neutral or positive. These words imply that the next idea will be negative. Unless the purpose is to place emphasis on negatives, such words as *denied, rejected,* and *disappointed* should not appear as the last words in a paragraph.

Likewise, the central idea of a written or spoken report appears in the introduction (the beginning) and the conclusion (the end). Good transition sentences synthesize ideas at the end of each major division.

Quantity and Placement

The various divisions of a report or spoken presentation are not expected to be of equal length, but an extraordinary amount of space devoted to a topic attaches special significance to that topic. Similarly, a topic that receives an exceedingly small amount of space is de-emphasized. The manner in which information is physically arranged affects the emphasis it receives and consequently the overall impact of the document. Generally, information that is presented first and last receives the most emphasis, since it is most likely to be remembered.

Improve Readability

This section discusses two elements of readability: the difficulty of the words and the complexity of the sentences and the visual presentation.

objective ⑤
Identify factors affecting readability, and revise messages to improve readability.

Understand Readability Measures

The grammar and style–checker feature of leading word processing software calculates readability measures to aid you in preparing writing that is quick and easy to read. The Fog Index, a popular

WRITING TO AN EXACT GRADE LEVEL DOESN'T GUARANTEE THAT YOUR WRITING WILL BE UNDERSTOOD. READERS OF ALL SKILL LEVELS APPRECIATE CLEAR, LUCID WRITING.

readability index developed by Robert Gunning in 1968, and the Flesch-Kincaid Grade Level available in Microsoft Word consider the length of sentences and the difficulty of words to produce the approximate grade level a person would need to understand the material. For example, a grade level of ten indicates a person needs to be able to read at the tenth-grade level to understand the material. Fortunately, you won't have to calculate readability manually, but understanding the manual calculation of the Fog index will illustrate how sentence length and difficulty of words affect readability calculations and guide you in adapting your own messages.

Trying to write at the exact grade level of the receiver is inadvisable. You may not know the exact grade level, and even those who have earned advanced degrees appreciate writing they can read and understand quickly and easily. Also, writing a passage with a readability index appropriate for the audience does not guarantee that the message will be understood. Despite simple language and short sentences, the message can be distorted at any stage of the communication process by imprecise words, biased language, jargon, and translations that ignore cultural interpretations, to name just a few. The value of calculating a readability measure lies in the valuable feedback you gain. Use this information about the average length of the sentences and the difficulty of the words to identify needed revisions. Recalculate the readability index and continue re-

cliché
overused expression common in our everyday conversations and in business messages

vising until you feel the reading level is appropriate for the intended audience.

Figure 9-3 shows how the use of readability measures can help you adjust your writing level.

Use Contemporary Language

Business messages should reflect correct, standard English and contemporary language used in a professional business setting. Outdated expressions and dull clichés reduce the effectiveness of a message and the credibility of a communicator.

Eliminate Outdated Expressions

Using outdated expressions will give your message a dull, stuffy, unnatural tone. Instead, substitute fresh, original expressions that reflect today's language patterns.

Outdated Expressions	Improvement
Pursuant to your request, the physical inventory has been scheduled for May 3.	As you requested, the physical inventory has been scheduled for May 3.
Enclosed please find a copy of my transcript.	The enclosed transcript should answer your questions.
Very truly yours (used as the complimentary close in a letter)	Sincerely

Eliminate Clichés

Clichés, or overused expressions, are common in our everyday conversations and in business messages. These handy verbal shortcuts are convenient, quick, and easy to use and often include simple metaphors and analogies that effectively communicate the most basic idea or emotion or the most complex business concept. However, writers and speakers who routinely use stale clichés may be perceived as unoriginal, unimaginative, lazy, and perhaps even disrespectful. Less frequently used words capture the receiver's attention because they are original, fresh, and interesting.

Cliché	Improvement
Pushed (or stretched) the envelope	Took a risk or considered a new option
Skin in the game	Committed to the project
Cover all the bases	Get agreement/input from everyone
That sucks!	That's unacceptable/needs improvement

Figure 9-3 Improving Readability Through Cautious Use of a Grammar and Style-Checker

Step 1:
Select grammar and style rules for the document.

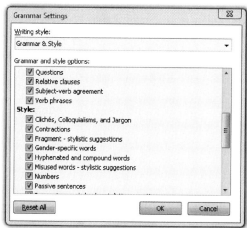

Step 2:
Evaluate and respond to advice given for grammar and style errors detected.

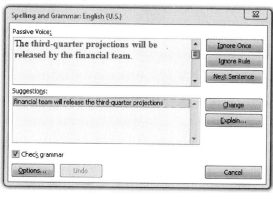

Step 3:
Use counts, averages, and readability indexes as guides for adjusting writing level appropriately.

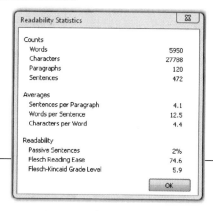

Clichés present another serious problem. Consider the scenario of shoppers standing in line at a discount store with the cashier saying to each "Thanks for shopping with us today; please come again." Because the last shopper has heard the words several times already, he or she may not consider the statement genuine. The cashier has used an expression that can be stated without thinking and possibly without meaning. A worn expression can convey messages such as "You are not special" or "For you, I won't bother to think; the phrases I use in talking with others are surely good enough for you." Original expressions convey sincerity and build strong human relations.

Use Simple, Informal Words

Business writers prefer simple, informal words that are readily understood and less distracting than more difficult, formal words. If a receiver questions the sender's motive for using formal words, the impact of the message may be diminished. Likewise, the impact would be diminished if the receiver questioned a sender's use of simple, informal

words. That distraction is unlikely, however, if the message contains good ideas that are well organized and well supported. Under these conditions, simple words enable a receiver to understand the message clearly and quickly.

To illustrate, consider the unnecessary complexity of a notice that appeared on a corporate bulletin board: "Employees impacted by the strike are encouraged to utilize the hotline number to arrange for alternative transportation to work. Should you encounter difficulties in arranging for alternative transportation to work, please contact your immediate supervisor." A simple, easy-to-read revision would be, "If you can't get to work, call the hotline or your supervisor."[10] For further illustration, note the added clarity of the following words:

Formal Words	Informal Words
terminate	end
procure	get
remunerate	pay
corroborate	support

Bullfighter is a program that helps business writers reduce jargon, corporate speak, and wordiness. Developed by the authors of *Why Business People Speak Like Idiots,* this free download is available at **http://fightthebull.com** and works as a convenient add-in to Microsoft Word and PowerPoint.

© Felipe Rodriguez/Alamy

Using words that have more than two or three syllables when they are the most appropriate is acceptable. However, you should avoid regular use of a long, infrequently used word when a simpler, more common word has the same meaning. Professionals in some fields often use specialized terminology, referred to as *jargon,* when communicating with colleagues in the same field. In this case, the audience is likely to understand the words, and using the jargon saves time. However, when communicating with people outside the field, professionals should select simple, common words to convey messages. Using clear, jargon-free language that can be readily understood by non-native recipients and be easily translated is especially important in international communication.

You should build your vocabulary so that you can use just the right word for expressing an idea and can understand what others have said. Just remember that the purpose of business messages is not to advertise your knowledge of infrequently used words but to transmit a clear and tactful message. For the informal communication practiced in business, use simple words instead of more complicated words that have the same meaning.

Communicate Concisely

Concise communication includes all relevant details in the fewest possible words. Abraham Lincoln's two-minute Gettysburg Address is a premier example of concise communication. Mark Twain alluded to the skill needed to write concisely when he said, "I would have written a shorter book if I had had time."

Some executives have reported that they read memos that are two paragraphs long but may only skim or discard longer ones. Yet it's clear that this

redundancy
a phrase in which one word unnecessarily repeats an idea contained in an accompanying word

survival technique can lead to a vital message being discarded or misread. Concise writing is essential for workers struggling to handle the avalanche of information that has been created by technological advances and other factors. Concise messages save time and money for both the sender and the receiver. The receiver's attention is directed toward the important details and is not distracted by excessive words and details.

The following techniques will produce concise messages:

- **Eliminate redundancies.** A **redundancy** is a phrase in which one word unnecessarily repeats an idea contained in an accompanying word. "Exactly identical" and "past history" are redundant because both words have the same meaning; only "identical" and "history" are needed. To correct "3 P.M. in the afternoon," say "3 P.M." or "three o'clock in the afternoon." A few of the many redundancies in business writing are shown in the following list. Be conscious of redundancies in your speech and writing patterns.

Redundancies to Avoid

Needless repetition: advance forward, it goes without saying, best ever, cash money, important essentials, each and every, dollar amount, pick and choose

Unneeded modifiers: actual experience, brief summary, complete stop, collaborate together, disappear from sight, honest truth, trickle down, month of May, pair of twins, personal opinion, red in color, severe crisis

Repeated acronyms: ATM Machine, PIN Number, SAT tests, SIC code

Redundancy is not to be confused with repetition. In a sentence or paragraph, you may need to use a certain word again. When repetition serves a specific purpose, it is not an error. Redundancy serves no purpose and is an error.

- **Use active voice to reduce the number of words.** Passive voice typically adds unnecessary words, such as prepositional phrases. Compare the sentence length in each of these examples:

Passive Voice	Active Voice
The documentation was prepared by the systems analyst.	The systems analyst prepared the documentation.
The loan approval procedures were revised by the loan officer.	The loan officer revised the loan approval procedures.

- **Review the main purpose of your writing and identify relevant details needed for the receiver to**

understand and take necessary action. More information is not necessarily better information. You may be so involved and perhaps so enthusiastic about your message that you believe the receiver needs to know everything that you know. Or perhaps you just need to devote more time to audience analysis and empathy.

- **Eliminate clichés that are often wordy and not necessary to understand the message.** For example, "Thank you for your letter," "I am writing to," "May I take this opportunity," "It has come to my attention," and "We wish to inform you" only delay the major purpose of the message.

- **Do not restate ideas that are sufficiently implied.** Notice how the following sentences are improved when ideas are implied. The revised sentences are concise, yet the meaning is not affected.

Wordy	Concise
She took the Internet marketing course and passed it.	She passed the Internet marketing course.
The editor checked the advertisement and found three glaring errors.	The editor found three glaring errors in the advertisement.

- **Shorten sentences by using suffixes or prefixes, making changes in word form, or substituting precise words for phrases.** In the following examples, the expressions in the right column provide useful techniques for saving space and being concise. However, the examples in the left column are not grammatically incorrect or forbidden from use. In fact, sometimes their use provides just the right *emphasis*.

Wordy	Concise
She was a manager who was courteous to others.	She was a courteous manager.
He waited in an impatient manner.	He waited impatiently.
The production manager disregards methods considered to be of no use.	The production manager disregards useless methods.
Sales staff with high energy levels . . .	Energetic sales staff . . .
. . . arranged according to the alphabet	. . . arranged alphabetically.

- **Use a compound adjective.** By using the compound adjective, you can reduce the number of words required to express your ideas and thus save the reader a little time.

Wordy	Concise
The document requires language that is gender neutral. . .	The document requires gender-neutral language.
B. J. Dahl, who holds the highest rank at Medder Enterprises, is . . .	B. J. Dahl, the highest-ranking official at Medder Enterprises, is . . .
His policy of going slowly was well received.	His go-slow policy was well received.

Apply Visual Enhancements to Improve Readability

The vast amount of information created in today's competitive global market poses a challenge to you as a business writer. You must learn to create visually appealing documents that entice a receiver to read rather than discard your message. Additionally, an effective design will enable you to highlight important information for maximum attention and to transition a receiver smoothly through sections of a long, complex document. These design techniques can be applied easily using word processing software. However, add visual enhancements only when they aid in comprehension. Overuse will cause your document to appear cluttered and will defeat your purpose of creating an appealing, easy-to-read document.

Chunking

Many times writers want to save space; however, cluttered text is unappealing and difficult to read. *Chunking*—a desktop publishing term—is an answer to the problem. Chunking involves breaking down information into easily digestible pieces or smaller paragraphs. It's the communication equivalent of a batch of cupcakes rather than one whole cake. The added white space divides the information into blocks, makes the page look more organized, and increases retention by 50 percent.[11]

Lists

To emphasize units in a series, place a number, letter, or bullet before each element in a sentence. Words preceded by numbers, bullets, or letters attract the receiver's special attention and are easier to locate when the page is reviewed.

Original	Highlighted
The human resources problems have been narrowed into three categories: absenteeism, tardiness, and pilferage.	The human resources problems have been narrowed into three categories: (1) absenteeism, (2) tardiness, and (3) pilferage.

Enumerated or bulleted lists can be used to chunk and add even greater visual impact to items in a series. Items appear on separate lines with numerals, letters, or various types of bullets (•, ◆, ❑, ✓, and so on) at the beginning. Multiple-line items often are separated by a blank line. This design creates more white space that isolates the items from other text and demands attention. Bullets also make a document easier to skim to locate the important points. Bullets are typically preferred over numerals unless the sequence of the items in the series is critical (e.g., steps in a procedure that must be completed in the correct order). In the following excerpt from a long analytical report, the four supporting reasons for a conclusion are highlighted in a bulleted list:

Original	Highlighted
For our needs, then, the most appropriate in-service training method is web-based instruction. This training is least expensive, allows employees to remain at their own workstations while improving their skills, affords constant awareness of progress, and lets employees progress at their own rates.	Web-based instruction is the most appropriate in-service training method because it • is least expensive. • allows employees to remain at their own workstations while improving their skills. • affords constant awareness of progress. • lets employees progress at their own rates.

Headings

Headings are signposts that direct the receiver from one section or topic of the document to another. Studies have shown that readers find documents with headings easier to grasp at a glance; readers also report they are more motivated to pay attention to the text, even in a short document, such as a half-page warranty.[12] You'll find that organizing the content of various types of doc-

uments will be more readable and appealing when you add logical, well-written headings. Follow these general guidelines for writing effective headings:

- Compose brief headings that make a connection with the receiver, giving clear cues as to the usefulness of the information, such as "How Do I Apply?". Consider using questions rather than noun phrases to let readers know they are reading the information they need: Choose "Who Is Eligible to Apply?" rather than "Eligible Loan Participants".[13] Consider informative headings that reveal the conclusions reached in the discussion rather than general topic headings or what are sometimes called "label" headings: For example, "Costs Are Prohibitive" is more informative than "Cost Factors."

- Strive for parallel structure of headings within a section. For example, mixing descriptive phrases with questions requires additional mental effort and distracts readers who may have been led to expect a particular pattern.

- Follow a hierarchy, with major headings receiving more attention than minor headings or paragraph headings. To draw more attention to a major heading, you might vary its placement on the page and use bolding and a larger font size.

Tables and Graphs

Tables and graphs are used to simplify and clarify information and to add an appealing variety to long sections of dense text. The clearly labeled rows and columns in a table organize large amounts of specific numeric data and facilitate analysis. Graphics, such as pie charts, line charts, and bar charts, visually depict relationships within the data. In Chapter 11, you will gain proficiency in selecting an appropriate graphic format for data and in designing effective and accurate tables and graphs.

Lines and Borders

Horizontal and vertical lines can be added to partition text or to focus attention on a specific line(s). For example, a thin line followed by a thick line effectively separates the identification section of a résumé from the qualifications. Placing a border around a paragraph or section of text sets that text apart; adding shading inside the box adds greater impact. For example, a shaded border might spotlight a testimonial from a satisfied customer in a sales letter, important dates to remember in a memorandum, or a section of a document that must be completed and returned.

Relevant Images

A variety of interesting shapes and lines can be used to highlight information and add appeal. Examples include creating a rectangular callout box highlighting a key idea with an arrow pointing to a specific number in a table, surrounding a title with a shaded oval for added impact, and using various shapes to illustrate the steps in a process. The applications are limited only by the writer's creativity. Clip art or photos can also be added to reinforce an idea and add visual appeal.

Project a Positive, Tactful Tone

© C Squared Studios/Photodisc/Getty

objective ⑥
Identify ways to project a positive, tactful tone.

Being adept at communicating negative information will give you the confidence you need to handle sensitive situations in a positive, constructive manner. The following suggestions reduce the sting of an unpleasant thought:

- **State ideas using positive language.** Rely mainly on positive words—words that speak of what can be done instead of what cannot be done, of the pleasant instead of the unpleasant. In each of the following pairs, both sentences are sufficiently clear, but the positive words in the improved sentences make the message more diplomatic and promote positive human relations.

Negative Tone	Positive Tone
Don't forget to submit your time and expense report.	Remember to submit your time and expense report.
We cannot ship your order until you send us full specifications.	You will receive your order as soon as you send us full specifications.
You neglected to indicate the specifications for Part No. 332-3.	Please send specifications for Part No. 332-3 so your order can be finalized.

Positive words are normally preferred, but sometimes negative words are more effective in achieving the dual goals of clarity and positive human relations. For example, addition of negative words can sharpen a contrast (and thus increase clarity):

Use an oil-based paint for this purpose; do not use latex.
Final copies are to be printed using a laser printer; ink-jet print is not acceptable.

When pleasant, positive words have not brought desired results, negative words may be justified. For example, a supervisor may have used positive words to instruct an accounts payable clerk to verify that the unit price on the invoice matches the unit price on the purchase order. Discovering later that the clerk is not verifying the invoices correctly, the supervisor may use negative words such as "*No, that's the wrong way*" to demonstrate once more and explain. If the clerk continues to complete the task incorrectly, the supervisor may feel justified in using even stronger negative words. The clerk may need the emotional jolt that negative words can provide.

- **Avoid using second person when stating negative ideas.** Avoid second person for presenting unpleasant ideas, but use second person for presenting pleasant ideas. Note the following examples:

Pleasant Idea (second person preferred)	
You substantiated your argument sufficiently.	*The person will appreciate the emphasis placed on his or her excellent performance.*

Unpleasant Idea (third person preferred)	
This report contains numerous mistakes.	*"You made numerous mistakes on this page" directs undiplomatic attention to the person who made the mistakes.*

However, use of second person with negative ideas is an acceptable technique on the rare occasions when the purpose is to jolt the receiver by emphasizing a negative.

- **Use passive voice to convey negative ideas.** Presenting an unpleasant thought emphatically (as active verbs do) makes human relations difficult. Compare the tone of the following negative thoughts written in active and passive voices:

Active Voice	Passive Voice Preferred for Negative Ideas
Melissa did not proofread the bid proposal carefully.	The bid proposal lacked careful proofreading.
Melissa completed the bid weeks behind schedule.	The bid was completed two weeks behind schedule.

Because the subject of each active sentence is the doer, the sentences are emphatic. Since the idea is negative, Melissa probably would appreciate being taken out of the picture. The passive voice sentences place more emphasis on the job than on who failed to complete it; they retain the essential ideas, but the ideas seem less irritating. For negative ideas, use passive voice. Just as emphasis on negatives hinders human relations, emphasis on positives promotes human relations. Which sentence makes the positive idea more vivid?

Passive Voice	Active Voice Preferred for Positive Ideas
The bid was completed ahead of time.	Melissa completed the bid ahead of schedule.

Because "Melissa" is the subject of the active-voice sentence, the receiver can easily envision the action. Pleasant thoughts deserve emphasis. For presenting positive ideas, use active voice.

- **Use the subjunctive mood.** Sometimes the tone of a message can be improved by switching to the subjunctive mood. *Subjunctive sentences* speak of a wish, necessity, doubt, or condition contrary to fact and employ such conditional expressions as *I wish, as if, could, would, might,* and *wish.* In the following examples, the sentence in the right column conveys a negative idea in positive language, which is more diplomatic than negative language.

Negative Tone	Subjunctive Mood Conveys Positive Tone
I <u>cannot</u> approve your transfer to our overseas operation.	If positions <u>were</u> available in our overseas operation, I <u>would</u> approve your transfer.
I am <u>unable</u> to accept your invitation to speak.	I <u>could</u> accept your invitation to speak only if our scheduled speaker <u>were</u> to cancel.
I <u>cannot</u> accept the consultant's recommendation.	I <u>wish</u> I <u>could</u> accept the consultant's recommendation.

Sentences in subjunctive mood often include a reason that makes the negative idea seems less objectionable and thus improves the tone. Tone is important, but clarity is even more important. The revised sentence in each of the preceding pairs sufficiently *implies* the unpleasant idea without stating it directly. If for any reason a writer suspects the implication is not sufficiently strong, a direct statement in negative terms is preferable.

- **Include a pleasant statement in the same sentence.** A pleasant idea is included in the following examples to improve the tone:

Negative Tone	Positive Tone
Your personnel ratings for communication ability and team skills were satisfactory.	Your personnel ratings for communication ability and team skills were satisfactory, but <u>your rate for technical competence was excellent</u>.
Because of increased taxes and insurance, you are obligated to increase your monthly payments.	Because of increased taxes and insurance, your monthly payments will increase by $50; however, <u>your home has increased in value at the monthly rate of $150</u>.

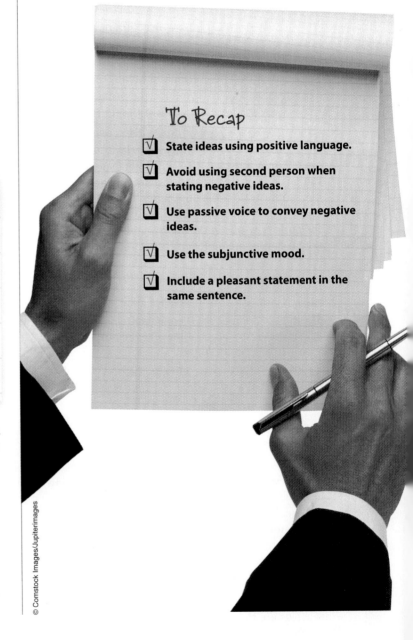

To Recap

☑ **State ideas using positive language.**

☑ **Avoid using second person when stating negative ideas.**

☑ **Use passive voice to convey negative ideas.**

☑ **Use the subjunctive mood.**

☑ **Include a pleasant statement in the same sentence.**

© Comstock Images/Jupiterimages

Be Sensitive to International Audiences

When writing for intercultural or international audiences, keep these suggestions in mind:

- **Avoid abbreviations, slang, acronyms, technical jargon, sports and military analogies, and other devices.** Such expressions help clarify an idea and personalize messages; however, they may be confusing to those unfamiliar with American usage. Those speaking English as a second language learned it from a textbook; therefore, they may have difficulty understanding "ASAP" (as soon as possible) or "WYSIWYG" (what you see is what you get). They may be mystified when you reject bid proposals that are "out of the ballpark" or "way off target," recruit job applicants who are "sharp as brass tacks," or refer to the supervisor as "the top gun."

- **Avoid words that trigger emotional responses, such as anger, fear, or suspicion.** Such words are often referred to as *red flag* words because they elicit the same response as a red flag waved in front of a raging bull. Using *hot buttons*—terms that make political judgments, show condescension, or make cultural judgments, for example—is a sure way to shut a reader's mind to your message.

- **Use simple terms, but attempt to be specific as well.** Some of the simplest words must be interpreted within the context of each situation in which they are used (e.g., *fast* has several meanings). Likewise, avoid the use of superlatives such as *fantastic* and *terrific* because they may be misinterpreted as overly dramatic or insincere. Also avoid overly formal and difficult words and expressions that may be confusing or considered pompous—for example, *pursuant to your request, ostentatious,* or *nebulous.*

- **Use figures for expressing numbers to avoid confusion with an international audience.** Be aware, however, of differences in the way numbers and dates are written. As a general rule, use figures for numbers, and keep in mind that most people in the world use the metric system. Note the following examples:

United States	Other Countries
$2,400.00	2400,00
January 29, 2008	29 January 2008

- **Write out the name of the month in international correspondence to avoid misunderstandings.** When using a number to represent the month, many countries state the day before the month as shown in the following examples:

United States	Other Countries
2/10/08	10.2 2008 or 10.2.08
March 26, 2008	26th of March 2008

- **Become familiar with the differing letter formats.** Different countries have different expectations regarding the formatting of letters, often in the formality of the salutation and the close. Germans, who prefer a formal salutation, such as "Very Honored Mr. Professor Jones," might be offended by your choice of an informal "Dear Jim," a salutation you believed was appropriate because you had met and done prior business with Professor Jones. You will also want to check the position of various letter parts, such as the letter address and the writer's name and title. For example, in German letters the company name follows the complimentary close and the typed signature block is omitted, leaving the reader responsible for deciphering the writer's signature.[14]

Understanding the Report Process and Research Methods

Characteristics of Reports

"Hello, Kristen. This is Abe in customer service. The boss wants to know how things are going with the 400-case Stanphill order. Are we going to make the 4 P.M. shipping deadline?"

objective ① Identify the characteristics of a report and the various classifications of business reports. "Oh hi, Abe. We are going to make the deadline, with time to spare. We have about 250 cases on the loading dock, 100 on the box line, and 50 going through the labeling process. They'll all be ready for the loader at two o'clock."

This brief exchange illustrates a simple reporting task. A question has been posed; the answer given (along with supporting information) satisfies the reporting requirement. Although Kristen may never have studied report preparation, she did an excellent job; so Abe, in turn, can report to his supervisor. Kristen's spoken report is a simple illustration of four main characteristics of reports:

- **Reports typically travel upward in an organization because they usually are requested by a higher authority.** In most cases, people would not generate reports unless requested to do so.

- **Reports are logically organized.** In Kristen's case, she answered Abe's question first and then supported the answer with evidence to justify it. Through your study of message organization, you learned the difference between deductive and inductive organiza-

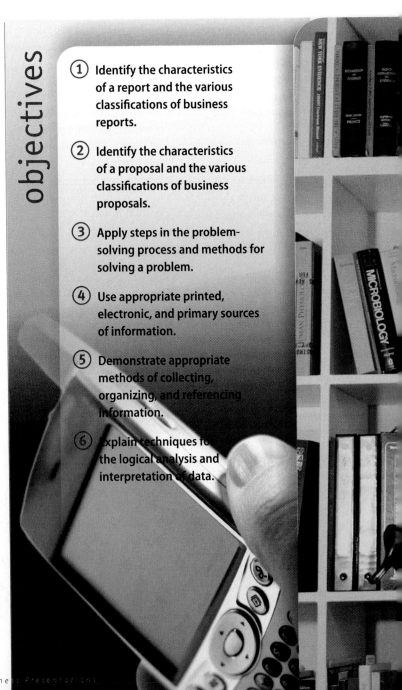

objectives

① Identify the characteristics of a report and the various classifications of business reports.

② Identify the characteristics of a proposal and the various classifications of business proposals.

③ Apply steps in the problem-solving process and methods for solving a problem.

④ Use appropriate printed, electronic, and primary sources of information.

⑤ Demonstrate appropriate methods of collecting, organizing, and referencing information.

⑥ Explain techniques for the logical analysis and interpretation of data.

tion. Kristen's report was deductively organized. If Kristen had given the supporting evidence first and followed with the answer that she would meet the deadline, the organization of her reply would have been inductive and would still have been logical.

- **Reports are objective.** Because reports contribute to decision making and problem solving, they should be as objective as possible; when nonobjective (subjective) material is included, the report writer should make that known.

- **Reports are generally prepared for a limited audience.** This characteristic is particularly true of reports traveling within an organization and means

that reports, like letters, memos, and emails, can be prepared with the receivers' needs in mind.

Types of Reports

Based on the four characteristics, a workable definition of a *report* is an orderly, objective message used to convey information from one organizational area to another or from one organization to another to assist in decision making or problem solving. Reports have been classified in numerous ways by management and by report-preparation authorities. The form, direction, functional use, and content of the report are used as

Figure 10-1 Report Formality Continuum

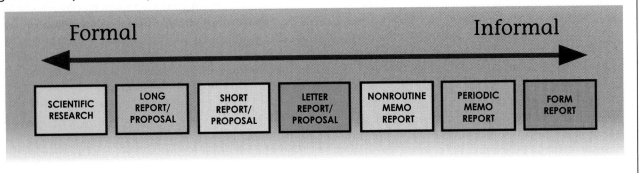

bases for classification. However, a single report might fit several classifications. The following brief review of classification illustrates the scope of reporting and establishes a basis for studying reports.

- **Formal or informal reports.** The formal/informal classification is particularly helpful because it applies to all reports. A **formal report** is carefully structured; it is logically organized and objective, contains much detail, and is written in a style that tends to eliminate such elements as personal pronouns. An **informal report** is usually a short message written in natural or personal language. An internal memo generally can be described as an informal report. All reports can be placed on a continuum of formality, as shown in Figure 10-1. The distinction among the degrees of formality of various reports is explained more fully in Chapter 12.

- **Short or long reports.** Reports can be classified generally as short or long. A one-page memo is obviously short, and a report of twenty pages is obviously long. What about in-between lengths? One important distinction generally holds true: As it becomes longer, a report takes on more characteristics of formal reports. Thus, the classifications of formal/informal and short/long are closely related.

formal report
a carefully structured report that is logically organized and objective, contains much detail, and is written without personal pronouns

informal report
a short message written in natural or personal language

informational report
a report that carries objective information from one area of an organization to another

analytical report
a report that presents suggested solutions to problems

upward-directed reports
reports made by subordinates to superiors

downward-directed reports
reports made by superiors for subordinates

internal report
a report that travels within an organization

external report
a report prepared for distribution outside an organization

periodic reports
reports issued on regularly scheduled dates

functional report
a report that serves a specified purpose within a company

- **Informational or analytical reports.** An **informational report** carries objective information from one area of an organization to another. An **analytical report** presents suggested solutions to problems. Company annual reports, monthly financial statements, reports of sales volume, and reports of employee or personnel absenteeism and turnover are informational reports. Reports of scientific research, real estate appraisal reports, and feasibility reports by consulting firms are analytical reports.

- **Vertical or lateral reports.** The vertical/lateral classification refers to the directions reports travel. Although most reports travel upward in organizations, many travel downward. Both represent vertical reports and are often referred to as **upward-directed** and **downward-directed reports**. The main function of vertical reports is to contribute to management *control,* as shown in Figure 10-2. Lateral reports, on the other hand, assist in *coordination* in the organization. A report traveling between units on the same organizational level, as between the production department and the finance department, is lateral.

- **Internal or external reports.** An **internal report**, such as a production or sales report, travels within an organization. An **external report**, such as a company's annual report to stockholders, is prepared for distribution outside an organization.

- **Periodic reports.** **Periodic reports** are issued on regularly scheduled dates. They are generally directed upward and serve management control purposes. Daily, weekly, monthly, quarterly, semiannual, and annual time periods are typical for periodic reports. Preprinted forms and computer-generated data contribute to uniformity of periodic reports.

- **Functional reports.** A **functional report** serves a specified purpose within a company. The functional classification includes accounting reports, marketing reports, financial reports, personnel reports, and a variety of other reports that take their functional designation from their ultimate use. For example,

Figure 10-2 The General Upward Flow of Reports

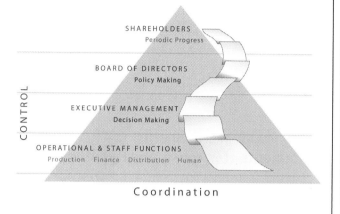

CONTROL

SHAREHOLDERS
Periodic Progress

BOARD OF DIRECTORS
Policy Making

EXECUTIVE MANAGEMENT
Decision Making

OPERATIONAL & STAFF FUNCTIONS
Production   Finance   Distribution   Human

Coordination

© Mike Kemp/Rubberball/Jupiterimages

a justification of the need for additional personnel or for new equipment is described as a *justification report* in the functional classification.

Proposals

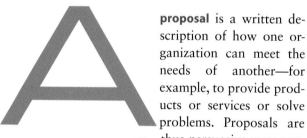

proposal is a written description of how one organization can meet the needs of another—for example, to provide products or services or solve problems. Proposals are thus persuasive messages. Businesses issue "calls for bids" that present the specifications for major purchases of goods and certain services. Most governmental agencies issue "requests for proposals," or **RFPs**. Potential suppliers prepare proposal reports telling how they can meet that need. Those preparing the proposal create a convincing document that will lead to their obtaining a contract.

objective ②
Identify the characteristics of a proposal and the various classifications of business proposals.

Managers prepare **internal proposals** to justify or recommend purchases or changes in the company—for instance, installing a new computer system, introducing telecommuting or other flexible work schedules, or reorganizing the company into work groups. An **external proposal** is a written description of how one organization can meet the needs of another by providing products or services. Written to generate business, external proposals are a critical part of the successful operation of many companies.

Proposals may be solicited or unsolicited. **Solicited proposals** are invited and initiated when a potential customer or client submits exact specifications or needs in a bid request or RFP. Governmental agencies, such as the Department of Education, solicit proposals and place orders and contracts based on the most desirable proposal. The bid request or RFP describes a problem to be solved and invites respondents to describe their proposed solutions.

An **unsolicited proposal** is prepared by an individual or firm that sees a problem to be solved and submits a proposal. For example, a business consultant is a regular customer of a family-owned retail store. On numerous occasions, she has attempted to purchase an item that was out of stock. Recognizing that stock shortages decrease sales and profits, she prepares a proposal to assist the business in designing a computerized perpetual inventory with an automatic reordering system. For the business to accept the proposal, the consultant must convince the business that the resulting increase in sales and profits will more than offset the cost of the computer system and the consulting fee.

proposal
a written description of how one organization can meet the needs of another
RFP
a request for a proposal
internal proposal
a report written to justify or recommend courses of action taken in the company
external proposal
a written description of how one organization can meet the needs of another by providing products or services
solicited proposal
a proposal that is invited and initiated
unsolicited proposal
a proposal prepared by an individual or firm that sees a problem to be solved and submits a proposal without invitation

In our information-intensive society, proposal preparation is a major activity for many firms. In fact, some companies hire consultants or designate employees to specialize in proposal writing. Chapter 12 presents proposal preparation in considerable detail.

The Problem-Solving Process

objective ③
Apply steps in the problem-solving process and methods for solving a problem.

The upward flow of reports provides management with data that someone may use to make a decision. The purpose is to use the data to solve a problem. Some problems are recurring and call for a steady flow of information; other problems may be unique and call for information on a one-time basis. A problem is the basis for a report. The following steps are used for finding a solution:

1. Recognize and define the problem.
2. Select a method of solution.
3. Collect and organize the data and document the sources.
4. Arrive at an answer.

Only after all four steps have been completed is a report written for presentation. Reports represent an attempt to communicate how a problem was solved. These problem-solving steps are completed *before* the report is written in final form.

STEP 1: Recognizing and Defining the Problem

Problem-solving research cannot begin until the researchers define the problem. Frequently, those requesting a report will attempt to provide a suitable definition. Nevertheless, researchers should attempt to state the problem clearly and precisely to ensure they are on the right track.

Using Problem Statements, Statements of Purpose, and Hypotheses

The **problem statement**, or **statement of the problem**, is the particular problem that is to be solved by the research. The **statement of purpose** is the goal of the study and includes the aims or objectives the researcher hopes to accomplish. Research studies often have both a problem statement and a statement of purpose. For example, a real estate appraiser accepts a client's request to appraise a building to determine its market value. The problem is to arrive at a fair market value for the property. The purpose of the appraisal, however, might be to establish a value for a mortgage loan, to determine the feasibility of adding to the structure, or to assess the financial possibility of demolishing the structure and erecting something else. Thus, the purpose may have much to do with determining what elements to consider in arriving at an answer. In other words, unless you know why something is wanted, you might have difficulty knowing what is wanted. Once you arrive at the answers to the what and why questions, you will be on your way to solving the problem.

A **hypothesis** is a statement to be proved or disproved through research. For example, a study of skilled manufacturing employees under varying conditions might be made to determine whether production would increase if each employee were part of a team as opposed to being a single unit in a production line. For this problem, the hypothesis could be formulated in this way:

Hypothesis: Productivity will increase when skilled manufacturing employees function as members of production teams rather than as single units in a production line.

problem statement (statement of the problem)
the particular problem that is to be solved by the research
statement of purpose
the goal of the study
hypothesis
a statement to be proved or disproved through research

Because the hypothesis tends to be stated in a way that favors one possibility or is prejudiced toward a particular answer, many researchers prefer to state hypotheses in the null form. The **null hypothesis** states that no relationship or difference will be found in the factors being studied, which tends to remove the element of prejudice toward a certain answer. The null hypothesis for the previous example could be written as follows:

> **Null hypothesis:** No significant difference will be found in productivity between workers organized as teams and workers as individual production line units.

Using the problem/purpose approach and/or the hypothesis approach is a choice of the researcher. In many ways, the purpose of a study is determined by the intended use of its results.

Limiting the Scope of the Problem

A major shortcoming that often occurs in research planning is the failure to establish or to recognize desirable limits. The *scope* of the report helps to establish boundaries in which the report will be researched and prepared. Assume, for instance, that you want to study salaries of office support staff. Imagine the enormity of such a task. Millions of people are employed in office support jobs. Perhaps a thousand or so different types of jobs fall into this classification. To reduce such a problem to reasonable proportions, use the *what, why, when, where,* and *who* questions to limit the problem. Here are the limits you might derive as the human resources manager at a metropolitan bank:

Now you can phrase the problem this way:

> **Statement of purpose:** The purpose of this study is to survey salaries of office support staff in local banks to determine whether our salaries are competitive and consistent.

Note that this process of reducing the problem to a workable size has also established some firm limits to the research. You have limited the problem to current salaries, the local area, and a particular type of business. Note, too, how important the why was in helping to establish the limits. Limiting the problem or defining its scope is "zeroing in on the problem."

In some reports, it is desirable to differentiate between the boundaries that were placed on the project outside the control of the researcher(s) and those that were chosen by the researcher(s). Boundaries imposed outside the control of the researchers are called **limitations**; they may include the assignment of the topic, allotted budget, and time for completion of the report. These boundaries affect how the topic can be researched. Boundaries chosen by the researcher(s) to make the project more manageable are called **delimitations**; they may include the sources and methods chosen for research.

Defining Terms Clearly

Words often have more than one meaning, and technical or special-use words may occur in the report that are not widely used or understood. Such terms would require a definition for the reader's understanding of the information presented. In the previously used example concerning the study of office support staff salaries, a comparison of one bank's salaries with those paid by others would be meaningful only if the information gathered from other banks relates to identical jobs. A job description defining the duties performed by an administrative assistant, for example, would help

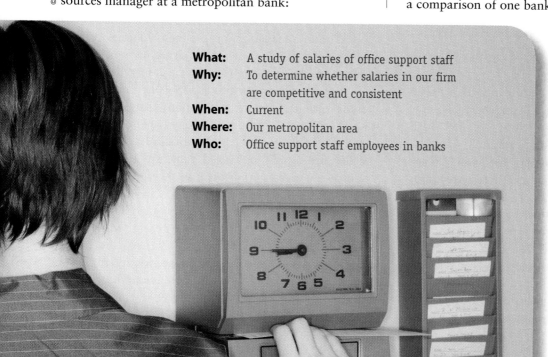

What:	A study of salaries of office support staff
Why:	To determine whether salaries in our firm are competitive and consistent
When:	Current
Where:	Our metropolitan area
Who:	Office support staff employees in banks

null hypothesis
the statement that no relationship or difference will be found in the factors being studied
limitations
boundaries imposed outside the control of the researchers
delimitations
boundaries chosen by the researcher(s) to make the project more manageable

ensure that all firms would be talking about the same job tasks regardless of the job title. In addition, the term *salary* requires definition. Is it hourly, weekly, monthly, or yearly? Are benefits included?

Documenting Procedures

The procedures or steps a writer takes in preparing a report are often recorded as a part of the written report. This **procedures** section, or **methodology**, adds credibility to the research process and also enables subsequent researchers to repeat, or replicate, the study in another setting or at a later time. Reports that study the same factors in different time frames are called **longitudinal studies.**

The procedures section of a report records the major steps taken in the research, and possibly the reasons for their inclusion. It may, for instance, tell the types of printed and electronic sources that were consulted and the groups of people interviewed and how they were selected. Steps in the procedures section are typically listed in chronological order so that the reader has an overall understanding of the timetable that existed for the project.

STEP 2: Selecting a Method of Solution

objective (4)
Use appropriate printed, electronic, and primary sources of information.

After defining the problem, the researcher will plan how to arrive at a solution. You may use secondary and/or primary research methods to collect necessary information.

Secondary Research

Secondary research provides information that has already been created by others. Researchers save time and effort by not duplicating research that has already been undertaken. They can access this information easily through the aid of electronic databases and bibliographic indexes. Suppose that a marketing manager has been asked to investigate the feasibility of implementing a strategic information system. The man-

methodology (procedures)
the procedures or steps a writer takes in preparing a report that are often recorded as a part of the written report
longitudinal study
a report that studies the same factors in different time frames
secondary research
information that has already been created by others

ager knows other companies are using this technology. By engaging in secondary research, the manager can determine the boundaries of knowledge before proceeding into the unknown.

Certain truths have been established and treated as principles reported in textbooks and other publications. However, because knowledge is constantly expanding, the researcher knows that new information is available. The job, then, is to canvass the literature of the field and attempt to redefine the boundaries of knowledge. Such secondary research accomplishes the following objectives:

- Establishes a point of departure for further research
- Avoids needless duplication of costly research efforts
- Reveals areas of needed research
- Makes a real contribution to a body of knowledge

Secondary research can be gathered by means of traditional printed sources or by using electronic tools.

Printed Sources. Major categories of published sources are books, periodicals, and government documents. Books are typically cataloged in libraries by call number, with most larger libraries using the Library of Congress classification system. The card catalog in most libraries has been replaced by an "online catalog," which allows the user to locate desired books by author, title, subject, or key word. A wide assortment of reference books is typically available for use within the library; these include dictionaries, encyclopedias, yearbooks, and almanacs. Some of these volumes contain general information on a wide array of topics, while others are designed for a specific field of study.

Periodicals, referred to as serials by librarians, include various types of publications that are released on a regular, periodic basis. Newspapers, magazines, and journals are all types of periodicals. Newspapers, which are usually published daily, are a good initial source for investigation because they give condensed coverage of timely topics. Magazines may be published weekly, monthly, bimonthly, or in some other interval. They are typically written for a general readership, providing expanded coverage in an easy-to-read format. Journals, on the other hand, are written for more specialized audiences and are more research oriented. Journal articles share the results of research studies and provide interpretive data that support their find-

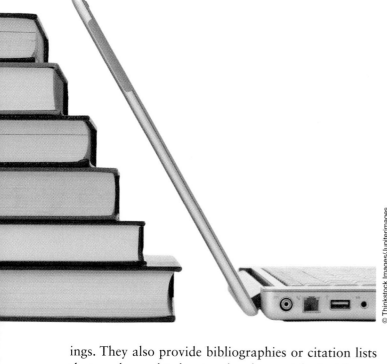

Electronic Sources. The availability of computer-assisted data searches has simplified the time-consuming task of searching through indexes, card catalogs, and other sources. Weekly and monthly updates keep electronic databases current, and they are easy to use. Databases such as Lexis-Nexis Academic Universe have full-text retrieval capability, meaning you can retrieve the entire article for reviewing and printing. Other databases offer only some articles in full text, with citations or abstracts provided for others. Note the list of electronic databases for business users listed in Figure 10-3.

The Internet and its subset, the World Wide Web, have made thousands of reference sources available in a matter of minutes. However, the vastness of this resource can be overwhelming to the novice researcher. The following tips will help to make your Internet search more productive:

- **Choose your search engine or database appropriately.** A *search engine* is a cataloged database of websites that allows you to search on specific topics. Several popular search engines exist, including Google,

ings. They also provide bibliographies or citation lists that can be used to locate related materials. Articles on specific topics can be located using both published and online indexes. A noninclusive list of these sources is shown in Figure 10-3.

Figure 10-3 Useful Reference Sources

Printed Indexes

Business Periodicals Index
Education Index
The New York Times Index
Readers' Guide to Periodical Literature
Social Science and Humanities Index
The Wall Street Journal Index

Electronic Databases

ABI/INFORM
Academic Search Elite
Business & Company Resource Center
Business Dateline
Business Source Premier
DIALOG Information Services
ERIC
First Search
FSI Online
General BusinessFile
Lexis-Nexis Academic Universe
Periodical Abstracts
ProQuest
Westlaw

Biography

Who's Who in America
Similar directories for specific geographic areas, industries, and professions

General Facts and Statistics

Statistical Abstract of the United States
Bureau of the Census publications
Dictionaries (general and discipline specific)
Encyclopedia (*Americana* or *Britannica*)
Fortune Directories of U.S. Corporations
World Atlas
Lexis-Nexis Statistics
Almanacs

Report Style and Format

American Psychological Association. (2001). *Publication Manual of the American Psychological Association* (5th ed.). Washington, DC: Author. [http://www.apastyle.org/about-apa-style.aspx]

Gibaldi, J. (2003). *MLA Handbook for Writers of Research Papers* (6th ed.). New York: Modern Language Association. [http://www.mla.org/style_faq]

Yahoo!, AltaVista, HotBot, and Ask. Megasearch engines such as Web Crawler and IxQuick, which index billions of web pages, search through a number of other engines to produce "hits."[1] (A hit is a located website that contains the word or words specified in the search.) You want to obtain a sufficient number of hits but not thousands. Although the variety of these larger engines is greater, they pose more difficulty in narrowing a search. Start with a small search engine and then move to a larger one, if necessary.

Electronic databases provide access to articles from newspapers, magazines, journals, and other types of publications. The database provider may charge to access articles either as a subscription fee or a document delivery fee. These types of databases are not accessible by a search engine and are often described as the **hidden Internet**. Many libraries provide access to these databases. Some databases are suited for topic searches of general interest; others are geared toward specialized fields. A topic search will produce a listing of references and abstracts for articles, or even full text of some. Databases available through your library might include Business Source Premier (an offering of information services company EBSCO), Academic Search Elite, Lexis-Nexis Academic Universe, ABI/INFORM, First Search, Business & Company Resource Center, General BusinessFile, and others.

- **Structure searches from broad to specific.** Use words for your topic that are descriptive and do not have multiple meanings. Once sites have been located for your general topic, you can use **Boolean logic** to narrow the selection. Boolean operands (*and, or, not*) serve to limit the identified sites. The following example shows how these delimiters can assist you in locating precisely what you want:

  - Using the key phrase *workplace productivity* will produce all sites that have either of the key words in the title or descriptors.

  - Placing *and* between key words will produce hits that have both words.

  - Keying *workplace productivity not United States* will eliminate hits that refer to the United States.

- **Use quotation marks when literal topics are desired.** Putting quotation marks around your topic words can drastically affect the number of hits. The quotation marks cause the search engine to look for the designated words as a phrase, thus producing only those sites that have the phrase present. Without the quotation marks, the search engine will treat the words individually and produce many more hits, most of which may not be useful. For instance, if you are looking for sites related to "international communication," placing quotation marks around the desired phrase would eliminate the sites that deal with international topics that are not communication oriented.

- **Look for web pages that have collections of links to other related topics.** Clicking on these hyperlinks will allow you to maximize your time investment in the data-gathering phase of your research.

- **Be adaptable to the various access format requirements.** Each search engine and database has its own particular format and instructions for use. Some require keyboard input and do not respond to your mouse. The method for specifying and narrowing your search will vary.

A final consideration when using the Internet for research is the quality of the information found there. The Internet has been likened to a wild, untamed frontier, open to all who desire to exercise their right to free speech. Because anyone with a computer can create a website and put him or herself off as an "expert," the serious researcher has several reasons for exercising caution in using information found there.

- **Internet resources are not always accurate.** Because the Internet is not centrally patrolled or edited, postings come from a wide variety of sources. Some of these sources are reliable and credible; some are not.

- **Certain uses of Internet sources may be illegal.** Some material available on the Internet is copyright protected and therefore not available for some uses by those who download the files. For instance, photograph files that are copyrighted may be viewed by Internet users but not incorporated into documents that have commercial use unless permission is granted by the copyright holder. Such permission often involves a royalty fee.

- **Internet resources are not always complete.** Selected text of articles and documents is often available via the Internet, while full text may be available only in published form. Additionally, Internet resources are not always updated to reflect current information.

- **Electronic periodicals are not always subjected to a rigorous review process.** Because most traditional magazines and journal articles are reviewed by an editorial board or peer reviewers, they are considered to be of more value than an article prepared by one or a few individuals that is not critiqued by other experts before its publication. Articles available over the Internet may not have benefited from such a review process.

electronic databases
articles from newspapers, magazines, journals, and other types of publications delivered electronically, usually for a fee

hidden Internet
databases that are not accessible by a search engine

Boolean logic
the use of Boolean operands (and, or, not) to narrow the selection and limit the identified sites

To ensure that the information you are finding on the Internet is credible, exercise these precautions:

- **Research the author.** Find out the author's educational background, his or her expertise as demonstrated in past publications on a particular topic, and his or her general standing as an expert in the topic.

- **Research the institution.** Find out the organization, institution, or company with which the person is associated, the goals of the organization, and whether the organization monitors published material and how. If the organization or institution supports a special interest or singular perspective on an issue, the information provided probably is one-sided and biased.

- **Timeliness of the publication.** Find out when the source was published and whether the date is current. Some information does not change significantly over time, but other data does. Therefore, it is important to be able to determine whether the data is up-to-date and thus accurate and relevant.

- **Research the publisher or producer.** Is the publisher of the material credible and reputable? For example, a university press or a government agency is likely to be a reputable source that reviews what it publishes. That helps to ensure some quality control over the material. The publisher should be recognized in the field as being an authority in the subject. Ask whether the publisher is likely to be an appropriate one for this kind of information. Or might the publisher or group have a particular bias on this topic? (For example, if you are looking at a website for a particular candidate for office, is the site sponsored by people trying to elect that person or opponents of that candidate?) Finally, find out whether there is any sort of review process or fact checking. (If a pharmaceutical company publishes data on a new drug it is developing, has there been outside review of the data?)

Primary Research

After reviewing the secondary data, you may need to collect primary data to solve your problem. **Primary research** relies on firsthand data—for example, responses from pertinent individuals or observations of people or phenomena related to your study. Recognized methods to obtain original information are observational studies, experimental research, and normative surveys.

Observational studies are those in which the researcher observes and statistically analyzes certain phenomena in order to assist in establishing new principles or discoveries. For example, market analysts observe buying habits of certain income groups to determine the most desirable markets. Executives analyze the frequency of ethical misconduct to determine the effectiveness of a comprehensive ethics program. Developing an objective system for quantifying observations is necessary to collect valid data. For example, to gain insight on the effect of a comprehensive ethics program, a researcher might record the number of incidents of ethical misconduct reported or the number of calls made to an ethics help line to seek advice about proper conduct. Observational studies typically involve no contact with the human subjects under study.

Experimental research typically involves the study of two or more samples that have exactly the same components before a variable is added to one of the samples. Any differences observed are viewed as due to the variable. Like scientists, businesses use experimental research to solve various problems. For example, a company conducts new employee training with all new hires. Two training methods are presently used: New hires in one regional office receive their training in a traditional classroom setting with other new employees, while employees at the other regional office take a web-based online training class. Management wants to determine whether one method is superior to the other in terms of learning success. During the period of the study, learning differences in the two study groups are noted. Because the training method is assumed to be the only significant variable, any difference is attributed to its influence. Experimental research requires very careful record keeping and can require informed consent from participants that are subjected to experimental methods.

Normative survey research is undertaken to determine the status of something at a specific time. Survey instruments such as questionnaires, opinion surveys, checklists, and interviews are used to obtain information from participants. Election opinion polls represent one type of normative survey research. The term *normative* is used to qualify surveys because surveys reveal "norms" or "standards" existing at the time of the survey. A poll taken two months before an election might have little similarity to one taken the week before an election.

Surveys can help verify the accuracy of existing norms. The U.S. Census is conducted every decade to establish an actual population figure, and each person is supposedly counted. In effect, the census tests the accuracy of prediction techniques used to estimate population during the years between censuses. A survey of what employees consider a fair benefits package would be effective only for the date of the survey. People retire, move, and change their minds often; these human traits make survey research of opinions somewhat tentative. Yet surveys remain a valuable tool for gathering information on which to base policy making and decision making.

Researchers normally cannot survey everyone, particularly if the population is large and the research budget is limited. **Sampling** is a survey technique that eliminates the need for questioning 100 percent of the population. Sampling is based on the principle that a sufficiently large number drawn at

primary research
data collected for the first time, usually for a specific purpose

observational studies
studies in which the researcher observes and statistically analyzes certain phenomena in order to assist in establishing new principles or discoveries

experimental research
the study of two or more samples that have exactly the same components before a variable is added to one of the samples

normative survey research
research to determine the status of something at a specific time

sampling
a survey technique that eliminates the need for questioning 100 percent of the population

© Winston Davidian/iStockphoto.com

random from a population will be representative of the total population; that is, the sample will possess the same characteristics in the same proportions as the total population. For example, a company collecting market research data before introducing a new low-fat food product would survey a small number of people. The data are considered *representative* if the sample of people surveyed has the same percentage of ages, genders, purchasing power, and so on as the anticipated target market. As a researcher, you must be cautious about drawing conclusions from a sample and generalizing them to a population that might not be represented by the sample. For example, early-morning shoppers may differ from afternoon or evening shoppers; young ones may differ from old ones; men shoppers may differ from women shoppers. A good researcher defines the population as distinctly as possible and uses a sampling technique to ensure that the sample is representative.

Whether a survey involves personal interviewing or the distribution of items, such as checklists or questionnaires, some principles of procedure and preplanning are common to both methods. These principles assure the researcher that the data gathered will be both valid and reliable.

Validity refers to the degree to which the data measure what you intend to measure. It generally results from careful planning of the questionnaire or interview questions or items. Cautious wording, preliminary testing of items to detect misunderstandings, and some statistical techniques are helpful in determining whether the responses to the items are valid. A **pilot test** of the instrument is often conducted prior to the full-scale survey so that a smaller number of participants can test the instrument, which can then be revised prior to wide-scale administration.

Reliability refers to the level of consistency or stability over time or over independent samples; that is, reliable data are reasonably accurate or repeatable. Reliability results from asking a large enough sample of people so that the researcher is reasonably confident the results would be the same even if more people were asked to respond or if a different sample were chosen from the same population. For example, if you were to ask 10 people to react to a questionnaire item, the results might vary considerably. If you were to add 90 more people to the sample, the results might tend to reach a point of stability where more responses would not change the results. Reliability would then be reasonably established.

Selecting an appropriate data collection method and developing a sound survey instrument are crucial elements of an effective research study.

STEP 3: Collecting and Organizing the Data

objective ⑤
Demonstrate appropriate methods of collecting, organizing, and referencing information.

Collecting the right data and ensuring that they are recorded appropriately is paramount to the success of a business report. Various techniques can assist in this process when collecting both secondary and primary research.

Collecting Secondary Data

When beginning to collect secondary data, beware of collecting too much information. Although you want to be thorough, you do not want to collect and record such a large amount of information that you will hardly know where to begin your analysis.

The availability of computer-assisted data searches has simplified the time-consuming task of searching through indexes, card catalogs, and other sources. For example, suppose you select an online database such as Business Source Premier or an Internet search engine such as Google to research the role of instant messaging in the workplace. By inputting the key term *instant messaging* in an online database, you receive the screen output in Figure 10-4 on the next page. The screen output contains information that will facilitate your research.

First, you can quickly evaluate the relevance of each reference by reading the title and brief summary and then clicking on the hyperlink (underlined title) of each reference that appears to have merit. The full text of the selected articles, which can then be saved or printed out, will be displayed. Retrieved articles can be read and analyzed for useful information. Be sure to obtain a full bibliographic citation for each reference you obtain to avoid the need to revisit the library or the online database.

After you have located the relevant sources, you can begin taking notes using various methods. Because your aim is to *learn*, not to accumulate, the following technique for taking notes is effective:

validity
the degree to which the data measure what you intend to measure
pilot test
implementation of the instrument conducted prior to the full-scale survey with a smaller number of participants
reliability
the level of consistency or stability over time or over independent samples

Figure 10-4 A Sample Computer Data Search Using an Online Database

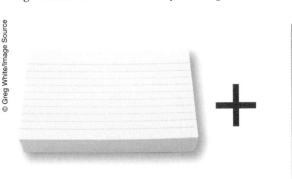

- Insert key search term.

- Alerts researcher of articles that can be viewed in full text.

1. Read an article rapidly.
2. Put the article aside.
3. List main and supporting points *from memory*.
4. Review the article to see whether all significant points have been included.

Rapid reading forces concentration. Taking notes from memory reinforces learning and reduces the temptation to rely heavily on the words of others. If you really learn the subject matter of one source, you will (as research progresses) see the relationship between it and other sources.

The traditional method of research involves reading articles and immediately writing notes on cards.

Another method is to highlight important points on a photocopy or printout of the articles and compose notes at the keyboard. Rather than spending time and money photocopying large volumes of information, researchers today compose notes at the keyboard in the library and then return the reference material to the shelf.

You can use two kinds of note taking: direct quotation or paraphrase. The **direct quotation method** involves citing the exact words from a source. This method is useful when you believe the exact words have a special effect or you want to give the impact of an expert. The **paraphrase method** involves summarizing information in your own words without changing the author's intended meaning. Put direct quotations in quotation marks as a reminder that the material is

direct quotation method
citing the exact words from a source

paraphrase method
summarizing information in your own words without changing the author's intended meaning

quoted, and indicate the page numbers of cited information. This information may save you time relocating the reference.

Plagiarism is the presentation of someone else's ideas or words as your own. To safeguard your reputation against plagiarism charges, be certain to give credit where credit is due. Specifically, provide a citation for each (1) direct quotation and (2) passage from someone else's work that you stated in your own words rather than using the original words (the words are your own, but the idea is not). After identifying the text that must be credited to someone else, develop complete, accurate citations and a reference page according to some recognized referencing method.

Collecting Data Through Surveys

The method of distribution and the makeup of the questionnaire are critical factors in successful survey research.

Selecting a Data Collection Method. Selecting an appropriate data collection method is crucial to effective research. Researchers must consider various factors when selecting an appropriate method for collecting data, as illustrated in Figure 10-5 on the next page.

Developing an Effective Survey Instrument. No matter which survey technique or combination of techniques is used, the way in which the survey instrument is designed and written has much to do with response validity and reliability, response rate, and quality of information received.

The construction of the survey instrument—usually a questionnaire or interview guide—is critical to obtaining reliable and valid data. Before developing items for a questionnaire or opinion survey, a researcher should visualize the ways responses will be compiled and included in a final report. Here are some suggestions for developing an effective questionnaire:

- **Provide brief, easy-to-follow directions.** Explain the purpose of the study in a cover message or in a brief statement at the top of the questionnaire so that the respondents understand your intent. While a screening question may be needed to determine whether the respondent is qualified to answer a set of questions, minimize confusing "skip-and-jump" instructions such as the following:

> If you answered Yes to item 4, skip directly to item 7; if you answered No, explain your reason in items 5 and 6.

Consider using electronic survey systems that advance respondents to the next question based on answers to screening questions.

- **Arrange the items in a logical sequence.** If possible, the sequence should proceed from easy to difficult items; easy, nonthreatening items involve respondents and encourage them to finish. You might group related items, such as demographic data or those that use the same response options (multiple choice, rating scales, open-ended questions).
- **Create an appealing, easy-to-comprehend design using word processing or desktop publishing software.** Use typefaces, bold, underline, and italics to emphasize important ideas. Use graphic lines and boxes to partition text so the reader can identify and move through sections quickly.
- **Use short items that ask for a single answer to one idea.** Include only the questions needed to meet the objectives of your study—long questionnaire length affects the return rate negatively.
- **Design questions that are easy to answer and tabulate.** Participants may not take the time to answer numerous open-ended questions that require essay-style answers. When open-ended questions are included, provide enough space for respondents to answer adequately.
- **Strive to write clear questions that all respondents will interpret in the same way.** Avoid words with imprecise meanings (e.g., several, usually) and specialized terms and difficult words that respondents might not understand. Use accurate translations for each concept presented if other cultures are involved. Provide examples for items that might be difficult to understand.
- **Ask for factual information whenever possible.** Opinions may be needed in certain studies, but opinions may change from day to day. As a general rule, the smaller the sample, the less reliable are any conclusions based on opinions.
- **Ask for information that can be recalled readily.** Asking for "old" information may not result in sound data.
- **Provide all possible answer choices on multiple-choice items.** Add an "undecided" or "other" category so that respondents are not forced to choose a nonapplicable response.
- **Decide on an optimal number of choices to place on a ranking scale.** Ranking scales, also called Likert scales, allow participants to indicate their opinion on a numbered continuum. When deciding the numbers to place on the scale, consider the tendency of some groups to choose the noncommittal midpoint in a scale with an odd number of response choices (i.e., choosing 3 on a scale from 1 to 5).
- **Avoid questions that may be threatening or awkward to the respondent.** For sensitive issues, such as age and income, allow respondents to select among ranges if possible. Ensure that

plagiarism
the presentation of someone else's ideas or words as your own

Figure 10-5 Selecting an Appropriate Data Collection Method

Method	Advantages	Limitations
Mailed surveys 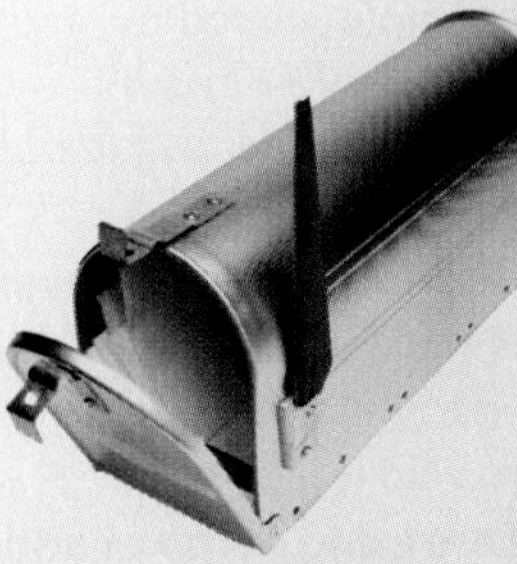	• Are relatively inexpensive to administer • Can reach a wide number of people who complete the survey at their convenience • Allow anonymity, which may produce more honest responses • Remove difference-in-status barriers	• Can be expensive if follow-up mailings are required • Yield a low response rate • Are not useful for obtaining detailed information
Telephone surveys 	• Provide inexpensive and rapid data collection • Allow personal contact between interviewer and respondent for clarification or follow-up questions	• Must be relatively short to minimize perceived intrusion and to increase typical small return rate • May exclude respondents with unlisted numbers and those without telephones
Personal interviews 	• Are useful to obtain in-depth answers and explore sensitive topics • Allow personal contact between interviewer and respondent for clarification and follow-up questions	• Are time-consuming and resource intensive • Require proper interviewer • Vary in value, depending on quality and consistency of interviewer
Email polling 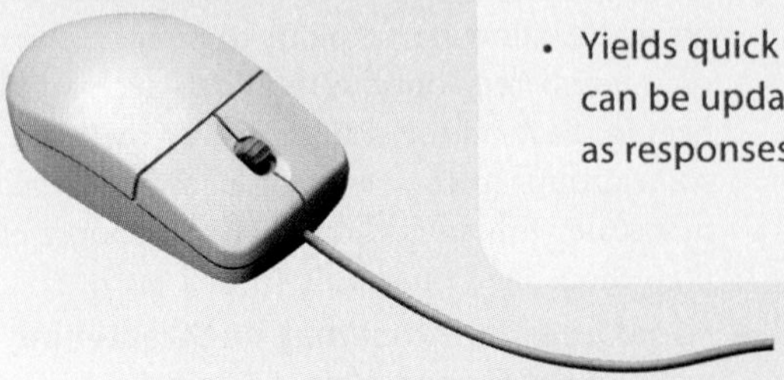	• Is inexpensive • Provides for easy response • Yields quick results that can be updated electronically as responses are received	• Is limited to respondents with computer access

© C Squared Studios/Photodisc/Getty Images

© Ryan McVay/Photodisc/Getty Images

© Duncan Smith/Photodisc/Getty Images

© Siede Preis/Photodisc/Getty Images

ranges do not overlap, and provide for all possible selections.

- **Consider the advisability of prompting a forced answer.** A forced answer question can be used to determine which factor is most critical to a respondent, as shown in the following example:

> Of all the problems listed, which is the *single* most critical problem for you personally?

When using forced choice items, avoid "leading questions" that cause people to answer in a way that is not their true opinion or situation. Rather, use neutral language that force respondents to choose a preference. The following items illustrate the distinction:

> Have you stopped humiliating employees who question your management decisions? **BAD**
>
> ☐ Yes   ☐ No
>
> Should city taxes be levied to fund a city recreational complex? **GOOD**
>
> ☐ Yes   ☐ No

- **Include a postage-paid envelope with a mailed questionnaire.** A higher response rate results when this courtesy is provided. Include your return information at the bottom of the questionnaire in the event the envelope is misplaced.

Various types of items can be used in questionnaire design, depending on your purpose and the characteristics of your participants. Figure 10-6 on page 182 illustrates the principles of effective questionnaire design.

Things to Avoid

- 🚫 Using samples that are too small
- 🚫 Using samples that are not representative
- 🚫 Using poorly constructed data-gathering instruments
- 🚫 Using information from biased sources
- 🚫 Failing to gather enough information to cover all important aspects of a problem
- 🚫 Gathering too much information (and then attempting to use all of it even though some may be irrelevant)

A final step in questionnaire design is to test the instrument by asking others to complete and/or critique the questionnaire. For surveys of major importance, researchers typically conduct a *pilot test,* sending out the questionnaire to a small group of the population involved. This process allows them to correct problems in clarity and design and typically leads to better response and quality of answers. A pilot study may uncover factors affecting your results, which you can address in the final research design and before conducting the actual survey.

Researchers must select from among the several formats available the one best suited to the situation. Criteria for selecting one alternative over the others might include the following: Which format leaves the least chance for misinterpretation? Which format provides information in the way it can best be used? Can it be tabulated easily? Can it be cross-referenced to other items in the survey instrument?

Avoiding Data-Gathering Errors

If acceptable data-gathering techniques have been used, data will measure what they are intended to measure (have validity) and will measure it accurately (have reliability). Some common errors at the data gathering stage seriously hamper later interpretation. Hopefully, a carefully designed research process will yield useful data for analysis.

Documenting Sources of Information

A crucial part of ethical research writing is documenting or referencing sources fairly and accurately. Although time-consuming and tedious, meticulous attention to documentation marks you as a respected, highly professional researcher. The *Publication Manual of the American Psychological Association* points out the importance of documentation with a forceful quote by K. F. Bruner: An inaccurate or incomplete reference "will stand in print as an annoyance to future investigators and a monument to the writer's carelessness."[2]

An important first step is to pledge that you will not, for any reason, present someone else's ideas as your own. Then, develop a systematic checklist for avoiding plagiarism. Carelessly forgetting to enclose someone else's words within quotation marks or failing to paraphrase another's words can cause others to question your ethical conduct. When you feel that the tedious work required to document sources fairly and accurately is not worth the time invested, remind yourself of the following reasons for documentation:

- **Citations give credit where it is due—to the one who created the material.** People who document demonstrate high standards of ethical conduct and responsibility in scholarship. Those exhibiting this

Figure 10-6 Example of an Effective Questionnaire

- Uses variety of items to elicit different types of responses.

- Uses clear, concise language to minimize confusion.

- Provides clear instructions for answering each item.

- Provides additional lines to allow for individual opinions.

- Provides even number of rating choices to eliminate "fence" responses.

- Asks for easily recalled information.

- Provides nonoverlapping categories of response and open-ended final category.

Format Pointers
Provides adequate space for answering open-ended item.

Keeps length as short as possible while meeting survey objectives.

Includes instructions for submitting completed questionnaire.

1. **Rank the following job factors in order of their importance to you. Add other factors important to you in the space provided.**

		1	2	3	4	5	6	7
a.	Wages	○	○	○	○	○	○	○
b.	Health and retirement benefits	○	○	○	○	○	○	○
c.	Job security	○	○	○	○	○	○	○
d.	Ability to maintain balance between work and family life	○	○	○	○	○	○	○
e.	Creativity and challenge of work assignment	○	○	○	○	○	○	○
f.	Perceived prestige of work	○	○	○	○	○	○	○
g.		○	○	○	○	○	○	○
h.		○	○	○	○	○	○	○

2. **Which of the following is the single job satisfaction factor that you feel needs more attention in our company? (Please select only one.)**
   - ○ Wages
   - ○ Health and retirement benefits
   - ○ Job security
   - ○ Ability to maintain balance between work and family life
   - ○ Creativity and challenge of work assignment
   - ○ Perceived prestige of work
   - ○ Other (specify) [_____▼]

3. **How would you rate your overall job satisfaction?**

Very unsatisfied 1	Somewhat dissatisfied 2	Neutral 3	Somewhat satisfied 4	Satisfied 5	Very satisfied 6
○	○	○	○	○	○

4. **How would you rate your overall job satisfaction 12 months ago?**

Very unsatisfied 1	Somewhat dissatisfied 2	Neutral 3	Somewhat satisfied 4	Satisfied 5	Very satisfied 6
○	○	○	○	○	○

5. **Indicate your age group:**
   - ○ 20–29
   - ○ 30–39
   - ○ 40–49
   - ○ 50–59
   - ○ 60–69
   - ○ 70 years and over

6. **Indicate your time with the company:**
   - ○ Less than 1 year
   - ○ 1–3 years
   - ○ 4–6 years
   - ○ 7–10 years
   - ○ Over 10 years

7. **What could the company do to enhance your satisfaction as a company employee?**

[text box]

Thanks for your participation. Click to submit your questionnaire.

[Submit]

professional behavior will gain the well-deserved trust and respect of peers and superiors.

- **Documentation protects writers against plagiarism charges.** Plagiarism occurs when someone steals material from another and claims it as his or her own writing. Besides embarrassment, the plagiarist may be assessed fines, penalties, or professional sanctions.

- **Documentation supports your statements.** If recognized authorities have said the same thing, your work takes on credibility; you put yourself in good company.

- **Documentation can aid future researchers pursuing similar material.** Documentation must be complete and accurate so that the researcher can locate the source.

Follow these general suggestions for preparing accurate documentation:

- **Decide which authoritative reference manual to follow for preparing in-text parenthetical citations or footnotes (endnotes) and the bibliography (references).** Some companies and most journals require writers to prepare reports or manuscripts following a particular reference manual. Once you are certain you have selected the appropriate style manual, follow it precisely as you prepare the documentation and produce the report.

- **Be consistent.** If you are carefully following a format, you shouldn't have a problem with consistency. For example, one style manual may require an author's initials in place of first name in a bibliography; another manual requires the full name. The placement of commas and periods and other information varies among reference manuals. Consult the manual, apply the rules methodically, and proofread carefully to ensure accuracy and consistency. If you cannot locate a format for an unusual source in the reference manual you are using, use other entries as a guide for presenting information consistently.

- **Follow the rule that it is better to include more than enough than too little.** When you are in doubt about whether certain information is necessary, include it.

Citations. Two major types of citations are used to document a report: source notes and explanatory notes. Depending on the authoritative style manual used, these notes may be positioned in parentheses within the report, at the bottom of the page, or at the end of the report.

- **Source notes acknowledge the contributions of others.** These citations might refer readers to sources of quotations, paraphrased portions of someone else's words or ideas, and quantitative data used in the report. Source notes must include complete and accurate information so that the reader can locate the original source, if desired.

- **Explanatory notes are used for several purposes:** (1) to comment on a source or to provide information that does not fit easily in the text, (2) to support a statistical table, or (3) to refer the reader to another section of the report. The following sample footnote describes the mathematics involved in preparing a table:

*The weighted opinion was derived by assigning responses from high to low as 5, 4, 3, 2, 1; totaling all respondents; and dividing by the number of respondents.

In this case, the asterisk (*) was used rather than a number to identify the explanatory footnote both in the text and in the citation. This method is often used when only one or two footnotes are included in the report. If two footnotes appear on the same page, two asterisks (**) or numbers or letters are used to distinguish the second from the first. An explanatory note that supports a visual or a source note that provides the reference from which data were taken appears immediately below the visual.

Referencing Methods. Various reference methods are available for the format and content of source notes: in-text parenthetical citations, footnotes, and endnotes. Note the major differences among the methods in the following discussion.

- **In-text parenthetical citations.** The *Publication Manual of the American Psychological Association, MLA Handbook,* and some other documentation references eliminate the need for separate footnotes or endnotes. Instead, an in-text citation that contains abbreviated information within parentheses directs the reader to a list of sources at the end of a report. The list of sources at the end contains all publication information on every source cited. This list is arranged alphabetically by the author's last name or, if no author is provided, by the first word of the article title.

Many style guides are available to advise writers how to organize, document, and produce reports and manuscripts. Figure 10-3 includes two of the most popular authoritative style manuals. The Publication Manual of the American Psychological Association *has become the most-used guide in the social and "soft" sciences and in many scholarly journals. The* MLA Handbook for Writers of Research Papers *is another authoritative source used in the humanities.*

The in-text citations contain the minimal information needed to locate the source in the complete list. In-text citations prepared using APA include the author's last name and the date of publication; the page number is included if referencing a direct quotation. An MLA citation includes the author's last name and the page number but not the date of publication.

- **Footnote citation method.** Placing citations at the bottom of the page on which they are cited is the footnote citation, or traditional, method. The reader can conveniently refer to the source if the documentation is positioned at the bottom of the page. Alternatively, a list of footnotes can be collected at the end of the document in the order they appeared in an *endnotes page*. Footnotes and endnotes are easily created with word processing software and automatically updated each time the report is revised. Footnotes and endnotes are not used in APA and MLA referencing, as these styles permit the use of in-text citations only.

- **References (or works cited).** This document is an alphabetized list of the sources used in preparing a report. Each entry contains publication information necessary for locating the source. In addition, the bibliographic entries give evidence of the nature of *sources the author consulted. Bibliography* (literally "description of books") is sometimes used to refer to this list. A researcher often uses sources that provide information but do not result in citations. To acknowledge that you may have consulted these works and to provide the reader with a comprehensive reading list, you might include them in the list of sources. The APA and MLA styles use different terms to distinguish between these types of lists.

STEP 4: Arriving at an Answer

objective ⑥
Explain techniques for the logical analysis and interpretation of data.

Even the most intelligent person cannot be expected to draw sound conclusions from faulty information. Sound conclusions can be drawn only when information has been properly organized, collected, and interpreted.

measures of central tendency
metrics that help describe distributions of quantitative data
range
the distribution of the scores

Analyzing the Data

Follow a step-by-step approach to the solution of your research problem. Plan your study, and follow the plan.

Question every step for its contribution to the objective. Keep a record of actions. In a formal research study, the researcher is expected to make a complete report. Another qualified person should be able to make the same study, use the same steps, and arrive at the same conclusion.

Suppose you have conducted a survey and collected several hundred replies to a 20- or 30-item questionnaire in addition to many notes from printed and electronic sources. What do you do next? You must carefully consider your notes for relevance and organize them for relationships among ideas. Then, you should apply appropriate statistical analysis to interpret survey results. *Tabulation* techniques should be used to reduce quantitative data, such as numerous answers to questionnaire items. For instance, you may want to tabulate the number of males and females participating in the study, along with the appropriate percentages for each gender.

For many kinds of studies, **measures of central tendency** may help in describing distributions of quantitative data. The **range** assists the researcher

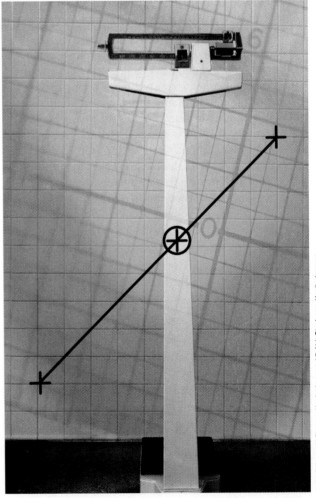

Figure 10-7 The Report Process

RESEARCH

Primary
· Surveys
· Observations
· Experiments

Secondary
· Review of printed and online sources
· Company records

CONDENSATION

Compiling using notes, cards, or inputting to a computer
· Direct quotations
· Paraphrased citations

COMBINATION

· Charts
· Tables
· Graphs
· Summaries

ASSIMILATION

Analysis
· Findings
· Conclusions
· Recommendations

WRITING

· Finished report

in understanding the distribution of the scores. The **mean, median, and mode** are descriptions of the average value of the distribution.

Other statistical techniques may be used. For example, **correlation analysis** might be used to determine whether a relationship exists between how respondents answered one item and how they answered another. Were males, for example, more likely to have chosen a certain answer to another item on the survey than were females?

The report process is one of reducing the information collected to a size that can be handled conveniently in a written message, as shown in Figure 10-7. Visualize the report process as taking place in a huge funnel. At the top of the funnel, pour

mean, median, and mode
different descriptions of the average value of the distribution

correlation analysis
a tool used to determine whether a relationship exists between how respondents answered one item and how they answered another

in all the original information. Then, through a process of compression within the funnel, take these steps:

1. Evaluate the information for its usefulness.
2. Reduce the useful information through organization of notes and data analysis.
3. Combine like information into understandable form through the use of tables, charts, graphs, and summaries. (See Chapter 11.)
4. Report in written form what remains. (See Chapter 12.)

Interpreting the Data

Your ethical principles affect the validity of your interpretations. Through all steps in the research process, you must attempt to maintain the integrity of the research. Strive to remain objective, design and conduct an unbiased study, and resist any pressure to slant research to support a particular viewpoint (e.g., ignoring, altering, or falsifying data). Some common errors that seriously hinder the interpretation of data include the following:

- **Trying, consciously or unconsciously, to make results conform to a prediction or desire.** Seeing predictions come true may be pleasing, but objectivity is much more important. Facts should determine conclusions.

- **Hoping for spectacular results.** An attempt to astonish supervisors by preparing a report with revolutionary conclusions can have a negative effect on accuracy.

- **Attempting to compare when commonality is absent.** Results obtained from one study may not always apply to other situations. Similarly, research with a certain population may not be consistent when the same research is conducted with another population.

- **Assuming a cause–effect relationship when one does not exist.** A company president may have been in office one year, and sales may have doubled.

However, sales might have doubled despite the president rather than because of the president.

- **Failing to consider important factors.** For example, learning that McDonald's was considering closing its restaurants in Kassel, Germany, a manager of an industrial supply company recommended that his firm reconsider its plans to expand its operation into Germany. The manager failed to recognize that the adverse impact of a new tax on disposable containers, not an unfavorable German economy or government, was the reason McDonald's was considering closing its restaurants.[3]

- **Basing a conclusion on lack of evidence.** The statement "We have had no complaints about our present policy" does not mean that the policy is appropriate. Conversely, lack of evidence that a proposed project will succeed does not necessarily mean that it will fail.

- **Assuming constancy of human behavior.** A survey indicating that 60 percent of the public favors one political party over the other in March does not mean the same will be true in November. Because some people paid their bills late last year does not mean a company should refuse to sell to them next year since reasons for slow payment may have been removed.

If you avoid common data collection errors, you are more likely to collect valid and reliable data and reach sound conclusions. However, if you interpret valid and reliable data incorrectly, your conclusions will still *not* be sound. Keep in mind the differences in meaning of some common research terms as you analyze your material and attempt to seek meaning from it.

- **Finding:** A specific, measurable fact from a research study
- **Conclusion:** Summation of major facts and evidence derived from findings
- **Recommendation:** A suggested action based on your research

Consider the following examples of conclusions and recommendations generated by analyzing research findings:

Example 1	Example 2
Finding: Nearly 75 percent of responding recruiters indicated they were more likely to hire a candidate who was involved in extracurricular activities.	Finding: Only 16 percent of the consumers interviewed knew that Hanson's Toy Company sells educational computer software.
Conclusion: Active involvement in extracurricular activities is an important job-selection criterion.	Conclusion: Few consumers are knowledgeable of our line of educational software.
Recommendation: Students should be involved in several extracurricular activities prior to seeking a job.	Recommendation: An advertising campaign focusing on educational software should be launched.

SPEAK UP!

THEY DID

BCOM2 was built on a simple principle: to create a new teaching and learning solution that reflects the way today's faculty teach and the way you learn.

Through conversations, focus groups, surveys, and interviews, we collected data that drove the creation of the version of BCOM2 that you are using today. But it doesn't stop there—in order to make BCOM2 an even better learning experience, we'd like you to SPEAK UP and tell us how BCOM2 worked for you.

What did you like about it? What would you change? Are there additional ideas you have that would help us build a better product for next semester's students?

At **4ltrpress.cengage.com/bcom** you'll find all of the resources you need to succeed – **videos, audio downloads, flash cards, interactive quizzes** and more!

Speak Up! Go to **4ltrpress.cengage.com/bcom.**

Managing Data and Using Graphics

Communicating Quantitative Information

Before you can interpret quantitative data, the elements must be classified, summarized, and condensed into a manageable size. This condensed information is meaningful and can be used to answer your research questions. For example, assume that you have been given 400 completed questionnaires from a study of employee needs for financial planning. This large accumulation of data is overwhelming until you tabulate the responses for each questionnaire item by manually inputting or compiling responses received electronically or optically scanning the responses into a computer. Then, you can apply appropriate statistical analysis techniques to the tabulated data.

objective ① Communicate quantitative information effectively.

The computer generates a report of the total responses for each possible answer to each item. For example, the tabulation of responses from each employee about his or her most important need in financial planning might appear like this:

Retirement Annuities	128
Traditional and Roth IRA	104
Mutual Funds	80
Internet Stock Trading	52
Effective Charitable Giving	36
	400

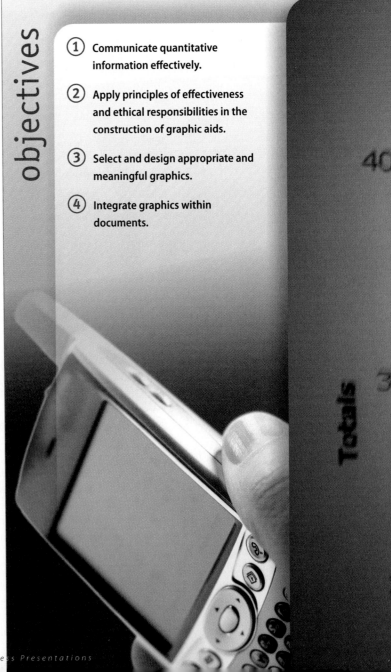

objectives

1. Communicate quantitative information effectively.
2. Apply principles of effectiveness and ethical responsibilities in the construction of graphic aids.
3. Select and design appropriate and meaningful graphics.
4. Integrate graphics within documents.

The breakdown reduces 400 responses to a manageable set of information. The tabulation shows only five items, each with a specific number of responses from the total of 400 questionnaires. Because people tend to make comparisons during analysis, the totals are helpful. People generally want to know proportions or ratios, and these are best presented as percentage parts of the total. Thus, the numbers converted to percentages are as follows:

Personal Development Need	Number	Percentage
Retirement Annuities	128	32
Traditional and Roth IRA	104	26
Mutual Funds	80	20
Internet Stock Trading	52	13
Effective Charitable Giving	36	9
	400	100%

Now analyzing the data becomes relatively easy. Of the survey participants, 13 percent selected Internet stock trading, and only 9 percent selected effective charitable giving. Other observations, depending on how exactly you intend to interpret percentages, could be that a fifth of the employees selected mutual funds. Combining data in two categories allows you to summarize that slightly more than one half of the employees selected retirement annuities and individual retirement accounts.

© Creatas Images/Jupiterimages

When tabulating research results of people's opinions, likes, preferences, and other subjective items, rounding off statistics to fractions helps paint a clear picture for readers. In actuality, if the same group of people were asked this question again a day or two later, a few probably would have changed their minds. For example, an employee who had not indicated a desire for retirement planning may have learned of the benefits of a Roth IRA during a civic club meeting. The next day, the employee might indicate a desire for training in IRAs and retirement annuities.

Fractions, ratios, and percentages are examples of **common language**. In effect, common language reduces difficult figures to the "common denominators" of language and ideas. Although "104 of 400 prefer traditional and Roth IRAs" is somewhat easy to understand, "26 percent prefer . . ." is even easier, and "approximately one out of four indicate a preference for traditional and Roth IRAs" is even more understandable.

Common language also involves the use of indicators other than actual count or quantity. The Dow Jones Industrial Average provides a measure of stock market performance and is certainly easier to understand than the complete New York Stock Exchange figures. Similarly, oil is counted in barrels rather than in the quart or gallon sizes purchased by consumers. Because of inflation, dollars are not accurate items to use as comparisons from one year to another in certain areas; for example, automobile manufacturers use "automobile units" to represent production changes in the industry. The important thing for the report writer to remember is that reports are communication media, and everything possible should be done to make sure communication occurs.

common language
reduces difficult figures to the "common denominators" of language and ideas

Using Graphics

Imagine trying to put in composition style all the information available in a financial statement. Several hundred pages might be necessary to explain material that could otherwise be contained in three or four pages of balance sheets and income statements. Even then, the reader would no doubt be thoroughly confused! To protect readers from being overwhelmed or simply bored with data, report writers must design a visually appealing graphic that is appropriate for the data being

objective ②
Apply principles of effectiveness and ethical responsibilities in the construction of graphic aids.

© PRNewsFoto/Green Giant Fresh

Using graphics appropriately can bolster sales for companies. In 2008, Green Giant redesigned its packaging to take advantage of the 96-percent consumer recognition rate of its larger-than-life icon, the Jolly Green Giant. The Fresh Produce line capitalizes on consumer association with the image of the Green Giant and top-quality produce by devoting more than a third of the package to the Green Giant and his valley.[1]

presented. Data reported in a table, graph, or picture will make your written analysis clearer to the reader.

The term *graphics* is used in this chapter to refer to all types of illustrations used in written and spoken reports. The most commonly used graphics are tables, bar charts, line charts, pie charts, pictograms, maps, flowcharts, diagrams, and photographs.

Effective and Ethical Use of Graphics

Graphics go hand in hand with the written discussion for three purposes: to clarify, to simplify, or to reinforce data. As you proceed through the remainder of this chapter, ask yourself if the discussion would be effective if the accompanying graphic figures were not included. Use the following questions to help you determine whether using a graphic presentation is appropriate and effective in a written or spoken report:

- **Is a graphic needed to clarify, reinforce, or emphasize a particular idea?** Or can the material be covered adequately in words rather than in visual ways? To maintain a reasonable balance between words and graphics, save graphics for data that are difficult to communicate in words alone.

- **Does the graphic presentation contribute to the overall understanding of the idea under discussion?** Will the written or spoken text add meaning to the graphic display?

- **Is the graphic easily understood?** Does the graphic emphasize the key idea and spur the reader to think intelligently about this information? Follow these important design principles:

  DO *avoid chartjunk.* This term, coined by design expert Edward Tufte, describes decorative distractions that bury relevant data.[2] Extreme use of color, complicated symbols and art techniques, and unusual combinations of typefaces reduce the impact of the material presented.

  DO *develop a consistent design for graphics.* Arbitrary changes in the design of graphics (e.g., use of colors, typefaces, three-dimensional (3D) or flat designs) within a written or spoken report can be confusing as the reader expects consistency in elements within a single report.

  DO *write meaningful titles that reinforce the point you are making.* For example, a reader can interpret data faster when graphics use a talking title—that is, a title that interprets the data. Consider the usefulness of the following graphic titles for a doctor browsing through a complex table in the middle of the night:[3]

Descriptive Title:	White-Cell Counts During April
Talking Title:	White-Cell Count Has Fallen Throughout April

Obviously, the talking title saves the physician time in reaching the writer's interpretation but also ensures the accuracy of the physician's interpretation and proper diagnosis and/or treatment. Similarly, poor business decisions may be averted if graphic titles reveal the key information. You will learn more about the appropriate use of descriptive and talking headings as you study the preparation of informational and analytical reports in Chapter 12.

- **Is the graphic honest?** Visual data can be distorted easily, leading the reader to form incorrect opinions about the data.

- **Can a graphic used in a spoken presentation be seen by the entire audience?** Flipcharts, whiteboards, overhead transparencies, and electronic presentations are the visual means most often used to accompany spoken reports. You will learn more about designing graphics for a business presentation in Chapter 13.

Professional communicators take care to make sure their visuals aren't misleading. That may sound obvious, but graphics designers can mislead their audiences either through lack of expertise or deliberate ambiguity. Distortion can occur in bar charts when the value scale starts at some point other than "0" and in bar charts when visually equal increments on the y-axis are used to represent varying values. Misuse of relative-size symbols in pictograms can also confuse or mislead a reader.

The key to preparing effective graphics is selecting an appropriate graphic for the data and developing a clean, simple design that allows the reader or audience to quickly extract needed information and meaning.

Tips for Creating Ethical Graphics

To check if you have a misleading graphic, ask yourself these questions:[4]

- Does the visual actually do what it seems to promise to do? Does the design cause false expectations?
- Is it truthful? Does it avoid implying lies?
- Does it avoid exploiting or cheating its audience?
- Does it avoid causing pain and suffering to members of the audience?
- Where appropriate, does it clarify text? Does the story told match the data?
- Does it avoid depriving viewers of a full understanding? Does it hide or distort information?

Types of Graphic Aids

objective ③
Select and design appropriate and meaningful graphics.

The greatest advantage of computer graphics is their value to the decision maker who formerly had to battle through a maze of computer-printed output. Using powerful software programs, managers can perform the data management functions discussed in this chapter to produce highly professional graphics. The information can be reproduced in a variety of ways for integrating into reports and for supporting highly effective presentations.

Selecting the graphic type that will depict data in the most effective manner is the first decision you must make. After identifying the idea you want your receiver to understand, you can choose to use a table, bar chart, line chart, pie chart, flowchart, organization chart, photograph, model, and so on. Use Figure 11-1 to

chartjunk
decorative distractions that bury relevant data

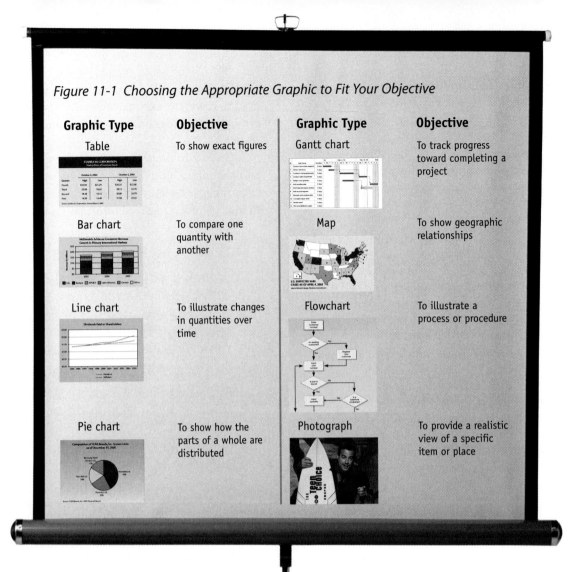

Figure 11-1 Choosing the Appropriate Graphic to Fit Your Objective

Graphic Type	Objective	Graphic Type	Objective
Table	To show exact figures	Gantt chart	To track progress toward completing a project
Bar chart	To compare one quantity with another	Map	To show geographic relationships
Line chart	To illustrate changes in quantities over time	Flowchart	To illustrate a process or procedure
Pie chart	To show how the parts of a whole are distributed	Photograph	To provide a realistic view of a specific item or place

help you choose the graphic type that matches the objective you hope to achieve.

A variety of graphics commonly used in reports is illustrated in Figures 11-2 through 11-13. These figures illustrate acceptable variations in graphic design: placement of the caption (figure number and title), inclusion or exclusion of grid lines, proper labeling of the axes, proper referencing of the source of data, and others. When designing graphics, adhere to the requirements in your company policy manual or the style manual you are instructed to follow. Then be certain that you design all graphics consistently throughout a report. When preparing a graphic for use as a transparency or on-screen display in a spoken presentation, you may wish to remove the figure number and include the title only.

Tables

table

data presented in columns and rows, which aid in clarifying large quantities of data in a small space

A **table** presents data in columns and rows, which aid in clarifying large quantities of data in a small space. Proper labeling techniques make the content clear. Guidelines for preparing an effective table follow and are illustrated in Figure 11-2:

- **Number tables and all other graphics consecutively throughout the report.** This practice enables you to refer to "Figure 1" rather than to "the following table" or "the figure on the following page."

- **Give each table a title that is complete enough to clarify what is included without forcing the reader to review the table.** Table titles may be quite long, as they may contain sources of data, numbers included in the table, and the subject. Titles may be written in either all capitals or upper- and lowercase letters. Titles that extend beyond one line should be arranged on the page so that they are balanced and do not extend into the margins.

- **Label columns of data clearly enough to identify the items.** Usually, column headings are short and easily arranged. If, however, they happen to be lengthy, use some ingenuity in planning the arrangement.

Figure 11-2 Effective Table Layout, Identifying Information, Labels, and Source

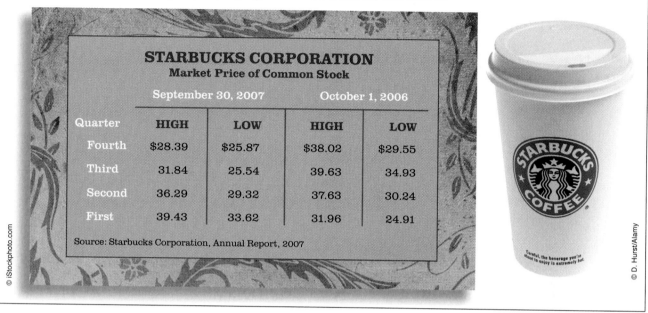

STARBUCKS CORPORATION
Market Price of Common Stock

| | September 30, 2007 | | October 1, 2006 | |
Quarter	HIGH	LOW	HIGH	LOW
Fourth	$28.39	$25.87	$38.02	$29.55
Third	31.84	25.54	39.63	34.93
Second	36.29	29.32	37.63	30.24
First	39.43	33.62	31.96	24.91

Source: Starbucks Corporation, Annual Report, 2007

- **Indent the second line of a label for the rows (horizontal items) two or three spaces.** Labels that are subdivisions of more comprehensive labels should be indented, as should summary labels such as total.

- **Place a superscript beside an entry that requires additional explanation, and include the explanatory note beneath the visual.**

- **Document the source of the data presented in a visual by adding a source note beneath the visual.** If more than one source was used to prepare a visual, use superscripts beside the various information references and provide the sources beneath the figure.

Bar Charts

A **bar chart** is an effective graphic for comparing quantities. The length of the bars, horizontal or vertical, indicates quantity. The simple bar chart in Figure 11-3 shows how the obstacles to proper

> **bar chart**
> *effective graphic for comparing quantities*

Figure 11-3 Simple Bar Chart (Horizontal)

Obstacles to Proper Hydration

- Worry too much about restroom breaks
- Can't leave desk for hydration break
- No bottled water available
- Don't feel thirsty
- Forget to drink
- Prefer other beverages
- Don't like the taste
- Lack of time/too busy

(scale: 0 5 10 15 20 25)

Source: International Bottled Water Association

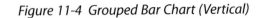

Figure 11-4 Grouped Bar Chart (Vertical)

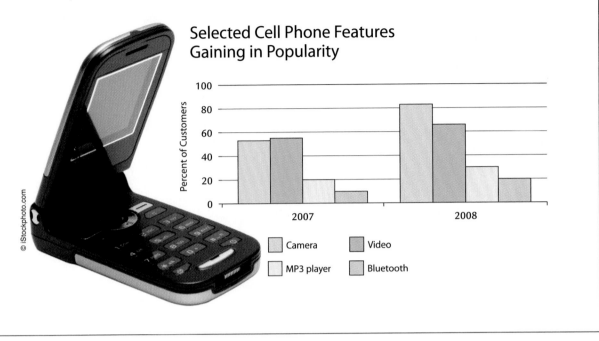

Selected Cell Phone Features Gaining in Popularity

Percent of Customers

- Camera
- Video
- MP3 player
- Bluetooth

hydration compare. Variations of the simple bar chart make it useful for a variety of purposes, as shown in Figures 11-3 through 11-7:

- *Grouped bar charts* (also called *clustered bar charts*) are useful for comparing more than one quantity. Figure 11-4 shows changes in the popularity of several cell phone features.

- *Segmented bar charts* (also called *subdivided, stacked bar,* or *100-percent bar charts*) show how

components contribute to a total figure. The segments in Figure 11-5 illustrate how McDonald's revenue has increased through consistent growth in every major international market.

- *Pictograms* use pictures to illustrate numerical relationships in a visually engaging way. A standard size image of a tree is used in Figure 11-6 to depict lumber production in the United States.

Figure 11-5 Segmented Bar Chart

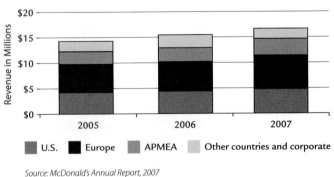

McDonald's Achieves Consistent Revenue
Growth in Primary International Markets

Revenue in Millions

- U.S.
- Europe
- APMEA
- Other countries and corporate

Source: McDonald's Annual Report, 2007

Figure 11-6 Pictogram

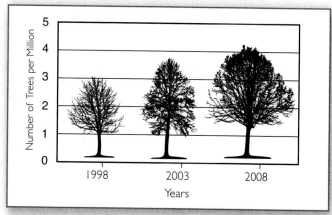

Number of Trees Harvested
United States, 1998-2008

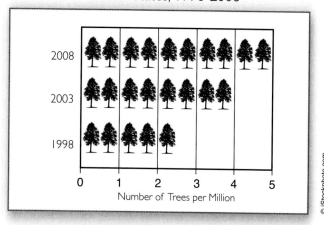

Number of Trees Harvested
United States, 1998-2008

© iStockphoto.com

In addition to the suggestions for developing tables, here are further suggestions related to constructing bar charts:

- **Begin the quantitative axis at zero, divide the bars into equal increments, and use bars of equal width.**

- **Position chronologically or in some other logical order.**

- **Use variations in color to distinguish among the bars when the bars represent different data.**

- **Avoid using 3D-type formatting that makes values more difficult to distinguish.**

- **Include enough information in the scale labels and bar labels for clear understanding.** Exclude nonessential information such as specific amounts, grids, and explanatory notes to reduce clutter and increase readability. To determine labeling needs, consider the audience's use of the data. For example, showing the specific dollar or quantity amount at the top of each bar can assist in understanding the graph, as readers tend to skim the text and rely on the graphics for details. Omit actual amounts if a visual estimate is adequate for understanding the relationships presented in the chart.

Another variation of the bar chart is the **Gantt chart**, developed by Henry L. Gantt. The Gantt chart is useful for tracking progress toward completing a series of events over time. The Gantt chart in Figure 11-7 on page 196, prepared using Microsoft Project, plots the output on the y-axis (activities involved in planning and implementing a research study) and the time (days planned to complete the activity) on the x-axis. This version of the Gantt chart not only schedules the important activities required to complete this research but also plots the *actual* progress of each activity with the *planned* progress.

Gantt chart
chart useful for tracking progress toward completing a series of events over time

Figure 11-7 Gantt Chart

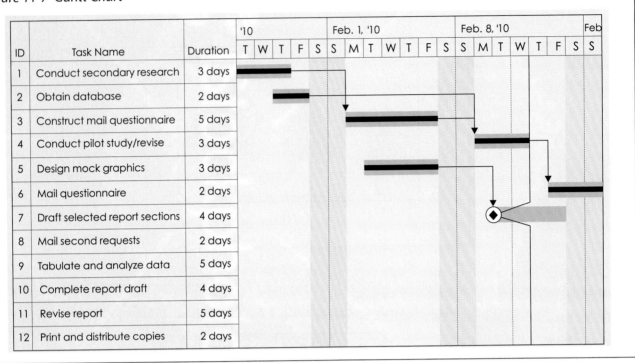

Figure 11-8 Simple Line Chart

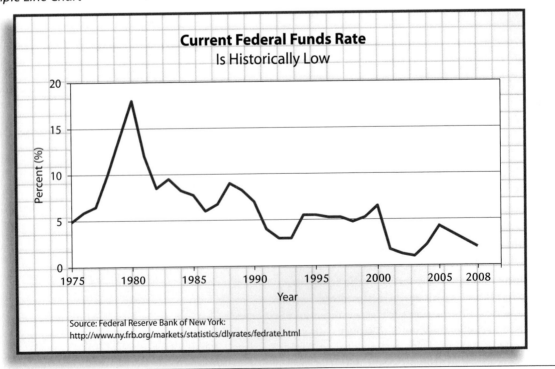

Figure 11-9 Multiple Line Chart

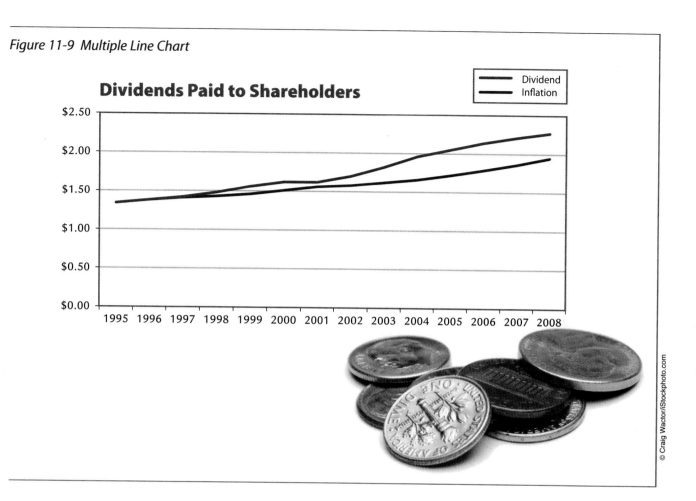

Dividends Paid to Shareholders

Line Charts

A **line chart** depicts changes in quantitative data over time and illustrates trends. The line chart shown in Figure 11-8 tracks changes in the discount rate of the Federal Reserve Bank of the United States. The two lines plotted in Figure 11-9 illustrate how the increase in a company's annual dividend has outpaced inflation.

When constructing line charts, keep these general guidelines in mind:

- **Use the vertical axis for amount and the horizontal axis for time.**

- **Begin the vertical axis at zero.**

- **Divide the vertical and horizontal scales into equal increments.** The vertical or amount increments, however, need not be the same as the horizontal or time increments so that the line or lines drawn will have reasonable slopes. (Unrealistic scales might produce startling slopes that could mislead readers.)

An **area chart**, also called a **cumulative line chart** or a **surface chart**, is similar to a segmented bar chart because it shows how different factors contribute to

a total. An area chart is especially useful when you want to illustrate changes in components over time. For example, the area chart in Figure 11-10 on page 198 illustrates changes in the actions of visitors to a company's website. A company decision maker can easily recognize the growth in the number of hits and orders placed. The cumulative total of the number of hits, registrations, and orders is illustrated by the top line on the chart. The amount of each component can be estimated by visual assessment.

Pie Charts

A **pie chart**, like segmented charts and area charts, shows how the parts of a whole are distributed. Pie charts are effective for showing percentages (parts of a whole), but they are inef-

line chart
chart that depicts changes in quantitative data over time and illustrates trends

area chart (cumulative line chart, surface chart)
bar chart that shows how different factors contribute to a total

pie chart
chart that shows how the parts of a whole are distributed

Figure 11-10 Area Chart

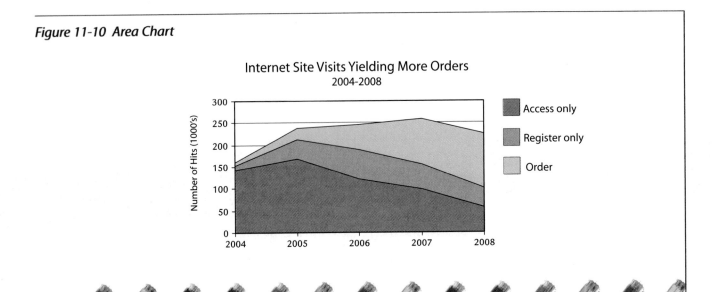

Internet Site Visits Yielding More Orders
2004-2008

Legend:
- Access only
- Register only
- Order

fective in showing quantitative totals or comparisons. Bars are better used for those purposes. The pie chart in Figure 11-11 shows the restaurant composition of the global restaurant chain YUM! Brands, Inc.

Here are some generally used guidelines for constructing pie charts:

- **Position the largest slice or the slice to be emphasized at the twelve o'clock position.** Working clockwise, place the other slices in descending order of size or some other logical order of presentation.

- **Label each slice, and include information about the quantitative size (percentage, dollars, acres, square feet, etc.) of each slice.** If you are unable to attractively place the appropriate labeling information beside each slice, use a legend to identify the color or pattern for each slice. Note the labeling in Figure 11-11.

- **Draw attention to one or more slices for desired emphasis.** Special effects include exploding the slice(s) to be emphasized (removing it from immediate contact with the pie) or displaying or printing only the slice(s) to be emphasized.

- **Avoid using 3D-type formatting that makes values more difficult to distinguish.**

Your software may limit your ability to follow rules explicitly, and the nature of the data or the presentation

may require slight deviations. For example, if you intend to explode the largest pie slice, placing it in the twelve o'clock position may not be desirable because the slice is likely to intrude into the space occupied by a title positioned at the top of the page.

Maps

A **map** shows geographic relationships. This graphic type is especially useful when a reader may not be familiar with the geography discussed in a report. The map shown in Figure 11-12 effectively presents the percentage of obese adults for each state in 2007. The map gives the information visually and thus eliminates the difficulty of explaining the information in words. In addition to being less confusing, a map is more concise and interesting than a written message.

Flowcharts

A **flowchart** is a step-by-step diagram of a procedure or a graphic depiction of a system or organization. A variety of problems can be resolved by using flowcharts to support written analyses. For example, most companies have procedures manuals to instruct employees in certain work tasks. Including a flowchart with written instructions minimizes the chance of errors. The flowchart in Figure 11-13 on page 200 illustrates the procedures for processing a telephone order in a series of simple steps. If this information had been presented only in a series of written steps, the

map
shows geographic relationships

flowchart
step-by-step diagram of a procedure or a graphic depiction of a system or organization

Figure 11-11 Pie Chart

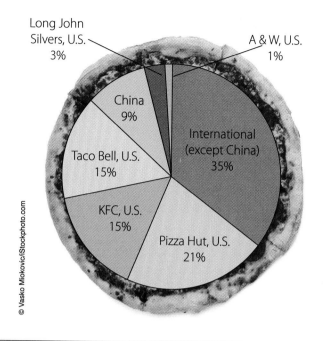

Composition of **YUM!**
Brands, Inc.
System Units
as of December 31, 2007

Long John
Silvers, U.S.
3%

A & W, U.S.
1%

China
9%

International
(except China)
35%

Taco Bell, U.S.
15%

KFC, U.S.
15%

Pizza Hut, U.S.
21%

© Vasko Miokovic/iStockphoto.com

Source: YUM! Brands, Inc.,
2007 Financial Report

Figure 11-12 Map Conveying Statistical Data

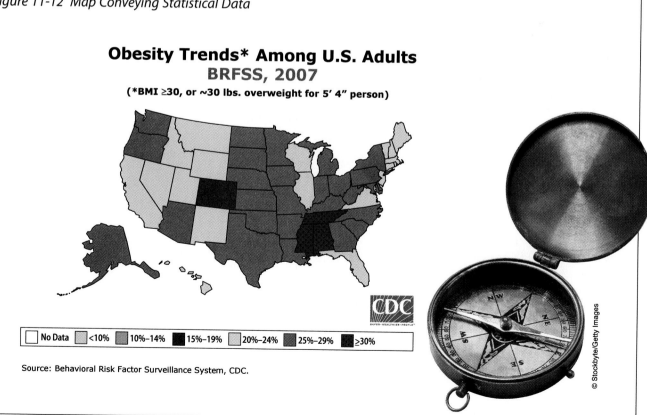

Obesity Trends* Among U.S. Adults
BRFSS, 2007
(*BMI ≥30, or ~30 lbs. overweight for 5′ 4″ person)

| No Data | <10% | 10%–14% | 15%–19% | 20%–24% | 25%–29% | ≥30% |

Source: Behavioral Risk Factor Surveillance System, CDC.

© Stockbyte/Getty Images

Figure 11-13 *Flowchart Simplifying Understanding of Work Tasks*

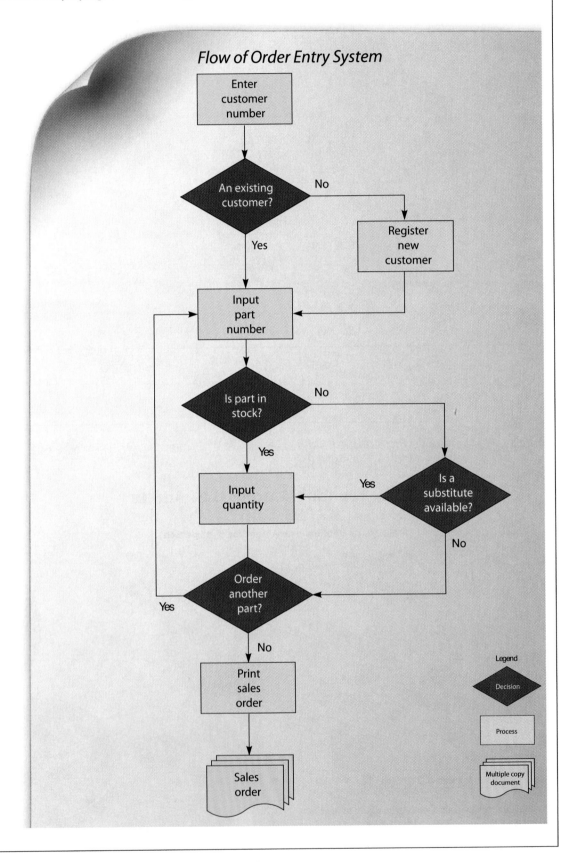

customer service manager would have to rely not only on the input operators' reading ability but also on their willingness to study the written procedures.

Organization charts, discussed in Chapter 1, are widely used to provide a picture of the authority structure and relationships within an organization. They provide employees with an idea of what their organization looks like in terms of the flow of authority and responsibility. When businesses change (because of new employees or reorganization of units and responsibilities), organization charts must be revised. Revisions are simple if the organization chart is prepared using graphics software.

Other Graphics

Other graphics, such as floor plans, photographs, cartoons, blueprints, and lists of various kinds, may be included in reports. The availability of graphics and sophisticated drawing software facilitate inclusion of these more complex visuals in reports and spoken presentations. Because managers can prepare these visuals themselves less expensively and more quickly than having them prepared by professional designers, sophisticated graphics are being used increasingly for internal reports. Photographs are used frequently in annual reports to help the general audience understand complex concepts and to make the documents more appealing to read. Frequently, you must include some graphic material in a report that would make the narrative discussion unwieldy. In this case, the material might be placed in an appendix and only referred to in the report.

Including Graphics in Text

Text and graphics are partners in the communication process. If graphics appear in the text before readers have been informed, they will begin to study the graphics and draw their own inferences and conclusions. For this reason, always give a text introduction to a graphic immediately preceding the positioning of the graphic. A graphic that follows an introduction and brief explanation will supplement what has been said in the report. Additional interpretation and needed analysis should follow the graphic.

objective ④
Integrate graphics within documents.

Pattern for Incorporating Graphics in Text

The pattern, then, for incorporating graphics in text is (1) introduce, (2) show, and (3) interpret and analyze.

Note how the language in the next set of examples below introduces graphic or tabular material.

Positioning of Graphics in Text

Ideally, a graphic should be integrated within the text material immediately after its introduction. A graphic that will not fit on the page where it is introduced should appear at the top of the following page. The

		Example	Rationale
X	Poor:	Figure 1 shows preferences for shopping locations.	Poor because it tells the reader nothing more than would the title of the figure.
✓	Acceptable:	About two thirds of the consumers preferred to shop in suburban areas rather than in the city. (See Figure 1.)	Acceptable because it interprets the data, but it places the figure reference in parentheses rather than integrating it into the sentence.
✓⁺	Better:	As shown in Figure 1, about two thirds of the consumers preferred to shop in suburban areas rather than in the city.	Better than the previous examples but puts reference to the figure at the beginning, thus detracting from the interpretation of the data.
✓⁺⁺	Best:	About two thirds of the consumers preferred to shop in suburban areas rather than in the city, as shown in Figure 1.	Best for introducing figures because it talks about the graphic and also includes introductory phrasing, but only after stressing the main point.

previous page is filled with text that would have ideally followed the graphic. In this chapter, figures are placed as closely as possible to their introductions in accordance with these suggestions. However, in some cases, several figures may be introduced on one page, making perfect placement difficult and sometimes impossible.

When interpreting and analyzing the graphic, avoid a mere restatement of what the graphic obviously shows. Instead, emphasize the main point you are making. This analysis may include summary statements about the data, compare information in the figure to information obtained from other sources, or extend the shown data into reasonably supported speculative outcomes. Contrast the boring style of the following discussion of graphic data with the improved revision:

Obvious Restatement of Data: Among the respondents, 35 percent are pleased with their rate of return from online investing, 12 percent are not pleased with their rate of return from online investing, 31 percent are not investing online but plan to begin, 8 percent only invest using a broker, and 15 percent do not trade stocks.

Emphasis on Main Point: Over one third of the respondents are pleased with their rate of return from online investing.

Strive to transition naturally from the discussion of the graphic into the next point you wish to make.

Throughout the discussion of tables and graphics, the term *graphics* has been used to include all illustrations. Although your report may include tables, graphs, maps, and even photographs, you will find organizing easier and writing about the illustrations more effective if you label each item as a "Figure" followed by a number and then number the items consecutively. Some report writers prefer to label tables consecutively as "Table 1," etc., and graphs and charts consecutively in another sequence as "Graph 1," etc. When this dual numbering system is used, readers of the report may become confused if they come upon a sentence saying, "Evidence presented in Tables 3 and 4 and Graph 2 supports. . . ." Both writers and readers appreciate the single numbering system, which makes the sentence read, "Evidence presented in Figures 3, 4, and 5 supports. . . ."

Strive to transition naturally from the discussion of the graphic into the next point you wish to make.

graphic → next point

© Image Source/Jupiterimages

© Jason Stitt/iStockphoto.com

REVIEW

HE DID

BCOM2 puts a multitude of study aids at your fingertips. After reading the chapters, check out these resources for further help:

• **Chapter in Review cards**, found in the back of your book, include all learning outcomes, definitions, and visual summaries for each chapter.

• **Online printable flash cards** give you three additional ways to check your comprehension of key concepts.

Other great ways to help you study include **interactive games, podcasts, audio downloads,** and **online tutorial quizzes with feedback**.

You can find it all at **4ltrpress.cengage.com/bcom**.

Organizing and Preparing Reports and Proposals

Parts of a Formal Report

Reports serve a variety of purposes, so the type of report you prepare depends on the subject matter, the purpose of the report, and the readers' needs. The differences between a formal report and an informal report lie in the format and possibly in the writing style. At one extreme, a brief, informal report could look exactly like a brief memorandum. At the other, a highly formal report might include many elements.

objective (1)
Identify the parts of a formal report and the contribution each part makes to overall effectiveness.

A business report rarely contains all of the parts shown in Table 12-1 on page 206 but may include any combination of them. The preliminary parts and addenda are organizational items that support the body of a report. The body contains the report of the research and covers the four steps in the research process. The organization of the body of a report leads to the construction of the contents page.

Because individuals usually write to affect or influence others favorably, they often add parts as the number of pages increases. When a report exceeds one or two pages, you might add a cover or title page. When the body of a report exceeds four or five pages, you might even add a finishing touch by placing the report in a ring binder or binding in a professional manner. Reports frequently take on the characteristics of the formal end of the continuum simply by reason of length. First, note how the preliminary parts and addenda items shown in

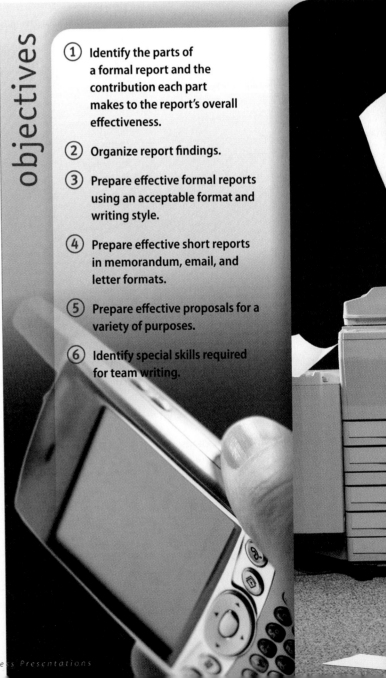

objectives

(1) Identify the parts of a formal report and the contribution each part makes to the report's overall effectiveness.

(2) Organize report findings.

(3) Prepare effective formal reports using an acceptable format and writing style.

(4) Prepare effective short reports in memorandum, email, and letter formats.

(5) Prepare effective proposals for a variety of purposes.

(6) Identify special skills required for team writing.

Figure 12-1 on page 207 increase in number as the report increases in length. Second, notice the order in which report parts appear in a complete report and the distribution of reports in print and electronic forms.

Memo and letter reports are often one page in length, but they can be expanded into several pages. As depicted, long reports may include some special pages that do not appear in short reports. The format you select—long or short, formal or informal—may help determine the supporting preliminary and addenda items to include.

To understand how each part of a formal report contributes to reader comprehension and ease of access to the information in the report, study the following explanations of each part shown in Table 12-1. The three basic sections—preliminary parts, report text, and addenda—are combined to prepare a complete formal report.

Preliminary Parts

Preliminary parts are included to add formality to a report, emphasize report content, and aid the reader in locating

preliminary parts
elements that add formality to a report, emphasize report content, and aid the reader in locating information in the report quickly and in understanding the report more easily

© Sии Stafford/Stone/Getty Images

Table 12-1 Parts of a Formal Report: Preliminary Parts, Report Text, and Addenda

Preliminary Parts

Half-title page (Title Fly)	Title page	Authorization	Transmittal	Table of contents	Table of figures	Executive summary
Contains report title; adds formality.	Includes title, author, and date; adds formality.	Provides written authorization to complete report.	Presents report to reader and summarizes main points or analysis.	Provides overview of report and order in which information will be presented; contains headings and page numbers.	Includes number, title, and page number of tables and graphics.	Summarizes essential elements in report.

Report Text

Introduction	Body	Analysis
Orients reader to topic and previews major divisions.	Presents information collected.	Reviews main points presented in body and may include conclusions and recommendations.

Addenda

References	Appendixes	Index
Includes alphabetical list of sources used in preparing report.	Contains supplementary information that supports report, but placing this information in report would make report bulky and unmanageable.	Includes alphabetical guide to subjects in report.

information in the report quickly and in understanding the report more easily. These parts might include a half-title page, title page, authorization, transmittal, table of contents, table of figures, and executive summary. The most frequently used preliminary parts are described here.

Title Page

The **title page** includes the title, author, date, and frequently the name of the person or organization that requested the report. A title page is often added when opting for a formal report format rather than a memorandum or letter arrangement.

The selected title should be descriptive and comprehensive; its words should reflect the content of the report. Avoid short, vague titles or excessively long titles. Instead, use concise wording to identify the topic adequately. For example, a title such as "Marketing Survey: Noncarbonated Beverages" leaves the reader confused when the title could have been "Noncarbonated Beverage Preferences of College Students in Boston." To give some clues for writing a descriptive title, think of the "Five W's": *Who, What, When, Where,* and *Why.* Avoid such phrases

title page
a page that includes the title, author, date, and frequently the name of the person or organization that requested the report

as "A Study of . . . ," "A Critical Analysis of . . . ," or "A Review of. . . ."

Follow company procedures or a style manual to place the title attractively on the page. Arrange the title consistently on the half-title page, title page, and the first page of a report.

Table of Contents

The table of contents provides the reader with an analytical overview of the report and the order in which information is presented. Thus, this preliminary part aids the reader in understanding the report and in locating a specific section of it. The list includes the name and location (beginning page number) of every report part except those that precede the contents page. Include the list of figures and the transmittal, executive summary, report headings, references, appendixes, and index. Placing spaced periods (leaders) between the report part and the page numbers helps lead the reader's eyes to the appropriate page number.

Table of Figures

To aid the reader in locating a specific graphic in a report with many graphics, the writer might include a list of fig-

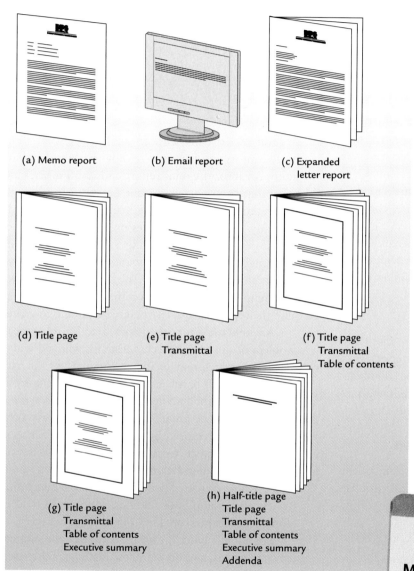

Figure 12-1 The Number of Assisting Parts Increases as the Length of a Report Increases

(a) Memo report

(b) Email report

(c) Expanded letter report

(d) Title page

(e) Title page
Transmittal

(f) Title page
Transmittal
Table of contents

(g) Title page
Transmittal
Table of contents
Executive summary

(h) Half-title page
Title page
Transmittal
Table of contents
Executive summary
Addenda

positioned before the first page of the report.

Typically, an executive summary is included to assist the reader in understanding a long, complex report. Because of the increased volume of information that managers must review, some managers require an executive summary regardless of the length and complexity of a report. The executive summary presents the report in miniature: the introduction, body, and summary as well as any conclusions and recommendations. Thus, an executive summary should (1) introduce briefly the report and preview the major divisions, (2) summarize the major sections of the report, and (3) summarize the report summary and any conclusions and recommendations.

> **executive summary (abstract, overview, précis)**
> *short summary of the essential elements in an entire report*

ures separate from the contents. The list should include a reference to each figure that appears in the report, identified by both figure number and name, along with the page number on which the figure occurs. The contents and the figures can be combined on one page if both lists are brief.

Executive Summary

The **executive summary** (also called the **abstract, overview,** or **précis**) summarizes the essential elements in an entire report. This overview simplifies the reader's understanding of a long report. The executive summary is

© Image Source

More Than Spell-Check

Word processing software simplifies the time-consuming, tedious task of preparing many of the preliminary and addenda report parts, including the table of contents, lists of figures, and the index. Before you compile these items manually, check your software for these capabilities. Because the software can generate these parts automatically, report writers can make last-minute changes to a report and still have time to update preliminary and addenda parts.

Pay special attention to topic sentences and to concluding sentences in paragraphs or within sections of reports. This technique helps you write concise executive summaries based on major ideas and reduces the use of supporting details and background information.

According to public relations consultant Cynthia Pharr, the executive summary is probably the most important part of a report being presented to top management. She advises that summaries be prepared with the needs of specific executive readers in mind. For instance, a technically oriented executive may require more detail; a strategist may want more analysis. An executive summary should "boil down" a report to its barest essentials without making the overview meaningless. Essentially, an executive summary should enable top executives to glean enough information and understanding to feel confident making a decision.

Preliminary pages are numbered with small Roman numerals (i, ii, iii, and so on). Table 12-1 provides more information about the purpose of each preliminary part.

Report Text

The report itself contains the introduction, discussion (also called the body), summary, and any conclusions and recommendations. Report pages are numbered with Arabic numerals (1, 2, 3, and so on).

discussion (body)
the main part of the report that presents the information collected and relates it to the problem
summary
a review of the main points presented in the body of the report
analytical report
a report designed to solve a specific problem or answer research questions
conclusions
inferences the writer draws from the findings
recommendations
the writer's opinions on a possible course of action based on the conclusions
addenda
materials used in the research that are not appropriate to be included in the report itself and so are placed at the end in a separate section
references
an alphabetical listing of the sources used in preparing the report that is included at the end of the report

Introduction

The introduction orients the reader to the problem. It may include the following items:

- What the topic is.
- Why the information is being reported.
- The scope and limitations of the research.
- Where the information came from.
- An explanation of special terminology.
- A preview of the major sections of the report to provide coherence and transitions:
  - How the topic is divided into parts.
  - The order in which the parts will be presented.

Discussion

The **discussion**, often called the heart of the report, presents the information collected and relates it to the problem. To increase readability and coherence, this section contains numerous headings to denote the various divisions within a report. Refer to "Organization of Formal Reports" in this chapter for an in-depth discussion of preparing the **body**.

Analysis

A good report ends with an analysis of what the reported information means or how it should be acted upon. An informational report ends with a brief **summary** that serves an important function: It adds unity to a report by reviewing the main points presented in the body. A summary includes only material that is discussed in a report. Introducing a new idea in the summary may make the reader wonder why the point was not developed earlier. It may suggest that the study was not completed adequately or that the writer did not plan the report adequately before beginning to write.

An **analytical report**, designed to solve a specific problem or answer research questions, will end with an "analysis," which may include a summary of the major research findings, particularly if the report is lengthy. Reviewing the major findings prepares the reader for the **conclusions**, which are inferences the writer draws from the findings. If required by the person/organization authorizing the report, recommendations follow the conclusions. **Recommendations** present the writer's opinion on a possible course of action based on the conclusions. Review the examples of findings, conclusions, and recommendations presented in Chapter 10 if necessary.

For a long report, the writer may place the summary, the conclusions, and the recommendations in three separate sections or in a section referred to as "Analysis." For shorter reports, all three sections are often combined.

Addenda

The **addenda** to a report may include materials used in the research that are not appropriate to be included in the report itself. The three basic addenda parts are the references, appendixes, and index. Addenda parts continue with the same page numbering system used in the body of the report.

References

The **references** (also called *works cited* or *bibliography*) section is an alphabetical listing of the sources used in preparing the report. Because the writer may be influenced by any information consulted, some reference manuals require all sources consulted to be included in the reference list. When the reference list includes sources not cited in the report, it is referred to as a **bibliography** or a list of **works consulted**. If a report includes endnotes rather than in-text parenthetical citations (author and date within the text), the endnotes precede the references. Using word processing software to create footnotes and endnotes alleviates much of the monotony and repetition of preparing accurate documentation.

© Radius Images/Jupiterimages

Appendix

An **appendix** contains supplementary information that supports the report but is not appropriate for inclusion in the report itself. This information may include questionnaires and accompanying transmittal letters, summary tabulations, verbatim comments from respondents, complex mathematical computations and formulas, legal documents, and a variety of items the writer presents to support the body of the report and the quality of the research. Placing supplementary material in an appendix helps prevent the body from becoming excessively long.

If the report contains more than one appendix, label each with a capital letter and a title. For example, the two appendixes (or appendices) in a report could be identified as follows:

Appendix A: Cover Letter Accompanying
              Customer Satisfaction Survey

Appendix B: Customer Satisfaction Survey

Each item included in the appendix must be mentioned in the report. A reference within the report to the two appendixes mentioned in the previous example follows:

> The cover message (Appendix A) and the customer satisfaction survey (Appendix B) were distributed by email to 1,156 firms on February 15, 2008.

Index

The **index** is an alphabetical guide to the subject matter in a report. The subject and each page number on which the subject appears are listed. Word processing software can generate the index automatically. Each time a new draft is prepared, a new index with revised terms and correct page numbers can be generated quickly and easily.

Organization of Formal Reports

objective ②
Organize report findings.

Tabloid authors typically have no valid documentation to support their claims, so they make up their own support. The result is entertaining reading, not hard, factual news. Reports, however, are writing to inform, not entertain, so the writer of a bona fide report must do a much more convincing and thorough job of reporting.

Writing Convincing and Effective Reports

Reports often require you to conduct research to find quotes, statistics, or ideas from others to back up the ideas presented. This support from outside sources bolsters the research and your credibility. Doing research and taking notes, however, are only parts of the process of putting together a well-documented, acceptable report. Careful

bibliography (works consulted)
a list at the end of the report that includes sources not cited in the report
appendix
a section placed at the end of the report that contains supplementary information that supports the report but is not appropriate for inclusion in the report itself
index
an alphabetical guide to the subject matter in a report

organization and formatting ensure that the reader will understand and comprehend the information presented. Many companies have their own style manuals that give examples of acceptable formats for reports, so this section presents only general organization guidelines.

Outlining and Sequencing

The content outline serves as a framework on which to build the report. In the development of the outline, the writer identifies the major and minor points that are to be covered and organizes them into a logical sequence. Outlining is an essential prerequisite to writing the report. The outline is a planning document and is thus subject to modification as the writer develops the report.

Developing an outline requires the writer to think about the information to be presented and how it can best be organized for the clear understanding of the reader. Assume, for instance, that you must select a smartphone (which integrates a cell phone with wireless email and web access and rich-media capabilities) from among three comparable brands—Palm, Hewlett-Packard (HP), and Motorola. You must choose the smartphone that will best serve the portable computing needs of a small office and present your reasons and recommendations in a **justification report**.

You gather all available information from the suppliers of the three smartphones, operate each smartphone personally, and compare the three against a variety of criteria. Your final selection is the Palm. Why did you select it? What criteria served as decision guides? When you write the report, you will have to tell the reader—the one who will pay for the equipment—how the selection was made so that he or she is "sold" on your conclusion.

If you organize your report so that you tell the reader everything about the Palm, the HP, and the Motorola each in a separate section, the reader may have trouble making comparisons. Your content outline might look like this:

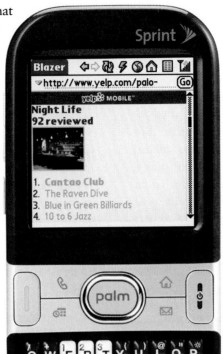

© AP Images /Palm Inc., Achille Bigliard

> I. Introduction
>> A. The Problem
>> B. The Method Used
> II. Palm
> III. HP
> IV. Motorola
> V. Conclusion

Note that this outline devotes three Roman numeral sections to the findings, one to the introduction that presents the problem and the method, and one to the conclusion. This division is appropriate because the most space must be devoted to the findings. However, the reader may have difficulty comparing the expansion capacity of the smartphones because the information is in three different places. Would discussing the expansion capacity of all three in the same section of the report be better? Would prices be compared more easily if they were all in the same section? Most reports should be divided into sections that reflect the criteria used rather than into sections devoted to the alternatives compared.

If you selected your smartphone based on cost, service/warranties, expandability, and availability of applications, these criteria (rather than the smartphone brands themselves) might serve as divisions of the findings. Then your content outline would appear this way:

> I. Introduction
>> A. The Problem
>> B. The Methods Used
> II. Product Comparison
>> A. Motorola Is Least Expensive
>> B. Service/Warranties Favor Palm
>> C. Expandability Is Best on Palm
>> D. Availability of Applications Is Equal
> III. Conclusion: Palm Is the Best Buy

The outline now has three major sections, with the product comparison consisting of four subsections. When the report is prepared in this way, the features of each smartphone (the evaluation criteria) are compared in the same section, and the reader is led logically to the conclusion.

Note the headings used in Sections II and III. These are called *talking headings* because they talk about the

justification report
a report that makes a recommendation based on research

content of the section and even give a conclusion about the section. Adding page numbers after each outline item will convert the outline into a contents page. Interestingly, the headings justify the selection of the Palm. As a result, a knowledgeable reader who has confidence in the researcher might be satisfied by reading only the content headings.

In addition to organizing findings for analytical reports by criteria, report writers can also use other organizational plans. When a report is informational and not analytical, you should use the most logical organization. A report on sales might be divided by geographic sales region, by product groups sold, by price range, or by time periods. A report on the development of a product might use chronological order. By visualizing the whole report first, you can then divide it into its major components and perhaps divide the major components into their parts.

A final caution: Beware of overdividing the sections. Too many divisions might make the report appear disorganized and choppy. On the other hand, too few divisions might cloud understanding for the reader.

When developing content outlines, some report writers believe that readers expect the beginning of the body to be an introduction, so they begin the outline with the first heading related to findings. In our example, then, Section I would be "Product Comparison." Additionally, when they reach the contents page, readers may eliminate the Roman numeral or other outline symbols.

The research process consists of inductively arranged steps as shown in Figure 12-2: (1) Problem, (2) Method, (3) Findings, and (4) Conclusion. Note how the four steps of research have been developed through headings in the Roman numeral outline and to a contents page for a report. When the report is organized in the same order, its users must read through the body to learn about the conclusions—generally the most important part of the report to users. To make the reader's job easier, report writers may organize the report deductively, with the conclusions at the beginning. This sequence is usually achieved by placing a synopsis or summary at the beginning:

REPORT TITLE IN DEDUCTIVE SEQUENCE REVEALS THE CONCLUSION

I. Conclusion Reported in the Synopsis
II. Body of the Report
   A. Problem
   B. Method
   C. Findings
III. Conclusion

This arrangement permits the reader to get the primary message early and then to look for support in the body of the report. The deductive arrangement contributes to the repetitious nature of reports, but it also facilitates understanding.

Using Headings Effectively

Headings are signposts informing readers about what text is ahead. Headings take their positions from their relative importance in a complete outline. For example, in a Roman numeral outline, "I" is a first-level heading, "A" is a second-level heading, and "1" is a third-level heading:

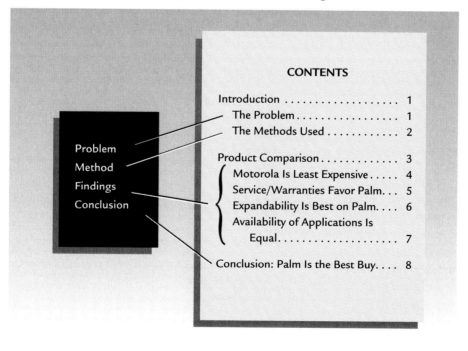

Figure 12-2 The Basic Outline Expands into a Contents Page

CONTENTS

Problem
Method
Findings
Conclusion

Introduction 1
   The Problem 1
   The Methods Used 2

Product Comparison 3
   Motorola Is Least Expensive 4
   Service/Warranties Favor Palm . . . 5
   Expandability Is Best on Palm 6
   Availability of Applications Is
      Equal 7

Conclusion: Palm Is the Best Buy 8

```
I.  First-Level Heading
    A.  Second-Level Heading
    B.  Second-Level Heading
        1.  Third-Level Heading
        2.  Third-Level Heading
II. First-Level Heading
```

Two important points about the use of headings also relate to outlines:

- **Because second-level headings are subdivisions of first-level headings, you should have at least two subdivisions (A and B).** Otherwise, the first-level heading cannot be divided—something divides into at least two parts or it is not divisible. Thus, in an outline, you must have a "B" subsection if you have an "A" subsection following a Roman numeral, or you should have no subsections. The same logic applies to the use of third-level headings following second-level headings.

- **All headings of the same level must be treated consistently.** Consistent elements include the physical position on the page, appearance (type style, underline), and grammatical construction. For instance, if Point A is worded as a noun phrase, Point B should be worded in the same manner. Or if Point I is a complete sentence, Points II and III should also be worded as sentences.

Appendix A provides further information about the placement and treatment of the various levels of headings. The method illustrated is typical but not universal. Always identify the format specified by the documentation style you are using, and follow it consistently. With word processing programs, you can develop fourth- and fifth-level headings simply by using boldface, underline, and varying fonts. In short reports, however, organization rarely goes beyond third-level headings; thoughtful organization can limit excessive heading levels in formal reports.

Choosing a Writing Style for Formal Reports

objective ③
Prepare effective formal reports using an acceptable format and writing style.

As you might expect, the writing style of long, formal reports is more formal than that used in many other routine business documents. The following suggestions should be applied when writing a formal report:

- **Avoid first-person pronouns as a rule.** In formal reports, the use of *I* is generally unacceptable. Because of the objective nature of research, the fewer personal references you use the better. However, in some organizations, the first person is acceptable.

Certainly, writing is easier when you can use yourself as the subject of sentences.

- **Use active voice.** "Authorization was received from the IRS" might not be as effective as "The IRS granted authorization." Subjects that can be visualized are advantageous, but you should also attempt to use the things most important to the report as subjects. If "authorization" were more important than "IRS," the writer should stay with the first version.

- **Use tense consistently.** Because you are writing about past actions, much of your report writing is in the past tense. However, when you call the reader's attention to the content of a graphic, remember that the graphic *shows* in the present tense. If you mention where the study *will take* the reader, use a future-tense verb.

- **Avoid placing two headings consecutively without any intervening text.** For example, always write something following a first-level heading and before the initial second-level heading.

- **Use transition sentences to link sections of a report.** Because you are writing a report in parts, show the connection between those parts by using transition sentences. "Although several advantages accrue from its use, the incentive plan also presents problems" may be a sentence written at the end of a section stressing advantages and before a section stressing problems.

- **Use a variety of coherence techniques.** Just as transition sentences bind portions of a report together, certain coherence techniques bind sentences together: repeating a word, using a pronoun, or using a conjunction. If such devices are used, each sentence seems to be joined smoothly to the next. These words and phrases keep you from making abrupt changes in thought.

Time Connectors	Contrast Connectors
at the same time	although
finally	despite
further	however
initially	in contrast
next	nevertheless
since	on the contrary
then	on the other hand
while	yet

Similarity Connectors	Cause-and-Effect Connectors
for instance/example	alternately
in the same way	because
just as	but
likewise	consequently
similarly	hence
thus	therefore

Other ways to improve transition include the following:

- **Use tabulations and enumerations.** When you have a series of items, bullet them or give each a number and list them consecutively. This list of writing suggestions is easier to understand because it contains bulleted items.

- **Define terms carefully.** When terms are not widely understood or have specific meanings in the study, define them. Definitions should be written in the term-family-differentiation sequence: "A dictionary *(term)* is a reference book *(family)* that contains a list of all words in a language *(point of difference).*" "A sophomore is a college student in the second year."

- **Check for variety.** In your first-draft stage, most of your attention should be directed toward presenting the right ideas and support. When reviewing the rough draft, you may discover certain portions with monotony in sentence length or construction. Changes and improvements in writing style at this stage are easy and well worth the effort.

Enhancing Credibility

Readers are more likely to accept your research as valid and reliable if you have designed the research effectively and collected, interpreted, and presented the data in an objective, unbiased manner. The following writing suggestions will enhance your credibility as a researcher:

- **Avoid emotional terms.** "The increase was fantastic" doesn't convince anyone. However, "The increase was 88 percent—more than double that of the previous year" does convince.

- **Identify assumptions.** Assumptions are things or conditions taken for granted. However, when you make an assumption, state that clearly. Statements such as "Assuming all other factors remain the same . . ." inform the reader of an important assumption.

- **Label opinions.** Facts are preferred over opinion, but sometimes the opinion of a recognized professional is the closest thing to fact. "In the opinion of legal counsel . . ." lends conviction to the statement that follows and lends credence to the integrity of the writer.

- **Use documentation.** Citations and references (works cited) are evidence of the writer's scholarship and honesty. These methods acknowledge the use of secondary material in the research.

The Annual Report

A company's annual financial report does much more than communicate just the accounting summary for the organization's performance. Three groups of vital partners scrutinize the report: the customers, the owners, and the employees. In addition to projecting profitability, many U.S. firms see the annual report as a vehicle for illuminating prevailing management philosophy, projecting corporate charisma, and humanizing themselves to their publics.

© Jan Stromme/Photodisc/Getty Images

Mastering
APA Style
Student's Workbook and Training Guide
A hands-on guide for learning the style rules of the *Publication Manual of the American Psychological Association,* Fifth Edition

Harold Gelfand, Charles J. Walker, & the American Psychological Association

© American Psychological Association

Write with Style

The APA style has guidelines for long reports. A sample long report following the APA style is at 4ltrpress.cengage.com/bcom. Keep in mind that a company's report-writing style manual may override the APA or any other established style guide you are used to using.

© Image Source

Short Reports

S hort reports incorporate many of the same organizational strategies as do long reports. However, most **short reports** include only the minimum supporting materials to achieve effective communication. Short reports focus on the body—problem, method, findings, and conclusion. In addition, short reports might incorporate any of the following features:

objective ④
Prepare effective short reports in memorandum, email, and letter formats.

- Personal writing style using first or second person.
- Contractions when they contribute to a natural style.
- Graphics to reinforce the written text.
- Headings and subheadings to partition portions of the body and to reflect organization.
- Memorandum, email, and letter formats when appropriate.

Memorandum, Email, and Letter Reports

Short reports are often written in memorandum, email, or letter format. The memorandum report is directed to an organizational insider, as are most email reports. The letter report is directed to a reader outside the organization. Short reports to internal and external readers are illustrated in Figures 12-3 and 12-4. The commentary in the left column will help you understand how effective writing principles are applied.

The memo report in Figure 12-3 communicates the annual activity of a company's on-site exercise facility. This periodic report is formatted as a memorandum because it is prepared for personnel within the company and is a brief, informal report. An outside consultant presents an audit of a company's annual bal-

short report
a report that contains only the minimum supporting materials to achieve effective communication
form report
a report designed to collect information easily, organize the data clearly, and be used repetitively

ance sheet and income in the letter report in Figure 12-4 on page 216.

The report in Figure 12-5 on pages 218 and 219 is written deductively. Implementation of an internal communication plan is described in an expanded letter report written by a consultant to a client (external audience). The consultant briefly describes the procedures used to analyze the problem, presents the findings in a logical sequence, and provides specific recommendations.

Form Reports

Form reports meet the demand for numerous, repetitive reports. College registration forms, applications for credit, airline tickets, and bank checks are examples of simple form reports. Form reports have the following benefits:

- When designed properly, form reports increase clerical accuracy by providing designated places for specific items.
- Forms save time by telling the preparer where to put each item and by preprinting common elements to eliminate the need for narrative writing.
- In addition to their advantages of accuracy and time saving, forms make tabulation of data relatively simple. The value of the form is uniformity.

Most form reports, such as a bank teller's cash sheet, are informational. At the end of the teller's work period, cash is counted and totals are entered in designated blanks. Cash reports from all tellers are then totaled to arrive at period totals and perhaps to be verified by computer records.

In addition to their informational purpose, form reports assist in analytical work. A residential appraisal report assists real estate appraisers in analyzing real property. With this information, the appraiser is able to determine the market value of a specific piece of property.

Many form reports are computer generated. For example, an automated hospital admission process expedites the repetitive patient reports that must be created. The admission clerk inputs the patient information using the carefully designed input screen beginning with the patient's social security number. If the patient has been admitted previously, the patient's name, address, and telephone number are displayed automatically for the clerk to verify. When the clerk inputs the patient's date of birth, the computer calculates the patient's age, eliminating the need to ask a potentially sensitive ques-

Figure 12-3 Short, Periodic Report in Memorandum Format

ETO Industries

233 State Boulvard
Kansas City, MO 64123-7600

TO: Candice Russell, Director, Human Resources
FROM: Tim Johnson, Manager, In-House Exercise Program
DATE: January 1, 2010
SUBJECT: Annual Report on In-House Exercise Program, 2009

The in-house exercise center has made significant gains in the past year. Data related to participation in our programs and current staffing follow:

Enrollment: 506 employees, up from 384 at end of 2008
Staff: One full-time trainer/manager and two part-time trainers

Our goal for the coming year is to increase our enrollment in the in-house exercise programs another 10 percent. We also have plans to create a nutrition program that will be rolled out next month. If that program is successful initially, we may need to hire a certified nutritionist. This person might also be used part-time in the company cafeteria to improve the nutritional value of the lunches and snacks provided there.

Employees report overall satisfaction with the quality of the current program. At the end of 2009, we asked program participants to complete a questionnaire. Eighty-eight percent indicated that they were very satisfied or extremely satisfied with our program. The most frequently mentioned suggestion for improvement was the extension of hours until 7 p.m. This change would allow employees to work late and still take advantage of the exercise facility. A copy of the questionnaire is provided for your review.

Call me should you wish to discuss the nutritional program, extended service hours, or any other aspects of this report.

Attachment

- *Includes header to serve formal report functions of transmittal and title page.*

- *Includes horizontal line to add interest and separate transmittal from body of memo.*

- *Uses deductive approach to present this periodic report requested by management on an annual basis.*

- *Uses headings to highlight standard information; allows for easy update when preparing subsequent report.*

- *Includes primary data from survey completed by program participants.*

- *Attaches material to memorandum, which would be an appendix item in formal report.*

Format Pointer
Uses memorandum format for brief periodic report prepared for personnel within company.

tion and ensuring accuracy when patients cannot remember their ages. All data are stored in a computer file and retrieved as needed to generate numerous reports required during a patient's stay: admissions summary sheet, admissions report, pharmacy profile, and even the addressograph used to stamp each page of the patient's record and the identification arm band.

Using the computer to prepare each report in the previous example leads to higher efficiency levels and minimizes errors because recurring data are entered only once. Preparing error-free form reports is a critical public relations tool because even minor clerical errors may cause patients or customers to question the organization's ability to deliver quality service.

Figure 12-4 Audit Report in Letter Format

- Letterhead and letter address function as title page and transmittal.

- Introduces overall topic and leads into procedures and findings.

- Uses side heading to denote beginning of body.

- Closes with appreciation for business and offer to answer questions.

Format Pointers
Uses letter format for short report prepared by outside consultant.

Includes reference initials of typist, who did not write message.

Paragon Accounting Group

767 RIVER ROAD, SUITE 216
BOSTON, MA 10812-0767
800-555-3000

January 30, 2010

Melinda Forrester, CEO
Randall and Associates
366 State Street
Boston, MA 10810-1796

Dear Ms. Forrester:

We have audited the accompanying balance sheet of Randall and Associates as of December 31, 2009, and the related statement of income, retained earnings, and cash flow for the year ended on that date. These financial statements are the responsibility of the company. Our responsibility is to express an opinion about these statements based on our audit.

PROCEDURES

We conducted our audit using generally accepted auditing standards. Those standards require that we plan and perform the audit to obtain reasonable assurance that the financial statements are free of material mistakes. An audit includes assessing whether generally accepted accounting principles are used and whether the significant estimates made by management and overall financial statement presentation are accurate. We believe that our audit provides a reasonable basis for our opinion on these matters.

FINDINGS

In our opinion, the financial statements referred to above present fairly, in all material aspects, the financial position of Randall and Associates as of December 31, 2009. The results of its operations and its cash flows for the year ended December 31, 2009, are in conformity with generally accepted accounting principles.

Thank you for the opportunity to serve your organization in this manner. Should you wish to discuss any aspects of this report, please call me.

Sincerely,

Karla Schmidt

Karla Schmidt
Senior Auditor

tsr

Parts of a Proposal

objective ⑤
Prepare effective proposals for a variety of purposes.

Recall from Chapter 10 that managers prepare proposals for a variety of reasons. Whether internal or external, solicited or unsolicited, proposals are a critical part of the successful operation of many companies.

Structure

A proposal includes (1) details about the manner in which the problem would be solved and (2) the price to be charged or costs to be incurred. Often, the proposal is a lengthy report designed to "sell" the prospective buyer on the ability of the bidder to perform. However, a simple price quotation also constitutes a proposal in response to a request for a price quotation.

The format of a proposal depends on the length of the proposal and the intended audience:

Format	Proposal Length and Intended Audience
Memo or email report	Short; remains within the organization
Letter report	Short; travels outside the organization
Formal report	Long; remains within the organization or travels outside the organization

Most work resulting from proposals is covered by a working agreement or contract to avoid discrepancies in the intents of the parties. In some cases, for example, users of outside consultants insist that each consultant be covered by a sizable general personal liability insurance policy that also insures the company. Many large firms and governmental organizations use highly structured procedures to ensure understanding of contract terms.

The following general parts, or variations of them, may appear as headings in a proposal: (1) Problem or Purpose, (2) Scope, (3) Methods or Procedures, (4) Materials and Equipment, (5) Qualifications, (6) Follow-Up and/or Evaluation, (7) Budget or Costs, (8) Summary, and (9) Addenda. In addition to these parts, a proposal may include preliminary report parts, such as the title page, transmittal message, and table of contents as well as addenda parts, such as references, appendix, and index.

Problem and/or Purpose

Problem and purpose are often used as interchangeable terms in reports. Here is the introductory purpose statement, called "Project Description," in a proposal by a firm to contribute to an educational project:

Project Description: Logan Community College has invited business and industry professionals to participate in the creation of *Business Communication,* a television course and video training package. These materials will provide effective training in business communication skills to enhance the performance of individuals in business and contribute to organizational skills and profitability. In our rapidly evolving information society, skill in communication is integral to success.

Note how the heading "Project Description" has been used in place of "Purpose." In the following opening statement, "Problem" is used as the heading:

Problem: The Board of Directors of Oak Brook Village Association has requested a proposal for total management and operation of its 1,620-unit permanent

residential planned development. This proposal demonstrates the advantages of using Central Management Corporation in that role.

The purpose of the proposal may be listed as a separate heading (in addition to "Problem") when the proposal intends to include objectives of a measurable nature. When you list objectives such as "To reduce overall expenses for maintenance by 10 percent," attempt to list measurable and attainable objectives and list only enough to accomplish the purpose of selling your proposal. Many proposals are rejected simply because writers promise more than they can actually deliver.

Scope

When determining the scope of your proposal, you can place limits on what you propose to do or on what the material or equipment you sell can accomplish. The term *Scope* need not necessarily be the only heading for this section. "Areas Served," "Limitations to the Study," and "Where *(specify topic)* Can Be Used" are examples of headings that describe the scope of a proposal. Here is a "Scope" section from a consulting firm's proposal to conduct a salary survey:

What the Study Will Cover: To assist Sun Valley Technologies in formulating its salary and benefits program for executives, Patterson Consulting will include an analysis of compensation (salary and benefits) for no fewer than 20 of Sun Valley's competitors in the same geographic region. In addition to salaries, insurance, incentives, deferred compensation, medical, and retirement plans will be included. Additionally, Patterson Consulting will make recommendations for Sun Valley's program.

Another statement of scope might be as follows:

Scope: Leading figures in business and industry will work with respected academicians and skilled production staff to produce fifteen 30-minute interactive video training courses that may be used in courses for college credit or as modules dealing with discrete topics for corporate executives.

Methods and/or Procedures

The method(s) used to solve the problem or to conduct the business of the proposal should be spelled out in detail. In this section, simply think through all of the steps necessary to meet the terms of the proposal and write them in sequence. When feasible, you should include a time schedule for implementation of the project.

Figure 12-5 Short Report in Expanded Letter Format, Page 1 of 2

Absolute Communications Solutions

592 River Road, Suite 240   Atlanta, GA 30360-2950   800-555-6700

April 3, 2010

Linda Ruiz
President, Massive Corp.
660 Western Avenue
Atlanta, GA 30360-1660

Dear Ms. Ruiz:

RECOMMENDATIONS FOR IMPLEMENTING
INTERNAL COMMUNICATION PLAN AT MASSIVE

Thank you for allowing us to assist you in the recent communication audit of your organization. Studies have shown that improved communication practices can minimize costly mistakes, improve morale, and improve customer relations, all of which can add to the corporate bottom line.

Procedures

In preparing this report, data were gathered using a variety of methods. Interviews were conducted with all management personnel regarding the flow and channels of communication used in the organization as well as their perceptions of communication effectiveness. Focus groups composed of employees from each of the company's departments were used to gather similar information and perceptions from the rank and file. To double-check the validity of these methods and the responses that we received to our questions, an online survey was disseminated to all employees. The responses from these methods of data gathering along with our proven knowledge of corporate communication policies and practices led to the recommendations in this report.

Findings

Research revealed useful information concerning Massive's current communication process and practices.

Results of Interviews with Management Personnel

Across the board, management stated that it did not see any problems with the communication flow and channels currently used at Massive. However, when specific questions were asked about productivity, efficiency, morale, and losses from mistakes and misunderstandings, a different picture emerged. Eighty-percent of management personnel answered affirmatively to the following questions:

- Have you witnessed or heard about mistakes being made by employees because the information or instructions provided to them was interpreted incorrectly?
- Have you ever had an employee express frustration to you because he or she believed that management did not know what was occurring in his or her department or at lower levels of the organization?
- Do you think that the current communication process used by your organization could be streamlined to help make task completion by employees faster?

From our interviews with management personnel, two pictures emerged: On the surface, they believed communication practices and processes at Massive were sufficient, but when pressed about particular issues, the majority believed improvements could be made.

Results of Focus Groups with Employees

Nine focus groups were conducted with employees from each of Massive's departments. Focus group size ranged from 8 to 12 persons. Unlike the responses we initially received from management, employees generally believed there were numerous areas for improvement in Massive's communication practices.

All participants said that management did not listen to employees at lower levels and did not solicit suggestions from them. The results, according to employees, were that management did not value employees, did not have the information it needed to make good decisions, and was reactive when dealing with problems rather than proactive.

Annotations (left margin):

- Letterhead, letter address, and subject line function as title page and transmittal.

- Uses deductive approach to present main idea to president.

- Provides research methods and sources to add credibility.

- Uses centered heading to denote major division of body; transition sentence leads reader to subpoint denoted by its own heading.

- Uses bullets to make it easier to find key points.

Format Pointer
Uses subject line to introduce topic of letter report.

Figure 12-5 Short Report in Expanded Letter Format, Page 2 of 2

- *Includes second page heading to show continuation; appears on plain matching paper.*

- *Uses side heading to denote minor section.*

- *Uses table to make information easy to access. Table immediately follows its introduction; no other table is used, so it is not numbered.*

- *Uses step list to make it easier to find recommendations.*

- *Closes with courteous offer to provide additional service.*

- *Includes enclosure notation to alert reader of enclosed appendix.*

Ms. Linda Ruiz
Page 2
April 3, 2009

Furthermore, employees said that they did not feel that management clearly communicated organizational goals, activities, and events. The result was that employees often felt disconnected and devalued because they were not seen as a source for solutions. Employees said that Massive did not have a team culture. In the words of one employee, Massive is "a collection of individuals, all going their own separate way."

Results of Companywide Questionnaire

Of the 405 questionnaires sent out via email, we received responses from 349 employees. The responses to the questionnaire closely followed the responses we received from employee focus groups. The results from the survey are summarized below. The questionnaire can be found in the Appendix.

Question	Always	Sometimes	Never
1	5 percent	34 percent	61 percent
2	10 percent	50 percent	40 percent
3	13 percent	47 percent	40 percent
4	16 percent	60 percent	24 percent
5	6 percent	42 percent	51 percent
6	20 percent	62 percent	15 percent
7	11 percent	34 percent	55 percent
8	19 percent	48 percent	31 percent

Recommendations

The primary recommendations for Massive are

1. Improve the upward flow of communication from employees to management. Not only does this recommendation require changes in the company's communication practices, it also requires changes in its organizational culture. Management needs to become more open to others' ideas and more informal in its interactions with employees. It also needs to become much more active in and present at daily operations throughout the company. More formally, departments need to have regular meetings to gather ideas from employees, and this information needs to be spread throughout the company by additional meetings with management throughout the organization. Management should encourage employees to send suggestions through all channels of communication.
2. Improved downward flow of communication from management to employees. Management needs to actively share corporate goals, strategies, activities, and events that affect the company and its employees. This can be done through a variety of channels, including regular email messages, weekly or monthly company meetings, and a monthly company newsletter posted on the company website.
3. Improved horizontal flow of communication. This issue has been addressed in step 1. Regular meetings between all department heads sharing departmental activities and concerns as well as those of employees can lead to better decision making through better coordination of solutions.

Advantages of Implementing Recommendations

Organizational studies have shown that implementing such a communication plan may result in a number of advantages:

- Improved attitudes. People who feel valued for their ideas and appreciated by management and colleagues generally have higher morale.
- Increased productivity. Enhanced, systematic communication plans can lead to higher-quality work, greater professional commitment, and increased company loyalty.
- Better decision making. Communication practices that enable companies to gather more information from knowledgeable parties often lead to better, more effective solutions.
- Greater profitability. Higher morale, increased productivity, and more effective solutions lead to greater profitability.

Thank you for the opportunity to audit Massive's internal communication practices and to provide our results and recommendations for improvement. Please let us know how we can assist you further with the implementation of our proposed plan and the monitoring of its effectiveness.

Sincerely,

Hasan Hassoud

Hasan Hassoud, Consultant
ksm
Enclosure: Appendix

Materials and Equipment

For large proposals, such as construction or research and development, indicate the nature and quantities of materials and equipment to be used. In some cases, several departments will contribute to this section. When materials and equipment constitute a major portion of the total cost, include prices. Much litigation arises when clients are charged for "cost overruns." When contracts are made on the basis of "cost plus XX percent," the major costs of materials, equipment, and labor/personnel must be thoroughly described and documented.

Qualifications

Assuming your proposal is acceptable in terms of services to be performed or products to be supplied, your proposal must convince the potential buyer that you have the expertise to deliver what you have described and that you are a credible individual or company. Therefore, devote a section to presenting the specific qualifications and special expertise of the personnel involved in the proposal. You may include past records of the bidder and the recommendations of its past customers, and the proposed cost. Note how the brief biography of the principal member in the following excerpt from a proposal contributes to the credibility of the proposer:

> Principal: Project Director: Charles A. McKee, M.B.A., M.A.I., Partner in Property Appraisers, Inc., consulting appraiser since 1974. Fellow of the American Institute of Appraisers, B.A., M.B.A., Harvard University. Phi Kappa Phi and Beta Gamma Sigma honorary societies. Lecturer and speaker at many realty and appraisal conferences and at the University of Michigan.

In another related section, the proposal might mention other work performed:

> Major Clients of Past Five Years: City of Tulsa, Oklahoma; Dade County, Florida; City of San Francisco, California; City of Seattle, Washington; Harbor General Corporation, Long Beach, California; Gulf Houston, Incorporated, Houston, Texas. Personal references are available on request.

Follow-Up and/or Evaluation

Although your entire proposal is devoted to convincing the reader of its merit, clients are frequently concerned about what will happen when the proposed work or service is completed. Will you return to make certain your work is satisfactory? Can you adjust your method of research as times change?

If you propose to conduct a study, do not promise more than you can deliver. Not all funded research proves to be successful. If you propose to prepare a study in your firm's area of expertise, you may be more confident. A public accounting firm's proposal to audit a company's records need not be modest. The accountant follows certain audit functions that are prescribed by the profession. However, a proposal that involves providing psychological services probably warrants a thoughtful follow-up program to evaluate the service.

© Stockbyte/Getty Images

Budget or Costs

The budget or cost of the program should be detailed when materials, equipment, outside help, consultants, salaries, and travel are to be included. A simple proposal for service by one person might consist of a statement such as "15 hours at $200/hour, totaling $3,000, plus mileage and expenses estimated at $550." Present the budget or costs section after the main body of the proposal.

Summary

You might conclude the proposal with a summary. This summary may also be used as the initial section of the proposal if a deductive sequence is desired.

Addenda

When supporting material is necessary to the proposal but would make it too bulky or detract from it, include the material as addenda items. A bibliography and an appendix are examples of addenda items. References used should appear in the bibliography or as footnotes. Maps, questionnaires, letters of recommendation, and similar materials are suitable appendix items.

A short, informal proposal that includes several of the parts previously discussed is shown in Figure 12-6 on pages 222 and 223. This proposal consists of two major divisions: "Purpose," and "Proposed Plan Implementation." The "Proposed Plan Implementation" section is divided into four minor divisions to facilitate understanding. Wanting to increase the chances of securing the contract, the writer made sure the proposal was highly professional and had the impact needed to get the reader's attention. In other words, the writer wanted the proposal to "look" as good as it "sounds." To add to the overall effectiveness of the proposal, the writer incorporated appealing, but not distracting, page design features. Printing the proposal with a laser printer using proportional fonts of varying sizes and styles resulted in a professional appearance and an appealing document. The reader's positive impression of the high standards exhibited in this targeted proposal is likely to influence his or her confidence in the writer's ability to execute the planned communication changes.

Proposal Preparation

Writers have much flexibility in preparing proposals. When they find a particular pattern that seems to be successful, they no doubt will adopt it as their basic plan. The ultimate test of a proposal is its effectiveness in achieving its purpose. The task is to assemble the parts of a proposal in a way that persuades the reader to accept it.

As with most report writing, first prepare the pieces of information that you will assemble later as the "whole" report. Determine the parts to include, select one part that will be easy to prepare, prepare that part, and then go on to another. When you have completed the parts, you can arrange them in whatever order you like, incorporate the transitional items necessary to create coherence, and then put the proposal in finished form. Allow adequate time after completing the research and writing for proofreading and editing. Figures should be checked carefully for accuracy, since underreporting costs can lead to a financial loss if the proposal is accepted and overreported costs may lead to refusal of the proposal. If you fail to allow sufficient time for proposal completion, you may miss the required deadline for proposal submission.

Collaborative Skills for Team Writing

f you become part of a collaborative writing team producing a proposal of major size, you probably will be responsible for writing only a small portion of the total proposal. For example, a proposal team of 16 executives, managers, and engineers might be required to prepare an 87-page proposal presenting a supplier's plan to provide parts to a military aircraft manufacturer.

objective ⑥
Identify special skills required for team writing.

After the group brainstorms and plans the proposal, a project director delegates responsibility for the research and origination of particular sections of the proposal. Finally, one person compiles all the sections, creates many of the preliminary and addenda parts, and produces and distributes the final product.

Many problems faced by organizations cannot be solved by an individual because no one person has all the experience, resources, or information needed to accomplish the task. Team writing produces a corporate document representing multiple points of view. Group support systems (GSS) are interactive computer-based environments that support coordinated team efforts. Numerous GSS products have been developed, and the style of the team-editing process dictates which GSS application will be most appropriate:

- **Sequential editing.** Collaborators divide the task so that the output of one stage is passed to the next writer for individual work. Software editors that support this process are called markup tools.

- **Parallel editing.** Collaborators divide the task so that each writer works on a different part of the document at the same time. Then the document is reassembled in an integration stage.

- **Reciprocal editing.** Collaborators work together to create a common document, mutually adjusting their activities in real time to take into account each other's changes.

Early attempts at collaborative writing typically used an unstructured process that often proved to be dysfunctional and frustrating to participants. Successful collaborative writing projects typically involve a multistage process:

1. **Open discussion.** Collaborators develop the objectives and general scope of the document using brainstorming or parallel-discussion software.

2. **Generation of document outline.** Collaborators develop main sections and subsections that will provide the structure for the document.

Figure 12-6 Short Proposal, Page 1 of 2

- Describes problem and presents proposed plan as solution to problem.

- Uses headings to aid reader in understanding proposal's organization. Boldface font adds emphasis.

- Divides "Proposed Plan Implementation" into five minor sections for easier comprehension. Describes implementation plan in detail.

Format Pointer
Incorporates page design features to enhance appeal and readability (e.g., print attributes, headings, bulleted lists, laser print on high-quality paper).

PROPOSAL FOR IMPLEMENTATION OF INTERNAL COMMUNICATION PLAN

for Massive Corp.
by Hasan Hassoun, Communications Consultant

May 1, 2010

Purpose

After careful study, the management of Massive Corp. has decided to implement the internal communication plan that was recommended last month. The internal communication plan is designed to improve communication at every level of Massive Corp.

Proposed Plan Implementation

The implementation of the internal communication plan will be directed by me, Hasan Hassoun. Three additional consultants, Jana Lowry, Teresa Warner, and Ted Mitchell, will complete the team involved with plan implementation.

Implementation Process

The implementation process will begin with a two-day retreat for all management personnel. This retreat will have a number of sessions, including "Bringing About Corporate Culture Change," "Creating and Sharing Corporate Visions," "Leading Effective Meetings," and "Managing by Walking Around." The retreat will conclude with the creation of a schedule for regular meetings to be held at all levels of the organization. These meetings are intended to impart the new cultural values to employees and to provide for the transmission of information from employees to management and vice versa.

The next step in the process will take place at the scheduled meetings. Our consultants will attend the first of each of these departmental meetings. Consultants will then meet with each manager to provide feedback and coaching (if necessary) to support him or her in effective transmission of the corporate message as well as the gathering of information from employees.

After the initial visit to each department meeting as well as those at the management and companywide level, our consultants will visit a second meeting to observe how well managers are implementing their new skills and provide any needed feedback. If certain managers need additional support, this can be arranged. Subsequent meeting visits will be provided monthly for a period of six months.

Plan Assessment

At the end of the six-month period, our consultants will assess how well the plan has been implemented and whether employees believe it has been successful. This assessment will be performed using two methods: two focus groups composed of a random selection of employees and a second online questionnaire disseminated to all employees. The findings from this assessment will be communicated to Massive's corporate team.

Figure 12-6 Short Proposal, Page 2 of 2

- *Includes heading to identify second page. Adds horizontal line for professional appearance.*

- *Itemizes costs so reader understands exactly how figure was calculated. Disclosing detailed breakdown gives reader confidence that cost is accurate.*

Staff Development Proposal   Page 2

Length of Plan Implementation

As outlined above, implementation of the plan will be performed over a six-month period, beginning with a two-day retreat and consisting of seven additional visits to all departmental, management, and companywide meetings. If desired, an assessment of the plan implementation will be conducted at the end of six months. This assessment will consist of two one-hour focus groups and the dissemination of an online questionnaire to all employees.

Number of Participants

The plan will serve all Massive employees, which is reportedly 405.

Cost

Exact cost figures are as follows:

Professional fees for retreat workshop	$ 2,400.00
Rental of retreat site and meals for 20 persons	3,500.00
Professional fees for meeting visits and coaching	10,000.00
Plan assessment	2,000.00
Total	$17,900.00

---

3. **Discussion of content within outline.** Collaborators interactively generate and discuss document content in each section using parallel discussions.

4. **Composing by sub-teams.** Sub-teams may consist of a few people (or sometimes only one person) who take the content entries from a section and organize, edit, and complete the section as a first draft.

5. **Online feedback and discussion.** The team reviews each section and makes suggestions in the form of annotations or comments. The section editors accept, reject, or merge suggestions to improve their own sections.

6. **Verbal walk-through.** Using a collaborative writing tool, the team does a verbal walk-through of the document.

Stages 1 through 3 are sequential and are undertaken only once. Stages 4 through 6 are circular in nature, and in some cases multiple loops are carried out before the document is finalized. As synchronous group time may be limited and valuable, it is used to add and refine document content. Formatting can be accomplished later by team members or an outside editor.

Disputes can arise when collaborative team members have incorrect or incomplete information or different philosophical approaches to an issue. In such cases, the disputing team members can be assigned to work together as a sub-team, negotiating their differences without an audience. When the sub-team returns to the group with compromised text, the group readily accepts it, knowing that multiple points of view went into its composition.

WARNING

When preparing a collaborative report, one person compiles all the sections, creates many of the preliminary and addenda parts, and produces and distributes the final product. Also make sure that one person reads the report (everyone's portion) in its entirety as the intended reader will do. Edit to make sure that the report prepared by many has only one voice.

Designing and Delivering Business Presentations

Planning an Effective Business Presentation

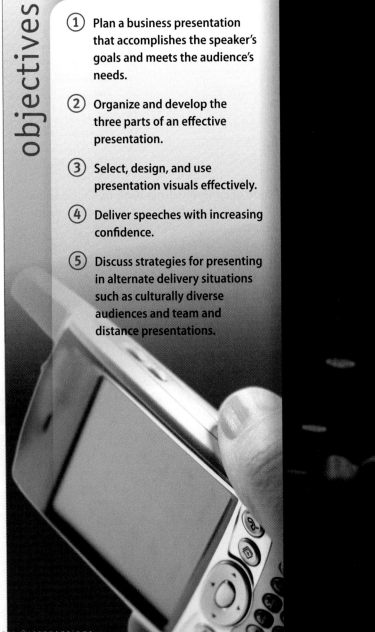

① Plan a business presentation that accomplishes the speaker's goals and meets the audience's needs.

② Organize and develop the three parts of an effective presentation.

③ Select, design, and use presentation visuals effectively.

④ Deliver speeches with increasing confidence.

⑤ Discuss strategies for presenting in alternate delivery situations such as culturally diverse audiences and team and distance presentations.

A business presentation is an important means of obtaining and exchanging information for decision making and policy development. Because several people receive the message at the same time, and the audience is able to provide immediate feedback for clarification, presentations can significantly reduce message distortion and misunderstanding.

objective ①
Plan a business presentation that accomplishes the speaker's goals and meets the audience's needs.

Many of the presentations you give will be formal, with sufficient time allowed for planning and developing elaborate visual support. You may present information and recommendations to external audiences such as customers and clients whom you've never met or to an internal audience made up of coworkers and managers you know well. You can also expect to present some less formal presentations, often referred to as **oral briefings**. An oral briefing might entail a short update on a current project requested during a meeting without advance notice or a brief explanation in the hallway when your supervisor walks past. Sales representatives give oral briefings daily as they present short, informal pitches for new products and services.

Regardless of the formality of the presentation, the time given to prepare, the nature of the audience

oral briefing
a less formal presentation delivered face-to-face

(friends or strangers), or the media used (live, distant, Web, or DVD delivery on demand), your success depends on your ability to think on your feet and speak confidently as you address the concerns of the audience. Understanding the purpose you hope to achieve through your presentation and conceptualizing your audience will enable you to organize the content in a way the audience can understand and accept.

Identify Your Key Message

Determining what you want to accomplish during a presentation is an important fundamental principle of planning an effective presentation. Some speech coaches recommend completing the following vital sentence to lay the foundation for a successful presentation: "At the end of my presentation, the audience will _____." In his book, *Do's and Taboos of Public Speaking,* Roger Axtell provides two excellent mechanisms for condensing your presentation into a brief, achievable purpose that will direct you in identifying the major points to be covered and the content to support those points:[1]

- Ask yourself, "What is my message?" Then, develop a phrase, a single thought, or a conclusion you want the audience to take with them from the presentation. This elementary statement likely may be the final

sentence in your presentation—the basic message you want the audience to remember.

- Imagine your audience is leaving the room and someone asks them to summarize the message they just heard in as few words as possible. Ideally, you want to hear them describe your central purpose.

Know Your Audience

A common mistake for many presenters is to presume they know the audience without attempting to find out about them. To be successful, you need to know your audience and focus your presentation on them—from planning your speech to practicing its delivery.

Generally, audiences *do* want to be in tune with a speaker, but people most want to listen to speeches about things of interest to *them*. A speech about acid rain to a farm group should address the farmers' problems, for example, and not focus on scientific causes of acid rain. Additionally, different strategies are needed for audiences who think and make decisions differently. For instance, different strategies are needed for making a successful presentation to sell software to a group of lawyers than to a group of doctors. Lawyers typically think quickly and are argumentative and decisive, while doctors are often cautious, skeptical, and don't make quick decisions.[2]

To deliver a presentation that focuses on the wants and expectations of an audience, you must determine who they are, what motivates them, how they think, and how they make decisions. Helpful information you can obtain about most audiences includes ages, genders, occupations, educational levels, attitudes, values, broad and specific interests, and needs. In addition, you should also consider certain things about the occasion and location. Patriotic speeches to a group of military veterans will differ from speeches to a group of new recruits, just as Fourth of July speeches will differ from Memorial Day speeches. When you discuss your speaking engagement with someone representing the group or audience, be sure to ask:

1. *Who* is the audience, and *who* requested the presentation? General characteristics of the audience should be considered as well as the extent of their knowledge and experience with the topic, attitude toward the topic (receptive or nonreceptive), anticipated response to the use of electronic presentation technology, and required or volunteer attendance.

2. *Why* is this topic important to the audience? What will the audience do with the information presented?

3. *What* environmental factors affect the presentation?

- How many will be in the audience?
- Will I be the only speaker? If not, where does my presentation fit in the program? What time of day?
- How much time will I be permitted? Minimum? Maximum?
- What are the seating arrangements? How far will the audience be from the speaker? Will a microphone or other equipment be available?

Answers to these questions reveal whether the speaking environment will be intimate or remote, whether the audience is likely to be receptive and alert or nonreceptive and tired, and whether you will need to develop additional motivational or persuasive techniques.

Organizing the Content

objective ②
Organize and develop the three parts of an effective presentation.

Once you understand the purpose of your business presentation—why you are giving it, what you hope to achieve—and know the size, interest, and background of the audience, you will be prepared to outline your presentation and identify appropriate content. First introduced by famous speech trainer Dale Carnegie and still recommended by speech experts today, the simple but effective presentation format includes an introduction, a body, and a close. In the introduction, tell the audience what you are going to tell them; in the body, tell them; and in the close, tell them again.

This design may sound repetitive; on the contrary, it works quite well. The audience processes information verbally and cannot slow the speaker down when information is complex. Thus, repetition aids the listener in processing the information that supports the speaker's purpose.

Introduction

What you say at the beginning sets the stage for your entire presentation and initiates your rapport with the audience. However, inexperienced

© C Squared Studios/Photodisc/Getty Images

Don't settle for an unoriginal opening like, "My name is . . ."

speakers often settle for unoriginal and overused introductions, such as "My name is . . . , and my topic is . . ." or "It is a pleasure . . . ," or negative statements, such as apologies for lack of preparation, boring delivery, or late arrival, that reduce the audience's desire to listen. An effective introduction accomplishes the following goals:

- **Captures attention and involves the audience.** Choose an attention-getter that is relevant to the subject and appropriate for the situation. Attention-getting techniques may include:

  - A shocking statement or startling statistic.
  - A quotation by an expert or well-known person.
  - A rhetorical or open-ended question that generates discussion from the audience.
  - An appropriate joke or humor.
  - A demonstration or dramatic presentation aid.
  - A related story or anecdote.
  - A personal reference, compliment to the audience, or reference to the occasion of the presentation.

To involve the audience directly, ask for a show of hands in response to a direct question, allow the audience time to think about the answer to a rhetorical question, or explain why the information is important and how it will benefit the listeners. Consider the following examples.

A drug awareness speech to young people might begin with a true story

I live in a quiet, middle-class, comfortable neighborhood. That is, until just a few months ago—when four young people from three different families were killed in an automobile accident following a party at which drugs were used.

A report presenting an information systems recommendation could introduce the subject and set the stage for

the findings (inductive sequence) or the recommendation (deductive sequence)

Inductive: When we were granted approval to adopt enterprise resource planning, we assigned a team to identify the optimal software to meet our information needs.

Deductive: By investing in enterprise resource planning, we can manage our information needs and support the future growth of our company.

- **Establishes rapport.** Initiate rapport with the listeners; convince them that you are concerned that they benefit from the presentation and that you are qualified to speak on the topic. You might share a personal story that relates to the topic but reveals something about yourself or you might discuss your background or a specific experience with the topic being discussed.

- **Presents the purpose statement and previews the points that will be developed.** To maintain the interest you have captured, present your purpose statement directly so that the audience is certain to hear it. Use original statements and avoid clichés such as "My topic today is . . ." or "I'd like to talk with you about . . . ." Next, preview the major points you will discuss in the order you will discuss them. For example, you might say,

"First, I'll discuss . . . , then . . . , and finally. . . ."

The acquisition and construction cost of all three sites were comparable. The decision to locate the new distribution facility in Madison, South Carolina, is based on three criteria: (1) quality of living, (2) transportation accessibility, and (3) availability of an adequate workforce.

Revealing the presentation plan will help the audience understand how the parts of the body are tied together to support the purpose statement, thus increasing the coherence of the presentation. For a long, complex presentation, you might display a presentation visual that lists the points in the order they will be covered. As you begin each major point, display a slide that contains that point and perhaps a related image. These divider slides partition your presentation just as headings do in a written report and thus move the listener more easily from one major point to the next.

Body

In a typical presentation of 20 to 30 minutes, limit your presentation to only a few major points (three to five)

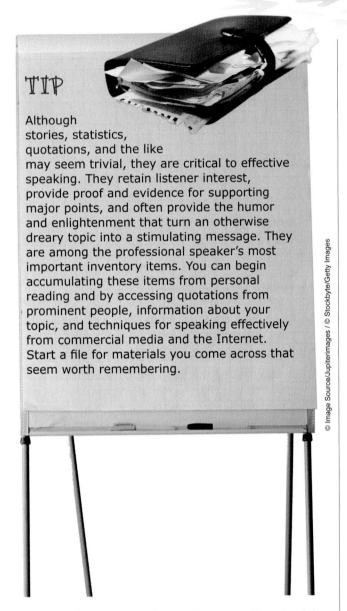

TIP

Although stories, statistics, quotations, and the like may seem trivial, they are critical to effective speaking. They retain listener interest, provide proof and evidence for supporting major points, and often provide the humor and enlightenment that turn an otherwise dreary topic into a stimulating message. They are among the professional speaker's most important inventory items. You can begin accumulating these items from personal reading and by accessing quotations from prominent people, information about your topic, and techniques for speaking effectively from commercial media and the Internet. Start a file for materials you come across that seem worth remembering.

because of time constraints and your audience's ability to concentrate and absorb. Making every statement in a presentation into a major point—something to be remembered—is impossible, unless the presentation lasts only two or three minutes.

Once you have selected your major points, locate your supporting material. You may use several techniques to ensure the audience understands your point and to reinforce it:

- **Provide support in a form that is easy to understand.** Two techniques will assist you in accomplishing this goal:

  1. *Use simple vocabulary and short sentences that the listener can understand easily and that sound conversational and interesting.* Spoken communication is more difficult to process than written communication; therefore, complex, varied vocabulary and long sentences often included in written documents are not effective in a presentation.

  2. *Avoid jargon or technical terms that the listeners may not understand.* Instead, use plain English that the audience can easily comprehend. Make your speech more interesting and memorable by using word pictures to make your points. Matt Hughes, a speech consultant, provides this example: If your message is a warning of difficulties ahead, you could say: "We're climbing a hill that's getting steeper, and there are rocks and potholes in the road."[3] Drawing analogies between new ideas and familiar ones is another technique for generating understanding. For example, noting that the U.S. blog-reading audience is already one fifth the size of the newspaper-reading population helps clarify abstract or complex concepts. When it became apparent that many Mississippi Gulf Coast residents intended to weather Katrina, a category 5 hurricane, Mississippi governor Haley Barbor instructed the news media to stress that this hurricane was predicted to be worse than Hurricane Camille, a destructive hurricane that most Mississippians still remember or have heard of in their families' stories. References to the portable FEMA trailers lining this area as "tumbleweeds" stress that early evacuation is critical for the upcoming hurricane season.

- **Provide relevant statistics.** Provide statistics or other quantitative measures available to lend authority and believability to your points. A word of warning: Do not overwhelm your audience with excessive statistics. Instead, use broad terms or word pictures that the listener can remember. Instead of "68.2 percent" say "over two thirds"; instead of "112 percent rise in production" say "our output more than doubled." Hearing that a flash drive can hold 35 times or more than a CD is less confusing and more memorable than hearing the exact number of megabytes for each medium.[4]

- **Use quotes from prominent people.** Comments made by other authorities are helpful in establishing credibility. Comments from top management of leading companies represent a credible source of quotations.

- **Use jokes and humor appropriately.** A joke or humor can create a special bond between you and the audience, ease your approach to sensitive subjects, disarm a nonreceptive audience, make your message easier to understand and remember, and make your audience more willing to listen. Plan your joke carefully so that you can (1) get the point across as quickly as possible, (2) deliver it in a conversational manner with interesting inflections and effective body movements, and (3) deliver the punch line effectively. If you cannot tell a joke well, use humor instead—amusing things that happened to you or someone you know, one-liners, or humorous quotations that relate to your presentation. Refrain from any humor that may reflect negatively on race, color, religion, gender, age, culture, or other personal areas of sensitivity.

- **Use interesting anecdotes.** Audiences like anecdotes or interesting stories that tie into the presentation. Like jokes, be sure you can get straight to the point of the story.

- **Use presentation visuals.** Presentation visuals, such as handouts, whiteboards, flipcharts, transparencies, electronic presentations, and demonstrations, enhance the effectiveness of the presentation. Develop presentation visuals that will enable your audience to see, hear, and even experience your presentation.

© iStockphoto.com

Close

The close provides unity to your presentation by "telling the audience what you have already told them." The conclusion should be "your best line, your most dramatic point, your most profound thought, your most memorable bit of information, or your best anecdote."[5] Because listeners tend to remember what they hear last, use these final words strategically. Develop a close that supports and refocuses the audience's attention on your purpose statement.

- **Commit the time and energy needed to develop a creative, memorable conclusion.** An audience is not impressed with endings such as "That's all I have" or "That's it." Techniques that can be used effectively include summarizing the main points that have been made in the presentation and using anecdotes, humor, and illustrations. When closing an analytical presentation, state your conclusion and support it with the highlights from your supporting evidence: "In summary, we selected the Madison, South Carolina, location because it had. . . ." In a persuasive presentation, the close is often an urgent plea for the members of the audience to take some action or to look on the subject from a new point of view.

- **Tie the close to the introduction to strengthen the unity of the presentation.** For example, you might answer the rhetorical question you asked in the opening, refer to and build on an anecdote included in the introduction, and so on. A unifying close to a drug awareness presentation might be "So, my friends, make your community drug free so you and your friends can grow up to enjoy the benefits of health, education, family, and freedom."

- **Use transition words that clearly indicate you are moving from the body to the close.** Attempt to develop original words rather than rely on standard statements such as "In closing" or "In conclusion."

- **Practice your close until you can deliver it without stumbling.** Use your voice and gestures to communicate this important idea clearly, emphatically, and sincerely rather than swallow your words or fade out at the end as inexperienced speakers often do.

- **Smile and stand back to accept the audience's applause.** A solid close does not require a "thank-you"; the audience should respond spontaneously with applause to thank you for a worthwhile presentation.[6]

Designing Compelling Presentation Visuals

objective ③
Select, design, and use presentation visuals effectively.

Speakers who use presentation visuals are considered better prepared and more persuasive and interesting. As well, they achieve their goals more often than speakers who do not use visuals. Presentation visuals support and clarify a speaker's ideas and help the audience visualize the message. A speaker using presentation visuals hits the listener (receiver) with double impact—through the eyes and the ears—and achieves the results quoted in an ancient Chinese proverb: "Tell me, I'll forget. Show me, I may remember. But involve me and I'll understand." Research studies have confirmed this commonsense idea that using visuals enhances a presentation.

The effective use of presentation visuals provides several advantages:[7]

- Clarifies and emphasizes important points.
- Increases retention from 14 to 38 percent.
- Reduces the time required to present a concept.
- Results in a speaker achieving goals 34 percent more often than when presentation visuals are not used.
- Increases group consensus by 21 percent when presentation visuals are used in a meeting.

© Image Source

Types of Presentation Visuals

A speaker must select the appropriate medium or combination of media to accomplish the purpose and to meet the needs of a specific audience. The most common presentation visuals are illustrated in Figure 13-1.

Design of Presentation Visuals

Computer technology has raised the standards for presentation visuals; however, inexperienced designers often use the power of the technology to make visuals overly complex and difficult to understand. Your goal is to create an appealing, easy-to-read design that supports your main points. Additionally, your presentation visuals should possess the same degree of professionalism as your delivery and personal appearance. You can create dynamic and useful presentation visuals, including slides, handouts, and notes pages, by composing effective slide content and applying basic design rules related to space usage, typography, and color.

Effective Slide Content

Well-organized, crisp slide content enhances the audience's ability to grasp the speaker's meaning and find immediate value in the information. Follow these simple rules for writing concise, meaningful slide content. Study the sample slides in Figures 13-2 and 13-3 on page 232 that illustrate basic design principles.

- **Limit the number of visual aids used in a single presentation.** While the audience values being able to "see" your points, they also welcome the variety provided by listening and the break from concentrating on visuals. Design compelling visuals that direct the audience's attention to major points and clarify or illustrate complex information. Integrate other strategies, such as precise, vivid language, that will involve the audience and enrich your message and delivery style.

- **Include engaging text that accurately describes one major idea on each visual.**

- **Include only core ideas the audience can scan quickly, understand, and remember.** Leave the explanations to the speaker. Good slides lead to an extemporaneous delivery rather than a speaker's monotonous reading of scripted slides. Short text lines are also easier for the eye to follow and open up the slide with appealing white space.

- **Develop powerful bulleted lists.** First, to eliminate confusion and rereading, use bulleted lists that are grammatically parallel and similar in meaning. One item appearing out of place weakens the emphasis given to each item in the list and may distract the audience's attention from the message. Be certain each major point relates to the key concept presented in the slide title and each subpoint relates to its major point. Second, limit the number of items in a bulleted list to increase audience retention and facilitate a smooth flow of ideas; in your draft, look for overlap and repetition that will allow you to collapse content into a short list that an audience can remember more easily.

- **Choose powerful visuals to reinforce ideas, illustrate complex ideas, and enliven boring content.** Images and shapes are more visually appealing and memorable than words, and they enable audiences to grasp information more easily. What's more, today's audiences expect media-rich, dynamic visuals, not a speaker's dense notes simply cleaned up, put on screen, and used as a crutch during a boring delivery. Note the power of visual design as you compare the slides illustrated in Figure 13-3.

- **Reflect legal and ethical responsibility in the design of presentation visuals.** Like the graphics you developed in Chapter 11, presentation visuals should be uncluttered, easily understood, and depict information honestly.

- **Proofread the visual carefully, following the same systematic procedures used for printed letters and reports and electronic communication.** Misspellings in visuals are embarrassing and diminish your credibility. When preparing visuals customized for a prospective client/customer, double-check to be certain that names of people, companies, and products are spelled correctly.

Figure 13-1 Selecting an Appropriate Presentation Visual

VISUAL	ADVANTAGES	LIMITATIONS
HANDOUTS	• Provide detailed information that audience can examine closely • Extend a presentation by providing resources for later use • Reduce the need for note taking and aid in audience retention	• Can divert audience's attention from the speaker • Can be expensive
 BOARDS AND FLIPCHARTS	• Facilitate interaction • Are easy to use • Are inexpensive if traditional units are used	• Require turning speaker's back to audience • Are cumbersome to transport, can be messy and not professional looking • Provide no hard copy and must be developed on-site if traditional units are used
 OVERHEAD TRANSPARENCIES	• Are simple to prepare and use • Allow versatile use; prepare beforehand or while speaking • Are inexpensive and readily available	• Are not easily updated and are awkward to use • Must have special acetate sheets and markers unless using a document camera • Pose potential for equipment failure
 ELECTRONIC PRESENTATIONS	• Meet audience expectations of visual standards • Enhance professionalism and credibility of the speaker • Provide special effects to enhance retention, appeal, flexibility, and reuse	• Can lead to poor delivery if misused • Can be expensive, require highly developed skills, and are time-consuming • Pose technology failure and transportability challenges
35MM SLIDES	• Are highly professional • Depict real people and places	• Require a darkened room • Creates a formal environment not conducive to group interaction • Lacks flexibility in presentation sequence
 MODELS OR PHYSICAL OBJECTS	• Are useful to demonstrate an idea	• Can compete with the speaker for attention

Figure 13-2 Writing Effective Slide Content: Poor (left) and Good (right) Examples

Humor

- Important element in any presentation
- Easy connection with the audience
- Gets attention
- Alleviates boredom
- Reduction of mental tension
- Discourages conflect
- Enhances comprehension
- Shouldn't embarrass people
  - Ethnic jokes are inappropriate
  - Profane language is definitely not recommended

Value of Humor in a Presentation

- Establishes a connection with the audience
- Increases audience's willingness to listen
- Makes message more understandable and memorable
- Alleviates negativity associated with sensitive subjects

The revised slide

- Includes a descriptive title that captures major idea of slide, in this case, the value of humor.
- Omits items unrelated to value of humor. Specifically, "important element in any presentation" is a verbal transition, not needed on slide; "shouldn't embarrass people" and related subpoints will appear on a separate slide focusing on tips for using humor.
- Collapses remaining content into a few memorable points that use parallel structure for clarity and grammatical accuracy (singular action verbs).
- Proofreads carefully to avoid misspellings that damage credibility, such as "conflect" in original slide.

Figure 13-3 Engaging Conceptual Slide Design: Poor (left) and Good (right) Examples

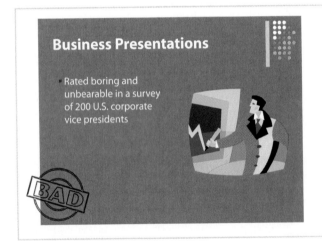

Business Presentations

- Rated boring and unbearable in a survey of 200 U.S. corporate vice presidents

How Well Do Business Presentations Measure Up?

Boring. Unbearable.

Survey of 200 corporate vice presidents, 2005

© Justin Horrocks/iStockphoto.com

The revised slide

- Uses descriptive title that captures central idea of dissatisfaction with typical business presentation.
- Selects images that imply intended message—ineffectiveness of business presenters; enlarges images for slide appeal and balance.
- Trims text to emphasize central idea and eliminates bullet, as bulleted list should have at least two items.
- Moves source to less prominent slide position to add credibility to research data while keeping focus on central idea.

Copyright Use—Or Abuse

When preparing presentations, you will probably want to use copyrighted materials to support your ideas. Your informed use of copyrighted materials may save you embarrassment and your company the cost of an expensive lawsuit.

To avoid copyright abuse when preparing presentation materials:

1. **Commit to learning the basics of copyright law.** Don't gamble that you won't get caught or that you will be safe if you plead ignorance.

2. **Assume that any pre-existing work is copyrighted and requires permission from the copyright owner to use or copy.** Plan ahead so you will have plenty of time to secure permissions and negotiate a fair price with the copyright owner.

3. **Note the precautions that relate to fair use.** The "fair use" defense is generally applicable in education, research, and scholarly uses and rarely applies in for-profit settings.[8]

4. **Acquire your own library of multimedia content by purchasing royalty-free multimedia content from reputable companies.** Royalty-free multimedia content provides unlimited use for a one-time fee because all copyrights have been cleared for the purchased content. (This photo is royalty free.) However, be wary of advertisers that sell "royalty-free" content but fail to clear the copyrights.

5. **Stay abreast of changes in the copyright law.** Owners and information users will continue to devise ways to make the copyright law work in an electronic environment.

Space Design and Typography

Follow these guidelines related to the use of space on the visual and the presentation of the text:

- **Limit the amount of text on the slide.** To avoid clutter and keep the audience's attention on important ideas, avoid filling more than 75 percent of the slide with text. Limit headings to four words and follow the 7 × 7 rule, which limits text to 7 lines per slide and 7 words per line.

- **Use graphic devices to direct the audience's attention and to separate items.** Options include borders, boxes, shadows, lines, and bullets. Unless sequence is important, use bullets—they add less clutter and are easier to follow than numbers.

- **Select a page layout orientation appropriate for the presentation visual you are creating:**

  - *Use landscape orientation for computer presentations and 35mm slides.* This horizontal placement provides a wide view that (1) creates a pleasing, soothing feeling similar to looking over the horizon, (2) provides longer lines for text and images, and (3) ensures that no text is included so low on the slide that it cannot be seen properly.

  - *Use portrait orientation for overhead transparencies.* This vertical placement positions the text to be read across the shortest side of the page, which makes additional lines available for text on an overhead transparency.

- **Use left alignment of text as a general rule.** Left alignment that begins flush at the left margin and ends at various points along the line creates an informal, personal appearance and easily leads the viewer's eyes consistently back to the same position for reading each item. Use centered alignment for positioning a few words on the slide and creating a formal look; use right alignment to format numerical data.

- **Follow these capitalization and punctuation rules for easy reading:**

  - *Use capital letters sparingly, as they are difficult to read from a distance.* Capitalize the first letter of important words in slide titles (initial caps) and the first letter of the first word and proper nouns in a bulleted list (sentence case).

  - *Omit punctuation at the end of bulleted lists.* Avoid punctuation elsewhere on the slide because punctuation is too small to be read from a distance. Consider inserting special characters when punctuation such as an exclamation point is needed.

  - *Avoid abbreviations and hyphenations that may cause confusion.*

Follow these guidelines concerning fonts to help ensure that your textual message supports the tone of your presentation and increases readability.

- **Choose interesting fonts that convey the mood of your presentation and are a fresh change from the fonts most commonly used.** For a less formal presentation, you might consider informal fonts such as Comic Sans MS over Arial and Times New Roman.

- **Limit the number of fonts within a single presentation to no more than three.** Choose a font for the (1) slide title, (2) bulleted list, and (3) other text.

- **Choose sturdy fonts that can be read easily from a distance.** Avoid delicate fonts with narrow strokes that wash out, especially when displayed in color, and italic, decorative, and condensed fonts that are difficult to read.

- **Emphasize specific content on a slide by varying the font face and font size.** A logical hierarchy of importance emerges when you apply the general guidelines illustrated in Figure 13-4. You'll need to know a few typography basics to apply these design rules:

Sans serif font: A font without short cross-strokes, known as *serifs,* that has a simple, blocky look appropriate for displaying text as in the headlines of newspaper or the title of a slide. Examples include **Arial** and **Univers**.

Serif font: A font with short cross-strokes that project from the top and bottom of the main stroke of a letter—the type that typically is read as the main print in books and newspapers. Examples include **Times New Roman** and **CG Times**.

Point: One point, the measurement scale used for text, equals 1/72 of an inch. A one-inch letter measured from the top of the highest part of the letter to the lowest part of the letter is 72 points.

Effective Use of Color

Color is the most exciting part of presentation design. The colors you choose and the way you combine them determine the overall effectiveness of your presentation and add a personal touch to your work. Your strategic choice of color will aid you in (1) conveying the formality of the presentation; (2) creating a desired tone; (3) associating your presentation with your company, a product, or the subject of the presentation; and (4) emphasizing important components of your slide.

Figure 13-4 Selecting Effective Fonts

- *For slide titles, choose sans serif font, 24 to 36 points: Arial.*

- *For bulleted list, choose serif font, 18 to 24 points: Times New Roman.*

- *For other text, choose a serif font no smaller than 18 points: Times New Roman.*

Slide Design Strategies

- Develop a simple design that
  - Sets the desired tone and reads easily
  - Adds flexibility and fosters audience interaction
- Develop simple, precise content that supports the speaker
- Use multimedia effects in moderation
- Practice for a smooth, seamless delivery

Source: Lehman, C. & DuFrene, D. (2005). "Making Business Slide Presentations Work for You," In: Business Communication (14th ed.).

Desired Effect	Guidelines
Formality	Choose conservative colors (blue) to add formality; choose brighter colors (yellow) for a less formal and perhaps trendy look.
Effect	Choose cool colors such as blues and greens to create a more relaxed and receptive environment. Use warm colors such as reds, oranges, and yellows in moderation to stimulate your audience.
Association	Reinforce an audience's natural color association with certain ideas and companies or products:

	Green	Money, go, the environment
	Red	Stop, danger, or financial loss
	White and blue	Cleanliness; crisp pure images
	Earth tones	Naturalness, stable, conservative, autumn
	Red and white	Coca-Cola
	Blue and white	Pepsi

	Because of a natural association of red with financial loss, red would be inappropriate in a table of numbers or a graph depicting growth or a healthy financial situation.
Differentiation	Use color to help the audience distinguish between different information or elements:

- Emphasizing the slide title over the bulleted list or key elements in a graph.
- Color coding related components in a table, line drawing, or organizational chart.
- Printing pages on different colors of paper to help the audience find a particular sheet in handouts.

Red and green should be avoided when differentiating important points, as almost 10 percent of the population is color impaired and cannot distinguish between red and green. The red and green bars in a graph would be seen as one large area.

To avoid an overwhelming, distracting design, limit colors to no more than three on a slide and follow these steps for selecting an effective color scheme for presentation visuals:

1. **Determine the medium you will use for displaying the visual.** The color scheme needed for optimal readability varies depending on your use of an electronic presentation, overhead transparencies, or a web page.

2. **Choose a background color that conveys the desired effect.** Consider the issues of formality and mood discussed previously.

3. **Choose complementary foreground colors that have high contrast to the background to ensure readability.** Choose a slightly brighter color for the slide title that distinguishes it from the color chosen for the bulleted list. Black text against a white background—the color scheme used traditionally in overhead transparencies—has the greatest contrast. A blue background with yellow text contrasts well, but a light blue background with white text would be difficult to read because of low contrast.

| High contrast | Low contrast | High contrast |

After you have chosen the background and foreground colors, evaluate the readability of the font(s) you have chosen. Colored text tend to wash out when projected; therefore, be certain that the fonts are sturdy enough and large enough to be read easily using the color scheme you selected.

4. **Choose the accent colors that complement the color scheme.** Accent colors are used in small doses to draw attention to key elements: bullet markers, bars/slices in graphs, backgrounds (fills) of shapes and lines, selected text, or drawings that are color coded for emphasis.

Output Medium	Background/Foreground
Overhead transparencies shown in a well-lit room	Light background Dark text
Electronic presentations and 35mm slides presented in a dark room	Medium to dark background Light text
Web page	Light background Dark text

Project your presentation ahead of time in the room where you are to present so you can adjust the color scheme. This process is essential because colors display differently on a computer monitor than on projection devices. You can also check the readability of the text and double-check for typographical errors at the same time.

The slides in Figure 13-5 provide an opportunity to review slide de-sign guidelines. First, study carefully the poor example (left) and identify design principles that you believe have been violated. Note changes needed in the following major areas: (1) content, (2) choice of template and graphics, (3) space usage and layout, (4) typography, and (5) color scheme. Then, compare your suggestions with the revised slide and the provided explanation of the principles violated.

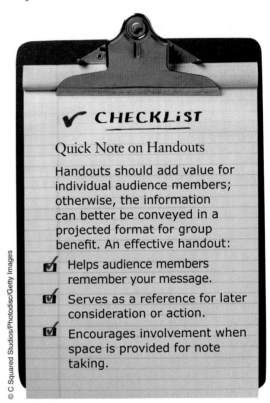

✔ **CHECKLiST**

Quick Note on Handouts

Handouts should add value for individual audience members; otherwise, the information can better be conveyed in a projected format for group benefit. An effective handout:

- ☑ Helps audience members remember your message.
- ☑ Serves as a reference for later consideration or action.
- ☑ Encourages involvement when space is provided for note taking.

© C Squared Studios/Photodisc/Getty Images

Refining Your Delivery

After you have organized your message, you must identify the appropriate delivery method, develop your vocal qualities, and practice your delivery.

objective ④ Delivery Method

Deliver speeches with increasing confidence.

Four presentation methods can be used: memorized, scripted, impromptu, and extemporaneous. Impromptu and extemporaneous styles are generally more useful for business presentations.

Memorized presentations are written out ahead of time, memorized, and recited verbatim. Memorization

memorized presentation
a presentation that is written out ahead of time, memorized, and recited verbatim

Figure 13-5 Effective Slide Design: Poor (left) and Good (right) Examples

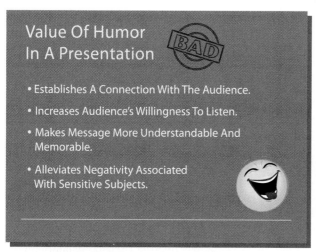

Here's why the good slide is better:

Template and Graphics
- Substitutes professional template for unrelated "Edge" template.
- Substitutes clip art of smiley face with relevant image of involved presenter.

Color Scheme
- Uses cool color that is more relaxing than warm color and fits topic's professional mood.
- Uses complementary foreground colors (slide title and bulleted list) and accent color (bullet) that have high contrast with background for easy readability. Placing brighter color in slide title pulls audience's eyes first to descriptive title, then to list.

Space Use and Layout
- Provides appropriate white space (no more than 75 percent coverage).
- Follows 7 × 7 rule by limiting content to value of humor.
- Balances size of clip art with text and two-line title.

Typography
- Selects fonts to create informal tone and to differentiate slide title from bulleted lists:

    Slide title: Sans serif font, Arial, 40 points.

    Bulleted list: Serif font, Times New Roman, 32 points.
- Uses initial caps in slide title and capitalizes only first word in bulleted list.
- Omits periods at end of bulleted items.

has the greatest limitations of the speech styles. Speakers are almost totally unable to react to feedback, and the speaker who forgets a point and develops a mental block may lose the entire speech. Memorized speeches tend to sound monotonous, restrict natural body gestures and motions, and lack conviction. For short religious or fraternal rites, however, the memorized presentation is often impressive.

Manuscript delivery, also known as **scripted,** involves writing the speech word for word and reading it to the audience. For complex material and technical conference presentations, manuscript presentations ensure content coverage. Additionally, this style protects speak-

ers against being misquoted (when accuracy is absolutely critical) and fits into exact time constraints, as in television or radio presentations. Speeches are sometimes read when time does not permit advance preparation or several different presentations are given in one day (e.g., the speaking demands of the President of the United States and other top-level executives). Manuscript presentations limit speaker–audience rapport, particularly when speakers keep their eyes and heads buried in their manuscripts. Tele-prompters that project the

manuscript (scripted) delivery
writing the speech word for word and reading it to the audience

manuscript out of view of the audience allow the speaker to appear to be speaking extemporaneously.

Impromptu delivery is frightening to many people because the speaker is called on without prior notice. Experienced speakers can easily analyze the request, organize supporting points from memory, and present a simple, logical response. In many cases, businesspeople can anticipate a request and be prepared to discuss a particular idea when requested (e.g., status report on an area of control at a team meeting). Because professionals are expected to present ideas and data spontaneously on demand, businesspeople must develop the ability to deliver impromptu presentations.

Extemporaneous presentations are planned, prepared, and rehearsed but not written in detail. Brief notes prompt the speaker on the next point, but the exact words are chosen spontaneously as the speaker interacts with the audience and identifies their specific needs. Extemporaneous presentations allow natural body gestures, sound conversational, and can be delivered with conviction because the speaker is speaking "with" the listeners and not "to" them. The audience appreciates a warm, genuine communicator and will forgive an occasional stumble or groping for a word that occurs with an extemporaneous presentation. Learning to construct useful notes will aid you in becoming an accomplished extemporaneous speaker.

Vocal Qualities

The sound of your voice is a powerful instrument used to deliver your message and to project your professional image. To maximize your vocal strengths, focus on three important qualities of speech—phonation, articulation, and pronunciation.

Phonation involves both the production and the variation of the speaker's vocal tone. You project your voice and convey feelings—even thoughts—by varying your vocal tones. Important factors of phonation are pitch, volume, and rate. These factors permit us to recognize other people's voices over the phone.

- **Pitch** is the highness or lowness of the voice. Pleasant voices have medium or low pitch; however, a varied pitch pattern is desirable. The pitch of the voice rises and falls to reflect emotions; for example, fear and anger are reflected in a higher pitch; sadness, in a lower pitch. Lower pitches for both men and women are perceived as sounding more authoritative; higher pitches indicate less confidence and suggest pleading or whining. Techniques to be discussed later in this section can help you lower the pitch of your voice.

- **Volume** refers to the loudness of tones. Generally, good voices are easily heard by everyone in the audience but are not too loud. Use variety to hold the audience's attention, to emphasize words or ideas, or to create a desired atmosphere (energetic, excited tone vs. quiet, serious one).

- **Rate** is the speed at which words are spoken. Never speak so quickly that the audience cannot understand your message or so slowly that they are distracted or irritated. Vary the rate with the demands of the situation. For example, speak at a slower rate when presenting a complex concept or emphasizing an important idea. Pause to add emphasis to a key point or to transition to another major section of the presentation. Speak at a faster rate when presenting less important information or when reviewing.

An inherent problem related to speaking rate is verbal fillers—also called *nonwords*. Verbal fillers, such as *uhhh, ahhh, ummm,* and *errr,* are irritating to the audience and destroy your effectiveness. Many speakers fill space with their own verbal fillers; these include *you know, I mean, basically, like I said, okay,* and *as a matter of fact.* Because of the conversational style of impromptu and extemporaneous presentations, a speaker will naturally grope for a word or the next idea from time to time. Become aware of verbal fillers you frequently use by critiquing a tape or video recording and then focus on replacing them with a three- to five-second pause. This brief gap between thoughts gives you an opportunity to think about what you want to say next and time for your audience to absorb your idea. Presenting an idea (sound bite) and then pausing briefly is an effective way to influence your audience positively. The listener will not notice the slight delay, and the absence of meaningless words will make you appear more confident and polished. Also avoid annoying speech habits, such as clearing your throat or coughing, that shift the audience's attention from the speech to the speaker.

The following activities will help you achieve good vocal qualities (medium to low pitch and audible, steady pace, with variations to reflect mood):

- **Breathe properly and relax.** Nervousness affects normal breathing patterns and is reflected in vocal tone and pitch. The better prepared you are, the bet-

impromptu delivery
being called on to speak without prior notice

extemporaneous presentation
a presentation planned, prepared, and rehearsed but not written in detail

phonation
the production and the variation of the speaker's vocal tone

pitch
the highness or lowness of the voice

volume
the loudness of tones

rate
the speed at which words are spoken

ter your phonation will be. Although relaxing may seem difficult to practice before a speech, a few deep breaths, just as swimmers take before diving, can help.

- **Listen to yourself.** A recording of your voice reveals much about pitch, intensity, and duration. Most people are amazed to find their voices are not quite what they had expected. "I never dreamed I sounded that bad" is a common reaction. Nasal twangs usually result from a failure to speak from the diaphragm, which involves taking in and letting out air through the larynx, where the vocal cords operate. High pitch may occur from the same cause, or it may be a product of speaking too fast.

- **Develop flexibility.** The good speaking voice is somewhat musical, with words and sounds similar to notes in a musical scale. Read each of the following sentences aloud, and emphasize the *italicized* word in each. Even though the sentences are identical, emphasizing different words changes the meaning.

I am happy you are here.	*Maybe I'm the only happy one.*
I *am* happy you are here.	*I really am.*
I am *happy* you are here.	*Happy best describes my feeling.*
I am happy *you* are here.	*Yes, you especially.*
I am happy you *are* here.	*You may not be happy, but I am.*
I am happy you are *here*.	*Here and not somewhere else.*

Articulation involves smooth, fluent, and pleasant speech. It results from the way in which a speaker produces and joins sounds. Faulty articulation is often caused by not carefully forming individual sounds. Common examples include:

- Dropping word endings—saying *workin'* for *working*.
- Running words together—saying *kinda* for *kind of*, *gonna* for *going to*.
- Imprecise enunciation—saying *dis* for *this*, *wid* for *with*, *dem* for *them*, *pin* for *pen*, or *pitcher* for *picture*.

These examples should not be confused with *dialect*, which people informally call an *accent*. A dialect is a variation in pronunciation, usually of vowels, from one part of the country to another. Actually, everyone speaks a dialect; speech experts can often identify, even pinpoint, the section of the country from where a speaker comes. In the United States, common dialects are New England, New York, Southern, Texan, Midwestern, and so forth. Within each of these, minor dialects may arise regionally or from immigrant influence. The simple fact is that when people interact, they influence each other even down to speech sounds. Many prominent speakers have developed a rather universal dialect, known as Standard American Speech or American Broadcast English, that seems to be effective no matter who the audience is. This model for professional language is the most widely used of all regional dialects in the United States, is used by major broadcasters, and is easily understood by those learning English as a second language because they likely listened to this speech pattern as they learned the language.[9]

You can improve the clarity of your voice, reduce strain and voice distortion, and increase your expressiveness by following these guidelines:

- **Stand up straight with your shoulders back and breathe from your diaphragm rather than your nose and mouth.** If you are breathing correctly, you can then use your mouth and teeth to form sounds precisely. For example, vowels are always sounded with the mouth open and the tongue clear of the palate. Consonants are responsible primarily for the distinctness of speech and are formed by an interference with or stoppage of outgoing breath.

- **Focus on completing the endings of all words, not running words together, and enunciating words correctly.** To identify recurring enunciation errors, listen to a recording and seek feedback from others.

- **Obtain formal training to improve your speech.** Pursue a self-study program by purchasing tapes that help you reduce your dialect and move more closely to a universal dialect. You can also enroll in a diction course to improve your speech patterns or arrange for private lessons from a voice coach.

Pronunciation involves using principles of phonetics to create accurate sounds, rhythm, stress, and intonation. People may articulate perfectly but still mispronounce words. A dictionary provides the best source to review pronunciation. Two pronunciations are often given for a word, the first one being the desired pronunciation and the second an acceptable variation. For example, to adopt a pronunciation commonly used in England such as *shedule* for *schedule* or *a-gane* for *again* could be considered affected speech. In other cases, the dictionary allows some leeway. The first choice for pronouncing *data* is to pronounce the first *a* long, as in *date;* but common usage is fast making pronunciation of the short *a* sound, as in *cat,* acceptable. Likewise, the preferred pronunciation of *often* is with a silent *t.* Good speakers use proper pronunciation and refer to the dictionary frequently in both pronunciation and vocabulary development.

When your voice qualities combine to make your messages pleasingly receptive, your primary concerns revolve around developing an effective delivery style.

Delivery Style

Speaking effectively is both an art and a skill. Careful planning and practice are essential for building speaking skills.

Before the Presentation

Follow these guidelines when preparing for your presentation:

- **Prepare thoroughly.** You can expect a degree of nervousness as you anticipate speaking before a group. This natural tension is constructive because it increases your concentration and your energy and enhances your performance. Being well prepared is the surest way to control speech anxiety. Develop an outline for your presentation that supports your purpose and addresses the needs of your audience. Additionally, John Davis, a successful speech coach, warned: "Never, never, never give a speech on a subject you don't believe in. You'll fail. On the other hand, if you prepare properly, know your material, and *believe* in it . . . your audience will not only hear but *feel* your message."[10]

- **Prepare effective presentation support**

tools. Follow the guidelines presented in the prior section to select and design presentation support tools appropriate for your audience and useful in delivering the presentation: visuals, handouts, and notes pages. Additionally, develop a contingency plan in the event of technical difficulties with computer equipment. Prepared presenters have backup overheads and hard copies of their presentations and may have a backup computer preloaded and ready. Arrive early so you can troubleshoot unexpected technological glitches. Despite your degree of planning, however, technical problems may occur during your presentation. Remain calm, and correct them as quickly and professionally as you can. Take heart in the fact that Bill Gates' computer once crashed when he introduced a new version of Windows!

- **Practice, but do not rehearse.** Your goal is to become familiar with the key phrases on your note cards so that you can deliver the presentation naturally as if you are talking with the audience—not reciting the presentation or acting out a role. Avoid overpracticing that may make your presentation sound mechanical and limit your ability to respond to the audience.

- **Practice the entire presentation.** This practice will allow you to identify (1) flaws in organization or unity; (2) long, complex sentences or impersonal expressions inappropriate in a presentation; and (3) "verbal potholes." Verbal potholes include word combinations that could cause you to stumble, a word you have trouble pronouncing ("irrelevant" or "statistics"), or a word you perceive accentuates your dialect ("get" may sound like "git" regardless of the intention of a southern speaker).

- **Spend additional time practicing the introduction and conclusion.** You will want to deliver these important parts with finesse while making a confident connection with the audience. A good closing serves to leave the audience in a good mood and may help overcome some possible mistakes made during the speech. Depending on the techniques used, consider memorizing significant brief statements to ensure their accuracy and impact (e.g., direct quotation, exact statistic, etc.).

- **Practice displaying presentation visuals so that your delivery appears effortless and seamless.** Your goal is to make the technology virtually transparent, positioned in the background to support you as the primary focus of the presentation. First, be sure you know basic commands for advancing through your presentation without displaying distracting drop-down menus. Develop skill in returning to a specific slide in the event of a computer glitch or a spontaneous question from the audience.

pronunciation
principles of phonetics to create accurate sounds, rhythm, stress, and intonation

© Fred Prouser/Reuters/Landov

- **Seek feedback on your performance that will enable you to polish your delivery and improve organization.** Critique your own performance by practicing in front of a mirror and evaluating a videotape of your presentation. If possible, present to a small audience for feedback and to minimize anxiety when presenting to the real audience.

- **Request a lectern to hold your notes and to steady a shaky hand, at least until you gain some confidence and experience.** Keep in mind, though, that weaning yourself from the lectern will eliminate a physical barrier between you and the audience. Without the lectern, you will speak more naturally. If you are using a microphone, ask for a portable microphone so that you can move freely.

- **Insist on a proper, impressive introduction if the audience knows little about you.** An effective introduction will establish your credibility as the speaker on the subject to be discussed and will make the audience eager to hear you speak. You may prepare your own introduction as professional speakers do, or you can provide concise, targeted information that answers these three questions: (1) Why is the subject relevant? (2) Who is the speaker? and (3) What credentials qualify the speaker to talk about the subject? Attempt to talk with the person introducing you to verify any information, especially the pronunciation of your name, and to review the format of the presentation (time limit, question-and-answer period, etc.). Be certain to thank the person who made the introduction. "Thank you, Mr. President" or "Thank you for your kind introduction, Ms. Garcia" are adequate. Then, follow with your own introduction to your presentation.

- **Dress appropriately to create a strong professional image and to bolster your self-confidence.** An audience's initial impression of your personal appearance—your grooming and clothing—affects their ability to accept you as a credible speaker. Because first impressions are difficult to overcome, take ample time to groom yourself immaculately and to select clothing that is appropriate for the speaking occasion and consistent with the audience's expectations.

- **Arrive early to become familiar with the setup of the room and to check the equipment.** Check the location of your chair, the lectern, the projection screen, and light switches. Check the microphone, and ensure that all equipment is in the appropriate place and working properly. Project your electronic presentation so you can adjust the color scheme to ensure maximum readability. Finally, identify the technician who will be responsible for resolving any technical problems that may occur during the presentation.

During the Presentation

The following are things you can do during your presentation to increase your effectiveness as a speaker:

- **Communicate confidence, warmth, and enthusiasm for the presentation and the time spent with the audience.** "Your listeners won't care how much you know until they know how much you care" is pertinent advice.[11] Follow these guidelines:

  - *Exhibit a confident appearance with alert posture.* Stand tall with your shoulders back and your stomach tucked in. Stand in the "ready position"— no slouching or hunching over the lectern or leaning back on your feet. Keep weight forward with knees slightly flexed so you are ready to move easily rather than rooted rigidly in one spot, hiding behind the lectern.

  - *Smile genuinely throughout the presentation.* Pause as you take your place behind the lectern, and smile before you speak the first word. Smile as you finish your presentation, and wait for the applause.

  - *Maintain steady eye contact with the audience in random places throughout the room.* Stay with one person approximately three to five seconds—long enough to finish a complete thought or sentence to convince the listener you are communicating individually with him or her. If the audience is large, select a few friendly faces and concentrate on speaking to them rather than a sea of nondescript faces.

  - *Refine gestures to portray a relaxed, approachable appearance.* Vary hand motions to emphasize important points; otherwise, let hands fall naturally to your side. Practice using only one hand to make points unless you specifically need two hands, such as when drawing a figure or showing dimensions or location. Eliminate any nervous gestures that can distract the audience (e.g., clenching hands in front or behind body, steepling hands in praying position, placing hands in pocket, jingling keys or change, or playing with a ring or pencil).

- *Move from behind the lectern and toward the audience to reduce the barrier created between you and the audience.* You may stand to one side and casually present a relaxed pose beside the lectern. However, avoid methodically walking from place to place without a purpose.

- **Exercise strong vocal qualities.** Review the guidelines provided for using your voice to project confidence and credibility.

- **Watch your audience.** They will tell you how you are doing and whether you should shorten your speech. Be attentive to negative feedback in the form of talking, coughing, moving chairs, and other signs of discomfort.

- **Use your visuals effectively.** Many speakers will go to a great deal of effort to prepare good presentation visuals—and then not use them effectively. Inexperienced speakers often ignore the visual altogether or fall into the habit of simply nodding their heads toward the visual. Neither of these techniques is adequate for involving the audience with the visual. In fact, if the material is complex, the speaker is likely to lose the audience completely.

  - *Step to one side of the visual so the audience can see it.* Use a pointer if necessary. Direct your remarks to the audience so that you can maintain eye contact and resist the temptation to look over your shoulder to read the information from the screen behind you.

  - *Paraphrase the visual rather than reading it line for line.* To increase the quality of your delivery, develop a workable method of recording what you plan to say about each graphic.

- **Handle questions from the audience during the presentation.** Questions often disrupt carefully laid plans. At the same time, questions provide feedback, clarify points, and ensure understanding. Often, people ask questions that will be answered later in the presentation. In these cases, you should say, "I believe the next slide will clarify that point. If not, we will come back to it." If the question can be answered quickly, the speaker should do so while indicating that it will also be covered later.

  Anticipate and prepare for questions that might be raised. You may generate presentation visuals pertaining to certain anticipated questions and display them only if the question is posed. An audience will appreciate your thorough and complete explanation and your willingness and ability to adjust your presentation to their needs—this strategy is much more professional than stumbling through an explanation or delaying the answer until the information is available. Speakers giving electronic presentations have ready access to enormous amounts of information that can be instantly displayed for audience discussion. Hyperlinks created within a presentation file will move a speaker instantaneously to a specific slide within the presentation, a different presentation, or even a spreadsheet file. The hyperlink can be used to play a music file embedded in a presentation, to start a CD, or to link to an Internet site.

- **Keep within the time limit.** Be prepared to complete the presentation within the allotted time. In many organizations, speakers have one or more rehearsals before delivering reports to a group such as a board of directors. These rehearsals, or dry runs, are made before other executives and are critiqued, timed, revised, and rehearsed again. Presentation software makes rehearsing your timing as simple as clicking a button and advancing through the slides as you practice. By evaluating the total presentation time and the time spent on each slide, you can modify the presentation and rehearse again until the presentation fits the time slot.

After the Presentation

How you handle the time following a presentation is as important as preparing for the presentation itself:

- **Be prepared for a question-and-answer period.** Encourage the audience to ask questions, recognizing an opportunity to ensure that your presentation meets audience needs. Restate the question, if necessary, to ensure that everyone heard the question, and ask the questioner if your answer was adequate. Be courteous even to hostile questioners to maintain the respect of your audience. Stay in control of the time by announcing that you have time for one or two more questions and then invite individual questions when the presentation is over.

- **Distribute handouts.** Distribute the handout when it is needed rather than at the beginning of the presentation. Otherwise, the audience may read the handout while you are explaining background information needed to understand the written ideas. If you expect the audience to take notes directly on the handout or if the audience will need to refer to the handout immediately, distribute the handout at the beginning of the presentation or before it begins. To keep control of the audience's attention, be sure listeners know when they should be looking at the handout or listening to you. If the handout is intended as resource material only, post the handout to a web page or place it on a table at the back of the room and on a table at the front for those who come by to talk with you after the presentation.

Special Presentation Situations

objective ⑤
Discuss strategies for presenting in alternate delivery situations such as culturally diverse audiences and team and distance presentations.

Certain situations may require additional considerations when preparing for and delivering a presentation. These include situations in which you may be presenting to a culturally diverse audience, presenting as a team, or delivering a presentation using distance technologies.

Speaking to Culturally Diverse Audiences

When speaking to a culturally diverse audience, you will want to be as natural as possible while adjusting your message for important cultural variations. Using empathy, you can effectively focus on the listener as an individual rather than a stereotype of a specific culture. Be open and willing to learn, and you will reap the benefits of communicating effectively with people who possess a variety of strengths and creative abilities. Additionally, follow these suggestions for presenting to people from outside your own culture:

- **Speak simply.** Use simple English and short sentences. Avoid acronyms and expressions that may be confusing to non-native English speakers—namely, slang, jargon, figurative expressions, and sports analogies.

- **Avoid words that trigger negative emotional responses such as anger, fear, or suspicion.** Such "red flag" words vary among cultures; thus, try to anticipate audience reaction and choose your words carefully.

- **Enunciate each word precisely and speak somewhat more slowly.** Clear, articulate speech is especially important when the audience is not familiar with various dialects. Avoid the temptation to speak in a loud voice, a habit considered rude in any culture and especially annoying to the Japanese, who perceive the normal tone of North Americans as too loud.

- **Be extremely cautious in the use of humor and jokes.** Cultures that prefer more formality may find your humor and jokes inappropriate or think you are not serious about your purpose. Asians, for instance, do not appreciate jokes about family members and the elderly.

- **Learn the culture's preferences for a direct or indirect presentation.** While North Americans tend to prefer directness, with the main idea presented first, many cultures, such as Japanese, Latin American, and Arabic, consider this straightforward approach tactless and rude.

- **Adapt to subtle differences in nonverbal communication.** The direct eye contact expected by most North Americans is not typical of Asian listeners, who keep their eyes lowered and avoid eye contact to show respect. Arab audiences may stare into your eyes in an attempt to "see into the window of the soul." Cultures also vary on personal space and degree of physical contact (slap on the back or arm around the other as signs of friendship).

- **Adapt your presentation style and dress to fit the degree of formality of the culture.** Some cultures prefer a higher degree of formality than the casual style of North Americans. To accommodate, dress conservatively; strive to connect with the audience in a formal, reserved manner; and use highly professional visuals rather than jotting ideas on a flipchart.

- **Seek feedback to determine whether the audience is understanding your message.** Observe listeners carefully for signs of misunderstanding, restating ideas

© Ryan McVay/Digital Vision/Getty Images

as necessary. Consider allowing time for questions after short segments of your presentation. Avoid asking "Is that clear?" or "Do you understand?" as these statements might elicit a "Yes" answer if the person perceives saying "No" to be a sign of incompetence.

Potential frustrations can also occur when presentations or meetings bring together people of cultures who are not time conscious and who believe that personal relationships are the basis of business dealings (e.g., Asian, Latin American) with North Americans, who see "time as money." When communicating with cultures that are not time driven, be patient with what you may consider time-consuming formalities and courtesies and lengthy decision-making styles when you would rather get right down to business or move to the next point. Recognize that the presentation may not begin on time or stay on a precise time schedule. Be prepared to allow additional time at the beginning of the presentation to establish rapport and credibility with the audience, and perhaps provide brief discussion periods during the presentation devoted to building relationships.

Be patient and attentive during long periods of silence; in many cultures, people are inclined to stay silent unless they have something significant to say or if they are considering (not necessarily rejecting) an idea. In fact, some Japanese have asked how North Americans can think and talk at the same time. Understanding patterns of silence can help you feel more comfortable during these seemingly endless moments and less compelled to fill the gaps with unnecessary words or to make concessions before the other side has a chance to reply.

Gaining competence in matters of cultural difference will enable you to concentrate on the presentation rather than agonizing over an awkward, embarrassing slip in protocol. Your audience will appreciate your willingness to learn and value their customs. Being sensitive to cultural issues and persistent in learning specific differences in customs and practices can minimize confusion and unnecessary embarrassment.

Team Presentations

Because much of the work in business today is done in teams, many presentations are planned and delivered by a team of presenters. Team presentations give an organization an opportunity to showcase its brightest talent while capitalizing on each person's unique presentation skills. Email, collaborative software, and other technologies make it easy to develop, edit, review, and deliver team presentations.

The potential payoff of many team presentations is quite high—perhaps a $200,000 contract or a million-dollar

RESIST the sure-to-fail strategies of many presenters who decide to "wing it" or "blow off" team presentations.

account. Yet, according to experts, team presentations fail primarily because presenters don't devote enough time and resources to develop and rehearse them.[12] Resist the sure-to-fail strategies of many presenters who decide to "wing it" or "blow off" team presentations. Instead, adapt the skills you already possess in planning and delivering an individual presentation to ensure a successful team presentation. Follow these guidelines:

- **Select a winning team.** Begin by choosing a leader who is well liked and respected by the team, is knowledgeable of the project, is well organized, and will follow through. Likewise, the leader should be committed to leading the team in the development of a cohesive strategy for the presentation as well as the delegation of specific responsibilities to individual members. Frank Carillo, president of Executive Communications Group, warns team presenters that the problem with "divvying up" work into pieces is that the "pieces don't fit together well when they come back."[13]

  The core team members, along with management, should choose a balanced mix of members to complete the team. Use these questions to guide team selection: What are this member's complementary strengths and style (e.g., technical expertise, personality traits, presentation skills)? Can this member meet the expectations of the audience (e.g., a numbers person, technical person, person with existing relationship with the audience)? Is this member willing to support the team strategy and commit to the schedule?[14]

- **Agree on the purpose and schedule.** The team should plan the presentation using the same process as for an individual presentation. Agreeing on the purpose to be achieved and selecting content that focuses on a specific audience will prevent the panic and stress caused by an individual's submitting material that does not support the presentation. The quality of the presentation deteriorates when material must be hastily redone in the final days before the deadline or when unacceptable material is included only because the presenter worked so hard on it. Mapping out a complete presentation strategy can also minimize bickering among team members because of uneven workloads or unfavorable work assignments.

  The team will also need to agree on a standard design for presentation visuals to ensure consistency in the visuals prepared by individual presenters. Assign a person to merge the various files, to edit for consistency in design elements and the use of jargon and specialized terminology, and to proofread carefully for grammatical accuracy.

Developing a rehearsal schedule ensures adequate time for preparation and practice. Many experts recommend five practice sessions to produce team presentations that are delivered with a unified look. Planning time in the schedule to present before a review team is especially useful for obtaining feedback on team continuity and adjustments needed to balance major discrepancies in the delivery styles of individual presenters.

- **Plan seamless transitions between segments and presenters.** A great deal of your rehearsal time for a team presentation should be spent planning and rehearsing appropriate verbal and physical transitions between team members. The transitions summarize each part of the presentation and make the whole presentation cohesive. This continuity makes your team look polished and conveys the tone that each member really cares about the team. Follow these suggestions for ensuring seamless presentations:

  - *Decide who will open and conclude the presentation.* The team member who knows the audience and has established rapport is a logical choice for these two critical sections of a presentation. If no one knows the audience, select the member with the strongest presentation skills and personality traits for connecting well with strangers. This person will introduce all team members and give a brief description of the roles they will play in the presentation.

  - *Build natural bridges between segments of the presentation and presenters.* A lead presenter must build a bridge between his or her presentation and that of the teammate who will immediately follow. If a lead presenter forgets to make the connection to the next section clear, the next person must summarize what's been said and then preview his or her section. These transitions may seem repetitive to a team that has been working with the material for a long time; however, audiences require clear guideposts through longer team presentations. Also, courtesies such as maintaining eye contact, thanking the previous speaker, and clearing the presentation area for the next speaker communicates an important message that the presenters are in sync—they know each other and work well together.[15]

  - *Deliver as a team.* You must present a unified look and communicate to the audience that you care about the team. Spend your time on the "sideline" paying close attention to team members as they are presenting and monitoring the audience for subtle hints of how the presentation is going. Be on guard to assist the presenter wherever needed—the presenter has not noticed that a wrong presentation visual is displayed but the audience has, equipment malfunctions, and so on.

- **Field questions as a team.** Decide in advance who will field questions to avoid awkward stares and silence that erode the audience's confidence in your team. Normally, the person presenting a section is the logical person to field questions about that section. You may refer questions to team members who are more knowledgeable, but avoid pleading looks for that person to rescue you. Rather, check visually to see if the person wants to respond and then ask if he or she would like to add information. Tactfully contradict other presenters only when the presenter makes a mistake that will cause major problems later. While you should be ready to help presenters having difficulty, resist the urge to tack on your response to a presenter's answer when the question has already been answered adequately.

Distance Presentations

Videoconferencing has been used for some time for large, high-exposure activities, such as quarterly executive staff presentations, companywide addresses, new product launches, and crisis management. The technology's decreased cost, improved quality, and increased ease of use have opened videoconferencing to myriad settings.

Substantial cost savings from reduced travel and time is a compelling reason for companies to use videoconferencing. Videoconferencing also leads to important communication benefits that result from:[16]

- Improving employee productivity by calling impromptu videoconferences to clear up issues.
- Involving more people in key decisions rather than limiting important discussions to those who are allowed to travel.
- Involving the expertise critical to the mission, regardless of geographic boundaries.
- Creating a consistent corporate culture rather than depending on memos to describe company policy.
- Improving employees' quality of life by reducing travel time that often cuts into personal time (e.g., Saturday night layovers for a reasonable airfare).

Internet conferencing or *webcasting* allows companies to conduct a presentation in real time over the Internet simultaneously with a conference telephone call. Because it runs on each participant's Internet browser, a presentation can reach hundreds of locations at once. While listening to the call, participants can go to a designated website and view slides or a PowerPoint pre-

sentation that is displayed in sync with the speaker's statements being heard on the telephone. Participants key comments and questions in chat boxes or press a keypad system to respond to an audience poll, thus giving valuable feedback without interrupting the speaker.

Major software products being used for live web presentations include Contigo Internet Conferencing System, Netpodium Interactive Broadcasting Suite, and Placeware Conference Center. Microsoft PowerPoint, in conjunction with Microsoft NetMeeting, can also be used for online presentations in real time.

Companies deliver live web presentations on issues ranging from internal briefings on new developments and organizational and procedural changes to product strategy and training presentations. For example, Ernst & Young uses Netpodium to announce organizational changes and has found it to be an effective alternative for memos and emails that weren't always remembered or understood. People most affected by an organizational change are able to interact with leaders in the firm who are announcing the change. Additionally, businesses using the web presentation method report that more questions are typically asked than in other meeting formats, resulting in more effective communication.

Follow these guidelines for adapting your presentation skills to videoconferences and web presentations:

- **Determine whether a distance delivery method is appropriate for the presentation.** Is the presentation purpose suited to the technology? Can costs in time, money, and human energy be justified? Are key people willing and able to participate? For example, a videoconference for a formal presentation such as an important speech by the CEO to a number of locations justifies the major expense and brings attention to the importance of the message. Distance delivery formats are inappropriate for presentations that cover highly sensitive or confidential issues, for persuasive or problem-solving meetings where no relationship has been established among the participants, and whenever participants are unfamiliar with and perhaps unsupportive of the technology.

- **Establish rapport with the participants prior to the distance presentation.** If possible, meet with or phone participants beforehand to get to know them and gain insights about their attitudes. This rapport will enhance your ability to interpret subtle nonverbal cues and to cultivate the relationship further through the distance format. Emailing or faxing a short questionnaire or posting presentation slides with a request for questions is an excellent way to establish a connection with participants and to ensure that the presentation is tailored to audience needs. Some enterprising distance presenters engage participants in email discussions before the presentation and then use this dialogue to develop positive interaction during the presentation.

- **Become proficient in delivering and participating through distance technology.** Begin by becoming familiar with the equipment and the surroundings. While technical support staff may be available to manage equipment and transmission tasks, your goal is to concentrate on the contribution you are to make and not your intimidation with the delivery method.

  - *Concentrate on projecting positive nonverbal messages.* Keep a natural, friendly expression; relax and smile. Avoid the tendency to stare into the lens of the camera. Instead of this glassy-eyed stare, look naturally at the entire audience as you would in a live presentation. Speak clearly with as much energy as you can. If a lag occurs between the video and audio transmission, adjust your timing to avoid interrupting other speakers. Use gestures to reinforce points, but avoid fast or excessive motion that will appear blurry. Avoid side conversations, coughing, and throat clearing, which could trigger voice-activated microphones. Pay close attention to other presenters to guard against easy distraction in a distance environment and to capture subtle nonverbal cues. You will need to judge the vocal tone of the person asking a question because you won't see faces.

  - *Adjust camera settings to enhance communication.* Generally, adjust the camera so that all participants can be seen, but zoom in more closely on participants when you wish to clearly observe nonverbal language. Project a wide-angle shot of yourself during rapport-building comments at the presentation's beginning and then zoom in to signal the start of the agenda or to emphasize an important point during the presentation. While some systems accommodate a split screen, others allow participants to view either you or your presentation visuals only. You will want to switch the camera between a view of you and your presentation visuals, depending on what is needed at the time.

- **Develop high-quality graphics appropriate for the particular distance format.** Even more than in a live presentation, you will need graphics to engage and maintain participants'

attention. Graphics are a welcome variation to the "talking head"—you—displayed on the monitor for long periods. Some companies provide assistance from a webmaster or graphics support staff in preparing slide shows specifically for distance presentations. Also, e-conferencing companies will develop and post presentation slides and host live web presentations, including managing email messages and audience polling. Regardless of the support you receive, you should understand basic guidelines for preparing effective visuals for videoconferencing and web presentations.

- *Videoconferences.* Readability of text will be a critical issue when displaying visuals during a videoconference because text becomes fuzzy when transmitted through compressed video. Select large, sturdy fonts, and choose a color scheme that provides high contrast between the background and the text. Stay with a tested color scheme such as dark blue background, yellow title text, and white bulleted list text to ensure readability. Projecting your visuals ahead of time so you can adjust the color scheme and other design elements (font face and size) is an especially good idea.

- *Web presentations.* In addition to considering overall appeal, clarity, and readability, web presentations must be designed for minimal load time and compatibility with various computers. For your first presentation, consider using a web template in your electronic presentations software and experiment with the appropriateness of other designs as you gain experience.

When Your Presentation Has to Deliver Itself

Stand-alone presentations designed specifically for web delivery require unique design strategies to compensate for the absence of a speaker.[17]

- Consider posting text-based explanations in the notes view area or adding vocal narration.
- Develop interactive slide formats that allow viewers to navigate to the most useful information in your presentation. For example, design an agenda slide that includes hyperlinks to the first slide in each section of the presentation.
- Select simple, high-quality graphics that convey ideas effectively.
- Plan limited animation that focuses audience attention on specific ideas on the slide.
- Consider adding video if bandwidth is not an issue.

Preparing Résumés and Application Messages

Preparing for the Job Search

objective ①
Prepare for employment by considering relevant information about yourself as it relates to job requirements.

Work isn't something that happens from 8 to 5, with life happening after 5 P.M. Life and work are interconnected, and true satisfaction comes from being able to fully express yourself in what you do. This means merging who you are—your values, emotions, capabilities, and desires—with the activities you perform on the job.[1]

An ideal job provides satisfaction at all human need levels, from basic economic to self-actualizing needs. The right job for you will not be drudgery; the work itself will be satisfying. It will give you a sense of well-being, and you will sense its positive impact on others. Synchronizing your work with your core beliefs and talents leads to enthusiasm and fulfillment. You will probably work 10,000 days of your life, not including time spent commuting and on other peripheral activities. Why spend all of this time doing something unfulfilling when you could just as easily spend it doing what you enjoy?

Students often devote too little time and thought to career goals, or they unnecessarily postpone making career decisions. Are you willing to spend the necessary time gathering, recording, and analyzing information that will lead to a satisfying career? Are you ready to

objectives

① Prepare for employment by considering relevant information about yourself as it relates to job requirements.

② Identify career opportunities using traditional and electronic methods.

③ Plan a résumé that reflects your qualifications and communicates your value to potential employers.

④ Prepare an organized, persuasive résumé that is adapted for print, scanning, and electronic postings.

⑤ Utilize employment tools other than the résumé that can enhance employability.

⑥ Write an application message that effectively introduces an accompanying print (designed) or electronic résumé.

start compiling information that will guide you to the best career for you? Finding a job is a process, not an event; it's not too early to get started.

Just as finding the right career is important to you, finding the right employees is important to employers. Before they can offer you a job, employers need information about you—in writing. Your résumé is a vital communication tool that provides a basis for judgment about your capabilities on the job. In preparing this document, your major tasks will be gathering essential information about yourself and the job using traditional and electronic resources, planning and organizing the résumé to showcase your key qualifications, and adapt-

ing the résumé for various types of delivery. You may also need to supplement your résumé with examples of your accomplishments and abilities. Finally, you'll prepare persuasive application messages appropriate for the delivery of your résumé.

Gathering Essential Information

The job search begins with research—collecting, compiling, and analyzing information—in order to assess your marketability. The key accomplishments that surface from this thoughtful analysis will be the main ideas touted in a résumé or an interview. The research phase of the job

search involves the steps shown in Figure 14-1 and is summarized as follows:

1. **Gather relevant information for decision making.** Complete a self-assessment to identify your own qualifications related to the job and an analysis of the career field that interests you and a specific job in that field. Follow up with an interview of a career person in your field to provide additional information.

2. **Prepare a company/job profile.** Compile the information you gathered into a format that allows you to compare your qualifications with the company and job requirements—to determine a possible match between you and the potential job.

3. **Identify unique selling points and specific support.** Determine several key qualifications and accomplishments that enhance your marketability. These are the key selling points you'll target in your résumé and later in a job interview.

Identifying Potential Career Opportunities

objective ②
Identify career opportunities using traditional and electronic methods.

Plan to begin your job search for prospective employers months beforehand. Waiting too long to begin and then hurrying through the job search process could affect your ability to land a satisfying job.

Before you begin, take the time to develop an organized strategy for your search efforts. You might download a template such as Microsoft's job search log (http://search. officeupdate.microsoft.com/ TemplateGallery) or invest in software such as WinWay Resume, WinWay Resume Deluxe, or Resumail Resume to

---

Figure 14-1 Process of Applying for a Job

STEP 1	STEP 2	STEP 3	STEP 4	STEP 5
Conduct research and analysis of self, career, and job	Identify a job listing using traditional and electronic sources	Prepare targeted résumé and application message in required formats	Consider supplementing the résumé: Portfolio (print or electronic) or video recording	Interview with companies

RÉSUMÉ PRESENTATION AND DELIVERY OPTIONS

Print (Designed)
- Mail to company accompanied by application letter
- Mail as follow-up to electronic submission

Scannable
- Print résumé formatted for computer scanning

Electronic Postings
- Email to network contacts, career and corporate sites, and career service centers
- Online form
- Electronic portfolio at personal website
- Beamer to PDA or cell phone

simplify the task of tracking your contacts. You'll need a record of the name, address, and telephone number of each employer with a job in which you have an interest. Later, record the date of each job call you make and receive (along with what you learned from the call), the date of each returned call, the name of the person who called, the date you sent a résumé, and so on. Maintaining this list alphabetically will enable you to find a name quickly and respond effectively to a returned telephone call.

Your search for potential career opportunities likely will involve traditional and electronic job search sources.

Using Traditional Sources

Traditional means of locating a job include printed sources, networks, career services centers, employers' offices, employment agencies and contractors, and professional organizations.

Printed Sources

Numerous printed sources are useful in identifying firms in need of employees. Responses to advertised positions in the employment sections of newspapers should be made as quickly as possible after the ad is circulated. If your résumé is received early and is impressive, you could get a favorable response before other applications are received. If an ad invites response to a box number without giving a name, be cautious. The employer could be legitimate but does not want present employees to know about the ad or does not want applicants to telephone or drop by the premises. However, you have a right to be suspicious of someone who wants to remain obscure while learning everything you reveal in your résumé. Other printed sources for job listings include company newsletters, industry directories, and trade and professional publications. Many of these sources are also available on the Internet.

Networks

The majority of job openings are never advertised. Therefore, developing a network of contacts may be the most valuable source of information about jobs. Your network may include current and past employers, guest speakers in your classes or at student organization meetings, business contacts you met while interning or participating in shadowing or over-the-shoulder experiences, and so on. Let these individuals know the type of job you are seeking, and ask their advice for finding employment in today's competitive market.

Career Services Centers

You will want to register with your college's career services center at least three semesters before you graduate. Typically, the center has a website and a browsing room loaded with career information and job announcement bulletins. Career counseling is available, including workshops on résumé writing, interviewing, and etiquette, mock interviews, "mocktail" parties for learning to mingle in pre-interview social events, and more. Through the center, you can attend job fairs to meet prospective employers and schedule on-campus interviews and video interviews with company recruiters.

Most career services centers, like companies, use electronic tracking systems. Rather than submitting printed résumés, students input their résumés into a computer file following the specific requirements of the tracking system used by the college or university. A search of the résumé database generates an interview roster of the top applicants for a campus recruiter's needs. Some centers assist students in preparing electronic portfolios to supplement the résumé, as discussed in a later section of this chapter.

Employers' Offices

Employers who have not advertised their employment needs may respond favorably to a telephone or personal inquiry. The receptionist may be able to provide useful information, direct you to someone with whom you can talk, or set up an appointment.

Employment Agencies and Contractors

Telephone directories list city, county, state, and federal employment agencies that provide free or inexpensive services. Some agencies offer online listings or a recorded answering service so that applicants can get information about job opportunities and procedures for using their services. Fees charged by private agencies are paid by either the employee or the employer. This fee usually is based on the first month's salary and must be paid within a few months. Some agencies specialize in finding high-level executives or specialists for major firms. Employment contractors specialize in providing temporary employees. Instead of helping you find a permanent job, a contractor may be able to place you in a position on a temporary basis until you find a full-time job.

Professional Organizations

Officers of professional organizations, through their contacts with members, can be good sources of information about job opportunities. Much job information is exchanged at meetings of professional associations. In response to job listings in journals or organization websites, interviews are sometimes conducted at conference locations.

In addition to the professional growth that comes from membership in professional organizations, active participation is a good way to learn about jobs. Guest speakers share valuable information about the industry, career, and job opportunities. Employers are often favorably impressed when membership and experiences gained are included on the résumé and discussed during an interview. They are even more impressed if the applicant has been an officer in the organization, indicating leadership, community commitment, willingness to exert effort without tangible reward, social acceptance, or high level of aspiration. By joining and actively participating in professional, social, and honorary organizations, you increase your opportunities to develop rapport with peers and professors and get an edge over less involved applicants.

Using Electronic Job Searches

An increasing number of companies and job hunters are harnessing the power of the Internet to assist in various stages of the job search pro-

cess. Convenience, speed, accessibility, and a tight labor market are reasons for the popularity of electronic job searches among cost-conscious human resources managers. The cost of electronic recruiting is lower than traditional methods, and applicants and employers can respond more quickly. Employment experts agree, however, that it is too early for applicants to rely solely on the Internet for locating a job. Instead, job seekers should use the Internet to complement rather than replace the traditional methods previously discussed.

Numerous printed sources and excellent online assistance are available for learning to tap into the power of online job hunting. In this chapter, you'll explore the vast availability of useful career information and job postings on job banks and corporate home pages that match your qualifications. Later, you'll apply effective techniques for online job searching, including ways to protect your privacy while job hunting in cyberspace.

Locating Career Guidance Information

According to one career consultant, "Most people in the old days could go into an organization [during a job interview] and not really know about it and hope for the best. Now, people can understand the organization before they even apply."[2] The Internet places at your fingertips a wealth of information that will prepare you for the job interview if you use it as a research tool. Suggestions follow for effectively using the career guidance information you can locate on the Internet:

- **Visit career sites for information related to various phases of the job search.** You'll find a wide range of timely discussions at career sites: planning a job search, finding a job you love, researching employers, working a career fair, crafting winning résumés and cover letters, negotiating a salary, and so on.

- **Visit corporate websites to learn about the company.** From the convenience of your computer, you can locate information you'll need to target your résumé appropriately and prepare for the job interview. Read mission statements or descriptions of services to see how the organization describes itself, and review the annual report and strategic plan to learn about the financial condition and predicted growth rates. Search for sections touting new developments on "What's New" or "News" links and career opportunities and job postings. Evaluating the development and professional nature of the website will give you an impression of the organization. Supplement this information with independent sources to confirm the company's financial health and other sensitive information, as negative news will likely not be posted on the website.

- **Identify specific skills companies are seeking.** Study the job descriptions provided on corporate home pages and job sites to identify the skills required for the job and the latest industry buzzwords. Use this information to target your résumé to a specific job listing and to generate key words for an electronic résumé.
- **Network electronically with prospective employers.** It's easy to network online by attending electronic job fairs, chatting with career counselors, participating in news groups and listservs applicable to your field, and corresponding by email with contacts in companies. The value of these electronic networking experiences is to learn about an industry and career, seek valued opinions, and uncover potential job opportunities. By applying effective communication strategies for an online community, you can make a good impression, create rapport with employment contacts online, and polish your interviewing skills.

Identifying Job Listings

You can use the Internet to locate job opportunities in several ways:

- Look in the employment section of companies' corporate web pages to see if they are advertising job openings.
- Search the electronic databases of job openings of third-party services.
- Access online job classifieds from daily and trade newspapers. CareerBuilder (**http://www.careerbuilder.com**) offers the classifieds of a number of major newspapers.
- Subscribe to a newsgroup through UseNeXT (**http://www.usenext.com**), which gives you access to jobs by geographic location and specific job categories.
- Subscribe to services such as America Online (**http://www.aol.com**), which provide job search sites and services by keying "Career."

Online and printed sources will help you learn to search particular databases. The following general suggestions will help you get started:

- Input words and phrases that describe your skills rather than job titles because not every company uses the same job title.
- Use specific phrases such as "entry-level job" or "job in advertising" rather than "job search."
- Start with a wider job description term, such as "pharmaceutical sales jobs," then narrow down to the specific subject, geographic region, state, and so forth.

- Don't limit yourself to just one search engine. Try several, and bookmark interesting sites.
- Don't get distracted as you go.

Searching for useful career sites among the hundreds available can be quite time-consuming. In addition to CareerBuilder and AOL, mentioned earlier, Monster.com (**http://www.monster.com**) is a major career site offering information and services. Independent ratings of the effectiveness of job sites are also helpful in untangling the web of choices. Ratings are prepared by *WebWeek, Internet World,* and others, including Richard Bolles, career expert and author of the longtime leading career guide *What Color Is Your Parachute?* His top ratings, "Parachute Picks: My Personal Rating System," and career advice are published at **http://www.jobhuntersbible.com**.

Planning a Targeted Résumé

targeted résumé
a résumé reflects the requirements of a specific job listing

n order to match your interests and qualifications with available jobs, you'll need an effective résumé. To win a job interview in today's tight market where job seekers outnumber positions, you need more than a general résumé that documents your education and work history. The powerful wording of a **targeted résumé** reflects the requirements of a specific job listing that you have identified through traditional and electronic job search methods.

objective ③
Plan a résumé that reflects your qualifications and communicates your value to potential employers.

An employer typically scans résumés quickly, looking for reasons to reject the applicant, schedule an interview, or place in a stack for rereading. This initial scan and a second brief look for those who make the cut give little time to explain why you are the best person for the job.[3] To grab an employer's attention in this brief time, your writing must be powerful and error free. In a phone interview with 150 executives, 76 percent said that one to two typos on a résumé would remove a candidate from consideration for the job.[4] A typo on a résumé reflects an applicant's attention to detail (or lack of) and gives the employer ample reason to cut one more résumé from the stack. You must selectively choose *what to say, how to say it,* and *how to arrange it* on the page so that it can be read quickly but thoroughly. A concise, informative, easy-to-read summary of your relevant qualifications will demonstrate that you possess the straightforward communication skills demanded in today's information-intensive society.

The goal of the résumé is to get an interview, so ask yourself this question: "Does including this information increase my chances of getting an interview?" If the answer is "Yes," include the information; if the answer is "No," omit the information and use the space to develop your qualifications. When selecting information to be included, you must also be wary of the temptation to inflate your résumé to increase your chances of being hired.

Standard Parts of a Résumé

A winning résumé contains standard parts that are adapted to highlight key qualifications for a specific job. An in-depth explanation of each standard part and sample résumés provided in Figures 14-2 to 14-5 will get you ready to prepare a résumé that describes your qualifications best.

Identification

Your objective is to provide information that will allow the interviewer to reach you. Include your name, current address, and telephone number. You may also include your email address and Internet address to facilitate an interviewer's communication.

To ensure that the interviewer can quickly locate the identification information, center it on the page or use graphic design elements to target attention to your name (e.g., change the font face and size, add graphic lines and borders, etc.). You may also include a permanent address (parent or other relative's address) if you are interviewing when classes are not in session. If you are unavailable to take calls during typical office hours (the time the interviewer is likely to call), provide a telephone number where messages can be left. Explain to those taking messages that prospective employers may be calling; thus, the accuracy of their messages and the impression they make while taking the message could affect your job search. Evaluate the personal message on your voice mail to be certain that it portrays you as a person serious about securing a job.

Job and/or Career Objective

Following the "Identification" section, state your job/career objective—the job you want. Interviewers can see quickly whether the job you seek matches the one they have to offer. A good job/career objective must be specific enough to be meaningful yet general enough to apply to a variety of jobs. The following example illustrates a general objective that has been revised to describe a specific job.

General Objective	Specific Objective
A position that offers both a challenge and a good opportunity for growth.	→ *Entry into management training program with advancement to commercial lending.*
A responsible position with a progressive organization that provides opportunity for managerial development and growth commensurate with ability and attitudes.	→ *Enter a challenging management position with special interest in mergers and acquisitions.*

Some experts argue that a statement of your job or career objective may limit your job opportunities. Your objective should be obvious from your qualifications, they say. In general, however, making your objective clear at the beginning assures the interviewer that you have a definite career goal.

Career Summary

To survive the interviewer's 40-second scan, you must provide a compelling reason for a more thorough review of your résumé. Craft a persuasive introductory statement that quickly synthesizes your most transferable skills, accomplishments, and attributes, and place it in a section labeled "Summary" or "Professional Profile."

In this synopsis of your key qualifications, communicate why you should be hired. Your answer should evolve naturally from the career objective and focus on your ability to meet the needs of the company you have identified from your extensive research. Combining the career objective with the career statement is an acceptable strategy, as noted in the following examples.

Separate Objective and Career Summary

Objective Obtain a challenging entry-level sales position for a high-growth consumer products company. Desire advancement into international sales management.
Career Summary Honors graduate with a bachelor's degree in marketing with strong international emphasis including study abroad; three semesters of related co-op experience with a large retail store; effective team worker and communicator.

Combined Objective with Career Summary

Professional Profile Sales position, leading to sales management. International sales/marketing manager with three years' experience in pharmaceutical sales, advertising, and contract negotiation with international suppliers. Strong technology, presentation, and interpersonal skills.

Linked Objective and Career Summary

Profile Position as sales representative where demonstrated commission selling and hard work bring rewards.

Accomplishments:
- Three years' straight commission sales
- Average of $35,000–$55,000 a year in commissioned earnings
- Consistent success in development and growth of territories

A high-impact career summary, once considered optional, has become a standard section of résumés in today's fast-paced information age. Develop your résumé to skillfully target the requirements of a specific position, then compose a career summary sure to interest any interviewer who instantly sees an applicant with exactly the skills needed.

Qualifications

The Qualifications section varies depending on the information identified in the self-, career, and job analyses. This information is used to divide the qualifications into appropriate parts, choose appropriate labels for them, and arrange them in the best sequence. Usually, qualifications stem from your education and work experience (words that appear as headings in the résumé). Arrange these categories depending on which you perceive as more impressive to the employer, with the more impressive category appearing first. For example, education is usually the chief qualification of a recent college graduate; therefore, education appears first. However, a sales representative with related work experience might list experience first, particularly if the educational background is inadequate for the job sought.

© Comstock Images/Jupiterimages

Education

Beginning with the most recent, list the degree, major, school, and graduation date. Include a blank line between schools so the employer can see them at a glance. The interviewer will probably want to know first whether you have the appropriate degree, then the institution, and then other details. Recent or near college graduates should omit high school activities because that information is "old news." However, include high school activities if they provide a pertinent dimension to your qualifications. For example, having attended high school abroad is a definite advantage to an applicant seeking employment in an international firm. In addition, high school accomplishments may be relevant for freshmen or sophomores seeking cooperative education assignments, scholarships, or part-time jobs. Of course, this information will be replaced with college activities when the résumé is revised for subsequent jobs or other uses.

Include overall and major grade-point averages (GPAs) if they are B or better—but be prepared to discuss any omissions during an interview. Some recruiters recommend that every candidate include GPAs, since an omission may lead the reader to assume the worst. Honors and achievements that relate directly to education can be incorporated in this section or included in a separate section. Listing scholarships, appearance on academic lists, and initiation into honor societies will be simple, but highlight business-relevant skills you developed in active classroom experiences, such as client projects, team building, field experiences, and so on. If honors and achievements are included in the "Education" section, be sure to include plenty of white space or use bullets to highlight these points (see Figures 14-2 and 14-4 later in this chapter).

The "Education" section could also include a list of special skills and abilities such as foreign language and computer competency. A list of courses typically required in your field is unnecessary and occupies valuable space. However, you should include any courses, workshops, or educational experiences that are not usual requirements. Examples include internships, cooperative education semesters, "shadowing," "over-the-shoulder" experiences, and study abroad.

Work Experience

The "Work Experience" section provides information about your employment history. For each job held, list the job title, company name, dates of employment, primary responsibilities, and key accomplishments. The jobs may be listed in reverse chronological order (beginning with the most recent) or in order of job relatedness. Begin with the job that most obviously relates to the job being sought if you have gaps in your work history, if the job you are seeking is very different from the job you currently hold, or if you are just entering the job market and have little, if any, related work experience.

Arrange the order and format of information about each job (dates, job title, company, description, and accomplishments) so that the most important information is emphasized—but format all job information consistently. If you have held numerous jobs in a short time, embed dates of employment within the text rather than surround them with white space. Give related job experience added emphasis by listing it first or surrounding it with white space.

Employers are interested in how you can contribute to their bottom line, so a winning strategy involves concentrating on accomplishments and achievements rather than rushing through a boring list of obvious duties. Begin with the job title and company name that provides basic information about your duties, then craft powerful descriptions of the quality and scope of your performance. These bullet points will provide deeper insight into your capability, ambition, and personality.

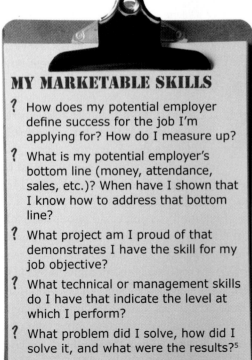

MY MARKETABLE SKILLS

? How does my potential employer define success for the job I'm applying for? How do I measure up?

? What is my potential employer's bottom line (money, attendance, sales, etc.)? When have I shown that I know how to address that bottom line?

? What project am I proud of that demonstrates I have the skill for my job objective?

? What technical or management skills do I have that indicate the level at which I perform?

? What problem did I solve, how did I solve it, and what were the results?[5]

Return to the in-depth analysis you completed at the beginning of the job search process to recall insights as to how you can add immediate value to this company. Did your personal involvement play a key role in the success of a project? Did you uncover a wasteful, labor-intensive procedure that was resolved through your innovation? Did you bridge a gap in a communication breakdown? In short, identify the marketable skills you've gained from your education, work, and community experiences.

Because interviewers spend such a short time reading résumés, the style must be direct and simple. Therefore, a résumé should use crisp phrases to help employers see the value of the applicant's education and experiences. To save space and to emphasize what you have accomplished, use these stylistic techniques:

1. Omit pronouns referring to yourself (*I, me, my*).

2. Use subject-understood sentences.

3. Begin sentences with action verbs as shown in the following examples:

Instead of	Use
I had responsibility for development of new territory.	*Developed* new territory.
My duties included designing computer systems and writing user documentation manuals.	*Designed* computer programs to monitor accounting systems including writing user documentation that enables users to operate these sophisticated system efficiently.
I was the store manager and supervised employees.	*Managed* operations of store with sales volume of $1,000,000 and supervised eight employees.
My sales consistently exceeded sales quota.	*Earned* average of $35,000 a year in commissioned earnings. *Received* service award for exceeding sales quota two of three years employed.
I was a member of the Student Council, Society for the Advancement of Management, Phi Kappa Phi, and Chi Omega Social Sorority.	*Refined* interpersonal skills through involvement in student organizations such as the Student Council . . . .

Because employers are looking for people who will work, action verbs are especially appropriate. Note the subject-understood sentences in the right column of the

© Image Source

previous example; action words used as first words provide emphasis. The following list contains action verbs that are useful in résumés:

achieved	drafted	participated
analyzed	increased	planned
assisted	initiated	recruited
compiled	managed	streamlined
developed	organized	wrote

To give the employer a vivid picture of you as a productive employee, you may find some of the following adjectives helpful as you describe your work experience:

adaptable/flexible	dependable	resourceful
analytical	efficient/productive	sensitive
conscientious	independent	sincere
consistent	objective	tactful
creative	reliable	team oriented

To avoid a tone of egotism, do not use too many adjectives or adverbs that seem overly strong. Plan to do some careful editing after writing your first draft.

Honors and Activities

Make a trial list of any other information that qualifies you for the job. Divide the list into appropriate divisions and then select an appropriate label. Your heading might be "Honors and Activities." You might include a section for "Activities," "Leadership Activities," or "Memberships," depending on the items listed. You might also include a separate section on "Military Service," "Civic Activities," "Volunteer Work," or "Interests." If you have only a few items under each category, use a more general term and combine the lists. If your list is lengthy, divide it into more than one category; interviewers prefer "bite-size" pieces because they are easier to read and can be remembered more readily.

Resist the urge to include everything you have ever done; keep in mind that every item you add distracts from other information. Consider summarizing information that is relevant but does not merit several separate lines—for example, "Involved in art, drama, and choral groups." To decide whether to include certain information, ask these questions: How closely related is it to the job being sought? Does it provide job-related information that has not been presented elsewhere?

Personal Information

Because a résumé should contain primarily information that is relevant to an applicant's experience and qualifications, you must be selective when including personal

information (not related to the job). The space could be used more effectively to include more about your qualifications or to add more white space. Personal information is commonly placed at the end of the résumé just above the "References" section because it is less important than qualifications (education, experience, and activities).

Under the 1964 Civil Rights Act (and subsequent amendments) and the Americans with Disabilities Act (ADA), employers cannot make hiring decisions based on gender, age, marital status, religion, national origin, or disability. Employers prefer not to receive information that provides information about gender, age, and national origin because questions could be raised about whether the information was used in the hiring decision.

- **Do not include personal information that could lead to discriminatory hiring.** Exclude height, weight, color of hair and eyes, and a personal photograph on the résumé.

- **Reveal ethnic background (and other personal information) only if it is job related.** For example, certain businesses may be actively seeking employees in certain ethnic groups because the ethnic background is a legitimate part of the job description. For such a business, ethnic information is useful and appreciated.

- **Include personal information (other than the information covered by employment legislation) that will strengthen your résumé.** Select information that is related to the job you are seeking or that portrays you as a well-rounded, happy individual off the job. Typically, include interests, hobbies, favorite sports, avocations, and willingness to relocate. You can also include the following topics if you have not covered them elsewhere in the résumé: spoken and written communication skills, computer competency, foreign-language or computer skills, military service, community service, scholastic honors, job-related hobbies, and professional association memberships.

- **Consider whether personal information might be controversial.** For example, listing a sport that an interviewer might perceive to be overly time-consuming or dangerous would be questionable. An applicant seeking a position with a religious or political organization may benefit from revealing a related affiliation.

When selecting information to be included, honestly ask yourself, "Does this information present my qualifications honestly and ethically, or does it inflate my qualifications to increase my chances of getting the job?" If you sense you're stretching the truth, omit the item. What you believe is a "career booster" could end your career.

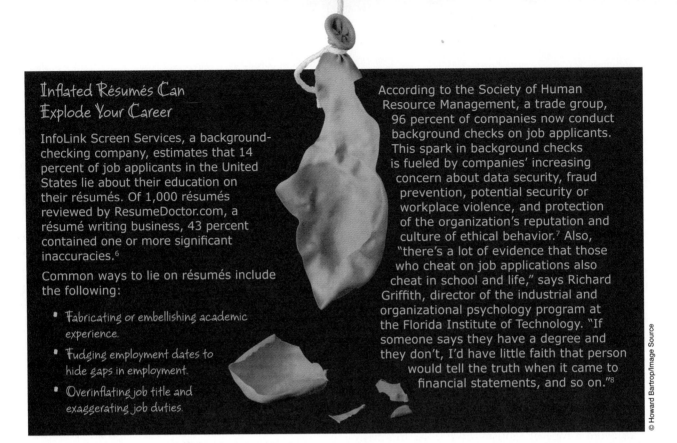

Inflated Résumés Can Explode Your Career

InfoLink Screen Services, a background-checking company, estimates that 14 percent of job applicants in the United States lie about their education on their résumés. Of 1,000 résumés reviewed by ResumeDoctor.com, a résumé writing business, 43 percent contained one or more significant inaccuracies.[6]

Common ways to lie on résumés include the following:

- Fabricating or embellishing academic experience.
- Fudging employment dates to hide gaps in employment.
- Overinflating job title and exaggerating job duties.

According to the Society of Human Resource Management, a trade group, 96 percent of companies now conduct background checks on job applicants. This spark in background checks is fueled by companies' increasing concern about data security, fraud prevention, potential security or workplace violence, and protection of the organization's reputation and culture of ethical behavior.[7] Also, "there's a lot of evidence that those who cheat on job applications also cheat in school and life," says Richard Griffith, director of the industrial and organizational psychology program at the Florida Institute of Technology. "If someone says they have a degree and they don't, I'd have little faith that person would tell the truth when it came to financial statements, and so on."[8]

References

Providing potential employers with a list of references (people who have agreed to supply information about you when requested) is an important component of your employment credentials. Listing names, addresses, telephone numbers, and email addresses of people who can provide information about you adds credibility to the résumé. Employers, former employers, instructors, and former instructors are good possibilities. Friends, relatives, and neighbors are not (because of their perceived bias in your favor). Some career experts recommend including a peer to document your ability to work as a member of a team, an important job skill in today's team-oriented environment.[9]

When preparing a separate list of references to be given after a successful interview, place the word *References* and your name in a visible position as shown in Figure 14-3 on page 263. Balance the list (name, address, telephone number, and relationship of reference to applicant) attractively on the page, and use the same paper used for printing the résumé. When asked for references at the end of a successful interview, you can immediately provide the references page to the interviewer. If you need additional time to consider the interview, you can send the references page within a day or so by postal or electronic mail. Whether it is handed to the interviewer personally or mailed, the references page professionally complements your ré-

chronological résumé
the traditional organizational format for résumés

sumé. Confident that you have a good message, you are now ready to put it in writing—to construct a résumé that will impress an employer favorably.

Types of Résumés

The general organization of all résumés is fairly standard: identification (name, address, telephone number, and email address), job objective, qualifications, personal information, and references. The primary organizational challenge is in dividing the qualifications section into parts, choosing labels for them, and arranging them in the best sequence. When you review your self-, career-, and job analyses data and company/job profile, you will recognize that your qualifications stem mainly from your education and your experience. Your task is to decide how to present these two categories of qualifications. Résumés usually are organized in one of three ways: reverse chronological order (most recent activity listed first), functional order (most important activity listed first), or chronofunctional, which combines the chronological and functional orders as the name implies. To determine which organizational plan to use, draft your résumé in each.

Chronological Résumé

The **chronological résumé** is the traditional organizational format for résumés. Two headings normally appear in the portion that presents qualifications:

"Education" and "Experience." Which one should appear first? Decide which one you think is more impressive to the employer, and put that one first. Within each section, the most recent information is presented first. Reverse chronological order is easier to use and is more common than functional order; however, it is not always more effective.

The chronological résumé is an especially effective format for applicants who have progressed up a clearly defined career ladder and want to move up another rung. Because the format emphasizes dates and job titles, the chronological résumé is less effective for applicants who have gaps in their work histories, are seeking jobs different from the job currently held, or are just entering the job market with little or no experience.[10]

If you choose the chronological format, look at the two headings from the employer's point of view, and reverse their positions if doing so is to your advantage. Under the "Experience" division, jobs are listed in reverse order. Assuming you have progressed typically, your latest job is likely to be more closely related to the job being sought than the first job held. Placing the latest or current job first will give it the emphasis it deserves. Include beginning and ending dates for each job.

Functional Résumé

In a **functional résumé**, points of primary interest to employers—transferable skills—appear in major headings. These headings highlight what an applicant can do for the employer—functions that can be performed well. Under each heading, an applicant could draw from educational and/or work-related experience to provide supporting evidence.

A functional résumé requires a complete analysis of self, career, and the job sought. Suppose, for example, that a person seeking a job as an assistant hospital administrator wants to emphasize qualifications by placing them in major headings. From the hospital's advertisement of the job and from accumulated job appraisal information, an applicant sees this job as both an administrative and a public relations job. The job requires skill in communicating and knowledge of accounting and finance. Thus, headings in the "Qualifications" section of the résumé could be (1) "Administration," (2) "Public Relations," (3) "Communication," and (4) "Budgeting." Under "Public Relations," for example, an applicant could reveal that a public relations course was taken at State University, from which a degree is to be conferred in June, and that a sales job at ABC

Store provided abundant opportunity to apply principles learned. With other headings receiving similar treatment, the qualifications portion reveals the significant aspects of education and experience.

Order of importance is probably the best sequence for functional headings. If you have prepared an accurate self- and job analysis, the selected headings will highlight points of special interest to the employer. Glancing at headings only, an employer could see that you have the qualities needed for success on the job. By carefully selecting headings, you reveal knowledge of the requisites for success.

Having done the thinking required for preparing a functional résumé, you are well prepared for a question that is commonly asked in interviews: "What can you do for us?" The answer is revealed in your major headings. They emphasize the functions you can perform and the special qualifications you have to offer.

If you consider yourself well qualified, a functional résumé is worth considering. If your education or experience is scant, a functional résumé may be best for you. Using "Education" and "Experience" as headings (as in a chronological résumé) works against your purpose if you have little to report under the headings; the format would emphasize the absence of education or experience.

Chrono-functional Résumé

The **chrono-functional résumé** combines features of chronological and functional résumés. This format can give quick assurance that educational and experience requirements are met and still use other headings that emphasize qualifications.

Preparing Résumés

Format requirements for résumés have changed significantly in recent years. Whether presented on paper or electronically, the arrangement of a résumé is

objective ④
Prepare an organized, persuasive résumé that is adapted for print, scanning, and electronic postings.

functional résumé
a résumé in which points of primary interest to employers—transferable skills—appear in major headings
chrono-functional résumé
a résumé that combines features of chronological and functional résumés

just as important as the content. If the arrangement is unattractive, unappealing, or in poor taste, the message may never be read. Errors in keyboarding, spelling, and punctuation may be taken as evidence of a poor academic background, lack of respect for the employer, carelessness, or haste. Recognize that résumés serve as your introduction to employers, and indicate the quality and caliber of work you'll produce. Imperfect résumés are unacceptable. Put forth your best effort to this important task—one that could open the door to the job you really want.

As in preparing other difficult documents, prepare a rough draft as quickly as you can and then revise as many times as needed to prepare an effective résumé that sells you. After you are confident with the résumé, ask at least two other people to check it for you. Carefully select people who are knowledgeable about résumé preparation and the job you are seeking and can suggest ways to present your qualifications more effectively. After you have incorporated those changes, ask a skillful proofreader to review the document.

To accommodate employers' preferences for the presentation and delivery of résumés, you'll need three versions of your résumé as shown in Figure 14-1: an enhanced résumé printed on paper, a scannable résumé to be read by a computer, and an electronic résumé accessible through email and websites.

Preparing a Print (Designed) Résumé

Your print (designed) résumé is considered your primary marketing document, and appearance is critical. To win out among hundreds of competing résumés, it must look professional and reflect current formatting and production standards while maintaining a distinctive conservative tone. Follow these guidelines for designing and producing a highly professional résumé with your own computer:

- **Develop an appealing résumé format that highlights your key qualifications and distinguishes your résumé from the many look-alikes created with résumé templates.** Use the power of your word processing software for style enhancements rather than settle for outdated, inflexible templates that are difficult to use when sequencing and reformatting. Study the example résumés in this chapter and models from other sources for ideas for enhancing the style, readability, and overall impact of the document. Then create a custom design that best highlights your key qualifications.
- **Format information for quick, easy reading.** To format your résumé so that it can be read at glance:

- *Use attention-getting headings to partition major divisions and add graphic lines and borders to separate sections of text.*
- *Use an outline format when possible to list activities and events on separate lines, and include bullets to emphasize multiple points.*
- *Use font sizes no smaller than 10 point to avoid reader eye strain.*
- *Use type styles and print attributes to emphasize key points.* For example, to draw attention first to the identification and then to the headings, select a bold sans serif font slightly larger than the serif font used for the remaining text. The blocky appearance of sans serif fonts (e.g., **Arial** or **Univers**) that do not have cross-strokes makes them easy to read and useful for displaying important text. Serif fonts such as **Times New Roman** or **New Century Schoolbook** have cross-strokes and are primarily used for large amounts of text to be read carefully. Capitalization, indention, and print enhancements (underline, italics, bold) are useful for adding emphasis. Limit the number of type styles and enhancements, however, so the page is clean and simple to read.
- *Include identification on each page of a multiple-page résumé.* Place your name and a page number at the top of the second and successive pages, with "Continued" at the bottom of the first page. The interviewer is re-exposed to your name, and pages can be reassembled if separated.
- **Create an appealing output to produce top professional quality.**
  - *Check for consistency throughout*

the résumé. Consistency in spacing, end punctuation, capitalization, appearance of headings, and sequencing of details within sections will communicate your eye for detail and commitment to high standards.

- *Balance the résumé attractively on the page with approximately equal margins.* Allow generous white space so the résumé looks uncluttered and easy to read.

- **Consider adding a statement of your creativity and originality.** Be certain, however, that your creativity will not be construed as gimmicky and consequently distract from the content of the résumé. Demonstrating creativity is particularly useful for fields such as advertising, public relations, and graphic design as well as in those requiring computer competency.

- *Select paper of a standard size (8¹/₂″ by 11″) neutral color (white, buff, or gray), and high quality (preferably 24-pound, 100-percent cotton fiber).* Because an application letter will accompany a résumé, use a large (No. 10) envelope. Consider using a mailing envelope large enough to accommodate the résumé without folding. The unfolded documents on the reader's desk may get favorable attention and will scan correctly if posted to an electronic database. (A detailed discussion of scannable résumés follows this section.)

- *Print with a laser printer that produces high-quality output.* Position paper so the watermark is read across the sheet in the same direction as the printing.

Some employers insist that the "best" length for a résumé is one page, stating that long résumés are often ignored. However, general rules about length are more flexible. Most students and recent graduates can present all relevant résumé information on one page. However, as employees gain experience, they may need two or more pages to format an informative, easy-to-read résumé. A résumé forced on one page will likely have narrow margins and large blocks of run-on text (multiple lines with no space to break them). This dense format is unappealing and complicates the interviewer's task of skimming quickly for key information.

The rule about length is simple. Be certain your résumé contains only relevant information presented as concisely as possible. A one-page résumé that includes irrelevant information is too long. A two-page résumé that omits relevant information is too short.

The résumé illustrated in Figure 14-2 demonstrates the organizational principles for the chronological résumé. A references page is illustrated in Figure 14-3 on page 263, and a functional résumé is depicted in Figure 14-4 on page 264. Study the various layouts illustrated in these print (designed) résumés to find the layout that will highlight your key qualifications most effectively.

Preparing a Scannable Résumé

In addition to the traditional résumé read by a person, your résumé may be uploaded from a variety of sources into an electronic database where it will be read by a computer. Companies of all sizes are using *electronic applicant-tracking systems* to increase efficiency of processing the volumes of résumés being submitted in a competitive market. The career services center at your college likely uses an academic tracking system to process résumés for campus recruiters.

Your efforts to adapt your traditional résumé will be more effective if you understand the demands of these tracking systems. The system processes incoming résumés in the following way:

1. **Stores incoming résumés in an electronic database.** Résumés are uploaded from a variety of sources: emailed or faxed résumés, or postings to Internet job banks or corporate websites. Because print résumés must first be scanned and converted into a digital format, they are often referred to as **scannable résumés**. However, any of these résumés is technically an **electronic résumé** because it will be read by the computer and not by a human.

2. **Compares the electronic résumés to a list of key words, and ranks applicants based on the number of key words.** The key words describe an ideal candidate and include mandatory and desired traits. The computer scans each résumé; the more matches of key words included in a résumé, the higher the ranking on the computer's short list of candidates.

3. **Prepares letters of rejection and interview offers.** This automation is beneficial to job seekers who may receive no communication from companies processing applications manually.

scannable résumé (electronic résumé)
a résumé that will be read by the computer and not by a human

Figure 14-2  Chronological Résumé

- *Includes email address that reflects professional image.*

- *Reveals type of work sought.*

- *Positions education as top qualification for recent graduate. Includes high GPA (B or better).*

- *Edges out competition reflecting related experience and work achievements.*

- *Uses separate section to emphasize language proficiencies listed in job requirements.*

- *Emphasizes activities that reflect service attitude, high level of responsibility, and people-oriented experiences.*

Format Pointers
Places name at top center, where it can be easily seen when employers place it in file drawer (top right is also acceptable).

Uses bold sans serif font to distinguish identification section and headings from remaining text in serif font.

Creates visual appeal through custom format rather than commonly used template, short readable sections focusing on targeted qualifications, and streamlined bulleted lists.

Diversity Challenges Constraint
Follows standard format and rules for résumés for application with U.S. companies. Specific job application formats are available for specific countries and federal government.

Omits references to use space for additional qualifications; references will be furnished when requested.

Cassandra Jensen
783 Ash Street
Palmdale, CA 83307
(204) 555-6789
cjensen@hotmail.com

CAREER OBJECTIVE
Challenging position in finance or investment banking with international promotion opportunities.

EDUCATION
California State University *August 2006–May 2010*
Bachelor of Science in Business Administration
Corporate Finance and International Business
GPA 3.6 on a 4.0 scale

RELATED EXPERIENCE
Intern, **Citicorp,** Los Angeles, CA *June 2009–Present*
- Assisted in the management of guided portfolio management accounts for high net-worth clients
- Interpreted statements and conducted money wire transfers
- Developed an understanding of secured financial transactions

Intern, **Financial Solutions,** *May 2008–*
Century City, CA *October 2008*
- Conducted research to create stock portfolios, including an organic food portfolio that grew 10% in 8 months.
- Assisted in the management of accounts for high net-worth clients

LANGUAGES
- English: Native fluency
- Spanish: Fluent (speaking, reading, writing, comprehension)

LEADERSHIP & HONORS
Order of Omega Honor Society, *Co-Vice President of Conference*
August 2009–Present
Organized a leadership conference for members of the CSU Greek System

CSU Panhellenic Council, *January 2008–December 2008*
Vice President of Communications
- Developed and produced content for a new Panhellenic website
- Representative at the Western Regional Greek Leadership Conference

Kappa Kappa Gamma, Sorority *August 2006–Present*
Representative at Kappa Kappa Gamma Province Leadership Convention

Matthew and Teresa S. Arnold *2008/2009 and 2009/2010*
Endowed Scholarship Recipient

Figure 14-3   References Page

- References include professor and immediate supervisors. List does not include friends, relatives, or clergy to avoid potential bias.

- Each reference includes full contact information, including email address if available, and relationship to job applicant.

Format Pointers
Reference page is prepared at same time as résumé and can be provided immediately after successful interview. Paper (color, texture, and size) and print type match résumé.

References are balanced attractively on page.

Cassandra Jensen
783 Ash Street
Palmdale, CA 83307
(204) 555-6789
cjensen@hotmail.com

REFERENCES

Clark Denton
Financial Services Manager
Citicorp
P.O. Box 813
Los Angeles, CA 90101-1801
213 555-9000
cdenton@citicorp.com
Relationship: Immediate supervisor during two-semester internship,
June 2008–Present

Francis Lupino
Customer Relations Manager
Financial Solutions
P.O. Box 5937
Culver City, CA 91032-5937
310 555-4382
rlupino@financialsolutions.com
Relationship: Immediate supervisor during extended internship,
May 2007–October 2007

Matthew Pearson, Professor
Finance Department
California State University
2150 West 21st Street
Los Angeles, CA 90790-2150
213 777-9090
mpearson@management.csu.edu
Relationship: Academic adviser, professor in two upper-level finance courses

4. **Stores the résumés, and accesses them for future openings.** The résumé remains in the system and is accessed whenever a new position is posted. A résumé is transferred into an employee tracking system when the applicant is hired to allow consideration for any job postings and internal promotions.

Computerized résumé searches provide several distinct advantages to job seekers. Applicants are considered for every position in the company (not just reviewed by the recruiter whose desk on which the résumé happens to land); therefore, an applicant's résumé may be matched with a position he or she would not have applied for otherwise. The résumé remains in the system and is accessed whenever a new position is posted.[11]

When seeking a job with a company that scans résumés into an electronic database, you will need to submit a scannable résumé that can be read by a computer and then follow up with a print (designed) résumé that will be read by a person if you are among the applicants selected to be interviewed. If you are unsure whether a company scans résumés, call and ask. If still in doubt, take the safe route and submit your résumé in both formats.

Formatting a Scannable Résumé

To ensure that the scanner can read your résumé accurately and clearly, you must prepare a plain résumé with no special formatting, often referred to as a "vanilla, no-frills" résumé.[12] Your objective is to use distinctive

Figure 14-4  *Functional Résumé*

Clarence Foster
715 Armadillo Circle
San Antonio, TX 78710-0715
(512) 555-1396
cfoster@hotmail.com

OBJECTIVE — Position in retail clothing sales with advancement to sales management.

CUSTOMER SERVICE
- Processed customer financial transactions within assigned limits and established guidelines.
- Provided excellent customer service in completing transactions efficiently and in a friendly, professional manner.
- Met sales and referral goals by identifying and selling financial products and services beneficial to the customer needs.
- Identified fraudulent activity to prevent potential losses to the bank.

SALES
- Provided quality customer service to store patrons.
- Handled cash transactions and daily receipt balances.
- Usually surpassed weekly goal of opening new credit accounts.
- Employee of the month.

COMMUNICATION SKILLS AND WORK ETHIC
- Ability to communicate effectively over the phone and in person.
- Ability to work well unsupervised.
- Experience working on team projects both at work and in courses.
- Report consistently and promptly when scheduled for work.

COMPUTER SKILLS
Proficient in spreadsheet and word processing software.

EMPLOYMENT HISTORY — Sales Associate, Claremont Department Store, 2006–Present

Customer Service Associate, Union Bank, 2005–2006

EDUCATION — B.S., Marketing, Claremont State College, Expected graduation, May 2010

REFERENCES — Clare Randall, Sales Manager, Claremont Department Store, 435 Main Street, Claremont, TX 78009, (818) 555-2345

Daniel Shore, Professor, Marketing Department, Claremont State College, 890 Alamo Street, San Antonio, TX 87003, (803) 555-8907

Lisa Cox, Senior Teller, Union Bank, 900 Main Street, Claremont, TX 87303, (818) 555-1234

- *Includes clear objective statement to grab attention and invite close reading.*

- *Uses headings that show applicant knows what skills are needed to succeed in sales.*

- *Arranges qualifications into sections that emphasize applicant's relevant skills and accomplishments.*

- *Uses employers' names and dates to match skills with work history.*

- *Lists references for employer convenience and to strengthen résumé.*

Format Pointers
Creates visual appeal with easy-to-read columnar format and balanced page arrangement.

Places name at top center, where it can be easily seen.

Uses bold font to distinguish identification section and headings from remaining text.

Lists education and work history as quick overview of basic qualifications and to accommodate employers' preference for chronological format.

print that can still be read after it has been mushed and run together in the scanning process, and to resist the temptation to add graphic enhancements that cannot be read by a scanner. Follow these guidelines to prepare an electronic résumé that can be scanned accurately:

- **Use popular, nondecorative typefaces.** Typefaces such as Helvetica, Univers, Times New Roman, and New Century Schoolbook are clear and distinct and will not lose clarity in scanning.

- **Use 10- to 14-point font.** Computers cannot read small, tight print well. With a larger font, your résumé may extend to two pages, but page length is not an issue because a computer is reading the résumé.

- **Do not include italics, underlining, open bullets, or graphic lines and boxes.** Use boldface or all capitals for emphasis. Italicized letters often touch, and underlining may run into the text above; therefore, the scanned image may be garbled. Design elements, such as graphic lines, shading, and shadowing effects, confuse equipment designed to read text and not graphics. Use solid bullets (●); open bullets (○) may be read as o's.

- **Use ample white space.** Use at least one-inch margins. Leave plenty of white space between the sections of a résumé so the computer recognizes the partitions.

- **Print on one side of white, standard-size paper with sharp laser print.** Send an original that is smudge free; the scanner may pick up dirty specks on a photocopy. Colored and textured paper scans poorly.

- **Use a traditional résumé format.** Complex layouts that simulate catalogs or newspaper columns are confusing to the scanner.

- **Do not fold or staple your résumé.** If you must fold, do not fold on a line of text. Staples, when removed, make the pages stick together.

Making a Scannable Résumé Searchable

A few significant changes must be made in a print résumé to make it computer-friendly. You have two concerns: (1) You want to be certain that information is presented in a manner the computer can read, and (2) you want to maximize the number of hits your résumé receives in a computerized résumé search and thus enhance your ranking in the computer's short list of candidates. You may use more than one page if needed to present your qualifications. The more information you present the more likely you are to be selected from the database of applicants, and computers can read your résumé more quickly than humans can. Be sure to send a cover letter to reinforce your electronic résumé.

Follow these guidelines for modifying the content of your print résumé to make it searchable:

- **Position your name as the first readable item on the page.** Follow with your address, telephone number, fax number (if any), and email below your name on separate lines to avoid possible confusion by the systems.

- **Add powerful key words in a separate section called "Key Words" or "Key Word Summary" that follows the identification.** To identify key words, highlight on a copy of your print (designed) résumé the nouns you think the computer might use as key words in the search. Ask yourself if these words describe your qualifications and continue looking for other words that label your qualifications. Make maximum use of industry jargon and standard, easily recognizable abbreviations (B.A., M.S.) in the key word summary and the body of the résumé, as these buzzwords will likely be matches with the computer's key words.

  Techniques for hammering out key words offered by Kennedy and Morrow, leading consultants in the electronic job revolution, include asking yourself "What achievements would I discuss with my supervisor if I were meeting to discuss a raise?" Consider a job-related problem and describe the solution and every step required to solve the problem; consider the results. Consider actions that if done poorly would affect goals of the job and then state them positively. For example, a negative action is "an employee not getting to work on time"; stated positively, it becomes "efficiency minded and profit conscious."[13]

- **Format the key word summary following these guidelines:** Capitalize the first letter of each word, and separate each key word with a period. Position the key words describing your most important qualifications first and move to the least important ones. Order is important because some systems stop scanning after the first 80 key words. The usual order is (1) job title, occupation, or career field; (2) education; and (3) essential skills for a specific position. Be certain to include key words that describe interpersonal traits important in your field. Examples of such key words are *adaptable, flexible, sensitive, team player, willing to travel, ethical, industrious, innovative, open-minded, and detail oriented.*

- **Support your key words with specific facts in the body of the résumé.** Keep the key word summary a reasonable length so that you have space to support your key words. Use synonyms of your key words in the body in the event the computer does not recognize the key word (e.g., use M.B.A. in the key word summary and Master of Business Administration in the body; use presentation graphics software in the key word summary and a specific program in the body).

One unfortunate applicant reported using "computer-assisted design" consistently throughout his résumé when the computer was searching for "CAD." Also, use a specific date of graduation in the education section. Some computer programs read two dates beside an institution to mean the applicant did not earn the degree (e.g., 2004–2008). If the degree is programmed as a requirement (rather than a desirable qualification), this applicant would be excluded from the search.

The scannable résumé Joseph Priestley prepared when seeking an entry-level audit position in a public accounting firm appears in Figure 14-5. Note how he presents qualifications that correspond to the company/job profile posted at the text support site. The scannable résumé is formatted so that it can be scanned into an electronic database, and the content is searchable for an employer attempting to match applicants with an entry-level audit position.

Adapting to Varying Electronic Submission Requirements

In addition to traditionally formatted résumés, in the digital age of instant information, there are various other online methods for applying for a job and presenting your qualifications to prospective employers.

The easiest and most common method of putting your résumé online is through emailing a résumé to a job bank for posting or to a networking contact who asked you to send a résumé. Many job banks, corporate sites, and career services centers require you to respond to specific openings by completing an online form that may require you to paste your résumé into a designated section of the form. Frequently, you may input information directly on the website or download the form to be submitted by email, fax, or mail. You may also choose to post your résumé on your personal web page as part of an electronic portfolio that showcases evidence of your qualifications. You may also need to develop a **beamer** or **beamable résumé**, a quick version of your résumé designed in a format suitable for broadcasting on a PDA or digital phone. Recruiting professionals predict that millions of these electronic résumés will be exchanged silently at conferences, business meetings, and power lunches, rather like exchanging business cards.[14]

Electronic submissions are quick and easy

beamer (beamable résumé)
a quick version of your résumé designed in a format suitable for broadcasting on a PDA or digital phone

but present new challenges and many opportunities to jeopardize your employment chances and compromise your privacy. Just consider recent struggles you may have faced in dealing with viruses and unwelcomed emails, attempting to access nonworking links, and more. Before sending your résumé into cyberspace, follow these suggestions to ensure that your electronic submission is both professional and technically effective:

- **Choose postings for your résumé with purpose.** Online résumé postings are not confidential. Once your résumé is online, anyone can read it, including your current employer. You may also begin to receive junk mail and cold calls from companies who see your résumé online; even more seriously, you could become a victim of identify theft. To protect your privacy online, limit personal information disclosed in the résumé and post only to sites with password protection, allowing you to approve the release of your résumé to specific employers. Dating your electronic résumé will also prevent embarrassment should your employer find an old version of your résumé, which could occur as result of exchange of résumés between career sites and delays in updating postings.

  Protect your references' privacy by omitting their names when posting online. Withholding this information will prevent unwelcome calls by recruiters needed to fill vacancies or other inappropriate contacts and threats to privacy. Although technology allows broadcast of your résumé to all available positions on a career site, read postings carefully and apply only to those that match your qualifications. This action improves the efficiency of the job selection process for the company and the applicant and depicts fair, ethical behavior.

- **Don't be in a hurry.** The speed, convenience, and informality of filling in online boxes or composing an email cover letter for an attached résumé can lead to sloppiness that reflects negatively on your abilities and attitude. Make sure every aspect of your electronic submission is top-notch, just as you would for a print résumé. Provide all information exactly as requested; write concise, clear statements relevant to the job sought; and proofread carefully for grammatical and spelling errors. Should you direct an employer to an electronic portfolio, devote necessary time to make it attractive, informative, and technically sound. Double-check your files to ensure they can be opened and will retain an appealing format. Finally, read the posting carefully to know how long your résumé will remain active, how to update it, and how to delete it from the site.

- **Include your résumé in the format requested by the employer or job bank.** You may be instructed to send the résumé as an attachment to the message or

Figure 14-5  *Scannable Résumé*

- *Positions name as first readable item.*

- *Includes "Professional Profile" section that identifies job sought and reason to hire.*

- *Includes "Keywords" section listing qualifications that match job description.*

- *Supports keywords with specific facts; uses nouns that might match those in description.*

- *Uses synonyms of keywords in body to ensure match with database.*

- *Emphasizes willingness to provide professional, more impressive document.*

- *Includes date of last revision to avoid confusion or embarrassment if résumé is accessed after position is accepted.*

Format Pointers
Keeps résumé simple and readable by computer: ample white space especially between sections; easy-to-read font within range of 10 to 14 points; solid bullets; and no italics, underlining, or graphic lines or borders.

Mails cover letter and print résumé unfolded and unstapled in large envelope.

JOSEPH PRIESTLEY
89 Lincoln Street
Santa Fe, NM 78285-9063
512 555-9823
jpriestley@hotmail.com

Professional Profile
- Technical proficiency in ERP systems, ACL, database, and spreadsheet software.
- Hands-on experience in accounting gained through internship with well-regarded local firm.
- Excellent interpersonal communication and teamwork skills developed through course projects and active involvement in student organizations.
- Ability to manage time effectively, excellent work ethic and dedication to high-quality work as demonstrated by part-time work to finance my education and 3.87 GPA.

Keywords
Bachelor's degree in accounting. Entry-level accounting experience. Knowledge of basic accounting principles and practices. Excellent communication skills. Personal characteristics include good work ethic, ability to manage time efficiently, and dedication to producing quality work.

Education
B.B.A., Accounting, University of New Mexico, May 2010, GPA 3.87
- Dean's List, 2006–2010
- Deanna D. Darling Academic Scholarship

Technical Skills
Proficient in Microsoft Office Suite, database and spreadsheet software, ERP systems, and ACL.

Related Employment
Intern, Gerald and Associates, CPAs, Santa Fe, NM June–August 2009
- Shadowed auditor and helped to write numerous auditing reports for corporate clients.
- Created and maintained spreadsheets and databases, containing client audit information.
- Worked with audit teams to hone communication skills and developed phone skills necessary to effectively interact with professional clientele.

Other Employment
- Server, Bubba's BBQ, Sante Fe, NM 2008–2010
- Stockperson, University of New Mexico Bookstore, Santa Fe, NM 2006–2008

Leadership Activities
Beta Alpha Psi, honorary accounting society, 2006–2010, chapter president, 2009–2010
Chess Team, 2007–2010, president, 2008–2009

An attractive and fully formatted hard copy version of this document is available upon request.

Last revised 1/1/10

include it in the body of email message, known as an **inline résumé**. The inline résumé is becoming the preferred choice as fear of computer viruses and daily email overload prevent employers from opening attachments.

Unless instructed to send your attachment in a specific format such as Word, save your résumé and cover letter in one file beginning with the cover letter as an ASCII or Rich Text Format (RTF) file with line length limited to 65 characters and spacing. This plain text version, referred to as a **text résumé**, removes formatting and lacks the appeal of your designed résumé; however, you can be confident that an employer can open the file and won't have to spend time "cleaning up" your résumé if it doesn't transmit correctly. For this reason, you'll also paste the text version of your résumé below your email message when sending an inline résumé.

As an added safeguard, send yourself and a couple of friends a copy of the résumé and see how it looks on different computers before sending it out to an employer. If you wish, follow up with a print résumé and cover letter on high-quality paper.

- **Include a key word summary after the identification section.** Just as you did in the scannable résumé, you'll want to grab the employer's attention by placing the key words on the first screen (within the first 24 lines of text). Providing this relevant information will motivate the employer to keep scrolling down to see how the key words are supported rather than click to the next résumé.

- **Email a cover message to accompany an online résumé.** Some companies consider this cover email message to be prescreening for a job interview. Write a formal, grammatically

Some possible items for inclusion in your portfolio:

- Sample speeches with digitized audio or video clips of the delivery.
- Performance appraisals.
- Awards.
- Certificates of completion.
- Reports, proposals, or written documents from classes.
- Brochures or programs describing workshops attended.
- Commendation messages, records, or surveys showing client or customer satisfaction with service.
- Attendance records.

correct message, just as you would if you were sending an application letter in the mail.

Supplementing a Résumé

Some candidates may feel their career accomplishments are not appropriately captured in a standard résumé. Two additional tools for communicating your qualifications and abilities are the portfolio and the employment video.

objective ⑤
Utilize employment tools other than the résumé that can enhance employability.

Professional Portfolios

The **professional portfolio** (also called the **electronic** or **e-portfolio** when presented in a digital format) can be used to illustrate past activities, projects, and accomplishments. It is a collection of artifacts that demonstrate your communication, people, and technical skills. Although portfolios were once thought of as only for writers, artists, or photographers, they are now seen as appropriate for other fields of work when the applicant wants to showcase abilities.

Many portfolios are now presented in digital format, making the portfolio easier to organize and distribute to prospective employers via a website or burned to a CD or

inline résumé
a résumé that is attached to or included in the body of an email message

text résumé
a résumé without formatting and lacking the appeal of your designed résumé

professional portfolio (electronic portfolio, e-portfolio)
a collection of artifacts that demonstrate your communication, people, and technical skills

other media. With the availability of user-friendly software, college campuses are offering e-portfolio systems that aid students in reflecting on their experiences and producing e-portfolios. Just as students are currently not asked if they have an email account, predictions are that soon they will also be expected to have "a web space that represents their learning and their assessment."[15]

A clear understanding of your audience's needs and your qualifications will allow you to develop a logical organizational structure for your portfolio.

After selecting the items for inclusion in your portfolio, you will need to select the appropriate software or binder you will use to showcase your accomplishments. Once you're organized, you can add items that demonstrate that you have the characteristics the employer is seeking. The portfolio should be continually maintained even after you are hired because it can demonstrate your eligibility for promotion, salary increase, advanced training, or even justify why you should not be laid off.[16]

For illustration purposes, take a look at Joseph Priestley's electronic portfolio shown in Figure 14-6 that was created using a Microsoft web template and posted to his personal website.

Employment Videos

A video recording may be used to extend the impact of the printed résumé visually. A video can capture your stage presence and ability to speak effectively and add a human dimension to the written process. The most current technology enables applicants to embed video segments into **multimedia résumés** created with presentation software such as Microsoft Producer or Camtasia Studio and sent to prospective employers on a CD or DVD, or posted on the applicant's personal web page.

multimedia résumé
a résumé created with presentation software such as Microsoft Producer or Camtasia Studio and sent to prospective employers on a CD or DVD or posted on the applicant's personal web page

Figure 14-6 Electronic Portfolio Posted to an Applicant's Personal Website

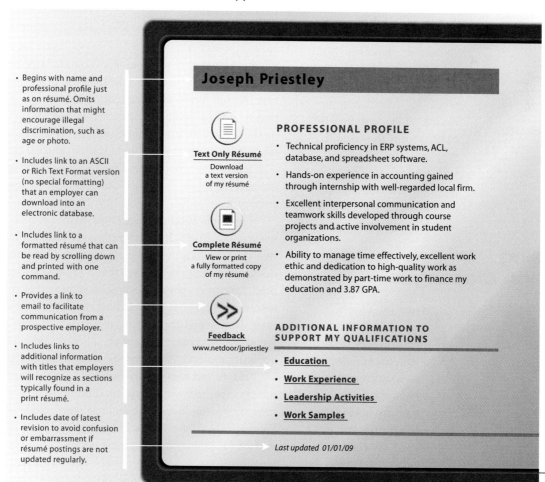

Employment videos are more commonly used to obtain employment in career fields for which verbal delivery or visual performance is a key element. These fields include broadcasting and the visual and performing arts. The following guidelines apply when preparing an employment video:

- Be sure the video makes a professional appearance and is complimentary to you. A "home movie" quality recording will be a liability instead of an asset to your application.

- Avoid long "talking head" segments. Include segments that reflect you in a variety of activities; shots that include samples of your work are also desirable.

- Remember that visual media (such as photographs and videos) encourage the potential employer to focus on your physical characteristics and attributes, which may lead to undesired stereotyping and discrimination.

Be sure to advertise the availability of your portfolio and employment video to maximize its exposure. List your URL in the identification section of your résumé. In your application letter, motivate the prospective employer to view your portfolio or video by describing the types of information included. Talk enthusiastically about the detailed supplementary information available during your job interview, and encourage the interviewer to view it when convenient.

Composing Application Messages

When employers invite you to send a résumé, they expect you to include an **application** or **cover message**—regardless of whether the résumé is sent by mail or electronically. A mailed paper résumé should be accompanied by an ap-

plication letter. When a résumé is submitted electronically, the application "letter" can take the form of an email message. As you have learned, a résumé summarizes information related to the job's requirements and the applicant's qualifications. An application message (1) seeks to arouse interest in the résumé, (2) introduces it, and (3) interprets it in terms of employer benefits. The application message is placed on top of the résumé so it can be read first by the employer.

The application message is persuasive, so it should be written inductively. It is designed to convince an employer that qualifications are adequate, just as a sales message is designed to convince a buyer that a product will satisfy a need. Like sales messages, application messages are either solicited or unsolicited. Job advertisements *solicit* applications. Unsolicited application messages have greater need for attention-getters; otherwise, solicited and unsolicited application messages are based on the same principles.

Unsolicited application messages are the same basic message (perhaps with slight modifications) sent to many prospective employers. By sending unsolicited messages, you increase your chances of locating potential openings and may alert employers to needs they had not previously identified for someone of your abilities. However, sending unsolicited messages has some disadvantages. Because the employer's specific needs are not known, the opening paragraph will likely be more general (less targeted to a specific

application (cover message)
a message placed on top of the résumé so it can be read first by the employer

unsolicited application message
an unrequested message sent to many prospective employers and containing the same basic message

objective ⑥
Write an application message that effectively introduces an accompanying print (designed) or electronic résumé.

position) than the opening paragraph in solicited messages. The process could also be expensive.

Joseph Priestley wrote the letter in Figure 14-7 to accompany a chronological résumé that he prepared after completing the company/job profile of an entry-level auditor posted at the text support site. The time Joseph devoted to analyzing the job, the company, and his qualifications was well spent.

Persuasive Organization

A persuasive message is designed to convince the reader to take action, which in this case is to read the résumé and invite you to an interview. Because an application message is persuasive, organize it as you would a sales message:

Sales Message	Application Message
Gets attention	Gets attention
Introduces product	Introduces qualifications
Presents evidence	Presents evidence
Encourages action	Encourages action
(sells a product, service, or idea)	(results in an interview)

Like a well-written sales message, a well-written application message uses a central selling feature as a theme. The central selling feature is introduced in the first or second paragraph and stressed in paragraphs that follow. Two to four paragraphs are normally sufficient for supporting evidence. Consider order of importance as a basis for their sequence, with the most significant aspects of your preparation coming first.

Gain the Receiver's Attention

To gain attention, begin the message by identifying the job sought and describing how your qualifications fit the job requirements. This information will provide instant confirmation that you are a qualified applicant for a position open in that company. An employer required to read hundreds of application letters and résumés will appreciate this direct, concise approach.

For a job that has been announced, you may indicate in the first paragraph how you learned of the position—for example, employee referral, customer referral, executive referral, newspaper advertising, or job fair. Your disclosure will not only confirm you are seeking a job the manager has open but also will facilitate evaluation of the company's recruiting practices. Note that the opening of the letter in Figure 14-7 on the next page indicates the applicant learned of the position through a posting on JOBTRACK.

An opening for an unsolicited message must be more persuasive: You must convince the interviewer to continue to read your qualifications even though a job may not exist. As in the opening of a solicited message, indicate the type of position sought and your qualifications but be more creative in gaining attention. The following paragraph uses the applicant's knowledge of recent company developments and an intense interest in the company's future to gain receiver attention.

> During the past few years, TelCom has experienced phenomenal growth through various acquisitions, mergers, and market expansion. With this growth come new opportunities, new customers, and the need for new team players to work in sales and marketing. While following the growth of TelCom, I have become determined to join this exciting team and am eager to show you that my educational background, leadership abilities, and internship experience qualify me for the job.

Provide Evidence of Qualifications

For graduates entering the world of full-time work for the first time, educational backgrounds usually are more impressive than work histories. They can benefit from interpreting their educational experiences as meaningful, job-related experiences. An applicant for an auditor's trainee program should do more than merely report having taken courses in auditing theory and practice:

> In my auditing theory and practice class, I could see specific application of principles encountered in my human relations and psychology classes. Questions about leadership and motivation seemed to recur throughout the course: What really motivates executives? Why are auditors feared at many levels? How can those fears be overcome? How can egos be salvaged? The importance of the human element was a central focus of many courses and my research report, "The Auditor as a Psychologist."

Because the preceding paragraph included topics discussed in a class, do not assume that your application message should do likewise. Recognizing that auditors must be tactful (a point on which the person reading the message will surely agree), the applicant included some details of a class. That technique is a basic in persuasion: Do not just say a product or idea is good; say what makes it good. Do not just say that an educational or work experience was beneficial; say what made it so.

By making paragraphs long enough to include interpretation of experiences on the present or previous job, you show an employer that you are well prepared

Figure 14-7  *Example of an Application Letter*

- *Addresses letter to specific person using correct name and job title.*

- *Reveals how applicant learned of position, identifies specific job sought, and introduces background.*

- *Discusses how education relates to job requirements.*

- *Uses bulleted list to highlight qualifications that correspond to job requirements.*

- *Introduces résumé for additional information.*

- *Encourages employer to take action without sounding pushy or apologetic.*

Format Pointers
Formats as formal business letter since message is accompanying print résumé. Abbreviated email message followed by inline résumé in ASCII or RTF format would be appropriate for electronic submission.

Uses same high-quality paper as for résumé (neutral color, standard size); includes writer's address and contact information.

Joseph Priestley • 89 Lincoln Street • Santa Fe, NM 78285-9063

March 15, 2010

Justine Hong, Partner
Clark and Clark, CPAs
100 Speedway Boulevard
Albuquerque, NM 78710-1000

Dear Ms. Hong:

I am applying for the entry-level accounting position advertised on JOBTRACK. Related work experience, a bachelor's degree in accounting, and my communication skills and excellent work ethic qualify me for this position.

My interest in tax issues led me to complete two courses where I learned about federal, state, and local tax systems, income and expense definitions, and the effect of property transactions, investing, and financing and operations on a company's tax obligations. I have also taken courses in managerial accounting, financial statement auditing, and performance management issues. The latter course helped me to understand management decision-making and control systems and how they can enhance the achievement of an organization's objectives.

My internship at Gerald and Associates has prepared me for entry-level accounting assignments in your firm:

- Prepared numerous auditing reports for corporate clients.
- Created and maintained spreadsheets and databases, containing client audit information.
- Worked with audit teams to hone communication skills and developed phone skills necessary to effectively interact with professional clientele.

Please review the enclosed résumé for additional information about my accounting education and related work experience. Please call or write so we can discuss my joining the staff at Clark and Clark.

Sincerely,

Joseph Priestley
Joseph Priestley

Enclosure

for your next job. For example, the following excerpt from an applicant whose only work experience was at a fast-food restaurant is short and general: *For three months last summer, I worked at Marketplace Bagel. While the assistant manager was on vacation, I supervised a crew of five on the evening shift. Evaluations of my work were superior.*

As the only reference to the Marketplace Bagel experience, the paragraph conveys one employer's apparent satisfaction with performance. Superior evaluations and some supervisory responsibility are evidence of that satisfaction, but added details and interpretation could make the message more convincing:

> In my summer job at Marketplace Bagel, I learned the value of listening carefully when taking orders, making change quickly and accurately, offering suggestions when customers seemed hesitant, and keeping a cheerful attitude. Supervising a crew of five while the assistant manager was on vacation, I appreciated the importance of fairness and diplomacy in working with other employees.

Apparently, the applicant's experience has been meaningful. It called attention to qualities that managers like to see in employees: willingness to listen, speed, accuracy, concern for clients or customers, a positive attitude, fairness, and tact. As a *learning* experience, the Marketplace Bagel job has taught or reinforced some principles that the employer sees can be transferred to the job being sought.

In this section, you can discuss qualifications you have developed by participating in student organizations, student government, athletics, or community organizations. Be specific in describing the skills you have gained that can be applied directly on the job—for example, organizational, leadership, spoken and written communication skills, and budgeting and financial management. You can also use your involvement as a vehicle for discussing important personal traits vital to the success of a business—interpersonal skills, motivation, imagination, responsibility, team orientation, and so forth.

> For the past year, I have served as state president of Phi Beta Lambda, a national business student organization. By coordinating various statewide meetings and leadership seminars, I have refined communication, organizational, and interpersonal skills.

Finally, end this section with an indirect reference to the résumé. If you refer to it in the first or second paragraph, readers may wonder whether they are expected to turn from the message at that point and look at the résumé. Avoid the obvious statement *"Enclosed please find my résumé"* or *"A résumé is enclosed."* Instead, refer indirectly to the résumé while restating your qualifications. The following sentence emphasizes that references can confirm applicant's qualifications:

> References listed on the enclosed résumé would be glad to comment on my accounting education and experience.

Encourage Action

Once you have presented your qualifications and referred to your enclosed résumé, the next move is to encourage the receiver to extend an invitation for an interview. The goal is to introduce the idea of action without apologizing for doing so and without being demanding or "pushy." If the final paragraph (action closing) of your message is preceded by impressive paragraphs, you need not press hard for a response. Just mentioning the idea of a future discussion is probably sufficient. If you have significant related experience that you have developed as a central selling feature, mentioning this experience in the action closing adds unity and stresses your strongest qualification one last time. Forceful statements about *when* and *how* to respond are unnecessary and irritating. Do avoid some frequently made errors:

- **Setting a date.** "May I have an appointment with you on March 14?" The date you name could be inconvenient, or even if it is convenient for the employer, your forwardness in setting it could be resented.

- **Expressing doubt.** "If you agree," "I hope you will," and "Should you decide" use subjunctive words that indicate lack of confidence.

- **Sounding apologetic.** "May I take some of your time" or "I know how busy you are" may seem considerate, but an apology is inappropriate when discussing ways you can contribute to a company.

- **Sounding overconfident.** "I know you will want to set up an appointment." This statement is presumptuous and egotistical.

- **Giving permission to call.** "You may call me at 555-6543." By making the call sound like a privilege ("may call") you could alienate the reader. Implied meaning: You are very selective about the calls you take, but the employer does qualify.

- **Reporting capability of response.** "You can call me at 555-6543." When a number or address is given, employers are aware they are capable of using it ("can call").

The following sentences are possible closing sentences that refer to an invitation to interview. They are not intended as model sentences that should appear in your message. Because finding the right job is so important, you will be well rewarded for the time and thought invested in original wording.

- **"When a date and time can be arranged, I would like to talk with you."** The statement does not indicate who will do the arranging, and the meeting place and the subject of the conversation are understood.

- **"I would appreciate an opportunity to discuss the loan officer's job with you."** The indirect reference to action is not forceful. However, if the applicant has impressive qualifications, the reader will want an interview and will not need to be pushed.

- **"I would appreciate an appointment to discuss your employment needs and my information systems experience."** The statement asks for the interview and re-emphasizes the applicant's strong related work experience.

General Writing Guidelines

Writing an excellent application message may be the most difficult message you ever attempt to write. The key to success is to avoid standard verbiage and make sure that your self-marketing connects *your* experiences to your future with a specific company and reflects *your* personality and values. The following writing techniques will help you craft an original and impressive message that distinguishes your application message from the competition:

- **Substitute fresh, original expressions that reflect contemporary language.** Overly casual expressions and overused statements will give your message a dull, unimaginative tone that may be perceived as disrespectful. Obvious ideas such as "This is an application," "I read your ad," and "I am writing to apply for" are sufficiently understood without making direct statements. With the application message *and* résumé in hand, a reader learns nothing from "I am enclosing my résumé for your review." Observe caution in choosing overused words such as *applicant, application, opening, position, vacancy,* and *interview.*

- **Avoid overuse of "I" and writer-focused statements.** Because the message is designed to sell your services, some use of "I" is natural and expected; however, restrict the number of times "I" is used, especially as the first word in a paragraph. Focus on providing specific evidence that you can meet the company's needs. The employer is not interested in reading about your need to earn more income, to be closer to your work, to have more pleasant surroundings, or to gain greater advancement opportunities.

- **Avoid unconvincing generalizations that may sound boastful.** Self-confidence is commendable, but overconfidence (or worse still, just plain bragging) is objectionable. Overly strong adjectives, self-judgmental terms, and unsupported generalizations damage your credibility. Instead of labeling your performance as "superior" or "excellent," or describing yourself as "an efficient, technically skilled team player," give supporting facts that show the interviewer you can deliver on what you're selling.

- **Tailor the message to the employer's need.** To impress the interviewer that your message is not a generic one sent to everyone, provide requested information and communicate an understanding of the particular company, job requirements, and field.

- **Provide requested information.** Job listings often request certain information: "Must provide own transportation and be willing to travel. Give educational background, work experience, and salary expected." Discuss these points in your application message. Preferably, the question of salary is left until the interview, allowing you to focus your message on your contributions to the company—not what you want from the company (money). Discussion of salary isn't meaningful until after a mutually successful interview; however, if an ad requests a statement about it, the message should address it. You may give a minimum figure or range, indicate willingness to accept a figure that is customary for work of that type, or indicate a preference for discussing salary at the interview.

- **Communicate knowledge of the company, job requirements, and language of the field.** Your statements about a company's rapid expansion or competitive advantage show that you really are interested in the company, read widely, do more than you are required to do, gather information before making decisions, and so on. However, phrase these statements carefully to avoid the perception of insincere flattery. For example, referring to the employer as "*the* leader in the field," "*the* best in the business," or "a great company" may appear as an attempt to get a favorable decision as a reward for making a complimentary statement. To reflect your understanding of the job requirements, use indirect statements that are informative and tactful. Direct statements such as "The requirements of this job are . . ." presents information the employer presumes you already know; "An auditor should be able to . . ." and "Sales personnel should avoid . . ." sound like a lecture and may be perceived as condescending. Discussing experiences related to a specific job requirement or your preference for work that requires this skill reveals your understanding without a direct statement. Including terminology commonly used by the profession allows you to communicate clearly in terms the reader understands; it also saves space and implies your background in the field.

- **Focus on strengths, and portray a positive attitude.** Concentrate on the positive aspects of your education or experience that have prepared you for the particular job. Apologizing for a shortcoming or admitting failure only weakens your case and raises questions about your self-esteem. Do not discuss your current employer's shortcomings. Regardless of how negatively you perceive your present employer, that perception has little to do with your prospective employer's needs. Also, if you speak negatively of your present employer, you could be perceived as someone who would do the same to the next employer.

Finishing Touches

The importance of professional formatting and careful proofreading of a print document is generally understood. However, proofing and formatting a "real" résumé and letter appears more important to some applicants than producing quality email submissions. Employers frequently voice concern with the sloppiness and unprofessional appearance and content of electronic submissions. To survive the skeptical eye of an interviewer scanning

Keep all your job application materials polished and professional, and remember that presentation (like with a gift) matters.

for ways to reject an applicant, allow yourself time to produce a professional-looking document regardless of the presentation or delivery option you've chosen. Include these steps in your finishing phase:

- Regardless of your delivery option, address your application letter or email message to the individual who is responsible for hiring for the position you are seeking rather than sending the document to the "Human Resources Department" or "To Whom It May Concern." If necessary, consult the company's annual report or website, or call the company to locate this information.

- Verify the correct spelling, job title, and address, and send a personalized message to the appropriate individual.

- Keep the message short and easy to read. A one-page letter is sufficient for most applications but especially for students and graduates entering the job market.

- Apply visual enhancements learned previously to enhance the appeal and readability of the message and to draw attention to your strengths.

- Definitely keep the paragraphs short, and consider listing your top four or five achievements or other important ideas in a bulleted list.

- Use paper that matches the résumé (color, weight, texture, and size). The watermark should be readable across the sheet in the same direction as the printing. Since you're using plain paper, include your street address and city, state, and ZIP Code above the date or formatted as a letterhead at the top of the page.

  - Include "Enclosure" below the signature block to alert the employer that a résumé is enclosed. The proper letter format is shown in the example in Figure 14-7.

- Get opinions from others, and make revisions where necessary.

When preparing an application message for email submission, career experts recommend formatting it as a business letter with the complete address of the company exactly as presented in a letter sent by mail. To compete with the high volumes of junk mail, daily messages, and fear of computer viruses, you must provide a motive for an interviewer to open an unexpected message from an unknown person. Messages with missing or vague subject lines are annoying and may be ignored or deleted immediately. To bring attention to your message, include the name of the person referring you to the position directly in the subject line or mention your email is a follow-up to a conversation (RE: Follow-up: Résumé for . . .). If the message is totally "cold," describe the specific value you can add to the company (Résumé for Forensics Accountant with Extensive ACL Skills). Stay away from tricks such as marking an email "urgent" or adding "re" to pass your message off as a reply to an earlier message. Typically, you will want to send a complete letter and copy of your résumé by regular mail as a follow-up to the email submission. These suggestions are illustrated in Figure 14-8, a sample application letter an applicant sent after talking with a prospective employer at a career fair.

Figure 14-8 Example of Application Message Sent by Email

- **Provides specific subject line that ensures message will be opened.**

- **Reveals how applicant learned of position, and confirms knowledge of and interest in company.**

- **Condenses content of persuasive application letter sent by mail into one screen. Avoids tendency to send impersonal message stating résumé is attached.**

- **Introduces résumé and reminds interviewer that submission was requested.**

- **Encourages employer to take action without sounding pushy or apologetic.**

Format Pointers
Formats as formal business letter with complete address exactly as done when job credentials are sent by mail.

Complete letter and printed copy of résumé will be sent as follow-up to email.

New Message

To: mtownsend@principle.com
From: mtrueblood@unj.edu
Subject: Career Fair Follow-up: Résumé for Melissa Trueblood

October 15, 2009

Margaret Townsend
Human Resources Manager
Principle Pharmaceuticals Ltd.
1208 West 34th Street
Newark, NJ 23140-1000

Dear Ms. Townsend:

It was a pleasure meeting you at the career fair this morning. The opportunities offered in pharmaceutical sales identify your company as a leader in today's global marketplace.

My education and related work experience in sales enable me to be a valuable asset to your company:

- A degree in communication with a minor in marketing from the University of New Jersey.
- Knowledge of the medical field gained as an administrative assistant at Dr. Joan Petti's internal medicine practice.
- Customer service skills gained as a sales associate at North Street Drug and Pharmacy.
- Excellent communication skills gained through numerous group projects in an academic setting and through three years' experience working with colleagues and customers in fast-paced retail and health care environments.

Please review the attached résumé that you requested for additional information about my education and work experience. Please contact me so we can discuss my joining Principle Pharmaceuticals.

Sincerely,

Melissa Trueblood

Attachment

LISTEN UP!

SHE DID

BCOM2 was designed for students just like you—busy people who want choices, flexibility, and multiple learning options.

BCOM2 delivers concise, focused information in a fresh and contemporary format. And...

BCOM2 gives you a variety of online learning materials designed with you in mind.

At **4ltrpress.cengage.com/bcom,** you'll find electronic resources such as **videos, audio downloads,** and **interactive quizzes** for each chapter.

These resources will help supplement your understanding of core concepts in a format that fits your busy lifestyle. Visit **4ltrpress.cengage.com/bcom** to learn more about the multiple resources available to help you succeed!

Interviewing for a Job and Preparing Employment Messages

Types of Employment Interviews

Most companies conduct various types of interviews before hiring a new employee. While the number and type of interviews vary among companies, applicants typically begin with a screening interview, an in-depth interview, an on-site interview with multiple interviewers, and sometimes a stress interview. Depending on the goals of the interviewer, interviews may follow a structured or an unstructured approach.

objective ①
Explain the nature of structured, unstructured, stress, team, and virtual interviews.

Structured Interviews

In a **structured interview**, generally used in the screening process, the interviewer follows a predetermined agenda, including a checklist of items or a series of questions and statements designed to elicit the necessary information or interviewee reaction. Because each applicant answers the same questions, the interviewer has comparable data to evaluate. A particular type of structured interview is the behavior-based interview, in which applicants are asked to give specific examples of

> **structured interview**
> *an interview in which the interviewer follows a predetermined agenda, including a checklist of items or a series of questions and statements designed to elicit the necessary information or interviewee reaction*

occasions in which they demonstrated particular behaviors or skills. The interviewer already knows what skills, knowledge, and qualities successful candidates must possess. The examples you provide will allow him or her to determine whether you possess them.[1]

Companies are finding computer-assisted interviews to be a reliable and effective way to conduct screening interviews. Applicants use a computer to provide answers to a list of carefully selected questions. A computer-generated report provides standard, reliable information about each applicant that enables an interviewer to decide whether to invite the applicant for a second interview. The report flags any contradictory responses (e.g., an applicant indicated he was terminated for absenteeism but later indicated that he thought his former employer would give him an outstanding recommendation), highlights any potential problem areas (e.g., an applicant responded that she would remain on the job less than a year), and generates a list of structured interview questions for the interviewer to ask (e.g., "Terrance, you said you feel your former employer would rate you average. Why don't you feel it would be higher?").

Research has shown that applicants prefer computer interviews to human interviews and that they respond more honestly to a computer, feeling less need

to give polite, socially acceptable responses. Because expert computer systems can overcome some of the inherent problems with traditional face-to-face interviews, the overall quality of the selection process improves. Typical interviewer errors include forgetting to ask important questions, talking too much, being reluctant to ask sensitive questions, forming unjustified negative first impressions, obtaining unreliable and illegal information that makes an applicant feel judged, and using interview data ineffectively.[2] Regardless of whether the interview is face-to-face or computer assisted, you will need to provide objective, truthful evidence of your qualifications as they relate to specific job requirements.

Unstructured Interviews

An **unstructured interview** is a freewheeling exchange that may shift from one subject to another, depending on the interests of the participants. Some experienced interviewers are able to make a structured interview seem unstructured. The goal of many unstructured interviews is to explore unknown areas to determine the applicant's ability to speak comfortably about a wide range of topics.

Stress Interviews

A **stress interview** is designed to place the interviewee in an anxiety-producing situation so an evaluation may be made of the interviewee's performance under stress. In all cases, interviewees should attempt to assess the nature of the interview quickly and adjust behavior accordingly. Understanding that interviewers sometimes deliberately create anxiety to assess your ability to perform under stress should help you handle such interviews more effectively. As the following discussion of different interviewer styles reveals, you, as an interviewee, can perform much better when you understand the interviewer's purpose.

Team Interviews

As organizations have increased emphasis on team approaches to management and problem solving, selecting employees who best fit their cultures and styles has become especially important. Involving key people in the organization in the candidate selection process has led to new interview styles. In a series interview, the candidate meets individually with a number of different interviewers. Each interviewer will likely ask questions from a differing perspective; for instance, a line manager may ask questions related to the applicant's knowledge of specific job tasks, while the vice president of operations may ask questions related to the applicant's career goals. Some questions will likely be asked more than once in the process. Team interviews are a popular trend in organizations that desire a broad range of input in the hiring decision but want to avoid the drawn-out nature of series interviews.

Virtual Interviews

Many companies, from IBM and Microsoft to Nike and Hallmark Cards, are now screening candidates through video interviews from remote locations and saving money and time in the process. **Virtual interviews** conducted via videoconferencing technology are a more productive use of a recruiter's valuable time. Companies may replay the taped interviews to take another look at a candidate. Positions are filled quickly after interviewing applicants from around the world and achieved with a significant reduction in travel costs.[3] The general consensus is that the video interview is excellent for screening applicants, but a "live interview" is appropriate for the important final interview.

Various companies have direct hookups with the career services centers of colleges and universities to interview students. These virtual interviews allow students to meet representatives from large companies who typically would not visit colleges with small applicant pools and to interview with companies who could not travel because of financial constraints or other reasons. Students simply sit in front of a camera, dial in, and interview with multiple interviewers; in some cases, several applicants are interviewed simultaneously. Some photocopy stores are now equipped for video interviews. Companies and executive search firms use higher-quality systems set up in specially equipped rooms for middle-level and senior management jobs.

As you would imagine, some candidates who interview well in person may fail on camera. Because of the additional stress of functioning under the glare of a camera, videoconferencing is an excellent method to screen out candidates who cannot work under pressure. Likewise, a candidate who can't operate the controls would likely be eliminated from a highly technical position.

You should prepare for a virtual interview in a different manner than you would for a traditional interview. First, suggest a preliminary telephone conversation with the interviewer to establish rapport. Arrive early and acquaint yourself with the equipment; know how to adjust the volume, brightness, and other camera functions so you can adjust the equipment for optimal performance after the interview begins. Second, concentrate on projecting strong nonverbal skills: Speak clearly, but do not slow down; be certain you are centered in the frame, sit straight; look up, not down; and use gestures to communicate energy and reinforce points while avoiding excessive motion that will appear blurry. Third, realize voices may be out of step with the pictures if there is a lag between the video and audio transmissions. You will need to adjust to the timing (e.g., slow down your voice) to avoid interrupting the interviewer.[4]

Preparing for an Interview

© Jon Feingersh/Image Source

Pre-interview planning involves learning something about the company or organization, doing some studying about yourself, and making sure your appearance and mannerisms will not detract from the impression you hope to make.

Study the Prospective Employer

Nothing can hurt a job candidate more than knowing little about the organization. No knowledge indicates insincerity, and the interviewer does not want to waste precious interview time providing the candidate with information that should have been gathered long before.

Companies that have publicly traded stock are required to publish annual reports that are available in school libraries or online. Other information can be obtained from the printed and electronic sources you consulted when preparing the company/job profile discussed in Chapter 14. Employees of the company or other students who have interviewed may be of help to the interviewee. Some universities have taped interviews with various company recruiters and make them available to students. Pertinent information about the company and the job sought needed for an interview includes the following:

objective ②
Explain the steps in the interview process.

College students frequently schedule on-campus interviews with representatives from various business organizations. Following the on-campus interviews, successful candidates often are invited for further interviews on the company premises. The purpose of the second interview is to give executives and administrators other than the human resources interviewer an opportunity to appraise the candidate. Whether on campus or on company premises, interview methods and practices vary with the situation.

Company Information

Be sure to research the following on the companies with which you interview:

- *Name.* Know, for example, that *Exxon* was a computer-generated name selected in the 1970s to identify the merged identity of an old, established oil company.
- *Status in the industry.* Know the company's share of the market, its *Fortune* 500 standing if any, its sales, and its number of employees.
- *Latest stock market quote.* Be familiar with current market deviations and trends.
- *Recent news and developments.* Read current business periodicals for special feature articles on the company, its new products, and its corporate leadership.
- *Scope of the company.* Is it local, national, or international?
- *Corporate officers.* Know the names of the chairperson, president, and chief executive officer.
- *Products and services.* Study the company's offerings, target markets, and innovative strategies.

Job Information

Be sure to know the following about the job you are seeking:

- *Job title.* Know the job titles of typical entry-level positions.
- *Job qualifications.* Understand the specific knowledge and skills desired.
- *Probable salary range.* Study salaries in comparable firms as well as regional averages.
- *Career path of the job.* What opportunities for advancement are available?

Study Yourself

When you know something about the company, you will also know something about the kinds of jobs or training programs the company has to offer. Next, review your answers to the company/job profile. This systematic comparison of your qualifications and job requirements helps you identify pertinent information

(strengths or special abilities) to be included in your résumé. If you cannot see a relationship between you and the job or company, you may have difficulty demonstrating the interest or sincerity needed to sell yourself.

Plan Your Appearance

An employment interviewer once said she would not hire a job applicant who did not meet her *extremities* test: fingernails, shoes, and hair must be clean and well kept. This interviewer felt that if the candidate did not take care of those details, the candidate could not really be serious about, or fit into, her organization. Other important guidelines include avoiding heavy makeup and large, excessive jewelry. Select conservative clothes, and be certain clothing is clean, unwrinkled, and properly fitted. Additionally, avoid smoking, drinking, or wearing heavy fragrance.

You can locate a wealth of information on appropriate interview dress from numerous electronic and printed

© Brand X Pictures/Jupiterimages

sources (many are listed in Chapter 14). Additionally, talk with professors in your field, professors of professional protocol (business etiquette), personnel at your career services center, and graduates who have recently acquired jobs in your field. Research the company dress code—real or implied—ahead of time. If you *look* and *dress* like the people who already work at the company, the interviewer will be able to visualize you working there.

Plan Your Time and Materials

One of the worst things you can do is be late for an interview. If something should happen to prevent your arriving on time, telephone an apology. Another mistake is to miss the interview entirely. Plan your time so that you will arrive early and can unwind and review mentally the things you plan to accomplish. Be sure to bring a professional portfolio that contains everything you will need during the interview. These items might include copies of your résumé, a list of references and/or recommendations, a professional-looking pen, paper for taking notes, highlights of what you know about the company, a list of questions you plan to ask, and previous correspondence with the company.

Practice for the Interview

objective ③

Prepare effective answers to questions often asked in job interviews, including illegal interview questions.

The job interview may be the most important face-to-face interaction you ever have. You will be selling yourself in competition with others. How you listen and how you talk are characteristics the interviewer will be able to measure. Your actions, your mannerisms, and your appearance will combine to give the total picture of how you are perceived. Added to the obvious things you have acquired from your education, experience, and activities, your interview performance can give a skilled interviewer an excellent picture of you. Practicing for an interview will help you learn to handle the nervousness that is natural when interviewing.

To prepare for an interview, gather all of the possible interview questions that you might find and think about how you might respond to each in such a way

as to showcase your best qualities and capabilities. You want to practice, but do not memorize verbatim answers that will sound rehearsed and insincere. Instead, think carefully about how your accomplishments match the job requirements, and practice communicating these ideas smoothly, confidently, and professionally. Additional steps in the preparation process include the following:

- **List five or six key points that you want to emphasize.** Likely, you will want to present your education as a major asset. You should point out its relationship to the job for which you are being considered. Even more important, the fact that you have succeeded in academics indicates that you have the ability to learn. Because most companies expect you to learn something on the job, your ability to learn and thus quickly become productive may be your greatest asset. Even lack of work experience may be an asset: You have acquired no bad work habits that you will have to unlearn.

  Additionally, be sure to provide evidence of your interpersonal skills. You will want to communicate that you can get along with others and are sensitive to diversity:

  - What did you do in college that helped you get along with others?

  - Were you a member, an officer, or president of an organization?

  - In regard to your organization, what did you accomplish? How did others perceive you? Were you a leader? How did your followers respond to your leadership style?

  - Can you organize projects?

  The extracurricular activities listed on your résumé give an indication of these traits, but how you talk about them in your interview helps. "I started as corresponding secretary and was subsequently elected to higher office for four semesters, eventually becoming president" is a statement that may prove your leadership qualities. If you can show your organization moved to greater heights, you will appear successful as well. You can also use questions about your extracurricular activities to show that you have broad, balanced interests rather than a single, time-consuming avocation that could lead to burnout and stress if carried to the job.

  What are other skills that graduating students need to succeed in a cross-cultural, interdependent workforce? While academic performance is weighted more heavily for some types of jobs than others, the ability to juggle a complicated schedule is weighed heavily by many employers as an important job-success factor. Additionally, a UNESCO report of employer

Figure 15-1 Skills Needed: Balance of Soft and Hard Skills

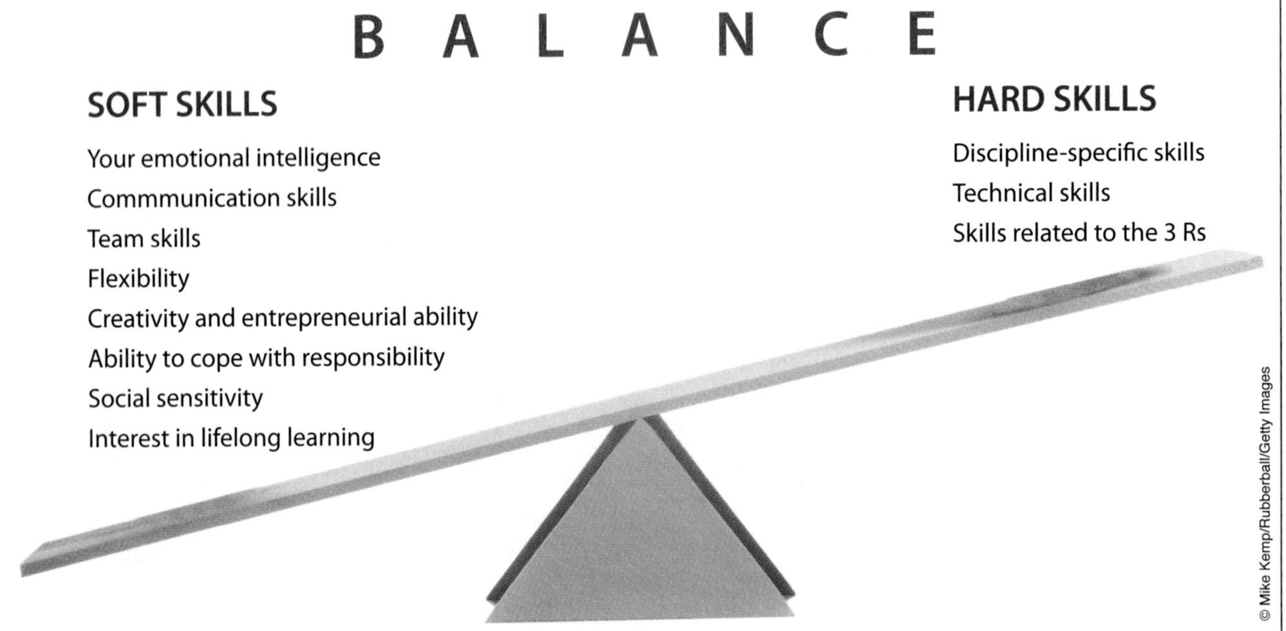

BALANCE

SOFT SKILLS

Your emotional intelligence

Commmunication skills

Team skills

Flexibility

Creativity and entrepreneurial ability

Ability to cope with responsibility

Social sensitivity

Interest in lifelong learning

HARD SKILLS

Discipline-specific skills

Technical skills

Skills related to the 3 Rs

© Mike Kemp/Rubberball/Getty Images

views revealed certain skills to be essential for workers in today's business climate, as shown in Figure 15-1.[5]

Consider these general job success traits and then use your knowledge of the job requirements and your own strengths to develop your "central selling features." These key points targeted to your audience are the central element of a winning argument: You are able and willing to add value to a company.

- **Be prepared to answer standard interview questions.** These questions are designed to show (1) why you want the job, (2) why you want to work for this organization, and (3) why the company should want you. Practice concise but fully developed answers that reflect your personality and your communication power. While one-word answers aren't adequate, long-winded answers may prevent interviewers from asking you other planned questions critical to making an informed decision. Many of the career sites and printed sources discussed in Chapter 14 include lists of frequently asked interview questions; some sources provide suggested answers to the more difficult questions.

- **Be prepared to answer behavioral questions.** These questions are designed to challenge you to provide evidence of your skills or the behaviors required to perform the job. Rather than asking applicants how they feel about certain things, interviewers are finding that asking potential employees for specific examples to illustrate their answers is a more objective way to evaluate applicants' skills. Behavioral questions include the following:

- Describe a time when you (1) worked well under pressure, (2) worked effectively with others, (3) organized a major project, (4) motivated and led others, (5) solved a difficult problem, and (6) accepted constructive criticism.

- What was the most difficult problem you had to overcome in your last job (or an academic or extracurricular activity)? How did you cope with it?

- Tell me about a time you had difficulty working with a supervisor or coworker (professor, peer in a team in a class setting). How did you handle the situation?

- Describe something you have done that shows initiative and willingness to work.

- How have your extracurricular activities, part-time work experience, or volunteer work prepared you for work in our company?

- Tell me about a time you hit a wall trying to push forward a great idea.

To prepare for answering behavioral questions, brainstorm to identify stories that illustrate how your qualifications fit the job requirements. These stories should show you applying the skills needed on the job. Career counselors recommend using the STAR method (Situation or Task/Action/Result) as a consistent format to help you present a complete answer to these open-ended questions. You first describe a situation or task you were involved in, the action you took, and finally the result of your effort.[6] Even if the interviewer doesn't ask behavioral questions, you can use this approach when answering standard interview questions.

- **Be prepared to demonstrate logical thinking and creativity.** Many companies ask applicants to solve brain teasers and riddles, create art out of paper bags, solve complex business problems, and even spend a day acting as managers of fictitious companies. These techniques are used to gauge an applicant's ability to think quickly and creatively and observe an emotional response to an awkward situation.[7] You cannot anticipate this type of interview question, but you can familiarize yourself with mind teasers that have been used. Most importantly, however, recognize the interviewer's purpose; relax, and do your best to showcase your logical reasoning, creativity, or your courage to even try.

- **Be prepared to discuss salary and benefits.** For most entry-level positions, the beginning salary is fixed. However, if you have work experience, excellent scholarship records, or added maturity, you may be able to obtain a higher salary. The interviewer should initiate the salary topic. What you should know is the general range for candidates with your qualifications so that your response to a question about how much you would expect is reasonable.

If you have other job offers, you are in a position to compare salaries, jobs, and companies. In this case, you may suggest to the interviewer that you would expect a competitive salary and that you have been offered X dollars by another firm. If you really want to know about it, simply ask courteously how much the salary would be for someone with your qualifications. If you really believe the job offers the nonmonetary benefits you seek, do not attempt to make salary a major issue.

Typically, an interviewer will introduce the subject of benefits without your asking about them. In some cases, a discussion of total salary and "perks" (perquisites) is reserved for a follow-up interview. If nothing has been said about certain benefits, you should take the liberty of asking, particularly

<<Tread lightly around salary issues: Asking questions in this area may imply that you're more interested in money than in your contribution to the company.

when an item may be especially important to you. Health insurance, for example, may be very important when you have children. Retirement planning, however, is less appropriate for a new graduate to discuss.

- **Be knowledgeable of interview questions that might lead to discriminatory hiring practices.** Surveys indicate that more than one third of applicants have been asked an illegal interview question pertaining to race, age, marital status, religion, or ethnic background.[8]

The Equal Employment Opportunity Commission (EEOC) and Fair Employment Practices Guidelines make it clear that an employer cannot legally discriminate against a job applicant on the basis of race, color, gender, age, religion, national origin, or disability. Interviewers must restrict questions to an applicant's ability to perform specific job-related functions essential to the job sought. Generally, the following topics should not be introduced during an interview or during the small talk that precedes or follows one:

- *National origin and religion.* "You have an unusual accent; where were you born?" "What religious holidays will require you to miss work?"

- *Age.* "I see you attended Metro High School; what year did you graduate?" "Could you provide a copy of your birth certificate?"

- *Disabilities, health conditions, and physical characteristics not reasonably related to the job.* "Do you have a disability that would interfere with your ability to perform the job? "Have you ever been injured on the job?" "Have you ever been treated by a psychiatrist?" "How much alcohol do you consume each week?" "What prescription drugs are you currently taking?"

- *Marital status, spouse's employment, or dependents.* "Are you married?" "Who is going to watch your children if you work for us?" "Do you plan to have children?" "Is your spouse employed?"

Additionally, employers may not ask the names or relationships of people with whom you live.

- *Arrests or criminal convictions that are not related to the job.* "Have you ever been arrested other than for traffic violations? If so, explain." Keep in mind that the arrest/conviction record of a person applying for a job as a law enforcement officer or a teacher could be highly relevant to the job, but the same information could be illegal for a person applying for a job as an engineer.

Since interviewers may ask illegal questions either because of lack of training or an accidental slip, you must decide how to respond. You can refuse to answer and state that the question is improper, though you risk offending the interviewer. A second option is to answer the illegal question, knowing it is illegal and not related to the job requirements. A third approach for responding to an illegal question is to provide a low-key response such as "How does this question relate to how I will do my job?" or to answer the legitimate concern that probably prompted the question. For example, an interviewer who asks "Do you plan to have children?" is probably concerned about how long you might remain on the job. An answer to this concern would be "I plan to pursue a career regardless of whether I decide to raise a family." If you can see no legitimate concern in a question, such as "Do you own your home, rent, or live with parents?" answer, "I'm not sure how that question relates to the job. Can you explain?"[9]

- **Be prepared to ask the interviewer questions.** The interview is not only an opportunity for the organization to determine whether it wants to hire you but also for you to figure out whether you would be a good fit and happy working for it. Nowadays, interviews should be two-way conversations aimed at both parties achieving these goals.

Good questions show the interviewer that you have initiative and are interested in making a well-informed decision. For that reason, be certain not to say "I don't have any questions." Focus on questions that help you gain information about the company and the job that you could not learn from published sources

or persons other than the interviewer. Do not waste the interviewer's time asking questions that show you are unprepared for the interview (e.g., questions about the company's scope, products/services, job requirements, new developments). Having committed a block of uninterrupted time to talk to you, the interviewer will resent this blatant lack of commitment and respect for the company. Avoid questions about salary and benefits that imply you are interested more in money than in the contribution you can make.

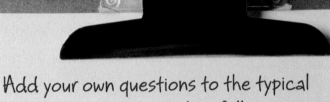

Add your own questions to the typical interviewee questions that follow:

- What is a typical day like in this job?
- What type of people would I be working with (peers) and for (supervisors)?
- Why do you need someone for this job (why can this job not be done by a current employee)?
- What circumstances led to the departure of the person I would be replacing? What is the turnover rate of people in this job? (or, How many people have held this job in the past five years?)
- Why do you continue to work for this company? (to an interviewer who has worked for the company for an extended time)
- Would you describe the initial training program for people in this position?
- What types of ongoing employee in-service training programs do you provide?
- How much value does your firm place on a master's degree?
- How do you feel this field has changed in the past ten years? How do you feel it will change in the next ten years?
- What advice do you wish you had been given when you were starting out?
- When do you expect to make your decision about the position?

© Image Sousrce

Conducting a Successful Interview

objective ④
Identify the parts of a job interview.

The way you handle an interview will vary somewhat depending on your stage in the hiring process. Regardless of whether you are being screened by a campus recruiter or have progressed to an on-site visit, an interview will have three parts: the opening formalities, an information exchange, and the close.

The Opening Formalities

Larry Hayes, president of Hayes Marketing Communication, emphasizes that skills missing during the interview are important because he assumes these same deficiencies will carry over during employment. "The good and the bad are obvious in the first five to ten seconds," says Hayes.[10] Clearly, since the impression created during the first few seconds of an interview often determines the outcome, you cannot afford to take time to warm up in an interview. You must come in the door selling yourself!

Common courtesies and confident body language can contribute to a favorable first impression in the early few seconds when you have not yet had an opportunity to talk about your qualifications:

- **Use the interviewer's name, and pronounce it correctly.** Even if the interviewer calls you by your first name, always use the interviewer's surname unless specifically invited to do otherwise.

- **Apply a firm handshake.** Usually, the interviewer will initiate the handshake, although you may do so. In either case, apply a firm handshake. You do not want to leave the impression that you are weak or timid. At the same time, you do not want to overdo the firm grip and leave an impression of being overbearing.

- **Wait for the interviewer to ask you to be seated.** If you aren't invited to sit, choose a chair across from or beside the interviewer's desk.

- **Maintain appropriate eye contact, and use your body language to convey confidence.** Sit erect and lean forward slightly to express interest. For a professional image, avoid slouching, chewing gum, and fidgeting.

© Thinkstock Images/Jupiterimages

- **Be conscious of nonverbal messages.** If the interviewer's eyes are glazing over, end your answer, but expand it if they are bright and the head is nodding vigorously. If the interviewer is from a different culture, be conscious of subtle differences in nonverbal communication that could affect the interviewer's perception of you. For example, a North American interviewer who sees eye contact as a sign of trust may perceive an Asian female who keeps her eyes lowered as a sign of respect to be uninterested or not listening.[11] Women should also be aware of typical "feminine behavior" during the interview. For instance, women nod more often than men when an interviewer speaks. Women are also likely to smile more and have a rising intonation at the end of sentences; such behaviors can convey a subservient attitude.[12]

Following the introductions, many interviewers will begin the conversation with nonbusiness talk to help you relax and to set the stage for the information exchange portion of the interview. Other interviewers may bypass these casual remarks and move directly into the interview.

The Information Exchange

With the appropriate preparation, the period of questions and answers should run smoothly. But it is important to remember to display a professional attitude throughout the interview.

First, communicate your sincere interest in the company; show that you are strongly interested in the company and not just taking an interview for practice. Reveal your knowledge of the company gained through reading published information, and refer to the people you have talked with about the working conditions, company achievements, and career paths.

Second, focus on the satisfaction gained from contributing to a company rather than the benefits you will receive. What's important in a job goes beyond financial reward. All applicants are interested in a paycheck; any job satisfies that need—some will pay more, some less. Recognize that the paycheck is a part of the job and should not be your primary concern. Intrinsic rewards such as personal job satisfaction, the feeling of accomplishment, and making a contribution to society are ideas to discuss in the interview. You should like what you are doing and find a challenging job that will satisfy these needs.

Third, show your humanness. If you are being interviewed by a representative of a successful company, do not suggest that you can turn the company around.

Interviewing Doesn't Stop— Even If You Get the Job

Effective interviewing skills continue to be valuable after you begin work. You will be involved in interviews with your supervisor for various reasons: to seek advice or information about your work and working conditions, to receive informal feedback about your progress, to receive a deserved promotion, and to discuss other personnel matters. In addition, your supervisor will likely conduct a performance appraisal interview to evaluate your performance. This formal interview typically occurs annually on the anniversary of your start of employment.

© image100/Jupiterimages

Similarly, telling an interviewer you have no weaknesses could make you sound shallow and deceptive. Instead, mention a real weakness, then talk about the steps you are taking to overcome it.

The Closing

The interviewer will provide cues indicating that the interview is completed by rising or making a comment about the next step to be taken. At that point, do not prolong the interview needlessly. Simply rise, accept the handshake, thank the interviewer for the opportunity to meet, and close by saying you look forward to hearing from the company. The tact with which you close the interview may be almost as important as the first impression you made. Be enthusiastic. If you really want the job, you might ask for it.

Preparing Other Employment Messages

objective ⑤
Compose effective messages related to employment (application forms, follow-up, thank-you, job acceptance, job refusal, resignation, and recommendation request).

Preparing a winning résumé and application letter is an important first step in a job search. To expedite your job search, you may need to prepare other employment messages: complete an application form, send a follow-up message to a company that does not respond to your résumé, send a thank-you message after an interview, accept a job offer, reject other job offers, and communicate with references. A career change will require a carefully written resignation letter.

Application Forms

Before going to work on a new job, you will almost certainly complete the employer's application and employment forms. Some application forms, especially for applicants who apply for jobs with a high level of responsibility, are very long. They may actually appear to be tests in which applicants give their answers to hypothetical questions and write defenses for their answers. Increasing numbers of companies are designing employment forms as mechanisms for getting information about a candidate that may not be included in the résumé. Application forms also ensure consistency in the information received from each candidate and can prevent decisions based on illegal topics that may be presented in a résumé.

© Tony Freeman/PhotoEdit

Have you been convicted of a crime in the past ten years other than misdemeanors and summary offenses?

Yes ☐   No ☐

If yes, explain circumstances and disposition of matter below.

Follow-Up Messages

When an application message and résumé do not elicit a response, a follow-up message may bring results. Sent a few weeks after the original letter, it includes a reminder that an application for a certain job is on file, presents additional education or experience accumulated, points out its relationship to the job, and closes with a reference to desired action. In addition to conveying new information, follow-up messages indicate persistence (a quality that impresses some employers). Figure 15-2 on the next page shows a good example of a follow-up letter.

Thank-You Messages

What purposes are served in sending a thank-you message, even though you expressed thanks in person after the interview or a discussion with a special employer at a career fair? After a job interview, a written message of appreciation is a professional courtesy and enhances your image within the organization. To be effective, it must be sent promptly. For maximum impact, send a thank-you message the day of the interview or the following day. Even if during the interview you decided you do not want the job or you and the interviewer mutually agreed that the job is not for you, a thank-you message is appropriate. As a matter of fact, if you've made a positive impression, interviewers may forward your résumé to others who are seeking qualified applicants.

The medium you choose for sending this message depends on the intended audience. If the company you've interviewed with prefers a traditional style, send a letter in complete business format on high-quality paper that matches your résumé and application letter. If the company is technologically savvy and has communicated with you extensively by email, follow the pattern and send a professional email. Choosing to send an email rather than slower mail delivery can give you a competitive edge over other candidates whose mailed letters arrive several days later than yours.

After an interview has gone well and you think a job offer is a possibility, include these ideas in the message of appreciation: express gratitude, identify the specific job applied for, refer to some point discussed in the interview **THANKS** (the strength of the interview), and close by making some reference to the expected call or message that conveys the employer's decision. The tone of this business message should remain professional regardless of the personal

Figure 15-2 GOOD *Example of a Follow-Up Letter*

- States main idea and clearly identifies position being sought.

- Refers to enclosed résumé; summarizes additional qualifications.

- Assures employer that applicant is still interested in job.

Format Pointers
Uses template to design professional personal letterhead and matching envelope.

Formats as formal business letter but could have sent message electronically if previous communication with employer had been by email.

Prints letter and envelope with laser printer on paper that matches résumé and application letter.

Dear Mr. Nguyen:

Recently, I applied for an information specialist position at TechPro and now have additional qualifications to report.

The enclosed, updated résumé shows that I have successfully passed the certification exam for Linux operating systems. In addition, I have learned a great deal about troubleshooting corporate computer systems in my recently completed internship with Crandon & Crandon Technology Systems, which I can immediately apply in a position with TechPro.

Mr. Nguyen, I would welcome the opportunity to visit your office and talk more about the contributions I could make as an information specialist at your firm. Please write or call me at (303) 555-8237.

relationship you may have developed with the interviewer and the informality encouraged by email. The message may be read by many others once it is placed in your personnel file as you complete annual appraisals and vie for promotions. Specific points to cover are outlined in Figure 15-3.

The résumé, application letter, and thank-you message should be stored in a computer file and adapted for submission to other firms when needed. Develop a database for keeping a record of the dates on which documents and résumés were sent to certain firms and answers were received, names of people talked with, facts conveyed, and so on. When an interviewer calls, you can retrieve and view that company's record while you are talking with the interviewer.

Job-Acceptance Messages

A job offer may be extended either by telephone or in writing. If a job offer is extended over the telephone, request that the company send a written confirmation of the job offer. The confirmation should include the job title, salary, benefits, starting date, and anything else negotiated.

Often, companies require a written acceptance of a job offer. Note the deductive sequence of the letter shown in Figure 15-4: acceptance, details, and closing (confirms the report-for-work date).

Job-Refusal Messages

Like other messages that convey unpleasant news, job-refusal messages are written inductively: a beginning that reveals the nature of the subject, explanations that lead to a refusal, the refusal, and a pleasant ending. Of course, certain reasons (even though valid in your mind) are better left unsaid: questionable company goals or methods of operation, negative attitude of present employees, possible bankruptcy, unsatisfactory working conditions, and so

NO THANKS

on. The applicant who prefers not to be specific about the reason for turning down a job might write this explanation: *After thoughtfully considering job offers received this week, I have decided to accept a job in the actuarial department of an insurance company.*

Figure 15-3 **Example of a Thank-You Message**

	New Message
To:	crosko@globalaerospace.com
From:	fmarshall@hotmail.com
Subject:	Appreciation for On-site Interview

Dear Mr. Rosko:

Thank you for the opportunity to visit Global Aerospace for an on-site interview yesterday. I enjoyed meeting you and appreciated the complete tour of your operation and the opportunity to learn about the exciting technological developments being made at Global Aerospace.

Global Aerospace's success in developing advanced munitions and smart weapons makes it the worldwide leader in military products. I was impressed with the many friendly, knowledgeable employees who were willing to speak with me about their work and their loyalty to Global Aerospace.

My visit to your plant reinforced my interest and assured me that my internship at Stark Technologies' engineering department would allow me to contribute immediately to Global Aerospace's munitions design efforts. My work at Stelland University on the drone project financed by the recent Homeland Security grant is particularly applicable to some of the projects being developed in your labs.

Mr. Rosko, I am eager to receive an offer from Global Aerospace for the entry-level engineering position. If you need additional information in the meantime, please contact me.

Thanks,

Frank Marshall

- *States main idea of appreciation for interview and information gained.*
- *Includes specific points discussed during interview, increasing sincerity and recall of applicant.*
- *Assures employer of continued interest in position.*
- *Politely reminds employer that applicant is awaiting reply.*

Format Pointer
Prepared as email message because all previous submissions have been completed by email.

Figure 15-4 **Example of a Job-Acceptance Message**

- *Begins by stating main idea— job offer is being accepted.*
- *Continues with any necessary details.*
- *Confirms beginning employment date.*

I accept your employment offer as a management trainee. Thank you for responding so quickly after our discussion on Tuesday.

As you requested, I have signed the agreement outlining the specific details of my employment. Your copy is enclosed, and I have kept a copy for my records.

If you should need to speak with me before I report to work on June 15, please call me at 555-4321.

Figure 15-5 **Example of a Job-Refusal Message**

- *Begins with neutral but related idea to buffer bad news.*

- *Presents reasons diplomatically that lead to refusal.*

- *Ends message on positive note that anticipates future association with company.*

I appreciate your spending time with me discussing the sales associate position.

Your feedback regarding my fit for your organization and the opportunities available to me were particularly valuable. Having received offers in both sales and marketing, I feel that a career in the latter field better suits my personality and long-term career goals. Today, I am accepting an entry-level marketing position with Fashion Trends, Inc.

Thank you for your confidence demonstrated by the job offer. When I hear about Marasol's continued success, I will think of the dedicated people who work for the company.

You may want to be more specific about your reasons for refusal when you have a positive attitude toward the company or believe you may want to reapply at some later date. The letter in Figure 15-5 includes reasons for refusal.

Resignations

Resigning from a job requires effective communication skills. You may be allowed to "give your notice" in person or be required to write a formal resignation. Your supervisor will inform you of the company's policy. Regardless of whether the resignation is given orally or in writing, show

RESIST THE URGE

to vent, rant, or tell your boss how to run the business. It's not professional.

© James Dawson/Image Farm/Jupiterimages

empathy for your employer by giving enough time to allow the employer to find a replacement. Because your employer has had confidence in you, has benefited from your services, and will have to seek a replacement, your impending departure is bad news. As such, the message is written inductively. It calls attention to your job, gives your reasons for leaving it, conveys the resignation, and closes on a positive note. A written resignation is shown in Figure 15-6.

A resignation is not an appropriate instrument for telling managers how a business should be operated. Harshly worded statements could result in immediate termination or cause human relations problems during your remaining working days. If you can do so sincerely, recall positive experiences you had with the company. Doing so will leave a lasting record of your goodwill, making it likely that your supervisor will give you a good recommendation in the future.

Recommendation Requests

Companies seek information from references at various stages. Some prefer talking with references prior to an interview and others after a successful interview. Specific actions on your part will ensure that your references are treated with common courtesy and that references are prepared for the employer's call.

- **Remind the reference that he or she had previously agreed to supply information about you.** Identify the job for which you are applying, give a complete address to which the letter is to be sent, and indicate a date by which the prospective employer needs the letter. By sharing information about job requirements and reporting recent job-related experiences, you may assist the reference in writing an effective message. Indicate your gratitude, but do not apologize for making the request. The reference

Figure 15-6   *Example of a Resignation Message*

- *Begins with appreciative comments to buffer bad news.*

- *Presents reasons that lead to main idea—the resignation.*

- *States resignation. Includes additional details.*

- *Conveys genuine appreciation for experience gained and ends on cordial note.*

SUBJECT: PLEASURE OF SERVING FIRST NATIONAL BANK

My job as a customer service associate at First National Bank over the past year has been a rewarding experience. It has taught me a great deal about the banking industry and providing excellent customer service.

Learning about the business of banking has been particularly exciting. From the time I declared a major in finance, I have wanted to work with investment products. Before I accepted my current position, that goal was discussed. Now, that goal is becoming a reality, as I have accepted a job as a sales trainee in the investment division of WideWorld beginning one month from today. If satisfactory with you, I would like June 1 to be my last day here.

Thank you for the confidence you placed in me, your support of customer service associates, and your feedback to help me continue growing as a valued employee. As I continue my career in investment banking, I will take with me many pleasant memories of my time with First National.

Figure 15-7   *Example of a Thank-You Message to a Reference*

- *States main idea of appreciation for recommendation. Informs reference of success in acceptance to academic program.*

- *Communicates sincere appreciation for assistance; uses specific examples and avoids exaggeration.*

- *Restates main idea and anticipates continued relationship; is original and sincere.*

Thank you so much for the letter of recommendation you prepared for my application to law school. I learned today that I have been accepted by Cleveland University for the fall semester.

Because of the rigor of that law program, I believe your comments about my work ethic, dedication to high-quality work, and willingness to seek out feedback for improvement carried a great deal of weight. The dean commented that she was impressed with the detailed evidence and examples you provided to support your statements, unlike the general recommendations she often receives.

Dr. Kenney, I appreciate your helping me secure a seat in a highly competitive academic discipline with such a well-regarded law program. Thanks for the recommendation and your outstanding instruction. I will keep you informed about my law school experience and hope to stop by your office next time I am in town to catch up.

has already agreed to write such a letter and will likely take pleasure in assisting a deserving person.

- **Alert the reference of imminent requests for information, especially if considerable time has elapsed since the applicant and reference have last seen each other.** Enclosing a recent résumé and providing any other pertinent information (e.g., name change) may enable the reference to write a letter that is specific and convincing. If the job search becomes longer than anticipated, a follow-up mes-

sage to references explaining the delay and expressing gratitude for their efforts is appropriate.

- **Send a sincere, original thank-you message after a position has been accepted.** This thoughtful gesture will build a positive relationship with a person who may continue to be important to your career. The message in Figure 15-7 is brief and avoids clichés and exaggerated expressions of praise but gives specific examples of the importance of the reference's recommendation.

Grammar and Usage Appendix

Polishing your language skills will aid you in preparing error-free documents that reflect positively on you and your company. This text appendix is an abbreviated review that focuses on common problems frequently encountered by business writers and offers a quick "refreshing" of key skills.

Grammar
Sentence Structure

1. **Rely mainly on sentences that follow the normal subject-verb-complement sequence for clarity and easy reading.**

   Jennifer and I withdrew for three reasons.
      (subject)   (verb)   (complement)

Original	**Better**
There are two reasons for our withdrawal.	Two reasons for our withdrawal are . . . .
	Jennifer and I withdrew for two reasons.
It is necessary that we withdraw.	We must withdraw.
Here is a copy of my résumé.	The enclosed résumé outlines . . . .

   There, it, and *here* are *expletives*—filler words that have no real meaning in the sentence.

2. **Put pronouns, adverbs, phrases, and clauses near the words they modify.**

Incorrect	**Correct**
Angie put a new type of gel on her hair, which she had just purchased.	Angie put a new type of gel, which she had just purchased, on her hair.
He only works in the electronics department for $8.50 an hour.	He works in the electronics department for only $8.50 an hour.
The clerk stood near the fax machine wearing a denim skirt.	The clerk wearing a denim skirt stood near the fax machine.

3. **Do not separate subject and predicate unnecessarily.**

Incorrect	**Clear**
He, hoping to receive a bonus, worked rapidly.	Hoping to receive a bonus, he worked rapidly.

4. **Place an introductory phrase near the subject of the independent clause it modifies.** Otherwise, the phrase dangles. To correct the dangling phrase, change the subject of the independent clause, or make the phrase into a dependent clause by assigning it a subject.

Incorrect	**Correct**
When a little boy, my mother took me through a manufacturing plant. [Implies that the mother was once a little boy.]	When I was a little boy, my mother took me through a manufacturing plant.
	When a little boy, I was taken through a manufacturing plant by my mother.
Working at full speed every morning, fatigue overtakes me in the afternoon. [Implies that "fatigue" was working at full speed.]	Working at full speed every morning, I become tired in the afternoon.
	Because I work at full speed every morning, fatigue overtakes me in the afternoon.
To function properly, you must oil it every hour. [Implies that if "you" are "to function properly," the machine must be oiled hourly.]	If the machine is to function properly, you must oil it every hour.
	To function properly, the machine must be oiled every hour.

5. Express related ideas in similar grammatical form (use parallel construction).

Incorrect	Correct
The machine operator made three resolutions: (1) <u>to be punctual</u>, (2) <u>following instructions carefully</u>, and third, <u>the reduction of waste</u>.	The machine operator made three resolutions: (1) <u>to be</u> punctual, (2) <u>to follow</u> instructions carefully, and (3) <u>to reduce</u> waste.
The human resources manager is concerned with the <u>selection</u> of the right worker, <u>providing</u> appropriate orientation and the <u>worker's progress</u>.	The human resources manager is concerned with <u>selecting</u> the right worker, <u>providing</u> appropriate orientation, and <u>evaluating</u> the worker's progress.

6. Do not end a sentence with a needless preposition.

Where is the plant to be <u>located</u> (not *located at*)?

The worker did not tell us where he was <u>going</u> (not *going to*).

End a sentence with a preposition if for some reason the preposition needs emphasis.

I am not concerned with what he is paying <u>for</u>. I am concerned with what he is paying <u>with</u>.

The prospect has everything—a goal to work <u>toward</u>, a house to live <u>in</u>, and an income to live <u>on</u>.

7. Avoid split infinitives. Two words are required to express an infinitive: *to* plus a *verb*. The two words belong together. An infinitive is split when another word is placed between the two.

Incorrect	Correct
The superintendent used <u>to</u> occasionally <u>visit</u> the offices.	The superintendent used <u>to visit</u> the offices occasionally.
I plan <u>to</u> briefly <u>summarize</u> the report.	I plan <u>to summarize</u> the report briefly.

Exercise 1

Identify the weakness in each sentence and write an improved version.

1. It is essential that you sign and return the enclosed form.
2. I am submitting an editorial to the newspaper, which I wrote last summer.
3. The work team wants to quickly bring the project to a conclusion.
4. To operate efficiently, you must perform periodic maintenance on your computer.
5. Protect your online privacy by use of effective password protection, clearing temporary menus regularly, and encryption of sensitive information.

Pronoun Reference

1. **Make a pronoun agree in number with its antecedent (the specific noun for which a pronoun stands).**

   a. Use a plural pronoun when it represents two or more singular antecedents connected by *and*.

   The secretary <u>and</u> the treasurer will take <u>their</u> vacations.
   ["The" before "treasurer" indicates that the sentence is about two people.]

   The <u>secretary</u> and <u>treasurer</u> will take <u>his</u> vacation.
   [Omitting "the" before "treasurer" indicates that the sentence is about one person who has two sets of responsibilities.]

   b. Parenthetical remarks (remarks that can be omitted without destroying the basic meaning of the sentence) that appear between the pronoun and its antecedent have no effect on the form of the pronoun.

   Michael Box, <u>not the secretaries</u>, is responsible for his correspondence.
   [Because "his" refers to Michael and not to "secretaries," "his" is used instead of "their."]

   c. Use a singular pronoun with *each, everyone, no*, and their variations.

   <u>Each</u> student and each teacher will carry <u>his or her</u> own equipment.

   <u>Everyone</u> is responsible for <u>her or his</u> work.

   d. Use a singular pronoun when two or more singular antecedents are connected by *or* or *nor*.

   <u>Neither</u> Brandon <u>nor</u> Will can complete <u>his</u> work.

   Ask <u>either</u> Mallory <u>or</u> Suzanne about <u>her</u> in-service training.

   e. Use pronouns that agree in number with the intended meaning of collective nouns.

   The <u>team</u> has been asked for <u>its</u> contributions. ["Team" is thought of as a unit; the singular "its" is appropriate.]

   The <u>team</u> have been asked for <u>their</u> contributions. ["Team" is thought of as more than one individual; the plural "their" is appropriate.]

2. **Place relative pronouns as near their antecedents as possible for clear understanding.** A relative pronoun joins a dependent clause to its antecedent.

Ambiguous	Clear
The <u>members</u> were given receipts <u>who</u> have paid.	The <u>members who</u> have paid were given receipts.

The agreement will enable you to pay <u>whichever</u> is lower, 6 percent or $50.

The agreement will enable you to pay 6 percent or $50, <u>whichever</u> is lower.

Restate a noun instead of risking a vague pronoun reference.

Vague

The officer captured the suspect even though <u>he</u> was unarmed.

Clear

The officer captured the suspect even though <u>the officer</u> was unarmed.

3. **Do not use a pronoun by itself to refer to a phrase, clause, sentence, or paragraph.** A pronoun should stand for a noun, and that noun should appear in the writing.

Incorrect

He expects to take all available accounting courses and obtain a position in a public accounting firm. <u>This</u> appeals to him.

Correct

He expects to take all available accounting courses and obtain a position in a public accounting firm. <u>This plan</u> appeals to him.

Exercise 2

Select the correct pronoun to use.

1. The president and the chief executive officer reported (his, their) earnings to the ethics committee.

2. Everyone (was, were) asked to contribute to the company blog.

3. The production manager, not the controller, presented (her, their) strongly opposing views.

4. Neither Stephen nor Lydia (was, were) recognized for their contribution.

5. The company is revising (its, their) mission statement.

6. The committee will present (its, their) recommendation at the next staff meeting.

7. Paige forgot to retain her expense vouchers; (this, this oversight) caused a delay in reimbursement.

Pronoun Case

1. **Use the correct case of pronouns.** *Case* tells whether a pronoun is used as the subject of a sentence or as an object in it.

   a. Use nominative-case pronouns (also known as subjective-case pronouns) (*I, he, she, they, we, you, it, who*) as subjects of a sentence or clause.

   <u>You</u> and <u>I</u> must work together. ["You" and "I" are subjects of the verb "work."]

   Those <u>who</u> work will be paid. ["Who" is the subject of the dependent clause "who work."]

   b. Use objective-case pronouns (*me, him, her, them, us, you, it, whom*) as objects of verbs and prepositions.

   Mrs. Kellum telephoned <u>him</u>. ["Him" is the object of the verb "telephoned."]

   The promotions are for the manager and <u>her</u>. ["Her" is the object of the preposition "for."]

   To <u>whom</u> should we send the report? ["Whom" is the object of the preposition "to."]

   TIP: Restate a subordinate clause introduced by *who* or *whom* to determine the appropriate pronoun.

   She is the type of manager <u>whom</u> we can promote. [Restating "whom we can promote" as "We can promote her (whom)" clarifies that "whom" is the object.]

   She is the type of manager <u>who</u> can be promoted. [Restating "who can be promoted" as "She (who) can be promoted" clarifies that "who" is the subject.]

   TIP: Change a question to a statement to determine the correct form of a pronoun.

   <u>Whom</u> did you call? [You did call *whom*.]

   <u>Whom</u> did you select for the position? [You did select *whom* for the position.]

   c. Use the nominative case when forms of the linking verb *be* require a pronoun to complete the meaning.

   It was <u>he</u> who received credit for the sale.

   It is <u>she</u> who deserves the award.

   ["It was he" may to some people sound just as distracting as the incorrect "It was him." Express the ideas in a different way to avoid the error and an expletive beginning.]

   He was the one who received credit for the sale.

   She deserves the award.

   d. Use the possessive form of a pronoun before a gerund (a verb used as a noun).

   We were delighted at <u>his</u> (not *him*) taking the job.

   ["Taking the job" is used here as a noun. "His" in this sentence serves the same purpose it serves in "We are delighted at his success."]

Exercise 3

Select the correct pronoun case to use in each example.

1. The instructor asked Franz and (I, me) to leave the room.
2. Stacey requested that proceeds be divided equally between Allison and (her, she).
3. It was (her, she) (who, whom) recommended revising the company's technology policy to include cell phones.
4. The speaker did not notice (me, my) leaving early.
5. She is an employee in (who, whom) we have great confidence.

Verb Agreement

1. **Make subjects agree with verbs.**

   a. Ignore intervening phrases that have no effect on the verb used.

   Good material <u>and</u> fast delivery <u>are</u> (not *is*) essential.

   <u>You</u>, not the carrier, <u>are</u> (not *is*) responsible for the damage. [Intervening phrase, "not the carrier," does not affect the verb used.]

   The <u>attitude</u> of these customers <u>is</u> (not *are*) receptive. [The subject is "attitude"; "of these customers" is a phrase coming between the subject and the verb.]

   b. Use a verb that agrees with the noun closer to the verb when *or* or *nor* connects two subjects.

   Only one or two <u>questions</u> <u>are</u> (not *is*) necessary.

   Several paint brushes or one paint <u>roller</u> <u>is</u> (not *are*) necessary.

   c. Use singular verbs with plural nouns that have a singular meaning or are thought of as singular units.

   The <u>news</u> <u>is</u> good.   <u>Economics</u> <u>is</u> a required course.

   Twenty <u>dollars</u> <u>is</u> too much.   Ten <u>minutes</u> <u>is</u> sufficient time.

   d. Use a singular verb for titles of articles, firm names, and slogans.

   "Taming Your Tongue" <u>is</u> an interesting article.

   Stein, Jones, and Baker <u>is</u> the oldest firm in the city.

   "Eat Smart for Hearts" <u>is</u> a campaign slogan directed at better nutrition for senior adults.

2. **Choose verbs that agree in person with their subjects.** *Person* indicates whether the subject is (1) speaking, (2) being spoken to, or (3) being spoken about.

   First person: I am, we are.
   [Writer or speaker]

   Second person: You are.
   [Receiver of message]

   Third person: He is, she is, they are.
   [Person being discussed]

   <u>She</u> <u>doesn't</u> (not *don't*) attend class regularly.

   <u>They</u> <u>don't</u> recognize the value of networking.

Verb Tense and Mood

1. **Use the appropriate verb tense.** *Tense* indicates time. Tense can be either simple or compound.

   Simple tenses:

   Present: I <u>see</u> you. [Tells what is happening now.]

   Past: I <u>saw</u> you. [Tells what has already happened.]

   Future: I <u>will</u> <u>see</u> you. [Tells what is yet to happen.]

   Compound tenses:

   Present perfect: I <u>have</u> <u>seen</u> you. [Tells of past action that extends to the present.]

   Past perfect: I <u>had</u> <u>seen</u> you. [Tells of past action that was finished before another past action.]

   Future perfect: I <u>will</u> <u>have</u> <u>seen</u> you. [Tells of action that will be finished before a future time.]

   a. Use present tense when something was and still is true.

   The speaker reminded us that Rhode Island <u>is</u> (not *was*) smaller than Wisconsin.

   The consultant's name is (not *was*) Ryan Abrams.

   b. Avoid unnecessary shifts in tense.

   The carrier <u>brought</u> (not *brings*) my package but <u>left</u> without asking me to sign for it.

   Verbs that appear in the same sentence are not required to be in the same tense.

   The contract that <u>was prepared</u> yesterday <u>will</u> <u>be</u> <u>signed</u> tomorrow.

2. Use subjunctive mood to express situations that are untrue or highly unlikely. Be sure to use *were* for the present tense of *to be* to indicate the subjunctive mood. Use *was* when the statement could be true.

I wish the story <u>were</u> (not *was*) true.

If I <u>were</u> (not *was*) you, I would try again.

Verb Voice

Exercise 4

Select the correct voice for each sentence.

1. Only one of the video clips (was, were) usable.

2. The typesetters, not the editor, (are, is) responsible for these errors.

3. Neither the manager nor the employees (was, were) aware of the policy change.

4. Both Corey and Stephen (was, were) promoted.

5. The news from the rescue mission (is, are) encouraging.

6. *Ten Steps to Greatness* (has, have) been placed in the company library.

7. The sales manager announced that Scottsdale, Arizona, (is, was) the site for the annual sales meeting.

8. Dylan (don't, doesn't) expect preferential treatment.

9. The client studied the financial analysis for a minute and (starts, started) asking questions.

10. If the applicant (was, were) experienced with databases, she would have been hired.

Adjectives and Adverbs

1. **Use an adjective to modify a noun or pronoun and an adverb to modify a verb, an adjective, or another adverb.**

   Adjective: Bryan developed an <u>impressive</u> slide show.

   Adverb: The new employee looked <u>enthusiastically</u> at the sales prospect. [The adverb "enthusiastically" modifies the verb "looked."]

   The team leader was <u>really</u> visionary. [The adverb "really" modifies the adjective "visionary."]

   Worker A progressed <u>relatively</u> <u>faster</u> than did Worker B. [The adverb "relatively" modifies the adverb "faster."]

2. **Use an adjective after a linking verb when the modifier refers to the subject instead of to the verb.** [A linking verb connects a subject to the rest of the sentence. "He is old." "She seems sincere."]

   The man entering the building looked <u>suspicious</u>. [The adjective "suspicious" refers to "man," not to "looked."]

3. **Use comparatives (to compare two) and superlatives (to compare three or more) carefully.**

   She is the <u>faster</u> (not *fastest*) of the two workers.

   Edwin is the <u>better</u> (not *best*) writer of the two team members.

   Exclude a person or thing from a group with which that person or thing is being compared.

   He is more observant than <u>anyone else</u> (not *anyone*) in his department. [As a member of his department, he cannot be more observant than himself.]

   The X-60 is newer than <u>any other machine</u> (not *any machine*) in the plant. [The X-60 cannot be newer than itself.]

Exercise 5

Select the correct modifier.

1. Our supply of parts is replenished (frequent, frequently).

2. Marcus looked (impatient, impatiently) at the new production assistant.

3. The server moved (quick, quickly) from table to table.

4. Of the numerous people I met during the recent speed networking event, Blair made the (better, best) impression.

5. Haley is more creative than (any, any other) advertising agent in the company.

Punctuation

Commas

1. **Use a comma**

   a. Between coordinate clauses joined by *and, but, for, or,* and *nor.*

   He wanted to pay his bills on time, <u>but</u> he did not have the money.

   b. To separate introductory clauses and certain phrases from independent clauses. Sentences that begin with dependent clauses (often with words such as *if, as, since, because, although,* and *when*) almost always need a comma. Prepositional phrases and verbal phrases with five or more words require commas.

Dependent clause:	If you can meet us at the airport, please plan to be there by six o'clock. [The comma separates the introductory dependent clause from the independent clause.]
Infinitive:	To get the full benefit of our insurance plan, just complete and return the enclosed card. [A verb preceded by "to" ("to get").]
Participial:	Believing that her earnings would continue to increase, she sought to borrow more money. [A verb form used as an adjective: "believing" modifies the dependent clause "she sought."]
Prepositional phrase:	Within the next few days, you will receive written confirmation of this transaction. [Comma needed because the phrase contains five words.] Under the circumstances we think you are justified. [Comma omitted because the phrase contains fewer than five words and the sentence is clear without the comma.]

c. To separate three or more words in a series.

You have a choice of gray, green, purple, and white. [Without the comma after "purple," no one can tell for sure whether four choices are available, the last of which is "white," or whether three choices are available, the last of which is "purple and white."]

You have a choice of purple and white, gray, and green. [Choice is restricted to three, the first of which is "purple and white."]

d. Between two or more independent adjectives that modify the same noun.

New employees are given a long, difficult examination. [Both "long" and "difficult" modify "examination."]

We want quick, factual news. [Both "quick" and "factual" modify "news."]

Do not place a comma between two adjectives when the second adjective modifies the adjective and noun as a unit.

The supervisor is an excellent public speaker. ["Excellent" modifies the noun phrase "public speaker."]

e. To separate a nonrestrictive clause (a clause that is not essential to the basic meaning of the sentence) from the rest of the sentence.

Mr. Murray, who is head of customer resource management, has selected Century Consulting to oversee the rollout of a new software. [The parenthetical remark is not essential to the meaning of the sentence.]

The man who is head of customer resource management has selected Century Consulting to oversee the rollout of a new software. [Commas are not needed because "who is head of customer resource management" is essential to the meaning of the sentence.]

f. To set off or separate dates, addresses, geographical names, degrees, and long numbers:

On July 2, 2008, Mr. Pearson made the final payment. [Before and after the year in month-day-year format]

I saw him in Tahoe City, California, on the 12th of October. [Before and after the name of a state when the name of a city precedes it]

Roy Murr, President [Between the printed name and the title on the same line beneath a signature or in a letter address]

Kathryn W. Edwards
President of Academic Affairs [No comma is used if the title is on a separate line.]

g. To separate parenthetical expressions or other elements interrupting the flow from the rest of the sentence.

Ms. Watson, speaking in behalf of the entire department, accepted the proposal. [Set off a parenthetical expression]

Cole, I believe you have earned a vacation. [After a direct address]

Yes, you can count on me. [After the words *No* and *Yes* when they introduce a statement]

Arun Ramage, former president of the Jackson Institute, spoke to the group. [Set off appositives when neutral emphasis is desired]

The job requires experience, <u>not formal education</u>. [Between contrasted elements]

Exercise 6

Insert needed commas. Write "correct" if you find no errors.

1. The applicant who arrived late has not been interviewed.

2. Emoticons which are created by keying combinations of symbols to produce "sideway faces" communicate emotion in electronic messages.

3. Sean Harrison a new member of the board remained silent during the long bitter debate.

4. Primary qualifications for graduates seeking a first job are education work experience and leadership activities.

5. The entire population was surveyed but three responses were unusable.

6. If you approve of the changes place your initials in the space provided.

7. To qualify for the position applicants must have technology certification.

8. We should be spending less money not more.

9. On November 20 2008 all required documents had been submitted.

10. Yes I agree that the theme meeting in St. Thomas should be scheduled for late May.

Semicolons and Colons

1. **Use a semicolon**

   a. To join the independent clauses in a compound sentence when a conjunction is omitted.

      Our workers have been extraordinarily efficient this year; they are expecting a bonus.

   b. To join the independent clauses in a compound-complex sentence.

      As indicated earlier, we prefer delivery on Saturday morning at four o'clock; but Friday night at ten o'clock will be satisfactory.

      We prefer delivery on Saturday morning at four o'clock; but, if the arrangement is more convenient for you, Friday night at ten o'clock will be satisfactory.

   c. Before an adverbial conjunction. Use a comma after the adverbial conjunction.

Adverbial conjunction:	The shipment arrived too late for our weekend sale; <u>therefore</u>, we are returning the shipment to you.

   Other frequently used adverbial conjunctions are *however*, *otherwise*, *consequently*, and *nevertheless*.

   d. Before words used to introduce enumerations or explanations that follow an independent clause.

Enumeration with commas:	Many factors affect the direction of the stock market; <u>namely</u>, interest rates, economic growth, and employment rates.
Explanation forming a complete thought:	We have plans for improvement; <u>for example</u>, we intend. . . .
	The engine has been "knocking"; that is, the gas in the cylinders explodes before the pistons complete their upward strokes.

   NOTE: The following exceptions require a comma to introduce the enumeration or explanation:

Enumeration without commas:	Several popular Internet browsers are available, <u>for example</u>, Firefox and Internet Explorer. [A comma, not a semicolon, is used because the enumeration contains no commas.]
Explanation forming an incomplete thought:	Many companies have used nontraditional methods for recruiting applicants, <u>for instance</u>, soliciting résumé postings to company websites. [A comma, not a semicolon, is used because the explanation is not a complete thought.]

e. In a series that contains commas.

Some of our workers have worked overtime this week: Smith, 6 hours; Hardin, 3; Cantrell, 10; and McGowan, 11.

2. Use a colon

a. After a complete thought that introduces a list of items. Use a colon following both direct and indirect introductions of lists.

Direct introduction:	The following three factors influenced our decision: an expanded market, an inexpensive source of raw materials, and a ready source of labor. [The word "following" clearly introduces a list.]
Indirect introduction:	The carpet is available in three colors: green, burgundy, and blue.

Do not use a colon after an introductory statement that ends with a preposition or a verb (*are, is, were, include*). The list that follows the preposition or verb finishes the sentence.

Incomplete sentence:	We need to (1) expand our market, (2) locate an inexpensive source of materials, and (3) find a ready source of labor. [A colon does not follow "to" because the words preceding the list are not a complete sentence.]

b. To stress an appositive (a noun that renames the preceding noun) at the end of a sentence.

His heart was set on one thing: promotion.

Our progress is due to the efforts of one person: Brooke Keating.

Exercise 7

Insert or change punctuation as needed. Write "correct" if you find no errors.

1. Receipts were not included, otherwise, the expenses would have been reimbursed.

2. The following agents received a bonus this month: Barnes, $400, Shelley, $450, and Jackson, $600.

3. The proposal was not considered it arrived two days late.

4. This paint does have some disadvantages for example a lengthy drying time.

5. Soon after the figures are received, they will be processed, but a formal report will not be released until June 1.

---

6. The program has one shortcoming: flexibility.

7. Our meetings are scheduled for: Monday, Tuesday, and Friday.

8. We are enthusiastic about the plan because: (1) it is least expensive, (2) its legality is unquestioned, and (3) it can be implemented quickly.

Apostrophes

1. Use an apostrophe to form possessives.

a. Add an apostrophe and s ('s) to form the posessive case of a singular noun or a plural noun that does not end with a pronounced s.

Singular noun:	Jenna's position firm's assets employee's benefits
Plural noun without a pronounced s:	men's clothing children's games deer's antlers

b. Add only an apostrophe to form the possessive of a singular or plural noun that ends with a pronounced s.

Singular noun with pronounced s:	Niagara Falls' site Ms. Jenkins' interview
Plural noun with pronounced s:	two managers' decision six months' wages

Exception: An apostrophe and s ('s) can be added to singular nouns ending in a pronounced s if an additional s sound is pronounced easily.

Singular noun with additional s sound:	boss's decision class's party Jones's invitation

c. Use an apostrophe with the possessives of nouns that refer to time (minutes, hours, days, weeks, months, and years) or distance in a possessive manner.

eight hours' pay	two weeks' notice
today's schedule	ten years' experience
a stone's throw	a yard's length

Exercise 8

Correct the possessives.

1. This companies mission statement has been revised since it's recent merger.

2. The night shift earned a bonus of three weeks wages for last months overtime.

3. The banks' had been negotiating a merger for several month's.

Hyphens

1. **Use a hyphen**

    a. Between the words in a compound adjective. (A *compound adjective* is a group of adjectives appearing together and used as a single word to describe a noun.)

    An <u>attention-getting</u> device

    A <u>two-thirds</u> interest

    Do not hyphenate a compound adjective in the following cases:

    (1) When the compound adjective follows a noun.

      A device that is <u>attention getting</u>.

      A lecture that was <u>hard to follow</u>.

      NOTE: Some compound adjectives are hyphenated when they follow a noun.

      The news release was <u>up-to-date</u>.

      The speaker is <u>well-known</u>.

      For jobs that are <u>part-time</u>, ...

    (2) An expression made up of an adverb that ends in *ly* and an adjective is not a compound adjective and does not require a hyphen.

      <u>commonly accepted</u> principle

      <u>widely quoted</u> authority

    (3) A simple fraction and a percentage.

Simple fraction:	<u>Two thirds</u> of the respondents
Percentage:	<u>15 percent</u> sales increase

    b. To prevent misinterpretation.

    <u>Recover</u> a chair [To obtain possession of a chair once more]

    <u>Re-cover</u> a chair [To cover a chair again]

    <u>Eight inch</u> blades [Eight blades, each of which is an inch long]

    <u>Eight-inch</u> blades [Blades eight inches long]

Quotation Marks and Italics

1. **Use quotation marks**

    a. To enclose direct quotations.

Single-sentence quotation:	The supervisor said, "We will make progress."
Interrupted quotation:	"We will make progress," the supervisor said, "even though we have to work overtime."
Multiple-sentence quotation:	The president said, "Have a seat, gentlemen. I'm dictating a letter. I should be finished in about five minutes. Please wait." [Place quotation marks before the first word and after the last word of a multiple-sentence quotation.]
Quotation within quotation:	The budget director said, "Believe me when I say 'A penny saved is a penny earned' is the best advice I ever had." [Use single quotation marks to enclose a quotation that appears with a quotation.]

    b. To enclose titles of songs, magazine and newspaper articles, lecture titles, and themes within text.

      "Candle in the Wind"   "Making an Impact"

      The chapter, "Cell Phone Etiquette," . . . .

    c. To enclose a definition of a defined term. Italicize the defined word.

      The term *downsizing* is used to refer to "the planned reduction in the number of employees."

    d. To enclose words used in humor, a word used when a different word would be more appropriate, slang expressions that need to be emphasized or clarified for the reader, or nicknames. These words can also be shown in italics.

Humor/ Different word:	Our "football" team. . . . [Hints that the team appears to be playing something other than football.]
	Our football "team" . . . . [Hints that "collection of individual players" would be more descriptive than "team."]
	. . . out for "lunch." [Hints that the reason for being out is something other than lunch.]
Slang:	With negotiations entering the final week, it's time "to play hardball."
Nicknames:	And now for some comments by Robert "Bob" Johnson.

2. Use italics

a. To indicate words, letters, numbers, and phrases used as words.

He had difficulty learning to spell *recommendation*.

b. To emphasize a word that is not sufficiently emphasized by other means.

Our goal is to hire the *right* person, not necessarily the most experienced candidate.

c. To indicate the titles of books, magazines, and newspapers.

Managing for Quality   *The New York Times*
Reader's Digest

Exercise 10

Add necessary quotation marks and italics.

1. Goleman presents an interesting theory of intelligence in his book Emotional Intelligence.

2. The article A Softer Side of Leadership appeared in the July 2006 issue of Training.

3. His accomplishments are summarized on the attached page. [Indicate that a word other than *accomplishments* may be a more appropriate word.]

4. Kent said the firm plans to establish a sinking fund. [Direct quotation]

5. The term flame is online jargon for a heated, sarcastic, sometimes abusive message or posting to a discussion group.

6. Read each email message carefully before sending to avoid flaming.

Dashes, Parentheses, and Periods

1. Use an em dash

a. To place emphasis on appositives.

His answer—the correct answer—was based on years of experience.

Compare the price—$125—with the cost of a single repair job.

b. When appositives contain commas.

Their scores—Reneé, 21; Tairus, 20; and Drew, 19—were the highest in a group of 300.

c. When a parenthetical remark consists of an abrupt change in thought.

The committee decided—you may think it's a joke, but it isn't—that the resolution should be adopted.

NOTE: Use an em dash (not two hyphens) without spaces before or after form a dash in computer-generated copy.

2. Use parentheses for explanatory material that could be left out.

Three of our employees (Kristen Hubbard, Alex Russo, and Mark Coghlan) took their vacations in August.

All our employees (believe it or not) have perfect attendance records.

3. Use a period after declarative and imperative sentences and courteous requests.

We will attend. [Declarative sentence]

Complete this report. [Imperative sentence]

Will you please complete the report today. [A *courteous request* is a question but does not require a verbal answer with requested action]

Exercise 11

Correct punctuation, adding or modifying dashes, parentheses, and end punctuation.

1. Additional consultants, programmers and analysts, were hired to complete the computer conversion. [Emphasize the appositive.]

2. The dividend will be raised to 15 cents a share approved by the Board of Directors on December 1, 2008. [Deemphasize the approval.]

3. Would you include the updated projections in tomorrow's presentation visuals?

Number Usage

1. Use figures

a. To provide deserved emphasis and make critical points easy for readers to locate. Regardless of whether a number has one digit or many, use figures to express dates, sums of money, mixed numbers and decimals, distance, dimension, cubic capacity, percentage, weights, temperatures, and chapter and page numbers.

May 10, 2008	165 pounds
$9 million	Chapter 3, page 29

5 percent (use % in a table)

over 200 applicants (or two hundred) [an approximation]

b. With ordinals (*th*, *st*, *rd*, *nd*) only when the number precedes the month.

The meeting is to be held on June 21.

The meeting is to be held on the 21st of June.

c. With ciphers but without decimals when presenting even-dollar figures, even if the figure appears in a sentence with another figure that includes dollars and cents.

Miranda paid $70 for the cabinet.

Miranda paid $99.95 for the table and $70 for the cabinet.

d. For numbers that represent time when *a.m.* or *p.m.* is used. Words or figures may be used with *o'clock*.

Please meet me at 10:15 p.m.

Please be there at ten o'clock (or 10 o'clock).

Omit the colon when expressing times of day that include hours but not minutes, even if the time appears in a sentence with another time that includes minutes.

The award program began at 6:30 p.m. with a reception at 7 p.m.

2. Spell out

a. Numbers if they are used as the first word of a sentence.

Thirty-two people attended.

b. Numbers one through nine if no larger number appears in the same sentence.

Only three auditors worked at the client's office.

Send 5 officers and 37 members.

c. The first number in two consecutive numbers that act as adjectives modifying the same noun;

write the second number in figures. If the first number cannot be expressed in one or two words, place it in figures also.

The package required four 39-cent stamps. [A hyphen joins the second number with the word that follows it, thus forming a compound adjective that describes the noun "stamps."]

We shipped 250 180-horsepower engines today. [Figures are used because neither number can be expressed in one or two words.]

Exercise 12

Correct the number usage in the following sentences taken from a letter or a report. Write "correct" if you find no errors.

1. The question was answered by sixty-one percent of the respondents.

2. The meeting is scheduled for 10:00 a.m. on February 3rd.

3. These 3 figures appeared on the expense account: $21.95, $30.00, and $35.14.

4. The MIS manager ordered 150 120-GB hard drives.

5. 21 members voted in favor of the $2,000,000 proposal.

6. Approximately 100 respondents requested a copy of the results.

7. Mix two quarts of white with 13 quarts of brown.

8. Examine the diagram on page seven.

Capitalization

Capitalize

1. **Proper nouns (words that name a particular person, place, or thing) and adjectives derived from proper nouns.** Capitalize the names of persons, places, geographic areas, days of the week, months of the year, holidays, deities, specific events, and other specific names.

Proper nouns	Common nouns
Lynn Claxton	An applicant for the management position
Bonita Lakes	A land development
Centre Park Mall	A new shopping center
Veteran's Day	A federal holiday
Information Age	A period of time

Proper adjectives: Irish potatoes, Roman shades, Swiss army knife, Chinese executives, British accent, Southern dialect

Do not capitalize the name of the seasons unless they are personified.

Old Man Winter

2. **The principal words in the titles of books, magazines, newspapers, articles, compact disks, movies, plays, television series, songs, and poems.**

Seven Habits of Highly Effective People [Book]

"Add Dimension to Presentations with a Document Camera" [Article]

Video Producer [Magazine]

Encarta Encyclopedia [Compact disk]

3. **The names of academic courses that are numbered, are specific course titles, or contain proper nouns.** Capitalize degrees used after a person's name and specific academic sessions.

Oscar Malone is enrolled in classes in <u>French</u>, <u>mathematics</u>, <u>science</u>, and <u>English</u>.

Students entering the MBA program must complete <u>Accounting 6093</u> and <u>Finance 5133</u>.

Allison O'Donnell, <u>M.S.</u>, will teach <u>Principles of Management</u> during <u>Spring Semester</u> 2008.

Professor O'Donnell earned a <u>master's</u> degree in business from Harvard.

4. **Titles that precede a name.**

Mr. Ronald Smith	Editor Franklin
Uncle Fred	Dr. Lauren Hobbs
President Lopez	Professor Senter

Do not capitalize titles appearing alone or following a name unless they appear in addresses.

The <u>manager</u> approved the proposal submitted by the <u>editorial assistant</u>.

Bryan Morris, <u>executive vice president</u>, is responsible for that account.

Russell has taken the position formerly held by his <u>father</u>.

Address all correspondence to Colonel Michael Anderson, <u>Department Head</u>, 109 Crescent Avenue, Baltimore, MD 21208.

5. **The main words in a division or department name if the official or specific name is known or the name is used in a return address, a letter address, or a signature block.**

Official or specific name known:	Return the completed questionnaire to the <u>Public</u> <u>Relations</u> <u>Department</u> by March 15.
Official or specific name unknown:	Employees in your information <u>systems</u> <u>division</u> are invited . . . .
Return or letter address, signature block:	Mr. Owen Rowan, <u>Manager</u>, <u>Public</u> <u>Relations</u> <u>Department</u> . . .

6. **Most nouns followed by numbers (except in page, paragraph, line, size, and verse references).**

Policy No. 8746826	Exhibit A	Chapter 7
page 97, paragraph 2	Figure 3-5	Model L-379
Flight 340, Gate 22	size 8, Style 319 jacket	

7. **The first word of a direct quotation.**

The program director said, "We leave for our London office tomorrow."

Do not capitalize the first word in the last part of an interrupted quotation or the first word in an indirect quotation.

"We will proceed," he said, "with the utmost caution." [Interrupted quotation]

He said that the report must be submitted by the end of the week. [Indirect quotation]

8. **The first word following a colon when a formal statement or question follows.**

Here is an important rule for report writers: Plan your work and work your plan.

Each sales representative should ask this question: Do I really look like a representative of my firm?

Exercise 13

Copy each of the following sentences, making essential changes in capitalization.

1. The first question professor Kellermanns asked me during interviewing 101 was "why do you want to work for us?"

2. The Summer season is much slower than the rest of the year according to the Sales Manager.

3. Inform the marketing department of our temporary shortage of AC adapters for laptop computers.

4. We recently purchased digital juice, an excellent source of copyright-free animated images.

5. Julie Gerberding, Director of the Center for Disease Control, is the agency's key communicator.

Words Frequently Misused

These words are frequently misused. If you're not certain of meaning or usage, check a dictionary or style guide.

1. Accept, except
2. Advice, advise
3. Affect, effect
4. Among, between
5. Amount, number
6. Capital, capitol
7. Cite, sight, site
8. Complement, compliment
9. Continual, continuous
10. Credible, creditable
11. Council, counsel
12. Different from, different than
13. Each other, one another
14. Eminent, imminent
15. Envelop, envelope
16. Farther, further
17. Fewer, less
18. Formally, formerly
19. Infer, imply
20. Its, it's
21. Lead, led
22. Lose, loose
23. Media, medium
24. Personal, personnel
25. Principal, principle
26. Reason is, because
27. Stationary, stationery
28. That, which
29. Their, there, they're
30. To, too, two

Exercise 14

Select the correct word.

1. Exactly how will the change (affect, effect) us?

2. The consultants' (advice, advise) is to downsize the organization.

3. The manager was astonished by the (amount, number) of complaints from the customer service staff.

4. Seeing Callye receive the top service award was an exhilarating (cite, sight, site).

5. I consider your remark a (compliment, complement).

6. The two panelists were constantly interrupting (each other, one another).

7. The issue will be discussed (further, farther) at our next meeting.

8. Limit your discussion to five or (fewer, less) points.

9. I (infer, imply) from Chad's statements to the press that he is optimistic about the proposal.

10. The storm seems to be losing (its, it's) force.

11. The chemical engineer (lead, led) the research team's investigation to eliminate (lead, led) from gas emissions.

12. Employees are entitled to examine their (personal, personnel) folders.

13. The system's (principal, principle) advantage is monetary.

14. (Their, There, They're) planning to complete (their, there, they're) strategic plan this week.

15. The (to, too, two) external auditors expect us (to, too, two) complete (to, too, two) many unnecessary reports.

Solutions to Exercises

Exercise 1—Sentence Structure

1. You must sign and return the enclosed form. [Sentence begins with an expletive.]

2. I am submitting an editorial, which I wrote last summer, to the newspaper. [Other words are placed between a pronoun and its antecedent.]

3. The work team wants to bring the project to a conclusion quickly (or quick conclusion). [The infinitive "to bring" is split.]

4. You must perform periodic maintenance on your computer to keep it operating efficiently. [The introductory phrase dangles.]

5. Protect your online privacy by using effective password protection, clearing temporary menus regularly, and encrypting sensitive information. [Units of a series are not stated in parallel form.]

Exercise 2—Pronoun Reference

1. their
2. was
3. her
4. was
5. its
6. its
7. this oversight

Exercise 3—Pronoun Case

1. me
2. her
3. she, who
4. my
5. whom

Exercise 4—Verb Agreement, Tense, and Mood

1. was
2. are
3. were
4. were
5. is
6. has
7. is
8. doesn't
9. started
10. were

Exercise 5—Adjectives and Adverbs

1. frequently
2. impatient
3. quickly
4. best
5. any other

Exercise 6—Commas

1. Correct.

2. Emoticons, which are created by keying combinations of symbols to produce "sideway faces," communicate emotion in electronic messages.

3. Sean Harrison, a new member of the board, remained silent during the long, bitter debate.

4. Primary qualifications for graduates seeking a first job are education, work experience, and leadership activities.

5. The entire population was surveyed, but three responses were unusable.

6. If you approve of the changes, place your initials in the space provided.

7. To qualify for the position, applicants must have technology certification.

8. We should be spending less money, not more.

9. On November 20, 2008, all related documents were submitted.

10. Yes, I agree that the theme meeting in St. Thomas should be scheduled for late May.

Exercise 7—Semicolons and Colons

1. Receipts were not included; otherwise, the expenses would have been reimbursed.

2. The following agents received a bonus this month: Barnes, $400; Shelley, $450; and Jackson, $600.

3. The proposal was not considered; it arrived two days late.

4. This paint does have some disadvantages, for example, a lengthy drying time.

5. Soon after the figures are received, they will be processed; but a formal report will not be released until June 1.

6. Correct

7. Our meetings are scheduled for Monday, Tuesday, and Friday.

8. We are enthusiastic about the plan because (1) it is least expensive, (2) its legality is unquestioned, and (3) it can be implemented quickly.

Exercise 8—Apostrophes

1. company's; its
2. weeks'; month's
3. banks; months

Exercise 9—Hyphens

1. self-confidence
2. State-of-the-art; timely business information
3. Correct
4. two-thirds; 5 percent
5. one half; highly educated

Exercise 10—Quotation Marks and Italics

1. Goleman presents an interesting theory of intelligence in his book *Emotional Intelligence*. [Italicizes a book title.]
2. The article "A Softer Side of Leadership" appeared in the July 2006 issue of *Training*. [Encloses the name of an article in quotation marks and italicizes the title of a magazine: Training.]
3. His "accomplishments" are summarized on the attached page. [Uses quotation marks to introduce doubt about whether "accomplishments" is the right label. His undertakings may have been of little significance.]
4. Kent said, "The firm plans to establish a sinking fund." [Uses quotations marks in a direct quotation.]
5. The term *flame* is online jargon for "a heated, sarcastic, sometimes abusive message or posting to a discussion group." [Italicizes a word used as a word and encloses a definition of a defined term.]
6. Read each email message carefully before you send it to avoid "flaming." [Uses quotation marks to emphasize or clarify a word for the reader.]

Exercise 11—Dashes, Parentheses, and Periods

1. Additional consultants—programmers and analysts—were hired to complete the computer conversion.
2. The dividend will be raised to 15 cents a share (approved by the Board of Directors on December 1, 2008).
3. Would you include the updated projections in tomorrow's presentation visuals. [Uses a period to follow courteous request that requires no verbal response.]

Exercise 12—Number Usage

1. The question was answered by 61 percent of the respondents.
2. The meeting is scheduled for 10 a.m. on February 3.
3. These three figures appeared on the expense account: $21.95, $30, and $35.14.
4. Correct.
5. Twenty-one members voted in favor of the $2 million proposal.
6. Approximately 100 respondents requested a copy of the results. [Approximations above nine that can be expressed in one or two words may be written in either figures or words, but figures are more emphatic.]
7. Mix 2 quarts of white with 13 quarts of brown.
8. Examine the diagram on page 7.

Exercise 13—Capitalization

1. The first question Professor Kellermanns asked me during Interviewing 101 was "Why do you want to work for us?"
2. The summer season is much slower than the rest of the year according to the sales manager.
3. Inform the Marketing Department of the temporary shortage of AC adapters for laptop computers.
4. We recently purchased Digital Juice, an excellent source of copyright-free animated images.
5. Julie Gerberding, director of the Center for Disease Control, is the agency's key communicator.

Exercise 14—Words Frequently Misused

1. affect
2. advice
3. number
4. sight
5. compliment
6. each another
7. further
8. fewer
9. infer
10. its
11. led; lead
12. personnel
13. principal
14. They're; their
15. two; to; too

LISTEN UP!

SHE DID

BCOM2 was designed for students just like you—busy people who want choices, flexibility, and multiple learning options.

BCOM2 delivers concise, focused information in a fresh and contemporary format. And...

BCOM2 gives you a variety of online learning materials designed with you in mind.

At **4ltrpress.cengage.com/bcom,** you'll find electronic resources such as **videos, audio downloads,** and **interactive quizzes** for each chapter.

These resources will help supplement your understanding of core concepts in a format that fits your busy lifestyle. Visit **4ltrpress.cengage.com/bcom** to learn more about the multiple resources available to help you succeed!

Chapter 1

1. The challenges facing workers in the future. (1999, August). *HR Focus*, 6.
2. Roth, D. (2000, January 10). My job at The Container Store. *Fortune*, 74–78.
3. Slayton, M. (1980). *Common sense & everyday ethics*. Washington, DC: Ethics Resource Center.
4. Slayton, M. (1991, May–June). Perspectives. *Ethics Journal*. Washington, DC: Ethics Resource Center.
5. When something is rotten. (2002, July 27). *Economist*, 53+.
6. A gift or a bribe? (2002, September). *State Legislatures*, 2(8), 9.
7. Mathison, D. L. (1988). Business ethics cases and decision models: A call for relevancy in the classroom. *Journal of Business Ethics, 10*, 781.
8. McGarry, M. J. (1994, June 9). Short cuts. *Newsday*, p. A50.
9. Felts, C. (1995). Taking the mystery out of self-directed work teams. *Industrial Management, 37*(2), 21–26.
10. Miller, B. K., & Butler, J. B. (1996, November/December). Teams in the workplace. *New Accountant*, 18–24.
11. Ray, D., & Bronstein, H. (1995). *Teaming up*. New York: McGraw Hill.
12. The trouble with teams. (1995, January 14). *Economist*, 61.
13. Frohman, M. A. (1995, April 3). Do teams . . . but do them right. *Industry-Week*, 21–24.
14. Zuidema, K. R., & Kleiner, B. H. (1994). New developments in developing self-directed work groups. *Management Decision, 32*(8), 57–63.
15. Barry, D. (1991). Managing the baseless team: Lessons in distributed leadership. *Organizational Dynamics, 20*(1), 31–47.
16. Mason, R. O. (1986). Four ethical issues of the information age. In Dejoie, R., Fowler, G., & Paradice, D. (1991). *Ethical issues in information systems* (pp. 46–55). Boston: Boyd & Fraser.

Chapter 2

1. Baumgardner, A. H. & Levy, P. E. (1988). Role of self-esteem in perceptions of ability and effort: Illogic or insight? *Personality and Social Psychology Bulletin, 14*, 429–438.
2. Evered, R. & Tannebaum, R. (1992). A dialog on dialog. *Journal of Management Inquiry, 1*, 43–55.
3. Ibid.

4. Barnlund, D.C. (1970). A transactional model of communication. In K. K. Sereno and C. D. Mortensen (Eds.), *Foundations of communication theory* (pp. 98–101). NY: Harper and Row.
5. Wood, J. T. (1997). *Communication theories in action*. Belmont, CA: Wadsworth.
6. DeVito, J. A. (1986). *The communication handbook: A dictionary*. NY: Harper and Row.
7. Shedletsky, L. J. (1989). The mind at work. In L. J. Shedletsky (Ed.), *Meaning and mind: An intrapersonal approach to human communication*. ERIC and The Speech Communication Association.
8. Gardner, H. & Krechevsky, M. (1993). *Multiple intelligences: The theory in practice*. New York: Basic Books.
9. Ibid.
10. Shoda, Y., Mischel, W. & Peake, P. K. (1990). Predicting adolescent cognitive and self-regulatory competencies from preschool delay of gratification: Identifying diagnostic conditions. *Developmental Psychology 26* (6) 978–986.
11. Eisenberg, E. M. & Goodall, Jr., H. L. (1993). *Organizational communication: Balancing creativity and constraint*. New York: St. Martin's Press.
12. Snyder, M. (1979). Self-monitoring processes. In L. Berkowitz (Ed.), *Advances in experimental social psychology*. New York: Academic Press.
13. Jablin, F. M. (2001). Organizational entry, assimilation, and disengagement/exit. *The new handbook of organizational communication* (pp. 732–818). Thousand Oaks, CA: Sage Publications.
14. Ibid.
15. Eisenberg, E. M. & Goodall, Jr., H. L. (1993). *Organizational communication: Balancing creativity and constraint*. New York: St. Martin's Press.
16. Pearson, J. C., Nelson, P. E., Titsworth, S., & Harter, L. (2003). *Human communication*. New York: McGraw-Hill.
17. Eisenberg, E. M. & Goodall, Jr., H. L. (1993), 252.
18. Orbe, M. P. (1996). Laying the foundation for co-cultural communication theory: An inductive approach to studying "nondominant" communication strategies and the factors that influence them. *Communication Studies, 47*, 157–176.
19. Infante, D., Trebling, J., Sheperd, P., & Seeds, D. (1984). The relationship of

argumentativeness to verbal aggression. *Southern Speech Communication Journal, 50*, 67–77.
20. Orbe, M. P. (1996), 170.
21. Eisenberg, E. M. & Goodall, Jr., H. L. (1993), 252.
22. Pearson, J. C., Nelson, P. E., Titsworth, S., & Harter, L. (2003). *Human communication*. New York: McGraw-Hill.
23. Wilson, S. R. (1998). Introduction to the special issue on seeking and resisting compliance: The vitality of compliance-gaining research, *Communication Studies, 49*, 273–275.
24. Miller, G. R., Boster, F. J., Roloff, M. E., & Seibold, D. (1977). Compliance-gaining message strategies: A typology and some findings concerning effects of situational differences. *Communication Monographs, 44*, 37–51.
25. Pearson, J. C., Nelson, P. E., Titsworth, S., & Harter, L. (2003). *Human communication*. New York: McGraw-Hill.
26. Saeki, M. & O'Keefe, B. (1994). Refusals and rejections: Designing messages to serve multiple goals. *Human Communication Research, 21*, 67–102.
27. Ifert, D. E. & Roloff, M. E. (1997). Overcoming expressed obstacles to compliance: The role of sensitivity to the expressions of others and ability to modify self-presentation. *Communication Quarterly, 45*, 55–67.
28. Burgoon, J. K, Johnson, M. L., & Koch, P. T. (1998). The nature and measurement of interpersonal dominance. *Communication Monographs, 65*, 308–335.
29. Keys, B. & Case, T. (1990). How to become an influential manager. *Academy of Management Executive, 4*, 38–50.
30. Ibid.
31. Ibid.
32. Ibid
33. Riley, P. & Eisenberg, E. (1991). The ACE model of management. Unpublished working paper, University of Southern California.
34. Mehrabian, A. (1971). *Silent messages*. Belmont, CA: Wadsworth.
35. Briggs, W. (1998, December). Next for communicators: Global negotiation. *Communication World, 16*(1), 12+.
36. Flannigan, T. (1990). Successful negotiating with the Japanese. *Small Business Reports, 15*(6), 47–52.
37. Salopek, J. J. (1999, September). Is anyone listening? *Training & Development, 53*(9), 58+.

Chapter 3

1. Hillkirk, J. (1993, November 9). More companies reengineering: Challenging status quo now in vogue. *USA Today*, p. 1b.
2. Zuidema, K. R., & Kleiner, B. H. (1994, October). Self-directed work groups gain popularity. *Business Credit*, 21–26.
3. Hunt, V. D. (1993). *Managing for quality: Integrating quality and business strategy*. Homewood, IL: Business One Irwin. (p. 121).
4. Stasser, G. (1992). Pooling of unshared information during group discussions. In S. Worchel, W. Wood, & J. A. Simpson (Eds.) *Group process and productivity* (pp. 48–67). Newbury Park, CA: Sage; Stasser, G., Taylor, L. A., & Hanna, C. (1989). Information sampling in structured and unstructured discussions of three- and six-person groups. *Journal of Personality and Social Psychology, 57*, 67–78; Wittenbaum, G. M. & Stasser, G. (1996). Management of information in small groups. In J. L. Nye & A. M. Brower (Eds.), *What's social about social cognition? Research on socially shared cognitions in small groups* (pp. 3–28). Thousand Oaks, CA: Sage.
5. Di Salvo, V. S., Nikkel, E., & Monroe, C. (1989). Theory and practice: A field investigation and identification of group members' perceptions of problems facing natural work groups. *Small Group Behavior, 20*, 551–567.
6. Myers, D. G. & Lamm, H. (1976). The group polarization phenomenon. *Psychological Bulletin, 83*, 602–627.
7. Clark, K. B. (1971). The pathos of power. *American Psychologist, 26*, 1047–1057; Myers, D. G. & Lamm, H. (1975). The polarizing effect of group discussion. *American Scientist, 63*, 297–303; Myers, D. G. & Lamm, H. (1976). The group polarization phenomenon. *Psychological Bulletin, 83*, 602–627; Goethals, G. R. & Zanna, M. P. (1979). The role of social comparison in choice shifts. *Journal of Personality and Social Psychology, 37*, 1469–1476; Myers, D. G. (1978). The polarizing effects of social comparison. *Journal of Experimental Social Psychology, 14*, 554–563; Sanders, G. S. & Baron, R. S. (1977). Is social comparison irrelevant for producing choice shifts? *Journal of Experimental Social Psychology, 13*, 303–314.
8. Davis, J. H., Kameda, T., & Stasson, M. (1992). Group risk taking: Selected topics. In J. F. Yates (Ed.), *Risk-taking behavior* (pp. 63–199). Chichester: Wiley; Laughlin, P. R. & Earley, P. C. (1982). Social combination models, persuasive arguments theory, social comparison theory, and choice shift. *Journal of Personality and Social Psychology, 42*, 273–280; Zuber, J. A., Crott, J. W., & Werner, J. (1992). Choice shift and group polarization: An analysis of the status of arguments and social decision schemes. *Journal of Personality and Social Psychology, 62*, 50–61.
9. Eisenberg, E. M. & Goodall, Jr., H. L. (1993). *Organizational communication: Balancing creativity and constraint*. New York: St. Martin's Press.
10. Hirokawa, R. & Rost, K. (1992). Effective group decision making in organizations. *Management Communication Quarterly, 5*, 267–388.
11. Ohbuchi, K., Chiba, S., & Fukushima, O. (1996). Mitigation of interpersonal conflicts: Politeness and time pressure. *Personality and Social Psychology Bulletin, 22*, 1035–1042.
12. Rosenbaum, M. E. (1986). The repulsion hypothesis: On the nondevelopment of relationships. *Personality and Social Psychology, 51*, 1156–1166.
13. Haythorn, W., Couch, A. S., Haefner, D., Langham, P., & Carter, L. F. (1956). The effects of varying combinations of authoritarian and equalitarian leaders and followers. *Journal of Abnormal and Social Psychology, 53*, 210–219.
14. Moreland, R. L., Levine, J. M., & Wingert, M. L. (1996). Creating the ideal group: Composition effects at work. In E. Witte & J. Davis (Eds.), *Understanding group behavior: Small group processes and interpersonal relations* (Vol. 2), (pp. 11–35). Mahwah, NJ: Erlbaum.
15. McGrath, J. E. (1984). Small group research, that once and future field: An interpretation of the past with an eye to the future. *Group Dynamics: Theory, Research, and Practice, 1*, 7–27.
16. Houle, C. O. (1989). *Governing boards: Their nature and nurture*. San Francisco: Jossey-Bass.
17. Franken, R. E. & Brown, D. J. (1995). Why do people like competition? The motivation for winning, putting forth effort, improving one's performance, performing well, being instrumental, and expressing forceful/aggressive behavior. *Personality and Individual Differences, 19*, 175–184; Franken, R. E. & Prpich, W. (1996). Dislike of competition and the need to win: Self-image concerns, performance concerns, and the distraction of attention. *Journal of Social Behavior and Personality, 11*, 695–712; Steers, R.M. & Porter, L.W. (1991). *Motivation and work behavior* (4th ed.). New York: McGraw-Hill; Tjosvold, D. (1995). Cooperation theory, constructive controversy, and effectiveness: Learning from crisis. In R. A. Guzzo, E. Salas, & Associates, *Team effectiveness and decision making in organizations* (pp. 79–112). San Francisco: Jossey-Bass.
18. Tjosvold, D. (1995). Cooperation theory, constructive controversy, and effectiveness: Learning from crisis. In R. A. Guzzo, E. Salas, & Associates, *Team effectiveness and decision making in organizations* (pp. 79–112). San Francisco: Jossey-Bass.
19. Kelley, H. H. (1997). Expanding the analysis of social orientations by reference to the sequential-temporal structures of situations. *European Journal of Social Psychology, 27*, 373–404.
20. Bonta, B. D. (1997). Cooperation and competition in peaceful societies. *Pyschological Bulletin, 121*, 299–320; Fry, D. P. & Bjorkqvist, K. (Eds.). (1997). *Cultural variations in conflict resolution: Alternatives to violence*. Mahwah, NJ: Erlbaum; Van Lange, P. A. M., De Bruin, E. M. N., Otten, W., & Joireman, J. A. (1997). Development of prosocial, individualistic, and competitive orientations: Theory and preliminary evidence. *Journal of Personality and Social Psychology, 37*, 858–864.
21. Lencioni, P. M. (2002). *The five dysfunctions of a team*. San Francisco: Jossey-Bass.
22. Blake, R. & Mouton, J. (1964). The managerial grid. Houston: Gulf Publishing; Kilmann, R. & Thomas, K. (1977). Developing a force-choice measure of conflict-handling behavior: The "MODE" instrument. *Educational and Psychological Measurement, 37*, 309–325.
23. Morrill, C. (1995). *The executive way*. Chicago: University of Chicago Press.
24. Wall, V. D., Jr. & Nolan, L. L. (1987). Small group conflict: A look at equity, satisfaction, and styles of conflict management. *Small Group Behavior, 18*, 188–211.
25. Chaney, L. H., & Lyden, J. A. (1998, May). Managing meetings to manage your image. *Supervision, 59*(5), 13–15.
26. Munter, M. (1998, June). Meeting technology: From low-tech to high-tech. *Business Communication Quarterly, 61*(2), 80–87.
27. Munter, M. (1998, June). Meeting technology: From low-tech to high-tech. *Business Communication Quarterly, 61*(2), 80–87.

Chapter 4

1. Canavor, N., & Meirowitz, C. (2005). Good corporate writing: Why it matters, and what to do; poor corporate writing—in press releases, ads, bro-

chures, websites and more—is costing companies credibility, and revenues. Here's how to put the focus back on clear communication. *Communication World, 22*(4), 30(4).

2. Conger, J. (1998). The necessary art of persuasion. *Harvard Business Review, 76,* 84–95.

3. Conger, J. (1998). The necessary art of persuasion. *Harvard Business Review, 76,* 86.

4. Ibid.

5. Ibid.

6. Pagano, B., Pagano, E., & Lundin, S. (2003). *The transparency edge: How credibility can make you or break you in business.* New York, NY: McGraw-Hill.

7. Conger, J. (1998).

8. Kraepels, R. H. & Davis, B. D. (2003). Designation of "communication skills" in position listings. *Business Communication Quarterly, 66* (2), 90.

9. Tyler, K. (2003). Toning up communications: Business writing courses can help employees and managers learn to clearly express organizational messages. *HR Magazine48* (3). Retrieved Jan. 9, 2008 from http://www.shrm.org/hrmagazine/articles/0303/0303agn-training.asp#kt.

10. Barnlund, D. C. (1986). Toward a meaning-centered philosophy of communication. In J. Stewart (Ed.), *Bridges not walls: A book about interpersonal communication* (pp. 36–42). NY: Newbury Award Records.

11. Larson I. (1995). The importance of context for exegesis. *Notes on Translation 9* (4): 29.

12. Ibid.

13. Dealing with emotions in the workplace (2002, November). *USA Today Magazine Online.* Retrieved December 13, 2003, from http://www.findarticles.com/cf_dls/m1272/2690_131/94384310/p1/article.jhtml.

14. (Manley, 2001

15. McCune, J. C. (n.d.) Managing emotions in the workplace. Retrieved September 15, 2004, from bankrate.com/brm/news/biz/tcb/20020927a.asp?prodtype=biz.

16. Arenofsky, J. (2001). Control your anger before it controls you! *Current Health 1,* 24 (7), 6–12.

17. Buhler, P. (1991). Managing in the 90's. *Supervision, 52,* 18.

18. Lencioni, P. M. (2002). *The five dysfunctions of a team.* San Francisco: Jossey-Bass.

19. Dennett, J. T. (1988). Not to say is better than to say: How rhetorical structure reflects cultural context in Japanese-English technical writing, 16-1998. In Subbiah, M. (1992). Adding a new dimension to the teaching of audience analysis: Cultural awareness. *IEEE, 35*(1), 14–17.

20. Olsen, L. A. & Huckin, T. N. (1991). *Technical writing and professional communication* (2nd ed.). New York: McGraw-Hill.

21. Mintzberg, H. (1975). The manager's job: Folklore and fact. *Harvard Business Review, 68,* 163–177.

22. Souther, J. W. (1985). What to report. *IEEE Transactions on Professional Communication, 28* (3), 6.

23. McIntosh, P. & Luecke, R. (2007). Interpersonal Communication Skills in the Workplace. New York: AMACOM Books.

Chapter 5

1. Letters: Email etiquette. (1996, July 26). *Information Week,* 6.

2. Mohan, S. (1998, June 29). New technology makes communication harder. *InfoWorld.* Retrieved July 13, 2000, from http://archive.infoworld.com/cgi-bin/displayStat.pl?/careers/980629comm.htm.

3. Lacy, S. (2006, January 6). IM security one tough sell. *Business Week Online,* 11.

4. Varchaver, N. (2003). The perils of e-mail. *Fortune, 147*(3), 96+.

5. Ibid.

6. Chase, N. (1999, April). Quality data on the Internet. *Quality, 38*(5), 122–126.

7. Framework Technologies. (2006). ActiveProject. Retrieved February 13, 2006, from http://www.frametech.com/pages/ap_activeproject.htm.

8. Dvorak, P. (1999, July 22). Automatic project web pages keep teams informed. *Machine Design, 71*(14), 88.

9. McAlpine, R. (2001). Web word wizardry: A guide to writing for the *Web and intranet.* Berkeley, Ten Speed Press.

10. Fichter, D. (2001, November/December). Zooming in: Writing content for intranets. *Online, 25*(6), 80+.

11. Weblog. (2005). Loosely coupled. Retrieved February 2, 2006, from http://www.looselycoupled.com/glossary/weblog.

12. Quible, Z. K. (2005). Blogs and written business communication courses: A perfect union. *Journal of Education for Business, 80*(6), 327–332.

13. Jones, D. (2005, May 10). CEOs refuse to get tangled up in messy blogs. *USA Today.* Retrieved February 6, 2006, from Academic Search Premier database.

14. DeBare, I. (2005, May 5). Tips for effective use of blogs in business. *San Francisco Chronicle,* p. C6.

15. Hutchins, J. P. (2005, November 14). Beyond the water cooler. *Computerworld, 39*(46), 45–46.

16. How to get the most out of voice mail (2000, February). *The CPA Journal, 70*(2), 11.

17. Leland, K., & Bailey, K. (1999). *Customer service for dummies* (2nd ed.). New York: Wiley.

18. Berkley, S. (2003, July). Help stamp out bad voicemail! *The Voice Coach Newsletter.* Retrieved July 25, 2003, from http://www.greatvoice.com/archive_vc/archiveindex_vc.html.

19. McCarthy, M. L. (1999, October). Email, voicemail and the Internet: How employers can avoid getting cut by the double-edged sword of technology. *Business Credit, 100*(9), 44+.

20. Cell phone etiquette (2001, March). *Office Solutions, 18*(3), 13.

21. McGrath, C. (2006, January 22). The pleasures of the text. *The New York Times,* p. 15.

Chapter 6

No references this chapter

Chapter 7

1. Sussman, S. W., & Sproull, L. (1999). Straight talk: Delivering bad news through electronic communication. *Information Systems Research, 10*(2), 150+. Retrieved April 12, 2006, from Business Source Premier database.

2. Jacobs, K. (2009, January 27). UPDATE 2—Best Buy plans layoffs at headquarters. *Thomson Reuters.* Retrieved July 22, 2009 from http://www.forbes.com/feeds/afx/2009/01/27/afx5973448.html; Vomhof Jr., J. (2008, December 15). Best Buy offers buyout to headquarters employees. *Minneapolis/St. Paul Business Journal.* Retrieved July 22, 2009 from http://www.bizjournals.com/twincities/stories/2008/12/15/daily9.html.

Chapter 8

1. Cooper, T., & Kelleher, T. (2001). Better mousetrap? Of Emerson, ethics, and postmillennium persuasion. *Journal of Mass Media Ethics, 16*(2/3), 176+.

2. Cody, S. (1906). *Success in letter writing: Business and social.* Chicago: A. C. McClurg, pp. 122–126.

3. Nelson, E. (1993). WordPerfect 6.0: 10 new things it does for you. *WordPerfect Magazine, 5*(7), 36–38, 40, 42–43. [p. 37].

4. Treadmill HQ. (2006). Body Solid Endurance 8K Treadmill. Retrieved April 23, 2006, from http://www.treadmillhq.com/product-detail~pid~{F87B200B-4805-40A6-A9AE-204C99C10992}.htm.

5. Bell, J. D. (1994). Motivate, educate, and add realism to business communication using the claim letter. *Business Education Forum, 48*(2), 42–43.
6. Green, J. & Naughton, K. (2009, February 24). Ford eliminates non-union bonuses, offers UAW buyouts (Update2). Retrieved July 24, 2009 from http://www.bloomberg.com/apps/news?pid=20601209&sid=azLTcot5Lhcg.

Chapter 9

1. Is email making bosses ruder? (2005). *European Business Forum, 21,* 72.
2. Rindegard, J. (1999). Use clear writing to show you mean business. *InfoWorld, 21*(47), 78.
3. Charlton, J. (Ed.) (1985). The writer's quotation book. Stamford, CT: Ray Freeman.
4. Wrong number. (1995). *Central New Jersey Business, 8*(13), 3.
5. Neuwirth, R. (1998). Error message: To err is human, but darn expensive. *Editor & Publisher, 131*(29), 4.
6. Jury sent message with huge reward in Vioxx drug case. (2005, August 24). *Gainesville Times.* Retrieved January 2, 2006, from http://www.gainesville-times.com.
7. Goldberg, C., & Allen, S. (2005, March 18). Researcher admits fraud in grant data. Global Healing Center. Retrieved January 2, 2006, from http://www.ghchealth.com.
8. Reinemund, S. S. (1992). Today's ethics and tomorrow's work place. *Business Forum, 17*(2), 6–9.
9. Telushkin, J. (1997). Avoid words that hurt. *USA Today,* p. 74.
10. Horton, T. R. (1990, January). Eschew obfuscation. *Security Management, 34*(1), 22+.
11. Dyrud, M. A. (1996). Teaching by example: Suggestions for assignment design. *Business Communication Quarterly, 59*(3), 67–70.
12. Redish, J. C. (1993). Understanding readers. In C. M. Barnum & S. Carliner, eds. *Techniques for technical communicators.* New York: Prentice Hall.
13. Redish, J. C. (1993). Understanding readers. In C. M. Barnum & S. Carliner, eds. *Techniques for technical communicators.* New York: Prentice Hall.
14. Varner, I. I. (1987). Internationalizing business communication courses. *Bulletin of the Association for Business Communication, 50*(4), 11+.

Chapter 10

1. Grimes, B. (2003, May 6). Fooling Google. *PC Magazine, 22*(8), 74.
2. Bruner, K. F. (2001). The publication manual of the American Psychological Association, (5th ed.). Washington, DC: American Psychological Association, p. 216.
3. Kinzer, S. (1994, August 22). Germany upholds tax on fast-food restaurants. *The New York Times,* p. 2.

Chapter 11

1. Hamner, S. (2006, July). Packaging that pays. *Business 2.0, 7*(6), 68–69.
2. Martin, M. H. (1997, November 27). The man who makes sense of numbers. *Fortune,* 273–275.
3. Wright, P., & Jansen, C. (1998). How to limit clinical errors in interpretation of data. *Lancet, 352*(9139), 1539–1543.
4. Kienzler, D. S. (1997). Visual ethics. *The Journal of Business Communication, 34*(2), 171–187. [p. 171].

Chapter 12

No references for this chapter.

Chapter 13

1. Axtell, R. E. (1992). *Do's and taboos of public speaking: How to get those butterflies flying in formation.* New York: John Wiley.
2. Britz, J. D. (1999, October). You can't catch a marlin with a meatball. *Presentations, 13*(10), A1–22.
3. Hughes, M. (1990). Tricks of the speechwriter's trade. *Management Review, 9*(11), 56–58.
4. Ibid.
5. Axtell, R. E. (1992). *Do's and taboos of public speaking: How to get those butterflies flying in formation.* New York: John Wiley.
6. Mayer, K. R. (1998). *Well spoken oral communication for business.* New York: Dryden.
7. Decker, B. (1992). *You've got to be believed to be heard.* New York: St. Martin's Press.
8. U.S. Copyright Office. (2000, September). What is copyright? Retrieved June 20, 2003, from http://www.copyright.gov/circs/circ1.html#wci; Zielinski, D. (2001, July). Stop! Thief! The great web copyright crackdown. *Presentations, 15*(7), 50(9); University of Texas System. Using materials from the Internet: What are the rules? Retrieved June 20, 2003, from http://www.templetons.com/brad/copymyths.html.
9. Newcombe, P. J. (1991). *Voice and diction,* (2nd ed.). Raleigh, NC: Contemporary Publishing Company.
10. Axtell, R. E. (1992). *Do's and taboos of public speaking: How to get those butterflies flying in formation.* New York: John Wiley.
11. Decker, B. (1992). *You've got to be believed to be heard.* New York: St. Martin's Press. [p. 137].
12. Hanke, J. (1998, January). Presenting as a team. *Presentations, 12*(1), 74–82.
13. Ibid.
14. Ibid.
15. Flett, N. (1998, March). Ensure you're on the same team. *Management,* 14.
16. Davids, M. (1999). Smiling for the camera. *Journal of Business Strategy, 20*(3), 20–24.
17. Turner, C. (1998, February). Become a web presenter! (Really it's not that hard). *Presentations, 12*(2), 26–27.

Chapter 14

1. Jackson, T. (2003). Find a job you love and success will follow. Career Journal *(The Wall Street Journal).* Retrieved July 1, 2003, from http://www.career-journal.com/jobhunting/strategies/20030415-jackson.html.
2. Riley, M. F. The Riley guide: Employment opportunities and job resources on the Internet. Retrieved September 27, 2006, from http://www.rileyguide.com.
3. Marcus, J. (2003). How to prompt employers to read your résumé. Career Journal from *The Wall Street Journal.* Retrieved July 3, 2003, from http://www.careerjournal.com/jobhunting/Résumés/20020130-marcus.html.
4. Smith, L. (2009, July 15). How typos on résumé can ruin your career prospects. *ABC report.* Retrieved July 27, 2009 from http://www.abc15.com/content/financialsurvival.
5. Ireland. S. (2002, July–August). A résumé that works. *Searcher, 10*(7), 98(12).
6. Cullen, L. T. (2006, May 1). Getting wise to lies. *Time, 167*(18), 59.
7. IOMA. (2006, June). How to ferret out instances of résumé padding and fraud. *Compensation & Benefits for Law Offices,* 06-06, 1, 4–12.
8. Cullen, L. T. (2006, May 1). Getting wise to lies. *Time, 167*(18), 59.
9. Harshbarger, C. (2003). You're out! *Strategic Finance, 84*(11), 46(4).
10. Crosby, O. (1999, Summer). Résumés, applications, and cover letters. *Occupational Outlook Quarterly,* 2–14.
11. Kennedy, J. L., & Morrow, T. J. (1994). *Electronic résumé revolution: Create a winning résumé for the new world of job seeking.* New York: John Wiley.
12. Kennedy, J. L., & Morrow, T. J. (1994). Electronic résumé revolution: *Create a winning résumé for the new world of job seeking.* New York: John Wiley.
13. Ibid.
14. Résumés you don't see everyday. Retrieved September 27, 2006, from

http://www.dummies.com/WileyCDA/ DummiesArticle/id-1610.html.

15. Young, J. (2002). 'E-portfolios' could give students a new sense of their accomplishments. *Chronicle of Higher Education, 48*(26), 31(2).

16. King, J. (1997, July 28). Point-and-click career service: Recruitingware does more than track résumés. *Computerworld*, p. 37.

Chapter 15

1. Vogt, P. (2006). Acing behavioral interviews. *CareerJournal.com*. Retrieved September 28, 2006, from http:// www.careerjournal.com/jobhunting/ interviewing/19980129-vogt.html.

2. Marion, L. C. (1997, January 11). Companies tap keyboards to interview applicants. *The News and Observer*, p. B5.

3. Vicers, M. (1997, April 14). Video interviews cut recruiting costs for many firms. *International Herald Tribune*, p. 15.

4. Ibid.

5. Kleiman, P. (2003, May). Armed for a multitude of tasks. *The Times Higher Education Supplement*, p. 4.

6. Eng, S. (1997, June 1). Handling "behavioral interviews." *The Des Moines Register*, p. 1.

7. Munk, N., & Oliver, S. (1997, March 24). Think fast! *Forbes*, 146–151.

8. Clarke, R. D. (1999). None of their business. *Black Enterprise, 30*(2), 65.

9. Smith, K. S. (1996, March 24). Interviewing tips for job seekers, managers. *Rocky Mountain News*, p. 6W.

10. Mueller, S. (1996). What skills will graduating students need to make it in the business world? *Business Journal–San Jose, 14*(8), 8.

11. Lai, P., & Wong, I. (2000). The clash of cultures in the job interview. *Journal of Language for International Business, 11*(1), 31–40.

12. Austin, N. K. (1996, March). The new job interview. *Working Woman*, 23, 24.

81% of students surveyed find that 4LTR Press Solutions help them prepare better for their exams.

REVIEW

HE DID

BCOM2 puts a multitude of study aids at your fingertips. After reading the chapters, check out these resources for further help:

- **Chapter in Review cards**, found in the back of your book, include all learning outcomes, definitions, and visual summaries for each chapter.

- **Online printable flash cards** give you three additional ways to check your comprehension of key concepts.

Other great ways to help you study include **interactive games, podcasts, audio downloads,** and **online tutorial quizzes with feedback**.

You can find it all at **4ltrpress.cengage.com/bcom**.

A

Abstract, 207
Accent, 239
Accommodation, 49
Acknowledgment message, 101
Active verbs, 155
Active voice, 155–156, 160, 299
Actual progress charting, 195
Adjectives, 161, 299
Adjustment messages, 94
Adverbs, 299
Advocacy, 29
Agenda, 51, 52
AIDA, 130
Airhead, 42
Allowing disruptions, 35
Analytical report, 168, 208
Anger management, 59–60
Annual report, 213
Anticipatory socialization, 26
Antivirus software program, 80
Apostrophes, 302
Appearance at interview, 282–283
Application forms, 289
Application messages, 270–276
    composing, 270–276
    encouraging action, 273–274
    finishing touches, 275–276
    follow-up messages, 289
    gaining receiver's attention, 271
    persuasive organization, 271–274
    qualifications, evidence of, 271–273
    sample letter, 272
    writing guidelines, 274–275
Appreciation messages, 93
Area chart, 197
Articulation, 239
Assertiveness, 27
Audience
    adapting message to, 70
    envisioning, 61–66
    international, 64, 165
    persuasive messages, 128
    presentations, 226, 243–244
    types of, 63–64
Avoidance, 26–27, 49

B

Baby boomers, 65
Bad-news messages
    the "bad-news" statement, 111–112

channel or medium, 106–109
closing positively, 114
constructive criticism in, 119–121, 122
cultural concerns, 108
denying a claim, 117–119, 120
denying credit, 118–119
developing, 109–114, 115
inductive organizational approach, 108–109
introductory paragraph, 110
job-refusal messages, 290, 292
organizational communications, 121–124
reasons section, 110–111
refusing a request, 115–116, 117
resignations, 292–293
"silver lining" idea, 113–114
Bar chart, 193–195, 196
Barriers, 5
    to intercultural communications, 16–18
Beamable résumé, 266
Beamer résumé, 266
Bibliography, 184, 208–209
Blog, 84
Bloggers, 84
Body language, 29
    cultural differences, 17
    interpreting, 30
Boolean logic, 174
Borders, 162
Brainstorming, 51
Breakdowns in communication, 4

C

Capitalization, 305–307
Career search. See Job search
Career service centers, 251
Casual listening, 33
Cell phone communication, 85–86
Channel or medium
    bad-news messages, 106–109
    cost of, 69
    good-/neutral-news messages, 88
    selection of, 4–5, 67–70
Chartjunk, 191
Charts
    bar, 193, 194, 196
    flow, 199, 200
    line, 195–198
    pie, 198

Chronemics, 16
Chrono-functional résumé, 259
Chronological context, 66
Chronological résumés, 258–259, 262
Chunking, 161
Citations, 183–184
Claims, 93, 134
    denying, 117–118
    persuasive claims, 93–94, 137–138
    routine claims, 93–96, 97
Clause, 154
Clichés, 158–159, 161
Code of ethics, 14
Coherence, 152
Collaboration, 49
Collaborative software, 20–21
Collectivism versus individualism, 15
Colons, 302
Commas, 299–301
Comma splice, 155
Commitment, 44
Common language, 190
Communication breakdowns, 4
"Communication," defined, 2
Communication process, 3–4
Competence and expertise, 58
Competition, 49
Competitors, 47
Complements, 154
Compliance-gaining, 28
Compliance-resisting, 28
Compound adjectives, 161
Compromise, 49
Computer hoaxes, 80
Concise communications, 160–161
Confidentiality in electronic communications, 75
Conflict
    group. See Group conflict resolution, 47–49
Consensus, 52
Constructive criticism, 119–121, 122
Contemporary language, use of, 158–159
Context, 10, 66–67
Contribution, 44
Control over message, 69–70
Conversational control and panache, 28
Cooperation, 44
Cooperators, 47
Copyright constraints, 233
Correlation analysis, 185
Counterproposal, 113–114
Cover message, 270
Credibility
    communicating to establish, 57–60
    enhancing in reports, 213

Credit
    denying, 118–120
    extension of, 101–104
    information requests, 101
Credo, 14
Cross-functional team, 18, 42
Cultural concerns/differences, 15–16
    bad-news messages, 108
    diversity challenges, 14–18
    international audiences, 165
    nonverbal communication, 31–32
    presentations, 243–244
    written messages, 165
Cultural context, 66
Culture, 61
Cumulative line chart, 197
Customer order acknowledgments, 101

D

Dashes, 304
Databases, 174
    advantages to, 20
    Internet research, 173–174
Decisional roles, 63
Decoding, 6
Deductive, 152
Deductive approach, 72–73, 88–90
De-emphasized ideas, 156
Delimitations, 171
Democratic strategy, 64
Denying a claim, 117–119
Denying credit, 118–119
Dependent clause, 154
Detractor, 42
Dialect, 239
Diction. See Word usage
Digresser, 42
Dimensions of business behavior, 13–14
Direct quotation method, 178
Direct sequence, 90
Dismissing subjects as uninteresting, 35
Distance presentations, 246–247
Diversity challenges. See Cultural concerns/differences
Diversity initiatives, 15
Diversity skills, 15
Document production software, 20
Dominator, 42
Downward communication, 7–8
Downward-directed report, 168

E

Economic level, 61
Editing. *See also* Revising text
  parallel, 221
  reciprocal, 221
  sequential, 221
Educational/occupational
  background, 61
Electronic applicant-tracking
  systems, 261
Electronic communications
  cell phone communication,
  85–86
  confidential information, 75
  email. *See* Email
  instant messaging, 80–81
  personal information, 75
  purpose of message, 74
  text messaging, 86
  voice mail communication,
  85
  Web page communications,
  82–84
Electronic databases. *See*
  Databases
Electronic job searches,
  252–253
Electronic portfolio, 268–269
Electronic presentations. *See*
  Presentations
Electronic résumé, 261
Electronic sources, 173–174
Email, 76–81
  advantages of, 76
  effective use of, 79–80
  graphic highlighting, 78–79
  guidelines for preparing,
  76–79
  heading, 77
  legal constraints, 81–82
  procedural, with
  attachment, 105
  sequencing ideas, 77–78
  subject line, 77
  topic, 77
  word usage, 78
Email report, 214
Emotional control, 59–60
Emotional intelligence, 25
Empathetic listening, 34–35
Empathy, 34
Emphasized ideas, 156
Employers' offices, 251
Employment agencies/
  contractors, 251–252
Employment interviews. *See*
  Job interviews
Employment search. *See* Job
  search
Employment videos, 269–270
Encoding, 4
Endnotes page, 184
E-portfolio, 268–269
Ethical constraints, 11–14
  graphics, 191
  revising text, 150–151
  technology and, 21
Ethics, 11
Ethnocentrism, 16
Ethos, 128
Evidence supporting claim, 134

Expectations, 61
Experimental research, 176
Expert audiences, 63–64
Expertise and competence, 58
Extemporaneous presentations,
  238
Extension of credit, 101–104
External influences, 10, 11
External messages, 6
External proposal, 169
External report, 168
Extranets, 20

F

Face-to-face meetings, 50
Facilitator, 42
Faking attention, 35
Favors, asking for, 139
Feedback, 6, 68
First drafts, 73
Flame, 79–80
Flat organizational structures,
  38–39
Follow-up messages, 289
Formal network flow, 7–9
Formal reports, 168 204–209
  addenda, 208–209
  analysis, 208
  appendix, 209
  discussion, 208
  enhancing credibility, 213
  executive summary,
  207–208
  headings, 211–212
  index, 209
  organization of, 209–213
  outlining, 210–211
  preliminary matter,
  205–208
  references, 208–209
  sequencing ideas, 210–211
  table of contents, 206
  table of figures, 206–207
  text of, 208–209
  title page, 206
  writing style, 212–213
Forming, 43
Form letter, routine responses,
  99–101
Form reports, 214–215
Fraud, 150
Free rider, 42
Free riding, 47
Functional report, 168–169
Functional résumés, 259, 264
Fundamental attribution error,
  47
Fused sentence, 155

G

Gantt chart, 195–196
Gatekeeper, 42
Gender differences, 32
  cultural differences, 15
  in nonverbal
  communication, 32–33
Generational differences, 65

Generation Xers, 65
Generation Yers, 65
Good-news messages, 89,
  90–93
  appreciation messages, 93
  channel or medium, 88
  deductive organizational
  approach, 88–90
  job-acceptance messages,
  290, 291
  positive news message, 90,
  92
  thank-you messages, 91
Goodwill, 60–61
  building through inductive
  approach, 108–109
Grammar
  adjectives, 299
  adverbs, 299
  pronoun case, 297–298
  pronoun reference, 296–297
  sentence structure, 295–296
  verb agreement, 298
  verb mood, 164, 298–299
  verb tense, 298
  verb voice. *See* Verb voice
Grant, 94
Graphics, 190–201
  charts. *See* Charts
  effective use of, 190–191
  ethical constraints, 191
  maps, 198–199
  photographs, 199
  table of figures, 206–207
  tables, 162, 192–193
  in text, 201–202
  types of, 191–201
Graphs, 162
Group(s), 18, 38, 40–42
  communications, 7. *See
  also* Organizational
  communications
  competitive *versus*
  cooperative orientation,
  46–47
  conflict. *See* Group conflict
  effective groups,
  characteristics of, 40–42
  social dilemmas, 47
  to teams, 42–44. *See also*
  Team(s)
Group conflict, 45–50
  resolution of, 47–49
Group cooperation, 40, 46–47
Group decision-making, 44–45
Grouped bar charts, 194
Group norms, 41
Group roles, 41–42
Groupthink, 41, 46, 49–50

H

Haptics, 16–17
Harmonizer, 42
Headings
  email, 77
  formal reports, 211–212
  and readability, 162
  talking, 210–211
Hidden Internet, 174
High self-monitors, 26

Honest answers, 121
Horizontal communication, 9
Hot buttons, 165
Hyphens, 303
Hypothesis, 170–171

I

Illegal conduct/
  communications, 12–13,
  121. *See also* Legal
  constraints
Implying refusal, 111–112
Impression management, 26
Impromptu delivery, 238
Independent clause, 154
Indirect refusal, 112
Individualism *versus*
  collectivism, 15
Individualists, 47
Inductive, 152
Inductive approach, 72–73
  bad-news messages,
  108–109
  persuasive messages,
  130–137
Ineffective example, 90
Influence, 28
Informal network flow, 7, 9–10
Informal report, 168
Informational messages, 56
Informational report, 168
Informational roles, 63
Information requests
  credit, 101
  persuasive, 139
Initiating communication, 115,
  121
Inline résumé, 268
Instant messaging (IM), 80–81
Integrity, 58
Intensive listening, 34
Interferences, 5
  to intercultural
  communications, 16–18
Internal messages, 6
Internal proposal, 169
Internal report, 168
International audiences, 63, 165
Internet, 20
Internet conferencing, 246
Internet job searches, 252–253
Internet research, 173–174
Interpersonal communication,
  7, 22, 67
  impression management, 26
  listening during. *See*
  Listening
  nonverbal, 29–33. *See also*
  Nonverbal communication
  self-concept and, 22–26
  styles, 26–28
Interpersonal dominance, 28
Interpersonal influence, 28–29
Interpersonal intelligence,
  24–25
Interpersonal roles, 63
Interviews. *See* Job interviews
Intranets, 20
Intrapersonal communication,
  6, 24

Intrapersonal intelligence, 24
Isolate, 42
Italics, 303–304

J

Jargon, 160
Job-acceptance messages, 290, 291
Job interviews
appearance at, 282–283
closing, 288
information exchange, 288
opening formalities, 287–288
practicing for, 283–286
preparing for, 281–283
stress interviews, 280
structured, 278–280
success at, 287–288
team interviews, 280
thank-you messages, 289–290
types of, 278–281
unstructured, 280
virtual, 280–281
Job-refusal messages, 290, 292
Job search
application forms, 289
applications. See Application messages
career service centers, 251
electronic, 252–253
employers' offices, 251
employment agencies/ contractors, 251–252
identification of opportunities, 250–253
information gathering, 249–250
networks, 251
preparing for, 248–250
printed sources, 251
professional organizations, 252
résumés. See Résumés
Justification report, 210

K

Kinesics, 17, 29, 30. See also Body language

L

Lateral communication, 9
Layered approach, 64
Leader, 42
Leadership, 41
Legal constraints, 11–14
copyright constraints, 233
email, 81–82
technology and, 21
Letter reports, 214, 216–219
Libel, 151
Lines, 162
Listening, 28, 33

casual, 33
effective listening suggestions, 36, 37
empathetic, 34
for information, 34
intensive, 34
poor habits, 35
Lists, 162
Logos, 128
Longitudinal studies, 172
Low self-monitors, 26

M

Managers, 63
Manuscript delivery, 237–238
Mature persons, 65
Mean, 185
Measures of central tendency, 184
Median, 185
Medium. See Channel or medium
Meetings
effective meetings, 51–52
electronic meetings, 51
face-to-face meetings, 50
Memorandum report, 214, 215
Memorized presentations, 236–237
Memos, 88
Messages, 54–55
adapting to audience, 70
audience. See Audience
context of, 66–67
control over, 69–70
decoding, 6
encoding, 4–5
external, 6
internal, 6
medium of. See Channel or medium
organization of, 71–73
permanent record, need for, 69
procedural, 104, 105
purposes of, 56–61
sequencing ideas, 72–73
transmission of, 4–5
types of, 56–61
Metacommunication, 29
Methodology, 172
Millennials, 65
Mixed audiences, 63–64
Mobile phone communication, 85–86
Mode, 185
Multicultural audiences, 63–64
Multimedia résumés, 269–270

N

Needs and concerns of the receiver, 61
Netiquette, 79–80
Networks
informal network flow, 9–10
job search, 251
Neutral-news messages

channel or medium, 88
deductive organizational approach, 88–90
Non-expert audiences, 63
Nonverbal communication, 29
cultural differences, 31–32
failing to observe cues, 35
gender differences, 32–33
kinesic messages. See Body language
metacommunication, 29
understanding, 30–31
Nonwords, 238
Norm, 41
Normative survey research, 176
Norming, 43
Norm of reciprocity, 47
Null hypothesis, 171
Number usage, 305

O

Observational studies, 176
100 percent bar charts, 194
One-way, not face-to-face communication, 5, 67–68
Oral briefings, 224
Organizational communications, 6, 7. See also Group(s)
bad-news messages, 121–124
communication flow, 7–10
levels of, 6–7
meeting management, 50–52
persuasive messages, 139–142
Organizational culture, 66
Organizational role(s), 63–64
Organizational structures, 38–39
Organize, 71
Outdated expressions, 158
Outlining, 71–72, 210–211
Overlistening, 35
Oversampling, 44

P

Paragraphs
coherency in, 152–154
length of, 153
topic sentences, 152
Parallel editing, 221
Paraphrase method, 178–179
Parentheses, 304
Passiveness, 27
Passive verbs, 155
Passive voice, 163–164, 299
Pathos, 128
PDAs, 87
Performing, 43
Periodic report, 168
Periods, 304
Personal agenda, 46
Personal conflict, 46
Personal Digital Assistants (PDAs), 87

Personal ethics, 58
Personal information
in electronic communications, 75
in résumés, 254, 257
Personality differences, 65–66
Persuasive claims, 93–94, 137–138
Persuasive messages, 56–57
action desired, 129
application messages, 271, 274–275
audience, 128
claims, 93–94, 137–138
creating desire, 133–136
favors, asking for, 139
gaining attention, 130–131
gaining interest, 132–133
inductive organizational approach, 130–137
information requests, 139
motivating to action, 136–137
organizational communications, 139–142
planning before writing, 127–129
requests, 96, 137–145
sales messages, 142–145
strategies, 126–130
writing principles, 129
Persuasiveness and poise, 28
Persuasive requests, 96, 137–145
Phonation, 238
Photographs, 199
Phrase, 154
Physical context, 66
Physical setting, 66
Pictograms, 194–195
Pilot test, 177, 181
Pitch, 238
Plagiarism, 179
Planned progress charting, 195
Pleasing message, 89
Posts, 84
Power distance, 15
Précis, 207
Presentations
audience concerns, 226, 243–244
body of, 227–229
close, 229
color, use of, 234–236
copyright constraints, 233
cultural concerns/ differences, 243–244
delivery method, 236–238
delivery style, 240–242
distance presentations, 246–247
handouts following, 242
introduction, 226–227
key message in, 225–226
organization of, 226–229
planning, 224–226
question-and-answer period, 242
slide content, 230–232
software, 20
space design, 234–236
team presentations, 244–246
typography, 234

visual enhancements, 229–236
vocal qualities, 238–240
Primary research, 176–177
  survey methods, 179–181
Printed sources
  job search, 251
  secondary research, 172–173
Print résumés, 260–261
Problem-solving process, 170–186
Problem statement, 170
Procedural conflict, 46
Procedural messages, 104, 105
Procedures, 172
Product development team, 42
Professional image, 60
Professional organizations, 252
Professional portfolio, 268–269
Pronoun case, 297–298
Pronoun reference, 296–297
Pronunciation, 240
Proposals, 169–170
  addenda, 220–221
  budget/costs, 220
  evaluation/follow-up, 220
  materials and equipment, 220
  methods/procedures, 217
  parts of, 216–220
  preparation of, 221
  purpose/problem, 217
  qualifications, 220
  sample, 222–223
  scope of, 217
  structure of, 216–221
  summary, 220
Proxemics, 16
Public communication, 7
Public web presence, 82
Punctuation
  apostrophes, 302
  colons, 302
  commas, 299–301
  dashes, 304
  hyphens, 303
  italics, 304
  parentheses, 304
  periods, 304
  quotation marks, 303–304
  semicolons, 301–302
Purposes of communication, 2

Q

Quality assurance team, 42
Quality circle, 42
Quantitative information, 188–190
  number usage, 305
Quotation marks, 303–304

R

Range of scores, 184
Rapport, 61
Rate words spoken, 238
Rational-explanation, 29
Readability
  conciseness, 160–161
  contemporary language, use of, 158–159
  improving, 157–163
  measures of, 157–158
  visual enhancements, 161–163
Reciprocal editing, 221
Recommendations, 292, 293
Record keeper, 42
Red flag, 165
Redundancies, elimination of, 160
Referencing methods, 183–184
Refusing a request, 115–116, 117
Refuting supporting details, 108
Relationships, importance of, 26
Reliability, 177
Reporter, 42
Reports
  analytical, 208
  annual, 213
  body, 208
  characteristics of, 166–169
  conclusions, 208
  discussion, 208
  formal. See Formal reports
  problem-solving process, 170–186
  process of creating, 185
  proposals. See Proposals
  recommendations, 208
  short, 214–216
  summary, 208
  types of, 167–169
  works cited, 208–209
Representative data, 177
Requests
  persuasive requests, 96, 137–145
  refusing, 115–116, 117
  RFPs, 169
  routine requests, 96–101
Resale, 94
Research
  data. See Research data
  documenting information sources, 181–184
  primary. See Primary research
  secondary. See Secondary research
Research data
  analyzing, 184–186
  errors, avoidance of, 181
  interpreting, 186
Resignations, 292, 293
Responsiveness, 27–28
Résumés
  career summary, 254–255

chrono-functional, 259
chronological, 258–259, 262
education, 255
electronic submission requirements, 266, 268
follow-up messages, 289
functional, 259, 264
honors and activities, 257
objective, 254
parts of, 254–258
personal information, 254, 257
planning, 253–259
preparing, 259–268
print, 260–261
qualifications, 255–258
references, 258, 263
scannable. See Scannable résumés
supplementing, 268–270
types of, 258–259
work experience, 256–257
Revising text, 146
  active voice, use of, 155–156, 160
  effective revising suggestions, 146–148
  emphasizing important ideas, 156–157
  ethical constraints, 150–151
  logical development and unity, 151–154
  paragraph coherency, 152–154
  readability concerns. See Readability
  sentence structure, 154–155, 156–157
  systematic procedures for, 148–150
  for tone, 163–165
RFP (request for proposal), 169
Routine claims, 93–96
Routine requests, 96–101
Routine responses, 99–101
Run-on sentence, 155

S

Sales messages, 143–145
Sales promotional material, 94, 96
Sampling, 176–177
Scannable résumés, 261, 263, 265–266
  formatting, 263–265
  sample, 267
  searchable, 265–266
Scripted delivery, 237–238
Search engine, 173–174
Secondary research, 172–174
  collecting data, 177–179
Segmented bar charts, 194
Self-assurance, 28
Self-awareness, 24
Self-concept, 22–25
Self-directed team, 18

Self-esteem, 24
Self-fulfilling prophecy, 24
Semicolons, 301–302
Senior citizens, 65
Sentence fragment, 154
Sentences
  active voice, 155–156, 160
  length of, 153–154
  shortening, 161
  structure of, 154–155, 156–157, 295–296
  topic sentences, 152
Sequencing ideas, 72–73
  email, 77–78
  formal reports, 210–211
Sequential editing, 221
Serifs, 234
Short reports, 214–216
"Silver lining" idea, 113–114
Slander, 151
Social context, 66
Social dilemmas, 47
Socializer, 42
Software technologies, 20–21
Solicited proposal, 169
Solicited sales letters, 130–131
Solicited sales message, 142–143
Stacked bar charts, 194
Stakeholders, 11
Standards of ethical conduct, 14
Statement of purpose, 170
Statement of the problem, 170
Status, 39
Stereotypes/stereotyping, 16, 35
Storming, 43
Stress interview, 280
Structured interview, 278–280
Subdivided bar charts, 194
Subject, 154
Subjective sentences, 163–164
Subjunctive mood, use of, 164, 298–299
Substantive conflict, 46
Supplementing résumés, 268–270
Surface chart, 197
Survey methods, 179–181
Survey questionnaire, 181, 182
Synergy, 18

T

Tables, 162, 192–193
Tabulation of data, 184
Talking headings, 210–211
Targeted résumés. See Résumés
Task focus, 28
Task force, 42
Team(s), 18, 42–45
  collaborative writing skills, 221, 223
  groups to, 42–44
Team effectiveness, 19
Team environment, 18
Team interviews, 280
Team presentations, 244–246
Technology
  appropriate use of, 74
  changes in, 19–21

electronic communications.
See Electronic
communications
software technologies,
20–21
Telecommuting, 20
Text messaging, 86
Text résumé, 268
Thank-you messages, 91
after job interviews,
289–290
Tone, 163–165
Topic sentence, 152
Trust, 47, 61
Two-way, not face-to-face
communication, 5, 67

Uncertainty avoidance, 15–16
Understanding claims, 117
Understanding supporting
details, 108
Unethical conduct/
communications, 11–14,
58, 59, 120, 135. *See also*
Ethical constraints
Unsolicited application
messages, 270–271

Unsolicited proposal, 169
Unsolicited sales message,
142–143
Unstructured interview, 280
Upward communication, 8–9
Upward-directed report, 168

Validity, 177
Verb, 154
Verb agreement, 298
Verbal fillers, 238
Verb mood, 164, 298–299
Verb tense, 298
Verb voice, 299
    active voice, 155–156, 160
    passive voice, 163–164
Videoconferencing, 247
Virtual interviews, 280–281
Virtual team, 42
Viruses, 80
Visual enhancements. *See also*
    Graphics
    presentations, 229–236
    readability, 161–163
Voice mail communication,
84–85
Volume, 238

Webcasting, 246
Weblogs, 84
Web page communications,
82–84
Web presentations, 247
Web publishing tools, 20
Who, what, when, where, why,
171, 206
Win/win philosophy, 40
Wireless communications
    cell phone communication,
    85–86
    future of, 86–87
    text messaging, 86
    voice mail communication,
    85
Word usage
    clichés, 158–159, 161
    contemporary language,
    use of, 158–159
    email, 78
    frequently misused words,
    307
    labels, words as, 157
    outdated expressions, 158
    position of words, 157
    repetition of words, 157,
    160

simple, informal words,
159–160
Work group, 18
Workplace productivity, 174
Work team, 18
Writer's pride of ownership,
148
Writing principles/skills
    collaborative skills for
    teams, 221, 223
    first drafts, 73
    persuasive messages, 129
    revision skills. *See* Revising
    text
    suggestions for improving,
    58
Weblogs, 84
Web sites, 83–84

"You Attitude," 71

82% of students surveyed on a 4LTR Press Solution find it is designed more closely to match the way they naturally study.

LISTEN UP!

SHE DID

BCOM2 was designed for students just like you—busy people who want choices, flexibility, and multiple learning options.

BCOM2 delivers concise, focused information in a fresh and contemporary format. And...
BCOM2 gives you a variety of online learning materials designed with you in mind.

At **4ltrpress.cengage.com/bcom,** you'll find electronic resources such as **videos, audio downloads,** and **interactive quizzes** for each chapter.

These resources will help supplement your understanding of core concepts in a format that fits your busy lifestyle. Visit **4ltrpress.cengage.com/bcom** to learn more about the multiple resources available to help you succeed!

SPEAK UP!

THEY DID

BCOM2 was built on a simple principle: to create a new teaching and learning solution that reflects the way today's faculty teach and the way you learn.

Through conversations, focus groups, surveys, and interviews, we collected data that drove the creation of the version of BCOM2 that you are using today. But it doesn't stop there—in order to make BCOM2 an even better learning experience, we'd like you to SPEAK UP and tell us how BCOM2 worked for you.

What did you like about it? What would you change? Are there additional ideas you have that would help us build a better product for next semester's students?

At **4ltrpress.cengage.com/bcom** you'll find all of the resources you need to succeed – **videos, audio downloads, flash cards, interactive quizzes** and more!

Speak Up! Go to **4ltrpress.cengage.com/bcom.**

Learning Objectives

LO¹: Define communication and describe the main purposes for communication in business.

Communication is the process of exchanging information and meaning between or among individuals through a common system of symbols, signs, and behavior. Managers spend most of their time in communication activities.

LO²: Explain the communication process model and the ultimate objective of the communication process.

People engaged in communication encode and decode messages while simultaneously serving as both senders and receivers. In the communication process, feedback helps people resolve possible misunderstandings and thus improves communication effectiveness. Feedback and the opportunity to observe nonverbal signs are always present in face-to-face communication, the most complete of the three communication levels.

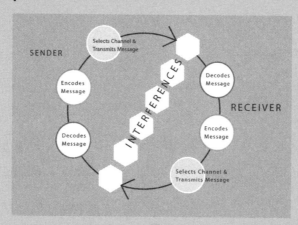

LO³: Discuss how information flows in an organization.

Communication takes place at five levels: intrapersonal (communication within one person), interpersonal (communication between two people), group (communication among more than two people), organizational (communication among combinations of groups), and public (communication from one entity to the greater public). Both formal and informal communication systems exist in every organization; the formal system exists to accomplish tasks, and the informal system serves a personal maintenance purpose that results in people feeling better about themselves and others. Communication flows upward, downward, and horizontally or laterally. These flows often defy formal graphic description, yet each is a necessary part of the overall communication activity of the organization.

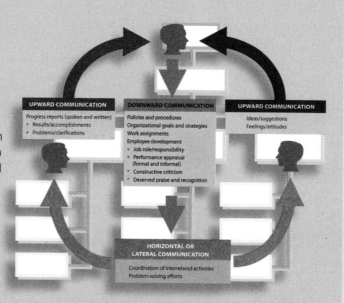

Key Terms

Encoding the process of selecting and organizing the message

Interferences (barriers) other factors that may hinder the communication process

Decoding the process of interpreting the message

Feedback the response the receiver gives to the sender of a message

Organizational communication communication concerned with the movement of information within the company structure

Internal messages messages intended for recipients within the organization

External messages messages directed to recipients outside the organization

Intrapersonal communication communication that occurs within oneself

Interpersonal communication communication that occurs between two people

Group communication communication that occurs among more than two people

Public communication communication intended to help the organization to reach out to its public to achieve its external communication goals

Formal network flow communication that often follows a company's formal organization chart

Informal network flow flow of communication that develops as people interact within the formal communication system

Downward communication communication from supervisor to employee

Upward communication communication from employees to supervisors

Horizontal (lateral) communication interactions between organizational units on the same hierarchical level

Stakeholders those affected by decisions

Ethics the principles of right and wrong that guide decision making

Code of ethics a written document summarizing the company's or profession's standards of ethical conduct

Diversity skills the ability to communicate effectively with both men and women of all ages and with people of other cultures or minority groups

Culture "the way of life" of a people, which includes a vast array of behaviors and beliefs

Power distance the extent to which less powerful people expect and accept the fact that power is unequal within the country or an organization

Ethnocentrism belief that the specific patterns of behavior desired in one's own culture are universally valued

Stereotype a mental picture of the main characteristics of another group, creating preformed ideas of what people in this group are like

Chronemics the study of how a culture perceives time and its use

Proxemics the study of cultural space requirements

Haptics the study of touch

Kinesics the study of body language

Team a small group of people with complementary skills who work together for a common purpose

Distributed leadership when the role of leader alternates among members, and more than one leadership style may be active at any given time

LO⁴: Explain how legal and ethical constraints, diversity challenges, team environment, and changing technology influence the process of business communication.

Communication occurs within an environment constrained by legal and ethical requirements, diversity challenges, team environment requirements, and changing technology.

- International, federal, state, and local laws impose legal boundaries for business activity, and ethical boundaries are determined by personal analysis that can be assisted by application of various frameworks for decision making.

- Communication is critically impacted by diversity in nationality, culture, age, gender, and other factors that offer tremendous opportunities to maximize talent, ideas, and productivity but pose significant challenges in interpretation of time, personal space requirements, body language, and language translation.

- Team environment challenges arise because communication in teams differs from communication in traditional organizational structures. The result of effective teams is better decisions, more creative solutions to problems, and higher worker morale.

- Significant strides have occurred in the development of tools for data collection and analysis, shaping messages to be clearer and more effective, and communicating quickly and efficiently over long distances. The use of technology, however, poses legal and ethical concerns in regard to ownership, access, and privacy.

LEGAL & ETHICAL CONSTRAINTS

- International Laws
- Domestic Laws
- Code of Ethics
- Stakeholder Interests
- Ethical Frameworks
- Personal Values

DIVERSITY CHALLENGES

- Cultural Differences
- Language Barriers
- Gender Issues
- Education Levels
- Age Factors
- Nonverbal Differences

TEAM ENVIRONMENT

- Trust
- Team Roles
- Shared Goals and Expectations
- Synergy
- Group Reward
- Distributed Leadership

CHANGING TECHNOLOGY

- Accuracy and Security Issues
- Telecommunications
- Software Applications
- "High-touch" Issues
- Telecommuting
- Databases

Grammar Quiz

Identify the weakness in each sentence and write an improved version.

1. It is essential that you sign and return the enclosed form.
2. I am submitting an editorial to the newspaper, which I wrote last summer.
3. The work team wants to quickly bring the project to a conclusion.
4. To operate efficiently, you must perform periodic maintenance on your computer.
5. Protect your online privacy by use of effective password protection, clearing temporary menus regularly, and encryption of sensitive information.

Quiz Solutions

1. You must sign and return the enclosed form. [Sentence begins with an expletive.]
2. I am submitting an article, which I wrote last summer, to the newspaper. [Other words are placed between a pronoun and its antecedent.]
3. The work team wants to bring the project to a conclusion quickly (or quick conclusion). [The infinitive "to bring" is split.]
4. You must perform periodic maintenance on your computer to keep it operating efficiently. [The introductory phrase dangles.]
5. Protect your online privacy by using effective password protection, clearing temporary menus regularly, and encrypting sensitive information. [Units of a series are not stated in parallel form.]

review card/ CHAPTER 2
FOCUSING ON INTERPERSONAL COMMUNICATION

Learning Objectives

LO¹: **Explain how the foundational element of intrapersonal communication is an understanding of ourselves.**

Communication with ourselves is called intrapersonal communication, which includes our perceptions, memories, experiences, feelings, interpretations, inferences, evaluations, attitudes, opinions, ideas, strategies, images, and states of consciousness.

- How you view yourself.
- How you view the other person.
- How you believe the other person views you.

- How the other person views himself or herself.
- How the other person views you.
- How the other person believes you view him or her.

LO²: **Describe the different communication styles.**

Self-concept, self-esteem, and self-awareness are relevant in affecting how we interact with others, thus determining our communication style. Styles of communication are separated into three types: (1) avoidance—passive whiners who complain, fret, and avoid engaging with people in the dominant group; (2) aggressive—hurtfully expressive, argumentative, self-promoting, and assume control over the choice of others; and (3) assertive—self-enhancing, expressive communicators that take into account both self and other's needs.

6 Steps to Communicating Assertively
1. **Describe how you view the situation.**
2. **Disclose your feelings.**
3. **Identify effects.**
4. **Wait for a response.**
5. **Paraphrase the other's response.**
6. **Ask for or suggest a solution.**

LO³: **Define the different types of influence in interpersonal communication.**

In interpersonal communication situations, influencing others is the goal of communication. Communicators who achieve influence or control over others have what is called interpersonal dominance. Types of influence are:

- Compliance-gaining—attempts made by a communicator to influence another to "perform some desired behavior that the [other person] otherwise might not perform."

- Compliance-resisting—the refusal to comply with influence attempts. When resisting requests, people tend to offer reasons or evidence to support their refusal. People who

6 Steps to Successful Advocacy
1. **Plan.**
2. **Determine why your boss should care.**
3. **Tailor your argument to the boss's style and characteristics.**
4. **Assess prior technical knowledge.**
5. **Build coalitions.**
6. **Hone your communication skills.**

Key Terms

Self-concept our subjective description of who we think we are

Self-esteem how you feel about yourself, how well you like and value yourself

Self-fulfilling prophecy the idea that you behave and see yourself in ways that are consistent with how others see you

Intrapersonal communication includes "our perceptions, memories, experiences, feelings, interpretations, inferences, evaluations, attitudes, opinions, ideas, strategies, images, and states of consciousness"

Intrapersonal intelligence the capacity to form an accurate model of one's self and to be able to use that model to operate effectively in life

Interpersonal intelligence the ability to understand other people such as what motivates them, how they work, and how to work cooperatively with them

Emotional intelligence an assortment of noncognitive skills, capabilities, and competencies that influence a person's ability to successfully cope with environmental demands and pressures

Impression management the control (or lack of control) of communication information through performance

High self-monitors individuals who are highly aware of their impression management behavior

Low self-monitors individuals who communicate with others with little attention to the responses to their messages

Anticipatory socialization the process through which most of us develop a set of expectations and beliefs concerning how people communicate in particular occupations and in formal and informal work settings

Avoidance a conscious attempt to avoid engaging with people in the dominant group

Assertiveness "self-enhancing, expressive communication that takes into account both self and others' needs"

Influence the power that a person has to affect other people's thinking or actions

Compliance-gaining attempts made by a communicator to influence another to "perform some desired behavior that the [other person] otherwise might not perform"

Compliance-resisting refusal to comply with influence attempts

Interpersonal dominance the achievement of influence or control over another via communication

Rational explanation a type of influence that includes some sort of formal presentation, analysis, or proposal

Advocacy the process of championing ideas, proposals, actions, or people to those above them in the organization

Metacommunication a message that, although not expressed in words, accompanies a message that is expressed in words

Empathy when a person attempts to share another's feelings or emotions.

are more sensitive to others and who are more adaptive are more likely to engage in further attempts to influence.

- Rational explanation—the most frequently used type of influence that subordinates use on superiors. Rational explanation includes some sort of formal presentation, analysis, or proposal.
- Advocacy—the process of championing ideas, proposals, actions, or people to those above them in the organization. Advocacy requires learning how to read superior's needs and preferences and designing persuasive arguments that are most likely to accomplish the influencer's goals.

LO⁴: Describe the role of nonverbal messages in communication.

Nonverbal communication conveys a significant portion of meaning and includes metacommunications, which are wordless messages that accompany words, and kinesic communications, which are expressed through body language. The meanings of nonverbal messages are culturally derived.

LO⁵: Identify aspects of effective listening.

Effective listening, which requires effort and discipline, is crucial to effective interpersonal communication and leads to career success. Various listening styles—casual listening, listening for information, intensive listening, and empathetic listening—require different strategies.

CHECK YOUR COMMUNICATION | Nonverbal Communication

Metacommunication

Metacommunication is a message that, although not expressed in words, accompanies a message that is expressed in words.

Grammar Quiz

Select the word that correctly completes the sentence.

1. The president and the chief executive officer reported (his, their) earnings to the ethics committee.
2. Everyone (was, were) asked to contribute to the company blog.
3. The production manager, not the controller, presented (her, their) strongly opposing views.
4. Neither Stephen nor Lydia (was, were) recognized for their contribution.
5. The company is revising (its, their) mission statement.
6. The committee will present (its, their) recommendation at the next staff meeting.
7. Paige forgot to retain her expense vouchers; (this, this oversight) caused a delay in reimbursement.

Quiz Solutions

1. their
2. was
3. her
4. was
5. its
6. its
7. this oversight

Kinesic Messages

Kinesic communication is an idea expressed through nonverbal behavior. In other words, receivers gain additional meaning from what they see and hear—the visual and the vocal:

- Visual—gestures, winks, smiles, frowns, sighs, attire, grooming, and all kinds of body movements.
- Vocal—intonation, projection, and resonance of the voice.

Understanding Nonverbal Messages

Metacommunications and kinesic communication have characteristics that all communicators should take into account. Nonverbal messages:

- Cannot be avoided.
- May have different meanings for different people.
- Vary between and within cultures.
- May be intentional or unintentional.
- Can contradict the accompanying verbal message, and affect whether your message is understood or believed.
- May receive more attention than verbal messages.
- Provide clues about the sender's background and motives.
- Are influenced by the circumstances surrounding the communication.
- May be beneficial or harmful.
- May vary depending upon the person's gender.

Learning Objectives

LO¹: Explain the factors influencing the increasing importance of group communication.

U.S. businesses are increasingly using groups to achieve organizational goals. Because flat organizational structures are becoming increasingly common, people in organizations are communicating with larger groups of colleagues than they did in more hierarchical organizations. Decision-making power is also being distributed throughout the organization, and cross-disciplinary teams now perform broad core processes and tasks.

LO²: Describe the characteristics of effective groups.

Communication in small groups leads to group decisions that are generally superior to individual decisions. The group process can motivate members, improve thinking, and assist attitude development and change. The emphasis that a particular group places on task and maintenance activities is based on several factors. Effective groups:

- Have participants who share a common goal, interest, or benefit.
- Have members who play a variety of necessary roles and seek to eliminate nonproductive ones.
- Members who assemble to achieve long-term goals rather than to do short-term tasks and activities.
- Are neither too small nor too large.
- Have members who have a variety of skills and qualifications and play a variety of roles in the group setting.
- Develop positive norms that guide the behavior of the group.

LO³: Explain the difference between groups and teams.

The main difference between groups and teams are in member attitudes and the levels of commitment. A team is typified by a clear identity and a high level of commitment on the part of members. Ways to organize workers into teams include task forces, quality assurance teams, cross-functional teams, product-development teams, and virtual teams. Groups go through four stages of team development: *forming*, when members become acquainted with each other; *storming*, when they deal with conflicting personalities, goals, and ideas; *norming*, when they develop strategies and outlines of behavior for promoting goal achievement; and *performing*, when the team reaches its optimal performance level.

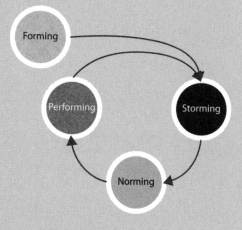

LO⁴: Outline the group decision-making process.

Groups process information in four stages: orientation, discussion, decision, and implementation. Members work through these stages as they identify problems, determine possible outcomes, and implement solutions. Challenges to group decision-making include the tendency of the group to spend too much time discussing information its members already know; the inability of group members to express themselves clearly; errors in judgment; and overlooking pertinent and sometimes important information.

Key Terms

Status formal position in the organizational chart

Norm a standard or average behavior

Task force a team given a single goal with a limited time to achieve it

Quality assurance team (quality circle) a team that focuses on product or service quality

Cross-functional team a team that brings together employees from various departments to solve a variety of problems

Product development team a team that concentrates on innovation and the development cycle of new products

Virtual team a team with members in more than one location

Forming the stage of team development when members become acquainted with each other and the assigned task

Storming the stage of team development when members deal with conflicting personalities, goals, and ideas

Norming the stage of team development during which members develop strategies and activities that promote goal achievement

Performing when the team reaches its optimal performance level

Oversampling the tendency of groups to examine information they already know

Norm of reciprocity cooperation begets cooperation while competition begets competition

Competitors individuals who view group disagreements as win-lose situations

Cooperators individuals who value accommodative interpersonal strategies

Individualists people concerned only with their own outcomes

Free riding the tendency of group members to not work as hard as when they are working for themselves

Fundamental attribution error the assumption that the other party's behavior is caused by personal rather than situational factors

Trust the confidence among group members that their peers' intentions are good

Groupthink when group members avoid conflict rather than pursue the best solution

Agenda a meeting outline that includes important information: date, beginning and ending time, place, and topics to be discussed and responsibilities of those involved

Brainstorming the generation of many ideas from among team members without judgment

Consensus the collective opinion of the group

LO⁵: Discuss group conflict and conflict resolution.

Lack of understanding about the nature and roles of other persons or groups is a possible cause of most conflict between or among groups. Substantive conflict arises from disagreements about the issues relevant to the group's real goals and outcomes. Procedural conflicts arise from disagreements about methods, goals, and decisional processes. Conflict is more likely when group members compete against each other for such resources as money, power, time, prestige, or materials. Cooperation enhances group performance, and most often motivations to compete and cooperate are blended. Groups often face social dilemmas related to free riding (slackers) and fundamental attribution error, of interpreting others' behaviors as deriving from personal choices rather than situational factors. Strategies for resolving conflict include collaborating, compromising, avoiding, and accommodating. Groupthink occurs because of the dislike of conflict and the need to promote cohesiveness.

LO⁶: Discuss aspects of effective meeting management.

Effective meetings present the opportunity to acquire and disseminate valuable information, develop skills, and make favorable impressions on colleagues, supervisors, and subordinates. Careful planning and attention to specific guidelines can help ensure the success of meetings, whether they are conducted in a face-to-face format or electronically.

CHECK YOUR COMMUNICATION | Meeting Management

Face-to-Face Meetings

Face-to-face meetings, the most-used meeting format, are appropriate in the following situations:

- When you need the richest nonverbal cues, including body, voice, proximity, and touch.
- When the issues are especially sensitive.
- When the participants don't know one another.
- When establishing group rapport and relationships are crucial.
- When the participants can be in the same place at the same time.
- When no other channel or medium of communication would suffice.

Electronic Meetings

Participants may communicate with one another through telephones, personal computers, or video broadcast equipment using groupware or meeting management software applications.

Electronic meetings offer certain advantages:

- They facilitate geographically dispersed groups.
- They speed up meeting follow-up activities.

Electronic meetings also have certain limitations:

- They cannot replace face-to-face contact, especially when group efforts are just beginning and when groups are trying to build group values, trust, and emotional ties.
- They may make it harder to reach consensus, because more ideas may be generated and because it may be harder to interpret the strength of other members' commitment to their proposals.
- The success of same-time meetings is dependent on all participants having excellent keyboarding skills to engage in rapid-fire, in-depth discussion. This limitation may be overcome as voice input systems become more prevalent.

Grammar Quiz

Select the correct pronoun to complete each sentence.

1. The instructor asked Franz and (I, me) to leave the room.
2. Stacey requested that proceeds be divided equally between Allison and (her, she).
3. It was (her, she) (who, whom) recommended revising the company's technology policy to include cell phones.
4. The speaker did not notice (me, my) leaving early.
5. She is an employee in (who, whom) we have great confidence.

Quiz Solutions

1. me
2. her
3. she, who
4. my
5. whom

Suggestions for Effective Meetings

- Limit meeting length and frequency.
- Make satisfactory arrangements.
- Distribute the agenda well in advance.
- Encourage participation.
- Maintain order.
- Manage conflict.
- Seek consensus.
- Prepare thorough minutes.

Learning Objectives

STEP 1	STEP 2	STEP 3	STEP 4	STEP 5	STEP 6	STEP 7
Determine the purpose and select an appropriate channel	Envision the audience	Consider the context	Choose a channel and the medium	Adapt the message to the audience's needs and concerns	Organize the message	Prepare the first draft

LO¹: Identify the purpose and type of message.

In the workplace, four purposes of communication exist: to inform, to persuade, to convey goodwill, and to establish credibility. The type of message is determined by the intent: delivery of good-, neutral-, or bad-news messages or messages to influence or change the attitudes or actions of the receiver.

LO²: Develop clear perceptions of the audience to enhance the impact of the communication and human relations.

Perceptual barriers limit the ability to see an issue from multiple perspectives and plan an effective message. To overcome those barriers, consider all you know about the receiver, including age, economic level, educational/occupational background, culture, existing relationship, expectations, and needs.

LO³: Consider the context of the message and any environmental influences that may affect its delivery.

The context of the message refers to the environmental influences that affect its content, style, and, in some cases, the decision as to whether to even send a message. Awareness of environmental factors such as legal and ethical constraints, considerations regarding technology, intercultural, financial, or diversity issues, and the team environment can determine how the message is perceived and the success of delivery.

LO⁴: Determine the appropriate channel and media for communicating the message.

Determine the appropriate channel for sending a particular message by considering the effect of the message on the receiver. Recall the channels for communication are two-way, face-to-face; two-way, not face-to-face; and one-way, not face-to-face. Media used to conduct the actual communication can be written, oral, or nonverbal including vocal cues, facial expressions, bodily movement, bodily appearance, and the use of space.

LO⁵: Apply techniques for adapting messages to the audience.

Messages should be adapted to fit the receiver's needs. Developing concise, sensitive messages that focus on the receiver's point of view will build and protect goodwill and demand the attention of the receiver. Communicating ethically and responsibly involves stating information truthfully and tactfully, eliminating embellishments or exaggerations, supporting viewpoints with objective facts from credible sources, and designing honest graphics.

LO⁶: Recognize the importance of organizing a message before writing the first draft and select the appropriate message outline (deductive or inductive) for developing messages to achieve the desired response.

Well-organized messages are easier to understand and promote a more positive attitude toward the sender. Outlining encourages brevity and accuracy, permits concentration on one phase at a time, saves writing time, increases confidence to complete the task, and facilitates appropriate emphasis of ideas.

A part of the outlining process is deciding whether the message should be deductive (main idea first) or inductive (explanations and details first). Good- and neutral-news messages should use deductive outlines; bad-news messages should use inductive outlines.

LO⁷: Prepare the first draft.

First drafts should be written rapidly, with the intent to rewrite certain portions, if necessary. Documents should be revised as many times as necessary to convey message effectively and be error free.

Key Terms

Goodwill the ability to create and maintain positive, productive relationships with others

Organizational culture a system of shared meanings and practices held by members that distinguish the organization from other organizations

Outlining the process of identifying ideas and arranging them in the right sequence

Deductive sequence when a message begins with the major idea

Inductive sequence when a message withholds the major idea until accompanying details and explanations have been presented

Grammar Quiz

Select the correct word.

1. Only one of the video clips (was, were) usable.
2. The typesetters, not the editor, (are, is) responsible for these errors.
3. Neither the manager nor the employees (was, were) aware of the policy change.
4. Both Corey and Stephen (was, were) promoted.
5. The news from the rescue mission (is, are) encouraging.
6. *Ten Steps to Greatness* (has, have) been placed in the company library.
7. The sales manager announced that Scottsdale, Arizona, (is, was) the site for the annual sales meeting.
8. Dylan (don't, doesn't) expect preferential treatment.
9. The client studied the financial analysis for a minute and (starts, started) asking questions.
10. If the applicant (was, were) experienced with databases, she would have been hired.

Quiz Solutions

1. was	5. is	9. started
2. are	6. has	10. were
3. were	7. is	
4. were	8. doesn't	

CHECK YOUR COMMUNICATION | Guidelines for Planning a Spoken or Written Message

Focus on the Receiver's Point of View

- Present ideas from the receiver's point of view, conveying the tone the message is specifically for the receiver.
- Give sincere compliments.

Communicate Ethically and Responsibly

- Present information truthfully, honestly, and fairly.
- Include all information relevant to the receiver.
- Avoid exaggerating or embellishing facts.
- Use objective facts to support ideas.
- Design graphics that avoid distorting facts and relationships.
- Express ideas clearly and understandably.
- State ideas tactfully and positively to preserve the receiver's self-worth and to build future relationships.

Build and Protect Goodwill

- Use euphemisms to present unpleasant thoughts politely and positively. Avoid using euphemisms when they will be taken as excessive or sarcastic.
- Avoid doublespeak or corporate speak that confuses or misleads the receiver.
- Avoid using condescending or demeaning expressions.
- Rely mainly on denotative words. Use connotative words that will elicit a favorable reaction, are easily understood, and are appropriate for the setting.
- Choose vivid words that add clarity and interest to your message.
- Use bias-free language.
- Do not use the pronoun *he* when referring to a group of people that may include women or *she* when a group may include men.
- Avoid referring to men and women in stereotyped roles and occupations, using gender-biased occupational titles, or differentiating genders in an occupation.
- Avoid referring to groups (based on gender, race and ethnicity, age, religion, and disability) in stereotypical and insensitive ways.
- Do not emphasize race and ethnicity, age, religion, or disability when these factors are not relevant.

Convey a Positive, Tactful Tone

- Rely mainly on positive words that speak of what can be done instead of what cannot be done, of the pleasant instead of the unpleasant. Use negative words when the purpose is to sharpen contrast or when positive words have not evoked the desired reaction.
- Use second person and active voice to emphasize pleasant ideas. Avoid using second person for presenting negative ideas; instead, use third person and passive voice to de-emphasize the unpleasant.
- Consider stating an unpleasant thought in the subjunctive mood.

Use Simple, Contemporary Language

- Avoid clichés and outdated expressions that make your language seem unnatural and unoriginal.
- Use simple words for informal business messages instead of using more complicated words that have the same meaning.

Write Concisely

- Do not use redundancies—unnecessary repetition of an idea.
- Use active voice to shorten sentences.
- Avoid unnecessary details; omit ideas that can be implied.
- Shorten wordy sentences by using suffixes or prefixes, making changes in word form, or substituting precise words for phrases.

Learning Objectives

LO¹: Identify the appropriate use of communication technology, including its legal and ethical implications.

Before using communication technology, consider the purpose of the message, confidentiality issues, and the human relation factors. Legal and ethical considerations should also be taken into account when communicating through technology: (a) Be certain that information technology does not violate basic rights of individuals and that you abide by all laws related to the use of technology; (b) understand that email is not private and can be monitored by a company; (c) develop and use procedures that protect the security of information; and (d) develop a clear and fair privacy policy.

   Other legal/ethical issues in using email include protecting copyright of materials downloaded from the Internet, not altering messages that you forward, getting permission to forward private messages, and responding to email promptly.

LO²: Discuss the effective use of email and instant messaging in business communication.

Email may be sent to receivers both inside and outside the organization. Email provides a fast, convenient way to communicate by reducing telephone tag and telephone interruptions, facilitating the transmission of a single message to multiple recipients, reducing telephone bills, eliminating time barriers, and fostering open communication among users in various locations. Email formats are less formal than business letter formats. With instant messaging or real-time email, abbreviations and online "shorthand" further reduce formality but increase speed.

LO³: Explain principles for writing effectively for the Web.

Web pages facilitate an organization's continual communication with a wide audience. HTML and a web browser turn ordinary text into a web page. Writing for web pages should be concise, jargon-free, and chunked to allow for scanning of content. Weblogs serve important needs in capturing information for further use but should be considered public and not confidential.

LO⁴: Discuss the effective use of voice and wireless technologies in business communication.

Voice recordings and messages should be clear and complete and considered as permanent records. Cell phones should be used with consideration for the receiver and the public. Cell phone communications should not be viewed as secure communications. Text messaging offers a limited avenue for exchanging quick, quiet messages. Applications and equipment to accommodate wireless communications continue to expand and offer flexibility for transmitting voice and data. Business decisions can be improved through the appropriate use of voice and wireless technologies.

Key Terms

Netiquette the buzzword for proper behavior on the Internet

Flame a sarcastic, sometimes abusive message or posting that may prompt a receiver to send a retaliatory response

Weblog (blog) a personal journal published on the Web that can take many forms

Grammar Quiz

Select the correct word.

1. Our supply of parts is replenished (frequent, frequently).
2. Marcus looked (impatient, impatiently) at the new production assistant.
3. The server moved (quick, quickly) from table to table.
4. Of the numerous people I met during the recent speed networking event, Blair made the (better, best) impression.
5. Haley is more creative than (any, any other) advertising agent in the company.

Quiz Solutions

1. frequently
2. impatient
3. quickly
4. best
5. any other

Email Messages

Organization, Content, Style, and Mechanics

- Provide a subject line that is meaningful to the recipient.
- Include only one main idea related to the receiver's needs.
- Show empathy and logic in determining the sequence of ideas.
- Use jargon, technical words, and shortened terms carefully.
- Use bulleted lists, tables, graphs, or images when they strengthen communication.
- Avoid flaming and use of overly emotional language.

Format

- Include an appropriate salutation, ending, and signature file (your name, address, phone, and other contact information).
- Keep lines no wider than the screen and message length to no longer than one screen. Use an attachment for longer messages.
- Single-space lines with a blank space between unindented paragraphs.
- Key the message using mixed-case letters. Use capital letters or quotation marks for emphasis, and omit specialized formatting (bold, clip art).
- Use emoticons and abbreviations in moderation only if the receiver understands them and the content is informal.

Instant Messages

Organization, Content, Style, and Mechanics

- Consider previously listed email guidelines when composing instant messages.
- Choose your message participants appropriately.
- Be certain that your conversation is free from unwanted eavesdropping.

Format

- Use understandable shorthand and abbreviations for frequent words and phrases.
- Focus more on efficiency and less on spelling and grammar.

Web Communications

Writing for a Website

- Create brief, simple documents designed for easy reading. Break longer documents into chunks that can be accessed easily.
- Use eye-catching headlines and other techniques to attract attention.
- Use jargon and technical terms cautiously.
- Avoid placing critical information in graphic form only that may be skipped by users of slow systems.

Writing for a Blog

- Consider previously listed email guidelines when writing in a blog.
- Communicate responsibly and ethically when writing anonymously.
- Develop a clear goal that leads to relevant content for the target audience when designing a corporate blog. Revise and update regularly and promote actively to attract and retain readers.

Voice and Wireless Communications

Voice Recordings

- Leave your email address, fax number, or mailing address on your greeting if this information might be helpful to callers.
- Encourage callers to leave detailed messages. If certain standard information is needed, use your greeting to prompt callers for it.
- Instruct callers how to review their messages or be transferred to an operator.
- Check voice mail regularly, and return all voice messages within 24 hours.

Voice Messages

- Speak slowly and clearly.
- Repeat your name and phone number at the beginning and end of the message, spelling your name if not well known to the recipient.
- Leave a detailed message; be specific about what you want.
- Keep your message brief, typically 60 seconds or less.
- Ensure that your message will be understandable; avoid calling from noisy environments and areas with a weak signal.

Text Messaging

- Choose for exchanging quick, quiet messages.
- Avoid using text messaging as a substitute for richer communication mediums.

Voice and Wireless Etiquette

- Exercise judgment about when to silence or turn off your phone.
- Respect others around you by speaking in low conversational tones and monitoring the content of your conversation.
- Practice safety when using wireless communication devices while driving.

Learning Objectives

LO¹: Describe the deductive outline for good news and routine information and its adaptations for specific situations.

When the receiver can be expected to be *pleased* by the message, the main idea is presented first and details follow. Likewise, when the message is *routine* and not likely to arouse a feeling of pleasure or displeasure, the main idea is presented first. The deductive approach is appropriate for positive news and thank-you and appreciation messages, routine claims, routine requests and responses to routine requests, routine messages, and responses about credit and orders.

LO²: Prepare messages that convey good news, including thank-you and appreciation messages.

Use the deductive approach for letters, memos, and email messages that contain positive news as the central idea. Thank-you messages express appreciation for a kindness or special assistance and should reflect sincere feelings of gratitude. Appreciation messages highlight exceptional performance and should avoid exaggerations and strong, unsupported statements that the receiver may not believe.

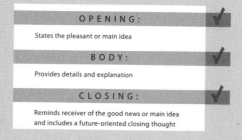

OPENING: ✓
States the pleasant or main idea

BODY: ✓
Provides details and explanation

CLOSING: ✓
Reminds receiver of the good news or main idea and includes a future-oriented closing thought

LO³: Write messages presenting routine claims and requests and favorable responses to them.

A routine claim requests the adjustment in the first sentence because you assume the company will make the adjustment without persuasion. It continues with an explanation of the problem to support the request and an expression of appreciation for taking the action. Responses to claims may include sales messages or futuristic comments indicating your confidence that the customer will continue doing business with a company that has a reputation for fairness. A routine request begins with the major request, includes details that will clarify the request, and alludes to the receiver's response. A response to a routine request provides the information requested and necessary details and closes with a personal, courteous ending.

Key Terms

Good-news message message that conveys pleasant information

Neutral message message of interest to the receiver but unlikely to generate an emotional reaction

Deductive sequence (direct sequence) when the message begins with the main idea

Claim a request for an adjustment

Routine claim claim granted quickly, willingly, and without persuasion

Persuasive claim claim granted only after explanations and persuasive arguments have been presented

Adjustment message message that adjusts the terms of a sale in the customer's favor

Resale a discussion of goods or services already bought

Sales promotional material statements made about related merchandise or service

Acknowledgment message a document that indicates the order has been received and is being processed

Grammar Quiz

Insert needed commas. Write "correct" if you find no errors.

1. The applicant who arrived late has not been interviewed.
2. Emoticons that are created by keying combinations of symbols to produce "sideway faces" communicate emotion in electronic messages.
3. Sean Harrison a new member of the board remained silent during the long bitter debate.
4. Primary qualifications for graduates seeking a first job are education work experience and leadership activities.
5. The entire population was surveyed but three responses were unusable.
6. If you approve of the changes place your initials in the space provided.
7. To qualify for the position applicants must have technology certification.
8. We should be spending less money not more.
9. On November 20 2009 all required documents had been submitted.
10. Yes I agree that the theme meeting in St. Thomas should be scheduled for late May.

Quiz Solutions

1. Correct.
2. Emoticons, which are created by keying combinations of symbols to produce "sideway faces," communicate emotion in electronic messages.
3. Margie Harrison, a new member of the board, remained silent during the long, bitter debate.
4. Primary qualifications for graduates seeking a first job are education, work experience, and leadership activities.
5. The entire population was surveyed, but three responses were unusable.
6. If you approve of the changes, place your initials in the space provided.
7. To qualify for the position, applicants must have technology certification.
8. We should be spending less money, not more.
9. On November 20, 2009, all related documents were submitted.
10. Yes, I agree that the theme meeting in St. Thomas should be scheduled for late May.

LO⁴: **Write messages acknowledging customer orders, providing credit information, and extending credit.**

Form or computer-generated acknowledgment messages or email messages assure customers that orders will be filled quickly. With individualized acknowledgments that confirm shipment and include product resale, the company generates goodwill and future business. When providing credit information, provide only verifiable facts to avoid possible litigation. A message extending credit begins with an approval of credit, indicates the basis for the decision, and explains credit terms. The closing may include sales promotional material or other futuristic comments. Credit extension messages must adhere to legal guidelines.

LO⁵: **Prepare procedural messages that ensure clear and consistent application.**

When preparing instructions, highlight the steps in a bulleted or numbered list or a flowchart and begin each step with an action statement. Check the accuracy and completeness of the document and incorporate changes identified by following the instructions to complete the task and asking another person to do likewise.

CHECK YOUR COMMUNICATION | Good- and Neutral-News Messages

Content

- Identify clearly the principal idea (pleasant or routine idea).
- Present sufficient supporting detail in logical sequence.
- Ensure accuracy of facts or figures.
- Structure the message to meet legal requirements and ethical dimensions.

Organization

- Place the major idea in first sentence.
- Present supporting details in logical sequence.
- Include final idea that is courteous and indicates a continuing relationship with the receiver; may include sales promotional material.

Style

- Ensure that the message is clear and concise (e.g., words will be readily understood).
- Use active voice predominantly and first person sparingly.
- Make ideas cohere by avoiding abrupt changes in thought.
- Use contemporary language; avoid doublespeak and clichés.
- Use relatively short sentences that vary in length and structure.
- Emphasize significant thoughts (e.g., position and sentence structure).
- Keep paragraphs relatively short.
- Adjust formality and writing style to the particulur medium of delivery (letter, memo, email, text message, etc.).

Mechanics

- Ensure that keyboarding, spelling, grammar, and punctuation are perfect.

Format

- Use a correct document format.
- Ensure the document is appropriately positioned.
- Include standard document parts in appropriate position and special parts as needed (subject line, enclosure, copy, etc.).

Cultural Adaptations

- Avoid abbreviations, slang, acronyms, technical jargon, sports and military analogies, and other devices peculiar to the United States.
- Avoid words that trigger emotional responses.
- Use simple terms but attempt to be specific.
- Consider the communication style of the culture when selecting an organizational pattern.
- Use graphics, visual aids, and forms when possible to simplify the message.
- Use figures for expressing numbers to avoid confusion.
- Be aware of differences in the way numbers and dates are written and write out the name of the month to avoid confusion.
- Adapt the document format for expectations of the recipient's country.

Learning Objectives

LO¹: Explain the steps in the inductive approach and understand its use for specific situations.

Because the receiver can be expected to be displeased by the message, the inductive approach is appropriate for messages denying an adjustment, refusing an order for merchandise, refusing credit, sending constructive criticism, or conveying negative organizational messages. The five steps in the inductive outline are explained to the right. While bad-news messages are typically expressed using paper documents or face-to-face means, electronic channels may be appropriate under certain circumstances.

The deductive approach can be used to communicate bad news when (a) the message is the second response to a repeated request; (b) a very small, insignificant matter is involved; (c) a request is obviously ridiculous, immoral, unethical, illegal, or dangerous; (d) a writer's intent is to "shake" the receiver; or (e) a writer–reader relationship is so close and long-standing that satisfactory human relations can be taken for granted.

LO²: Discuss strategies for developing the five components of a bad-news message.

The introductory paragraph should buffer the bad news and tactfully identify the subject. Following the introduction should be a logical discussion of the reasons for the refusal or bad news. The bad-news statement itself should be positioned strategically and (a) use the inductive approach, (b) not be set in a paragraph by itself, and (c) should sit in a dependent clause of a complex sentence. A counterproposal or silver lining should follow the bad-news statement, and the concluding paragraph of the message should demonstrate empathy.

LO³: Prepare messages refusing requests and claims.

A message refusing a request begins with a neutral idea and presents the reasons before the refusal. The close may offer a counterproposal—an alternative to the action requested.

A message denying a claim begins with a neutral or factual sentence that leads to the reason for the refusal. In the opening sentence you might include resale to reaffirm the reader's confidence in the merchandise or services. Next, present the explanation for the refusal and then the refusal in a positive, nonemphatic manner. Close with a positive thought such as sales promotion that indicates you expect to do business with the customer again.

LO⁴: Prepare messages handling problems with customers' orders and denying credit.

A message refusing an order implies receipt of the order and uses resale to reaffirm the customer's confidence in the merchandise or service. Continue with reasons for your procedures or actions and benefits to the customer. Close with information needed for the customer to reorder or anticipate later delivery.

Credit refusal messages must comply with laws related to fair credit practices and should be reviewed carefully by legal counsel. Begin the message by implying receipt of an order and using resale that could convince the applicant to buy your merchandise on a cash basis when he or she learns later that credit has been denied. You must provide an explanation for the refusal (in writing or verbally) and may encourage the customer to apply for credit later or offer a discount on cash purchases. Your legal counsel may advise that you omit the explanation and invite the applicant to call or come in to discuss the reasons or to obtain more information from the credit reporting agency whose name, address, and telephone number you provide in the message.

LO⁵: Prepare messages providing constructive criticism and negative organizational news.

Because of the importance of maintaining goodwill with employees and outside parties, convey constructive criticism and negative organizational news in a sensitive, honest, and timely manner; use the inductive approach. The motive for delivering constructive criticism should be to help, not to get even. The message includes verifiable facts and omits evaluative words, allowing the recipient to make logical judgments based on facts. Negative information about an organization includes negative decisions related to declining financial position and major changes in the organization and its policies.

"Five Steps"

There are no key terms introduced in this chapter. Instead, please focus on these five important steps for organizing bad-news messages.

Opening

1. Begin with a neutral statement that logically leads to the refusal or bad news.

Body

2. Present facts, analysis, and reasons for the refusal or bad news.
3. State bad news using positive tone and de-emphasis techniques.
4. Include a counterproposal or "silver lining" idea.

Closing

5. Provide information that shifts the focus away from the refusal or bad news and to a continuing relationship with the receiver.

Grammar Quiz

Using semicolons, colons, or commas, correct the following sentences. (Sometimes punctuation needs to be removed to make the sentence correct.) Write "correct" if you find no errors.

1. Receipts were not included, otherwise, the expenses would have been reimbursed.
2. The following agents received a bonus this month: Barnes, $400, Shelley, $450, and Jackson, $600.
3. The proposal was not considered it arrived two days late.
4. This paint does have some disadvantages for example a lengthy drying time.
5. Soon after the figures are received, they will be processed, but a formal report will not be released until June 1.
6. The program has one shortcoming: flexibility.
7. Our meetings are scheduled for: Monday, Tuesday, and Friday.
8. We are enthusiastic about the plan because: (1) it is least expensive, (2) its legality is unquestioned, and (3) it can be implemented quickly.

Quiz Solutions

1. Receipts were not included; otherwise, the expenses would have been reimbursed.
2. The following agents received a bonus this month: Barnes, $400; Shelley, $450; and Jackson, $600.
3. The proposal was not considered; it arrived two days late.
4. This paint does have some disadvantages, for example, a lengthy drying time.
5. Soon after the figures are received, they will be processed; but a formal report will not be released until June 1.
6. Correct
7. Our meetings are scheduled for Monday, Tuesday, and Friday.
8. We are enthusiastic about the plan because (1) it is least expensive, (2) its legality is unquestioned, and (3) it can be implemented quickly.

CHECK YOUR COMMUNICATION | Bad-News Messages

Content

- Be sure the principal idea (the unpleasant idea or the refusal) is sufficiently clear.
- Use sufficient supporting details, and present them in a logical sequence.
- Verify accuracy of facts or figures.
- Structure the message to meet ethical and legal requirements.
- Make cultural adaptions (e.g., organizational pattern, format, language usage).

Organization

- Structure the first sentence to introduce the general subject
  - without stating the bad news.
  - without leading a receiver to expect good news.
  - without including obvious statements (e.g., "I am replying to your letter").
- Precede the main idea (bad news) with meaningful discussion.
- Follow up the bad news with a counterproposal or silver lining statement that moves discussion into a positive mood.
- Use a closing sentence that is positive (an alternative, resale, or sales promotion).

Style

- Write clearly and concisely (e.g., words are easily understood).
- Use techniques of subordination to keep the bad news from emerging with unnecessary vividness. For example, bad news may
  - appear in a dependent clause.

- be stated in passive voice.
- be revealed through indirect statement.
- be revealed through the use of subjunctive mood.
- Use first person sparingly or not at all.
- Make ideas cohere by avoiding abrupt changes in thought.
- Keep sentences and paragraphs relatively short, and vary length and structure.
- Use original expression (sentences are not copied directly from the definition of the problem or from sample documents in the text); omit clichés.

Mechanics

- Ensure that keyboarding, spelling, grammar, and punctuation are perfect.

Format

- Use a correct document format.
- Ensure that the document is appropriately positioned.
- Include standard document parts in appropriate position.
- Include special parts if necessary (subject line, enclosure, copy, etc.).

Learning Objectives

LO¹: Develop effective outlines and appeals for messages that persuade.

The purpose of a persuasive message is to influence others to take a particular action or to accept your point of view. Effective persuasion involves understanding the product, service, or idea you are promoting; knowing your audience; presenting convincing evidence; and having a rational response to anticipated resistance to your arguments.

Effective persuasive communications build on a central selling point interwoven throughout the message. The receivers, rather than the product, serve as the subject of many of the sentences. Therefore, receivers can envision themselves using the product, contracting for the service, or complying with a request. Persuasive messages are written inductively.

LO²: Explain how the inductive approach can be used to create persuasive messages.

A sales message is written inductively following the four-point AIDA steps for selling:

- **Gain attention.** Use an original approach that addresses one primary receiver's benefit (the central selling point) in the first paragraph.
- **Introduce the product, service, or idea.** Provide a logical transition to move the receiver from the attention-getter to information about the product, service, or idea. Hold the receiver's attention by using action-oriented sentences to stress the central selling point.
- **Provide convincing evidence.** Provide specific facts and interpretations that clarify the nature and quality of a feature, nonexaggerated evidence people will believe, and research and testimonials that provide independent support. De-emphasize the price by presenting convincing evidence first but not in the final paragraph, showing how money can be saved, stating price in small units, illustrating that the price is reasonable, and placing the price in a sentence that summarizes the benefits.
- **Motivate action.** State confidently the specific action to be taken and the benefits for complying. Present the action as easy to take, and provide a stimulus for acting quickly.

LO³: Write effective persuasive requests (claim, favor, and information request, and persuasion within an organization).

A persuasive request is written inductively, is organized around a primary appeal, and is longer than a typical routine message because you must provide convincing evidence of receiver benefit.

- **Persuasive claim.** When an adjuster must be convinced that a claim is justified, gain the receiver's attention, develop a central appeal that emphasizes an incentive for making the adjustment, and end with the request for an adjustment you consider fair.
- **Request for a favor or information.** Gain the receiver's attention, build interest by emphasizing the reward for taking action, and encourage the receiver to grant the favor or send the information.
- **Persuasion within an organization.** When persuading employees or supervisors to take specific actions, gain the receiver's attention, introduce and build interest and support for the proposed idea, address any major resistance, and encourage the receiver to take a specific action.

Key Terms

Logos a logical appeal that consists of such information as facts and statistics

Ethos an appeal based on information or an association that provides credibility for ourselves, our product, or position

Pathos an emotional appeal that works by eliciting an emotional response from the audience

AIDA a four-step inductive process that involves gaining attention, generating interest, creating desire, and motivating action

Claim a general or abstract statement

Evidence specific, supportive statement

Grammar Quiz

Correct the possessives.

1. This companies mission statement has been revised since it's recent merger.
2. The night shift earned a bonus of three weeks wages for last months overtime.
3. The banks' had been negotiating a merger for several month's.
4. During yesterdays conference call, the company reported their earnings and revised their forecast for the next quarter.
5. The management team decided to change their direction and investigate their companies waste stream.

Quiz Solutions

1. company's; its   2. weeks'; month's   3. banks; months   4. yesterday's; its; its   5. its; company's

Sales Messages

Content

- Convince reader that product or service is worthy of consideration.
- Include sufficient evidence of usefulness to purchaser.
- Reveal price (in the message or an enclosure).
- Make central selling point apparent.
- Identify specific action that is desired.
- Ensure that message is ethical and abides by legal requirements.

Organization

- Use inductive sequence of ideas.
- Ensure that first sentence is good attention-getter.
- Introduce central selling point in first two or three sentences, and reinforce it through rest of message.
- Introduce price only after receiver benefits have been presented.
- Associate price (what receiver gives) directly with reward (what receiver gets).
- End with final paragraph that includes (1) specific action desired, (2) receiver's reward for taking action, and (3) an inducement for taking action quickly. Present action as easy.

Style

- Use objective language.
- Ensure that active verbs and concrete nouns predominate.
- Keep sentences relatively short but varied in length and structure.
- Place significant words in emphatic positions.
- Make ideas cohere by avoiding abrupt changes in thought.
- Frequently call central selling point to receiver's attention through repeated reference.
- Use original expression (sentences that are not copied directly from the definition of problem or from sample documents in text). Omit clichés.
- Achieve unity by including in the final paragraph a key word or idea (central selling point) that was introduced in first paragraph.

Mechanics

- Ensure that keyboarding, spelling, grammar, and punctuation are perfect.

Format

- Use correct document format.
- Ensure document is appropriately positioned.
- Include standard document parts in appropriate position.
- Include special parts if necessary (subject line, enclosure, copy, etc.).

Persuasive Requests

Content

- Convince receiver that idea is valid, that proposal has merit.
- Point out way(s) in which receiver will benefit.
- Incorporate primary appeal (central selling feature).
- Identify specific action desired.

Organization

- Use inductive sequence of ideas.
- Use first sentence that gets attention and reveals subject of message.
- Introduce major appeal in first two or three sentences and reinforce it throughout rest of message.
- Point out receiver benefits.
- Associate desired action with receiver's reward for taking action.
- Include final paragraph that makes reference to specific action desired and primary appeal. Emphasize easy action, and (if appropriate) include incentive for quick action.

Style

- Use language that is objective and positive.
- Ensure that active verbs and concrete nouns predominate.
- Keep sentences relatively short, but vary them in length and structure.
- Place significant words in emphatic positions.
- Make ideas cohere by ensuring that changes in thought are not abrupt.
- Call primary appeal to receiver's attention frequently through repeated reference.
- Use original expression (sentences that are not copied directly from directions or model documents). Omit clichés.
- Achieve unity by including in final paragraph a key word or idea (the primary appeal) that was used in first paragraph.

Mechanics

- Ensure that keyboarding, spelling, grammar, and punctuation are perfect.

Format

- Use correct document format.
- Ensure document is appropriately positioned.
- Include standard document parts in appropriate position.
- Include special parts if necessary (subject line, enclosure, copy, etc.).

reviewcard/ CHAPTER 9
REVISING WRITTEN MESSAGES

Learning Objectives

LO¹: List the steps in the systematic revision process.

Revise a document as many times as necessary to be certain that it conveys the message effectively and is error free. Use the spell-check to locate keying errors; then follow systematic procedures for proofreading a printed copy of the document. Proofread once for content, organization, and style and a second time for mechanics, format, and layout.

LO²: Discuss ways to communicate ethically and responsibly.

Adapt the message to fit the receiver's needs. Developing concise, sensitive messages that focus on the receiver's point of view will build and protect goodwill and demand the attention of the receiver. Communicating ethically and responsibly involves clarity, truthfulness, and consideration.

LO³: Identify ways to develop logical and unified messages.

Unified and coherent paragraphs will help the receiver understand the message clearly and respond favorably. To write effective paragraphs, develop deductive or inductive paragraphs consistently, link ideas to achieve coherence, keep paragraphs unified, and vary sentence and paragraph length.

LO⁴: Apply techniques for developing effective, powerful sentences.

Well-written sentences help the receiver understand the message clearly and respond favorably. To craft powerful sentences, use correct sentence structure, rely on active voice, and emphasize important points that affect the clarity and human relations of the message.

LO⁵: Identify factors affecting readability, and revise messages to improve readability.

The readability of a message is affected by the length of the sentences and the difficulty of the words. A readability index in the eighth-to-eleventh grade range is appropriate for most business writing. Creating concise professional writing using standard English and contemporary language and visually appealing documents that entice the reader to read on are two of the many ways to improve readability.

LO⁶: Identify ways to project a positive, tactful tone.

Handle sensitive situations by projecting a positive, tactful tone. Consider the following suggestions: (1) state ideas using positive language; (2) avoid using second person when stating negative ideas; (3) use passive voice to convey negative ideas; (4) use the subjunctive mood; and (5) include a pleasant statement in the same sentence. Special consideration should be paid when writing for an intercultural or international audience.

Key Terms

Libel written defamatory remarks

Slander spoken defamatory remarks

Topic sentence the one sentence that identifies the portion of the topic being discussed and presents the central idea of the paragraph

Deductive an organizational approach in which the topic sentence precedes the details

Inductive an organizational approach in which the topic sentence follows the details

Complements additional words in a sentence that help complete the meaning

Phrase (clause) a group of words that is not a complete sentence

Dependent clause a clause that does not convey a complete thought

Independent clause a clause that conveys a complete thought and could be a complete sentence if presented alone

Sentence fragment a portion of a sentence which when presented as a separate sentence causes receivers to become confused and distracted

Run-on sentence (fused sentence) when no punctuation or coordinating conjunction appears between clauses

Comma splice when clauses are joined only with a comma instead of a comma and coordinating conjunction or a semicolon

Active verbs when the subject is the doer of action

Passive verbs when the subject is the receiver of action

Cliché overused expression common in our everyday conversations and in business messages

Redundancy a phrase in which one word unnecessarily repeats an idea contained in an accompanying word

Grammar Quiz

Add necessary hyphens. Write "correct" if you find no errors.

1. The new hire's self confidence was crushed by the manager's harsh tone.

2. State of the art computers provide quick access to timely-business information.

3. Surveys indicate that a majority of today's consumers are convenience driven.

4. A two thirds majority is needed to pass the 5-percent increase in employee wages.

5. Nearly one-half of the respondents were highly-educated professionals.

6. Our company's decision making process is slow because key decision makers are traveling on business.

Quiz Solutions

1. self-confidence
2. State-of-the-art; timely business information
3. Correct
4. two-thirds; 5 percent
5. one half; highly educated
6. decision-making

Systematic Proofreading

- Use the spell-check to locate simple keying errors.
- Proofread once concentrating on content, organization, and style and a second time on mechanics, format, and layout.

Ethical Content

- Present information truthfully, honestly, and fairly.
- Include all information relevant to the receiver.
- Avoid exaggerating or embellishing facts.
- Use objective facts to support ideas.
- Design graphics that avoid distorting facts and relationships.
- Express ideas clearly and understandably.
- State ideas tactfully and positively to preserve the receiver's self-worth and to build future relationships.

Coherent Paragraphs

- Write deductively if a message will likely please or at least not displease. If a message will likely displease or if understanding the major idea is dependent on prior explanations, write inductively.
- Make sure the message forms a unit with an obvious beginning, middle, and ending and that in-between paragraphs are arranged in a systematic sequence (deductively or inductively).
- Avoid abrupt changes in thought, and link each sentence to a preceding sentence. Place transition sentences before major headings.
- Vary sentence and paragraph length to emphasize important ideas.
- Limit paragraphs in letters, memos, and email messages to six lines and paragraphs in reports to eight to ten lines.

Powerful Sentences

- Use correct sentence structure and avoid run-on sentences and comma splices.
- Use active voice to present important points or pleasant ideas. Use passive verbs to present less significant points or unpleasant ideas.
- Emphasize important ideas.

Readability

- Use simple words and short sentences for quick, easy reading (and listening).
- Strive for short paragraphs but vary their lengths.
- Create appealing, easy-to-read documents by incorporating bulleted and numbered list and using headings, tables, and graphs.

Goodwill

- Use euphemisms to present unpleasant thoughts politely and positively. Avoid using euphemisms when they will be taken as excessive or sarcastic.
- Avoid doublespeak or corporate speak that confuses or misleads the receiver.

- Avoid using condescending or demeaning expressions.
- Rely mainly on denotative words. Use connotative words that will elicit a favorable reaction, are easily understood, and are appropriate for the setting.
- Add clarity and interest to your message with vivid words.
- Use bias-free language.
- Do not use the pronoun *he* when referring to a group of people that may include women or *she* when a group may include men.
- Be sensitive and avoid gender, race, age, religion, and disability stereotyping.
- Do not emphasize race and ethnicity, age, religion, or disability when these factors are not relevant.

Positive Tone

- Rely mainly on positive words that speak of what can be done instead of what cannot be done. Use negative words when the purpose is to sharpen contrast or when positive words have not evoked the desired reaction.
- Use second person and active voice to emphasize pleasant ideas. Avoid using second person for presenting negative ideas; instead, use third person and passive voice to de-emphasize the unpleasant.
- Consider stating an unpleasant thought in the subjunctive mood.

Simple, Contemporary Language

- Avoid clichés and outdated expressions that make your language seem unnatural and unoriginal.
- Use simple words for informal business messages instead of using more complicated words that have the same meaning.

Conciseness

- Do not use redundancies—unnecessary repetition of an idea.
- Use active voice to shorten sentences.
- Avoid unnecessary details; omit ideas that can be implied.
- Shorten wordy sentences by using suffixes or prefixes, making changes in word form, or substituting precise words for phrases.

Learning Objectives

LO¹: Identify the characteristics of a report and the various classifications of business reports.

The basis of a report is a problem that must be solved through data collection and analysis. Reports are usually requested by a higher authority, are logically organized and highly objective, and are prepared for a limited audience. Reports can be classified as formal/informal, short/long, informational/analytical, vertical/lateral, internal/external, or a proposal.

LO²: Identify the characteristics of a proposal and the various classifications of business proposals.

Proposals are persuasive written messages describing how one organization can meet the needs of another. Internal proposals are written by employees to justify or recommend purchases or changes in the company. External proposals are written as a means to generate business by providing products or services or solve problems.

LO³: Apply steps in the problem-solving process and methods for solving a problem.

The four steps in the problem-solving process are: (a) Recognize and define the problem; (b) select an appropriate secondary and/or primary method for solving the problem; (c) collect and organize data, using appropriate methods; and (d) interpret the data to arrive at an answer.

LO⁴: Use appropriate printed, electronic, and primary sources of information.

Location of secondary sources of information involves appropriate use of printed indexes and application of electronic search techniques that can lead the researcher to books, periodicals, and other documents needed for topic exploration. Methods for collecting survey data include mailed questionnaires, telephone surveys, email polling, personal interviews, interviews, and participant observation. Developing an effective survey instrument is critical to obtaining valid and reliable data. Surveys should be administered to a sample that is representative of the entire population.

Key Terms

Formal report a carefully structured report that is logically organized and objective, contains much detail, and is written without personal pronouns

Informal report a short message written in natural or personal language

Informational report a report that carries objective information from one area of an organization to another

Analytical report a report that presents suggested solutions to problems

Upward-directed reports reports made by subordinates to superiors

Downward-directed reports reports made by superiors for subordinates

Internal report reports made by superiors for subordinates

External report a report prepared for distribution outside an organization

Periodic reports reports issued on regularly scheduled dates

Functional report a report that serves a specified purpose within a company

Proposal a written description of how one organization can meet the needs of another

Internal proposal a report written to justify or recommend courses of action taken in the company

External proposal a written description of how one organization can meet the needs of another by providing products or services

Solicited proposal a proposal that is invited and initiated

RFP a request for a proposal

Unsolicited proposal a proposal prepared by an individual or firm that sees a problem to be solved and submits a proposal

Problem statement (statement of the problem) the particular problem that is to be solved by the research

Statement of purpose the goal of the study

Hypothesis a statement to be proved or disproved through research

Null hypothesis the statement that no relationship or difference will be found in the factors being studied

Limitations boundaries imposed outside the control of the researchers

Delimitations boundaries chosen by the researcher(s) to make the project more manageable

Grammar Quiz

Add necessary quotation marks and italics.

1. Goleman presents an interesting theory of intelligence in his book Emotional Intelligence.

2. The article A Softer Side of Leadership appeared in the July 2006 issue of Training.

3. His accomplishments are summarized on the attached page. [Indicate that a word other than *accomplishments* may be a more appropriate word.]

4. The term flame is online jargon for a heated, sarcastic, sometimes abusive message or posting to a discussion group.

Quiz Solutions

1. Goleman presents an interesting theory of intelligence in his book *Emotional Intelligence*. [Italicizes a book title.]

2. The article "A Softer Side of Leadership" appeared in the July 2005 issue of *Training*. [Encloses the name of an article in quotation marks and italicizes the title of a magazine; *Training*.]

3. His "accomplishments" are summarized on the attached page. [Uses quotation marks to introduce doubt about whether "accomplishments" is the right label. His undertakings may have been of little significance.]

4. The term *flame* is online jargon for "a heated, sarcastic, sometimes abusive message or posting to a discussion group." [Italicizes a word used as a word and enclose a definition of a defined term.]

LO⁵: Demonstrate appropriate methods for collecting, organizing, and referencing information.

Information from published sources should be carefully read and interpreted. To avoid plagiarism, both direct quotes and paraphrases must be referenced. Survey instruments should be carefully designed to solicit information that is needed, avoid ambiguity and confusion, and reflect accurate information. Documenting sources accurately is crucial to professional researchers. Three acceptable reference methods are: (1) in-text parenthetical citations, (2) footnote citation method and (3) references (or works cited).

LO⁶: Explain techniques for the logical analysis and interpretation of data.

Measures of central tendency and correlation analysis are two common methods for analyzing data. To maintain the integrity of the research, the interpretation of data should be objective and unbiased and avoid making assumptions about areas unsupported by the data.

Methodology (procedures) the procedures or steps a writer takes in preparing a report that are often recorded as a part of the written report

Longitudinal study a report that studies the same factors in different time frames

Secondary research information that has already been created by others

Electronic databases articles from newspapers, magazines, journals, and other types of publications delivered electronically, usually for a fee

Hidden Internet databases that are not accessible by a search engine

Boolean logic the use of Boolean operands (and, or, not) to narrow the selection and limit the identified sites

Primary research data collected for the first time, usually for a specific purpose

Observational studies studies in which the researcher observes and statistically analyzes certain phenomena in order to assist in establishing new principles or discoveries

Experimental research the study of two or more samples that have exactly the same components before a variable is added to one of the samples

Normative survey research research to determine the status of something at a specific time

Sampling a survey technique that eliminates the need for questioning 100 percent of the population

Validity the degree to which the data measure what you intend to measure

Pilot test implementation of the instrument conducted prior to the full-scale survey with a smaller number of participants

Reliability the level of consistency or stability over time or over independent samples

Direct quotation method citing the exact words from a source

Paraphrase method summarizing information in your own words without changing the author's intended meaning

Plagiarism the presentation of someone else's ideas or words as your own

Measures of central tendency metrics that help describe distributions of quantitative data

Range the distribution of the scores

Mean, median, and mode different descriptions of the average value of the distribution

Correlation analysis a tool used to determine whether a relationship existed between how respondents answered one item and how they answered another

CHECK YOUR COMMUNICATION | Report Process and Research Methods

Problem Formation

- Decide what type of report is required.
- Formulate the problem statement.
- Determine boundaries for the research.
- Define specialized terms used in the report.

Research Methodology

- Select appropriate methods of solution, including relevant secondary and primary resources.
- Gather appropriate published and electronic sources.
- Plan appropriate primary research, using observational, experimental, or normative techniques.

Data Collection and Organization

- Document all quoted and paraphrased information using appropriate referencing method.
- Develop effective data collection instruments; pilot test and refine prior to conducting research.

- Avoid data collection errors that can minimize your research effort.

Data Interpretation

- Analyze data accurately and ethically.
- Interpret data to reach logical conclusions.
- Make recommendations that are well supported by the data presented.
- Avoid over generalizing results of the research conducted in one setting to another group or setting.

Learning Objectives

Key Terms

LO¹: Communicate quantitative information effectively.

Graphics complement text by clarifying complex figures and helping readers visualize major points. Tabulating data and analyzing data using measures of central tendency aid in summarizing or classifying large volumes of data into manageable information you can interpret. You can then communicate this meaningful data using common language—fractions, ratios, and percentages—that the reader can easily understand.

LO²: Apply principles of effectiveness and ethical responsibilities in the construction of graphic aids.

A graphic aid should clarify, reinforce, or emphasize a particular idea and should contribute to the overall understanding of the idea under discussion. It should be uncluttered, easily understood, and depict information honestly. Graphic aids used in spoken presentations should be large enough to be seen by the entire audience.

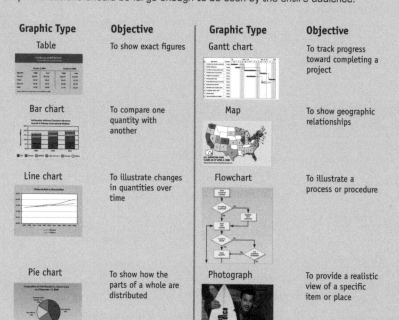

Graphic Type	Objective	Graphic Type	Objective
Table	To show exact figures	Gantt chart	To track progress toward completing a project
Bar chart	To compare one quantity with another	Map	To show geographic relationships
Line chart	To illustrate changes in quantities over time	Flowchart	To illustrate a process or procedure
Pie chart	To show how the parts of a whole are distributed	Photograph	To provide a realistic view of a specific item or place

Common language reduces difficult figures to the "common denominators" of language and ideas

Chartjunk decorative distractions that bury relevant data

Table data presented in columns and rows, which aid in clarifying large quantities of data in a small space

Bar chart effective graphic for comparing quantities

Gantt chart chart useful for tracking progress toward completing a series of events over time

Line chart chart that depicts changes in quantitative data over time and illustrates trends

Area chart (cumulative line chart, surface chart) bar chart that shows how different factors contribute to a total

Pie chart chart that shows how the parts of a whole are distributed

Map shows geographic relationships

Flowchart step-by-step diagram of a procedure or a graphic depiction of a system or organization

LO³: Select and design appropriate and meaningful graphics.

The type of graphic presentation should be chosen based on the ability to communicate the information most effectively. Tables present data in systematic rows and columns. Bar charts (simple, grouped, and stacked) compare quantities for a specific period. Line charts depict changes in quantities over time and illustrate trends. Pie charts, pictograms, and segmented and area charts show the proportion of components to a whole. Gantt charts track progress toward completing a series of events over time. Maps help readers visualize geographical relationships. Flowcharts visually depict step-by-step procedures for completing a task; organization charts show the organizational structure of a company. Floor plans, photographs, cartoons, blueprints, and lists also enhance reports.

LO⁴: Integrate graphics within documents.

A graphic should always be introduced in text before it is presented. The graphic will then reinforce your conclusions and discourage readers from drawing their own conclusions before encountering your ideas. An effective introduction for a graphic tells something meaningful about what is depicted in the graphic and refers the reader to a specific figure number. The graphic should be placed immediately after the introduction if possible or positioned at the top of the next page after filling the previous page with text that ideally would have followed the graphic. Analysis or interpretation follows the graphic, avoiding a mere repetition of what the graphic clearly shows.

CHECK YOUR COMMUNICATION | Types of Graphic Aids

Tables

- Number tables and all other graphics consecutively throughout the report.

- Give each table a title that is complete enough to clarify what is included without forcing the reader to review the table.

- Label columns of data clearly enough to identify the items.

- Indent the second line of a label for the rows (horizontal items) two or three spaces.

- Place a superscript beside an entry that requires additional explanation and include the explanatory note beneath the visual.

- Document the source of the data presented in a visual by adding a source note beneath the visual.

Bar Charts

- Begin the quantitative axis at zero, divide the bars into equal increments, and use bars of equal width.

- Position chronologically or in some other logical order.

- Use variations in color to distinguish among the bars when the bars represent different data.

- Avoid using 3D-type formatting that makes values more difficult to distinguish.

- Include enough information in the scale labels and bar labels for clear understanding.

Line Charts

- Use the vertical axis for amount and the horizontal axis for time.

- Begin the vertical axis at zero.

- Divide the vertical and horizontal scales into equal increments.

Pie Charts

- Position the largest slice or the slice to be emphasized at the twelve o'clock position.

- Label each slice and include information about the quantitative size (percentage, dollars, acres, square feet, etc.) of each slice.

- Draw attention to one or more slices for desired emphasis.

- Avoid using 3D-type formatting that makes values more difficult to distinguish.

Maps

- Use to show geographic information visually.

Flowcharts

- Use to show step-by-step procedures or graphic depiction of a system or organization.

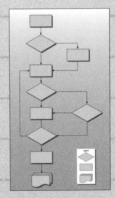

Learning Objectives

LO¹: Identify the parts of a formal report and the contribution each part makes to the report's overall effectiveness.

Formal reports can have three basic sections—preliminary parts, report text, and addenda. *Preliminary parts* add formality, emphasize content and ease of understanding, and provide quick reference for information in the report. The *report text* contains the body and any conclusions and recommendations. The three basic *addenda* parts are the references, appendixes, and index. As reports increase in length and formality, the addition of introductory and addenda items are appropriate.

LO²: Organize report findings.

Organizing the content of a report involves seeing the report problem in its entirety and then breaking it into its parts. After the research or field work has been completed, the writer creates an outline to identify the major and minor points and organize the report into logical sequence. Writers determine the format and style best able to communicate the intended message.

LO³: Prepare effective formal reports using an acceptable format and writing style.

In preparing effective long reports, outlining assists the writer with logical sequencing. Appropriate headings lead the reader from one division to another. The writing style should present the findings and data interpretation clearly and fairly. Opinions should be clearly identified as such.

LO⁴: Prepare effective short reports in memorandum, email, and letter formats.

Short reports are typically written in a personal writing style and in memorandum, email, or letter format. Form reports provide accuracy, save time, and simplify tabulation of data when a need exists for numerous, repetitive reports.

LO⁵: Prepare effective proposals for a variety of purposes.

Proposals can be written for both internal and external audiences. Proposals call for thorough organization and require writing methods that will be not only informative but also convincing. Because they have discrete parts that can be prepared in any order and then assembled into whole reports, they are conducive to preparation by teams.

LO⁶: Identify special skills required for team writing.

Team writing produces a corporate document representing multiple points of view and can be achieved using sequential, parallel, or reciprocal editing techniques. In sequential editing, collaborators work in order; with parallel editing, all collaborators work on their own individual parts and then put them together; and with reciprocal editing, collaborators work together in real time to create a common document.

Key Terms

Preliminary parts elements that add formality to a report, emphasize report content, and aid the reader in locating information in the report quickly and in understanding the report more easily

Title page a page that includes the title, author, date, and frequently the name of the person or organization that requested the report

Executive summary (abstract, overview, précis) short summary of the essential elements in an entire report

Discussion (body) the main part of the report that pre-sents the information collected and relates it to the problem

Summary a review of the main points presented in the body of the report

Analytical report a report designed to solve a specific problem or answer research questions

Conclusions inferences the writer draws from the findings

Recommendations the writer's opinions on a possible course of action based on the conclusions

Addenda materials used in the research that are not appropriate to be included in the report itself and so are placed at the end in a separate section

References an alphabetical listing of the sources used in preparing the report that is included at the end of the report

Bibliography (works consulted) a list at the end of the report that includes sources not cited in the report

Appendix a section placed at the end of the report that contains supplementary information that supports the report but is not appropriate for inclusion in the report itself

Index an alphabetical guide to the subject matter in a report

Justification report a report that makes a recommendation based on research

Short report a report that contains only the minimum supporting materials to achieve effective communication

Form report a report designed to collect information easily, organize the data clearly, and be used repetitively

Grammar Quiz

Correct the number usage in the following sentences taken from a letter or a report.

1. The question was answered by sixty-one percent of the respondents.
2. The meeting is scheduled for 10:00 a.m. on February 3rd.
3. These 3 figures appeared on the expense account: $21.95, $30.00, and $35.14.
4. The MIS manager ordered 150 120-GB hard drives.

Quiz Solutions

1. The question was answered by 61 percent of the respondents.
2. The meeting is scheduled for 10 a.m. on February 3.
3. These three figures appeared on the expense account: $21.95, $30, and $35.14.
4. The MIS manager ordered 150 120-GB hard drives.

Transmittal Letter or Memorandum

(Use a letter-style transmittal in reports going outside the organization. For internal reports, use a memorandum transmittal.)

- Transmit a warm greeting to the reader.
- Open with a "Here is the report you requested" tone.
- Establish the subject in the first sentence.
- Follow with a brief summary and expand the discussion if a separate summary is not included in the report.
- Acknowledge the assistance of those who helped with the study.
- Close the message with a thank-you and a forward look.

Title Page

- Include the title of the report, succinctly worded.
- Provide full identification of the authority for the report (the person or organization for whom the report was prepared).
- Provide full identification of the preparer(s) of the report.
- Provide the date of the completion of the report.
- Use an attractive layout.

Table of Contents

- Use *Table of Contents* or *Contents* as the title.
- Use indention to indicate the heading degrees used in the report.
- List numerous figures separately as a preliminary item called *Table of Figures* or *Figures.* (Otherwise, figures should not be listed because they are not separate sections of the outline but only supporting data within a section.)

Executive Summary

- Use a descriptive title, such as *Executive Summary, Synopsis,* or *Abstract.*
- Condense the major report sections.
- Use effective, generalized statements that avoid detail available in the report itself.

Report Text

- Avoid the personal *I* and *we* pronouns in formal writing. Minimize the use of the *writer, the investigator,* and *the author.*
- Use active construction to emphasize the *doer* of the action; use passive voice to emphasize the *results* of the action.
- Use proper tense.
- Avoid ambiguous pronoun references. They hinder clarity.
- Avoid expletive beginnings, such as *This is* and *There are.*
- Use bulleted or enumerated lists for three or more items.
- Incorporate transition sentences to ensure coherence.
- Apply formatting consistently and use parallel construction.
- Number consecutively and title report graphics.
- Question each statement for its contribution to the solution of the problem.
- Use units of production, percentages, or ratios to express large numbers.
- Use objective reporting style that avoids emotional terms, assumptions and opinions, and unwarranted judgments and inferences.
- State your conclusions carefully and clearly, and be sure they grow out of the findings.

Citations

- Include a citation (in-text reference, footnote, or endnote) for material quoted or paraphrased from another source.
- Adhere to an acceptable, authoritative style or company policy.
- Present consistent citations, including adequate information for readers to locate the source in the reference list.

References

- Include an entry for every reference cited in the report.
- Adhere to an acceptable, authoritative style or company policy.
- When in doubt, include more information than might be necessary.

Appendix

- Include cover messages and all other items that provide information but are not important enough to be included in the report body.
- Subdivide categories of information beginning with Appendix A, Appendix B, and so on.
- Identify each item with a title.

reviewcard/ CHAPTER 13
DESIGNING AND DELIVERING BUSINESS PRESENTATIONS

Learning Objectives

LO¹: Plan a business presentation that accomplishes the speaker's goals and meets the audience's needs.

Determine what you want to accomplish in your presentation and direct your presentation to the specific needs and interests of the audience. Identify the general characteristics (age, gender, experience, etc.), size, and receptiveness of the audience.

LO²: Organize and develop the three parts of an effective presentation.

An effective presentation has an introduction, body, and close. The introduction should capture the audience's attention, involve the audience and the speaker, present the purpose statement, and preview major points. The body is limited to a few major points that are supported and clarified with relevant statistics, anecdotes, quotes from prominent people, appropriate humor, presentation visuals, and so forth. The close should be a memorable idea that supports and strengthens the purpose statement.

LO³: Select, design, and use presentation visuals effectively.

Using visual aids reduces the time required to present a concept and increases audience retention. Available aids include handouts, models and physical objects, whiteboards, flip-charts, overhead transparencies, electronic presentations, videotapes, and audiotapes. Each type provides specific advantages and should be selected carefully. An effective visual presents one major idea in a simple design large enough for the audience to read. Permissions should be obtained for the use of copyrighted multimedia content.

LO⁴: Deliver speeches with increasing confidence.

Business speakers use the impromptu and extemporaneous speech methods more frequently than the memorized or scripted methods. Professional vocal qualities include a medium or low voice pitch, adequate volume, varied tone and rate, and the absence of distracting verbal fillers. Articulate speakers enunciate words precisely and ensure proper pronunciation. Preparation, professional demeanor, and staying in tune with the audience are keys to a successful speech.

LO⁵: Discuss strategies for presenting in alternate delivery situations such as culturally diverse audiences and team and distance presentations.

When communicating with other cultures, use simple, clear speech. Consider differences in presentation approach, nonverbal communication, and social protocol that may require flexibility and adjustments to your presentation style. Effective team presentations result from the selection of an appropriate leader and team members with complementary strengths and styles who plan ahead and rehearse thoroughly. When delivering a distance presentation, determine which delivery method is appropriate for the presentation, attempt to establish rapport with the participants prior to the distance presentation, become proficient in delivering and using distance technology, and develop high-quality graphics appropriate for the distance format being used.

Key Terms

Oral briefing a less formal presentation delivered face-to-face

Memorized presentation a presentation that is written out ahead of time, memorized, and recited verbatim

Manuscript (scripted) delivery writing the speech word for word and reading it to the audience

Impromptu delivery being called on to speak without prior notice

Extemporaneous presentation a presentation planned, prepared, and rehearsed but not written in detail

Phonation the production and the variation of the speaker's vocal tone

Pitch the highness or lowness of the voice

Volume the loudness of tones

Rate the speed at which words are spoken

Pronunciation principles of phonetics to create accurate sounds, rhythm, stress, and intonation

Grammar Quiz

Copy each of the following sentences, making essential changes in capitalization.

1. The first question professor Kellermanns asked me during interviewing 101 was "why do you want to work for us?"
2. The Summer Season is much slower than the rest of the year according to the Sales Manager.
3. Inform the marketing department of our temporary shortage of AC adapters for laptop computers.
4. We recently purchased digital juice, a source of copyright-free animated images.
5. Julie Gerberding, Director of the Center for Disease Control, is the agency's key communicator.

Quiz Solutions

1. The first question Professor Kellermanns asked me during Interviewing 101 was "Why do you want to work for us?"
2. The summer season is much slower than the rest of the year according to the sales manager.
3. Inform the Marketing Department of the temporary shortage of AC adapters for laptop computers.
4. We recently purchased Digital Juice, a source of copyright-free animated images.
5. Julie Gerberding, director of the Center for Disease Control, is the agency's key communicator.

CHECK YOUR COMMUNICATION | Presentation Skills

Planning and Organizing a Presentation

- **Identify your purpose.** Understand exactly what you hope to accomplish and choose content to support your purpose.
- **Analyze your audience.** Identify characteristics common to audience and speech setting (number in audience, seating arrangements, time of day).
- **Develop an effective opening.** Assure that the opening captures attention, initiates rapport with audience, presents the purpose, and previews the main points.
- **Develop the body.** Select a few major points and locate support for each point. Use simple, nontechnical language and sentences the listener can understand; avoid excessive statistics and use word pictures when possible; and use jokes or humor appropriately.
- **Develop an effective close.** Call for the audience to accept your idea or provide a conclusion with recommendations.

Selecting an Appropriate Presentation Visual

- Select a presentation visual that is appropriate for audience and topic.
- Use whiteboards and flipcharts for small audiences in an informal setting and when no special equipment is available. Prepare flipcharts in advance.
- Use overhead transparencies for small, informal audiences and to write audience comments that can be displayed.
- Use slides for presentations requiring photography; arrange in a planned sequence and show in a darkened room.
- Use electronic presentations for large audiences and to enliven the topic and engage the audience.
- Use video and audio files to illustrate major points in an engaging manner.
- Use models and physical objects to allow the audience to visualize and experience the idea being presented.

Designing and Using Presentation Visuals

- Limit the number of visual aids used in a single presentation.
- Clear all copyrights for multimedia content.
- Write descriptive titles and parallel bulleted lists.
- Create a standard design for each visual following these slide design principles on pages 236–238 of Chapter 13.
- Avoid graphics that distort facts.
- Proofread the visual carefully to eliminate any errors.
- Paraphrase rather than reading line for line and step to one side of the visual so the audience can see it.

Delivering a Presentation

Before the Presentation

- Prepare thoroughly to minimize natural nervousness.
- Prepare easy-to-read note cards or pages.
- Practice to identify any organizational flaws or verbal potholes; do not rehearse until your delivery is mechanical.
- Request a lectern to steady your hands but not to hide behind.
- Insist on a proper, impressive introduction.
- Dress appropriately to create a professional image.
- Arrive early to familiarize yourself with the room.

During the Presentation

- Use clear, articulate speech and proper pronunciation.
- Use vocal variety and adjust volume and rate to emphasize ideas.
- Avoid irritating verbal fillers and other annoying speech habits.
- Maintain steady eye contact with many audience members.
- Smile genuinely to communicate confidence and warmth.
- Watch your audience for important feedback and adjust your presentation accordingly.
- Handle questions from the audience politely.
- Keep within the time limit.

After the Presentation

- Be prepared for a question-and-answer period.
- Distribute handouts.

Adapting to a Culturally Diverse Audience

- Use simple English and short sentences.
- Use a straightforward, direct approach with the main idea presented first.
- Adjust presentation style to reflect differences in nonverbal communication.

Delivering a Team Presentation

- Select a leader who will lead the team in developing a cohesive presentation strategy and team members with complementary strengths and styles.
- Plan the presentation as a team.
- Rehearse thoroughly for cohesion and uniformity.

Delivering a Distance Presentation

- Determine whether a distance delivery method is appropriate for the presentation.
- Attempt to establish rapport with the participants prior to the distance presentation.
- Become proficient in delivering and participating using distance technology.
- Develop high-quality graphics appropriate for the distance format being used.

Learning Objectives

LO¹: Prepare for employment by considering relevant information about yourself as it relates to job requirements.

A job candidate should complete systematic self-, career, and job analyses. Candidates should gather information, ask questions about themselves, about possible careers, and about specific jobs in the chosen field. Recording and analyzing this information will aid in selecting a satisfying career and preparing an effective résumé.

LO²: Identify career opportunities using traditional and electronic methods.

The job candidate can use traditional and electronic methods for the employment search. Names and addresses of possible employers may be obtained from networks, career services centers at schools, employers' offices, employment agencies and contractors, online databases and printed sources, professional, electronic job fairs, news groups, and chat sessions.

LO³: Prepare for employment by considering relevant information about yourself as it relates to job requirements.

A résumé typically includes identification, objective, career summary, qualifications, personal information, and references. Résumés are chronological, functional, or chrono-functional. Chronological résumés list experiences in reverse chronological order and are for applicants with the apparent qualifications for the job. Functional résumés show applicant qualifications as headings and are used when the applicant lacks the appropriate education and experience. The chrono-functional résumé lists education and experience as headings and uses functional headings that emphasize qualifications.

LO⁴: Prepare an organized, persuasive résumé that is adapted for print, scanning, and electronic postings.

Effective print (designed) résumés concisely highlight key qualifications and are formatted for quick, easy reading. Scannable résumés are designed so that the information can be scanned and processed by an applicant-tracking system. An effective key word section summarizes qualifications and helps ensure that the résumé is identified during a search for matching requirements. Electronic résumé posting varies considerably, with popular options including a job bank posting, a website entry, a link to a personal web page, an email attachment, and an inline résumé within the body of an email message.

LO⁵: Utilize employment tools other than the résumé that can enhance employability.

Content for a professional portfolio or a video recording of the applicant should be carefully chosen to reflect skills necessary for effective job performance and should complement information in the résumé.

LO⁶: Write an application message that effectively introduces an accompanying print (designed) or electronic résumé.

The purposes of the application message are to introduce the applicant and the résumé, arouse interest in the information given on the résumé, and assist an employer in seeing ways in which the applicant's services would be desirable. As such, it is a persuasive message.

Key Terms

Targeted résumé a résumé reflects the requirements of a specific job listing

Chronological résumé the traditional organizational format for résumés

Functional résumé a résumé in which points of primary interest to employers—transferable skills—appear in major headings

Chrono-functional résumé a résumé that combines features of chronological and functional résumés

Scannable résumé (electronic résumé) a résumé that will be read by the computer and not by a human

Beamer (beamable résumé) a quick version of your résumé designed in a format suitable for broadcasting on a PDA or digital phone

Inline résumé a résumé that is attached to or included in the body of an email message

Text résumé a résumé without formatting and lacking the appeal of your designed résumé

Professional portfolio (electronic portfolio, e-portfolio) a collection of artifacts that demonstrate your communication, people, and technical skills

Multimedia résumé a résumé created with presentation software such as Microsoft Producer or Camtasia Studio and sent to prospective employers on a CD or DVD, or posted on the applicant's personal web page

Application (cover message) a message placed on top of the résumé so it can be read first by the employer

Unsolicited application message an unrequested message sent to many prospective employers and containing the same basic message

Quiz Solutions

1. affect
2. advice
3. number
4. sight
5. compliment
6. each another
7. further

CHECK YOUR COMMUNICATION | Résumés and Application Messages

Print (Designed) Résumé

Content

- Include relevant qualifications compatible with the job.
- Present qualifications truthfully and honestly.

Organization

- Choose organizational pattern that highlights key qualifications: chronological, functional, or chrono-functional.
- Arrange headings in appropriate sequence.
- List experiences consistently, either in time sequence or in order of importance.

Style

- Omit personal pronouns.
- Use simple words, positive language, and parallel structure.
- Use action verbs in past tense for previous jobs; present tense for present job.
- Place significant words in emphatic positions.

Mechanics

- Ensure there are *no* keying, grammar, spelling, or punctuation errors.
- Balance elements on the page.
- Use ample margins even if a second page is required.
- Include a page number on all pages except the first.
- Position headings consistently throughout.
- Use an outline or a bulleted list to emphasize multiple points.
- Use indention, underlining, capitalization, font changes, and graphic lines and borders to enhance overall impact.
- Laser print on high-quality (24-pound, 100-percent cotton-fiber content), neutral-colored paper.

Scannable Résumé

Content

- Position name as the first readable item on each page.
- Include "Objective" section to identify the job sought (same as a print résumé).
- Include "Key Word Summary" listing qualifications that match the job description.

Mechanics

- Use nondecorative font with size range of 10 to 14 points.
- Omit design elements that could distort the text.
- Allow ample white space, especially between sections.

Electronic Résumés

Content

- Adapt general guidelines for résumé preparation to fit the particular requirements of the submission.
- Place "Key Word Summary" listing qualifications within first 24 lines of text.
- Include link or reference to electronic portfolio.

Mechanics

- Save résumé in appropriate format for transmitting as an attachment, or paste into email message.

Professional Portfolio

Content

- Include items that showcase abilities and accomplishments.

Mechanics

- Choose an appropriate traditional or electronic format.
- For electronic formats, include links to print résumé, plain text version of résumé, email address, and appropriate supplementary documents.

Application Message

Content

- Identify the message as an application for a certain job.
- Emphasize significant qualifications and exclude nonessential ideas.
- Make reference to enclosed or attached résumé.
- End with action closing that is neither apologetic nor pushy.

Style

- Use simple language.
- Use relatively short sentences with sufficient variety.
- Place significant words and ideas in emphatic positions.

Mechanics

- Ensure that there are *no* keying, grammar, or spelling errors.
- Follow proper letter formatting techniques.
- Use equal side margins to balance the page.
- Keep first and last paragraphs relatively short; hold others to six or seven lines.

Learning Objectives

LO¹: Explain the nature of structured, unstructured, stress, team, and virtual interviews.

Interviewers and interviewees can be considered buyers and sellers: Interviewers want to know whether job candidates can meet the needs of their firms before making a "purchase"; interviewees want to sell themselves based on sound knowledge, good work skills, and desirable personal traits. Structured interviews follow a preset, specific, format; unstructured interviews follow no standard format but explore for information. Computer-assisted interviews provide standard, reliable information on applicants during the preliminary interview stages. Stress interviews are designed to reveal how the candidate behaves in high-anxiety situations. Team interviews involve various personnel within the organization in the candidate interview process.

LO²: Explain the steps in the interview process.

Successful job candidates plan appropriately for the interview so that they will know basic information about the company, arrive on time dressed appropriately for the interview, and present a polished first impression following appropriate protocol. During the interview, the candidate presents his or her qualifications favorably and obtains information about the company to aid in deciding whether to accept a possible job offer.

LO³: Prepare effective answers to questions often asked in job interviews, including illegal interview questions.

The successful job candidate effectively discusses key qualifications and skillfully asks questions that show initiative and genuine interest in the company. The candidate recognizes issues that fall outside the bounds of legal questioning. Refusing to answer an illegal question could be detrimental to your chances of securing a job, but answering the question may compromise your ethical values. An effective technique is to answer the legitimate concern behind the illegal question rather than to give a direct answer.

LO⁴ Identify the parts of a job interview.

Interviews have three parts: the opening formalities, an information exchange, and the close. The confidence and courtesy an applicant displays during the opening formalities set the tone for the information exchange which revolves around questions and answers. The close involves the same courtesies as the opening formalities and should not be prolonged unnecessarily.

LO⁵: Compose effective messages related to employment (application forms, follow-up, thank-you, job-acceptance, job refusal, resignation, and recommendation request).

The job applicant should: complete application forms accurately, neatly, and completely, and should only send a follow-up message after a few weeks of no response to an application. Applicants should send a prompt thank-you message following an interview as a professional courtesy. If a job offer is extended, write a deductive job-acceptance message that includes the acceptance, details, and a closing that confirms the date the employee will begin work; or an inductive job-refusal message that includes a buffer beginning, reasons that lead to the refusal, a tactful decline to the offer, and a goodwill closing. Resignation notices should confirm that termination plans are definite and emphasize positive aspects of the job. Requests for recommendations should include specific information about the job requirements and the applicant's qualifications.

Key Terms

Structured interview an interview in which the interviewer follows a predetermined agenda, including a checklist of items or a series of questions and statements designed to elicit the necessary information or interviewee reaction

Unstructured interview a freewheeling exchange that may shift from one subject to another, depending on the interests of the participants

Stress interview an interview designed to place the interviewee in an anxiety-producing situation so an evaluation may be made of the interviewee's performance under stress

Virtual interview interviews conducted via videoconferencing technology

Grammar Quiz

Select the correct word.

1. Limit your discussion to five or (fewer, less) points.
2. I (infer, imply) from Chad's statements to the press that he is optimistic about the proposal.
3. The storm seems to be losing (its, it's) force.
4. The chemical engineer (lead, led) the research team's investigation to eliminate (lead, led) from gas emissions.
5. Employees are entitled to examine their (personal, personnel) folders.
6. The system's (principal, principle) advantage is monetary.
7. (Their, There, They're) planning to complete (their, there, they're) strategic plan this week.
8. The (to, too, two) external auditors expect us (to, too, two) complete (to, too, two) many unnecessary reports.

Quiz Solutions

1. fewer
2. infer
3. its
4. led, lead
5. personnel
6. principal
7. They're, their
8. two, to, too

Inteviews

Planning Stage

- Learn as much as you can about the job requirements, range of salary and benefits, and the interviewer.
- Research the company with whom you are interviewing (products/services, financial condition, growth potential, etc.).
- Identify the *specific* qualifications for the job and other pertinent information about the company.
- Plan your appearance, including clean, well groomed, and appropriate clothing.
- Arrive early with appropriate materials to communicate promptness and organization.
- Try to identify the type of interview you will have (structured, unstructured, virtual, stress, or team).

Opening Formalities

- Greet the interviewer by name with a smile, direct eye contact, and a firm handshake.
- Wait for the interviewer to ask you to be seated.
- Sit erect and lean forward slightly to convey interest.

Body of the Interview

- Adapt your responses to the type of interview situation.
- Explain how your qualifications relate to the job requirements using multiple specific examples.
- Identify illegal interview questions; address the concern behind an illegal question or avoid answering the question tactfully.
- Ask pertinent questions that communicate intelligence and genuine interest in the company. Introduce questions throughout the interview where appropriate.
- Allow the interviewer to initiate a discussion of salary and benefits. Be prepared to provide a general salary range for applicants with your qualifications.

Closing the Interview

- Watch for cues the interview is ending; rise, accept the interviewer's handshake, and communicate enthusiasm.
- Express appreciation for the interview and say you are eager to hear from the company.

Employment Messages

Application Forms

- Read the entire form before completing it and follow instructions precisely.
- Complete the form neatly and accurately.
- Respond to all questions; insert N/A for questions that do not apply.
- Retain a copy for your records.

Follow-Up Messages

- Remind the receiver that your application is on file and you are interested in the job.

- Present additional education or experience gained since previous correspondence; do not repeat information presented earlier.
- Close with a courteous request for an interview.

Thank-You Messages

- Express appreciation for the interview and mention the specific job for which you have applied.
- Refer to a specific point discussed in the interview.
- Close with a reference to an expected call or document conveying the interviewer's decision.

Job-Acceptance Messages

- Begin by accepting the job offer; specify position.
- Provide necessary details.
- Close with a courteous ending that confirms the date employment begins.

Job-Refusal Messages

- Begin with a neutral, related idea that leads to the explanation for the refusal.
- Present the reasons for refusal.
- Close positively, anticipating future association with the company.

Resignation Messages

- Begin with a positive statement about the job to cushion the bad news.
- Present the explanation, state the resignation, and provide any details.
- Close with an appreciative statement about experience with the company.

Recommendation Requests

- Begin with the request for the recommendation.
- Provide necessary details including reference to an enclosed résumé.
- End with an appreciative statement for the reference's willingness to aid in the job search.
- Send a follow-up letter explaining delays and expressing appreciation for extended job searches.

Thank-Yous for a Recommendation

- Begin with expression of thanks for the recommendation.
- Convey sincere tone by avoiding exaggerated comments and providing specific examples of the value of the recommendation.
- End courteously, indicating future association with the reference.

Decisions about page format impact the effectiveness of the message. Many companies have policies that dictate the page layout, letter and punctuation style, and other formatting issues. In the absence of company policy, make your format choices from among standard acceptable options illustrated on this style card.

Page Layout, Punctuation, and Letter Style

The default margins set by word processing software typically reflect the standard line length to increase the efficiency of producing business correspondence. Letters are balanced on the page with approximately equal margins on all sides of the letter, a placement often referred to as fitting the letter into a picture frame. Short letters (one or two paragraphs) are centered on the page; all other letters begin 2 inches from the top of the page. Side margins may be adjusted to improve the appearance of extremely short letters.

Current word processing software has increased the default line spacing and space between paragraphs for easier on-screen reading. If you prefer the tighter, traditional spacing, simply adjust the line spacing to 1.0. Also, to conserve space but keep the fresh, open look, try reducing the line spacing in the letter address but retain the wider line and paragraph spacing in the body of the letter. Another new default is a crisp, open font such as Calibri (replacing the common Times New Roman) designed for easy reading on monitors.

New Document Look

July 24, 2008   **Tap Enter 2 times**

Mr. Bert A. Pittman
1938 South Welch Avenue
Northwood, NE 65432-1938   **Tap Enter 1 time**

Dear Mr. Pittman   **Tap Enter 1 time**

Your recent article, "Are Appraisers Talking to Themselves?" has drawn many favorable comments from local real estate appraisers.

Tap Enter 1 time

The Southeast Chapter of the Society of Real Estate Appraisers . . .

Traditonal Spacing

July 24, 2008   **Tap Enter 4 times (QS)**

Mr. Bert A. Pittman
1938 South Welch Avenue
Northwood, NE 65432-1938   **Tap Enter 2 times (DS)**

Dear Mr. Pittman   **Tap Enter 2 times (DS)**

Your recent article, "Are Appraisers Talking to Themselves?" has drawn many favorable comments from local real estate appraisers.

Tap Enter 2 times (DS)

The Southeast Chapter of the Society of Real Estate Appraisers . . .

Punctuation Styles. Two punctuation styles are customarily used in business letters: mixed and open. Letters using mixed punctuation style have a colon after the salutation and a comma after the complimentary close. Letters using open punctuation style omit a colon after the salutation and a comma after the complimentary close. Mixed punctuation is the traditional style; however, efficiency-conscious companies are increasingly adopting the open style (and other similar format changes), which is easier to remember.

Letter Styles. Business letters are typically formatted in either block or modified block letter styles. The Sample Letter card has examples of these two styles:

- **Block.** Companies striving to reduce the cost of producing business documents adopt the easy-to-learn, efficient block format. All lines (including paragraphs) begin at the left margin.

- **Modified Block.** Modified block is the traditional letter format still used in many companies. The dateline, complimentary close, and signature block begin at the horizontal center of the page. Paragraphs may be indented one-half inch if the writer prefers or the company policy requires it. However, the indention creates unnecessary keystrokes that increase the production cost. All other lines begin at the left margin.

Standard Letter Parts

Professional business letters include seven standard parts. Other parts are optional and may be included when necessary.

1

Heading. When the letterhead shows the company name, address, telephone and/or fax number, and logo, the letter begins with the dateline. Use the month-day-year format (September 2, 2008) for most documents prepared for U.S. audiences. When preparing government documents or writing to an international audience, use the day-month-year format (2 September 2008). Company policy may require another format.

2

Letter Address. The *letter address* includes a personal or professional title (e.g., Mr., Ms., or Dr.), the name of the person and company receiving the letter, and the complete address.

3

Salutation. The *salutation* is the greeting that opens a letter. To show courtesy for the receiver, include a personal or professional title (for example, Mr., Ms., Dr., Senator). Refer to the *first line* of the letter address to determine an appropriate salutation. "Dear Ms. Henson" is an appropriate salutation for a letter addressed to Ms. Donna Henson (first line of letter address). "Ladies and Gentlemen" is an appropriate salutation for a letter addressed to "Wyatt Enterprises," where the company name is keyed as the first line of the letter address.

4

Body. The *body* contains the message of the letter. Because extra space separates the paragraphs, paragraph indention, which requires extra setup time, is not necessary. However, for organizations that require paragraph indention as company policy, the modified block format with indented paragraphs is the appropriate choice.

5

Complimentary Close. The *complimentary close* is a phrase used to close a letter in the same way that you say good-bye at the end of a conversation. To create goodwill, choose a complimentary close that reflects the formality of your relationship with the receiver. Typical examples are "Sincerely," "Cordially," and "Respectfully." Using "yours" in the close has fallen out of popularity (as in "Sincerely yours" and "Very truly yours"). "Sincerely" is considered neutral and is thus appropriate in a majority of business situations. "Cordially" can be used for friendly messages, and "Respectfully" is appropriate when you are submitting information for the approval of another.

6

Signature Block. The *signature block* consists of the writer's name keyed below the complimentary close, allowing space for the writer to sign legibly. A woman may include a courtesy title to indicate her preference (e.g., Miss, Ms., Mrs.), and a woman or man may use a title to distinguish a name used by both men and women (e.g., Shane, Leslie, or Stacy) or initials (E. M. Goodman). A business or professional title may be placed on the same line with the writer's name or directly below it as appropriate to achieve balance.

Title on the Same Line	Title on the Next Line
Ms. Leslie Tatum, President	Ms. E. M. Goodman
Perry Watson, Manager	Assistant Manager
Quality Control Division Head	Richard S. Templeton
	Human Resources Director

7

7 Reference Initials. The *reference initials* consist of the keyboard operator's initials keyed in lowercase below the signature block. The reference initials and the signature block identify the persons involved in preparing a letter in the event of later questions. Reference initials are frequently omitted when a letter is keyed by the writer. However, company policy may require that the initials of all people involved in preparing a letter be placed in the reference initials line to identify accountability in the case of litigation. For example, the following reference initials show the indicated level of responsibility. The reference line might also include department identification or other information as required by the organization.

SF:lm:cd

| Person who signed document | Person who wrote document | Person who keyed document |

Optional Letter Parts

Delivery and Addressee Notations.
A *delivery notation* provides a record of how a letter was sent. Examples include *Air Mail, Certified Mail, Federal Express, Registered Mail,* and *Fax Transmission.* Addressee notations such as *Confidential* or *Personal* give instructions on how a letter should be handled.

Attention Line.
An *attention line* is used for directing correspondence to an individual or department within an organization while still officially addressing the letter to the organization. The attention line directs a letter to a specific person *(Attention Ms. Laura Ritter),* position within a company *(Attention Human Resources Director),* or department *(Attention Purchasing Department).* Current practice is to place the attention line in the letter address on the line directly below the company name and use the same format for the envelope address. The appropriate salutation in a letter with an attention line is "Ladies and Gentlemen."

Reference Line.
A *reference line (Re: Contract No. 983-9873)* directs the receiver to source documents or to files.

Subject Line.
A *subject line* tells the receiver what a letter is about and sets the stage for the receiver to understand the message. For added emphasis, use initial capitals or all capitals, or center the subject line if modified block style is used. Omit the word *subject* because its position above the body clearly identifies its function.

Second-Page Heading.
The second and succeeding pages of multiple-page letters and memorandums are keyed on plain paper of the same quality as the letterhead. Identify the second and succeeding pages with a *second-page heading* including the name of the addressee, page number, and the date. Place the heading one inch from the top edge of the paper using either a vertical or horizontal format as illusrated. The horizontal format is more time-consuming to format but looks attractive with the modified block format and may prevent the document from requiring additional pages.

Vertical Format

Communication Systems, Inc.

Page 2

January 19, 2008

Horizontal Format

Communication Systems, Inc.   2   January 19, 2008

Company Name in Signature Block. Some companies prefer to include the *company name* in the signature block, but often it is excluded because it appears in the letterhead. The company name is beneficial when the letter is prepared on plain paper or is more than one page (the second page of the letter is printed on plain paper). Including the company name also may be useful to the writer wishing to emphasize that the document is written on behalf of the company (e.g., a letter establishing an initial customer contact).

Enclosure Notation. An *enclosure notation* indicates that additional items (brochure, price list, résumé) are included in the same envelope. Key the plural form (Enclosures) if more than one item is enclosed. You may identify the number of enclosures (Enclosures: 3) or the specific item enclosed (Enclosure: Bid Proposal). Avoid abbreviations (Enc.) that may give the impression that your work is hurried and careless and may show disrespect for the recipient. Some companies use the word "Attachment" on memorandums when the accompanying items may be stapled or clipped and not placed in an envelope.

Copy Notation. A *copy notation* indicates that a courtesy copy of the document was sent to the person(s) listed. Include the person's personal or professional title and full name, after keying "c" for copy or "cc" for courtesy copy. Key the copy notation below the enclosure notation, reference initials, or signature block (depending on the optional letter parts used).

Postscript. A *postscript,* appearing as the last item in a letter, is commonly used to emphasize information. A postscript in a sales letter, for example, is often used to restate the central selling point; for added emphasis, it may be handwritten or printed in a different color. Often handwritten postscripts of a personal nature are added to personalize the printed document. Postscripts should not be used to add information inadvertently omitted from the letter. Because its position clearly labels this paragraph as a postscript, do not begin with "PS."

Computer File Notation. A *computer file notation* provides the path and file name of the letter. Some companies require this documentation on the file copy to facilitate revision. Place the computer file notation a single space below the last keyed line of the letter.

stylecard/ SAMPLE LETTERS

Block Letter Style with Open Punctuation

Begin 2" from top or 1/2" below letterhead

- Dateline

July 24, 2008

Tap Enter 2 times

- Letter address

Mr. Bert A. Pittman
1938 South Welch Avenue
Northwood, NE 65432-1938

Tap Enter 1 time

- Salutation

Dear Mr. Pittman

Tap Enter 1 time

Your recent article, "Are Appraisers Talking to Themselves?" has drawn many favorable comments from local real estate appraisers.

Tap Enter 1 time

- Body

The Southeast Chapter of the Society of Real Estate Appraisers has felt a strong need for more information about appraisal report writing. About 200 members will attend our annual seminar. They would be glad to meet you and are interested in hearing you discuss "Appraisal Report Writing." The meeting will be at the Tilton Hotel on Thursday, August 23, at 7 p.m. We promise you a pleasant evening and an attentive audience.

Tap Enter 1 time

Along with your acceptance, we would appreciate a photograph by August 7 so that we can include your picture in the program.

Tap Enter 1 time

- Complimentary close

Sincerely

Jennifer Malley **Tap Enter 2 times leaving space for signature**

Jennifer Malley
Program Chair

- Signature block
- Reference initials

tw

Tap Enter 1 time

SOCIETY REAL ESTATE APPRAISERS
763 Collins Avenue ■ Lansing, MI 48909-0763 ■ (517) 555-9073 ■ Fax (517) 555-9108

- Begins all lines at left margin; uses easy-to-read jagged right margin and single-spaced, unindented paragraphs.

- Omits colon after salutation and comma after complimentary close in open punctuation style.

- Signs legibly in available space and identifies writer.

- Identifies person keying document.

The document illustrates contemporary spacing with 1.15 spaces between lines. If using traditional single spacing (1.0), tap Enter 2 times to double-space between paragraphs and 4 times to quadruple space after the dateline and the complimentary close.

STEPHEN'S SMALL ENGINES

158 Cedar Bluff Road / Montgomery, AL 36119-0158 / Tel. (334) 555-1497

Begin 2" from top or 1/2" below letterhead

- *Dateline*

October 15, 2008

Tap Enter 2 times

> *Begins dateline, complimentary close, and signature block at horizontal center.*

- *Letter address*

Mr. Saunders Greyson, Manager
Tropical Importers, Inc.
1240 Coastal Lane
Miami, FL 33140-1000

Tap Enter 1 time

- *Salutation*

Dear Mr. Greyson:

> *Includes colon after salutation in mixed punctuation style.*

Tap Enter 1 time

It was a pleasure meeting you at the career fair this morning. The opportunities offered in logistics management identifies your company as being a leader in today's international marketplace.

Tap Enter 1 time

- *Body*

My experience and knowledge of logistics management enable me to be a valuable asset to your company:

- Realistic international experience with a delivery company.
- Demonstrated commitment to developing an appreciation for international cultures and business practices.
- Excellent performance evaluations, including special recognition for troubleshooting transportation problems to remote locations.

> *Uses single-spaced, unindented paragraphs, but indentions are acceptable with modified block style.*

Tap Enter 1 time

Please message me so we can discuss my joining Tropical Importers.

Tap Enter 1 time

- *Complimentary close*

Sincerely,

Brandon Shaw

Tap Enter 2 times leaving space for signature

> *Includes comma after complimentary close in mixed punctuation style.*

- *Signature block*

Brandon Shaw

> *Signs legibly in available space and identifies writer.*

> *Omits reference initials since writer keyed document*

Document illustrates contemporary spacing. If using traditional spacing (1.0) between lines, tap Enter 2 times to double space between paragraphs and 4 times to quadruple space after the dateline and the complimentary close.

Envelopes

An envelope should be printed on the same quality and color of paper as the letter and generated using the convenient envelope feature of your word processing program. Adjust defaults as needed to adhere to the recommendations of the United States Postal Service (USPS). To increase the efficiency of mail handling, use the two-letter abbreviations for states, territories, and Canadian provinces. USPS official state abbreviations are available at **www.USPS.gov.**

Most companies today do not follow the traditional USPS recommendation to key the letter address in all capital letters with no punctuation. The mixed case format matches the format used in the letter address, looks more professional, and allows the writer to generate the envelope automatically without rekeying text. No mail handling efficiency is lost as today's optical character readers that sort mail can read both upper- and lowercase letters easily. Proper placement of the address on a large and a small envelope generated using an envelope template available with word processing software is shown here:

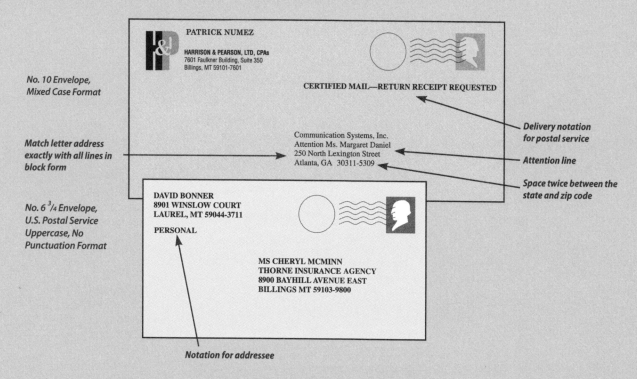

No. 10 Envelope, Mixed Case Format

Match letter address exactly with all lines in block form

No. 6 3/4 Envelope, U.S. Postal Service Uppercase, No Punctuation Format

Delivery notation for postal service

Attention line

Space twice between the state and zip code

Notation for addressee

PATRICK NUMEZ

HARRISON & PEARSON, LTD, CPAs
7601 Faulkner Building, Suite 350
Billings, MT 59101-7601

CERTIFIED MAIL—RETURN RECEIPT REQUESTED

Communication Systems, Inc.
Attention Ms. Margaret Daniel
250 North Lexington Street
Atlanta, GA 30311-5309

DAVID BONNER
8901 WINSLOW COURT
LAUREL, MT 59044-3711

PERSONAL

MS CHERYL MCMINN
THORNE INSURANCE AGENCY
8900 BAYHILL AVENUE EAST
BILLINGS MT 59103-9800

Additionally, to create a highly professional image, business communicators should fold letters to produce the fewest number of creases. Here are the proper procedures for folding letters for large (No. 10) and small (6³/₄) envelopes:

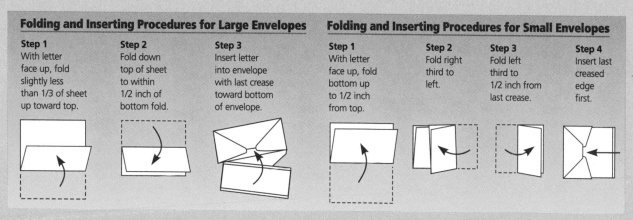

Folding and Inserting Procedures for Large Envelopes

Step 1
With letter face up, fold slightly less than 1/3 of sheet up toward top.

Step 2
Fold down top of sheet to within 1/2 inch of bottom fold.

Step 3
Insert letter into envelope with last crease toward bottom of envelope.

Folding and Inserting Procedures for Small Envelopes

Step 1
With letter face up, fold bottom up to 1/2 inch from top.

Step 2
Fold right third to left.

Step 3
Fold left third to 1/2 inch from last crease.

Step 4
Insert last creased edge first.

Memorandum Formats

To increase productivity of memorandums (memos), which are internal messages, companies use formats that are easy to input and that save time. Most companies use customized or standard memo templates found in most word processing software that include the basic headings (TO, FROM, DATE, SUBJECT) to guide the writer in providing the needed transmittal information. Memos may be printed on memo forms, plain paper, or letterhead depending on the preference of the company. Follow the guidelines for formatting a memo illustrated here.

Memo Format

- **Heading**

- **Body**

- **Enclosure notation**

Litton Best Foods, Inc.
6285 Northwest Blvd.   Laurel, MS 37450
(800)734-5291 Fax: (713)555-9214

Begin 2" from top of page or 1/2" below letterhead

TO: Erin W. Lutzel, Vice President

FROM: Isako Kimura, Marketing Director IK

DATE: July 15, 2008

SUBJECT: Marketing Activity Report, June 2008

Tap Enter 1 time

The marketing division reports the following activities for June.

Tap Enter 1 time

Advertising

Three meetings were held with representatives at the Bart and Dome agency to complete plans for the fall campaign for Fluffy Buns. The campaign will concentrate on the use of discount coupons published in the Thursday food section of sixty daily newspapers in the Pacific states. Coupons will be released on the second and fourth Thursdays in June and July.

Estimated cost of the program is $645,000. That amount includes 2.2 million redeemed coupons at 20 cents each ($440,000).

A point-of-sale advertising display, shown on the attached sheet, was developed for retail grocery outlets. Sales reps are pushing these in their regular and new calls. The display may be used to feature a different product from our line on a weekly basis.

Sales Staff

We have dropped one sales rep from the northern California section and divided the area between the southern Oregon and Sacramento reps.

Call me should you wish to discuss the information presented.

Attachment

- Omits courtesy titles in informal document.

- Includes writer's written initials.

- Keys subject line in mixed case or all capitals for added emphasis.

- Uses headings to divide message into easy-to-read sections.

- Uses single spaced, unindented, paragraphs and left justified margins for easy reading.

References (APA Version)

The *references* page located at the end of your document contains an alphabetized list of the sources used in preparing a report, with each entry containing publication information necessary for locating the source. A researcher often uses sources that provide information but do not result in citations. If you want to acknowledge that you have consulted these works and provide the reader with a comprehensive reading list, include these sources in the list of references and refer to your list as *Bibliography*. Your company guidelines may specify whether to list works cited only or works consulted. If you receive no definitive guidelines, use your own judgment. If in doubt, include all literature cited and read, and label the page with the appropriate title so that the reader clearly understands the nature of the list.

To aid the reader in locating sources in lengthy bibliographies, you may include subheadings denoting the types of publications documented; for example, books, articles, unpublished documents and papers, government publications, and websites. Check your reference manual to determine if subheadings are allowed.

Formats for Print and Recorded References

Reference styles for a variety of print and recorded sources prepared using the APA style are shown in Figure 1. Note that the following rules apply for APA references.

Indention and spacing	Begin first line of each entry at left margin and indent subsequent lines one-half inch. Paragraph indent is also permitted. While the APA style manual specifies double spacing within and between entries, common practice in preparing reports is to single space each entry and double space between entries.
Author names	List last names first for all authors. Use initials for first and middle names. Use an ampersand (&) before final author's last name.
Date	Place date in parentheses after author name(s). Months are spelled out.
Capitalization	In titles of books and articles, capitalize only first word of title, first word of subtitle, and proper names. All other words begin with lowercase letters. In titles of periodicals, capitalize all significant words.
Italicizing and quotation marks	Italicize titles of books, journals, and other periodicals, as well as periodical volume numbers. Do not use quotation marks around titles of articles.
Page notations	Use p. or pp. with page numbers for newspapers only.

Formats for Electronic References

Referencing Internet and other electronic sources can be somewhat challenging, since electronic information and publication environments continue to evolve. Figure 2 shows some examples of electronic referencing styles. The American Psychological Association offers an online update to its style manual that is amended regularly and provides guidelines for citing and referencing electronic sources; see **http://www.apastyle.org/elecref.html**.

A number of additional websites are available that provide information about electronic citations in various styles. One of the more comprehensive ones is the OWL site developed by Purdue University, which also provides general guidelines for using APA style and referencing various types of sources. You can access this site at **http://owl.english.purdue.edu/owl/resource/560/01/**.

When referencing an electronic source, include as many of the following items as possible:

1. Author (if given)
2. Date of publication
3. Title of article and/or name of publication
4. Electronic medium (such as online or CD-ROM)
5. Volume; series; page, section, or paragraph; and Internet address
6. Date you retrieved or accessed the resource

Figure 1 Guide to Preparing References for Print and Recorded Sources in APA (5th Edition) Style

Book reference with subtitle and two authors
Meshel, J. W., & Garr, D. (2005). *One phone call away: Secrets of a master networker*. New York: Penguin Group.

Edited book
Webster, S., & Connolly, F. W. (Eds.). (2003). *The ethics kit*. New York: McGraw Hill.

Chapter in a book or section within a reference book
Clark, J. L., & Clark, L. R. (2006). Electronic messaging. In How 11: *A handbook for professionals* (11th ed., pp. 285–300). Mason, OH: South-Western College Publishing.
Standard & Poor's. (2006). Unisys Corporation. In *Standard & Poor's standard corporation descriptions* (p. 439). New York: Author.

Report, brochure, or book from a private organization, corporate author
Wal-Mart Stores, Inc. (2007). *Annual report*. Bentonville, AR: Author.
Asahi Japan Collectibles. (2006). *Communication habits of Americans and Japanese*. [Brochure]. Kensington, CT: Author.
Note: When author and publisher are identical, use Author as name of publisher.

Article in a scholarly journal with separate pagination for each issue
Moe, W. W. (2006). A field experiment to assess the interruption effect of pop-up promotions. *Journal of Interactive Marketing, 20*(1), 34–44.
Note: 20(1) signifies volume 20, issue 1; volume number is italicized or underlined along with publication title.

Article in a scholarly journal with multiple authors and continuous pagination (page numbers do not start over with each issue)
Kirkman, B. L., Rosen, B., Tesluk, P. E., & Gibson, C. B. (2006). Enhancing the transfer of computer-assisted proficiency in geographically distributed teams. *Journal of Applied Psychology, 91*, 706–716.
Note: After the sixth author's name, use et al. to indicate remaining authors. Issue number is omitted when page numbers continue across issues.

Periodical article without an author
On hold. (2006, August 8). *PC Magazine, 25*, 20.
Note: For magazines, include volume number, but not issue.

Article in a newspaper
Solnik, C. (2005, July 29). Events that will float your boat. *Long Island Business News*, p. B47.
Note: For newspapers, include p. or pp. with page number(s).

Government publication
U.S. Department of Education. (2006). *Federal student financial aid handbook*. (Report No. ED 1.45/4:998-99). Office of Student Financial Assistance. Washington, DC: Student Financial Assistance Programs.

Unpublished interviews, memos, and letters
Note: Do not include in reference list; cite in text only. Example: . . . internal communications at NASA have improved (J. D. Arceneaux, personal communication, July 9, 2007).

Computer software
Practica Musica 5 [Computer software]. (2006). Redmond, WA: Ars Nova Software, LLC.
Note: Reference entries are not needed for standard off-the-shelf software such as Microsoft Word, Java, Adobe, SAS, or SPSS. Do provide reference entries for specialized software. If an individual has proprietary rights, name him/her as the author; otherwise, treat as unauthored. Names of software, programs, or languages are not italicized.

Films, filmstrips, slide programs, and video recordings
Breaking the barriers: Improving communication skills [CD-ROM]. (2006). Princeton: Films for the Humanities and Sciences.

Figure 2 Guide to Preparing References for Electronic Sources in APA (5th edition) Style

Article from an organization's website
Microsoft Corporation. (2005, October 25). Windows XP and Office XP: Collaborate in real time to perfect a presentation. Redmond, WA: Microsoft Corporation. Retrieved July 27, 2006, from http://www.microsoft.com/windowsxp/officexp/messenger.asp

Article from online periodical
Pirttiaho, L. (2003). Sound engineering practices and ethics in technology business. Electronic Journal of Business Ethics and Organization Studies, 8(1). Retrieved July 29, 2006, from http://ejbo.jyu.fi/index.cgi?page=articles/0701_3

Article from online database
January, J. (2006, April). Simple best practices for podcasts. B to B, 91(4), 52. Retrieved July 29, 2006, from Business & Company Resource Center database.

Article on CD
Microsoft Corporation. (2003). Fiber optics. Encarta Encyclopedia Plus 2003 [CD-ROM]. Redmond, WA: Author.

Message posted to online forum or discussion group
Bridges, K. (2007, August 1). Top ten rules of international communication. Discussions on international business communication [Msg 20]. Message posted to http://groups.yahoo.com/group/internationalcommunication/message/31

Email message
Note: Email is treated as a personal communication and, therefore, not cited in the reference list. The format in text is as follows: DuFrene (personal communication, January 23, 2007) said . . . .

References Styles (MLA Version)

A number of widely used reference styles are available for documenting the sources of information used in report writing. Two of the more popular style manuals for business writing are as follows:

Publication Manual of the American Psychological Association, 5th ed., Washington, DC: American Psychological Association, 2001.

Joseph Gibaldi, *MLA Handbook for Writers of Research Papers*, 6th ed., New York: Modern Languages Association of America, 2003. The *MLA Handbook* is designed for high school and undergraduate college students; the *MLA Style Manual and Guide to Scholarly Publishing*, 2nd ed. (1998) is designed for graduate students, scholars, and professional writers.

These sources, commonly referred to as the APA and MLA styles, provide general rules for referencing and give examples of the citation formats for various types of source materials. This style card reflects the rules along with examples for the MLA style. Whenever you are not required to use a particular documentation style, choose a recognized one and follow it consistently. Occasionally, you may need to reference something for which no general example applies. Choose the example that is most like your source and follow that format. When in doubt, provide more information, not less. Remember that a major purpose for listing references is to enable readers to retrieve and use the sources. This style card illustrates citation formats for some common types of information sources and refers you to various electronic sites that provide further detailed guidelines for preparing electronic citations.

In-Text Parenthetical Citations

The *MLA Handbook* supports the use of **in-text citations.** Abbreviated information within parentheses in the text directs the reader to a list of sources at the end of a report. The list of sources at the end contains all bibliographic information on each source cited in a report. This list is arranged alphabetically by the author's last name or, if no author is provided, by the first word of the title.

The in-text citations contain minimal information needed to locate the source in the complete list. The *MLA style* includes the author's last name and the page number for both quotes and paraphrases, but not the date of publication. Note the format of the in-text parenthetical citations shown below.

One author not named in the text, direct quotation

"A recent survey . . . shows that more and more companies plan to publish their annual reports on the Internet" (Prinn 13).

Direct quotation, no page number on source

According to James, "traditional college students have a perspective that is quite different from adult consumers"
Use par. 2 in place of missing page number only if paragraphs are numbered in original text.

Multiple authors for sources not named in the text wording

Globalization is becoming a continuous challenge for managers . . . (Tang and Crofford 29).
"For all its difficulty, teamwork is still essential . . ." (Nunamaker et al. 163).
For sources by more than three authors, use et al. after the last name of the first author or include all last names. Do not underline or italicize et al.

More than one source documenting the same idea

. . . companies are turning to micromarketing (Heath 48; Roach 54).

More than one source by the same author documenting the same idea

Past research (Taylor, "Performance Appraisal" 6, "Frequent Absenteeism" 89) shows . . .

Reference to author(s) or date in the text wording

Kent Spalding and Brian Price documented the results . . .
In 2006, West concluded . . . (E2).
Omit a page number when citing a one-page article or nonprint source.

No author provided

. . . virtues of teamwork look obvious ("Teams Triumph in Creative Solutions" 61).
Include full title or shortened version of it.

Works Cited

The **works cited** page located at the end of your document contains an alphabetized list of the sources used in preparing a report, with each entry containing publication information necessary for locating the source. A researcher often uses sources that provide information but do not result in citations. If you want to acknowledge that you have consulted these works and provide the reader with a comprehensive reading list, include these sources in the list of works cited and refer to list as Works Consulted. Your company guidelines may specify whether to list works cited only or works consulted. If you receive no definitive guidelines, use your own judgment. If in doubt, include all literature cited and read, and label the page with the appropriate title so that the reader clearly understands the nature of the list.

To aid the reader in locating sources in lengthy bibliographies, you may include several subheadings denoting the types of publications documented, for example, books, articles, unpublished documents and papers, government publications, and nonprint media. Check your reference manual to determine if subheadings are allowed.

Formats for Print and Recorded References

Reference styles for a variety of print and recorded sources prepared using the MLA style are shown in the box at the bottom of this side. Note that the following rules apply for MLA works cited.

Indention and spacing	Begin first line of each entry at at left margin and indent subsequent lines one-half inch. While the MLA style manual specifies double spacing within and between entries, common practice in preparing reports is to single space each entry and double space between entries.
Author names	List last name first for first author only. Use "and" before final author's name.
Date	Place date at end of citation for books and after periodical title and volume for articles. Months are abbreviated.
Capitalization	In titles of books, periodicals, and article titles, capitalize all main words.
Italicizing and quotation marks	Italicize titles of books, journals, and periodicals (or underline if directed). Place titles of articles within quotation marks.
Page notations	Omit the use of p. or pp. on all citations.

MLA (6th Edition Style)

Writer's Last Name   5

Works Cited

"Best Business Attire." Executive Communications Group. 2003. 30 May 2006 <http://ecglink.com>.

Brody, Mary. "Dress codes: 'Business Conservative' is Making a Comeback." *HR Briefing* 1 Mar. 2003: 7.

Egodigwe, Laura, and Sonya Alleyne. "Here Come the Suits." *Black Enterprise* Mar. 2003: 59–60.

Hudson, Repps. "'Business Casual' on the Wane." *St. Louis Post Dispatch* 15 Apr. 2002. 30 May 2006 <http://seattlepi.nwsource.com>.

Jones, Clark. "Experts Discuss Ways to Dress in Business Attire for Summer." *Las Vegas Review* 8 June 2003.

Business and Company Resource Center. University of Houston Lib. 29 July 2006 <http:bcrc.college.com/>.

Koestner, Maury. "What Exactly is Business Casual?" *The News-Herald* 7 May 2005.

General Businessfile. Texas A & M lib. 31 May 2006 <http://www.epnet.com/>.

Molloy, John T. "Executives Find as Dress Gets Sloppier, Attitudes Slip." *The Houston Chronicle* 9 December 2005: D2.

White, Ronald. D. "Clashing Dress Styles." *Careerbuilder* 26 Aug. 2001. 12 June 2006 <http://www.latimes.com>.

Email Format

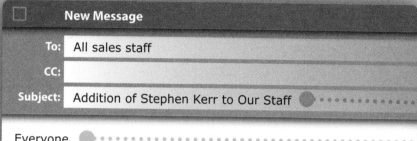

New Message

To: All sales staff

CC:

Subject: Addition of Stephen Kerr to Our Staff ·········· • **Includes descriptive subject line.**

Everyone, • ············· • **Includes appropriate salutation for group of coworkers.**

I'm pleased to announce the appointment of Stephen Kerr as communications specialist in the corporate communications department. He will fill the position vacated by Kenneth Shaw and will begin work on May 6.

FYI, Steve comes to us from Gynco Industries, where he was in charge of mass media relations. His duties with us will include long-range planning and acting as liaison with our ad agency. He has degrees in public relations and marketing.

• **Uses emoticon and email abbreviation in informal message to coworkers who understand and approve of this shorthand.**

Steve merits your full support. We wish him much success and extend a sincere welcome to our organization. :-)

Thanks,

Jenny

Jenny Veitch, Vice President of Operations
Franklin Corporation
875 Marshall Freeway, Suite 4500
Atlanta, GA 30304
(404) 555-3000, Extension 6139 Fax: (404) 555-9759

• **Includes signature file that identifies writer.**

Format Pointers
Includes single spaced, unindented paragraphs and short lines for complete screen display.

Uses mixed case for easy reading.

Keeps format simple for quick download and compatibility.

Email Format

While certain email formats are standard, some degree of flexibility exists in formatting email messages. Primarily, be certain your message is easy to read and represents the standards of formality that your company has set. The following guidelines and the model email illustrated above will assist you in formatting professional email messages:

- ***Include an appropriate salutation and closing.*** You might write "Dear" and the person's name or simply the person's first name when messaging someone for the first time. Casual expressions such as "Hi" and "Later" are appropriate for personal messages but not serious business email. A closing of "Sincerely" is considered quite formal for email messages; instead, a simple closing such as "best wishes" or "thank you" provides a courteous end to your message.

- ***Include a signature file at the end of the message.*** The signature file (known as a .sig) contains a few lines of text that include your full name and title, mailing address, telephone number, and any other information you want people to know about you. You might include a clever quote that you update frequently.

- ***Format for easy readability.*** Following these suggestions:
  - Limit each message to one screen to minimize scrolling. If you need more space, consider a short email message with a lengthier message attached as a word processing file. Be certain the recipient can receive and read the attachment.

- Limit the line length to 60 characters so that the entire line is displayed on the monitor without scrolling.
- Use short, unindented paragraphs. Separate paragraphs with an extra space.
- Use mixed case for easy reading. Typing in all capital letters is perceived as shouting in email and considered rude online behavior.
- Emphasize a word or phrase by surrounding it with quotation marks or keying in uppercase letters.
- *Use emoticons or email abbreviations in moderation when you believe the receiver will understand and approve.* *Emoticons*, created by keying combinations of symbols to produce "sideways" faces, are a shorthand way of lightening the mood, adding emotion to email messages, and attempting to compensate for nonverbal cues lost in one-way communication:

| :-) | smiling, indicates humor or sarcasm | %-(| confused |
| :-(| frowning, indicates sadness or anger | :-O | surprised |

Alternately, you might put a "g" (for grin) or "smile" in parentheses after something that is obviously meant as tongue-in-cheek to help carry the intended message to the receiver. Abbreviations for commonly used phrases save space and avoid unnecessary keying. Popular ones include BCNU (be seeing you), BTW (by the way), FYI (for your information), FWIW (for what it's worth), HTH (hope this helps), IMHO (in my humble opinion), and LOL (laugh out loud).

Some email users feel strongly that emoticons and abbreviations are childish or inappropriate for serious email and decrease productivity when the receiver must take time for deciphering. Before using them, be certain the receiver will understand them and that the formality of the message and your relationship with the receiver justify this type of informal exchange. Then, use only in moderation to *punctuate* your message.

Good Example of an Email Message

New Message

To:	Rodney Spurlin, Software Compliance Officer
From:	Claire Henderson, Director of Legal Services
Subject:	Legal Liability for Downloaded Music

Rodney,

Your immediate attention is needed to address the company's liability for employees' downloading copyrighted music.

The recording industry has announced its intent to prosecute organizations that allow their employees to download and store music files without proper authorization. This threat is real; one company has already agreed to a $1 million settlement.

The Recording Industry Association of America and the Motion Picture Association of America recently sent a six-page brochure to Fortune 1000 corporations. Please review the suggested corporate policies and sample communication to employees and determine whether you believe our corporation is at risk.

Please contact me when you are ready to discuss potential changes to our corporate code of conduct. I'll be online all week if you want to instant message once you've reviewed the brochure.

Later,

Claire

- *Provides subject line that is meaningful to reader and writer.*

- *Includes salutation and closing to personalize message.*

Format Pointers
Composes short, concise message limited to one idea and one screen.

Good Example of an Apology

New Message

To: Allen Melton <amelton@meltonpr.com>

CC:

Subject: Yesterday's Advertising Presentation

Allen:

Please accept my apology for the inconvenience you experienced yesterday because of the unavailability of computer equipment. Fortunately, you saved the day with your backup transparencies and gave an effective presentation of the new advertising campaign.

The next time you make a presentation at our company, I'll be sure to schedule the LGI room. This room has the latest technology to support multimedia presentations. Just call and let me know the date.

Later,

Thomas Lee Raferty
Administrative Assistant

- States the apology briefly without providing an overly specific description of the error.

- Reports measures taken to avoid repetition of such incidents, which strengthens the credibility of the apology.

- Closes with a positive statement.

Format Pointers

Limits the message to a single idea—the apology.

Composes a short, concise message that fits on one screen.

Includes a salutation and closing to personalize the message.

Good Example of an Appreciation Message

- Extends appreciation for employee's efforts to improve departmental communication.

- Provides specific evidence of worth of experience without exaggerating or using overly strong language or mechanical statements.

- Assures writer of tangible benefits to be gained from the training session.

Format Pointers
Uses short lines, mixed case; omits special formatting such as emoticons and email abbreviations for improved readability.

New Message

To: Ellen Meyer <emeyer@techno.com>

From: Martha Riggins <mriggins@techno.com>

Subject: Appreciation for Outstanding Contribution

Ellen,

Thank you for spearheading the initiative to improve interpersonal communication within the office and for arranging for the training sessions to achieve that goal. It was a big commitment on your part in addition to your regular duties.

Your efforts are already paying off. I have observed the techniques we learned in the training sessions being used in the department on several occasions already. In times of uncertainty, anxiety can often spill over into people's professional lives, so the seminar was very timely in helping to ensure a collaborative and civil workplace where everyone is treated respectfully.

You have proven yourself a dedicated and insightful employee, a true asset to the continued success of our organization.

Best regards,
Martha

Developing the Components of a Bad-News Message

Audited financial statements will improve your ability to negotiate contracts with suppliers, banks, and customers, as well as provide your stockholders with confidence regarding their investment. For this reason, the auditor you select must be capable of providing quality audit services.

To eliminate the appearance of a conflict of interest, Rule 101 of the AICPA Code of Professional Conduct requires auditors to be independent of their clients. One of our audit partners, Patrick Rackley, is a significant stockholder in the First National Bank, which currently has loaned a large amount of money to your company. Because of this indirect financial interest, we recommend that you seek another firm to perform the 2006 financial statement audit.

Since the independence rule applies only to audits of financial statements, we are available to provide other professional services. Our tax accountants are ready to assist you in finding methods to reduce your income tax liability. Please call me at 501-555-1245 to discuss these services.

Note the closing paragraph is a positive, forward-looking statement that includes sales promotion of other services the accounting firm can offer.

- **Begins with statement with which both can agree. Sets stage for reasons by presenting importance of quality audit.**
- **Reveals subject of message and transitions into reasons.**
- **Provides rule from authoritative literature to support refusal and clearly applies the rule to situation.**
- **States refusal positively and clearly using complex sentence and positive language.**
- **Includes counterproposal as alternative.**
- **Closes with sales promotion for other services inferring a continuing business relationship.**

Party Time
Unlimited

2937 Fox Cove Lane ☖ **Conway PA 76032-2937 (501) 555-1129 Fax (501) 555-3900**

June 3, 2008

Ms. Dena Marcum
Accounting and Budget
SPL Industries
7821 South Third Street
Conway, AR 72032-7839

Dear Ms. Marcum:

PartyTime Limited was pleased to be part of your staff/alumni banquet and
appreciated your staff's compliments on the quality of the food, service, and
decorations.

You are correct that the amount of the invoice is more than the price
specified by the contract. The contract price was based on the 250-guest
estimate provided by your administrative assistant. The estimate considered
the amount of food to be served and the number of servers required to serve
250 guests, as well as the cost of decorating the banquet hall.

Your invoice includes an additional $200 for the cost of food served to the 25
unexpected guests of your alumni. Although we typically prepare extra food
for large, formal affairs such as yours, we did not anticipate the large number
of additional guests that arrived that evening. I was relieved our staff was
able to obtain additional food from our warehouse to serve these guests.

Had these 25 guests been included in the original estimate, we would have
added $200 to the food cost estimate. We would also have included $80 for
the cost of two additional servers. Although we were short-handed, our staff
provided your guests with quality service. Your invoice does not include any
additional charges for service.

Ms. Marcum, as you begin planning festivities for the upcoming holidays,
keep our famous specialty desserts in mind for an extraordinary change from
the traditional catered turkey lunch.

Sincerely,

Jared Harrelson
Jared Harrelson
Manager

- Begins with a statement with
  which the reader can agree to
  get the message off to a good
  start.

- Presents a clear explanation
  for the additional charge.

- Continues the explanation.

- Uses the subjunctive mood to
  de-emphasize the refusal.

- Shifts emphasis away from
  the refusal by presenting sales
  promotion on other services.

Format Pointer
*Illustrates block format—all
lines begin at the left margin.*

Good Example of a Persuasive Claim

GOOD

VideoSolutions
A leader in entertainment video production

3109 Overlook Terrace / Beverly Hills, CA 90213-8120 / (213) 555-3120 Fax (213) 555-3129

May 20, 2008

Mr. Chris Ragan
Creative Director
Harrelson Producers
3674 Elmhurst Avenue
Los Angeles, CA 90052-3674

Dear Chris

When Thunderbolt negotiated with your firm to produce our first music video, we were impressed with the clips of other Harrelson videos and your proven performance record. Especially intriguing to us was your video of the Indigos, with its subtle use of symbolism in the graphic images along with creative shots of the musicians.

In our meeting with your creative team, we focused on the methods used in the Indigos video and specifically asked for graphic symbolism juxtaposed with shots of the band. After viewing the first draft of our video, we find the level of artistic expression disappointing. This video closely resembles a concert tape, focusing primarily on live-concert footage of the band and will have little appeal with our customers, the MTV set, who demand innovative and exciting new approaches in entertainment.

With Harrelson's reputation for creative productions, we are confident the video can be revised to meet our expectations. The band will do its part to assist in reshooting footage and will meet with the creative director at a mutually convenient time to discuss the kind of graphic imagery appropriate for interpreting our music and its message. Please call me at 555-3920 to schedule this meeting.

Sincerely

Cole Gallant

Cole Gallant
General Manager

- **Seeks attention by giving sincere compliment that reveals subject of message.**
- **Continues central appeal—commitment to creative production—while providing needed details.**
- **Presents reasoning that leads to request and subtle reminder of central appeal.**
- **Connects specific request with firm's commitment to develop creative productions.**

Legal and Ethical Considerations Uses letter rather than less formal email format to emphasize importance of these differences regarding contractual agreement.

Down-Home Restaurants

83 South Pass Road • Chattanooga TN 37426-2723 • (423) 555-5320

March 15, 2008

Mrs. Joyce Smith
976 Thompson Road
Crossville, TN 38555-0976

Dear Mrs. Smith:

Meeting you and touring the building on your property last week was a pleasure. That little building provided me with a fascinating glimpse of the past. You must have found it convenient using the building as a big "attic," storing all your canned goods and old farm implements over the years.

As the manager of the Down-Home Barbeque in Mena, I am constantly looking for items to build and display in our restaurants. Our restaurants are constructed of weathered wood to create a genuine rustic atmosphere, which we think complements our "down-home" menu.

As I toured your building, I couldn't help but notice some of the unique items inside and the old weathered boards hanging outside. The wood from the building and its contents would enable us to build and furnish a new restaurant in Clarksville and refurbish our Jackson location. Marc Lane, owner of Down-Home Restaurants, has asked me to extend you the offer explained in the enclosed proposal.

Naturally, no amount of money can compensate you for a building that holds so many memories for you. However, we would be happy to purchase the entire contents of the building, excluding any special items of sentimental value that you may want to keep.

Although the thought of selling the building may sadden you, think of the "second life" that the old farm equipment, dishes, washboards, seed bags, and weathered boards would have in our restaurants. People who would otherwise never see such Americana will have the opportunity to learn a little about its rich past.

After you have reviewed the proposal, please call me at 555-3253 to discuss our offer to display your treasures in our restaurants.

Sincerely,

Karla Ash

Karla Ash, Manager
Chattanooga Store

Enclosure

- Opens with a compliment that introduces an appeal to the owner's pride in the old property.

- Introduces the writer's interest in acquiring property and continues the primary appeal (desire to preserve the past).

- Offsets reluctance to sell by acknowledging the sentimental value and suggesting options.

- Stresses benefits of selling property in terms of the primary appeal.

- Connects the specific request for action with the reward for saying "Yes."

Format Pointers
Illustrates modified block format—the date and closing lines (complimentary close and signature block) begin at the horizontal center.

Uses mixed punctuation—a colon follows the salutation, and a comma follows the complimentary close.

Uses an enclosure notation to alert the reader that something is included.

Rough Draft of a Letter, Excerpt

September 14, 2007

FAX Transmission

Mr. Brent M. Weinberg
Production Manager
Worldwide Enterprises, Inc.
1635 Taylor Road
Baltimore, ~~Maryland~~ *MD* 21225-~~1635~~

Dear Mr. W~~i~~enberg:

With your proven ability to produce precision-quality electronic parts, our entrance into the DVD market is certain to be successful. *We're excited about other ways our companies can benefit through sharing our expertise.*

One of the objectives of our recent merger ~~are~~ *is* to increase your competitiveness by updating your information systems. The first step of this process is to form a steering committee ~~whose rudimentary~~ *The committee's primary* function is to direct the development of the new system and to ensure that it incorporates the information needs of the user and the organization. To accomplish this goal, committee members must represent inventory control, shipping, purchasing, accounting, and marketing, ~~Further, the group must~~ *(a)* consist of members from a variety of organizational levels, and ~~members must~~ *(c)* possess varying degrees of computer proficiency. *(b)*

Brent, because of your knowledge of company operations, we ~~need~~ *is essential* your input. Your serving on this committee will be clear ~~tangible~~ evidence of management's commitment to this significant change. Please ~~advise~~ *let* me ~~whether or not~~ *know by September 30 that* you will serve on the Information Systems Steering Committee. A meeting will be scheduled as soon as all members have been selected.

- Adds mailing notation.
- Uses two-letter state abbreviation.
- Corrects spelling of name.
- Adds a smooth transition to next paragraph.
- Corrects grammatical error.
- Replaces with simple word for clarity.
- Divides into two sentences to enhance readability.
- Enumerates list for emphasis and reduces wordiness.
- Recasts from receiver's viewpoint.
- Inserts comma to separate compound adjectives.
- Eliminates cliché and includes specific action ending.
- Eliminates redundancy.
- Corrects grammatical error.

Errors Undetectable by Spell-Check
Verify spelling of receiver's name, "Weinberg."

Correct word substitutions: "to" for "too" and "your" for "you."

Contrast the Readability and Appeal of Bulky Versus Broken Text

New Message

To: All employees
From: JoNell Lewis, HR Manager
Subject: Training Available through Podcasts

Can you image the convenience of upgrading your management skills as you make the daily commute to your office? It's possible with podcast training set to begin this week with an intriguing segment on leadership communication. All required training seminars, previously available via streaming video over the company intranet, are now available to be downloaded to your iPod. To encourage you to take advantage of this innovative learning method, you can purchase the latest generation iPod for $100—a substantial discount to the retail price. Simply order directly from the vendor's website and input LC413 for the discount code. Call technology support should you need assistance in downloading your first podcast. When you're not advancing your management skills to the next level, use your iPod to enjoy your favorite tunes and movies.

New Message

To: All employees
From: JoNell Lewis, HR Manager
Subject: Training Available through Podcasts

Can you image the convenience of upgrading your management skills as you make the daily commute to your office? It's possible with podcast training set to begin this week with an intriguing segment on leadership communication.

All required training seminars, previously available via streaming video over the company intranet, are now available to be downloaded to your iPod. To encourage you to take advantage of this innovative learning method, you can purchase the latest generation iPod for $100—a substantial discount to the retail price. Simply order directly from the vendor's website and input LC413 for the discount code.

Call technology support should you need assistance in downloading your first podcast. When you're not advancing your management skills to the next level, use your iPod to enjoy your favorite tunes and movies.

Passive Voice	Active Voice
The documentation was prepared by the systems analyst.	The systems analyst prepared the documentation.
The loan approval procedures were revised by the loan officer.	The loan officer revised the loan approval procedures.

Wordy	Concise
She <u>took</u> the Internet marketing course and <u>passed</u> it.	She <u>passed</u> the Internet marketing course.
The editor <u>checked</u> the advertisement and found three glaring errors.	The editor <u>found</u> three glaring errors in the advertisement.

Negative Tone	Positive Tone
<u>Don't forget</u> to submit your time and expense report.	Remember to submit your time and expense report.
We <u>cannot</u> ship your order until you send us full specifications.	You will receive your order as soon as you send us full specifications.
You <u>neglected</u> to indicate the specifications for Part No. 332-3.	Please send specifications for Part No. 332-3 so your order can be finalized.

Example of an Effective Questionnaire

- Uses variety of items to elicit different types of responses.

- Uses clear, concise language to minimize confusion.

- Provides clear instructions for answering each item.

- Provides additional lines to allow for individual opinions.

- Provides even number of rating choices to eliminate "fence" responses.

- Asks for easily recalled information.

- Provides nonoverlapping categories of response and open-ended final category.

Format Pointers
Provides adequate space for answering open-ended item.

Keeps length as short as possible while meeting survey objectives.

Includes instructions for submitting completed questionnaire.

---

1. **Rank the following job factors in order of their importance to you. Add other factors important to you in the space provided.**

		1	2	3	4	5	6	7
a.	Wages	○	○	○	○	○	○	○
b.	Health and retirement benefits	○	○	○	○	○	○	○
c.	Job security	○	○	○	○	○	○	○
d.	Ability to maintain balance between work and family life	○	○	○	○	○	○	○
e.	Creativity and challenge of work assignment	○	○	○	○	○	○	○
f.	Perceived prestige of work	○	○	○	○	○	○	○
g.		○	○	○	○	○	○	○
h.		○	○	○	○	○	○	○

2. **Which of the following is the single job satisfaction factor that you feel needs more attention in our company? (Please select only one.)**
   - ○ Wages
   - ○ Health and retirement benefits
   - ○ Job security
   - ○ Ability to maintain balance between work and family life
   - ○ Creativity and challenge of work assignment
   - ○ Perceived prestige of work
   - ○ Other (specify) [_____▼]

3. **How would you rate your overall job satisfaction?**

Very unsatisfied 1	Somewhat dissatisfied 2	Neutral 3	Somewhat satisfied 4	Satisfied 5	Very satisfied 6
○	○	○	○	○	○

4. **How would you rate your overall job satisfaction 12 months ago?**

Very unsatisfied 1	Somewhat dissatisfied 2	Neutral 3	Somewhat satisfied 4	Satisfied 5	Very satisfied 6
○	○	○	○	○	○

5. **Indicate your age group:**
   - ○ 20–29
   - ○ 30–39
   - ○ 40–49
   - ○ 50–59
   - ○ 60–69
   - ○ 70 years and over

6. **Indicate your time with the company:**
   - ○ Less than 1 year
   - ○ 1–3 years
   - ○ 4–6 years
   - ○ 7–10 years
   - ○ Over 10 years

7. **What could the company do to enhance your satisfaction as a company employee?**

   [_____]

   Thanks for your participation. Click to submit your questionnaire.

   [Submit]

Sample References in APA (5th Edition) Style

References

Barlow, J. (2000, May 7). Intranet replaces office grapevine. Houston Chronicle, Business, p.1.

Bartlett, J. E. (1998). Using an intranet in business education. In Integrating the intranet into the business curriculum, 1998: NBEA Yearbook, No. 36, pp. 139–147. Reston, VA: National Business Education Association.

Curtin, C., & Canterucci, J. (1997, February). Getting off to a good start on intranets. Training & Development, 42–46.

Greengard, S. (1998, September). Ten ways to protect intranet data. Workforce, 78–82.

Holtz, S. (2003). The intranet advantage. San Francisco: International Association of Business Communicators.

Intranet Road Map. (2003). Growth of intranet development. Retrieved April 16, 2004, from http://www.intranetroadmap.com/growth.cfm

Lampron, F. (2003, January). Intranet development requires teamwork: Before rollout, make sure tech support can handle employee self-service glitches. HR Magazine, 48(1), 67(3). Retrieved April 16, 2004, from Business Source Premier database.

Marlow, E. (1997). Web visions: An inside look at successful business strategies on the Net. New York: Van Nostrand Reinhold.

McCluskey-Moore, N. (2000). Untangling Web content management. Intranet Journal. Retrieved April 16, 2004, from http://www.intranetjournal.com/articles/200004/im_04_18_00a.html

Murray, W. E. (2002, October 10). Empowering staff through the intranet. New Media Age, 21. Retrieved April 16, 2004, from InfoTrac College database.

National Computer Security Center. (1985). Personal computer security considerations. (Report No. NCSC-WA-002-85). Fort Meade, MD: NCSC.

Guide to Preparing In-Text Citations in APA (5th Edition) Style

One author not named in the text, direct quotation
"A recent survey . . . shows that more and more companies plan to publish their annual reports on the Internet" (Prinn, 2006, p. 13).
Include page number only when referencing a direct quotation. Precede page numbers with p. (one page) or pp.(multiple pages).

Direct quotation, no page number on source
"Traditional college students have a perspective that is quite different from adult consumers" (James, 2006, Discussion and Conclusions section, ¶2).

Multiple authors for sources not named in the text wording
Globalization is becoming a continuous challenge for managers . . . (Tang & Crofford, 2005).
"For all its difficulty, teamwork is still essential . . ." (Nunamaker et al., 2006, p. 163).
For works by six or more authors, use et al. after the last name of the first author. For works by fewer than six authors, cite all authors the first time the work is referenced; use the first author's last name and et al. for subsequent references. Do not underline or italicize et al.

More than one source documenting the same idea
. . . companies are turning to micro-marketing (Heath, 2005; Roach, 2004).

More than one source by the same author documenting the same idea
Past research (Taylor, 2001, 2005) indicated . . .

Reference to author(s) or datein the text wording
Spalding and Price (2005) documented the results . . .
In 2006, West concluded . . .

No author provided
. . . virtues of teamwork look obvious ("Teams Triumph," 2005).
Include first two or three words of title, placed in quotation marks.

One of two or more works by the same author(s) in the same year
Zuidema and Kleiner (2004a) advocated . . .
Assign a, b, c, etc. after year.

Effective Table Layout, Identifying Information, Labels, and Source

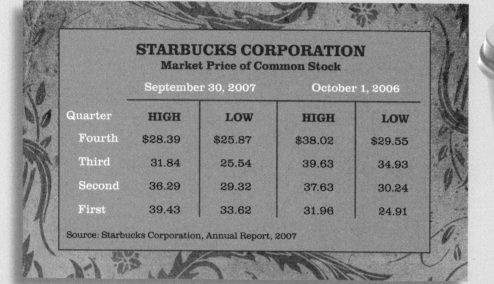

STARBUCKS CORPORATION
Market Price of Common Stock

Quarter	September 30, 2007		October 1, 2006	
	HIGH	LOW	HIGH	LOW
Fourth	$28.39	$25.87	$38.02	$29.55
Third	31.84	25.54	39.63	34.93
Second	36.29	29.32	37.63	30.24
First	39.43	33.62	31.96	24.91

Source: Starbucks Corporation, Annual Report, 2007

© D. Hurst/Alamy

Simple Bar Chart (Horizontal)

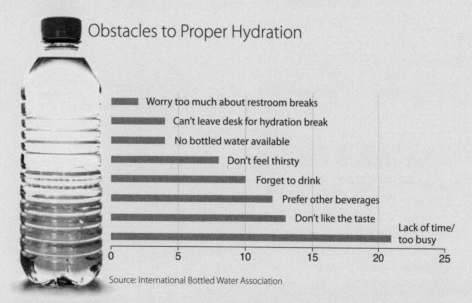

Obstacles to Proper Hydration

Worry too much about restroom breaks
Can't leave desk for hydration break
No bottled water available
Don't feel thirsty
Forget to drink
Prefer other beverages
Don't like the taste
Lack of time/ too busy

0   5   10   15   20   25

Source: International Bottled Water Association

Grouped Bar Chart (Vertical)

Selected Cell Phone Features Gaining in Popularity

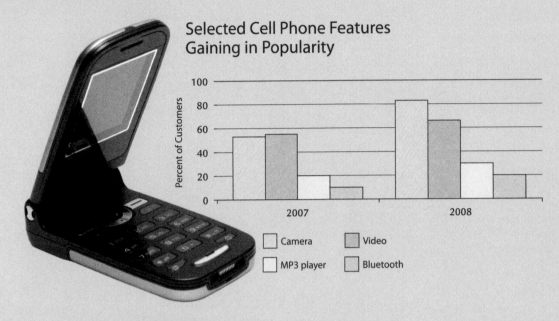

- ☐ Camera
- ☐ Video
- ☐ MP3 player
- ☐ Bluetooth

Segmented Bar Chart

McDonald's Achieves Consistent Revenue
Growth in Primary International Markets

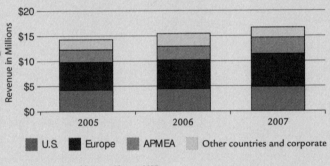

- ■ U.S.
- ■ Europe
- ■ APMEA
- ☐ Other countries and corporate

Source: McDonald's Annual Report, 2007

Short, Periodic Report in Memorandum Format

THE PLAY STATION (*Child Care and Learning Center*)

1560 Kingsbury Lane / Arlington, VA 22922 / (703)555-6412 FAX (703)555-0919

TO: Tracey E. Bricka, Director, Human Resources
FROM: Russ Huff, Coordinator, Child Care Services RH
DATE: September 14, 2008
SUBJECT: Quarterly Report on In-House Child Care Center, Second Quarter, 2008

The in-house child care center experienced a successful second quarter. Data related to enrollment and current staffing follow:

Enrollment: 92 children, up from 84 at end of first quarter.
Staff: Ten full-time staff members, including six attendants, three teachers, and one registered nurse.

Registration for the upcoming school year is presently underway and is exceeding projected figures. Current staff size will necessitate an enrollment cap of 98. Further increases in enrollment will be possible only if additional personnel are hired.

The payroll deduction method of payment, instituted on January 1, has ensured that operations remain profitable. It has also eliminated the time and expense of billing. Parents seem satisfied with the arrangement as well.

Full license renewal is expected in August as we have met and/or exceeded all state and county requirements for facilities, staff, and programs.

Favorable results were obtained from the employee satisfaction poll, which was administered to parents participating in the child care program. Ninety-one percent indicated that they were very satisfied or extremely satisfied with our in-house child care program. The most frequently mentioned suggestion for improvement was the extension of hours until 7 p.m. This change would allow employees time to run necessary errands after work, before picking up their children. We might consider this addition of services on a per-hour rate basis. A copy of the survey instrument is provided for your review.

Call me should you wish to discuss the extended service hours idea or any other aspects of this report.

Attachment

GOOD

- Includes headings to serve formal report functions of transmittal and title page.
- Includes horizontal line to add interest and separate transmittal from body of memo.
- Uses deductive approach to present this periodic report requested by management on quarterly basis.
- Uses headings to highlight standard information; allows for easy update when preparing subsequent report.
- Includes primary data from survey completed by parents.
- Attaches material to memorandum, which would be appendix item in formal report.

Format Pointer
Uses a memorandum format for brief periodic report prepared for personnel within company.

GSI Technology Consulting Group

290 RBC Parkway, West • Los Angeles, CA 90046-9439
(213)555-9087 • Fax (213)555-3872 • www.gsi.com

- *Letterhead and letter address function as title page and transmittal.*

April 3, 2008

Ms. Kerry Tang, CEO
Pacific Systems Design Centre
P. O. Box 17963
Long Beach, CA 90810-1796

Dear Ms. Tang:

- *Introduces overall topic and leads into procedures and findings.*

The personal computer software audit for Spectrum Analysis has been completed according to the procedures recommended by Software Publishers Association. These procedures and our findings are summarized below.

- *Uses side heading to denote beginning of body.*

PROCEDURES
Specific procedures involved

- *Uses bulleted list to add emphasis to important information.*

- Reviewing the software policy of the organization and its implementation and control.
- Reviewing the organization's inventory of software resources, including a list of all personal computers by location and serial number. Using SPAudit, we obtained a list of all the software on the hard disk of each computer.
- Matching purchase documentation with the software inventory record we had established. This procedure included reviewing software purchase records, such as invoices, purchase orders, check registers, canceled checks, manuals, disks, license agreements, and registration cards.

Format Pointer
Uses letter format for short report prepared by outside consultant.

FINDINGS
In the area of software policy and controls, we found that the organization owns a total of 432 copies of 11 applications from seven vendors. No record of registration with the publisher was available for 81 of the programs owned. In addition, we identified 65 copies of software programs for which no corresponding purchase records existed. These copies appear to be illegal.

Of the 113 personal computers, we found 14 machines with software that had been brought from home by employees.

Selecting an Appropriate Presentation Visual

VISUAL	ADVANTAGES	LIMITATIONS
HANDOUTS	• Provide detailed information that audience can examine closely • Extend a presentation by providing resources for later use • Reduce the need for note taking and aid in audience retention	• Can divert audience's attention from the speaker • Can be expensive
BOARDS AND FLIPCHARTS	• Facilitate interaction • Are easy to use • Are inexpensive if traditional units are used	• Require turning speaker's back to audience • Are cumbersome to transport, can be messy and not professional looking • Provide no hard copy and must be developed on-site if traditional units are used
OVERHEAD TRANSPARENCIES	• Are simple to prepare and use • Allow versatile use; prepare beforehand or while speaking • Are inexpensive and readily available	• Are not easily updated and are awkward to use • Must have special acetate sheets and markers unless using a document camera • Pose potential for equipment failure
ELECTRONIC PRESENTATIONS	• Meet audience expectations of visual standards • Enhance professionalism and credibility of the speaker • Provide special effects to enhance retention, appeal, flexibility, and reuse	• Can lead to poor delivery if misused • Can be expensive, require highly developed skills, and are time-consuming • Pose technology failure and transportability challenges
 35MM SLIDES	• Are highly professional • Depict real people and places	• Require a darkened room • Creates a formal environment not conducive to group interaction • Lacks flexibility in presentation sequence
MODELS OR PHYSICAL OBJECTS	• Are useful to demonstrate an idea	• Can compete with the speaker for attention

Writing Effective Slide Content: Poor (left) and Good (right) Examples

Humor

- Important element in any presentation
- Easy connection with the audience
- Gets attention
- Alleviates boredom
- Reduction of mental tension
- Discourages conflict
- Enhances comprehension
- Shouldn't embarrass people
  - Ethnic jokes are inappropriate
  - Profane language is definitely not recommended

Value of Humor in a Presentation

- Establishes a connection with the audience
- Increases audience's willingness to listen
- Makes message more understandable and memorable
- Alleviates negativity associated with sensitive subjects

The revised slide

- Includes a descriptive title that captures major idea of slide, in this case, the value of humor.
- Omits items unrelated to value of humor. Specifically, "important element in any presentation" is a verbal transition, not needed on slide; "shouldn't embarrass people" and related subpoints will appear on a separate slide focusing on tips for using humor.
- Collapses remaining content into a few memorable points that use parallel structure for clarity and grammatical accuracy (singular action verbs).
- Proofreads carefully to avoid misspellings that damage credibility, such as "conflect" in original slide.

Engaging Conceptual Slide Design: Poor (left) and Good (right) Examples

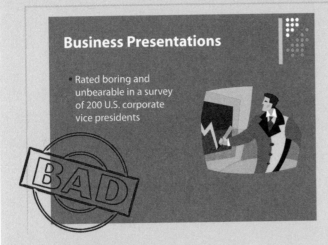

The revised slide

- Uses descriptive title that captures central idea of dissatisfaction with typical business presentation.
- Selects images that imply intended message—ineffectiveness of business presenters; enlarges images for slide appeal and balance.
- Trims text to emphasize central idea and eliminates bullet, as bulleted list should have at least two items.
- Moves source to less prominent slide position to add credibility to research data while keeping focus on central idea.

Example of Application Message Sent by Email

New Message

To: sgreyson@tropicalimporters.com

From: bshaw@netdoor.com

Subject: Career Fair Followup: Résumé for Brandon Shaw

October 15, 2007

Mr. Saunders Greyson
Human Resources Manager
Tropical Importers
1240 Coastal Lane
Miami, FL 33140-1000

Dear Mr. Greyson:

It was a pleasure meeting you at the career fair this morning. The opportunities offered in logistics management identifies your company as being a leader in today's international marketplace.

My experience and knowledge of logistics management enable me to be a valuable asset to your company:

• Realistic international experience with a delivery company.

• Demonstrated commitment to developing an appreciation for international cultures and business practices.

• Excellent performance evaluations, including special recognition for troubleshouting transporation problems to remote locations.

Please review the attached résumé that you requested for additional information about my education and related work experience. Please message me so we can discuss my joining Tropical Importers.

Sincerely,

Brandon R. Shaw

Attachment

• *Provides specific subject line that ensures message will be opened.*

• *Reveals how applicant learned of position and confirms knowledge of and interest in company.*

• *Condenses content of persuasive application letter sent by mail into one screen. Avoids tendency to send impersonal message stating résumé is attached.*

• *Introduces résumé and reminds interviewer that submission was requested.*

• *Encourages employer to take action without sounding pushy or apologetic.*

Format Pointers
Formats as formal business letter with complete address exactly as done when job credentials are sent by mail. Complete letter and printed copy of résumé will be sent as follow-up to email.

- Positions name as first readable item. Entices employer to email or visit website for additional qualifications.

- Includes "Professional Profile" section that identifies job sought and reason to hire.

- Includes "Keywords" section listing qualifications that match job description.

- Supports keywords with specific facts; uses nouns that might match those in description.
    Uses synonyms of keywords in body to ensure match with database.

JEANNE FULTON
89 Lincoln Street
San Antonio, TX 78285-9063
512 555-9823
jfulton@netdoor.com
www.netdoor/jfulton

Professional Profile
- First-year audit staff with an international accounting firm with an interest in forensic accounting.
- Technical proficiency in ERP systems, ACL, database, and spreadsheet software.
- Realistic audit experience through an internship with a regional CPA firm.
- Superior leadership abilities and team orientation developed through active involvement in student organizations; strong written and spoken communication skills.
- Fluency in Spanish.

Keywords
Entry-level audit position. Master's and bachelor's degrees in accounting. Sam Houston State University. 3.5 GPA. Beta Alpha Psi. Professional internship. Inventory control. Spanish fluency. Traveled Mexico. Analytical ability. Computer proficiency. Communication skills. Team player. Ethical. Creative. Adaptable. Willing to relocate. Windows. Software applications. Word, Excel, Access, PowerPoint. ACL. ERP Systems. Internet Explorer. Netscape. Web design.

Education
M.P.A., Accounting, Systems Emphasis, Sam Houston State University, August 2007, GPA 3.8.
B.B.A., Accounting, Sam Houston State University, May 2006, GPA 3.6.

- President's Scholar, 2002–2006
- Beta Alpha Psi (honorary accounting society)
- Lloyd Markham Academic Scholarship

Technical Skills
- Proficient in Windows, database, spreadsheet, ERP systems, ACL, Internet browsers (Netscape, Internet Explorer), and web design.
- Fluent Spanish; have traveled to Mexico.

Related Employment
Professional Internship, Smith & Lewis, CPAs, Dallas, Texas, June–August, 2007

- Participated in the rollout of a client's supply chain management system.
- Participated in audits of companies in the oil and gas, retail, and nonprofit sectors.
- Developed time management, team building, and communication skills while completing independent projects with diverse work teams.
- Demonstrated ability to accept and respond to criticism, learn job tasks quickly, and perform duties with minimal supervision.

Example of a Follow-Up Letter

Dear Mr. Franklin:

Recently I applied for an audit staff position at Foster & Daniel and now have additional qualifications to report.

The enclosed, updated résumé shows that I have passed the Auditing and Practice and Law sections of the CPA exam; I will take the final section at the next sitting. In addition, the internship I've just completed with Smith & Lewis, CPAs, has enhanced my formal education and confirmed my interest in working as an auditor.

Mr. Franklin, I would welcome the opportunity to visit your office and talk more about the contributions I could make as an auditor for Foster & Daniel. Please write or call me at (512) 555-9823.

- • States main idea and clearly identifies position being sought.

- • Refers to enclosed résumé; summarizes additional qualifications.

- • Assures employer that applicant is still interested in job.

Format Pointers
Uses template to design professional personal letterhead and matching envelope.

Formats as formal business letter, but could have sent message electronically if previous communication with employer had been by email.

Prints letter and envelope with laser printer on paper that matches résumé and application letter.

Example of a Job-Acceptance Message

I accept your employment offer as a market analyst. Thank you for responding so quickly after our discussion on Thursday.

As you requested, I have signed the agreement outlining the specific details of my employment. Your copy is enclosed, and I have kept a copy for my records.

If you should need to communicate with me before I report to work on May 14, please call me at 555-6841.

- • Begins by stating main idea—job offer is being accepted.

- • Continues with any necessary details.

- • Confirms beginning employment date.

 Example of a Thank-You Message

New Message

To:	wrfann@viking.com
From:	mperkins@hotmail.com
Subject:	Appreciation for Plant Interview

Dear Mr. Fann:

Thank you for the opportunity to visit Viking Range for a plant interview yesterday. I enjoyed meeting you and appreciated the complete tour of the operation and the opportunity to learn about the exciting research efforts underway at Viking.

Viking's success in developing higher quality products than its competitors after such a short time in the refrigeration market is impressive. Additionally, I was impressed with the many friendly, enthusiastic employees who were willing to share with me their knowledge and commitment to Viking.

After visiting your plant on Thursday, I am confident that my interest and previous experience in research and development at the DIAL labs in Starkville would allow me to contribute to Viking's important research efforts in the refrigeration area. I would also gain valuable real-world experience needed to enhance the mechanical engineering degree I'm pursuing at Mississippi State.

Mr. Fann, I am eager to receive an offer from Viking for the co-op position. If you need additional information in the meantime, please contact me.

Thanks,

Matt Perkins

- *States main idea of appreciation for interview and information gained.*

- *Includes specific points discussed during interview, increasing sincerity and recall of applicant.*

- *Assures employer of continued interest in position.*

- *Politely reminds employer that applicant is awaiting reply.*

Format Pointer
Prepared as email message because all previous submissions have been completed by email.

 Example of a Job-Refusal Message

I appreciate your spending time with me discussing the loan officer's job.

Your candid comparison of my background and opportunities in finance and insurance was especially helpful. Having received job offers in both fields, I am now convinced that a career in insurance is more consistent with my aptitudes and goals. Today, I am accepting a job in the actuarial department of States Mutual.

Thank you for your confidence demonstrated by the job offer. When I receive reports of Lincoln's continued success, I will think of the dedicated people who work for the company.

- *Begins with neutral but related idea to buffer bad news.*

- *Presents reasons diplomatically that lead to refusal.*

- *Ends message on positive note that anticipates future association with company.*